THE UNITED STATES
AND THE INDEPENDENCE OF
LATIN AMERICA
1800-1830

BY

ARTHUR PRESTON WHITAKER
University of Pennsylvania

The Norton Library
W · W · NORTON & COMPANY · INC ·
NEW YORK

First published in the Norton Library 1964 by
arrangement with the Johns Hopkins Press.

The Albert Shaw Lectures on Diplomatic History, 1938
The Walter Hines Page School of International Relations

*Published simultaneously in
Canada by George J. McLeod Limited, Toronto*

Books That Live

The Norton imprint on a book means that in the publisher's
estimation it is a book not for a single season but for the years.

W. W. Norton & Company, Inc.

SBN   393   00271   3

PRINTED IN THE UNITED STATES OF AMERICA

3 4 5 6 7 8 9 0

100008

PREFACE TO THIS EDITION

Since this book first appeared 23 years ago, many of the problems discussed in it have been placed in a new light by the exploitation of additional sources, the lifting of restrictions on the use of the highly important papers of John Quincy Adams, and the publication of numerous articles and books. The latter include my own book, *The Western Hemisphere Idea: Its Rise and Decline* (1954), which deals more specifically than its predecessor with the crucial importance of the period 1800–1830 for the formulation of that half-mystical, half-practical, and remarkably persistent idea.

Nevertheless, in my opinion, these subsequent accretions do not require major surgery on my study as published in 1941. Consequently, I was happy to agree with the publisher of the present edition that it should be identical with the first except for the correction of typographical errors. Agreement was all the easier since the subject will be treated within the broad context of U.S. foreign relations in the same period in a book which I am preparing for a series edited by Armin Rappaport of the University of California, Berkeley, to be published by Macmillan.

The introduction to the first edition of the present work pointed out certain resemblances as well as differences between the critical period covered in it and the one through which the United States was passing in 1941. The comparison could now be extended to the current situation. In saying this, my intention is to suggest, not that the past is worth studying only as prologue to the present, but that in the relations of the United States with Latin America since the early nineteenth century there have been some very durable factors, of which the Western Hemisphere idea is only one.

May 1964   A. P. W.

ABBREVIATIONS

AGN, BA: Archivo General de la Nación, Buenos Aires
AGN, Mvdo: Archivo General de la Nación, Montevideo
AHN, Est.: Archivo Histórico Nacional (Madrid), Sección de Estado
HSP: Historical Society of Pennsylvania (Philadelphia)
LC: Library of Congress (Washington, D.C.)
SD: State Department Archives (in the National Archives, Washington, D.C.)

INTRODUCTION

No one can read the records of the critical period covered in this book without noticing its similarity to the one through which we are now passing. Then, as now, the Atlantic world was divided into rival camps and the issues between them were confused by the intricate interplay of ideologies, national interests, and geographical concepts. With the substitution of "totalitarian" for "monarchical" and "democracy" for "republicanism," much that was said on both sides of the Atlantic in that period could be applied verbatim to the present situation; and it was then that the idea of hemisphere solidarity—and hemisphere defense—first took definite shape in the New World.

Then, too, Latin America was the danger zone in this hemisphere and during a large part of its struggles for independence the threat came from a kind of "axis," called the Holy Alliance, which dominated the Continent of Europe and was regarded as the enemy of free institutions everywhere. It was feared that Europe would reconquer Latin America not merely by force of arms but also by the force of ideas supported by trade. Actually, two of the new states did adopt Europe's form of government, monarchy—Mexico for a year, Brazil for the better part of a century. The United States, the leading exponent of liberty, undertook to defend Latin America from European aggression, and to promote its commercial and cultural, as well as political, relations with the new states to the south of it. Anglo-American cooperation was seriously discussed, though it never materialized. Britain, after following a policy of "appeasement" toward the "continental despots" for several years, finally cut loose from them and took a decisive stand in favor of Latin American independence, but continued its rivalry with the United States, which was one of the main themes of the period. In Latin America itself there were the now familiar conflicts between democracy and dictatorship, and between the partisans of European connections on the one hand and of inter-American solidarity on the other. Indeed, throughout the "two Americas" (the phrase was a common one even then) inter-American relations were discussed in the language of the twentieth century, and towards the close of the period, in 1826, an international congress was held at Panama which has often been called the first Pan American conference.

In the United States "isolationists" and "internationalists" (to use the jargon of our own day) debated the national, the continental, and the ideological bases of policy in modern terms. Henry Clay, seeking a "counterpoise" to the Holy Alliance, advocated the formation of an "American system" distinct from that of Europe. Daniel Webster, more conscious of his country's classical heritage and its living ties with Europe, thought the United States had at least as much in common with the Greeks as with the inhabitants of the Andes. James Monroe, devoted to the cause of liberty everywhere, wanted to encourage those struggling for freedom in both Greece and Latin America. John Quincy Adams said the United States already had the American system and was the whole of it; and he warned his countrymen never to engage in foreign wars of any kind, even wars for freedom, lest they destroy the foundations of our own freedom.

There are of course important differences between the situation then and now. To name only two, at that time Britain was undisputed mistress of the seas and the United States was not a great world power and had few manufactured goods to export and little capital to invest abroad. Consequently we must be careful not to read the present situation into the earlier one; but the resemblances between them are numerous and important and they enable us to understand that earlier world crisis better, perhaps, than it has been understood at any time in the past century. They also remind us that many of the issues of the present day are not new, that we are still living in the phase of history opened in the day of Monroe and Adams. Politically, the phase was marked by the emancipation of America from Europe and by the emergence of the American system of international cooperation. Only a tentative beginning of the system was made in the period of the present study; but already European publicists, impressed by its possibilities, were telling their fellow countrymen that unless they adopted it and formed some kind of federation of Europe, that continent would be ruined by the incessant wars to which its own system of international rivalry inevitably led.

The development of policy and opinion in the United States in this period is all the more interesting because at the beginning of it both the people at large and even the authorities at Washington were woefully ignorant in regard to Latin America. Let Thomas Jefferson speak to this point. In 1804 Baron Alexander von Humboldt passed through the United States on his return to Paris from Spanish America, where he had spent the past five years. Congratulating him on his safe arrival in this country after his long and hazardous "tour" through that remote region, Jefferson wrote:

The countries you have visited are of those least known
and most interesting, and a lively desire will be felt generally to receive the information you will give. No one will
feel it more strongly than myself. . . .

Five years later, Humboldt sent Jefferson a copy of his *Essai politique
sur le royaume de la Nouvelle Espagne,* which contained a large part
of the voluminous store of information that he had gathered in
Spanish America, and in thanking him for the book Jefferson described
New Spain (Mexico) as "one of the most singular and interesting
countries on the globe, one almost locked up from the knowledge of
man hitherto."

Though the ever courteous Jefferson may have sought to please
the author by exaggerating the novelty of his subject matter, what he
said was essentially true. To the great mass of the people of the
United States—to practically all but a handful of scholars and seamen
who had a special interest in it—Latin America was at this time
terra incognita, a Dark Continent.

Two decades later, the achievement of independence had converted
the continental colonies of Spain and Portugal into a dozen states
forming a recognized part of the family of nations and had thrown
them wide open to the gaze of all who might care to look at them.
In this score of years, a host of writers of many nations—diplomats,
businessmen, naval officers, scientists and others, natives of the region
as well as foreigners—had described almost every aspect of Latin
American life in newspapers, pamphlets, and books in many languages.
Much of this work of revelation was done in English and much of
it was done by and for the people of the United States. Whether this
consisted of fugitive items, such as an indignant Boston merchant's
letter to the editor about his maltreatment in some Latin American
port, or of works of broad interest and enduring worth, such as
Humboldt's massive "essay" on New Spain or Poinsett's *Notes on
Mexico in 1822,* it all added up to a vast body of information which,
by the end of the period, made it possible for the intelligent reader
in the United States to know Latin America better than any other part
of the world except his own country and a few countries in western
Europe.

So great was the advancement of knowledge in this field that it
might be said with little exaggeration that for the people of the
United States the period from 1810 to 1830 witnessed the discovery
of Latin America. The discovery was due to a combination of factors,

mainly, of course, to the dramatic character of the long struggle for Latin American independence, to the final destruction of the barriers raised around Latin America by Spain and Portugal, and to the political concern of the United States over the fate of the new nations. It was also due, however, to other considerations, such as the economic possibilities opened up by the destruction of the Spanish and Portuguese colonial monopolies and to the fact that Latin America promised to furnish rich materials for students of geography, archaeology, chemistry, medicine, and other branches of knowledge in which intellectual leaders in the United States as well as Europe were taking an increasingly keen interest in this period.

In other words, by the 1820's the *terra incognita* of 1810 had become the happy hunting ground not only of businessmen, politicians, and statesmen, but also of natural and social scientists; but since the core of the interest of the United States in Latin America was political, the growth of that interest can perhaps be indicated best by the fact that of the ten legations provided for by the State Department's budget for 1824, five were in Europe (London, Paris, St. Petersburg, Madrid, and Lisbon), and the remaining five were in Latin America (Buenos Aires, Bogotá, Santiago de Chile, Mexico City, and Lima). It is hardly necessary to add that, by the same time, Monroe's famous message of December 2, 1823 had made Latin America the subject of the most important single pronouncement in the history of American foreign policy. In the course of the next few years, the Monroe Doctrine was subjected to important definitions and interpretations, the diplomatic relations of the United States with Latin America were extended and clarified, and its knowledge of the region was further enriched.

About 1830, however, it was apparent that the end of an era had been reached, for there then occurred a very perceptible slowing down in the process of expansion in its various aspects—in the extension of knowledge and of commercial and cultural relations, and in the development of policy. There was even some contraction of ideas and policy. For some years past, the horizon of interest of the United States had extended as far South as Cape Horn; but in the next generation it was so effectively bounded by Cuba, Mexico, and Panama that the flagrant intervention of France and England in the Plata region between 1838 and 1850 excited little interest in this country.

The year 1830 may therefore be taken as marking the end of a well-defined period in the relations between the United States and Latin America. At the other end, a proper starting point is suggested by the statement already made, that the period was characterized not only by the establishment of Latin American independence but also by the discovery of Latin America by the United States. From this point of view the period begins not with the Latin American wars of independence but with the disintegration of Spain's system of commercial monopoly and exclusion at the close of the eighteenth century, which was followed a few years later by a similar development in Portuguese Brazil. These developments rapidly multiplied the contacts of the United States and other foreign nations with Latin America, promoted the Latin American wars of independence, and laid the groundwork of knowledge and interest on which public opinion and policy in the United States were built up in the next generation.

Consequently, from the point of view of the relations of the United States with Latin America, the period from the close of the eighteenth century to about 1830 possesses unity, completeness, and character in sufficiently high degree to warrant isolating it for special study, as has been done in this volume. Although the main outlines of the story are, of course, already familiar, the present study is the first synthesis of the subject which brings together the results of the many monographs published in the past generation and is also based upon an extensive study of the sources. It also presents a broader view of the subject than has been given before, by adding to the conventional narrative of diplomacy an account of economic interests, political ideas, and cultural relations, in an effort to recreate the climate of opinion in which Thomas Jefferson, James Monroe, John Quincy Adams, Henry Clay, and their contemporaries fashioned the policies and attitudes which still so largely govern the conduct of the United States in relation to Latin America.

April 16, 1941   A. P. W.

ACKNOWLEDGMENT

I wish to make grateful acknowledgment to the University of Pennsylvania and the Social Science Research Council for grants in aid of this study; to the authorities of the libraries and archives that I have consulted for placing their resources at my disposal; to Dr. Emilio Ravignani of Buenos Aires for copies of documents in the Archivo General de la Nación of that city; to Dr. Juan E. Pivel Devoto of Montevideo for important aid during my studies there; to Professor Samuel Flagg Bemis for an opportunity to read the galley proof of his monograph on the early missions from Buenos Aires; to Mr. Charles Lyon Chandler for enlightenment on many aspects of our early relations with Latin America; to Mr. Benjamin Rush for the use of the Richard Rush Papers, which are described elsewhere in these pages; and to Mr. Owen Lattimore, Director of the Page School of International Relations in the Johns Hopkins University, and Mr. C. W. Dittus, Manager of the Johns Hopkins Press, for their aid in getting this book through the press.

April 16, 1941   A. P. W.

CONTENTS

CHAPTER ONE

OPENING THE DOOR TO LATIN AMERICA

The invasion of the Iberian peninsula by the armies of Napoleon in 1807 and 1808 exercised a powerful influence upon the subsequent course of relations between the United States and the new states that soon emerged in Latin America. In the time-honored phrase, Napoleon shook the tree of liberty in the American colonies of Spain and Portugal. He drove the royal house of Braganza from Portugal to Brazil, forced the abdication of the Spanish Bourbons, and installed his brother Joseph on the throne of Spain. If he had had his way, he would have seized the transatlantic colonies as well; but since the British victory at Trafalgar in 1805 had reduced the navies of France and her ally, Spain, to insignificance, he was unable to exercise effective control over any part of the Spanish and Portuguese empires except Spain and Portugal themselves, and the net result of his invasion of the mother countries was to hasten the emancipation of their colonies in America.

The emancipation of these colonies was a commercial and cultural as well as a political emancipation; it was already under way for some time before Napoleon's armies moved southward across the Pyrenees; and while it possessed great interest for England, France, and Russia, none of these powers was as deeply concerned in it as the United States. In order to understand how the latter regarded the crisis that Napoleon's invasion of the Iberian peninsula precipitated in Latin America, we must first review the developments of the preceding decade, during which the government and people of the United States formed their first extensive contacts with the American colonies of Spain and Portugal.

I

The direct contacts of the United States with Spanish and Portuguese America at the beginning of the wars of the French Revolution were relatively few and they were confined largely to Spanish Louisiana, Florida, and Cuba. By 1808 they had been multiplied many times over and had been extended to every part of Latin America.

In this process the part played by commercial relations was of the utmost importance; indeed, in many cases they formed the only point of contact between the two Americas. Their economic value, which was already considerable in the closing years of the eighteenth century, increased rapidly in the course of the next decade. They led to the establishment of the first government agencies of the United States, which were of a quasi-consular character, in the Spanish colonies, and later they provided both a pretext and part of the personnel for the establishment of quasi-diplomatic relations with the revolutionary governments of that region. They were also one of the principal factors in promoting knowledge and shaping opinion in the United States about Latin America.

The growth of American commerce with that region was only one aspect of a much larger development, namely, the breakdown of the Spanish and Portuguese monopolies of commerce with their American colonies. Both economically and politically this was one of the most important of the many changes that occurred during the long upheaval of the French Revolution and the Napoleonic era, for it was one of the most far reaching and enduring.[1] Economically, it was important because it threw open to the world at large a region which was the world's chief source of supply of gold and silver, which was known to possess great undeveloped natural resources, and whose commerce rivaled that of England's great empire in value. Politically it was important because this economic liberation greatly stimulated the movement for political independence in Latin America. While other changes of this revolutionary age, especially in Europe, were wiped out after Napoleon's final overthrow, the change in Latin America continued to gain momentum; and even today its major consequences are still apparent in map and lawbook. By 1830, thirteen independent governments had been established in Latin America; all of these still exist, and seven others have since been added. As for the regime of international economic freedom, that, too, still exists in its main outlines and such limitations as it now suffers from have been imposed upon it by the Latin American nations themselves.

Until near the end of the eighteenth century the commerce of Latin America was, with some relatively minor exceptions, monopolized by Spain and Portugal. By the Ordinance of Free Commerce of 1778,[2] Spain had made

[1] The importance of commerce in preparing the way for the emancipation of Spanish America is stressed in the first chapter of the useful survey of the movement by Domingo Amunátegui Solar, *La Emancipación de Hispano-América* (Universidad de Chile (Santiago), 1936), p. 1-9.

[2] Emilio Ravignani, *El virreinato del Río de la Plata* (Buenos Aires, 1938, reprinted from *Historia de la nación argentina,* IV), p. 145-148.

sweeping changes in its regulation of colonial commerce, opening many new ports of entry in both Spain and the colonies and permitting an indirect commerce between foreign nations and the Spanish colonies by way of Spain; but the monopoly was still rigorously maintained in the sense that as a general rule the commerce had to be carried on in Spanish ships and through Spanish ports and that foreign ships and foreign travelers were still jealously excluded from the Spanish colonies. In time of war, this rule was often suspended; but otherwise the exceptions to it were rare. Thus, in time of peace, United States flour could legally reach Havana only by being taken across the Atlantic to Cadiz and then shipped back across the Atlantic to Havana. Under this system smuggling was, of course, extensive.

A similar system was set up by Portugal for Brazil, with England supplying, via Lisbon, most of the goods needed by the colony.[3] An occasional interloper from the United States or some other foreign country carried on a precarious trade with Brazil; but thanks to its long-standing alliance with England, which controlled the seas, Portugal was able to maintain its system virtually intact through all the vicissitudes of the European war until 1808.

Spain, on the other hand, was soon drawn into the orbit of France and went to war with England in 1796; and within a year it had to throw its colonies open to neutral trade by a royal order dated Nov. 18, 1797.[4] As we shall see, this toleration of neutral trade with the Spanish colo-

---

[3] Roberto Simonsen, *Historia economica do Brasil, 1500-1820* (2 vols., São Paulo, etc., 1937), II, 175-200.

[4] Ravignani, *op. cit.,* p. 148.

nies was continued under one form or another throughout the next decade.

The chief beneficiary under the system established by the Spanish royal order of 1797 was the United States, which was the leading maritime nation among the neutral powers; and the United States was able to derive great and immediate advantage from the new system because of certain limited but important connections which it had already established with the three parts of Spanish America: with contiguous Louisiana and the Floridas, with nearby Cuba, and with remote Chile.[5] Closely related to this was the trade that the United States carried on with the French colony of St. Domingue (the present Haiti), which, during the first decade after the establishment of American independence, provided the United States with one of its most valuable channels of communication with Spanish America.

The oldest commercial relations of the United States with Spanish America were those with Havana and New Orleans (which was Spanish until 1803). The trade with them dated from the period when the United States themselves were still colonies, and by 1797 it had been maintained for more than a generation. It was speculative; but its cash value was considerable, and—what is more important—it served as a stepping stone for the commercial expansion of the United States to other parts of Latin America and as a

[5] Louisiana and Florida: Arthur P. Whitaker, *Documents Relating to the Commercial Policy of Spain in the Floridas* (Deland, Fla., 1931), Historical Introduction. Cuba: Roy F. Nichols, "Trade Relations and the Establishment of the United States Consulates in Spanish America, 1779-1809," *Hispanic Am. Hist. Rev.,* XIII (1933), p. 290, 293, 295; Chile: Eugenio Pereira Salas, *Buques norteamericanos en Chile a fines de la era colonial (1788-1810),* (Universidad de Chile (Santiago), 1936; reprinted from *Anales de la Universidad de Chile*).

training school for the merchants, masters and supercargoes
who were to lead that expansion.[6]

The role of St. Domingue in our commercial relations
with Spanish America was, so to speak, confined to the first
scene of the first act; but it was an important one, for it
created interests that were worth preserving, and it gave
concrete evidence that Spanish colonial trade was well
worth cultivating by other means when this corridor was
closed. So it is not surprising that the Philadelphia merchant prince, Stephen Girard, who was heavily interested in
the trade with St. Domingue in the 1790's, was one of the
first of the more responsible American merchants to engage
in large-scale trade with continental Spanish America at
the beginning of the wars of independence.[7] The trade
with Chile was not, at the outset, a large one, but it possessed considerable importance because of the persons engaged
in it and because it marked the extension of American commerce into a new and remote quarter of Latin America,
gave Americans direct access, for the first time, to important
sources of supply of Spanish gold and silver, and soon
became an integral part of the rich trade with Asia and
the whaling and sealing trade in the South Pacific.

American ships doubtless entered many other Spanish
American ports in this early period; but the conditions
under which they did so makes it difficult to speak with any

[6] Samuel Eliot Morison, *Maritime History of Massachusetts,
1783-1860* (Boston, 1922), contains a fascinating account of one
aspect of the great expansion of commerce and navigation in this
period, with many scattering references to Latin America.

[7] Ludwell Lee Montague, *Haiti and the United States, 1714-1938*
(Durham, N. C., 1940), p. 32; John Bach McMaster, *Life and
Times of Stephen Girard, Mariner and Merchant* (2 vols., Phila-
delphia, 1918), I, 49 ff.

assurance on the subject. Enforcement of the law was lax and Spanish officials, in the United States as well as the colonies, were obliging—for a consideration.[8] Ships in these seas often carried two sets of papers, neither of which would necessarily reveal its true nationality; so that a ship entered as Spanish might also carry a set of American papers and yet in fact be British property.

By the time the Spanish royal order of 1797 admitted neutrals to the ports of Spanish America, seamen and merchants of the United States had already familiarized themselves with the mechanism of trade in Havana, New Orleans, and Valparaiso, and had thus established contact with important commercial zones in the Caribbean and the Gulf of Mexico, and on the western coast of South America. They were, moreover, already performing the main functions of that commerce as it was to operate when fully developed: they were carrying the wares of Europe and their own country to Spanish America, they were supplying it with foodstuffs, they were obtaining specie from it, they were using it as a way-station in their trade with the Far

[8] For example, in 1794 and 1795 the two Spanish *encargados de negocios* (chargé d'affaires) in the United States, Josef de Jáudenes and Josef de Viar, actually entered into a contract whereby they sold permits for the shipment of 20,000 barrels of flour to Havana. The permits were sold at the rate of three dollars a barrel; at least 10,000 barrels were shipped; and the two *encargados* received over $1800 each as their share of the graft. One of the parties to the contract was Thomas Stoughton, Jáudenes's father-in-law and Spanish consul at Boston, who took part of the flour in the ship *Governor Mifflin* from Philadelphia to Havana. New York Historical Society, *Letter Book of John Stoughton*, vol. 1 (1794-1795) relates mainly to this affair; vol. 2 (1795-1800) contains two important letters relating to it: John Stoughton to Thomas Stoughton (his brother, Spanish consul at New York), July 10, 1796, and March 24, 1797.

East, and they were undermining the loyalty of the colonists to Spain.

II

The Spanish royal order of Nov. 18, 1797, which opened the ports of Spanish America to neutral shipping, was a concession wrung from a reluctant court by grinding necessity and it was an emergency, war-time measure explicitly limited to the duration of the war whose disasters had compelled the court to adopt it. When Spain was drawn into the war with Britain in 1796 in consequence of her alliance with France, she was promptly cut off from regular communication with her American colonies. In order to preserve the latter from economic ruin, neutral ships were now permitted by this measure to enter their ports with foodstuffs, lumber, naval stores, manufactured goods, and slaves, and to take off the produce of the colonies, such as sugar, coffee, tobacco, indigo, cacao, and hides. These neutral ships also took large amounts of specie from the Spanish colonial ports, though the exportation of it was prohibited under severe penalties.

This abuse, together with others, led the court to revoke the permission to neutrals (April 18, 1799) ; but an important exception was made in favor of foodstuffs, some of the colonial officials refused, on the ground of urgent necessity, to enforce the order of revocation at all, and from every quarter the clamor of protest was so great that in 1801 the court instituted a system of special licenses which were sold to neutrals and which permitted them to enter Spanish American ports for purposes of general trade. With the restoration of peace in 1802 this system was abolished and the old Spanish monopoly restored—that is to say, the monopoly as regulated by the Ordinance of Free Commerce of 1778. This happy return to the good old days was short-lived, for war soon broke out again between France and England, in 1804 Spain was again involved in it in the wake of France and again the Spanish colonies had to be thrown open to neutral trade (December, 1804). This time the court tried still a third expedient, the contract system, whereby the right to issue licenses for neutral trade with the Spanish colonial ports was in effect farmed out to a number of court favorites and other individuals, who, generally acting through sub-contractors, sold the licenses for what the traffic would bear.[9] This was the system that prevailed until Napoleon's invasion of Spain in 1808 created a wholly new situation and, in the end, brought about the collapse of the monopoly and indeed of all uniform regulation of Spanish colonial commerce.

III

Commerce between the United States and Spanish America received a great impulse from the system established by the Spanish order of 1797 and continued to grow apace despite the subsequent restrictions of license and contract imposed by the court in 1799, 1801 and 1804.

The advantages that the United States, as a neutral, enjoyed under these regulations and in the carrying trade between Spanish America and Continental Europe were to a considerable extent offset by the free port system estab-

[9] Archivo de Indias, Seville, América en general, legajo 1, Consejo de Indias to the King, Aug. 22, 1818 (LC transcript), report reviewing the history of the regulation of colonial commerce by the Spanish government since 1797.

lished by Great Britain in the West Indies and the Caribbean at the turn of the century. Kingston, Jamaica, Port of
Spain, Trinidad, and other ports in this region were designated free ports and permitted to trade with the enemy,
and from them the British built up a thriving trade with the
Spanish colonists in the West Indies, northern South America, Central America, and Mexico.[10] The rivalry of the
United States and Great Britain in Spanish American trade
at this time provided one of the principal motives for a
famous British blast against the United States, James Stephen's *War in Disguise*. The views maintained by Stephen
prevailed at London; there was a general tightening of
British restrictions on neutral commerce, beginning with the
Essex decision of 1805; and the result was the imposition
of serious handicaps on the United States in its competition
with Britain for the commerce of Spanish America.[11]

Occasionally, still other handicaps were imposed upon the
commerce of the United States with Spanish America—for
example, by the undeclared naval war of 1798-1799 with
France;[12] but on the whole it flourished until it was cut off

[10] Dorothy Burne Goebel, "British Trade to the Spanish Colonies, 1796-1823," *Am. Hist. Rev.*, XLIII (1938), 288-320, makes
an original contribution of great value, though additional sources
in Spanish (especially for the River Plate region) might have
been used with profit. The period to 1808 is discussed on p. 289-
297, 304-310, and 315-316, where it is pointed out that the free
port system was based on the Free Ports Act of 1766, and that
Kingston in Jamaica and Port of Spain in Trinidad were the busiest
ports.

[11] Stephen's book and the *Essex* decision are discussed in *ibid.*,
p. 296, 297.

[12] Dudley W. Knox, ed., *Naval Documents Related to the Quasi-
War between the United States and France* (5 vols., Washington,
D. C., 1937), contains a mass of information (rendered accessible

by Jefferson's embargo of December 1807, which remained in force for more than a year. By that time Spain had ceased to exercise any important control over the commerce of its colonies.

The Spanish government's toleration of neutral trade with its colonies, under the royal order of 1797 and subsequent orders, did not extend to the ports on the Pacific coast of America. There seem to have been a number of reasons why this exception was made. For one thing, the war had brought less disturbance to Spanish colonial trade in that quarter and there was consequently less need of neutral aid. For another, the monopoly of the Philippine Company of Spain was one that could not be lightly disturbed,[13] all the more since Spain had, if possible, been even more jealous of foreign intrusion in the Pacific than in the Atlantic and, since the Tupac Amaru rebellion of 1780 in Peru, particularly apprehensive of seditious intrigue by foreigners in that part of the empire.[14]

Yet even in this quarter the commerce of the United States, building on the foundation already laid in Chile, grew by leaps and bounds at the turn of the century. Those who engaged in it had to trust to luck, their own astuteness, and the gullibility or venality or impotence of the local officials; but they were greatly aided by the breakdown

---

by a detailed index) relating to the vicissitudes of American commerce, mainly in the West Indies and the Caribbean, during this period.

[13] See below, Chap. 4, note 27.

[14] The unrest in Peru disturbed the Conde de Aranda so deeply that in 1786 he advised the Spanish court to cede Peru to the House of Braganza in exchange for Portugal: Modesto de Lafuente, *Historia general de España* (30 vols., Madrid, 1850-1869), XXI, 171-174.

of the Spanish administrative system under the stress of war. An illustration of this was furnished by the case of the American frigate *Hazard* at Valparaiso, Chile, in 1805.[15] The Spanish authorities, suspecting its captain, one Rowan, of planning to engage in contraband trade, took steps to forestall him, whereupon he mobilized his crew and offered armed resistance. Though ultimately subdued and arrested, he was soon released and permitted to go about his business—which, there is good reason to believe, actually was smuggling. In explaining to the court why Rowan had been treated so tenderly, the captain general said that it was because the court had never replied to his frequent requests for instructions as to how to deal with the *Bostoneses* (a term which many Spaniards applied indiscriminately to all American citizens) who frequented the coasts of Chile and were very dangerous because of their false religion and general unreliability. The court's reply merely approved what the Chilean colonial officials had done, which was practically nothing.

Aided by such administrative laxity, the commerce of the United States with Chile grew rapidly after 1797. The number of American ships entering Chilean ports increased from twenty-six in the nine years from 1788-1796 to two hundred and twenty-six in the thirteen years from 1797-1809. Of these, twenty-two were prosecuted for illicit trade and twelve condemned; but there can be little question that some of those that were released and many others that were never brought to trial were smugglers.[16] One of those that were prosecuted, the *Belle Savage* of Boston, the prop-

[15] Archivo del Ministerio de Estado, Madrid, Estados Unidos, legajo 213, Cevallos to Casa Irujo, Feb. 6, 1806 (LC transcript).

[16] Pereira Salas, *op. cit., supra*, note 5, p. 11.

erty of S. C. Coolidge, was released in 1800 " in consideration of the treaty of peace between Spain and the United States " (the treaty of San Lorenzo, ratified in 1796). The *Belle Savage* promptly relapsed into her evil ways, persisted in them with impunity, and at the end of two years sailed for Canton with $81,000 worth of specie that she had obtained by contraband trade on the coast of Chile.[17]

That these *Bostoneses* contributed to the rise of the independence spirit in Spanish America can hardly be questioned. At any rate, a loyal cleric in Chile, Melchior Martínez, regarded them as highly dangerous enemies of both royal and ecclesiastical authority and made their subversive activities the subject of a letter of warning to the Spanish court which has been quoted time and again in accounts of the rise of the revolutionary movement.[18] Since, in the nature of the case, this propaganda was carried on quite unobtrusively, we can find few authenticated instances of it; but one of unusual interest is recorded in Richard Cleveland's well-known *Narrative of Voyages and Commercial Enterprises* [19] and in the journal of his companion, William Shaler. In 1802 these men, who had already made a venture to Montevideo and Buenos Aires in 1799, sailed from Hamburg to Valparaiso by way of the Canaries and Rio de Janeiro, intending to exchange their cargo for furs on the Pacific coast and then go on to Canton. Already warned

[17] *Ibid.*, p. 23.

[18] J. Fred Rippy, *Latin America in World Politics* (New York, 1938, 3rd ed.), p. 29-30, and Bernard Moses, *The Intellectual Background of the Revolution in South America* (New York, 1926), p. 39-41.

[19] (Cambridge, Mass., 1842), p. 120-248, summarized in Roy F. Nichols, "William Shaler, New England Apostle of Rational Liberty," *New England Quarterly,* IX (1936), p. 73-74.

against them by letters from Hamburg, the local authorities prevented them from engaging in trade; but in the two months that they spent at Valparaiso Shaler talked with many discontented creoles, fanned their discontent by pointing out the relation between independence and prosperity, with the United States as an object lesson, and gave them a copy of the Constitution of the United States and a Spanish translation of the Declaration of Independence. When the authorities forced them to leave Valparaiso, they sailed up to San Blas, Mexico, where Shaler repeated his lectures on independence and prosperity. This episode is significant because it is probably typical of the way in which American traders sowed seeds of sedition in Latin America; and it should be noted that Cleveland returned many times to trade in Latin American ports and Shaler later served as an agent of the United States government in revolutionary Spanish America.

It was only in the Caribbean and on the Atlantic coast of South America that the Spanish toleration of neutral trade with its colonies was directly beneficial to the United States. One of the most important of the new regions that this system opened up to its commerce was the Plata estuary, in which the principal ports were Montevideo and Buenos Aires. Both of these ports had achieved commercial importance only in the last quarter of the eighteenth century. Until then, neither possessed nearly so much importance in the eyes of foreigners as did Vera Cruz, Callao, and Havana, for neither of them served as large a market or gave such ready access to the gold, silver, and copper mines of Spanish America, or could furnish cargoes of the most highly prized colonial products, such as sugar, tobacco, indigo, and cacao. Since the creation of the viceroyalty of the Rio de la Plata in 1776, however, new commercial regulations had diverted the flow of silver from the Potosí mines to Buenos Aires and Montevideo. There it could be had in exchange for foreign merchandise, such as assorted manufactures from Europe and the United States and spices and silks from the Far East. Flour was also much in demand at these ports, for much of the Plata hinterland was still cow country. Accordingly, a lively trade developed in which flour from Baltimore and Philadelphia was sold in return for jerked beef, which was taken to Havana, and hides, which were taken to the United States, mainly, it seems, for the use of the thriving boot and shoe trade in Philadelphia.[20]

Earlier studies [21] have already revealed many of the details of the commerce of the United States with these two ports, but the port records of Montevideo [22] show that the volume of its commerce with the United States on the eve of the wars of independence was considerably larger than has hitherto been realized. They also point to the rather novel conclusion that the African slave trade was an important factor in the early development of United States commerce with this part of South America. The latter conclusion is particularly interesting when set beside such other aspects of American commercial expansion as the Chilean activities of that traveling salesman of rational liberty, William Shaler.

In the calendar year 1805, 22 vessels of American regis-

[20] Emilio Ravignani, *op. cit.*, p. 127, 152-167. Also, see below, note 47.

[21] Especially Charles Lyon Chandler, "United States Merchant Ships in the Río de la Plata (1801-1808), "*Hispanic Amer. Hist. Rev.*, II (1919), 26-54.

[22] AGN, Mvdo., Fondo ex-" Archivo Administrativo," Libro No. 95, " Libro maestre de entradas de buques, 1805-1818."

try entered the port of Montevideo; of these, 11 brought cargoes of slaves from Africa. In 1806, the total number of American ships entered was 30; of these, 20 were slavers, which brought some 2500 slaves (this does not include those who died on the voyage from Africa, some 500 in number). According to the Montevideo records, most of the principal Atlantic ports of the United States, but especially those from Baltimore northward, were interested in this traffic. The American ships engaged in general commerce likewise represented the whole Atlantic coast of the United States, with a similar concentration in the ports from Baltimore northward; and they brought assorted cargoes in which important items were rum, brandy, wine, salt, naval stores, dry goods, and furniture, with occasionally a coach, a set of drawing instruments, saddles, and horseshoes.

IV

Because of its novelty and for other reasons that have already been stated, the development of the United States commerce with Southern South America—Chile and the Plata region—has so far received most of our attention; but the bulk of American commerce with the Spanish colonies was still concentrated in the West Indies and the Caribbean, in which it had now been extended to Venezuela. For example, it was in 1798 that the first ship clearing from a Venezuelan port (La Guaira) arrived at Philadelphia; but in 1807 the number of arrivals at that port from Venezuela was 29 as compared with 138 from Cuba, 18 from Puerto Rico, seven from Vera Cruz, and only two from the Plata, where the British invasion had disrupted commerce.[23] In

[23] Roy F. Nichols, "Trade Relations," *loc. cit.*, p. 296-297, note 25 and p. 310-311, note 67.

Puerto Rico and on the Spanish Main respectively the Americans were aided by the proximity of Cuba, where they were already well established, and of Dutch Curaçao, to which they had free access, as well as by the great demand for their relatively cheap foodstuffs; and they were able to outdistance their British competitors even after the latter established their free port system.[24]

The case of Mexico calls for special comment. By and large, the United States developed its commerce with its next-door neighbor more slowly than with the other parts of Spanish America. That was probably because in this case the British effort to develop an undercover trade with Spanish America met with considerable success, and also because Mexico, far from needing the American foodstuffs that had served as an open sesame in other parts of Spanish America, was a competitor of the United States—though, to be sure, not a very successful competitor—in the production of flour for the export market.

Even with Mexico important commercial connections sprang up and flourished mightily in the years 1806 and 1807 in connection with the famous scheme of Napoleon's agent, the French banker Ouvrard, for bringing some fifty million dollars' worth of silver from Mexico to Europe.[25]

[24] Goebel, "British Trade to the Spanish Colonies, 1796-1823," *loc. cit.*, p. 298, 299. In 1793 Jefferson sent a commission as consul at Curaçao to B. H. Phillips, who wrote several letters from that place to the State Department between 1793 and 1801, though he was never recognized as consul by the local authorities (National Archives, SD, Consular Despatches, Curaçao, vol. 1, 1793-1838). For further information about Curaçao, see below, chap. 3.

[25] The following account is based mainly on Vincent Nolte, *Fifty Years in Both Hemispheres* (New York, 1854, "Translated from the German"), especially chaps. 4-6. Since Vincent Nolte has seemed a rather shadowy person, the following letter from

While the period was brief and participation in the scheme was confined to a relatively small number of American merchants and ship owners, the latter were so influential and the scheme was, at least from their point of view, so successful that the episode deserves a prominent place in any account of early relations between the United States and Latin America.

Ouvrard's extraordinary scheme was a product of the war then raging in Europe. Under a treaty of 1804, His Catholic Majesty of Spain, Charles IV, had agreed to pay Napoleon an annual subsidy of $36,000,000. The subsidy had never been paid and there existed in Spain no means of paying it. In Mexico, the abundant output of mines and

---

David Parish to Stephen Girard, dated London, Aug. 12, 1811 (Stephen Girard Papers, Girard College Library, Philadelphia, Letters Received in 1811, No. 306) is worth quoting because it tends to confirm Nolte's story of the Mexican enterprise and to show that Nolte's part in it was as important as he claimed. It also harmonizes with Nolte's statement, *op. cit.*, p. 175, that he sailed from Liverpool for New York in September 1811. "This letter," wrote Parish, "will be delivered or forwarded to you by my very particular friend, Mr. Vincent Nolte, who is about crossing the Atlantic with a view of forming a commercial establishment at New Orleans. This gentleman having already during a former residence with me in America been charged with an important agency for my friends Messrs. Hope & Co. of Amsterdam & myself, has acquired our entire confidence & that of our mutual friends Messrs. Baring Brothers & Co. of London, & secured to his contemplated establishment the benefit of their particular patronage & support." See also note 26, below; André Fugier, *Napoléon et l'Espagne* (2 vols., Paris, 1930), II, 8-60, and John Rydjord, "Napoleon and Mexican Silver," *Southwestern Social Science Quarterly,* XIX (1938), 171-182. Henry Adams, *History of the United States* (New York, 1930), III, 372-379, discusses the affair mainly in relation to Europe and diplomacy, noting François Barbé Marbois's connection with it.

mint had accumulated to an amount far greater than that of the subsidy; but in 1805 Nelson's great victory over the allied French and Spanish fleets at Trafalgar had destroyed almost the last remnant of direct communication between Spain and her American colonies.

Ouvrard's problem was how to get this silver safely transported from Mexico to France across an ocean controlled by the navy of Great Britain, which was still at war with Spain as well as France. His solution was as bold as it was simple: to obtain the cooperation of Great Britain herself, as well as that of the neutral United States. The first part of the plan might well have seemed harebrained, since the whole project was obviously designed for the benefit of Britain's mortal enemy, Napoleon. Yet the cooperation of the British was obtained, and this was done by the simple expedient of sharing the benefits with them. Briefly, this was done in the following way: In the first place, Ouvrard entrusted the execution of the plan to the great mercantile house of Amsterdam, Hope and Company, and the latter took into partnership the great English mercantile house of Baring Brothers; in the second place, it was stipulated that part of the silver should be brought direct from Vera Cruz to England in English ships; and in the third place, the support of the British government was obtained by stressing the English merchants' dire need for specie with which to carry on their East India trade.

It was a relatively easy matter to obtain the cooperation of the United States, which was important both because of the protection afforded by a neutral flag and also because of the United States' proximity to Mexico. In this case, the only serious difficulty arose from the reluctance of the more substantial merchants on the Atlantic seaboard to take part in an enterprise which in the early stages appeared so irregular and hazardous. At first, therefore, it was carried on through New Orleans, which was not only the closest port in the United States to Mexico but also possessed other obvious qualifications for the task in hand. Until 1803 the town had been under the rule of Spain, it had maintained constant communication with Vera Cruz, its commerce had been founded on fraud throughout the Spanish period, and since its annexation to the United States it had become a rendez-vous for adventurers. To the New Orleans of 1806 Ouvrard's scheme must have seemed safe and respectable. At any rate, it was conducted from that base with considerable success for several months. There Hope Brothers was represented by Vincent Nolte, a young Italian-born German whose memoirs, written nearly a century ago, are still our best source of information about the undertaking. In Vera Cruz the company was represented by a former employee in its Amsterdam office, one A. P. Lestapis, who operated there under the name of José Gabriel de Villanueva.

It soon developed that, whatever other advantages New Orleans might possess, its commercial and financial facilities were too limited for so large and complex an enterprise as this, and the main operations were consequently shifted to Philadelphia, New York, and Baltimore. The chief American agent of Hope and Baring was David Parish, a Scottish merchant of Antwerp who was a friend of Talleyrand's and whose father, John Parish, had been the American consul at Hamburg and a friend of that able exponent of the art of mixing business with politics and diplomacy, Gouverneur Morris of Philadelphia and New York.[26]

[26] Nolte, *Fifty Years,* p. 80, 137. Another letter tending to confirm the account in Nolte's book is in the Stephen Girard

One of the first contacts that Parish made in the United States was with the well-established firm of Archibald Gracie and Company of New York; but his first large-scale operations were carried on through the younger firm of Robert and John Oliver of Baltimore and their brother-in-law James Craig of Philadelphia. The spectacular success of their early expeditions disarmed the skepticism of the more conservative merchants, and Parish soon had more business on his hands than he could take care of. The imposition of the embargo at the end of 1807 threatened him with ruin; but he succeeded in persuading Albert Gallatin, the Secretary of the Treasury, to let him send out ships in ballast to bring back the money due him on account of previous shipments.[27] It appears that when the business was wound up in 1811, the profits amounted to more than four million

---

Papers, Letters Received in 1806, David Parish to Stephen Girard, New York, Jan. 18, 1806. Parish wrote: " I have the honor of transmitting [to] you inclosed two introductory Letters from Messrs. Hope & Co. of Amsterdam & Mr. Alexr. Baring of London; you will observe thereby that my voyage to the U. S. is undertaken with a view to attend to the concerns of my own establishment at Antwerp, as well as to those of the house at Amsterdam." Parish further stated that he had arrived in New York " a week ago " from London; that letters should be addressed to him in care of " Mr. Arch[ibal]d Gracie " of New York; and that this letter would be delivered by " Mr. Lestapis," who had been with Messrs. Hope & Co. for several years.

[27] Nolte, *Fifty Years*, p. 139, 140. Parish apparently maintained very friendly relations with the administration. On May 13, 1810, as he was about to sail for Europe, he wrote President Madison offering to take " the deeds you wish to transmit to General Lafayette, with whom I plan to spend some days at La Grange in July or August," and expressing his best thanks to Madison " for the attention & civility I have experienced from you during my stay in America " (Madison Papers, LC, vol. 41).

dollars over and above all expenses and after a considerable sum had been set aside to provide for certain eventualities.[28]

In the history of relations between the United States and Latin America, this episode is important because on the very eve of the wars of independence in Spanish America it quickened the interest of many American political and commercial leaders in that region and multiplied their contacts with it. Interesting evidence on this point is contained in a letter written to Secretary of the Treasury Gallatin in 1807 by Samuel Smith, Baltimore merchant, pillar of the Republican party, and brother of the secretary of the navy Robert Smith. The letter also throws some light on the way in which the plan was carried out.

> You are probably informed [wrote Smith] that Messrs. Hope-Baring & Co., and a House in Nantz, made a purchase from Spain of nine milions to be received at *La Vera Cruz,* payable by six millions in Holland, to enable them to get the silver from thence, further permission was given them of immense advantage—*to wit,* permissions to carry goods to that port subject to the usual Duties. The Silver has already been *all* received, a part brought to the U. S. *in the* following way—Mr. Parish the Agent sold to individuals Bills for the Dollars, the purchasers undertaking all the Expence & Risque at a discount of 17 p c, that is Mr. Parish received 83 here for every 100 in La Vera Cruz— very fast sail[in]g schooners in Ballast have been employed and not one has ever yet been taken.[29]

---

[28] Nolte, *Fifty Years,* p. 172, 173.   On Feb. 12, 1812 Littleton W. Tazewell wrote Secretary of State Monroe from Norfolk giving him information about Parish's manipulation of foreign exchange to the disadvantage of the United States (Monroe Papers, NYPL).

[29] Samuel Smith Papers (LC), draft of letter from Samuel Smith to Albert Gallatin, July 19, 1807, replying to Gallatin's letter of July 17.

V

A comparison of the statistics of the export trade of the United States in 1795-1796, 1800-1801, and 1805-1806 [30] yields some interesting facts about the growth of United States commerce with Spanish America, its value compared with other related branches of commerce, and the shift of United States commerce from the French West Indies to Spanish America, to which allusion has already been made.

These figures show that exports from the United States to Spanish America were four times as great in the year 1800-1801 as they had been five years earlier (that is, as they were just before Spain opened her colonial ports to neutral trade) ; that this trade increased in the next five years in the same proportion as did the total trade of the United States with all foreign countries, despite the fact that during this period the United States acquired Louisiana, which had accounted for one-eighth of its trade with Spanish America in 1800-1801; and that whereas the exports of the United States to the French West Indies declined from $8,409,000 in 1795-96 to $6,745,000 ten years later, United States exports to the Spanish West Indies increased from $1,821,000 at the former period to $10,867,000 at the latter.

Finally, it is a striking fact that in 1805-1806 re-exported foreign goods constituted 60% of the total exports of the United States to all countries, but only 23% of its exports to Spanish America. To put it another way, domestic products of the United States constituted more than twice as large a proportion of its exports to Spanish America as of

[30] *Am. State Papers, Commerce and Navigation*, I, 362 (1795-1796), 489 (1800-1801), and 693-696 (1805-1806).

its exports to all other countries. That is to say, in other fields of foreign commerce the advantages accruing to the United States from the war-time dislocation of world commerce were confined largely to the carrying trade, were in the nature of things transient, and must be expected to lapse with the end of the war; but in the Spanish American field the gains were shared to a much greater extent by American producers—farmers and manufacturers—and they were made in a region—the nearby colonies of a decadent European power—in which the apparent drift towards economic and political liberation warranted the Americans in hoping that a sufficiently sustained and determined effort might make the gains permanent.

The rapid growth of United States trade with Spanish America soon brought about the establishment of the first governmental agencies in that region. During the American Revolution Congress and its committees had appointed a few agents to New Orleans and the West Indies, and because of the emergency, they had been tolerated by Spain, though never formally recognized. At the close of the Revolution they were all either withdrawn or expelled and for nearly fifteen years thereafter the United States had no accrédited agents in any part of Spanish America. Now their presence again became necessary not only for the ordinary despatch of a business that was growing by leaps and bounds but also for its protection against arbitrary and capricious exactions by local officials, who in these chaotic times were becoming difficult to control through diplomatic representations to Madrid, and against the privateers who had begun to swarm in the West Indies.

Appropriately enough, the establishment of these agencies began in 1797, the year in which Spain gave the trade a great impetus by opening its colonial ports to neutrals, and the first agencies were established in New Orleans and Havana, which were then the principal focal points of American commercial and political interest in the Spanish colonies. This was followed in 1798 by the appointment of a consul to Santiago, Cuba, and in 1800 of a consul to La Guaira, Venezuela—the first consul appointed by the United States to South America.[31] Spain still refused to recognize these consuls, declaring as was substantially true, that it was contrary to her settled policy to admit the agents of any foreign government to any of her colonies. She persisted in this refusal even in the case of New Orleans, where the establishment of the American deposit and free navigation of the Mississippi by the treaty of 1795 would have made it prudent as well as just to make an exception to the rule.[32] Again, however, as during the American Revolution, Spain tolerated the presence of these American agents in her colonial ports and her local officials actually permitted them to exercise their functions unofficially.

Thus by the end of 1807 the United States had in large measure realized the hopes of such of its statesmen, financiers, and diplomats as Alexander Hamilton, Robert Morris, and Thomas Pinckney, who had looked forward to the opening of a commercial intercourse with Spanish America that would enrich the United States and enlighten the Spanish Americans. The agents who had carried on this good work were of many diverse kinds, including at one

[31] Roy F. Nichols, " Trade Relations," *loc cit.*, p. 303.

[32] Arthur P. Whitaker, *The Mississippi Question, 1795-1803* (New York, 1934), p. 96, 97. One of many refusals was contained in an order of 1806 relating to Cuba: Archivo del Ministerio de Estado, Madrid, Estados Unidos, legajo 213, Cevallos to Casa Irujo, Jan. 11, 1806 (LC transcript).

extreme African slave traders and at the other apostles of
rational liberty. As a result of their enterprise, mainly in
the past ten years, the contacts between the United States
and Latin America had been greatly increased and vastly
extended; mutual understanding had been promoted and
enticing possibilities of further fruitful enterprise had been
revealed. United States government agencies had been established in some of the colonies, and, either as government
agents or in the prosecution of private ventures, many
Americans—such as William Shaler and Condy Raguet [33]—
who were later to render important service as consular or
diplomatic representatives in Latin America, had already
acquired a first-hand knowledge of that part of the world.
In one way or another, every section of the Union and
most of its principal occupational groups were the gainers
by what was in effect a revolution in the commerce of
Spanish America; and presumably they had an interest in
defending their gains.

VI

It would be a great mistake, however, to think that there
was any approach to unanimity of opinion in the United
States about Latin America, that the United States government had any settled, well defined policy in regard to
Latin America, or even that it had a clear-cut picture of
the region and its people. In the past generation Spanish
studies had made rather rapid progress in the United States
and in part they were directed towards Spanish America;

---

[33] For Shaler, see above in this chapter. Raguet, who was later
to serve the government in Brazil, visited Haiti in 1804, and in
1809 published "Memoirs of Haiti" in the *Portfolio*, vol. I,
series 2, No. 5 (May), and No. 6 (June).

but on the whole the results were meagre. In 1809 Jefferson described Mexico as " almost locked up from the knowledge of man hitherto "; [34] and in 1806 the publication of Washington Irving's translation of Depons' description of Venezuela provided the first modern and trustworthy account in English of any part of northern South America.[35]

In regard to the policy of the United States government towards Latin America in the decade before 1808, that was determined in large measure by the relations of the United States with the mother countries, Spain and Portugal, and with the two great European powers, France and England, that had important interests in America.

Montesquieu is reported to have said that God created the Turks and the Spaniards to hold great empires with insignificance.[36] The phrase suggests the belief, which was widespread on both sides of the Atlantic, that Spain was the sick man of America. From the point of view of the United States, this sick man had from earliest colonial times been an uncommonly disagreeable neighbor. With a zeal for its own imperial interests which was entirely natural but was as naturally resented in the United States, the Spanish government had withheld the recognition of American independence until its recognition no longer mattered; had

[34] See Introduction.

[35] Harry Bernstein, " Las primeras relaciones intelectuales entre New England y el mundo hispánico (1700-1815)," *Revista Hispánica Moderna,* V (1938), p. 8; also see below, Chap. 5, note 1.

[36] In 1789 the Consejo de Indias refused to permit the publication of Clavigero's history of Mexico in Spain unless he removed certain objectionable passages, including one in which he compared " the Spanish with the Turks and the Mexicans with the Greeks oppressed by the Mohammedans " (Lillian Estelle Fisher, *The Background of the Revolution for Mexican Independence* (Boston. 1934), p. 306).

stubbornly contested the American claim to territory on the border of Spanish Florida, and to the navigation of the Mississippi, which reached the Gulf of Mexico through Spanish Louisiana, and had sent the southern Indians to plunder and scalp the frontiersmen of Georgia and Tennessee; had, under heavy pressure, given the United States satisfaction on these points, together with the right of free deposit at New Orleans, by the treaty of 1795, but had then delayed the execution of the treaty for two years; and in 1802 had suppressed the New Orleans deposit in flagrant violation of the treaty, only to restore it a few months later under threat of war.

Although this " Mississippi Question " was at length set at rest by the Louisiana Purchase of 1803, Spain's conduct during the twenty-year controversy over it [37] had only increased the dislike, heavily tinged with contempt, that Americans generally felt for Spain; and while the Louisiana Purchase settled one group of controversies, it immediately raised another group, since the treaty defined the boundaries of Louisiana so vaguely that the United States was able to claim and Spain to deny, that the purchase included Texas and most of West Florida.[38] Indeed, Spain at first denounced the whole transaction as fraudulent; and

[37] Various aspects of the controversy are discussed in the following monographs: Samuel Flagg Bemis, *Pinckney's Treaty* (Baltimore, 1926) ; E. Wilson Lyon, *Louisiana in French Diplomacy, 1759-1804* (Norman, Okla., 1934) ; Arthur P. Whitaker, *The Spanish American Frontier, 1783-1795* (Boston, 1927), and *The Mississippi Question, cit. supra.*

[38] Various aspects of this boundary dispute, and related questions are discussed in the following monographs: Isaac Joslin Cox, *The West Florida Controversy, 1798-1813* (Baltimore, 1918), and Philip Coolidge Brooks, *Diplomacy and the Borderlands: The Adams-Onís Treaty of 1819* (Berkeley, 1939).

although it soon withdrew its protest and delivered Louisiana to France for transfer to the United States, it did so
only under pressure from Paris. On the heels of this came
the passage of the Mobile Act, by which the United States
asserted (though it did not for the time being attempt to
exercise) jurisdiction over a part of West Florida in pursuance of the Louisiana Purchase. The Spanish court's indignation boiled over and it prepared for war, even going so
far as to issue contingent instructions for the seizure of
American ships at Havana in advance of the declaration of
war.[39]

In 1804 Spain was again dragged into war on the side of
France against England, with results that further increased
the tension between the governments of Spain and the
United States. Briefly, the situation was this: The renewal
of the Anglo-Spanish war revived the prospect, which had
seemed so fair in 1798, that British sea-power might
be used to conquer or to revolutionize Spain's American
colonies and again the prospect stirred into action many
Americans who hoped to share in the gold and glory of the
enterprise. The two most important episodes that grew out
of this situation were Francisco de Miranda's use of New
York as the starting-point for his revolutionary expedition to
northern South America [40] and Aaron Burr's transformation

[39] Archivo del Ministerio de Estado, Madrid, Estados Unidos,
legajo 213, Cevallos to Casa Irujo, April 12, 1806 (LC transcript).
This order was based on a recent letter from Valentín de Foronda,
consul general of Spain in the United States, stating that 600 ships
from the United States entered the port of Havana every year
(AHN, Est., legajo 5543, extract of Foronda's letter and draft of
the order of April 12, 1806 to Casa Irujo and a similar order to
Captain General Someruelos of Cuba).

[40] William Spence Robertson, *The Life of Miranda* {2 vols.,

of the purpose of his protean conspiracy from the disruption of the Federal Union into an attack on Spanish Florida, Texas, and Mexico.

Neither scheme was officially endorsed by the government of the United States; but both won considerable support among its people, since they appealed not only to adventurers, but also to patriots, at a time when the outbreak of war between the United States and Spain was momentarily expected. Thus, William Smith, son-in-law of a former president, John Adams, was implicated in Miranda's scheme; and Andrew Jackson, whose loyalty to the United States cannot be seriously questioned, openly conferred with Burr about the projected attack on the hated Dons, at whose hands Jackson and his fellow westerners had suffered so much in the past two decades. While the United States government discountenanced such activities, the measures it took to suppress them were so tardy and, on the whole, ineffectual that the Spanish minister Marqués de Casa Irujo protested against its course with a violence which provoked Secretary of State Madison into severing relations with him.[41] Though the Spanish court warmly approved of what he had done, it had to transfer him, and during the rest of the period before the Napoleonic intrusion Spain's only official channels of communication in the United States were through the Spanish consul general and the French Minister.

Chapel Hill, N. C., 1929), I, 293-327. The same author's earlier study is still useful: *Francisco de Miranda and the Revolutionizing of Spanish America* (*American Historical Association Annual Report*, 1907 (Washington, 1909), I, 189-540).

[41] Charles E. Hill, " James Madison," in Samuel Flagg Bemis, ed., *The American Secretaries of State and their Diplomacy* (10 vols., New York, 1927-1929), III (1927), 69, 70.

Relations between the United States and Spain thus remained in a dangerous state of tension throughout most of the period from the Louisiana Purchase to Napoleon's invasion of Spain five years later; but neither side really wanted war. This was partly because they had their hands full with the problems that already confronted them as a result of the titanic struggle betwen France and England. It was also because of the keen but equivocal interest that both France and England took in Spanish American affairs, for this made it likely that Spain and the United States would expose themselves to incalculable risks if they took up arms against each other.

The risk to Spain was obvious. From 1796 to 1802 and again from 1804 to 1808, she was allied with France in the war against England, whose increasing preponderance at sea was crowned by Nelson's crushing defeat of the allied navies at Trafalgar. Thereafter the French alliance, which was already unsatisfactory from many other points of view, was worthless for the defence of Spanish America. Consequently, if Spain went to war with the United States and the latter decided, in Jefferson's phrase of 1802, to marry itself to the British fleet and nation, there was little or nothing Spain could do to prevent them from appropriating as much of Spanish America as they chose and emancipating the rest.

For the United States, a war with Spain at that time seemed almost equally hazardous. Whether or not it led to an open alliance with Great Britain, it would array the United States against Napoleon, and if he should defeat the British—as then seemed entirely possible—the United States would have to face him single-handed in his hour of victory. Of course it was equally possible that the British might win; but the bitter memories of the American Revolution were still so fresh and the subsequent relations between the mother country and its former colonies had been so troubled that many Americans distrusted Great Britain quite as much as they did Napoleon.

Strong though this Anglophobia was, an alliance with Great Britain had much to recommend it to the United States from the point of view of power politics, if only because it would have given the United States reasonable assurance of acquiring the Floridas, for which Hamiltonians as well as Jeffersonians had been clamoring for many years past. It was never adopted, however, for most of the American people realized that their country was too weak to play the game of power politics. In this case it could not even have begun to play the game without running counter to its own predilections and policies—for one thing, to Jefferson's passion for peace, and, for another, to his earlier dictum that decadent Spain should be left in possession of her American colonies, since they could not be in better hands until the United States was ready to take those that it needed. Above all, the game was open to the objection that it would in all probability result in the transfer of a considerable part of Spanish America to mighty Britain and thus postpone indefinitely that expulsion of Europe from America to which Americans were already looking forward.

And so, despite a keen mutual antagonism that was sharpened by a multitude of irritating incidents on land and at sea, the United States and Spain avoided war with each other and kept their duel on the plane of diplomatic bickering. On this plane the main question at issue was that of the boundaries of Louisiana and the most important stake seemed to be the favor of Napoleon. His influence was paramount at Madrid and, since it was he who had procured

Louisiana from Spain and sold it to the United States, he might be presumed to be the best authority on the territorial extent of the property thus conveyed. For several years Napoleon played the two rivals off against each other. How and why he did so need not be told here, for the growing preponderance of British sea power gave an increasing air of unreality to this whole transoceanic negotiation between France, Spain, and the United States, until its utter hollowness was exposed and the terms of the problem were profoundly altered by Napoleon's invasion of the Iberian peninsula.

In the period brought to a close by that epochal event, the diplomatic relations between the United States and Spain had not been marked by the settlement of any of the outstanding issues between them or indeed by any new development of enduring significance. Confused and inconclusive as they were, however, these relations brought out more clearly than ever before one fact of great importance in shaping opinion and policy in the United States, namely, the fact that Spanish America, which was a region of increasing concern to the United States, was closely bound to Europe, not only to Spain but also, through Spain's European alliances and rivalries, to the greatest powers in Europe—to England as well as to France. In other words, Spanish America was not a mere colonial dominion of a third-rate European power but an integral part of the European system—a system from which American policy under Washington, Adams, and Jefferson was clearly tending to remove the United States. That the republic should now be brought back within that system through the back door of Spanish America was not a pleasant prospect and yet the revolutionary changes which were clearly impending in that region seemed to show that the only alternative to this reinvolvement would be for the United States to isolate itself from Spanish America as well as from Europe. Until 1808 the policy-makers at Washington were not forced to face this dilemma, but events were making it increasingly probable that they would have to do so before long.

The relations of the United States with Portugal in this period can be described more briefly, for they involved no great controversy and they were much less important to the United States than its relations with Spain and Spanish America, despite the fact that it carried on a not inconsiderable trade with Portugal and that the latter's huge colony of Brazil was potentially one of the most attractive fields for American enterprise in all Latin America. To be sure, formal diplomatic relations did exist between the two countries. Though the United States had only half a dozen legations in all Europe in 1807, one of these was at Lisbon, and it was one of the very first established by the new republic, dating from Washington's first administration.[42] Nevertheless, it was the least important diplomatic post in the foreign service of the United States, partly because British influence was still paramount at Lisbon, as it had been for a century past. Another obstacle to closer relations was the language difficulty, for while Thomas Jefferson, James Monroe and many other Americans knew Spanish, very few of them understood Portuguese. For our present

[42] The first American minister to Portugal was David Humphreys, who was sent there in 1790 as a special agent and was appointed minister resident in 1791—the first diplomat of that grade appointed under the Constitution, the others being chargés d'affaires. He was sent to Lisbon partly in order " to obtain a right of sending flour there ": Frank L. Humphreys, *Life and Times of David Humphreys* (2 vols., New York, 1917), II, 22, 93-96.

purpose, perhaps the most important fact about the diplomatic relations between the two countries down to 1807 was that they had been maintained continuously and on a friendly footing for some time past, with the result that when the Portuguese court fled to Rio de Janeiro late in that year it was an easy and natural thing for the United States to send a minister to the new capital in Brazil; and this minister [43] was the first formal diplomatic agent of the United States who ever resided in Latin America.

VII

Of Jefferson's Latin American policy as it had developed by 1808, we can say little more than that he had begun to cast speculative glances at Florida, Cuba, and even Mexico, that he was ready to oppose the transfer of an American colony from one European power to another, and that he was more disposed to use government agencies for the promotion of foreign commerce than adherents of the agrarian-capitalist hypothesis seem willing to admit. But peace was still his passion and even, we might say, his policy. The extensive interests that the United States had built up in Latin America were the result of a situation which, though it had lasted for the better part of ten years, was highly abnormal and must come to an end some day. No one could say what new situation might arise in its place, and without such knowledge it would have been very difficult to frame any policy, even if Jefferson's administration had had a less compelling passion for peace and had not shared the general inclination of democratic governments to let the future take care of itself. Even the simple policy of preserving the

[43] Thomas Sumter, Jr., who in March 1809 was commissioned to the Portuguese court residing at Rio de Janeiro. Manning, *Dip. Cor.*, I, 5, note 2.

status quo in Latin America would not have been altogether satisfactory to the United States, for throughout the period under consideration it had been excluded from direct contact with the largest of all the Latin American colonies— Portuguese Brazil.

The situation would hardly have been clarified if Jefferson had made a thorough canvass of public opinion as a guide to national policy. As the experience of the next few years was to prove, there was no simple division of opinion on economic lines, such as " agrarian " and " capitalist-commercial," [44] for the sharpest conflicts occurred within the agricultural group and the commercial group. Nor was there any clear-cut division on party lines, for debates on Latin American policy found Federalist arrayed against Federalist and Republican against Republican.

The confusion was increased by the clash between the few rudimentary ideas that the people of the United States had about the political and social character of their strange southern neighbors. For lack of a better basis, most of these ideas were based on tradition, prejudice, and inference. On the one hand, the " Black Legend " of Spanish cruelty, despotism, and duplicity, so generally accepted in the United States since early colonial times, created a widespread prejudice against the Spanish Americans, who were, it was noted, Spanish as well as American; and they were as overwhelmingly Roman Catholic as the people of the United States were Protestant, and at that time Protestants in the United States regarded Roman Catholicism and obscuran-

[44] As is well known, the agrarian-capitalist antithesis runs through *The Rise of American Civilization* (New York, 1927) by Charles A. Beard and Mary Beard. The former subsequently made a specific application of it to the history of the territorial expansion of the United States in his book, *The Idea of National Interest* (New York, 1934), Chap. 3.

tism as virtually interchangeable terms. John Adams doubtless voiced the opinions of many of his countrymen when,
apropos of Francisco de Miranda's plan of 1797-1798 for
liberating Spanish America, he remarked contemptuously
that you might as well talk about establishing democracies
among the birds, beasts, and fishes as among the Spanish
American people.[45]

On the other hand, many of Adams's countrymen believed
that the Latin Americans, like the rest of mankind, were
naturally good and needed only to be free in order to
reveal their innate virtue. Many also believed that there was
a special virtue in the New World and all its people—a
special virtue which, again, would reveal itself as soon as
the shackles of bondage to Europe were struck off.[46]

The problem of policy itself contained a confusing
dilemma presented by the world situation. If the status
quo in Latin America were disturbed, the result might only
be to transfer the Spanish and Portuguese colonies to
France or England. In 1797 the latter actually seized the
strategically and commercially important Spanish island of
Trinidad near the coast of Venezuela, and in 1806 and
1807 tried to seize the Plata region as well, occupying
Buenos Aires and Montevideo for a considerable period.
The transfer of the Latin American colonies to either
France or England would from many points of view be a
decided change for the worse; but if the status quo were

---

[45] Robertson, *Life of Miranda*, II, 246, quoting Adams. Another hostile view was expressed by Timothy Pickering (leading
New England Federalist and secretary of state under Washington
and Adams) who wrote in 1799 that the Spanish Americans were
" corrupt and effeminate beyond example ": " Historical Index to
the Pickering Papers," *Mass. Hist. Soc. Collections,* 6th series, VIII
(Boston, 1896), 471, index of letter from Pickering to J. Trumbull.

[46] For a further discussion of this question, see below, Chap. 6.

maintained, the restoration of peace in Europe might be expected to bring with it the restoration of the Spanish monopoly (the Portuguese monopoly had never been broken). That in turn would mean the destruction of a branch of the United States' trade, which, between 1796 and 1806, had grown from three per cent to twelve per cent of its total export trade, had become an important link in the trade to China, the East Indies, and Smyrna,[47] was the principal source of supply of specie, and provided employment for scores of ships and important markets for the products of both farm and factory.

In short, by 1807 the United States knew that it had a large stake and a great opportunity in Latin America, but it did not yet know how to go about protecting the one or exploiting the other.

[47] The importance of this Latin American trade and its ramifications constituted one of the reasons for the rejection of the treaty negotiated with England in December 1806 by James Monroe and William Pinckney. Samuel Smith, who was then in the good graces of the administration, was consulted about the treaty by Secretary Madison. Replying in two letters of April 3 and 15, 1807, he pointed out how the treaty would injure the trade of the United States with the Spanish colonies and, through them, with other parts of the world, for example, between China and the French and Spanish colonies; between Buenos Aires and Havana; between the French and Spanish colonies and the Mediterranean, especially Smyrna; and between Asia and Manila, whence Asiatic goods, brought in American ships, were forwarded to Peru. He also spoke of the value of Spanish America as a source of specie for the China trade of the United States, and said that "the export from the U. S. to the Spanish Islands and to their possessions on the Pacific & Atlantic, of E. India goods is important, the loss of which would be felt." Smith's slashing attack on the treaty may help explain why it was not even submitted to the Senate. See Edward Channing, *History of the United States,* III (New York, 1917), 359-362 for a discussion of the negotiation, and further references. For the Smyrna trade, see Samuel Eliot Morison, "Forcing the Dardanelles in 1810," *New England Quarterly,* I (1928), 208-225.

CHAPTER TWO

THE LARGE POLICY OF 1808

Napoleon's invasion of the Iberian peninsula was quickly followed by developments that offered the United States great political and commercial advantages in Latin America. When Napoleon placed his own brother, Joseph Bonaparte, on the throne at Madrid, many Spaniards flew to arms against the "intruder King" and, encouraged by their resistance, England sent an army to join them in driving the French out of the Iberian peninsula. Thus was begun in 1808 the Peninsular War which started Wellington on the road to fame and Napoleon on the road to St. Helena.

I

For the next five years Spain was riven by a struggle that was both an international conflict between France and England and also a civil war between two factions of the Spanish people. One of these factions, the so-called *afrancesado* or "Frenchified" party, supported Joseph Bonaparte and was supported by the French army. The other, the patriot party, supported a government set up in the name of Ferdinand VII and was supported by the British army. Both of these rival governments claimed authority over the Spanish American colonies, but neither exercised it effectively and the chief result of this conflict of authority in Spain and consequent turmoil in America was the inauguration of a period of unprecedented freedom, both political

39

and commercial, for the orphaned Spanish colonies.[1] For all practical purposes, this period of divided loyalties and new-found freedom marks the beginning of the independence movement in Spanish America.

For Brazil, too, this period marked the beginning of the process of liberation; but here the process followed a very different pattern, for it was carried out under the auspices of the old ruling house of Portugal—the house of Braganza—and it was more gradual and far more orderly and peaceful than in Spanish America. On the approach of Napoleon's army the Portuguese Prince Regent, more prudent than the Spanish Bourbons, fled to America, under British protection. Taking the court and the machinery of government with him, he established his capital at Rio de Janeiro, where it remained until several years after Napoleon's downfall. Under the force of these circumstances and British persuasion, the Prince Regent signalized his arrival in Brazil by throwing it open to trade with all friendly nations. Thus at one stroke was destroyed the old Portuguese monopoly, which was never revived; and this measure was followed by others which, little by little, struck off the remaining badges of colonial servitude until in 1815 the process was virtually completed by the formal elevation of Brazil to the rank of a kingdom on a footing of equality with Portugal, to which it was henceforth bound only by common subjection to the same king.[2] The final step, the

[1] A comprehensive but compact account of this subject is contained in a recent work by a leading Chilean scholar, Domingo Amunátegui Solar, *La Emancipación de Hispano-América, cit. supra.* For an extended account of the background and early stages, see vol. V of the cooperative *Historia de la Nación Argentina,* ed. Ricardo Levene (Buenos Aires, 1936–, in progress).

[2] Manoel Oliveira Lima, *Dom João VI no Brazil, 1808-1821*

severance of the personal union with Portugal, was not taken until 1822; but from the beginning of its gradual emancipation in 1808, the situation in Brazil, as well as in Spanish America, developed along lines that were favorable to the interests and policy of the United States—lines that tended towards greater economic and political freedom and the identification of Brazil with the American rather than the European system.

It was not in Brazil but in the orphaned colonies of Spain that the authorities at Washington first sensed the golden opportunity created for their country by Napoleon's invasion of the Iberian peninsula. That the earthquake in Spain and the responsive tremors in Spanish America created a great opportunity for the United States is no new discovery: Jefferson and his cabinet were not slow to recognize the fact and record their recognition of it, and fifty years ago Henry Adams gave this part of the intricate Jeffersonian record a prominent place in his classic history of that period. But did he give it its proper place?

According to Adams, when Jefferson was confronted by the great events of 1808 in Spain, his first thought was that they might enable the United States to force a favorable settlement of its bitter dispute with Spain over the Louisiana Purchase and other questions. In Adams's own words, Jefferson was " so deeply mired . . . in the ruts of his

---

(2 vols., Rio de Janeiro, 1908), is still the standard account of this subject. See especially vol. I, chap. XI, " Elevação do Brasil a reino." The relations of Brazil with Britain and the United States in this period are discussed in two standard works of a more general character: Lawrence F. Hill, *Diplomatic Relations between the United States and Brazil* (Durham, N. C., 1932), and Allen K. Manchester, *British Preeminence in Brazil* (Chapel Hill, N. C., 1933).

Spanish policy and prejudices that he could not at once understand the revolution which had taken place in Spain . . . his first thought was selfish," and this thought was: " Should England make up with us, while Bonaparte continues at war with Spain, a moment may occur when we may without danger of commitment with either France or England seize to our own limits of Louisiana as of right, and the residue of the Floridas as reprisals for spoliations." [8]

That was in August 1808. Two months later, says Adams, Jefferson had been brought " to wider views," and on October 22 he and his cabinet agreed to authorize the agents of the United States to say unauthoritatively to influential persons in Cuba and Mexico:

". . . Should you choose to declare your independence, we cannot now commit ourselves by saying we would make common cause with you, but must reserve ourselves to act according to the then existing circumstances; but in our proceedings we shall be influenced by friendship to you, by a firm feeling that our interests are intimately connected, and by the strongest repugnance to see you under subordination to either France or England, either politically or commercially."

A week later Jefferson rounded out his policy by instructing Governor Claiborne of Louisiana:

[8] Henry Adams, *History,* IV, 339, 340. Jefferson's letter to the Secretary of War (Henry Dearborn), dated Aug. 12, 1808, from which this passage is quoted is in the Jefferson Papers (LC), vol. 180, which also contains a similar letter of the same date from Jefferson to the Secretary of State (James Madison) and the Secretary of the Navy (Robert Smith). The course had been suggested in a letter that Albert Gallatin, Secretary of the Treasury, wrote Jefferson from New York on Aug. 5, 1808. The letter is printed in Henry Adams, *Writings of Albert Gallatin* (3 vols., Philadelphia, 1879), I, 400.

" If they [the Spanish patriots] succeed [in their resistance to Napoleon], we shall be well satisfied to see Cuba and Mexico remain in their present dependence, but very unwilling to see them in that of France or England, politically or commercially. We consider their interests and ours as the same, and that the object of both must be to exclude all European influence from this hemisphere." [4]

Jefferson's concluding statement—that the object of both the United States and the advocates of independence in Spanish America " must be to exclude all European influence from this hemisphere "—is one of the most important made by any American statesman in the whole period covered by this book. We shall have occasion to recall it more than once in the following pages, and, as we shall see, in 1823 the idea suggested by it emerged full-fledged in the Monroe Doctrine.

Here, however, our immediate concern is with Henry Adams's critique, and the first thing we note about it is that he misunderstood the passage, for he understood Jefferson to say that it was the object of both the United States

[4] Adams, *History*, IV, 340-341; Isaac J. Cox, " The Pan-American Policy of Jefferson and Wilkinson," *Miss. Valley Hist. Rev.*, I (1914), 212-239; Louis Martin Sears, *Jefferson and the Embargo* (Durham, N. C., 1927), p. 117-118. On Oct. 1, 1808, shortly before Jefferson made this statement to Claiborne, General James Wilkinson wrote him from Carlisle, Pa., that the " grandest spectacle in nature " would be the " liberation of the American continent " from European shackles and the formation of a " distinct community." The letter is in Jefferson Papers (LC), vol. 181. Earlier in the year the administration had considered and rejected the idea of promoting a revolution in Spanish America, which, it seemed at that time, would play into the hands of Great Britain: National Archives, SD, Instructions to Ministers, Madison to John Armstrong (Minister to France), July 22, 1808. These instructions are not printed in Manning, *Dip. Cor.*

and *the Spanish patriots* to exclude all European influence from this hemisphere. A careful reading of the passage makes it perfectly plain that Jefferson was not guilty of any such absurdity. He was addressing himself not to the Spanish patriots but to their antagonists in America who were seeking to emancipate the colonies from control by any authority in Spain—from the authority of the Spanish patriots as well as that of the rival Spanish government under Joseph Bonaparte. Jefferson's statement referred directly to the advocates of independence in Cuba and Mexico, and, by implication, to those in the rest of Spanish America. What he was saying to them was in effect that the new states of Spanish America should not be content merely to win their independence from Spain, and that they had a common interest with the United States in making all of America independent of all of Europe.

Adams had even less sympathy with Jefferson's policy than understanding of it. " In private," he complains, " Jefferson avowed that American interests rather required the failure of the Spanish insurrection. . . . In truth, Jefferson and the Southern interest cared nothing for Spanish patriotism."

" In the Eastern States [he continues], the Democratic and Southern indifference toward the terrible struggle raging in Spain helped to stimulate the anger against Jefferson. . . . The New England conscience, which had never submitted to the authority of Jefferson, rose with an outburst of fervor toward the Spaniards, and clung more energetically than ever to the cause of England,—which seemed at last, beyond the possibility of doubt, to have the sanction of freedom. Every day made Jefferson's position less defensible, and shook the confidence of his friends." [5]

[5] Adams, *History*, IV, 342-343.

Brilliant though this analysis is, it does not carry conviction. There is something bizarre about the picture of Puritan New England bursting with fervor for Roman Catholic Spain, and even the invocation of the New England conscience leaves some room for doubt whether the freedom of Spain had a higher claim to the support of the United States than did the freedom of Spanish America. The question raised by the analysis is all the more interesting because, either directly or by inference, the statements of Jeffersonian policy quoted with no little disapproval by Adams anticipate several of the policies that won widespread acceptance in the United States in Jefferson's lifetime and have continued to enjoy it to this day. These policies were encouragement to Latin America in establishing and maintaining its independence, opposition to the transfer of an American colony from one European power to another, resistance to the extension of the commercial as well as the political influence of any European power in America, and, as the ultimate object, the exclusion of all European influence from the western hemisphere.

The best that Adams could find to say for these policies was that " to President Jefferson the Spanish revolution opened an endless vista of democratic ambition "; and that this was not said in praise of Jefferson's folly is evident from Adams's concluding observation that " every ·day made Jefferson's position less defensible and shook the confidence of his friends." It would be no difficult matter to show that Jefferson's position was at least as defensible as that of his New England critics, for, as everyone knew, the Spanish patriots on whose side they were so eager to throw the influence of the United States were fighting to restore to the throne of Spain an absolute monarch of the decadent Spanish House of Bourbon. How the restoration of the Spanish Bourbons would advance the cause of freedom even in Spain was not self-evident. That it would deal a heavy blow to freedom in Spanish America could hardly be doubted; and it was as certain as anything could be that it would do serious harm to the national interests of the United States, if only by strengthening the hand of Spain in the boundary disputes in which the two powers had been engaged since the Louisiana Purchase and by severing the many commercial contacts that the United States had established in the ports of Spanish America from Havana and Vera Cruz to Buenos Aires and Valparaiso.

The really remarkable thing is not that Jefferson preferred his own Spanish American policy to the one endorsed by the New England conscience and Henry Adams, but that, having adopted this policy, Jefferson and his chosen successor, Madison, did not follow it. This fact Adams failed to note. His failure is rather surprising, for he fully appreciated, and even exaggerated, the importance that Jefferson attached to this matter. " The independence of the Spanish colonies," said Adams, " was the chief object of American policy [at the end of Jefferson's administration] "; [6] and he was aware that Madison's administration was fully committed to Jefferson's Spanish American policy, since Madison himself was the chief member of the cabinet that had unanimously agreed to that policy as recently as October 1808.

As every schoolboy knows, neither Jefferson nor Madison carried out the large policy of 1808; rather, they followed a course which sacrificed most of the continental interests envisaged in it as well as many of the national interests that

[6] *Ibid.*, p. 342.

the United States had built up in Spanish America in the decade from 1797 to 1807. Indeed, the United States was so far from profiting by the golden opportunity of 1808 that, by the time peace was restored in 1815, it had lost much ground not only in Spanish America but in the whole of Latin America. Why it failed to seize an opportunity so clearly perceived by its leaders, why it failed to follow the large policy designed by them for this occasion, and what alternative course it followed in relation to Latin America until the end of the European struggle that had created the opportunity, are the questions to which the rest of this chapter and the following chapter will be addressed.

The main factors which prevented the fulfilment of the large policy of 1808 were the embargo, the growth of the Peninsular grain trade, the Madison administration's flirtation with the project of cooperation with France in revolutionizing Latin America, the rise of the War Hawks, and the War of 1812. Though these measures and developments have been named approximately in the chronological order in which they occurred, there was some overlapping in point of time and a close causal relationship between them; and they are less important in themselves than because they represent certain deep-seated divisions of interest and opinion in the United States which profoundly affected its policy towards Latin America.

II

The first of these factors, Jefferson's embargo, was, of course, already in effect when the president and his cabinet formulated their large policy towards Latin America in October 1808. The significance of the embargo in relation to this policy lies mainly in the fact that the upheaval in the Iberian peninsula created a situation full of potentialities for harm as well as for advantage to the United States; that by an unlucky coincidence, Jefferson's embargo went into effect just as Napoleon was beginning the invasion which caused this upheaval; and that both in the United States and in Latin America the embargo tended to develop the potentialities for harm contained in the Iberian upheaval and to prevent Jefferson from reaping its advantages. His large policy might have been crowned with success if he had pursued it energetically, if he had had the united support of the American people and if, in this crucial period, the United States had been in a position to extend the numerous contacts that it had already made with Latin America; but none of these conditions was fulfilled. In the United States the embargo strengthened and embittered the existing hostility to Jefferson's administration—a hostility that almost inevitably involved his Latin American policy in its condemnation of all things Jeffersonian—while in Latin America the embargo greatly reduced American contacts at the very moment when they most needed to be multiplied; and yet Jefferson clung tenaciously to this untimely measure. Under its influence the revolution in the Iberian peninsula contributed to the defeat of the policy which it had done so much to call forth.

If, as Henry Adams asserted, the independence of the Spanish colonies had been " the chief object of American policy " in these concluding months of Jefferson's administration, the administration would surely have done all it could to hasten the repeal of the embargo; but it did nothing of the sort. Though this policy was clearly formulated by October 1808, the embargo was not repealed until February 1809 and even then the policy was not an appreciable factor in bringing about the repeal.   Thus at the very time when the relations of the United States with Latin America most needed to be multiplied, the administration stubbornly adhered to a measure which, if enforced, would have severed them almost completely.   To make matters worse, Great Britain was rapidly extending its relations with Latin America at this very time.   The new market compensated in large measure for the market temporarily lost in the United States and to this extent deprived the embargo of effect.[7]

The net result of Jefferson's course, which he adhered to until the very end of his administration, was that, instead of forwarding his professed purpose of excluding European influence from Latin America, it tended strongly to transfer control of Latin America from two of the weakest powers in Europe, Spain and Portugal, to the most formidable of them all, Great Britain.   It is hardly necessary to say that Jefferson did not do this out of love for the British.   He did it because, contrary to Henry Adam's assertion, his chief interest lay not in Spanish America but in domestic problems in the United States and its relations with France and England.   Next after these came his interest in the border dispute with Spain over Florida and Texas.   Whatever he may have said, and whatever thought he may have had about the future, his deeds shows that for the present Spanish America trailed far behind these other interests in his estimation.

The course of Jefferson's administration in this crisis can not be attributed to its failure to see how adversely the

[7] Sears, *Jefferson and the Embargo*, p. 192, 193, 282-285, 299.

embargo was affecting its policy towards Latin America
and the whole nexus of American interests in that region,
for the point was made abundantly clear by members of
Congress in the debate on the embargo that began in November 1808, the month after the policy was formulated.
Timothy Pitkin of Connecticut, James Lloyd of Massachusetts, and other senators and representatives told how
the embargo had wiped out the lucrative carrying trade of
the United States to Latin America; how it had kept large
supplies of American beef, flour, meal, and cotton from
reaching their accustomed markets in the West Indies as
well as England; and how the continuation of the embargo
was theatening to make this injury to American interests
permanent by teaching the West Indies and England to
obtain from Latin America the foodstuffs and raw materials
that they had formerly obtained from the United States.[8]

It remained for Barent Gardenier, New York representative, to sketch the largest and most sombre view of the
pernicious effects of the embargo and the whole policy of
Jefferson's administration on the relations of the United
States with Spanish America. Speaking on December 13,
1808, he warned that if Napoleon should conquer Spain,
the Spanish colonies in America would at once become independent and, thanks to Jefferson's bungling, the new states
would be cordial allies of Great Britain.

We shall have in them, of consequence [he continued]
hostile and dangerous neighbors; while Great Britain will
monopolize their trade, and if our present difficulties continue, perpetually instigate them to hostility against us. All
this might have been prevented, if, in relation to Spain only
[i. e., the Spanish empire] our government had pursued the

[8] *Annals of Congress,* 10 Cong., 2 Sess., p. 21, 23, 24, 32-33,
134-135, 184-185, 809, 1215, 1217-1219.

proper course. The merchants applied for leave to resume their commerce with Spain, but a deaf ear was turned to them. Disposed as Great Britain is to do us harm, she may yet make use of the Spaniards on this continent for that purpose. And though the Spaniards have long been considered as contemptible, let it be remembered that a nation is always regenerated by a revolution. . . . It is not perhaps even now too late to retrieve the advantages the Administration have overlooked. A change of conduct may regain us the affections and friendship [of Spanish America] which have been unnecessarily lost. And this, sir, is to be more desired, when we look forward to what is likely to be the situation of the European continent if Spain is conquered. It will then be subject to the will and despotism of Napoleon. . . . It will be here, then, on this regenerated continent [that " the arts of peace "] may hope to find repose and protection.[9]

Long though it is, this passage is well worth quoting. It expresses a belief in the coming independence of Spanish America, a realization of the importance of that event to the United States, indignation at Jefferson's failure to take advantage of the opportunity that the situation offered the United States, and fear of Great Britain as the chief rival of the United States in Latin America. It also expresses a nascent sense of the solidarity of the regenerated American continent—regenerated by the revolution in Spanish America—and of the essential difference between this emergent New America, dedicated to the arts of peace, and war-torn, dictator-ridden Europe. Gardenier's words are particularly interesting because they were spoken at so early a stage of the independence movement in Latin America— another two years was to elapse before the first formal

[9] *Ibid.*, col. 848-849. This speech was made on December 13, 1808. A year earlier, a letter believed to have been written by Gardenier and published in the *New York Evening Post* " began the cry of French influence " (Adams, *History*, IV, 203).

declaration of independence was made there. His words are also interesting because, while he was a Federalist and was speaking in opposition to an administration that was accused of subservience to France, he himself voiced as strong an antagonism to Great Britain as to France, and because his antagonism to the British was based on their rivalry with the United States in Latin America.

When the embargo was at last repealed early in 1809, the revival of the foreign commerce of the United States led to the resumption and extension of its relations with Latin America. At the same time, however, the revival had the rather unexpected result of building up an important branch of trade which diverted enterprise from Latin America and tended to divide opinion and weaken policy in regard to that region.

This new development was the rise of the Peninsular grain trade—a term used to denote the shipment of foodstuffs from the United States to the Iberian peninsula for the use of civilians and the French and British armies, mainly the latter. The peninsular route was also used to screen an indirect trade with Great Britain and France when direct trade with them was forbidden by one or another of the British orders, French decrees, and acts of Congress that signalized the commercial warfare of that period.[10] The increase in the United States exports to Spain and Portugal was very great both in dollar value and in proportion to its exports to other regions. In the year ending

[10] Anna C. Clauder, *American Commerce as Affected by the Wars of the French Revolution and Napoleon, 1793-1812* (Philadelphia, 1932), p. 228-229; W. F. Galpin, "The American Grain Trade to the Spanish Peninsula, 1810-1814," *Am. Hist. Rev.*, XXVIII (1922), 24-44, and *The Grain Supply of England during the Napoleonic Period* (New York, 1925), chap. 8.

in October 1807 (just before the embargo went into effect) the value of its exports to Spain and Portugal was about $2,000,000; in 1811, it was about $12,400,000—a six-fold increase. In 1806, the domestic exports (excluding foreign goods re-exported) of the United States to Spain were worth less than one-fifth as much as its exports to Spanish America (figures for Brazil are not available, since its ports were not open to foreign trade); in 1811, domestic exports from the United States to Spain and Portugal were worth more than three times as much as those to Latin America (Brazil and the Spanish colonies, including the Spanish West Indies and Florida as well as the continental colonies).[11]

No less important than the money value of this trade was the nationwide distribution of its sources of supply in the United States. The principal articles were flour, corn and corn meal, and rye meal; and rice, beans, pork, and tobacco were sometimes included. The flour and corn came mainly through Philadelphia and Baltimore from their hinterlands in Pennsylvania, Maryland and Virginia, and through New Orleans from the Ohio Valley; the rice from South Carolina and Georgia; and many of the ships that carried these cargoes came from New York and New England. This gave every quarter of the union a direct interest in the lucrative Peninsular trade.[12]

---

[11] Am. State Papers, *Commerce and Navigation*, I, 696 (1807), I, 892 (1811).

[12] On Nov. 21, 1808, Senator James Lloyd, Jr., of Massachusetts discussed the trade with Spain and Portugal and concluded that it was "more equally divided among the different portions of the Union, than any other trade which is prosecuted from the United States to any part of Europe" (*Annals Cong.*, 10 Cong., 2 Sess., p. 34).

Moreover, the trade was invested with a moral grandeur seldom associated with traffic in flour and pork. Most of these foodstuffs were destined for the stomachs of Wellington's British soldiers and their Spanish and Portuguese allies who, it was easy to believe, if you had these things to sell, were fighting for the freedom of mankind against Napoleon's tyranny. This view of the Peninsular War was probably strongest in maritime New England, but it also existed in the other commercial centers of the United States. For example, in 1809 a New York writer [13] declared, " If Spain should ultimately succeed in baffling the attempts of the usurper [Bonaparte], the benefits resulting to herself, to Europe, and to the world would be incalculable." Specifying these benefits, he said that the victory of the Anglo-Spanish forces would " augment the aggregate of productive industry and commercial enterprise throughout the whole world " and " most materially " promote the cause of civil liberty.

This writer went on to say that the war in Spain would very probably promote the independence of Spanish America; [14] but as time passed it became increasingly apparent that a sharp antagonism existed between those in the United States who were mainly concerned with the Iberian peninsula and those who were mainly concerned with Latin America. Whether consciously or not, the former were drawn towards a policy of peace, friendship, and cooperation with England and its ally, the patriot government in Spain; while the latter were drawn towards rivalry with England in Latin America, encouragement of

[13] John Bristed, *Hints on the National Bankruptcy of Britain, and on Her Prospects to Maintain the Present Contest with France* (New York, 1809), p. 393-394.

[14] *Ibid.*, p. 398-399.

Spanish American independence, and conflict with the patriot government in Spain which claimed the allegiance of the Spanish Americans.

III

Out of this situation there arose in James Madison's first term (1809-1813) a divergence between the national administration and a large part of what was known as the commercial interest (which included farmers producing for the export market). This interest, forgetting the opportunities in Latin America that its spokesmen had so eloquently described in the debates preceding the repeal of the embargo, concentrated more and more on the Peninsular trade, with the implications for foreign policy noted above. Madison's administration, on the other hand, took up the Jeffersonian policy towards Latin America where Jefferson had left off and by 1811 had carried it to a more advanced point than it was to reach again for another decade. Madison, too, accepted the implications of his position for foreign policy, and, as we shall see, one of the most interesting consequences of this was a tendency towards cooperation with France in Latin America—a cooperation that almost developed into concerted action with France in promoting Latin American independence.

When Madison became president he was already committed to the large policy of 1808, which he had approved while secretary of state, and he apparently accepted it unreservedly. Once in office, he was pushed farther along the same road by the character of his chief advisers on foreign affairs, as well as by the logic of events. These advisers were his two secretaries of state, Robert Smith and James Monroe, and his secretary of the treasury, Albert Gallatin.

The unaided force of Robert Smith's talents and personality might have had little influence with Madison; but his brother Samuel Smith was a power in the Republican party at that time and a Baltimore merchant who was engaged in trade with Latin America.[15] This family connection may help explain why the first agents of the United States to the insurgent governments of Spanish America were sent while Robert Smith was secretary of state.[16]

James Monroe, who followed him in that office, represented another of the important factors shaping the forward policy of that period towards Latin America, for Monroe was a devout republican and was fired by a missionary zeal for propagating the republican faith in foreign parts. When he was in Spain on a special mission in 1805 he learned the Spanish language, but that was about all he gained by his mission; and his unhappy experience with the Spanish Bourbon court at that time had given him no reason to like official Spain or to look with favor on the maintenance of Bourbon authority in Spanish America.

Albert Gallatin had experienced a change of heart since 1798 when, in one of the great speeches of that generation,[17] he made a slashing attack on the whole system of commercial treaties and diplomatic connections. For now he cooperated whole-heartedly in sending commercial and other agents of the United States to Latin America to obtain

[15] See above, Chap. 1.

[16] See below, Chap. 3.

[17] Henry Adams, *Life of Gallatin* (Philadelphia, 1879), p. 197. The speech was made on March 1, 1798, nominally in answer to Federalist attacks on Jefferson's Mazzei letter. Adams regards this speech and Fisher Ames's speech on the Jay treaty as representing the high-water mark of Republican and Federalist oratory (*ibid.*, p. 198).

commercial treaties and occasionally he took the initiative in suggesting new diplomatic missions. Perhaps this was only a logical consequence of the idea of the separation of America from Europe, which he had made the main theme of his speech of 1798 [18] and which, as further developed, was to appear as the doctrine of the two spheres in Monroe's message of December, 1823. At any rate he continued under Madison, as he had commenced under Jefferson, to encourage trade with Latin America and to play an important part in shaping the policy of the United States towards that region.[19]

One of the first important questions that Madison's administration had to decide was whether the United States should insist upon the right of its citizens to continue to trade with the insurgent Spanish Americans. The question first arose in 1809 with reference to the colonies that resisted the authority of the Bonapartist government of Joseph I, mainly because it was feared that, in the interest of his brother, Napoleon would insist upon the suppression of such commerce, as he had already tried to suppress the commerce of the United States with the rebellious French colony of Haiti. Without waiting for the demand to be made, Robert Smith informed General John Armstrong, the American Minister at Paris, that it would be worse than useless for France to make it, since it would only endanger

[18] *Ibid.,* p. 269.

[19] For one illustration of this, see above, note 3. For another, see Adams, *Writings of Gallatin,* I, 483-484, letter from Madison to Gallatin, Aug. 22, 1810, in which the former states that the latter's hints in regard to Sumter and the relations between Brazil and Spanish South America have been attended to. Thomas Sumter, Jr., was the first minister of the United States to the Portuguese court at Rio de Janeiro. See above, chap. 1, note 43.

the peace of the two countries.[20]   A few days later he stated his position even more uncompromisingly, informing Armstrong that France need not hope to obtain the prohibition of United States trade with Spanish America even by offering to arrange a favorable settlement of the Florida-Texas boundary controversy for it.[21]

This soon proved to be an academic question, for France and Bonapartist Spain found the United States the best channel for communication with Spanish America.   Their agents [22] made so much use of it for that purpose that as early as January 1810 Luis de Onís,[23] the unrecognized

[20] Manning, *Dip. Cor.*, I, 3, Smith to Armstrong, April 27, 1809.   The original instructions (National Archives, S. D., Instructions to Ministers, vol. 7) contain a paragraph, omitted in Manning's extract, which begins: " The ground on which such a pretension, in relation to St. Domingo was combatted, will appear in the copies herewith forwarded. . . ."

[21] Manning, *Dip. Cor.*, Smith to Armstrong, May 1, 1809.

[22] According to Onís, early in 1810 there were fifty of these agents in Baltimore: William Spence Robertson, *France and Latin-American Independence* (Baltimore, 1939), p. 69. Further information on this subject is contained in *ibid.*, chaps. III and IV, *passim*, especially p. 79-85, on the mission of Jacques d'Amblimont.

[23] For a brief account of Onís's previous career, see Philip C. Brooks, *Diplomacy and the Borderlands: The Adams-Onís Treaty of 1819* (Berkeley, Cal., 1939), p. 13-14.   His career in the United States is discussed at length in this book, and more briefly in Charles C. Griffin, *The United States and the Disruption of the Spanish Empire, 1810-1822* (New York, 1937).   In 1816 George W. Erving wrote that Felix Merino, his former secretary in Seville, who was now employed in a Philadelphia counting house, had made it his business to gather information about the character of Onís (who lived a large part of the time in Philadelphia), and that " the anecdotes which he (Merino) has related to me go to prove that Onís is as *wicked* as a man in his situation can be." Erving then told of an attempt that had been made some eighteen months earlier to assassinate Manuel Torres (see below, Chap. 5) and said that, incredible as it might seem, the circumstances sug-

minister of the Spanish patriot government in the United
States, wrote the officers of that government in South
America warning them to be on their guard against all
ships coming from this country and suggesting that they
make an example of a few in order to put the fear of God
into the rest.[24]

A month later Onís went so far as to charge that the
American government itself was conniving with these Bonapartist agents in an effort to make Joseph the master of
Spanish America and was determined to form an alliance
with France, Russia, Denmark, and Sweden, and to go to
war with England.   Perhaps, he said, the alliance had
already been formed; at any rate, it explained John Quincy
Adams's mission to Russia, whither he was going by way
of Stockholm and Copenhagen.[25]

---

gested that Onís was implicated in the attempt (Monroe Papers,
NYPL, Erving to Monroe, Jan. 4, 1816, letter marked " Private &
confidential ").

[24] AGN, BA, Archivo del Gobierno de Buenos Aires, *tomo* 42,
Onís to the Viceroy of Buenos, Jan. 5, 1810, *duplicado*.   Onís
repeated this advice in a letter of Jan. 26, 1810, and asked the
Viceroy of Buenos Aires to pass it on to the Viceroy of Peru and
the Captain General of Chile, to whom, said Onís, he himself had
no means of communicating it (*ibid.*).   Somewhat milder measures to this effect had already been taken at Buenos Aires (*ibid.*,
Viceroy to the Marqués de Casa Irujo, Spanish ambassador at Rio
de Janeiro, Jan. 5, 1810, draft).

[25] *Annals Cong.*, 11 Cong., 3 Sess., p. 1273-1274, message from
Madison to Congress, enclosing a translation of a letter from Onís
to the Captain General of Caracas, Feb. 2, 1810.   According to
Onís, Gallatin, mistaking a certain loyal Spanish colonial official
for a revolutionary agent of France, merely because he had come to
the United States by way of Mexico and Havana, offered him
certain revolutionary documents and tried to employ him as an
agent in uniting the Spanish American insurgents with the United
States, with the promise that if the union were effected the seat
of government would be moved near them or even located among
them.

Mistaken though it was in some details, Onís's account of Madison's policy was essentially correct, for Madison was following a policy in relation to Latin America which tended towards cooperation with France in that region,[26] and this cooperation in turn carried the administration farther along the road that led to war with England in 1812. Even with regard to Russia, Onís's account was not wholly belied by subsequent events for in 1812 the American consul at St. Petersburg, Levett Harris, made a strong bid for Russian support of the cause of Latin American independence. Harris not only transmitted to the Russian foreign secretary an appeal for aid from Luis López Méndez, deputy of the Caracas government at London, but also inspired him with enthusiasm for the cause. In this he was aided by an American merchant then residing at the Russian capital, Cortland L. Parker, who had lived at Caracas for several years and was later to be American consul at Curaçao.[27] The Russian minister communicated his enthusiasm to the Tsar Alexander I who—according to Harris— was restrained only by the cautious advice of his council of state from taking immediate action in favor of the Spanish American patriots.[28]

[26] Robertson, *France and Latin-American Independence*, p. 84, 86, 93-95.

[27] See Chap. 4.

[28] Monroe Papers (NYPL), Levett Harris to James Monroe, Secretary of State, St. Petersburg, May 1-13, 1812, enclosing a copy of a letter from Harris to " Louis Lopez Mendez Esqr. Deputy of the independent Provinces of South America at the Court of London," March 19-31, 1812.   Monroe received the despatch on Dec. 27, 1813.   As early as 1808 Madison wrote that Harris " is considered as standing well [in St. Petersburg] and has received more than ordinary marks of attention even from the Emperor himself " (National Archives, SD, Instructions to Ministers, Madison to William Short, Sept. 8, 1808).

CHAPTER THREE

CROSS CURRENTS

Onís's prophetic analysis of American policy was written early in 1810. Its early fulfillment seemed to be indicated by the great quickening of American interest in Latin America that occurred in the same year. The increase was a natural consequence of developments in the Spanish colonies. The independence movement, which had unfolded hesitantly so long as the outcome of Napoleon's invasion of Spain seemed in doubt, now gained many adherents as his armies overran province after province until by 1810 the patriot government held only a small corner of southern Spain. With one of the two governments of Spain thus reduced to impotence and the other cut off from direct communication with America, the Spanish American colonies had to shift for themselves. The results were bewilderingly diverse. For instance, in Mexico a government loyal to the Spanish Bourbons was maintained in spite of a spectacular uprising of the Indians led by Miguel Hidalgo y Costilla; in Venezuela and Chile independence was openly declared and briefly achieved under creole leadership, only to be suppressed after a short interval by royalist reactions; and in Buenos Aires creole leadership overthrew Spanish authority definitively in 1810, although the independence of that city and the rest of modern Argentina was not formally declared until 1816.

I

In the period 1810-1812, the events that have attracted most attention from historians are those relating to the border region in dispute between Spain and the United States. Among these events were Madison's seizure of the Baton Rouge district of West Florida in 1810, and the filibustering and revolutionary activities that kept the Louisiana-Texas frontier in a turmoil throughout the period.[1] More important in the larger perspective of policy, however, were two other developments: the extension of United States agencies in Latin America, and a strong trend towards rivalry with Great Britain, and cooperation with France, in Latin America.

The year 1810 was signalized by the first systematic effort of the United States to extend its agencies in Latin America. Such agencies were badly needed, for at this time it had only one formal diplomatic representative in that region, its minister to the Portuguese court at Rio de Janeiro, Thomas Sumter, Jr.; and even in Brazil it had only one consul, Henry Hill at São Salvador (Bahia).[2]   The

[1] For example, Adams, *History*, V, 305, after describing briefly the chaos in Spain in 1810 and its disastrous effect on the Spanish empire, says: " England and the United States, like two vultures, hovered over the expiring empire . . . England pursued her game over the whole of Spanish America . . . while the United States for the moment confined their activity to a single object "—that is, to the acquisition of West Florida, to which Adams devotes the remainder of this chapter (p. 305-315). The agents sent to South America in this year are not discussed; the name of the most important of them, Joel Poinsett, does not appear in the index. The same thing is true of the sketch of Robert Smith, Secretary of State 1809-1811, by Charles C. Tansill, in Bemis, ed., *American Secretaries of State*, III, 151-197. Julius W. Pratt's sketch of Monroe, Secretary of State 1811-1817, *ibid.*, p. 201-277, broadens the view somewhat, but only to note that Monroe was "deeply interested" in the Spanish colonies and gave some encouragement to revolutionary agents in the West Indies and Mexico (*ibid.*, p. 247).

[2] *Am. State Papers, Commerce and Navigation*, I, 820, list of

need was greatest in Spanish America and it was here that Madison's attention was now focussed.

In this period three types of agents were employed by the United States in Latin America: special agents, agents for commerce and seamen,[3] and consuls. Those in the first group were appointed to perform some specific mission, usually of brief duration. To this group belonged General James Wilkinson, who in 1809 was instructed to stop at Havana on his way by sea from New Orleans to Baltimore and inform the captain general of Cuba that the United States would take appropriate steps to prevent either Cuba or Florida from being used for military purposes by any of the European belligerents except Spain herself.[4] If the mission was also intended to promote the independence movement among the Cubans, the results did not encourage the extension or repetition of it. Other special agents were General George Mathews and Colonel John McKee who in 1811 were authorized to accept, in behalf of the United States, that part of West Florida still remaining in the hands of Spain, if the Spanish governor were disposed to

---

" consular or commercial agents " of the United States in foreign countries, transmitted by Secretary of State Robert Smith on April 26, 1810, in accordance with a resolution of the House of Representatives of April 23, 1810. This Henry Hill should not be confused with another of the same name who served as vice-consul in Chile. The latter was the author of *Recollections of an Octogenarian* (Boston, 1884), and *Incidents in Chili, South America, 1817-1821* (Weymouth, Mass., n. d., c. 1895). His career in Chile is described in Eugenio Pereira Salas, *Henry Hill, comerciante, vice-consul y misionero* (Santiago, Chile, 1940).

[3] Henry M. Wriston, *Executive Agents in American Foreign Relations* (Baltimore, 1929), *passim*, discusses the various types of agents with great learning. The functional classification that I have adopted differs somewhat from his.

[4] *Ibid.*, p. 531-533; Cox, *West Florida Controversy*, p. 289-293.

surrender it peaceably, and to seize East Florida if a foreign power seemed likely to attempt its occupation.[5]   Obviously, both of these missions departed widely from ordinary diplomatic and consular procedure; the Florida mission was a consequence of the determination of President Madison, supported by an act of Congress, that this neighboring Spanish colony should not be transferred to any foreign power; and Wilkinson's Cuba mission was in part an earlier and less formal expression of the same policy.

The second group, agents for commerce and seamen, was substantially identical with the group of agents that the United States had maintained in the Spanish colonies—at Havana, New Orleans, and La Guaira, Venezuela—during the American Revolution and again in the period beginning with the Spanish toleration of neutral commerce in 1797.   Agents of this class were appointed under an act of Congress of 1796 for the protection of American seamen in foreign ports; and, as John Quincy Adams later said, they were sent to ports to which regular consuls were not admitted—in other words, they were consuls in a very thin disguise.[6]   With the beginning of the independence movement in Spanish America, they also took on a quasi-diplomatic character.

In 1810 the growing interest of the United States in

[5] Wriston, op. cit., p. 533-537.

[6] Worthington C. Ford, ed., Writings of John Quincy Adams (7 vols., New York, 1913-1917), VII, 478, Adams to R. C. Anderson, May 27, 1823: "This office of commercial agent is a substitute for that of consul in ports where consuls cannot be admitted, or to which from whatever cause they cannot be sent." For the employment of such agents in the period before 1808, see the brief discussion in Chap. I and the excellent detailed account in the article by R. F. Nichols cited in note 5 of that chapter.

Latin America led to the appointment of three agents who were ostensibly of this kind: William Shaler to Havana and Vera Cruz, Robert K. Lowry to La Guaira, and Joel Roberts Poinsett to Buenos Aires, Chile, and Peru. As their instructions [7] show, their first duty was to foster the commercial interests of the United States; but Shaler and Poinsett were also instructed, in view of the possibility that Spanish America might " dissolve altogether its colonial relations to Europe " to " diffuse the impression that the United States cherish the sincerest good will towards the People of Spanish America as Neighbors " and that it would " coincide with the sentiments and policy of the United States to promote the most friendly relations, and the most liberal intercourse between the inhabitants of this hemisphere." The Secretary of State who sent these first commercial agents of the United States to Latin America was Robert Smith, brother of the Baltimore merchant, Samuel Smith.

To the third group, regular consular agents to Spanish America, belonged Joel Poinsett, whose original appointment was changed in 1811 to that of consul general to Buenos Aires, Chile, and Peru,[8] and the vice-consuls who

[7] Manning, *Dip. Cor.*, I, 6-7, Secretary of State Robert Smith to Joel Poinsett, June 28, 1810. Manning, unable to find the original instructions, reproduced a copy of them contained in a report of the House of Representatives. The original is in the Poinsett Papers in the Historical Society of Pennsylvania. It contains a reference to West Florida omitted from the copy in Manning. Shaler's appointment is discussed in Roy F. Nichols, " William Shaler, New England Apostle of Rational Liberty," *New England Quarterly*, IX (1936), 75-77. Lowry appears to have been a mere commercial agent without political function (Wriston, *Executive Agents*, p. 413).

[8] Poinsett did not present his commission as consul general to the

were appointed to assist him in Buenos Aires and Chile. The appointment of these consular officials at this early date is all the more interesting because, at a later period, Adams refused to receive a consul from one of the unrecognized Latin American countries on the ground that such action might seem to commit the United States to recognition.[9]

It was unquestionably a great advantage to the United States to have its agents in Brazil and Spanish America, for their presence was both an aid to American commerce and a positive, though moderate, expression of political sympathy that was not forgotten by Latin America when independence was established. But they were on the whole unsuccessful in their rivalry with British agents; some of them, especially Shaler and Poinsett, were guilty of serious indiscretions.[10]   Moreover, it was soon charged that some of these agents were making improper use of their official positions to enrich themselves and their associates.   The

Buenos Aires government until Sept. 3, 1814; but in the meanwhile his title had been the subject of controversy between that government and the American vice-consul, W. G. Miller.   The objections of the former were based partly on the fact that the commission (including Chile and Peru as well as Buenos Aires) was too vague and general (AGN, BA, S1-A2-A4, No. 8, Spanish translation of a letter from W. G. Miller to the "Exma. Junta," etc., Dec. 28, 1811, and ensuing correspondence; *ibid.*, Spanish translation of Poinsett's commission as consul general, with a notation to the effect that it was presented to the Ministry of State, etc., on Sept. 3, 1814).

[9] Manning, *Dip. Cor.*, I, 88, Adams to Monroe, January 28, 1819.   The case referred to by Adams was complicated by other considerations: see Samuel Flagg Bemis, *Early Diplomatic Missions from Buenos Aires to the United States, 1811-1824* (Worcester, Mass., 1940, reprinted from *Proc. Am. Antiquarian Soc.*), p. 83.

[10] For Shaler, see the article by Roy F. Nichols cited above, note 7.   For Poinsett, see below in this chapter.

charge was almost inevitable; for the consular agents, both regular and disguised, received no salary but only the fees of the office,[11] with the result that such posts usually had to be filled with men who had business interests in Latin America. Even after its revival under Madison's administration, the large policy was still starved by republican frugality.

Madison also permitted revolutionary agents from Spanish America to reside in the United States, held unofficial correspondence with them and did not prevent them—any more than he prevented the unrecognized Spanish minister Onís [12]—from purchasing munitions in this country and shipping them to their respective governments. From Buenos Aires came Diego de Saavedra and Juan Pedro de Aguirre; from Venezuela, Telésforo de Orea and Juan Vicente Bolívar, brother of the future liberator, Simón Bolívar, who was in England at the same time on a similar mission; from Mexico, José Bernardo Gutiérrez de Lara; from Cuba, José Alvarez de Toledo; and from Cartagena (in what is now Colombia), Manuel Palacio Fajardo.[13]

[11] *Annals Cong.*, 11 Cong., 1 Sess., p. 1998, April 27, 1810, report from Secretary of State Smith showing that salaries were paid only to the consuls in Algiers, Tripoli, Tunis, and Morocco, and stating that all the other consuls and commercial agents were allowed to receive only the fees of office established by Congress.

[12] As early as Sept. 6, 1810, the first United States agent to Venezuela, Robert K. Lowry, transmitted to the State Department a protest from the revolutionary government of that country against the shipment of arms by Onís from Philadelphia to the Spanish authorities at Maracaibo (Manning, *Dip. Cor.*, II, 1145).

[13] Charles C. Griffin, *The United States and the Disruption of the Spanish Empire*, p. 50-55, where these missions are discussed in some detail, with references. Important additional information about some of them is contained in the following: Nichols, "Wil-

The experiences of the agents from Buenos Aires and Venezuela provide an interesting illustration of the connection between United States commerce and the independence movement in Latin America. In March 1811 Joel Poinsett wrote the State Department from Buenos Aires recommending the appointment of one William G. Miller as resident consul at that place. He described Miller as a young man of very respectable connections in Philadelphia; and from other sources we know that these connections were mercantile.[14] When the Buenos Aires agents, Saavedra and Aguirre, left for the United States three months later (June 1811), they carried with them Miller's draft on John Allen of Philadelphia for $3515, and they arrived at New York in the sloop *Tiger*, the cargo of which was consigned to John Jacob Astor, subject to the order of this John Allen.[15]

The main purpose of these Buenos Aires agents was to

liam Shaler," cited above, note 7, for Gutiérrez de Lara; Robertson, *France and Latin-American Independence,* for Palacio Fajardo; and Samuel Flagg Bemis, *Early Diplomatic Missions,* for Saavedra and Aguirre. For Orea and J. V. Bolívar, see Carraciolo Parra-Pérez, *Historia de la primera república* (2 vols., Caracas, 1939), p. 328-330, 349.

[14] Poinsett Papers, HSP, vol. I, Poinsett to Secretary of State Smith, March 9, 1811; *ibid.,* Poinsett to Gallatin, same date and tenor, adding that Miller " possesses the language and is a good merchant."

[15] AGN, BA, S1-A2-A4, No. 9, copy of the instructions to Saavedra and Aguirre, June 5, 1811, and several letters from them to the Junta, the first dated Philadelphia, Oct. 19, 1811, and the last, Buenos Aires, May 19, 1812. A penetrating account of the mission, based on the foregoing sources and others, is contained in Bemis, *Early Diplomatic Missions,* p. 8-16. He points out that the first communication from the Buenos Aires government to the United States government was dated two days before Poinsett's arrival in Buenos Aires (*ibid.,* p. 8).

obtain military supplies for their government. They first got in touch with Manuel Torres, a Spaniard with Colombian connections who had been living in Philadelphia since 1796, and with the merchant prince Stephen Girard and the Venezuelan agent, Telésforo de Orea. The three agents from South America now formed a kind of joint purchasing agency and tried to obtain a large credit from Girard for the purchase of 20,000 muskets. He had already furnished Orea and his associate, Vicente Bolívar, with supplies to the value of a cargo of coffee and indigo that they had brought with them; but that account was now balanced and Girard would do nothing more than write James Monroe, who was now Secretary of State, asking whether the United States government would help provide the muskets desired by the South Americans. When Monroe failed to reply Girard dropped the matter.[16] The Buenos Aires agents then decided to go it alone. Employing the Philadelphia mercantile house of Miller and Van Beuren— which doubtless represented the "very respectable connections" in that city of young William G. Miller of Buenos Aires—they purchased 1000 muskets from "sundry gunsmiths" in Philadelphia. In May 1812 they returned to Buenos Aires with these muskets and a generous supply of 372,050 flints as the principal fruit of their long and expensive mission to the United States.[17]

Several of the missions from the United States to Spanish America and vice versa have an interesting history; but space does not permit them to be described in detail here. They were important mainly because they paved the way for closer relations in the future; and their immediate signifi-

[16] McMaster, *Stephen Girard*, II, 163-171.
[17] See note 15.

cance lay mainly in the light that they threw on the attitude of the government and people of the United States toward Latin America in this early stage of the independence movement and on the conditions affecting the relations between the two regions. For this purpose the mission of the Buenos Aires agents to the United States and Poinsett's mission to South America were probably the most enlightening, although conditions varied so greatly from one region of Latin America to another that each of these missions illuminated some fresh aspect of the problem and all of them would have to be considered in a complete account of it.

The mere fact that these missions were sent exhibited a tendency on the part of the United States and Spanish America to draw together as soon as the ties that bound the latter to Spain were relaxed. Yet almost without exception the experience of the missions revealed the obstacles in the way of a closer rapprochement. Thus, while the United States government wanted Spanish America to become independent, it would not supply the Buenos Aires government with guns with which to win its independence. Again, while such American merchant princes as Astor and Girard were eager to develop trade relations with independent Spanish America, they were loath to take the risks involved in doing so. Even Girard, who professed deep sympathy for the Spanish American patriots and advertised his liberalism by giving his ships such names as *Voltaire* and *Rousseau,* excused himself from extending further credit to Vicente Bolívar on the ground that to do so would be contrary to his business principles.[18]   And when Gutiérrez de

[18] McMaster, *Girard,* II, 167. For information about Girard's ventures in the *Rousseau, Voltaire,* and *Montesquieu* to Buenos

Lara came to the United States seeking recruits for the army that was to liberate Mexico, only a handful of the many who had proclaimed their devotion to the cause of Mexican independence joined his standard.

Conversely, the agents of the United States in Latin America suffered a variety of disappointments. For an example of these we may again turn to Poinsett's South American experience.[19] In Chile, where most of his time was spent, he gave military aid to the patriots in their war with the royalists although he was the agent of a government that was neutral in the contest. His conduct may perhaps be excused on the ground of hypothetical verbal instructions or advice from the authorities at Washington before his departure; but he made the worse mistake of taking part in the factional strife among the patriots, with

---

Aires, Montevideo, and Valparaiso in 1810 and 1811, see *ibid.*, p. 111, 146-161. These ventures related in part to the Canton trade. Some additional information about them is contained in the Girard Papers (Girard College Library, Philadelphia). The card index of these papers indicates that Girard's trade with Latin American ports was most active in the period 1809-1811, but also continued through the War of 1812 and the decade following it. Among the places with which he had commercial connections and correspondence were Havana, Vera Cruz, Rio de Janeiro, Montevideo, Buenos Aires, Valparaíso, Santiago, and Callao.

[19] See J. Fred Rippy, *Joel Roberts Poinsett, Versatile American* (Durham, N. C., 1935), Dorothy M. Parton, *The Diplomatic Career of Joel Roberts Poinsett* (Washington, D. C., 1934), and references in these two works. Another account of the subject, by Charles Lyon Chandler and Edwin J. Pratt, based on a very thorough study of the sources, is in course of publication in the *Revista chilena de historia y geografía* (Santiago), which has already published two instalments of it in LXVII (1935), 37-52, and LXXXVIII (1940), 295-309, bringing the narrative down to 1811.

the result that his mission ended in failure and left a heritage of widespread dislike of the United States in that part of Latin America. Ill considered though his action was, it illustrated the difficulties that lay in the way of any American agent in that remote region, where it was difficult to obtain advice, and almost impossible to obtain support, from the home government.

II

Another result of Poinsett's experience, which was still more disquieting because it was shared by other American agents in Latin America at this time, was his discovery that Great Britain was winning from the patriot governments commercial favors that were not shared by the United States. Her success in this respect was all the more impressive and disturbing because she was already the well-rewarded friend and ally of the regency in Spain against which the Spanish American patriots were rebelling.

Thus, in 1811 Poinsett protested against the recent action of the Buenos Aires government in according preferential treatment to British ships; whereupon that government replied acknowledging the discrimination and stating plainly that it had been granted to Great Britain as a reward for the resolute refusal of the British naval forces in the Plata to tolerate the blockade of Buenos Aires which the royalists at Montevideo were trying to maintain.[20] Later in the same year, the United States agent at La Guaira, Venezuela, reported that in this region, too, British commerce enjoyed preferential treatment, which took the form

[20] AGN, BA, S1-A2-A4, No. 8, Poinsett to " The Most Excellent Junta at Buenos Aires," Feb. 18, 1811, and draft of the Junta's reply, Feb. 25, 1811.

of a 25% reduction of all import and export duties.[21] In Brazil, which formed the third of the three grand divisions of Latin America at that time—the other two being insurrectionary and royalist Spanish America—the British were already consolidating an ascendancy which was almost complete and which endured for many years. In short, it was by now apparent that the British were extending their influence in every quarter of Latin America, at the expense of the United States as well as all other foreign nations. This development was so contrary to the large policy of 1808 and to the hardly less ambitious policy which Madison was now following that we must pause to see how it had been accomplished and how it affected the subsequent course of Madison's administration in regard to Latin America.

For Great Britain as well as for the United States, Napoleon's invasion of Spain spelled a golden opportunity. The Spanish upheaval converted Britain from the worst enemy of the Bourbon monarchy into its best friend, and, with an ingenuity that commands admiration, Britain contrived to play the difficult double role of best friend to Spanish America as well. In both roles, as we have had occasion to note, she was aided by her chief rival in America, the United States, which obligingly gave her a head start by keeping the embargo in force for a year after Napoleon's intrusion began.

For our present purpose, special interest attaches to the extension of British contacts with insurgent Spanish America. These were multiplied through the free port system

[21] Manning, *Dip. Cor.*, II, 151, Robert K. Lowry to Monroe, Aug. 21, 1811.

already established in the Caribbean region [22] and through the British warships stationed in other Spanish American waters, such as the Plata basin, between Buenos Aires and Montevideo. There British naval officers not only broke blockades and otherwise protected British merchant ships on the high seas (which they liberally interpreted as extending up the Plata estuary to within gunshot of the shore at all points) but also intervened with the local authorities to obtain alterations of municipal law in favor of British commerce.[23] British merchants, shut out of the European continent and the United States, grasped at these opportunities eagerly and sometimes with more zeal than foresight or knowledge of local conditions. For example, they soon glutted the Buenos Aires market with their wares, among which, in apparent imitation of the Darien Company and forgetfulness of its famous fiasco, they included warming pans and skates.[24]

Such incidents, however, were not of a kind to displease Spanish American purchasers and were only temporary and very minor interruptions of the forward sweep of British

[22] See discussion of this system in Chap. 1.

[23] For example, letters to this effect were addressed to the Buenos Aires authorities by Robert Ramsay, commanding H. M. S. *Mistletoe,* and by Captain P. Heywood of H. M. S. *Nereus* on July 10, 1810, and June 28, 1811, respectively (AGN, BA, S1-A2-A3, No. 3, *carpeta* "1811 a 1848: Inglaterra. Varios "). On Heywood, see Edward Tagart, *A Memoir of Peter Heywood* (London, 1832, cited in J. Fred Rippy, *Rivalry of the United States and Great Britain over Latin America, 1808-1830* (Baltimore, 1929), p. 10), and C. K. Webster, *Britain and the Independence of Latin America, 1812-1830* (2 vols., London, 1939), I, 83-85.

[24] AGN, BA, S1-A2-A3, No. 3, copy of petition (in Spanish) by certain British merchants of Buenos Aires, dated June 28, 1811, and addressed to the President and members of the provisional *Junta de gobierno* of Buenos Aires.

influence. Evidence of this was given by the commercial privileges which the British obtained at Buenos Aires, La Guaira, and elsewhere, and which, in most cases, they kept for many years to come. For reasons that are easy to understand, the insurgents encouraged the multiplication of contacts with Great Britain, sometimes with so much zeal as to embarrass the latter, and at the same time that they sent agents to the United States, they also sent agents—who were often persons of greater distinction—to London.

One case [25] of this kind furnished an opportunity for an admirable exhibition of tight-rope walking on the part of the British government in its dual role of best friend to both the patriot government in Spain and the insurgents in America. In the winter of 1810-1811 Matías Irigoyen came to London on behalf of the Buenos Aires government seeking aid for the revolutionists of the Plata region. To please the Spanish government, the British refused to receive or aid him officially; but to please the insurgents they permitted him to obtain arms and money from private sources and the foreign secretary, Viscount Wellesley, even gave him a letter recommending him to the protection of Lord Strangford, British minister at Rio de Janeiro.

Irigoyen probably owed his life, and certainly his freedom, to this letter, for upon his arrival at Rio the Portuguese authorities arrested him and were about to turn him

---

[25] The following account of the case is based on transcripts from the Public Record Office (London), preserved in the Instituto de Investigaciones Históricas, Buenos Aires. The principal documents are: F. O., Portugal and Brazil, 63/101, Marquis Wellesley to Lord Strangford Jan. 19, 1811; *ibid.*, 63/103, Lord Strangford to Marquis Wellesley, July 3, 1811; *ibid.*, same to same, Oct. 6, 1811; and F. O. Spain, Capt. P. Heywood to Vice Captain General Elío (Montevideo), Aug. 8, 1811, enclosing copies of two letters from Elío to Heywood, dated July 31 and Aug. 2, 1811.

over to the Spanish viceroy at Montevideo for punishment as a deserter from the Spanish army when Strangford persuaded them to release him and let him proceed to Buenos Aires. This was done, said Strangford, in order that Irigoyen might have an opportunity to convince the people of Buenos Aires of the fallacy of expecting Britain to aid them in their system of separation from Spain. The fallacy seems to have escaped their attention when Irigoyen reached home safely with his cargo of British arms. What they did not fail to note was that he had received aid from the British people and protection from the long arm of the British government.

In Brazil, even more than in Spanish America, the events of 1808 conspired to promote the commercial and political influence of Britain. Until then, the British along with all other foreigners had been denied direct contact with Brazil; British goods had reached the Brazilian market only by way of Lisbon, and the Portuguese court had made at least a feeble effort to maintain its political independence by playing off French against British influence. All this was changed by the flight of the Braganzas to Rio de Janeiro, where they were far beyond the reach of Napoleon and were held in a firmer grasp than ever by Britain.

As we have already seen,[26] the refugee court signalized its arrival in Brazil early in 1808 by opening the ports of that country, which was still a colony, to commerce with all friendly powers. This measure was adopted not only because it accorded with the liberal economic ideas entertained by the Portuguese court [27] as well as in Brazil at that

[26] Chap. 1.
[27] Oliveira Lima, *D. João no Brazil,* I, 62-63, where Abbé Raynal is represented as the main source of these ideas.

time and because it seemed an excellent means of consolidating colonial sentiment in favor of the court, but also
because it was demanded by Britain. And, indeed, while
the proclamation opened the ports of Brazil to all friendly
powers, the power chiefly benefited by it was Britain, for
the commercial connections which she had long since
maintained with Brazil by way of Lisbon gave her a head
start over all other competitors in the newly opened market.

This advantage was greatly increased by the commercial
treaty negotiated at Rio in 1810 by the British minister,
Lord Strangford. He was a formidable champion of British
imperial interests and his career in Brazil has been compared to that of more recent British pro-consuls, such as
Cromer [28] in Egypt and Curzon in India. The comparison
is probably a just one; at any rate, his treaty of 1810 [29]
obtained for his nation extensive privileges which, though
not fully appreciated at the moment, formed a firm basis for
its hegemony in Brazil. This was done at the expense of all

[28] *Ibid.*, I, 374. Enrique Ruiz Guinazú, *Lord Strangford y la
revolución de Mayo* (Buenos Aires, 1937) is a thorough study of
his mission in relation to Buenos Aires. Beginning with 1812, his
mission is discussed, and some of his correspondence printed, in
Webster, *Britain* (consult index).

[29] Oliveira Lima, *op. cit.*, I, 376-391, 395-397. Two important
advantages obtained by the British in this treaty were (1) preferential tariff treatment (they paid a 15% duty on European goods
imported into Brazil; all other nations paid 24%), and (2) an
extra-territorial court ("*Juiz Conservador da Nação Britannica*").
Sumter reported that the treaty was more favorable to Brazil than
to England (Manning, *Dip. Cor.*, II, 674, Sumter to Smith, Feb. 5,
1811), and Oliveira Lima, *op. cit.*, I, 395-397, points out that
its operation was less advantageous to Britain than had been expected; but the fact remains that under it Britain consolidated her
economic predominance in Brazil. See also Roberto Simonsen,
Historia economica do Brasil, II, 244-261, and references there.

foreign nations, including the United States, and even of Portugal itself; and the hegemony thus established was maintained for more than thirty years, until in 1844 the imperial Brazilian government made a revolutionary change in the foreign trade policy of that country.

These developments had an important bearing on the Latin American policy of the United States, for, in the Latin American scene as viewed from Washington, Brazil occupied a position that was often prominent and sometimes pre-eminent. It was the largest of all the Latin American countries in area and the second largest in population; and its great land mass occupied then, as it does now, a position of great strategic importance, for the Spanish countries of South America form a fringe around its northern, western, and southern borders, and at its eastern extremity, which juts far out into the Atlantic, it is closer to the Old World than any other country in America.

At that time Brazil was close to the Old World politically as well as geographically. It was still linked to Portugal and governed by the old Portuguese house of Braganza, which in turn was linked by marriage to other royal families of Europe—principally the Spanish Bourbons and the Austrian Hapsburgs—and had been accompanied in its flight to America by a swarm of Portuguese noblemen and their families. A decade after the period with which we are now concerned, Brazil was to become a supporter of the American system and inter-American solidarity; but at this time it was one of the main strongholds of European influence in America and its ties with Europe were being reinforced by the success of Strangford's efforts to bring it under the hegemony of Britain.

III

The case of Brazil has been discussed at considerable length because it provides a vivid illustration of the way in which, from the point of view of Washington, the whole Latin American situation was deteriorating in the early years of Madison's administration, and because of the effect that his realization of this painful fact had on the development of his Latin American policy from 1810 until he wrecked it by going to war with England in 1812. What Madison realized was that, while the United States stood by with folded arms, its British rivals were rapidly extending their influence over the whole of Latin America—directly over those parts of it which were in rebellion, and indirectly, through their ties with the Spanish regency and the house of Braganza, over those which were still loyal. By 1810 it seemed clear that the United States must either bestir itself in Latin America or else reconcile itself not merely to the abandonment of all idea of excluding Europe from America but also to the intensification of European influence in America through the transfer of the effective control of Latin America to a European power which was far stronger than Spain and Portugal. That power, of course, was Britain, and the United States had always had, and seemed likely to continue to have, more trouble with Britain than with any other power in the world.

This situation, together with the rapid spread of the revolutionary movement in Latin America in 1810 goes far to explain why, as described above, Madison intensified the action of the United States in regard to Latin America in that year and soon began to move towards cooperation with Britain's chief enemy, France, in the Latin American field. The reports of his new agents in that field tended to confirm him in his new course. They made it ever clearer that the chief rival was not France or Spain or even Portugal-in-Brazil, but Britain, which was the only power besides the United States that was in a position to pursue an independent policy through direct contact with Latin America. They also indicated that, despite the inroads which Britain was making, the United States might still salvage a great deal if it acted quickly and vigorously.

One of the factors in the situation which was most favorable to the United States was the traditional antagonism between Englishmen and Spaniards, including Spanish Americans. This antagonism might be laid aside in time of stress, but it was not easily forgotten. As recently as 1806 and 1807 it had been fed fresh fuel by the British attack on Buenos Aires and Montevideo; and, though the British had professed a change of heart since the events of 1808 and played their difficult double role with skill, their ambiguous policy of open alliance with the Spanish regency and covert friendship for the Spanish American insurgents tended to breed distrust in both camps.

How this feeling, which was widespread in Spanish America, could be turned to the advantage of the United States, was described by Robert K. Lowry in a letter written to Secretary of State James Monroe from La Guaira, Venezuela, in August 1811. The leaders in that country, he said, now felt that Britain had deceived them and was rather an enemy than a friend to them; the success of their revolution depended largely upon aid from abroad and their only remaining hope was in the United States; but if the United States contemplated giving them any aid at all, it ought to act promptly and decisively: halfway measures would be futile.[30]

Within a few weeks after this was written, both the executive department and Congress were showing a disposition to take prompt and decisive action in regard to Spanish America. The immediate occasion was the receipt of a copy of the declaration of independence adopted by Venezuela in July, 1811, but the scope of the action contemplated by the authorities at Washington extended far beyond Venezuela.

On November 23, 1811, Secretary of State Monroe wrote to John Quincy Adams, recently appointed minister to Russia, and to other ministers of the United States in Europe, that for various reasons the United States was looking with a favorable eye upon the revolution now in progress in " South America " (meaning Spanish America). " Several of the Provinces," he continued, " have sent deputies to this country, to announce a complete revolution in some, and the approach of it in others, but as yet a formal recognition of a minister from neither has been made, nor has it been urged." [31]

A few days before this letter was written, the House of Representatives had appointed a " Committee on the Spanish American Colonies," with the well-known physician-scientist-politician, Samuel Latham Mitchill, as its chairman. Early in December, Mitchill wrote Monroe on behalf of the committee asking him whether the government was informed that any of the Spanish American colonies had

[30] Manning, *Dip. Cor.,* II, 1151, Lowry to Monroe, Aug. 21, 1811. Lowry wrote Monroe another letter to the same effect on Feb. 2, 1812 (*ibid.,* 1155-1156).
[31] *Ibid.,* I, 12.

declared their independence or that "material changes" had taken place in their relations. Monroe replied a few days later enclosing a copy of the Venezuelan declaration of independence and stating that, while it was not known whether any of the other Spanish American provinces had as yet made such a declaration, it was known that most if not all of those on the continent were in a revolutionary state.[32]

On December 10 Mitchill's committee made a preliminary report, which was based upon Monroe's letter and upon a number of other documents bearing upon relations between the United States and Spain, chiefly upon the Florida question, in the period 1806-1811. It took the form of a proposed "public declaration" to the following effect: Whereas (it began) several of the Spanish American provinces represent to the United States that it has been found expedient for them to form federal governments upon the elective and representative plan and to declare themselves free and independent, therefore be it resolved by the Senate and House of Representatives that they behold with friendly interest the establishment of independence by the Spanish American provinces; that, as neighbors and inhabitants of the same hemisphere, the United States feel great solicitude for their welfare; and that when those provinces shall have attained the condition of nations by a just exercise of their rights, Congress will unite with the executive in establishing with them such amicable relations and commercial intercourse as may require the exercise of the legislative authority.[33]

[32] Mitchill's letter and Monroe's reply were published with the report cited in the following note.

[33] *Annals Cong.*, 12 Cong., 1 Sess., p. 427-428.

This guarded but definite declaration of sympathy for the cause of Spanish American independence is interesting because it was the first statement of the kind publicly made by any organ of the United States government. It is also interesting because it expressed some of the ideas that were to play an important part in the development of policy and opinion in the United States for many years to come. Chief among these were the idea of " hemisphere solidarity " and the suggestion that the adoption of republican institutions by the new Spanish American states was an important condition of the United States' sympathy for their cause. The declaration was also linked to the future policy of the United States by the prominence that it gave to the development of commerce with Spanish America and by its omission of any statement that might be interpreted as a denial of the authority of Spain or as an incitement to rebellion against it.

This note of cautious regard for the rights of Spain is one of the most important features of the declaration. Its presence may seem surprising, since the whole declaration was based on the assumption that Spain was moribund and that the new revolutionary governments represented not the overthrow of Spanish authority but the efforts of the colonists to fill the void left by the collapse of Spanish authority. If, then, Spain was so weak, why this cautious regard for its rights? The explanation lies partly in the unwillingness of many Americans at that time to foment revolution in Spanish America, either because they distrusted the self-governing talents of the Spanish Americans or else because they opposed all such intervention in the domestic affairs of other peoples. The explanation lies still more in the fact that, while Spain herself was weak, she had a powerful

ally in Britain.[34] Caution about Latin American affairs on
this score—the fear of provoking some interested European
power or powers—remained one of the most constant
motives of American foreign policy for more than a decade
to come.

Despite the tentative, guarded character of the statements of the executive department as well as Congress in
regard to Latin America, the impression got abroad at this
time that the United States was about to recognize the new
Spanish American states, if, indeed, it had not already done
so. Early in December the *New York Gazette* stated that
according to a letter from Washington, " The administration have come to a determination of formally recognizing
the Independence of South America." How, asked another
editor, will Bony relish this? [35] " Bony "—Napoleon
Bonaparte to his friends—seemed to relish it greatly, for
on February 2 he himself informed the American minister
that the United States had recognized the independence of
the rebellious colonies of Spain in South America.[36]

These reports were, of course, false, but they indicate a
realization, which was widespread, of the direction in which

[34] Speaking of this alliance, a leading authority writes that it
" was an uneasy one, but it never faltered on either side in its
main objective," which was the defeat of Napoleon, and that
Britain " could not view with indifference any threat of interference by any other power in the relations between Spain and her
colonies or between Portugal and Brazil " (Webster, *Britain,* I,
9-10).

[35] *Poulson's Daily American Advertiser,* Dec. 6, 1811.

[36] Samuel Smith Papers (LC), J. S. Smith to Samuel Smith
(his father), Paris, Feb. 2, 1812. Young Smith disapproved. The
Spanish colonists, he wrote, " will taste the cup of liberty and
will like the French become inebriated with its contents, and like
the French will wade through scenes of blood and horrors. . . ."

the United States was moving, and they also suggest the extent to which the United States' encouragement of Latin American independence had become bound up with its policy towards France. To what extent the latter development was responsible for widening the breach with England and thus bringing on the War of 1812, it is impossible to say; but we are safe in saying that the Latin American interests of the United States in the period from 1808 to 1812 at least tended to encourage cooperation with France and rivalry with England and so to bring on war with the latter and preserve peace with the former at a time when the policies of those two nations were almost equally offensive to the United States in every field of their relations except Latin America.

Further progress along the lines indicated in the closing weeks of 1811 by Monroe's instructions to Adams and the resolution drafted by Mitchill's committee was delayed by a number of circumstances in the first half of the following year. In April word was received of the terrible earthquake that had devastated the city of Caracas, crippling and demoralising the independence forces in Venezuela. Since Venezuela had been regarded as the strongest and most promising of the new states, its heavy reverses checked the movement in favor of Spanish American independence in the United States, which was also retarded by the failure of the revolutionists in other parts of Spanish America to march forward as quickly and boldly as had been expected at the close of 1811. For example, Buenos Aires, which seemed most capable of winning independence, still refrained from asserting it, and was content with an ambiguous autonomy.

In view of this situation, it is understandable that the most important measure relating primarily to Latin America adopted by the American government in this six-month period was an act appropriating $50,000 for the purchase of provisions for the relief of Venezuela. This was a fine, humanitarian measure, but it had a most practical side too, as was shown by one member (John Rhea of Tennessee) who, in explaining why he voted for this measure but against a similar measure for the relief of the starving people of Teneriffe, said that he was " actuated by a regard to the interests of the United States, which peculiarly required them to cultivate amity with and conciliate the South American provinces." [37] Whether the measure served either purpose well is rather doubtful, for by the time the provisions arrived in Venezuela the revolutionary government had collapsed and it appears that the provisions, or at least a part of them, fell into the hands of the royalists and were sold by them at a handsome profit.[38]

These opening months of 1812 saw the passage of one measure that was ominous for the administration's Latin American policy. This was another embargo, which not only cut off commerce with Latin America at this critical juncture but also—and, from our point of view, this was even worse—was understood to be only a prelude to a declaration of war on Britain. That is, of course, just what it proved to be, for the War Hawks, the expansionists of 1812,[39] were in the saddle and would not be denied the war with England.

[37] *Annals Cong.,* 12 Cong., 1 Sess., p. 1350.

[38] *Aurora,* Feb. 25, 1819. Alexander Scott was sent in charge of the shipment, with an appointment as special agent and a copy of the instructions given Poinsett (Wriston, *Executive Agents,* p. 410-413; Manning, *Dip. Cor.,* I, 14-16). See also Parra Pérez, *op. cit.,* II, 351.

[39] Julius W. Pratt's excellent study, *The Expansionists of 1812* (New York, 1925), is concerned with domestic politics and border relations.

IV

The rise of the expansionist spirit and the resultant war with England illustrate the complexity of the major forces shaping American foreign policy in that period and the way in which some of these forces checked the development of its policy towards Latin America. As we have already seen, the growth of the Peninsular grain trade interest after 1808 tended to defeat the large policy towards Latin America outlined by Jefferson's cabinet in October 1808. As every one knows, the Peninsular trade interest in turn, along with all the other commercial and agricultural interests dependent upon the maintenance of peace with England and trade with Europe, was overborne by the rise of the expansionist urge.

The intricate interplay of the forces shaping foreign policy in these years vividly illustrates a point which has already been mentioned, namely, the internal divisions within the agrarian class and the capitalist-commercial class. The following case is a good example of these divisions. In December 1812 the House of Representatives was discussing an appropriation bill for increasing the navy, partly in order to protect commerce. Samuel McKee of Kentucky, who claimed to speak for the "American agriculturists," asserted that they would have to pay "nine-tenths of the tax which this expenditure will create," and questioned whether "our great agricultural interest should be taxed for the interest of merchants trading with specie to Abyssinia or China." "Do [the farmers] derive equal advantage from [this measure] with the merchants?" he asked, and answered his question with an unqualified "no." To this, a New York member, Thomas R. Gold, replied:

" It is now said that agriculture, the farming interest, is not concerned in the question of a navy. . . . This is strange language. . . . What may be the sentiments of farmers in the gentleman's state [Kentucky], I cannot say, but the farmers of New York, not a little exceeding in numbers and falling not short, I trust in knowledge of their interests, call loudly for a navy . . ." [40]

As this suggests, opinions among the agricultural interest on questions of foreign policy were determined not so much by status as by function, and the same could be said of the commercial interest. Opinion on these questions depended largely upon whether agricultural production served the domestic market or a foreign market, and upon whether commerce and commercialized agriculture served England and the Iberian Peninsula, or the French West Indies, or the revolutionary states of Spanish America, or some other part of the world. In each case a special set of interests was involved, which could best be served by a foreign policy often distasteful if not positively injurious to those who had other interests. Thus, some farmers wished to build up a navy capable of protecting American commerce, which was spread over the seven seas, while others wished at most a navy capable of defending the shores of the United States; and some merchants wished to preserve peace with England and the Spanish regency, while others preferred to foster commerce with insurgent Spanish America at the risk of war with both powers.

The existence of a two-party political system did not simplify the situation, but rather tended to complicate it, since each party contained both agrarian and capitalist-commerical interests. The Republican party, which was the more

[40] *Annals Cong.,* 12 Cong., 2 Sess., p. 411-413, 416.

important of the two because it controlled the federal government throughtout the whole period covered in this book, was even farther from being a simon-pure agrarian party than it had been in 1800. Since then, by the operation of a familiar process, its long tenure of power had attracted to it many men of means who had once been hostile to it but who concluded that they could serve their interests best by coming to terms with a party so firmly entrenched in office. These converts, some of whom came from the commercial classes, in turn modified the spirit of Republicanism, diluted the high-octane agrarianism of the party-in-opposition of the 1790's, and hastened the defection of a large part of the party from the older ideals of strict construction and the diminished state to the " new nationalism " of the years immediately following the restoration of peace. Nor should it be forgotten that since the closing years of the eighteenth century the outlook of the agricultural interest itself had been altered by the increase in the foreign demand for American produce, which had brought about a corresponding increase in the importance of commercialised agriculture in relation to domestic agriculture.[41]

The effect of these changes on the spirit and leadership of the party is indicated by the fact that by the period of Madison's administration, representatives of the commercial interest were in positions of influence in it. Among those

[41] In the debate referred to in note 40, Burwell Bassett (Virginia) argued that the cotton of the South, the sugar of Louisiana, and the hemp and canvas of Kentucky (all of which had been " commercialized " only recently), as well as the manufacturing and fishing interests of the East, were dependent on water-borne transportation: " Thus East, West, North and South, will feel as if the palsy was on them, the moment you abandon the ocean " (*Annals Cong.*, 12 Cong., 2 Sess., p. 125).

who held important public office were Benjamin Crownin-shield [42] of Salem, Massachusetts, who was secretary of the navy, and the Baltimore brothers, Samuel Smith, a leader of the party in Congress, and Robert Smith, successively Secretary of the Navy and of State.[43] Merchant princes who held no public office but were close to those who held the highest offices were John Jacob Astor and Stephen Girard.[44] A striking illustration of the change is furnished by the transformation that came over one of the most influential members of the Republican high command, Albert Gallatin. At the beginning of his career, Gallatin emerged as a champion of the Pennsylvania farmers against the commercial junta of Philadelphia and as late as 1798 he made a typically agrarian attack on the maintenance of an extensive foreign service and the whole system of commercial treaties. As we have already noted,[45] however, by the period 1806-1810 he was using his influence and powers as secretary of the treasury to extend the foreign service of the United States, to obtain commercial treaties, and to promote the ventures of mercantile and financial magnates in Latin

[42] Before his appointment as Secretary of the Navy, he became a partner in the "world-renowned firm" of George Crowninshield & Sons (DAB, article on Benjamin Crowninshield).

[43] See above in this chapter, also Chap. 1.

[44] Neither Astor nor Girard took a direct part in national politics, but both men gave important financial support to the government during the war of 1812; Girard was one of the first five government directors of the Second United States Bank appointed by President Madison in 1816; and Astor's influence at Washington was great. See articles on Astor and Girard in *Dictionary of American Biography*, references there; Adams, *History*, VI, 301; Kenneth Porter, *John Jacob Astor, Business Man* (Cambridge, Mass., 1931), II, 1060, 1061.

[45] See above, Chaps. 1, 2.

America and elsewhere; and after the War of 1812 one of the most significant facts in the career of this former agrarian was his intimate association with the great mercantile and banking house of Baring Brothers of London.[46]

The point here is not that the Republican party had been transformed into a capitalist-commercial party, for it certainly had not, but that the relative increase of the capitalist-commercial element in the party added to the confusion of counsels already divided by the divergences of interest and opinion within the dominant group in that party, which was a heterogeneous agglomeration of farmers and planters speciously united under the name of the agricultural interest. Striking proof of this inner diversity of opinion on fundamental questions of foreign policy is afforded by the following letter, written in November 1811 by John Taylor of Caroline, the intellectual leader of the Republican party,[47]

[46] For example, in 1818 it was through Alexander Baring that the plenipotentiaries at Aix-la-Chapelle received an important " intimation " from Gallatin about the probable recognition of the Buenos Aires government by the United States (Webster, *Britain,* II, 62, Castlereagh to Bathurst, Nov. 2, 1818). On May 12, 1819, William Duane remarked suspiciously in the *Aurora*: " It seems . . . that Mr. *Gallatin,* who was not to remain in Paris an hour after President Monroe's *ascent*—is doomed to *do penance* one year more at Paris—the correspondence of our minister with the *Barings* in *London,* continues to be *frequent and voluminous.*" See also Edward Channing, *History of the United States,* VI (New York, 1917), 404, note. In 1810 the Baltimore *Whig,* edited by Baptis Irvine (a supporter of Robert Smith) denounced Gallatin as " that *arch-apostate*" who had " gone over to the Philistines " and was drawing up Treasury reports designed to favor " rapacious speculators " (Bernard Mayo, *Henry Clay, Spokesman of the New West* (Boston, 1937), p. 352).

[47] Samuel Eliot Morison and Henry Steele Commager, *The Growth of the American Republic* (New York, 1937, revised ed.), I, 244.

and addressed to James Monroe, Secretary of State in Madison's Republican administration.

" I do not think [wrote Taylor] that my opinions accord with those of the government. . . . France seems to me to have vastly over-reached both the United States and England. . . . Bonaparte must consider the United States as an enemy and a rival for reasons as strong or stronger than those which govern his conduct towards England. They [the United States] are adverse to his conquest of Spain and Portugal, more deeply interested against his acquisition of South America than England herself, of a form of government more hostile to his, and destined, should England fall, to succeed her as his political rival; therefore he vexes their commerce and by every artifice obstructs their growth." [48]

The facts and opinions cited above have an obvious bearing upon certain specific aspects of the Latin American policy of the United States; but they have been given not so much for that reason as because they illustrate the conditions under which the whole foreign policy of the United States was developed at this time. The first impression that they produce is one of increasing disagreement on policy, which tended to prevent the government from following consistently and vigorously any given line of action. They suggest that the fumbling and irresolute course of Madison's administration in its early years was due not, as some writers hold, to his personal defects of character, such as lack of courage and firmness, but to the fact that his party was suffering from an acute case of schizophrenia.

The case was all the more acute because the conflict of wills proceeded from a diversity not only of economic interest, but also of political thought and emotional attitudes.

[48] Monroe Papers (NYPL), Taylor to Monroe, Nov. 24, 1811.

For example, there were few if any Americans, whether interventionist or non-interventionist, who did not want their government to follow a foreign policy which would, at least indirectly, favor the cause of liberty in the great struggle then in progress in Europe and Spanish America; but there was the sharpest possible diversity of opinion as to the policy that would serve that purpose best. Some saw in England the last bulwark against Napoleon's tyranny, while others regarded Napoleon as the only counterpoise to the overweening power of an imperialistic and politically reactionary England; and while some lauded the Spanish regency as the champion of Spanish liberty against Napoleon, others denounced it as the agent of Bourbon absolutism in Spanish America.

For the first three years of Madison's administration these opposing thrusts kept American foreign policy in a condition of unstable equilibrium. If occasionally—as in the case of Latin America in 1810—a move was made which seemed to promise vigorous action in one direction or another, it was less likely to be sustained than to be followed or even accompanied by similar action in another and perhaps the opposite direction. It would certainly be difficult to reconcile the administration's course in relation to the two great conflicts then in progress (between France and England, and between Spain and Spanish America), with any comprehensive, consistent policy. Cooperation with France in promoting Spanish American independence was accompanied by the protection of a trade with Spain that gave important aid to the enemies of France and Spanish American independence; and the administration's Latin American policy, by sharpening the rivalry with England, tended to defeat its sincere effort to keep the peace with that nation.

V

The lack of logical consistency in the administration's policy might never have caused serious dissatisfaction; but its fumbling and inglorious course could not be tolerated for long by so vigorous and self-confident a people as those of the United States.[49] The situation seemed made to order for a pressure group with a positive plan of action that promised release for pent-up energy, glory to salve the injured pride of the nation, and tangible rewards for many of its people.

The expansionists of 1812 constituted a pressure group that met these specifications. Their program called for war with Britain in defense of the nation's maritime rights and for the conquest of Canada from Britain and of Florida from Britain's ally, Spain. From start to finish the war met with strong opposition in the United States, for opinions on foreign relations were too deeply divided to be completely reconciled by any program whatsoever; but at any rate the expansionist program reconciled them to the extent of obtaining a substantial majority in both houses of Congress for the declaration of the war on England in June 1812, and the war thus begun virtually monopolized the attention of the government and suspended action along other lines of foreign policy until the restoration of peace two and a half years later.

The reverses of the war had a sobering effect on the expansionist spirit itself. On the Louisiana-Texas frontier, earlier filibustering and revolutionary enterprises directed

[49] A somewhat different view, stressing the prevalence of what is called, in modern jargon, the psychology of fear, is brilliantly presented in Adams, *History*, IV, 375-380.

against Spanish authority had merged with the war on England. For a time they throve under the new impulse and San Antonio itself was captured. In June 1813, however, William Shaler, who had transferred his consular and apostolic ministrations to this field, was given strict orders by Monroe " not to interfere in the affairs of those provinces, or to encourage any armaments of any kind against the existing government." The administration did not want to give the Spaniards any pretext for aiding the British.

One of the chief victims of the war of 1812 was the Latin American policy of the United States. Not the least ironical circumstance in this curious situation is the fact that Henry Clay, who was already sympathetic towards the ideas embodied in the large policy of 1808 and who was to come forth, upon the restoration of peace, as their most ardent champion, was one of the chief promoters of the expansionist war with England that did so much to defeat that policy.[50]

This was by no means the last time that the interests of the United States in Latin America as a whole were sacrificed to its desire for territory; but in the present case, the sacrifice was at least understandable. Latin America was a

[50] Clay's interest in Latin American independence was publicly expressed at least as early as January 1813: *Annals Cong.,* 12 Cong., 2 Sess., p. 663. In September 1815 the liberator-to-be Simón Bolívar commented publicly on the unfortunate effect that the War of 1812 had had on the independence movement in Spanish America by interrupting its commerce with the United States and thus depriving the patriots of war materials. " Sin esto," he wrote, " Venezuela sola habría triunfado, y la América del Sur no habría sido asolada por la crueldad española ni destrozada por la anarquía revolucionaria." Vicente Lecuna, *Cartas del Libertador* (10 vols., Caracas, 1929), I, 208.

remote and, to most people in the United States, still an inaccessible and fabulous region,[51] which was pictured as a kind of combination of penal colony and El Dorado, whereas Canada and Florida were not only familiar, but also contiguous to the United States, so that the full force of the republic could be exerted upon them. Their acquisition would confer tangible benefits by promoting agriculture, peace on the frontiers, and national defense; whereas all that could be expected of the Latin American policy for some time to come was closer relations with nations still in the making, whose trade, though valuable, was only a small fraction of the total trade of the United States and whose commercial and political future was highly problematical, if only because of the pronounced predilection of the Latin American people for England and their lack of preparation for self-government.

The war did not completely sever relations between the United States and Latin America, for American agents remained at their posts in Rio de Janeiro, Buenos Aires, and elsewhere, and managed to keep up a precarious corres-

---

[51] In 1809, in a letter to Baron von Humboldt quoted above in the introduction, Jefferson spoke of Mexico as a country "almost locked up from the knowledge of man hitherto" (Jefferson, *Writings*, XII, 263-264). In 1812 the best source of information about "the province of Carthagena" (Colombia) that Niles could find was William Robertson's twenty-three-year old *History of America*. Complaining that the information contained in it regarding the situation even in that remote period was "very slight indeed," Niles continued: "As heretofore observed, it has been the constant policy of Spain to keep from the world everything relative [to] her colonies. . . . Hence our want of knowledge of the geography of these extensive countries" (*Register*, I, 399, footnote). Niles could have found more information than he did; but his keen interest in Spanish America makes his ignorance about it all the more significant.

pondence with their government by means of the ships
which still, though less frequently than formerly, sailed
between the two regions. The volume of commerce was,
however, greatly reduced, for it was harried by the British
navy both along the coast of the United States and in Latin
American waters. In the Plata River, for instance, where
even before the outbreak of hostilities, American shipping
had almost disappeared for lack of naval protection, British
ships now pounced upon the few Americans who ventured
there, seizing them even in the outer port of Buenos
Aires.[52] In 1813 the frigate *Essex*, commanded by Commodore David Porter, was sent around Cape Horn to the South
Pacific, where it protected American commerce and captured
many British whalers; but in 1814 it was cornered and put
out of action by the British at Valparaiso.[53] At best, the
Essex was only a lone commerce raider, and for the most
part the British had things very much their own way in
South America as well as in the Caribbean region throughout the war.[54] The American ships that escaped them owed

[52] AGN, BA, S1-A2-A4, No. 8, W. G. Miller, American vice
consul, to Juan Manuel de Luca, Secretary, etc., June 30, 1813;
same to Nicolás de Herrera, Secretary, etc., May 21, 1814; Manley
Hall Dixon (British admiral, commanding H. M. S. *Nereus*) to
Herrera, May 30, 1814, in regard to the case of the American ship
Hope. I have been unable to find any reference to this case, or the
problem of which it is a part, in Webster, *Britain*.

[53] Eugenio Pereira Salas, *La actuación de los oficiales navales
norte-americanos en nuestras costas* (1813-1840) (Santiago, Chile,
1935), p. 10-21, gives an account of this episode based partly on
David Porter's own story, *Journal of a Cruise Made to the Pacific
Ocean in the Years 1812, 1813 and 1814* (2 vols., Philadelphia,
1815), and other well known works, and partly on printed and
manuscript sources in the United States and Chile.

[54] Timothy Pitkin, speaking in the Senate in December 1813,
said that the trade of " the Brazils, the Spanish West Indies, and

their immunity mainly to the sheer vastness of the region, which made the maintenance of a completely effective patrol impossible.

Consequently, from the point of view of the Latin American policy of the United States, the War of 1812 made a bad situation worse by giving the British an almost entirely free hand in consolidating their political and economic influence in Latin America. Another result of the war, which was less important but by no means negligible, was the aggravation of the already serious controversy between Spain and the United States. Though they remained technically at peace with each other, the United States tried to annex Spanish Florida, and did annex the Mobile district of West Florida, which it claimed under the Louisiana Purchase; [55] and Spain tried, with British aid, to recover Louisiana from the United States.[56] These efforts, together with Spanish resentment at the encouragement given to the independence movement in Spanish America by the United States,[57] and with difficulties arising from border incidents,

the whole of Spanish America," added to that of the East and China, was "entirely in her [Britain's] possession and under her controul" (*Poulson's Daily American Advertiser,* Jan. 5, 1814).

[55] These efforts are discussed in Cox, *West Florida Boundary Controversy,* and Pratt, *Expansionists of 1812.*

[56] Rippy, *Rivalry,* p. 45; Brooks, *Diplomacy and the Borderlands.* p. 25.

[57] AHN, Est., legajo 5559, "Bosquejo de las relaciones de la España con los Estados Unidos," Nov. 6, 1816, drawn up as a basis for instructions to Onís. The writer said, in part, that the United States "nos han puesto al punto de perder las Americas desde el momento en que . . . se cedió á los Estados Unidos la posesion de la Luisiana"; and that ever since Napoleon's invasion of Spain the United States, "siempre atentos á promover la rebelion y la perfidia," had been giving surreptitious aid to the rebels in Spanish America.

prize cases, and other sources, greatly increased the existing tension between the two powers. Spain, emerging from the war with a new sense of the strategic importance of Florida, especially the naval base at Pensacola,[58] was determined not to yield to the United States in their now multiple controversy. She was confirmed in this determination by the fact that the intruder King Joseph Bonaparte had been driven out and the whole country was once more united under a single government, which was allied with Britain. The situation created by this turn of events was to hamper the development of the United States' policy towards Latin America long after the termination of the War of 1812 enabled it to renew the free flow of its intercourse with that region.

[58] Archivo de Indias, Seville, 146-3-8, " Observaciones " written by the *oficial de la mesa* at the end of the extract of a very secret note from Secretary of State Cevallos to the Colonial Secretary, Nov. 25, 1814: " . . . Pansacola es muy importante que se mantenga en nuestro poder . . . si bien es cierto que la venta de la Nueva Orleans á los Estados Unidos, proporciona á estos un camino abierto para sus miras ambiciosas de ocupar las Provincias limitrofes á Nueva Espana, teniendo nosotros á Pansacola podremos hacer diversiones en contra de aquellas ideas."

CHAPTER FOUR

THE UNITED STATES FACES SOUTH

It has often been said that after the close of the War of 1812 the United States turned its back on Europe and its face towards the West. It would be more accurate to say that the United States turned its side to Europe and its face to the south, towards Latin America, and there, not unexpectedly, found itself face to face with Europe again.

Throughout the next decade the problems it encountered there formed one of the major themes of public discussion both at Washington and in the rest of the country. To judge by the newspapers and magazines and the correspondence of men prominent in public affairs at that time, this theme was one of even more widespread and sustained interest than the West. On at least four occasions in this decade, Latin America held the center of the national stage for weeks or months at a time: in 1817-18 and again in 1821-22, when neutrality and recognition were discussed with much heat and some light in Congress, the cabinet, and the press; in 1823-24, when the Holy Alliance, Cuba, and the Monroe Doctrine engrossed public attention; and in 1825-26, when the Panama Congress was the subject of a prolonged, heated, and nation-wide debate.

Aside from these major crises, in which attention was focussed directly upon Latin America, there were several other occasions when it was involved in questions that attracted widespread attention—such questions as those raised by Andrew Jackson's invasion of Florida, the long-drawn-out negotiation of the so-called Florida treaty with

Spain, privateering and piracy, and the transportation of specie by United States naval vessels in Latin American waters. Compared with all this, the one great controversy over the West in this decade, the Missouri Compromise, was a mere flash in the pan. One never heard much about Texas and Oregon except when a Jackson or a Benton grumbled about their neglect or abandonment, and California was hardly ever mentioned except in connection with Latin America, of which, to be sure, it was nominally a part because of its rather precarious dependence upon Mexico.

In order to understand the policy of the United States towards Latin America in this decade, one would have to know the conditions under which the policy developed, the nature of the economic and political interests that formed the solid basis of policy, the articulate and inarticulate premises of its makers and would-be makers, and the picture that the people of the United States were forming of Latin America and its people—of their character and talents, and the probable destiny of their part of the continent in relation to the rest of it. The inner diversity that characterized both of the Americas was so great that a discussion of these topics on the scale of the present study must deal largely in approximations and generalities; but even these ought to contribute to an understanding of the problem. Consequently, the present chapter will first sketch the international significance of Latin America as it appeared to observers on both sides of the Atlantic just after the close of the Napoleonic Wars and the War of 1812, and will then describe in some detail the growth of the economic interests of the United States, which were so closely intertwined with its political interests, in Latin America. The next two chapters will describe the picture of Latin America that was taking shape in the minds of the people of the United States in the early post-war years.

I

After the restoration of peace in Europe and the United States in 1815, observers on both sides of the Atlantic showed a keen awareness of the importance of the role that Latin America seemed destined soon to play in international affairs. One of the first and most articulate of these observers was the French publicist, Abbé de Pradt,[1] whose prolific, widely read and rather Olympian disquisitions on the world politics of that day made him a kind of prototype of the newspaper columnists of our time. Shrewd and penetrating in many of his comments, he showed a remarkably quick and just appreciation of Europe's interests in the new order that was emerging in Latin America. Perhaps

[1] Dominique de Pradt was a French ecclesiastic of liberal leanings who had been Archbishop of Malines and a baron of the Empire under Napoleon. Though he made his peace with the Restoration, the comparative liberalism (and, it appears, the sciolism) of his numerous books irritated the government and the subservient press of Paris. He wrote more than forty books, most of them after 1815; and many of them related to America. As we shall see, he influenced Jefferson and, perhaps, through Jefferson, the Monroe Doctrine. He was highly esteemed in Buenos Aires (see the following note), and the Liberator Simón Bolívar spoke of him with respect in his famous Jamaica Letter of 1815 (Vicente Lecuna, ed., *Cartas del Libertador,* 10 vols., Caracas, 1929-1930, I, 197) and many times subsequently, offering Pradt a pension in 1823 (*ibid.,* IV, 209, 210). The foregoing is based mainly on Carlos Alberto Pueyrredon, *Dominique de Pradt* (Buenos Aires, 1935). Other sketches of his life are listed in T. R. Schellenberg, "The Jeffersonian Origins of the Monroe Doctrine," *Hispanic Am. Hist. Rev.,* XIV (1934), 3, note 5. For Bolívar and de Pradt, see also Víctor Andrés Belaúnde, *Bolivar and the Political Thought of the Spanish American Revolution* (Baltimore, 1938), p. 35, 36.

this was partly because he was in close touch with Bernardino Rivadavia, talented representative in France of the government of Buenos Aires, which treasured its European heritage and affiliations; [2] but however that may be, there was no writer who hammered away at the point more persistenly or emphatically than he did.

Shortly after the close of the Congress of Vienna de Pradt published a book [3] in which he gave a sympathetic account of its achievements and then went on to discuss the most urgent problems still confronting Europe. In his opinion there were only three such problems, and one of them related to Latin America. They were, first, general disarmament and the curbing of militarism; second, the strengthening of the forces of law and order in Europe's focal point of revolutionary infection, which was France; and third, the termination of the current strife in Spanish America, which he proposed to bring about through the intervention of the great powers of Europe in favor of Spanish American independence.

[2] C. A. Pueyrredon, *op. cit.,* p. 41-42; Mario Belgrano, *La Francia y la Monarquia en el Plata (1818-1820)* (Buenos Aires, 1933), p. 16, note 1; Bartolomé Mitre, *Historia de Belgrano* (Buenos Aires, 1887, 4th ed.), III, 90. Although the Buenos Aires government had propagandists in its pay in England at this time (see below, chap. 6), de Pradt was apparently not on its payroll (he was receiving a comfortable pension as former Archbishop of Malines). It bought 25 copies of a book that he published in 1817, paying for them the modest sum of 50 pesos, and had a translation of a chapter from another book of the same year published in the official newspaper *Gaceta de Buenos Aires* (Pueyrredon, p. 44, 60).

[3] *Du congrès de Vienne* (2 vols., Paris, 1815). Highly favorable comments on this book and selections from it were published in the Buenos Aires newspaper *El Censor,* nos. 36 and 37, May 1816.

This startling proposal that the champions of legitimacy in Europe should become the patrons of revolution in America was made, de Pradt explained, not because he sympathized with the revolutionary principle in Spanish America or anywhere else but because he thought there was no other way in which Europe could preserve its interests and influence in the New World. Convinced that monarchical, legitimist Europe and the republican and essentially revolutionary United States represented two mutually antagonistic systems, he regarded Latin America as Europe's frontier in the New World, which must be fortified against the expanding political and commercial influence of the United States. Convinced also that Spain's dominion in America was doomed to early and complete destruction, he felt that the gravity of the crisis justified the sacrifice of the rights of that single European power to the higher claims of the concert of European powers, which, if they intervened promptly, would be able to establish Spanish American independence on such terms that the new states would remain attached to Europe and would not be drawn into the American system represented by the United States.

When these observations were made, Europe had just been reunited after a twenty-years' schism and the United States had only recently had a narrow escape from disunion in the course of its war with England and had not formed any kind of union with the revolutionary governments of Latin America. Yet already de Pradt perceived that, in the years just ahead, the concepts of European solidarity and American solidarity were to be highly important factors in the international relations of the Atlantic world; and he also perceived that these two concepts would find expression in conflicting policies and that Latin America would be deeply involved in the conflict. Thus early did de Pradt adumbrate the idea of a clash between the American system and the European system, with Latin America as their battleground.

Though the idea was not original with him, neither was it yet a commonplace of public discussion; it was less familiar on his side of the Atlantic than in America; and no prominent writer on either side had stated it with such clarity and forcefulness. If he oversimplified the issues, at least he sensed the main lines that international relations tended to follow in the next decade. He even helped to push them further along those lines, for, since he was widely —though not always respectfully [4]—read on both sides of the Atlantic, his writings promoted that divergence between the European and American systems and their rivalry over Latin America which he described as already in progress.

De Pradt gave most of his attention to political questions and to the common interests of the concert of Europe. It remained for others to give full expression to the economic theme and to those national interests of the several powers that often militated against cooperation by the concert of Europe in Latin American affairs. In both France and England, the economic and nationalistic aspects of European interest in Latin America were set forth by a host of publicists, merchants, politicians, and diplomats in the period following the overthrow of Napoleon. France, for example, resumed its commerce with Latin America as soon as the

[4] For favorable opinions of Pradt, see above, notes 1 and 3, and *El Censor* (Buenos Aires), no. 149, July 25, 1818. On the other hand, the Philadelphia *National Gazette* of July 3, 1823, editorial, said of a recent work of de Pradt's that " It contains, like the other productions of the Abbé, some useful information and ingenious ideas, with much *verbiage* and random speculation."

end of the war with England reopened the Atlantic to its shipping, sent one of its most distinguished peers as ambassador to Brazil to challenge the commercial and political hegemony of Britain in that country,[5] and engaged in a secret intrigue with the revolutionary government of Buenos Aires for much the same purpose.[6] An important impulse to these governmental activities came from writers representing the commercial interests of France, whose writings in newspapers, pamphlets, and books, poured forth in increasing volume in this decade.[7]

One of these productions deserves special notice because, though by no means the first, it was one of the best. This was M. Peuchet's *Etat des colonies des européens dans les deux Indes depuis 1783 jusqu'en 1821*, published in 1821,[8] which was designed as a sequel to Abbé Raynal's

[5] Oliveira Lima, *João VI no Brazil*, I, 63-64, 396.

[6] See below, chap. 11.

[7] Robertson, *France and Latin-American Independence*, p. 181, 204, 205.

[8] At Paris in two volumes, " pour faire suite à l'histoire philosophique et politique . . . de Raynal " (title page). Peuchet (p. 6, 7) stressed the great changes that had taken place since Raynal's day, especially the pressure of expanding industry among the nations of the continent and its need for new markets. " Mais, au lieu de les recontrer, il ne trouve souvent que des peuples qui, précédemment habitués à lui demander ses marchandises, en fabriquent aujourd'hui, et les lui offrent meme à des prix inférieurs aux siens." Here lay the importance of Spanish America, which, " par la nature de sa position et ses richesses, doit offrir de vastes dédommagemens aux pertes qu'elles [les nations continentales de l'Europe] ont fait ailleurs " (p. 8). The relative importance of Spanish America was shown by the fact that whereas the annual value of the products of all the colonies of Europe was 1,290,000,-000 francs, obtained by the outlay of 500,000,000 francs worth of European goods, the annual value of the products of Spanish America alone was 400,000,000 francs (one-fourth in precious

famous work of half a century earlier on the same subject. Peuchet produced a great array of statistics to prove that the trade of Latin America was one of the richest branches of trade in the world, yielding profits far greater even than those obtained from Britain's immense colonial empire. He argued that the dislocation of this trade caused by the struggle for independence in Latin America constituted an economic revolution of the first order, which promised rich rewards to the nations that should gain control of it; and he specified the many benefits that could be obtained from it and described these in detail, stressing the fact that Latin America would afford the kind of outlet needed by French manufacturers, who were finding the home market saturated.

In an earlier discussion of the same question from the British point of view, a writer in the London *Morning Chronicle* of April 24, 1819,[9] complained that since 1810 British manufacturers had suffered heavy losses because the wars of independence had closed old avenues of trade in Spanish America and the British government had failed to take advantage of the opportunities that these wars had offered it. Before 1810, he said, the annual value of European goods exported to Spanish America was $56,000,000, and the annual value of the gold and silver mined in Spanish America (all of which flowed into, or at least through, European hands), was $42,000,000; but since 1810 the

---

metals, the rest in produce), against an outlay of 120,000,000 francs worth of European goods (p. 15, 16). Peuchet also observed that colonies had contributed to the progress "des lumières et des connaissances" and had furnished liberty with "un auxiliaire contre la perpétuité du despotisme Européen" (p. 19).

[9] Clipped in the Philadelphia *Aurora*, June 25, 1819.

figure had been only about one-third as large in each case. So, he concluded, since that year the manufacturing nations of Europe had lost a " vent " for some $330,000,000 worth of manufactures and had been deprived of an " influx " of some $252,000,000 worth of specie.

England, he declared, had suffered more from these losses than any other nation; and the scarcity of bullion was all the more painful to it because in these very same years the rapid spread of " luxury " had brought about a ten-fold increase in its use of gold and silver. After drawing a sharp contrast between the shrinkage of English and other European trade with the colonies still subject to Spain (such as Mexico, which, though formerly a valuable market, had " for years been a nonentity ") and the three-fold increase in British trade with Buenos Aires,[10] which had been virtually independent since 1810, our British writer pointed the moral of his tale.

So far [he wrote] we have supinely neglected a great opportunity. The time is however come, when the clamors of the nation are raised against this apathy and supineness, at a moment when the aggrandizing views of our own rivals begin to display themselves, and will no longer bear disguise.

That the *Morning Chronicle,* like Abbé de Pradt, was a

[10] The British early developed a special interest in Buenos Aires. In 1814 Lord Strangford wrote Castlereagh that " the mass of British property which is now collected there is exceedingly great " and alluded to the fact that British trade with Buenos Aires was dependent on the maintenance of the revolutionary government there and that it was protected by naval convoys provided by the British government (although the latter, as is well known, had not recognized the Buenos Aires government): Webster, *Britain,* I, 94, 95.

mouthpiece for the government of Buenos Aires [11] only shows how receptive important European channels of publicity were to the efforts of that enterprising government to demonstrate the vital importance of Latin America to Europe.

II

After remaining in a state of suspended animation during the war of 1812, the interest of the United States in Latin America revived quickly at the end of the war. In many respects this interest followed the same pattern as in the pre-war period; but it was sharpened by the realization that the emergence of the concert of Europe had altered the terms of the Latin American problem, and that the United States no longer had to contend only with the rivalry of individual powers, such as Britain and the mother countries, Spain and Portugal, but that it must reckon with a united Europe. This prospect in turn tended to promote sympathy for the cause of the revolutionists and to strengthen the belief, which had not been widely held before the war, that the United States itself had an important stake in their success.

[11] See below, chap. 6, where it is shown that some of the writers for the *Morning Chronicle,* unlike Abbé de Pradt, were on the payroll of the Buenos Aires government. This fact, not noted by Webster, may be compared with the passage in which he cites the *Morning Chronicle* in support of his statement, *op. cit.,* II, 11, that while British policy towards Latin America in this period was partly directed by self-interest, there were " other forces in Britain on the side of the emancipators. The growing liberal movement was from the first deeply interested in their success. In debates in the House and in the pages of the *Morning Chronicle,* their cause was sustained by followers of the same men who had defended the right of the North Americans to revolt."

The new state of mind can be illustrated by the statements of two prominent Americans who represented widely different sectors of opinion. These were John Quincy Adams, Secretary of State under Monroe, and William Duane, Irish immigrant, Republican politician, editor of the Philadelphia newspaper *Aurora,* and merciless critic of the administration of which Adams was a member.

In 1819 a new map of Mexico was published at Philadelphia. To most of Duane's fellow-countrymen, this might have seemed an interesting fact but it could hardly have been an exciting one; but Duane, himself, who had long been fighting for Latin American freedom with printer's ink, burned with an incandescent zeal that could find matter for eloquent discourse in the most prosaic text if only it gave him an excuse to talk about his cause. " A more valuable map," he exploded in the columns of the *Aurora,*

" has not appeared for half a century, at least more interesting to the *American people*—who must, after all, and notwithstanding the infatuated policy pursued for three years past by the public administration of this republic—who *will after all* have to look to the regions south on the same continent, as the source of their *future prosperity, commerce,* and *security.* There it is that the *northern republics* of the American continent, will find the corrective of European jealousy, and the resources with which to defeat and counterplace the intolerant and malignant selfishness of European nations." [12]

Adams took a very different view of the Latin American problem and was, indeed, partly responsible for the " infatu-

[12] *Aurora,* May 8, 1819, item captioned " Geography." The map was made by the " celebrated *Dr. J. H. Robinson,* the friend and fellow traveller of the late gallant and good General Pike." Robinson had also taken an active part in the disturbances on the Louisiana-Texas border in the period of the War of 1812.

ated policy " that Duane denounced; and yet he, too, testified freely to the intense interest that the people of the United States were taking in the Spanish American struggle for independence. Writing to his father from Washington in December 1817, he quoted the opinion recently expressed by Abbé de Pradt [13] to the effect that South America had now taken the place in world affairs that the French revolution had occupied during the preceding twenty years.

" It is very much so here [continued Adams]. The republican spirit of our country not only sympathizes with people struggling in a cause, so nearly if not precisely the same which was once our own, but it is working into indignation against the relapse of Europe into the opposite principle of monkery and despotism. And now, as at the early stage of the French Revolution, we have ardent spirits who are for rushing into the conflict, without looking to the consequences."

In the nation at large this generous ardor was tempered by a disposition to consider the question in terms of national interest, and many of those who discussed it showed an engaging frankness in coupling idealism with the profit motive. Thus, in 1817, Isaac Briggs, addressing a committee of Congress in favor of a protective tariff for manufactures, said:

" But where shall we find a market for our manufactured cotton and woollen goods? I answer, in Mexico and South America. . . . I am not an advocate for an improper interference in the concerns of another nation; but I wish for the rational freedom of the human race. I think we ought to stand prepared to avail ourselves of a passing

---

[13] Adams, *Writings*, VI, 275-276. Adams's reference was not to de Pradt's *Du Congrès de Vienne* (1815), but to his *Les trois derniers mois de l'Amérique méridionale* (1817), where the idea was repeated.

good, when it can be *lawfully* offered to our acceptance. We shall have a jealous and watchful rival [i. e., Britain]. A *first* possession will be a very strong point—those whom I address can understand me." [14]

The equation " United States textiles plus rational liberty equals the exclusion of European influence from Latin America" was an interesting and persuasive one, and it was to be written on the blackboard of public opinion many a time in the course of the next decade.

The observations by Adams, Duane, and Briggs, which we have quoted, were made from two to four years after the restoration of peace; but we have the testimony of the watchful and uneasy Spanish minister Onís to the promptness with which many American people turned their attention to the struggle in Spanish America as soon as their own war with England was ended. As early as March and April 1815 he was able to give his superiors at Madrid many concrete illustrations which showed the wide extent and many-sidedness of this interest. In nearly every city in the United States, he reported,[15] army officers who had been

[14] *Aurora*, Feb. 24, 1817, "Statements and Remarks Addressed to Thomas Newton, chairman of the Committee of Commerce and Manufactures," signed Isaac Briggs, dated Jan. 25, 1817. Timothy Pitkin, *A Statistical View of the Commerce of the United States* (New York, 1817), p. 230, was impressed mainly by the value of Spanish America as a source of supply of "large quantities of precious metals by which they are enabled to carry on a trade with China and the East Indies, as well as to pay the balances due, in Europe and elsewhere." He also noted that the restoration of peace had brought about a revival of "old commercial systems" by the European nations and had "left Great-Britain in possession of almost every place, which commands every sea" (*ibid.*, p. 292. 293).

[15] AHN, Est., Legajo 5640, Onís to the Duque de San Carlos, March 28, 1815, no. 25, and to Cevallos, four despatches in 1815:

thrown out of employment by the conclusion of peace were meeting to decide whether to join the insurgent armies in Mexico and South America. Already nearly two hundred officers in Boston and a large number in Baltimore had decided to do so; and a shipload of such volunteers were actually on their way, having sailed from New York in the schooner *Comet* for Cartagena (Colombia), and similar expeditions were preparing in other ports of the United States. Many American privateers also had been thrown out of employment by the end of the war with England, and as these ships were designed for speed and had too little cargo space to be commercially profitable, their owners were selling them to the insurgents, who were in the market for naval vessels to be used against Spain. Merchants of Philadelphia, Baltimore, and New York had formed a company to purchase 30,000 surplus army rifles from the United States government for the use of the insurgents in various parts of Spanish America; and last but not least, a Philadelphia printer was on the point of leaving for Mexico to offer his services to the insurgents there.

As Onís realized, these isolated incidents were significant because, when added together, they revealed the feeling of the American people and their government towards Spain and Spanish America. The United States was certainly not observing the " good neighbor " policy [16] that ought to

---

March 31, no. 27; April 16, no. 33; April 17, no. 34; April 23, no. 35 (photostat copies, LC).

[16] The term " good neighborhood " (*buena vecindad*) as applied to international relations was a common one in the Spanish correspondence of that period. On this occasion Onís wrote that it was important for Spain to make the United States " adoptar con la España un plan mas analogo à la buena vecindad, que debe existir entre dos Potencias amigas . . . " (*ibid.*, Onís to the Duque de San Carlos, March 15, 1815, no. 17).

govern the relations between two friendly powers; on the contrary, he warned the court, a war with Spain would be popular with all factions in the United States, because they counted upon obtaining support among the inhabitants of Spanish America and upon finding "mountains of gold" with which to enrich themselves. They were also confident that such a war would enable them to make good their claim to Florida and Texas and to forward "their ambitious design of dominating the whole continent." [17]

The steps that Onís took in these premises will be discussed in a later chapter in connection with the development of the policy of the United States government; but one of the measures that he proposed to the court at this time requires notice here because of its relevance to our present purpose of sketching the background of United States interest in Latin America. The proposal in question related to commerce between the United States and Spanish America. Onís would have liked to cut off the connection completely; but since he admitted that political considerations might make it impossible for the court to do this, he contented himself with advising it to take drastic steps to reduce the volume of this commerce and render the remnant politically innocuous. This could be done, he suggested, by imposing heavy discriminating duties on the ships and goods of the United States in Spanish American ports and by punishing as spies all American citizens who were found to have gone to any part of Spanish America without proper authorization from the Spanish government.[18]

[17] *Ibia.*
[18] *Ibid.*, Onís to Cevallos, March 31, 1815, no. 27.

III

These were indeed drastic measures, but from the Spanish point of view they were not only justifiable but necessary. For ocean-borne commerce (which was what Onís had in mind) both formed the basis of the economic interest of the United States in Latin America and also provided the means by which all kinds of relations between the two regions—political and cultural, as well as economic, relations—were maintained. In spite of all that was said in those days about the common interests of the United States, Spanish America and Brazil, as parts of one great continent, in actual fact the United States was connected with its southern neighbors in precisely the same way in which it was connected with Europe—by sea. Mexico was the only exception to this rule, and this exception was unimportant, for overland travel through Texas and New Mexico was so difficult, dangerous, and expensive that here, too, most communications were carried on by water, through the Gulf of Mexico. The United States government itself was mainly dependent upon merchant ships for maintaining contact with its agents in Latin America, though it occasionally made use of naval vessels for that purpose; and, with one or two exceptions,[19] the use of naval vessels for unofficial purposes was out of the question. In short, commerce was the most important factor in all the relations of the United States with Latin America, and we must therefore observe how it was carried on in the decade after the war of 1812.

A comparison of the commerce of the United States with Latin America and the rest of the world just before and just

[19] The most important exception was the transportation of specie on private account. This is discussed below in chap. 10.

after the war of 1812 reveals some rather striking changes, which had a direct bearing upon the development of its foreign policy. The return of peace in 1815 was followed by a quick revival of the export trade of the United States. In the first full year after the war, its total exports were about one-third larger than in the last year before the war, amounting to approximately $61,000,000 in 1811 and $82,000,000 in 1816.[20] This increase, however, was by no means evenly distributed among its principal customers. Four-fifths of the increase was accounted for by Britain and her dominions, and a large part of the remainder by France and her dominions. The increase in these cases was partly offset by a sharp decrease in the cases of Spain and Portugal. In 1816, exports to Spain were worth only half as much, and exports to Portugal only one-seventh as much, as in 1811. There was also a great shrinkage in the case of Brazil, where the value of imports from the United States sank from $1,700,000 in 1811 to a paltry $410,000 in 1816. Compared with these heavy losses, the United States export trade to Spanish America stood up very well, for its value declined only about 25% in the same period (from $8,310,000 in 1811 to $6,385,000 in 1816). Combining these figures, we find that Brazil and Spanish America took about 16% of the total exports of the United States in 1811 and about 8% in 1816.

The tendencies shown by the export figures for 1816 appear even more clearly in those for 1821. The panic of 1819 and the ensuing depression (which was part of a general depression felt throughout Europe and America)

[20] The figures in the text are taken from *American State Papers, Commerce and Navigation,* I, 892 (1811), II, 55 (1816), and II, 575, 600 (1821). In each case they are for the year ending Sept. 30.

brought about a decline of the total exports of the United States from $82,000,000 in 1816 to $65,000,000 in 1821. In the latter year England was still by far the best customer, taking nearly 40% of the total exports. The decline of trade with Spain and Portugal had been accelerated by the revolutionary disturbances that began in both countries in 1820, so that Spain now took only $440,000 worth of American exports and Portugal only $148,000 worth.

The export trade to Latin America, on the other hand, showed an increase in this period. The increase was only moderate in the case of Spanish America (from $6,385,000 to $6,770,000) but very considerable in the case of Brazil (from $413,000 to $1,381,000), and the combined exports to both had risen from 8% of the total exports of the United States in 1816 to 13% in 1821.

These figures tell only a part of the story, but they indicate the outlines of the rest of it. The once thriving trade of the United States to the Iberian peninsula, which in the period from 1808 to 1812 had proved a serious obstacle to the development of Jefferson's large policy towards Spanish America, had been reduced almost to insignificance by this time, and was now worth only one-thirteenth as much as the export trade of the United States to Brazil and Spanish America. Moreover, the Latin American trade of the United States had not only resisted the general downward trend of world commerce but had actually shown a substantial increase. This development occurred at a crucial period in the evolution of our foreign policy, it coincided with important gains in the movement for Latin American independence, and it seemed to confirm the belief that the progress of rational liberty in Latin America would have a considerable cash value for the United States.

John Quincy Adams, who was secretary of state from 1817 to 1825, was keenly alive to the economic importance of Latin America to his own country, and he now declared, as explicitly as Jefferson had declared in 1808, that it was the policy of the United States to exclude the commercial as well as the political influence of Europe from America. A detailed study of our Latin American trade at this period shows that Adams was on the whole well informed about it, but that he labored under some misapprehensions about the relative importance of its various branches—misapprehensions which may have been a not unimportant factor in determining his attitude and his government's policy towards Latin America. What those misapprehensions were will appear in the following sketch of the trade in the decade following the restoration of peace. This sketch will indicate only the main outlines of the subject—the legal status of the trade, the policy of the United States government towards it, and the interests and regions mainly concerned in it. Further details regarding special aspects of it, such as the munitions trade, the sale of warships, and the use of the navy for the protection of American shipping and the transportation of specie, will be given in later chapters.

At the very beginning of the decade now under consideration American commerce with Latin America was encouraged by a Treasury Department order of July 3, 1815 admitting ships flying the flags of the insurgent governments to the ports of the United States.[21] As the State

[21] John Bassett Moore, *Digest of International Law* (8 vols., Washington, 1906), I, 170-171, Secretary of the Treasury Dallas to the Collector of Customs at New Orleans, July 3, 1815. In an interesting survey of the relations between the United States and Latin America, *America: Or a General Survey of the Political*

Department explained in answer to Spain's protest, this measure did not involve recognition of the independence of the insurgent governments; it merely applied to the present case the interpretation of international law for which the United States had contended in its own struggle for independence and instrumented the policy of strict and impartial neutrality adopted by the United States in the conflict between the Spanish American insurgents and Spain, permitting both parties access to the ports of the United States on equal terms.[22] Though subsequent acts of Congress (1817 and 1818) made it more difficult for belligerents to procure munitions and warships in the United States, and though these acts operated chiefly to the disadvantage of the insurgents, the Treasury order of 1815 was never revoked or substantially altered. On the whole, it undoubtedly promoted the growth of commerce between the United States

---

Situation of the Several Powers of the Western Continent, with Conjectures on their Future Prospects (Philadelphia, 1827), p. 280, Alexander H. Everett wrote that this measure was a "much more important one than it has sometimes been considered" and that "whenever the public law upon this subject shall be fully settled, it is probable that this [measure], and not the interchange of diplomatic agents, which is a merely formal thing, will be looked upon as the real and substantial acknowledgment of the independence of a new government. Such, however, is not the case at present." The historian Webster, commenting on the adoption of a similar measure by the British government in 1822, takes substantially the same view, for he writes that the recognition of the flags of South American vessels "was in a sense *de facto* recognition [of their governments] . . . and the first step towards full recognition had been taken" (Webster, *op. cit.,* I, 16). As noted by Everett, however, this was not the generally accepted view at the time.

[22] Neutrality policy and legislation are discussed below, chaps. 7 and 8.

and Latin America, although occasionally it had the opposite effect, since it facilitated the operations of the insurgent privateers, which took a heavy toll of neutral merchant shipping, including that of the United States, in the Caribbean and elsewhere.[23]

Most of the commerce between the United States and Latin America was carried on in ships flying the American flag. Again after 1815, as in the period before it was disrupted by the War of 1812, this commerce stood on a different legal footing in different parts of Latin America. In Brazil, the United States continued to enjoy general fredom of commerce under the decree of 1808; but the British still retained the favored position that they had won by the treaty of 1810.[24]

In Spanish America there was the greatest diversity in the legal status of United States commerce throughout this period. The main line of division was between the loyal colonies and those in rebellion; but even within these two groups there was a great diversity as between one colony and another and between one independent or quasi-independent state and another. Added to this was the fact that the line of division between the two groups was constantly shifting; Buenos Aires was the only government that maintained its independence throughout this period and Mexico was the only colony whose ports remained uninterruptedly in loyal-

[23] Charles C. Griffin, " Privateering from Baltimore during the Spanish American Wars of Independence," *Maryland Hist. Mag.,* XXXV (1940), 1-25, an excellent article, based on a careful study" of court records and other sources; T. S. Currier, *Los Corsarios del Río de la Plata* (Buenos Aires, 1929) ; Lewis W. Bealer, *Los Corsarios de Buenos Aires: sus actividades en las guerras hispano-americanas de independencia, 1815-1821* (Buenos Aires, 1937).

[24] See above, chap. 3.

ist hands until independence was established. In the region fronting on the Caribbean and the Pacific, alternating tides of rebellion, reconquest, and ultimate liberation swept over one country and another until, by the end of 1824, the last important Spanish force in continental America had been defeated. Even commerce with Buenos Aires was harassed almost incessantly by the kaleidoscopic changes in the province on the other side of the great Plata estuary, the modern Uruguay. There, patriot and royalist, federalist and unitarist, Argentine, Portuguese, and Brazilian, kept Montevideo and its hinterland in an uproar until at the end of a three years' war (1825-28) between Buenos Aires and Brazil, the independence of Uruguay was definitely established. Thus a period of peace on the Plata—almost the first it had known since the British invasion of 1806—was ushered in, in 1828, only to be ushered out again almost at once by the outbreak of another civil war in Argentina.[25]

While it would obviously be difficult to frame any statement of the legal status of American commerce with all of this chaotic Spanish America at any given time, still more throughout the whole period under consideration, two useful generalizations can be made. The first is that at no time was the United States admitted to free general commerce with the colonies loyal to Spain, but that nevertheless it contrived to carry on some kind of commerce with all of them, under conditions that varied not only from colony to colony but often also from port to port within the same colony and that tended to become more and more favorable to the United States, with the passage of time. In theory,

[25] For a convenient account of this turbulent period, see Ricardo Levene, *History of Argentina* (Chapel Hill, N. C., 1939, English translation by W. S. Robertson)

the Spanish court still maintained the old system of commercial monopoly; [26] but in practice—as we have had occasion to note in connection with Onís's advice to the court early in 1815—the United States, along with other foreign nations, carried on an extensive commerce with the colonies controlled by Spain. The court itself made many exceptions to its rule of monopoly, granting licenses to foreigners, including citizens of the United States, to take munitions, foodstuffs, and even general merchandise to the loyal ports of Spanish America. The colonial officials also, using their rather wide discretionary powers, frequently admitted American commerce on the plea of an emergency; and there was as usual the forbidden but broad and inviting avenue of contraband trade, the volume of which is, naturally, indeterminate, but seems to have been considerable.

As a rule, the exceptions in favor of American commerce with the loyal colonies were most numerous in those in which the need for munitions and foodstuffs was most pressing or where at any rate the local officials, who commonly accepted honoraria from foreign merchants, could allege the need without unduly straining the credulity of the court. Also, as a rule, exceptions in favor of the United States were most numerous in the colonies nearest to it and least numerous in those that were most remote. The working of these two rules gave the United States an exceptionally favorable position in Cuba and Puerto Rico, a less favorable but still advantageous position in Colombia and Venezuela, and a weak and uncertain one in Mexico; whereas in remote Ecuador (called, in colonial times, the Presidency of Quito) and Peru, the Spanish monopoly was

[26] It was not abandoned until 1824.

on the whole maintained with considerable rigor,[27] and United States commerce gained admission mainly through smuggling conducted from a base in independent Chile. Only with the final victory of the patriots were these barriers removed and the ports of this region thrown open to general commerce with the United States and other foreign nations.[28]

The second generalization is that, with all the independent and quasi-independent states of Spanish America, as with Brazil, the United States enjoyed general freedom of commerce, but under widely different tariff and port regulations, and that in some of these states, again as in Brazil, it suffered from unfavorable legislation. Sometimes this took the form of discrimination in favor of Great Britain, as in the case of a customs law enacted by Colombia which gave a 5% advantage to goods brought direct from Europe over goods brought from the United States.[29] Sometimes it took the form of legislation which was ostensibly general and undiscriminatory in character but which actually bore solely, or at least most heavily, on the commerce of the United States—as in the case of the Buenos Aires tariff imposing heavy duties on naval stores, fish, tobacco, and rum, against which consul Halsey protested in 1815,[30] and in the

[27] Goebel, " British trade to the Spanish Colonies, 1796-1823," loc. cit., p. 318, 319, and R. A. Humphreys, ed., British Consular Reports on the Trade and Politics of Latin America (London, 1940), p. 127, note 2.

[28] William Spence Robertson, Hispanic-American Relations with the United States (New York, 1923), p. 188-192, gives some information about this early trade.

[29] Manning, Dip. Cor., II, 1218, Lowry to Adams, March 20, 1822.

[30] AGN, BA, S1-S2-A4, No. 8, Halsey to Gregorio Tagle, Secretary, etc., July 31, 1015.

case of another Buenos Aires law, enacted in 1825, prohibiting the importation of flour, a measure which the American chargé d'affaires, J. M. Forbes, declared was " manifestly, and almost exclusively, injurious to the commerce of the United States." [31] Whether such unfavorable legislation was inspired by British agents or British merchants, or whether, as in the case of the Buenos Aires law forbidding the importation of flour, it was the result of the demand of the local interests for protection against foreign competition, is not the question here. The point is that the United States was placed at a disadvantage with respect to its competitors in some of the Latin American countries, whereas in none of them does it appear to have enjoyed any advantage conferred by law over its competitors.

IV

That the commerce of the United States with Latin America was able to make any progress at all under these conditions was due mainly to the individual enterprise of its people and to the fact that it possessed one of the largest and most efficient merchant marines in the world, that it found in Latin America a needed outlet for the surplus products of farm and workshop (an outlet needed more now than ever before, since the end of the war in Europe had closed other outlets),[32] that it obtained in Latin America the specie increasingly demanded by its own rapidly

---

[31] *Ibid.*, S1-A2-A4, No. 11, Forbes to M. J. García, Minister, etc., Aug. 22, 1825.

[32] H. M. Brackenridge, *South America: A Letter on the Present State of that Country, to James Monroe, President of the United States.* By an American (Washington, D. C., 1817), p. 33. This pamphlet is discussed below, chap. 6.

growing business community, and that it was able to make Latin America, especially South America, an important adjunct to its whaling and sealing industry in the South Pacific and its rich trade with Asia.[33]

The United States government did little to promote this development. Consular agents, and, later, diplomatic representatives were sent first to one part of Latin America and then to another to afford American seamen and merchants what protection they could, and soon the United States navy began to render important services to the national commerce in that part of the world; [34] but that was all.

On the one hand, the government did not give financial aid to the commerce of its people with Latin America by subsidies, loans, or any of the other devices with which we are now familiar. Even at the height of the wave of so-called nationalism following the war of 1812, when the dominant Republicans were adopting many of the loose-constructionist principles which they had condemned in the days of Federalist ascendancy, constitutional scruples still limited the scope of federal action so narrowly that the granting of such aid was not even seriously considered. The importance of this self-imposed limitation for the foreign policy of the United States, especially in relation to Spanish America, was noted by Onís early in 1815. Bitterly

[33] Manning, *Dip. Cor.,* I, 456, 457, Poinsett's report of Nov. 4, 1818; Jeremy Robinson Papers (LC), Diary, entries for June 6 and 23, 1818. Morison, *Maritime History,* p. 46, speaking of this period, says, " To find something salable in Canton, was the riddle of the China trade. Boston and Salem found it "—i. e., by developing the fur trade on the Northwest coast. It should be added that the development of the specie trade with South America was also a part of the solution of the riddle.

[34] These topics are discussed below, chaps. 7-10.

disappointed by Andrew Jackson's victory over the British at New Orleans, of which he had just learned, Onís wrote his government that if England had only had sense enough to take the war seriously, she could have reduced the United States to "the most complete nullity," and continued, "Now, however, the United States is going to become a great nation, full of pride, presumption, and the ambition to conquer, and the only hope that it will be checked lies in the absurdity of its constitution"[35]—the absurdity consisting in the fact that constitutional limitations made it impossible for the federal government to obtain the funds necessary for any great enterprise. Onís found further comfort in the reflection that political and financial power in the United States was divided between the "Democrats" (the Republican party), who controlled the government, and the Federalists, who had all the money. Onís was a better constitutional than politico-financial analyst; but on the whole his analysis was sound.

On the other hand, the United States government obtained no special favors for its commerce from the new states. In this case the reasons lay not in constitutional limitations but in the commercial policy of the United States, which was one of reciprocity and the open door. The American government did not seek any such favors and said that it would not accept them.[36] The idea that

[35] AHN, Est., Legajo 5640, Onís to the Duque de San Carlos, Feb. 13, 1815, no. 8 (photostat copy, LC): "En el dia va [los Estados Unidos] a constituirse en una gran Nacion, llena de orgullo, de presuncion, y de ambicion de conquistas, y ninguna otra esperanza queda de poderla contener, sino lo absurdo de su constitucion. . . . "

[36] Vernon G. Setser, *The Commercial Reciprocity Policy of the United States, 1774-1829* (Philadelphia, 1937), p. 244, 245. Setser

rational liberty should be made to pay dividends was a favorite one with people who had ships to charter and goods to sell; but it was never made the basis of national policy.

The main focus of the Latin American trade of the United States during this decade was neither in the liberated regions of Spanish America nor in Brazil, the only Latin American country in which the United States had regular diplomatic and consular representation throughout most of the decade, but in the colony which was the citadel of Spanish power in America, the ever-faithful island of Cuba. " Cuba almost in sight of our shores, from a multitude of considerations has become an object of transcendent importance to the political and commercial interests of our Union," wrote Adams in April 1823.[37] It possessed great strategic value, for it commanded the West Indies and communications with the Gulf of Mexico. It possessed great economic value because the United States carried on a direct commerce with it which was, said Adams, " immensely profitable and mutually beneficial." These and other considerations, he concluded, " give [Cuba] an importance in the sum of our national interests, with which that of no other foreign territory can be compared, and little inferior to that which binds the different members of this Union together." In January 1819 Calhoun stated one of the principal reasons why Cuba possessed transcendent economic importance for the United States: " The trade

---

points out that " the Latin American policy of the Monroe and Adams administration had its origins, to a considerable extent, in the same considerations which dictated the [commercial] reciprocity program " (*ibid.*, p. 243, 244).

[37] Adams, *Writings*, VII, 372.

to the Havanna alone," he said, "was now almost the only resource we had for procuring specie, and if it should be cut off it would greatly increase the embarrassments of our circulating medium." [38]

The great economic value of Cuba to the United States had already received widespread recognition in the United States—for instance, in 1818 it was used as one of the chief arguments against going to war with Spain over the Florida question [39]—and other commentators had amplified Adams's description of the American interests involved in it. The *St. Louis Enquirer,* in an article reproduced with evident approval by the New Orleans *Louisiana Courier* of March 15, 1820, declared that the annexation of Cuba by the United States was necessary in order to maintain the union of the western and the Atlantic states, protect the commerce of the Mississippi Valley, command that of Mexico, and "furnish coffee to the Republic." The Boston *Columbian Centinel* of March 22, 1823, published an article on the "invaluable island" of Cuba, in which it said: "The island owes its present prosperity to the great influx of

[38] C. F. Adams, ed., *Memoirs of John Quincy Adams* (12 vols., Philadelphia, 1874-1877), IV, 205. Although Adams's report is not entirely clear on the question, it seems reasonably certain that the statement was made by Calhoun. The important point is that it was made in a cabinet meeting and its accuracy does not seem to have been questioned by any of those present.

[39] Notably in (James Yard), *Spanish America and the United States; or Views of the Actual Commerce of the United States with the Spanish Colonies: and of the Effects of a War with Spain on that Commerce. . . . By a Merchant of Philadelphia* (Philadelphia, 1818). This 58-page pamphlet, commonly called "Yard's Pamphlet," aroused widespread discussion, which was favorable in the *Boston Daily Advertiser,* April 13, 1818, "Miscellany," and unfavorable in the *City of Washington Gazette,* April 2 and 4, 1818.

foreigners, *of which the United States claims the greatest
proportion.* Her citizens are to be found here as Merchants,
Agriculturists, Artizans, Mechanics, and a numerous body
who itinerate to and from the Island." In the vicinity of
Matanzas alone there were some forty or fifty United States
agriculturalists owning plantations worth about three million
dollars; and in the neighborhood of Havana the number
was even greater. "The United States," continued the
writer, "have by far the greatest proportion of the carrying trade [of Cuba]; and the number of voyages made
under her [the United States'] flag, to different ports in the
island, is not far from one thousand annually." Then he
put his finger on one of the most important points, declaring that Cuba was valuable to the United States not only
for its own trade but also because " it is the key to many
important commercial ports, West and South of this "—
that is, to many ports in continental Latin America.

On April 2, 1823, the *Columbian Centinel* published
another article in which it stressed the special interest of
New England in the trade with Cuba.

The *New England* States [said the Centinel], if this
cession [the cession of Cuba to England] should take place,
will be the greatest sufferers; for with the exception of Rice
and Flour, Cuba is nearly supplied from this section; and
by far the greatest proportion of tonnage employed in the
trade belongs to New England.

The customs records and other sources of information
bear out most of these statements about the great economic value of Cuba to the United States in the decade
following the War of 1812.[40] It will be recalled that this

---

[40] Conversely, the importance of United States trade to Cuba is
stressed in Ramiro Guerra y Sánchez, "Las primeras crisis de

was nothing new, for Cuba had for a long time past been most important to the United States both for its own trade and also as a point of commercial contact between the United States and Latin America; but after 1815 two new factors combined to bring out its special value in high relief. One of these was the fact that Cuba was loyal to Spain and relatively orderly and prosperous at a time when much of the rest of Spanish America was involved in a rebellion and civil war that seriously handicapped ordinary commerce. The other new factor was that now for the first time the published trade reports of the Treasury Department distinguished between Cuba and the rest of Spanish America and thus showed more clearly than ever before how great was the preponderance of our trade with that island. For instance, they showed that in 1821 the United States exported commodities to the value of $6,770,000 to the whole of Spanish America, of which $4,541,000 worth or more than two-thirds of the total, went to Cuba alone.[41]

Great as was the value of Cuba to the United States, however, Calhoun exaggerated it in one very important respect. His statement that Havana was now almost the only resource the United States had for procuring specie was flatly contradicted by the Treasury Department's next general report of specie imports. This was its report for the year 1821-

---

Cuba y sus relaciones con el comercio de los Estados Unidos," *Proceedings of the Second General Assembly, Pan American Institute of Geography and History* (Washington, D. C., 1937), p. 452-458. See also Herminio Portell Vilá, *Historia de Cuba en sus relaciones con los Estados Unidos y España* (3 vols., Havana, 1938-1939), I, 195.

[41] *American State Papers, Commerce and Navigation*, II, 575, 600.

22,[42] which showed that Cuba, so far from being the United States' sole source of supply of specie, was not even the principal source. In that year, the United States received from Cuba $283,421 in bullion and $306,748 in gold and silver coin, or a total of $590,169, whereas from "the Spanish South American Colonies" it received $12,-871 in bullion and $648,246 in gold and silver coin, or a total of $661,117—an amount which was $71,000, or 12%, larger than that received from Cuba.

The disparity indicated by these figures is increased by an item that they do not take into account, namely, the specie which United States vessels obtained in South American ports and then took straight to Asia, where it was used to buy silks, tea, and spices for the United States market. The amount obtained and used in this way is impossible to ascertain, but it was certainly large; it was an essential factor in an important branch of our foreign trade, and while it did not directly increase the "circulating medium" in the United States, which it never entered, it reduced the volume of that drainage of specie from the United States to Asia of which there was so much complaint at this period, or at least it made it possible to expand trade with Asia without increasing the drainage.

Even without this invisible item, Spanish South America was a more important source of specie supply than Cuba; with it, Spanish South America was far more important than Cuba. The contrary opinion was expressed by Calhoun, but it was apparently shared by the rest of the cabinet, including Adams.

[42] *House Doc.* 62, 17 Cong., 2 Sess., table no. 1, p. 6, 7,

V

This is not the only indication that Adams failed to appreciate the true character and importance of the commerce of the United States with South America. For one thing, he described Montevideo as the principal port in that part of America, whereas, in fact, Buenos Aires, with its great Argentine hinterland, was considerably more important than Montevideo, both actually and potentially. For another, he considerably underestimated the value of both ports to the United States. His instructions of May 17, 1823, to Caesar A. Rodney, who was about to go out as the first diplomatic representative of the United States to Buenos Aires, contain the remarkable statement that " Our commercial intercourse itself with Buenos Aires cannot for ages, if ever, be very considerable; and while Montevideo remains under the authority of another government, must be altogether trifling." [43]

Actually, the United States had already built up a brisk trade with both ports. In 1824 (figures for 1823 are not available) 118 United States merchant vessels entered the port of Buenos Aires, 73 of these coming from ports of the United States (mainly from Philadelphia, New York, Boston and Baltimore) and 45 from other foreign ports (mainly in Spain, France, England, and Brazil). From the United States, these vessels brought flour, furniture, saddles, rum, and general merchandise; from Europe, wines and liquors, salt, and general merchandise. It is important to note that when these ships left Buenos Aires, the majority of them (74) cleared for ports outside of the United States, many of them clearing for the West Indies (mainly

[43] Adams, *Writings*, VII, 433.

Havana) with cargoes of jerked beef, and many others for Valparaiso and the Pacific with specie and what remained of their original cargoes of merchandise. The cargoes to the United States consisted principally of skins, horns, and hides.[44]

In the same year (1824), 80 United States vessels arrived at Montevideo, 51 of these from ports of the United States (again mainly from Philadelphia, New York, Baltimore, and Boston, with a few from Portsmouth and Salem), 9 from Buenos Aires, 17 from other foreign ports (mainly Gibraltar and Tarragon), and 3 from ports not stated in the record.[45]

Altogether, 198 United States vessels entered Montevideo and Buenos Aires in 1824; and, while this number was small compared with the thousand or so that entered the ports of Cuba, it was certainly not "trifling," as Adams called it. This American commerce with the twin cities of the Plata not only gave employment to American ships and seamen; it also provided a market for American products such as flour, rum, shoes, and furniture, facilitated the trade with China and India, and even promoted that trade with Cuba which was so highly prized by Adams.

John Jacob Astor, who had already tried his hand at commerce in the Pacific by founding ill-fated Astoria in the Oregon country in 1811, sent his ships to the west coast as well as the east coast of South America after the restoration of peace.[46] Neither he nor many of his fellow

---

[44] Information compiled from reports published in the newspaper *Gaceta Mercantil* (Buenos Aires), 1824.

[45] AGN, Mvdo., *Capitanía de Puerto*, Libro 99, "Entrada de Buques, 1818-1824."

[46] Porter, *Astor*, II, 646, 648-653, 663. The case of one of these

countrymen, except the Nantucket and New Bedford whalers in the South Pacific,[47] seem to have got much profit out of their ventures on the west coast.[48] Chile, independent after 1816, admitted foreign commerce freely, but import duties were high, British competition was too keen, and many American seamen deserted to the Chilean navy.[49] In Spanish-dominated Peru the general prohibition of foreign commerce continued, though with many exceptions, and the Philippine Company still enjoyed its old monopoly.[50] Both Spaniards and insurgents were ready enough to use foreign ships for their own ends; but each, naturally enough, tried to wipe out foreign commerce with the ports controlled by the other. The United States was the

---

ships, the *Beaver*, is discussed below, in chap. 10. Astor also traded, though less actively, with the Caribbean region (the Danish West Indies, Havana, La Guaira) and Brazil. His biographer believes that the specie which formed such a large part of his cargoes from the West Indies was employed in his trade with Canton.

[47] A list drawn up in 1818 showed that 46 United States ships (34 from Nantucket, 10 from New Bedford, and 2 from New York) were then employed in the whale fishery in the Pacific: Jeremy Robinson Papers (LC), Box 1818-1820, Joseph Allen to Jeremy Robinson Callao, Aug. 20, 1818.

[48] There were important exceptions. Morison, *Maritime History,* p. 269, note, mentions among others Richard Alsop, of Alsop, Wetmore, and Cryder at Valparaíso, who was making $100,000 a year by 1827.

[49] Jeremy Robinson Papers, LC, Box 1808-1817, copy of a protest by Charles Carey, master of the *Levant* of Boston, Valparaíso, May 1, 1818, stating that the Chilean officials at that port had encouraged the desertion of his crew and those of other United States ships at Valparaíso in order to man the Chilean warship *Lautaro,* and that he had lost half his crew in this way and was unable to continue his voyage.

[50] Astor was one of those who suffered from it. See Porter, *Astor,* II, 652, 653.

chief sufferer from this commercial warfare, for the Chilean navy, commanded by Lord Cochrane, soon gained the upper hand over the royalists and used it to promote British commerce at the expense of the United States.[51]

While the intervention of the United States navy checked such depredations, it never entirely ended them. In one way or another American commerce with the west coast remained under serious handicaps throughout this decade and failed to continue the rapid expansion begun in the decade just before 1808. The first agents of the United States government in Chile, Joel Poinsett and J. B. Prevost, waxed lyrical over the promise of the immense advantages held out to their country by the "incalculable sources" of Chilean wealth;[52] but the promise was not fulfilled. Great Britain far outdistanced the United States and all other nations in trade with Chile. In the three years 1821-1823, goods from Great Britain and British India accounted for approximately 80% of the duties on all foreign importations into Chile.[53] Maria Graham, a British traveler who visited Valparaiso in 1822, found it thronged with her fellow countrymen, and she observed that "the preponderance of the English language over every other spoken in the chief streets would make one fancy Valparaiso a coast town in Britain."[54] In 1823 the preponderance of British influence throughout Chile was described by an American citizen, Jeremy Robinson, who wrote to Secretary Adams from Valparaiso:

[51] See below, chap. 10.
[52] Manning, *Dip. Cor.*, II, 920, 921. See also note 33, above.
[53] Humphreys, *British Consular Reports*, p. 92.
[54] *Ibid.*, p. 91, note 1, quoting Maria Graham, *Journal of a Residence in Chile, during the year 1822* (London, 1824), p. 131.

It is due to candor to state that there has been a leaning towards European connexions and habits, English and French, particularly the former, generated in their extensive intercourse (manufactures, numbers and power) with this people. . . . The English will take the lead of every other nation. . . . The trade of the United States on this side of the Andes will be very limited and comparatively inferior to that of the British. . . . Things must continue in this state until the United States can manufacture and send commodities which this people want, as cheap and as good as the Europeans—especially the English.[55]

In the case of Mexico, several circumstances conspired to prevent the rapid development of American commerce that might have been expected in view of its proximity to the United States and of the fact that for many years before 1808 its mines had been the greatest producers of precious metals in the world. Chief among these circumstances was the maintenance of Spanish authority over most of Mexico until 1821. During that period foreign commerce was tolerated only in special cases, the concentration of commerce at Vera Cruz made it relatively easy to control, and such foreign trade as was permitted fell largely to the British, who retained the initial advantages that they had won in the earlier period. There was some smuggling from the United States overland and along the Gulf coast, but the great distance and difficult character of the terrain between the chief centers of population in the two countries kept this down to a mere driblet compared with the stream of regulated commerce that flowed through Vera Cruz.

Under these conditions, American commerce with Mexico was irregular when it was not illegal, and it was generally precarious. It consisted mainly of such shipments as

[55] National Archives, SD, Special Agents, vol. 5, Jeremy Robinson to the Secretary of State, Feb. 18, 1823.

those sent from the United States under a six-months permission granted by the court in 1816 for the importation at Vera Cruz of all kinds of provisions,[56] or the contraband shipment of 300 muskets which Alexander Brown and Sons of Baltimore sent to Matanzas in 1819,[57] or the consignments of specie "to a considerable amount" which were brought from Campeche in 1817 by two American brigs and were taken away from them by a Venezuelan privateer.[58] Even after the establishment of Mexican independence in 1821, a Spanish garrison retained possession of the island fortress of San Juan de Ulúa, in Vera Cruz harbor, for five years and made no end of trouble for the ships trading at that port; and again it was the Americans, rather than their British rivals, who were the chief sufferers.

All these risks and uncertainties to which American commerce with Mexico was exposed help to explain why, until the publication of Joel Poinsett's *Notes on Mexico* in 1824, the American people knew less about this next-door neighbor than about almost any important country or region

[56] *Aurora,* Feb. 5, 1817, "Spanish Consul's Office, Norfolk, Jan. 27th, 1817."

[57] Alexander Brown & Co. (Baltimore), Letter Book, "Alexander Brown & Sons to M. and J. Brown, 1819-1821," letter of Aug. 2, 1819: ". . . 200 of them [the muskets] are without Bayonetts & one with & we don't expect them to produce much of anything."

[58] Navy Archives, Captain's Letters, vol. 3, Commodore Daniel T. Patterson to Secretary Crowninshield, July 28, 1817. On the other hand, in 1824 the British agent at Vera Cruz noted certain advantages enjoyed by the United States, and expressed the fear that "the Americans may engross the greater part of the carrying trade of this country": Humphreys, *British Consular Reports,* p. 314.

in the West Indies or South America. They also help to explain why in the early years of the independence movement the American people focused their economic interest on the other, better-known, more promising regions of Latin America and why American interest in Mexico was confined mainly to projects for revolutionizing it or colonizing or conquering its provinces bordering on the United States.

In northern South America, too—the modern Venezuela and Colombia—American commerce was exposed to many risks and uncertainties; but the situation here was very different from that in Mexico, and much more favorable. Two geographical factors were mainly responsible for the difference. In the first place, access to the important centers of population on the " Spanish Main " was gained not through a single port, such as Vera Cruz, but through several ports on the Caribbean (Cartagena, La Guaira, Puerto Cabello) ; and during Simón Bolívar's Orinoco campaigns that river served as another important highway for foreign commerce with this region. The other factor was the existence of islands near the mainland that were owned by foreign nations and that served as relatively safe bases for trade—both lawful and contraband—with royalists and insurgents alike. Among these islands were British Trinidad and Jamaica and Dutch Curaçao. For instance, the United States consulate at Curaçao, first established in 1793,[59] was administered by the same official from 1819 to 1825; he maintained close contact with the insurgent

[59] National Archives, SD, Consular Despatches, Curaçao, vol. 1, 1793-1838, B. H. Phillips to Thomas Jefferson, June 7, 1793. Only a sporadic correspondence was maintained before the appointment of Cortland L. Parker in 1819.

leaders of the mainland, and in 1824 he showed how
important a rôle Curaçao had played in their foreign commerce while the war was at its height by reporting that
" the commerce of this Island with the United States and
the Mother Country is rapidly declining as the Columbian
provinces in our neighborhood become more tranquil. . . ." [60]

Finally, the very fact that the turmoil was greater here
than in Mexico—for Colombia and Venezuela were the
main theatre of the protracted and ferocious struggle
between Bolívar's army of liberation and the Spanish royalist forces—was in one respect an advantage to American
commerce, since both sides required supplies of foodstuffs
and munitions from the United States. Royalists as well
as insurgents tapped this source. According to one American newspaper, the " richest and most favored merchants " of the United States were supplying the Spaniards
in South America from New York and Baltimore with " all
sorts of arms, accoutrements, stores, and munitions."
" Shall the resources of this *republic*," asked the indignant
editor, " be applied in this manner to support the cause of
tyranny? " [61]

In asking this question, the editor put his finger on one
of the most difficult and insistent questions that faced the
people and government of the United States when, with
the return of peace to their own country, they turned to
face the problem created by the epochal conflict developing

---

[60] *Ibid.*, Cortland L. Parker to J. Q. Adams, Sept. 10, 1824. In
1812 Parker had aided Levett Harris in his efforts to obtain the
Russian government's support of Spanish American independence.
See above, chap. 3.

[61] *Aurora*, Feb. 5, 1817. " Quere," clipped from the *Columbian*,

in Latin America. Before we can understand how they answered the question, we must first examine the image they had formed of Latin America. This was still in process of formation in the early post-war period, as they added and rearranged fragments of information and ideas drawn from many sources—from books, newspapers, letters and legends; from merchants, whalers, scientists, and public officials; from statesmen, philosophers, propagandists and crackpots; and the whole picture was colored by their conception of their own rôle in world affairs, in relation to Europe quite as much as to Latin America.

CHAPTER FIVE

THE LATIN AMERICAN PICTURE
AND ITS PAINTERS

(PART I)

It is astonishing how indifferent the great body of the people of the United States appear as to the events in these extensive regions [Spanish America]. This may partly arise from our ignorance of their real situation and of what is going on. It is strange that the feelings of the nation should have been so excited for the ' deliverance ' of old *Spain* from Bonaparte, when so little interest is excited for the *real* deliverance of the new world from the dominion of a knave, fool and bigot [Ferdinand VII of Spain]. The freedom of *Mexico* alone, is indeed, fifty times more important to the United States than the rescue of Spain from the hands of Napoleon was, in a commercial point of view, independent of those desires which, as republicans, we ought to have for its emancipation. . . .

Thus wrote Hezekiah Niles in his *Register* of November 4, 1815. By that time, the war with England had been over for nearly a year. The *Register* was published at Baltimore, one of the chief centers of trade with Latin America, and yet Niles, who took a keen and intelligent interest in the independence movement in Spanish America, found the great body of his fellow countrymen still indifferent to it. Though he exaggerated their indifference, he was right in attributing it partly to their ignorance of what the countries to the south of them were like and of what was going on there.

141

I

Although the past two decades had witnessed a marked increase of interest in Latin America and a rapid multiplication of contacts with it, it still presented a blurred picture to the government as well as to the people of the United States when they turned their attention to it again upon the restoration of peace in 1815. The publication of such works as Humboldt's voluminous "essay" on New Spain and Washington Irving's translation of Depons' travels in northern South America had clarified some of the details; [1] but even these comparatively recent works were based on observations made before the beginning of the revolutionary upheaval in 1808, and the more famous of the two, Humboldt's work, was the result of a mission patronized by the

---

[1] For example, in writing to Humboldt in December 1813 Jefferson said: "I think it most fortunate that your travels in those countries [of Spanish America] were so timed as to make them known to the world in the moment they were about to become actors on its stage . . . in truth we have little knowledge of them to be depended on, but through you" (P. L. Ford, ed., *The Writings of Thomas Jefferson* (New York, 1905, "Federal Edition"), XI, 351-352; see also *ibid.,* XII, 68). François R. J. Depons, *Voyage à la partie orientale de la Terre-Ferme* (3 vols., Paris, 1806), was translated by Washington Irving and published at New York in 1806, with a foreword by Samuel Latham Mitchill, under the title *History of Caraccas.* Announcing its sale, the New York *Daily Advertiser* of May 1, 1807, said that "our extensive commercial intercourse with Caraccas and our present political situation with regard to Spain equally demand that we should possess a perfect knowledge of the former." I am indebted for this citation to Mr. Harry Bernstein of the College of the City of New York. Manuel Segundo Sánchez, *Bibliografía venezolanista* (Caracas, 1914), says that Depons' book "surpasses all praise, since it is the most adequate description" of the region.

Spanish government and was therefore liable to the suspicion of bias in favor of the Spanish regime.[2]

For the rest, readers in the United States who wished to inform themselves about their southern neighbors had to rely upon such works as Jorge Juan and Antonio de Ulloa's *Voyage to South America*,[3] which, though written in 1748 and never revised, still contained the best account in English of a large part of that continent. Some of the many Americans who had visited Latin America in the past decade had published accounts of their experiences and observations; but, besides being fragmentary, most of these were buried in

[2] William D. Robinson, in his *Cursory View of Spanish America* (Georgetown, D. C., 1815), p. 22, 23, complained that Humboldt appeared " to have directed his pursuits to the study of nature, to scientific observation, and to fixing the latitude and longitude of certain spots, [rather] than to have examined a beautiful and luxuriant country with a political and commercial eye." Similarly, the *Aurora*, June 14, 1817, " Political Views, No. II," said that many people believed Humboldt had been imposed on by the Spanish government in regard to the population of Spanish America and had consequently underestimated it. There is a brief but interesting discussion of this problem in H. M. Brackenridge, *A Voyage to South America* (2 vols., London, 1820), I, vii-ix. He said that there was a surprisingly large number of excellent works on colonial " South America," but admitted the lack of information about its " actual state " and the events since 1810.

[3] The demand for this classic is indicated by the fact that it was republished at London in 1806 and again in 1807. A large part of it was again printed in John Pinkerton's *Voyages* (17 vols., London, 1808-1814). Other old standbys were William Robertson's *History of America* and Abbé Raynal's *Histoire philosophique et politique des établissements des européens dans les deux Indes*, in one of the many editions, in the original French or the English translation, through which this famous work had passed since its publication in 1770. It was from these and similar works that the information about Spanish America in Jedidiah Morse, *The American Gazetteer* (Boston, 1797), was drawn.

newspapers and periodicals, which had only a local circulation.[4] As for books, not one written by an American writer and giving a comprehensive and up-to-date account of Latin America or any of its principal regions was published before 1815.[5]

A few specialists in the United States, either individually or through learned societies such as the American Philosophical Society of Philadelphia and the New York Historical Society, had acquired a respectable store of information about Latin America.[6] Their work, in turn, had

[4] Examples are Condy Raguet's "Letters on Hayti," 1808 (cited in chap. 1), and William Shaler's "Journal of a Voyage between China and the North-Western Coast of America made in 1804," *American Register* (Philadelphia, 1808), which contains *inter alia,* "the first account of California in English" (Nichols, "William Shaler," *loc. cit.,* p. 74). Two books were published by participants in Miranda's Venezuela expedition of 1806: James Biggs, *The History of Don Francisco de Miranda's Attempt to Effect a Revolution in South America* (Boston, 1808), and John N. Sherman, *A General Account of Miranda's Expedition* (New York, 1808).

[5] Aside from the works of Humboldt and Depons, the most important foreign work made easily accessible to readers in the United States was Juan Ignacio Molina's *Geographical, Natural and Civil History of Chile* (Middletown, Conn., 1808), translated from the Spanish by William Shaler and Richard Alsop. Felix de Azara, *Voyages dans l'Amérique meridionale . . . depuis 1781 jusqu'en 1801* (4 vols., Paris, 1809), was not translated into English and appears to have attracted little attention in the United States at this time. Of the Englishman William Walton's *Present State of the Spanish Colonies* (2 vols., London, 1810), the *Edinburgh Review* remarked that the second volume "outrageously pillaged" Humboldt and the *Mercurio Peruano* (Lima), and the London *Quarterly Review* described it as written in a "vague, inaccurate, and desultory mode." For further information about Walton, see below in this chapter.

[6] Except as otherwise noted, the information in this paragraph was taken from the valuable article by Harry Bernstein, "Las

become known to scholars and scientists in that region. Thus, the works of Benjamin Franklin on electricity and of Alexander Garden on cochineal and tobacco were known in Mexico, and that of Zabdiel Boylston on small-pox inoculation was known in Peru.[7] North American science was, in fact, highly respected in Latin America at this time and played an important part in promoting contacts between the two regions.[8] For our present purpose, the importance

---

primeras relaciones intelectuales entre New England y el mundo hispánico (1700-1815)," *Revista hispánica moderna,* V (1938), 1-17. "New England" in this title is misleading, for the article contains a great deal of information about the Middle Atlantic region as well. An important pioneering work in this field is Charles Lyon Chandler, *Inter-American Acquaintances* (Sewanee, Tenn., 1915).

[7] Two additional illustrations may be given. The first comes from a letter written in 1818 by the distinguished Peruvian scholar José Hipólito Unánue: "The illustrious names of Mitchell [Samuel Latham Mitchill] and [Felix] Pascalis have long been known to me having often quoted in my observations on the climate of Lima [*El Clima de Lima*] the valuable periodical work entitled Medical Repository, in which these and other learned Americans have manifested the advancement of the natural sciences in their happy country" (Jeremy Robinson Papers, L. C., Box 1818-1820, Unánue to Robinson, Oct. 17, 1818, English translation). The other occurs in a letter written in the same year by José Gregorio Paredes, also of Peru, in which he said, "Several years ago came on my notice the profound knowledge of Mr. Nathaniel Bowditch," and went on to explain how he had found in a Spanish nautical almanac Bowditch's method for correcting the distances from the moon to the sun and stars (*ibid.,* Paredes to "Sir J. Robinson," Nov. 4, 1818).

[8] Evidence of personal contacts before 1815 is scanty. To Bernstein's authorities for the discussion of education in Mexico that President Ezra Stiles of Yale had with Francisco de Miranda in 1784 should be added *The Diary of Francisco de Miranda, Tour of the United States, 1783-1784* (New York, 1928), ed. William Spence Robertson. On Feb. 6, 1810, Dr. Benjamin Rush of Philadelphia wrote Walter Jones, a member of the House of Representatives, introducing José Roxas [Rojas], "a native of the

of these contacts lies in the contribution that they made to the promotion of knowledge of Latin America in the United States. In this connection, special mention should be made of Samuel Latham Mitchill of New York. In 1813 he delivered before the New York Historical Society an address in which he showed his familiarity with the most important books on Spanish and Portuguese colonization published up to that time; and in 1817 he made an interesting effort on behalf of the *Medical Repository* (a journal) and the New York Lyceum of Natural History, of which he was one of the founders, to promote cultural relations with Latin America.[9] His case is all the more important because he took an active part in public life and, as we have seen, was chairman of the committee of the House of Representatives that drew up the report of 1811 on Spanish America.

City of Mexico," as a gentleman of excellent character and great literary and scientific attainments, who had been introduced to him by Dr. Alexander Watkins of New Orleans. Rush spoke of the high opinion he had formed of Rojas during a personal acquaintance of several months' duration; pointed out that, as a friend to liberty and an enemy to " superstition in Religion," he was now a voluntary exile from his native country; and suggested that President Madison might extract " something useful " from his minute knowledge of the population, commerce, manners, and opinions of the people of New Spain (Mexico). The letter is now in the Madison Papers, L. C., vol. 40. Thus again, as in Samuel Latham Mitchill's case, was science the handmaiden of international politics.

[9] This effort was made through Jeremy Robinson in connection with his trip to South America (see below in this chapter). Many documents relating to it are in the Jeremy Robinson Papers, L. C., Box 1808-1817 and Box 1818-1820. They were utilized by Eugenio Pereira Salas in his article " Jeremías Robinson, agente norteamericano en Chile (1818-1823)," *Revista chilena de hist. y geog.*, LXXXII (1937), 201-236.

Aside from this handful of specialists, however, there were very few people in the United States who had anything more than a rudimentary knowledge of their southern neighbors. Except incidentally through the published debates of Congress and the reports of committees and administrative officers, the federal government did nothing to supply this grievous want of information about a region whose importance to the United States had been officially recognized as early as 1808. Indeed, in 1815 the government had little reliable information of this sort to give; and it is a striking fact that of the three men—James Monroe, John Quincy Adams, and Henry Clay—who were to play the leading roles in shaping American policy and opinion about Latin America in the next decade, not one possessed any special training or qualifications for the task. None of them had ever been in Latin America, and only one of them, Monroe, had a good reading and speaking knowledge of Spanish. As for Portuguese, as late as 1824 Adams admitted that the State Department had no one competent to translate even a written communication in that language.[10]

While Monroe's mission to Spain in 1805 had taught him to read and speak its language [11] and to dislike its government, he does not appear to have developed a special interest in or sympathy for Spanish America until he became Secretary of State in 1811; and since that time most of his attention had been absorbed by the war with England. Adams was impartially prejudiced against Spaniards and Spanish Americans alike, for he had swallowed whole the

[10] Arthur P. Whitaker, " José Silvestre Rebello," *Hispanic Am. Hist. Rev.,* XX (1940), 388.

[11] Carlos Ibarguren, *En la penumbra de la historia argentina* (Buenos Aires, 1932), p. 88.

"Black Legend" of the inveterate cruelty, faithlessness and fanaticism of the Spanish people, and he still regarded the Spanish Americans as Spaniards even after they began their struggle for independence against Spain.[12] At the outset, he showed as little interest in the Spanish Americans as liking for them. When he went to London in 1815, he had occasion to confer with the Spanish American agents there, but subsequently the only Iberian acquaintance of his London days whom he seems to have recalled with pleasure was the minister from the Portuguese-Brazilian court;[13]

[12] A great deal has been written about the "Black Legend" (*leyenda negra*) by historians in Spain and Spanish America. A convenient introduction to the literature of the subject, with some references to the period of the wars of independence in Latin America, is furnished by Lewis Hanke, "Dos Palabras on Antonio de Ulloa," *Hispanic Am. Hist. Rev.,* XVI (1936), 490. Adams, of course, did not know the "Black Legend" by name, but his belief in it is shown by an extraordinary diatribe in his instructions of May 27, 1823, to Richard C. Anderson (Adams, *Writings,* VII, 441-442). His application of it to the Spanish Americans is indicated by his letter of Dec. 29, 1817, to Alexander H. Everett (*ibid.,* VI, 280-283) congratulating Everett on his "excellent article" in the *Boston Patriot* questioning the expediency and justice of the United States' aiding the South Americans against Spain. Adams said he would like to see the same train of thought carried still further. By what right, he asked, could we take sides or judge which of the parties had the righteous cause? Was the South American cause, as its authors alleged, the same as our own in the late American Revolution? We fought for independence only as a means of securing civil rights; but in South America civil rights "appear to have been equally disregarded and trampled upon by all parties." These ideas lay behind Adams's famous observation, made apropos of a conversation with Abbe Corrêa: "As to an American system, we have it; we constitute the whole of it; there is no community of interests or of principles between North and South America" (Adams, *Memoirs,* V, 176).

[13] Adams, *Writings,* VI, 342, Adams to Richard Rush, May 29, 1818. This minister was Count Palmella.

and so far as his published writings show, he took no more than a tepid interest in Humboldt's much discussed essay on New Spain.[14]

As for Henry Clay, who was the foremost champion of Spanish American independence in Congress, his chief qualification for that role was that, as a Kentuckian, he came honestly by the settled antagonism that he manifested towards Spain. Except in connection with the War of 1812 and the negotiation of the Treaty of Ghent, in which he participated, he had shown little familiarity or concern with anything that lay beyond the borders of the United States, and he had no first-hand knowledge whatever of the colonies whose cause he was soon to plead with so much fervor and whose future he was to predict with so much assurance. Most of his information and ideas about them probably came from their agents and the propagandists whom we shall discuss below. A few years later (in 1824) he admitted that he was much indebted to Joel Poinsett in this respect.[15]

In short, as these examples suggest, in 1815 the government as well as the people of the United States still needed to be educated about Latin America. In the course of the next few years this need was supplied by a flood of information and ideas about Latin America that flowed in from many sources. The three principal sources were, first, letters and reports from American citizens who had visited Latin America or were residing there; second, the writings of propagandists in the United Statets; and third, foreign newspapers, books, and magazines.

[14] Adams had, however, met Humboldt in Europe (Adams, *Memoirs*, II, 494, and III, 158-163).

[15] *Annals Cong.*, 18 Cong., 1 Sess., vol. 2, p. 1968, in Clay's speech on the tariff bill, March 31, 1824.

II

The first group, American citizens in Latin America, included private individuals (merchants, seamen, travelers, and soldiers who had joined the patriot armies) as well as government agents (consular and special agents and naval officers.) Many letters from the former were published in the local newspapers all along the Atlantic coast from New Orleans to Portsmouth, New Hampshire, and sometimes reprinted in other parts of the country, and they gave many intimate glimpses of life in the vast, strange region to the south of the United States.[16] They were, however, a less important source of information than the letters and reports of the government agents, which were usually more comprehensive, more widely circulated, and presumably more reliable. In the latter connection, we may note a statement made by J. B. Prevost, a special agent of the United States who had spent several years in South America.

Our countrymen generally [he wrote to Secretary Adams from Chile in 1821] have not been of a class to claim respect, the few who are so have been and are cherished, the majority are adventurers, who have either been engaged in privateering or in devising some other mode of livelihood alike disgraceful.[17]

The immediate target of Prevost's broadside was one

[16] Examples are letters from Buenos Aires (March 2 and 3, 1818) and Rio de Janeiro (April 30, 1818), published in the *Delaware Watchman,* Wilmington, and republished in Niles, *Register,* XIV, 209-211, May 23, 1818; and an extract of a letter from Santiago, Chile (Jan. 27, 1819) published in the *Louisiana Courier,* June 7, 1819.

[17] National Archives, SD, Special Agents, vol. 6, J. B. Prevost to Adams, Jan. 6, 1821.

Jeremy Robinson,[18] whose case may be taken as an illustration of these sources of private information. In 1817 Robinson obtained a commission as special agent to South America and at the same time tried to form business connections with John Jacob Astor, Stephen Girard, and other merchants trading to that region. Though his commission was revoked and all the merchants seem to have turned him down, he nevertheless sailed for South America and spent several years in Chile and Peru. While there he bombarded Secretary Adams with long letters full of information and advice. For about two years Adams was strongly influenced by these letters, which he regarded as unusually impartial, accurate, and valuable.[19] That his confidence in Robinson was subsequently shaken seems to have been due to persistent charges that Robinson was associated with shady business deals.[20]

The best early example of the information that came from the more reliable class of American citizens, government agents, is furnished by the detailed reports of the commissioners sent to Buenos Aires and Chile in 1817.[21] First published at Washington, they were reproduced in

[18] See above, note 9 and Wriston, *Executive Agents*, p. 419-420.

[19] Adams, *Writings*, VII, 67, 68, Adams to Monroe, Aug. 26, 1820.

[20] Prevost's letter to Adams cited above, note 17; Jeremy Robinson Papers, LC, Box 1821-1832, Michael Hogan to Robinson, Jan. 12, 1822; *ibid.*, Leverett Saltonstall to (Robinson), May 1, 1826. Poinsett's confidence in Robinson was not shaken (*ibid.*, Poinsett to Secretary of State Edward Livingston, Feb. 2, 1832). For Robinson's mission to Cuba in 1832-1834, in connection with the archives of Florida, see Wriston, *op. cit.*, p. 555.

[21] Caesar A. Rodney, John Graham, Theoderick Bland, and their secretary, H. M. Brackenridge (Buenos Aires and Montevideo), and J. B. Prevost (Chile). These missions are discussed below, chaps. 0, 9.

whole or in part by many newspapers all over the United States, and there can be no question that they played an important part in shaping policy and opinion in regard to Spanish America.

It is important to note, however, that for the most part the effect of communications from government agents in Latin America was confined to government circles in Washington, since many of the communications—especially the regular letters—were not made public. It should also be noted that even for the executive department to which they were addressed, they were not by any means a wholly satisfactory source of information. For one thing, in the whole critical period from 1815 to 1823 the United States had only one full-fledged diplomatic representative in all Latin America—its minister at Rio de Janeiro—and even he was withdrawn upon the return of the Portuguese court to Lisbon in 1821 and was not replaced at Rio until after the independence of Brazil was recognized in 1824. The great majority of these communications, therefore, came from consular and commercial agents and special agents, whose personal as well as official character often made it impossible to give full faith and credit to their reports.

To be sure, many of these agents were men of high character and considerable experience and ability. For example, Joel Poinsett, who served successively at Buenos Aires, Valparaiso, and Mexico City, was a South Carolina gentleman, a member of the American Philosophical Society of Philadelphia, and something of a globe-trotter, and he was subsequently a member of Congress and secretary of war.[22] Condy Raguet, who served at Rio de Janeiro for

[22] See above, chap. 3.

several years, was also a member of the American Philosophical Society and in later years won some repute as a writer on economic questions.[23] John Murray Forbes, special agent and chargé at Buenos Aires, was a classmate of John Quincy Adams's at Harvard and had already served as consul at Hamburg and Copenhagen before he was sent to Buenos Aires. William Tudor, special agent and consul at Lima, had been a founder and the first editor of the *North American Review* and one of the leading literary lights of Boston before he was sent to Lima.[24]

Most of the other agents, however, stood on a considerably lower level than these men, and many of them continued to maintain commercial connections and other private business interests that diminished the reliability of their official reports. Thus, in 1818 Henry Hill, American consul at Valparaíso, joined with Lynch and Zimmerman, one of the principal mercantile houses of Buenos Aires, in establishing a partnership to do business at Valparaíso and Santiago under the name of Lynch, Hill and Company.[25] This practice was common throughout the whole consular service, and even the better class of agents engaged in it. William Tudor formed a partnership with Nixon and McCall of Lima; [26] and in 1816, before he went to South America, John Murray Forbes published a printed circular in which he coupled the announcement of his appointment as consul at Copenhagen with the statement that he had

[23] See below, chap. 15.
[24] Herbert Baxter Adams, *Jared Sparks* (2 vols., Boston, 1893), I, 220, 221, 224-227, and 229, note 2; Wriston, *op. cit.,* p. 423.
[25] Jeremy Robinson Papers, LC, Henry Hill to Robinson, Sept. 24, 1818.
[26] Manning, *Dip. Cor.,* III, 1766.

" already selected correspondents of the first standing and respectability, at Hamburg, Gottenburg, and St. Petersburg, making one concern, and also a house of character and credit at Copenhagen," and that it was his " intention to establish in the other ports of the Baltic such connexions as shall merit the confidence of my American friends." [27]

There was nothing secret or dishonorable about this practice, which was, indeed, almost a necessary consequence of the failure of the government to pay salaries to its consular and commercial agents, who generally received no compensation except the fluctuating and often inadequate fees of their office.[28] Yet the practice was undesirable from every point of view, except perhaps that of economy at Washington, and it was largely responsible for the unsatisfactory character of the whole consular service at that time. How unsatisfactory it was in Latin America—where, it will be recalled, the consular service, in the absence of a diplomatic service, constituted almost the whole regular foreign service of the United States—was made clear at an early date by one of the consuls themselves. This was Henry Hill of Rio de Janeiro (not to be confused with the consul of the same name at Valparaíso), who, in writing to Secretary Adams in 1818 about the misconduct of the former American consul at Buenos Aires, Thomas L. Halsey, said:

The moral defalcation of this man . . . illustrates in a strong point of view, the importance of a change in your Consular establishment, at least in these distant and immoral countries . . . a change which will afford a greater choice of applicants, and place those appointed above the necessities

[27] A copy of the printed circular, signed by Forbes, dated Washington, Jan. 23, 1816, and addressed to " J. Robertson [sic], Esq.," is in Jeremy Robinson Papers, LC, Box 1808-1817.

[28] See above, chap. 3.

or suspicions, attached to Chevaliers d'Industrie, and mere adventurers.[29]

No such reform could have been effected without the support of Congress, which was not forthcoming in our period; but it must be confessed that Adams himself paid little heed to such advice as Hill's and did less than he might have done to improve the personnel under the existing system. Thus, in 1820 he agreed to appoint, sight unseen, a man who wanted a consular appointment somewhere in South America and whose only important qualification appears to have been the fact that he was a protégé of the already politically influential Martin Van Buren; all Adams asked was that the man should name the post he would like to have.[30] Yet it was from such sources as these that Adams and his colleagues obtained a large part of their information about a region whose struggle for independence he compared in importance to the fall of the Roman Empire.[31]

It is hardly surprising, therefore, that greater confidence was often placed in a different kind of source—the reports of American naval officers in Latin American waters. Thus, one of a rather small number of authorities cited by Adams in the course of a highly important discussion of Latin American affairs in 1823 was Captain Charles Stewart, who was then in command of the Pacific Station on the coast of Chile and Peru.[32] As we shall see, naval officers as

[29] Manning, *Dip. Cor.*, II, 704, Hill to Adams, Dec. 21, 1818.

[30] Adams, *Memoirs*, VI, 462.

[31] Adams, *Writings*, VII, 471, in the instructions of May 27, 1823, to Richard C. Anderson.

[32] Adams, *Memoirs*, VI, 111, Nov. 28, 1822. It appears from the context that Adams was more inclined to credit Stewart's account of conditions in Chile than that of J. B. Prevost.

well as consuls were under fire in our period for exploiting public office for private gain; but this did not seriously impair the great prestige that the navy still enjoyed as a result of its heroic actions in the War of 1812, and its officers were socially a cut above the average consul. Hence their word carried greater weight, and this was rather important, for on the whole they seem to have been more critical of the Latin American patriots than were the consular and special agents, and they also showed a greater readiness to cooperate with the British in Latin America.[83]

III

Propagandists in the United States also provided a varied diet of fact and opinion about Latin America. They fell into two main groups, citizens of the United States and foreigners. The former group consisted almost entirely of those who sympathized with the independence cause and its leaders, for the few who opposed it were seldom articulate. The latter group, on the other hand, was sharply divided into the rival camps of apologists for the existing Spanish and Portuguese regimes and champions of Latin American independence.

Though the word was not then used in this sense, propaganda as we know it today was already a highly developed weapon and it was a matter of common knowledge that it was being used extensively by both sides in

[83] Captain James Biddle, testifying at the court martial of Commodore Charles Stewart in 1825 and referring to his own cruise in the *Ontario* on the coast of Chile and Peru in 1818, said, " I knew the British officers in those seas had shown a disposition to aid American citizens, and I was always disposed to reciprocate it " (*Am. State Papers, Naval Affairs*, II, 512).

the international conflict over Latin America. Commenting in 1819 on steps recently taken by the Spanish General Pablo Morillo to have a work directed against the Spanish American revolutionists published at Philadelphia, Duane's *Aurora* remarked, "This *system* of employing the *press* by the enemies of liberty, to impose upon the world, has become common to all governments. . . ." [34] Taking a larger view of the problem, Robert Walsh's *National Gazette* of the same city observed the following year that both royalists and patriots were tainting the news and expressed the opinion that "to the Patriots, and to their auxiliaries in this country and elsewhere, the palm of false-hood, fustian and effrontery, is unquestionably due." [35]

Both sides poured forth a stream of propaganda, and while their activities extended to Latin America and Europe as well, they probably reached their maximum development in the United States, where the freedom of the press was greater than in any other country. Foreign agents had long since learned how to exploit this freedom for their purpose, and as early as the 1790's the Spanish minister himself, Carlos Martínez de Irujo, had bombarded the people of the United States with anonymous newspaper articles and pamphlets designed to shake their faith in their own government's conduct of foreign relations. Irujo's example was followed, with less effort at concealment or none at all, by his successor, Luis de Onís, and the same game of propaganda was played by many other foreigners, such as the Portuguese minister, Abbe Corrêa, and the agent of the Republican revolutionists in Pernambuco, Brazil, Antonio Gonçalves da Cruz. It was also played by the agents of the

[34] *Aurora*, Sept. 18, 1819, "A Flagrant Imposture."
[35] *National Gazette*, Dec. 7, 1820, "South America.

Latin American governments and the exiled Argentine patriots in the United States. Among the latter was Vincente Pazos, author of the well known *Letters on the United Provinces of South America,* addressed to Henry Clay, which were written in Spanish and published in an English translation (1819).[36]

Two of the propagandists on behalf of Spanish America deserve special notice both because we possess more information about them than about most of the rest and also because, while they were exceptionally successful, we are probably safe in assuming that their methods were typical of the propaganda of that period. One of these was a foreigner, the Venezuelan agent Manuel Torres; the other, an American citizen and naval officer, David Porter.

In October 1814 Duane of the *Aurora* gave Manuel Torres letters of introduction to two members of Congress, William Branch Giles and John W. Eppes, and to the Secretary of State, James Monroe, with the suggestion that Monroe introduce him to President Madison and the Secretary of the Treasury.[37] There can be little question that

[36] The translator was Platt H. Crosby. Pazos had served earlier as secretary to the Buenos Aires agent Manuel de Sarratea in London. A notice of his *Letters* published in the *Aurora,* March 29, 1819, described the book as containing "*facts* and *circumstances* of a mercantile nature, sufficient, in the mind of a merchant or practical statesman of discernment, to answer, most satisfactorily, the frequent enquiries—' What has South America to send to the United States, should relations of commerce and friendship be established between the two countries? And is there not danger if she have the sinews of commerce, that she may rival us in the commerce of the rest of the world? And what could we *gain* by manifesting our good wishes for the freedom of South America?'"

[37] "Letters of William Duane," *Mass. Hist. Soc. Proceedings,* XX (1907), 375, Duane to Monroe, Oct. 25, 1814.

Duane thereby contributed to the revival of interest in Latin America that was soon manifested by Congress and the Executive Department. As he told Monroe, Torres was "a gentleman from South America who has resided here [Philadelphia] for a considerable number of years and is attached to our government and country . . . a man of practical experience and [of] principles and views perfectly in the Spirit of our Government." More than that, however, Torres was an active champion of Spanish American independence and was regarded as so dangerous by loyal Spaniards in the United States that in 1814 an attempt was made to assassinate him and it was suspected that Onís himself was implicated in the attempt.

The esteem that Torres had long enjoyed in Philadelphia and that he soon won at Washington gave exceptional importance to his activities as a propagandist; and these were numerous. He published two books, *An Exposition of the Commerce of Spanish America* (1816) and *An Exposition of South America, with some Observations upon its Importance to the U[nited] States* (1819), and he was personally acquainted with at least two newspaper editors, Duane, of the *Aurora*, and Baptis Irvine,[38] of the Balti-

---

[38] Irvine's interest in Spanish American independence bore an interesting relation to political, economic, and sectional rivalries in the United States—"this 'war of triangles,' between planters, merchants and the advocates of internal commerce," as he expressed it. To Mathew Carey, the Philadelphia publisher and advocate of a protective tariff, he wrote in 1821: "In my report on Venezuela, made above two years ago, I . . . showed—incontestibly, I think—the immense value of S. American commerce to us, and how it would nourish our manufactures," and in 1822: "From the *cotton* and *tobacco planters* [in control at Washington] little fair play can be expected, until South American and Mexican products begin *sensibly* to rival ours in the English market. Hence

more *Whig,* the *New York Columbian,* and the *City of Washington Gazette,* whom he provided with news and views about Spanish America. He apparently never lost the contact with Monroe that he formed in 1814 and he soon formed another with John Quincy Adams. While we have no way of measuring his influence on the general public, we can at least be sure that he exerted a good deal of influence over Adams. That was no mean achievement; nor was it unimportant, for, as we have seen, until he became secretary of state, Adams had shown little interest in Latin America or sympathy for its people. Now Torres read him many a lesson on its importance to the United States and fed his fears of British designs upon it. The impression that all this made upon Adams is indicated by the fact that a considerable part of his important instructions of 1823 to the first American minister to Colombia was little more than a paraphrase of a communication that he had received from Torres some eighteen months previously.[39]

I repeat what I said three years ago,—that ' the emancipation of Spanish America will effect our emancipation ' from the shackles of the South " (E. C. Gardiner Collection (HSP), Carey Correspondence, Irvine to Carey, Nov. 25, 1821, and Feb. 15, 1822.) Irvine's report on Venezuela, referred to above, was written as the result of his special mission to that country in 1818-1819 (see below, chap. 10). To his great mortification, it was not published, but it is briefly described in Lewis Hanke, " Baptis Irvine's Reports on Simón Bolívar," *Hispanic Am. Hist. Rev.,* XVI (1936), p. 361, note 6. His early connection with Duane (*ibid.,* p. 360) may explain the beginning of his interest in Latin America; it was probably increased by his contact with José Miguel Carrera of Chile when the latter visited the United States (Griffin, *United States,* p. 125).

[39] Part of Adams's instructions of May 27, 1823, to Richard C. Anderson (Manning, *Dip. Cor.,* I, 202-204) follows very closely

Captain David Porter, U. S. N.,[40] waged his propaganda campaign on behalf of Spanish American independence while he was a member of the Navy Board at Washington. Though he and Torres were serving the same cause at the same time, it does not appear that they cooperated with each other. They were connected with different parts of South America, worked with different groups in the United States, and reached the public in different ways. Since there was no conflict between them, this was an advantage to their cause, for it gave the people of the United States a broader view of Spanish America and advertized Spanish America more widely in the United States.

Porter's chief connection in South America was with the Carrera family, which headed one of the important patriot factions in Chile and which he had met during his naval service on the west coast of South America in the War of 1812.[41] After his return to the United States he kept up a correspondence with his Chilean friends, maintained a friendly and at times anxious oversight over the children that some of them sent to school in the United States, and conferred with J. M. Carrera when the latter

---

a letter of Nov. 30, 1821, from Torres to Adams (*ibid.*, II, 1212-1216). There are, however, at least three differences: (1) Adams, unlike Torres, speaks of the Amazon as a river of Colombia; (2) Adams takes exception to Torres's use of " empire " in the phrase " the centre and the empire of the human family "; (3) whereas Torres spoke of the United States and Colombia as economically complementary to each other, Adams said that in certain respects they would be " rather competitors and rivals than customers to each other." For Torres and the Monroe Doctrine, see below, chap. 16.

[40] See article on David Porter in DAB and references there.

[41] See chap. 3, note 53.

came to this country in 1816 in search of aid for the patriot cause.[42] The most intense period of Porter's activities as a propagandist began in 1817 and lasted through the following year.

Among the propagandists who were associated with him in this period were H. M. Brackenridge,[43] whose book, *South America: A Letter on the Present State of that Country, to James Monroe,* published in October 1817 and reprinted in England the following year, was one of the best of its kind and will be discussed below, and Joseph H. Skinner, postmaster at Baltimore, whose newspaper articles signed " Lautaro " [44] created a sensation in South America [45] as well as the United States. Neither writer appears to have been on Carrera's pay-roll, and in Skinner's case, at least, that relationship was reversed, for he made

[42] Poinsett Papers, HSP, vol. 2, David Porter to Joel Poinsett, April 19, 1817; Monroe Papers, NYPL, J. M. de Carrera to David Porter, Aug. 24, 1818; *ibid.,* Xaviera de Carrera to Porter, Aug. 26, 1818. Bemis, *Early Diplomatic Missions,* p. 30-33, gives a succinct account of Carrera's " self-sustained mission " to the United States, utilizing fresh sources as well as familiar studies such as Benjamín Vicuña Mackenna, *El ostracismo de los Carrera* (Santiago, 1857, and later editions), and William Miller Collier and Guillermo Feliú Cruz, *La primera Misión de los Estados Unidos en Chile* (Santiago, 1926).

[43] See Porter's reference to Brackenridge in his letter of Oct. 23, 1817, quoted below in the text.

[44] Since there has been some question about the authorship of the " Lautaro " letters, it may be noted that, in the margin of Porter's letter of Oct. 23, 1817, quoted below in the text, he wrote, " Confidentially: Mr. J. Skinner post master in Baltimore is the author of Lautaro as he is of many other publications on the same subject."

[45] For example, the letters were frequently mentioned, extracted, and discussed in *El Censor* of Buenos Aires from December 1817 to March 1818.

Carrera a loan of four thousand dollars.[46] His " Lautaro " letters also illustrate the way in which factional politics in Latin America occasionally affected propaganda in the United States, for the Buenos Aires government, which was hostile to the Carrera faction in Chile, was described in these letters as too subservient to Britain to merit recognition by the United States as an independent power. Joel Poinsett, former agent to Buenos Aires and Chile, was a frequent correspondent of Porter's at this time, but does not appear to have taken any part in the latter's campaign of propaganda. The newspapers of Washington, Richmond, and, above all, Baltimore were the chief media for the publications of the group. Of one of these newspapers Porter wrote in 1818: " The columns of the *Maryland Censor* [47] are open to me. They teem with S[outh] A[merican] affairs and the Editor is devoted to the Patriotic cause." [48]

The nature and extent of the activities of this group,

[46] Bemis, *op. cit.*, p. 32, note 2, says that Skinner entrusted to Theoderick Bland, for collection, Carrera's note for this debt, when Bland went to South America on the mission of 1817. He also cites a petition from Bland to the Buenos Aires government dated April 4, 1818, asking it to pay the note (agn, BA, S1-A2-A4, No. 8), and adds, " I found no evidence of action on this petition." There is, however, in the same bundle of documents a draft of the reply of the Buenos Aires government to Bland, dated April 16, 1818, to the effect that as it was understood that Skinner had presented this same claim to the Chilean government and General San Martín had offered his mediation to remove any possible difficulties, the Buenos Aires government could do nothing in the matter.

[47] This Baltimore newspaper was established Aug. 19, 1818, and the last issue located by Brigham was that of Jan. 20, 1819; copies of it are very rare: Clarence S. Brigham, " Bibliography of American Newspapers, 1690-1820," *American Antiquarian Society Proceedings*, 1915, p. 157.

[48] Poinsett Papers (HSP), Porter to Poinsett, Oct. 19, 1818.

and the strong Anglophobe bias of Porter's own writings about the Spanish American question are vividly described in the following letter, which he wrote to Poinsett from Washington on October 23, 1817.[49]

I had intended to have written you fully agreeable to promise on S[outh] A[merican] affairs but the plot thickened so rapidly that I knew not where to begin, and left you therefore to gather a knowledge of what was going on from the newspapers. In most of what you have seen, I have had a hand, and I take on myself to say that I first started this host of writers in favor of our taking a decided stand in the affairs of S. America. The pieces in defense of Carrera . . . were some written by myself some by a friend of mine—and that same friend is the author of Lautaro.[50] . . . I find that [this subject, Spanish America] is now brought to view as a matter of deep import what was once (and not long since) treated with indifference. We want to make it appear that the interests of the U. S. are jeopardized by the machinations of England through their [England's] agents, that we are the *natural* allies of S. America, that unless we aid them they will throw themselves into the arms of our worst enemy (our natural enemy), that no time is to be lost, that England has been long at work to effect her object &c &c &c. With these views we have taken some pains to heat the public mind as well as to enlighten it, and by doing so we hoped to produce some effect on both Congress & Govt. The views of the latter [the Executive Department] I believe to be in some degree (to a great degree) in conformity with our own. There are some of the best writers in this country engaged in the business. Brackenridge is here and at this moment is writing a pamphlet on the subject. . . . I should like very much to have your opinion of things in general. They would be of great service in the good cause.

These are only a few examples of the way in which the friends and foes of Spanish American independence in the

---

⁴⁹ *Ibid.*   ⁵⁰ See above, note 44.

United States sought " to heat the public mind as well as to enlighten it " in the period just following the War of 1812. Many others might be given and some of these, especially the speeches of Henry Clay and other members of Congress, will be discussed later in another connection. From what has already been said on the subject, and from the other available evidence, we may conclude that the friends of Spanish American independence were more active and much more articulate than its foes; that the former included important nuclei in several cities, such as Duane and Torres at Philadelphia, Irvine at New York and Washington, and Porter, Brackenridge and Skinner at Washington and Baltimore, who undertook a systematic campaign of propaganda in order to create a public opinion that would force Congress and the Executive Department to aid the Spanish American cause; that at least two of them (Duane and Torres) anticipated Clay in undertaking this campaign; that Brazil was completely overshadowed in it by Spanish America; and that one of the chief emotional devices of the propagandists was to capitalize on the traditional, deep-seated antagonism towards Great Britain in the United States by stressing the theme of Anglo-American rivalry over Latin America—a rivalry which did, in fact, exist, and had existed from the very beginning of the independence movement in that region.

In view of the subsequent development of policy and opinion in the United States, the importance of this strong Anglophobe motif in the propaganda on behalf of Spanish American independence can hardly be overemphasized. Porter was by no means the only one who played up the " machinations of England " in that quarter. Skinner's " Lautaro " letters described Buenos Aires as a mere factory " or trading post of Great Britain. Carrying the same idea several steps further, Duane in the *Aurora* warned that Buenos Aires in British hands might become a center of counter-revolution and anti-republicanism in that part of South America, and a base from which Britain might some day threaten the United States as it was already threatening China from its Bengal base.

Possibly [he continued] if England was to occupy Buenos Ayres alone, and was capable of limiting her views to the trade of that place, we might have nothing to care about ourselves; but—the same agency is at work nearer home, at the mouth of the Oronooko [Orinoco], [and] on the Mosquito shore; and there is Woodbine and Arbuthnot at this moment with the *Seminoles* . . . on the Florida frontier.[51]

---

[51] *Aurora,* June 7, 1817, item captioned " Very good news—if true."

CHAPTER SIX

THE LATIN AMERICAN PICTURE
AND ITS PAINTERS

(PART II)

I

While England served as chief bogeyman for propagandists of the Spanish American cause in the United States, English publications also served them and other writers of all shades of opinion as an important source of information about Latin America. This was partly because a vestigial colonialism still infected many educated Americans and made them stand in awe of any printed page that came from an English press. It was partly also for the very good reason that England's wider contacts and superior sources of information both in Latin America and also among those European nations that were interested in Latin American affairs entitled the publications of its comparatively free press to respectful attention. The most valuable of these in the years with which we are immediately concerned were periodicals, of which the four that appear to have been the most widely read and quoted in the United States were three newspapers, *Bell's Weekly Messenger,* which was primarily a journal of commerce, the *London Morning Chronicle,* and the *Times,* which were designed for the general newspaper reader, and a quarterly, *The Edinburgh Review,* which in addition to serving as supreme arbiter in the field of literature also specialised in *haute politique,* and of which we shall have occasion to speak more particularly in a later chapter.

A peculiar interest attaches to the part played by British periodicals in shaping American opinion about Latin America, for a considerable portion of what the British periodicals published on this subject was fed to them by the paid propagandists of the independent government of Buenos Aires. This propaganda was arranged for through the financial agents of the Buenos Aires government in London, Hullett Brothers,[1] who disguised themselves under the name Anti-Igyptus & Co.; it seems to have been carried on mainly in the period 1817-1820, though it may have been begun earlier and continued later; and it reached the public through the medium of such respectable journals as the *Times,* the *Morning Chronicle*, and the *British Review*.

Sometimes, apparently, these journals opened their columns to this propaganda free of charge, as in the case of an article defending the Spanish American cause which was published in the *British Review* in 1819. In at least one conspicuous case, however, there was a quid pro quo, if we may believe Hullett Brothers, for early in 1819 they reported that they had taken into their pay James Murray, foreign affairs editor of the *Times*.[2] Though the arrange-

[1] According to the index, this firm is mentioned only once in Webster, *op. cit.,* I, 158, a despatch from the British minister in Buenos Aires, Oct. 20, 1826, in which he deplores the "act of folly" of the government at that place in taking its "money business" out of the hands of Alexander Baring and placing it in the hands of "Messrs. Hullett & Co." Hullett Brothers had by this time been doing business with the Buenos Aires government for about a decade. This included the propaganda agency mentioned in the text. A great deal of correspondence regarding it is in AGN, BA, S1-A2-A2, nos. 12 and 14, and A3, no. 3. See also Humphreys, *British Consular Reports,* p. 99, note 2, and p. 127, note 2.

[2] AGN, BA, S1-A2-A2, no. 12, Hullett Hermanos y Cia. to Gregorio Tagle, *Primer Ministro,* etc., Feb. 2, 1819.

ment was kept a secret from the editor-in-chief lest it offend his "well known sense of delicacy," it served its purpose quickly and well, for in April, soon after it was concluded, the *Times*, which had hitherto been cool towards the Spanish American patriots, published a series of articles so favorable to them that it created a sensation in England.[3]

Whether their publication was paid for or not, these articles were prepared by writers employed by Hullett Brothers, among whom, in addition to Murray of the *Times*, were James Russell, law student and tutor to the eldest son of Viscount Lascelles, and William Walton,[4]

[3] *Ibid.*, "Anti-Igyptus y Cia." (Hullett Brothers) to Tagle, April 23, 1819. James Murray joined the staff of *The Times* before 1815, served it ably in the organization of its foreign correspondence, was its special correspondent at the Congress of Aix-la-Chapelle, bought one-half of one-sixteenth of a share of *The Times* for £1400 in 1819, and became its Foreign Director in 1827. See *The History of The Times, "Thunderer in the Making, 1785-1841"* (London, 1935), p. 174, 419-420. From 1818 to 1822 there was a great deal of gossip about the subsidies *The Times* and other London newspapers were supposed to be receiving from foreign governments. Replying to an inquiry from Castlereagh on this score, the British ambassador in Paris, Sir Charles Stuart, reported on June 23, 1818: "It would seem that most of our public prints are now in the pay of M. de Cazes [Decazes, French Minister of the Interior]. *The Times,* indeed, receives with both hands, from the Duke de St. Carlos [San Carlos, Spanish ambassador in London] with one, and from M. de Cazes with the other" (*ibid.*, p. 218).

[4] AGN, BA, S1-A2-A3, no. 3, folder marked "1817-1818. Inglaterra. Comisionado en Londres, D. Guillermo Walton," contains many documents on the subject, including a letter from Walton to the Buenos Aires government, Feb. 26, 1817, in which he gives an account of his publications and his services to the Spanish American cause. He was employed by the Buenos Aires government from the beginning of 1818 at a salary of 1500 pesos (£300), but was dropped before the end of the year for talking too much about the connection.

author of the well known *Exposé of the Dissentions in Spanish America*,[5] who had already been employed by the agent of Venezuela in London, Luis López Méndez, to write on behalf of that government. Most of their writing was done for the *Morning Chronicle*, whose editor, James Perry, was an enthusiastic supporter of the Spanish American cause, as is evidenced by a letter that he addressed to the head of the Buenos Aires government, Juan Martín de Pueyrredon, on January 17, 1818.

> Your gallant efforts [he wrote] are viewed with delight by every liberal man in Europe; and no doubt is entertained of your final and complete success. I have not failed in my humble but useful profession, as Editor of an independent journal devoted to the principles of freedom, justice and humanity, to endeavor to keep alive in this country the holy flame so gloriously kindled in South America. . . .[6]

These facts are highly important for our purpose, because the *Morning Chronicle* displayed no greater devotion to the principles of freedom, justice, and humanity than it did to the interests of British commerce in Spanish America; it also displayed a keen awareness that these interests were in conflict with those of the United States; and there was probably no British journal which contributed more towards shaping opinion in the United States about Latin America

[5] In this book Walton made free use of Servando Teresa de Mier's *Historia de la revolución de Nueva España* (2 vols., London, 1813). See Ballesteros, *Historia de España*, VII, 446, note 57. Cf. chap. 5, note 5.

[6] AGN, BA, S1-A2-A3, no. 3, Perry to Pueyrredon, dated " Morning Chronicle Office." James Perry acquired control of the *Morning Chronicle* in 1789, made it " the most influential journal [in England] for thirty years," and as an editor was " conspicuously independent—as journalistic independence went in those years " (*The History of The Times*, p. 33, 215).

than the *Morning Chronicle*. It was an article in this newspaper that provided the text for Niles's article of 1815 on Spanish America from which the quotation at the beginning of the present chapter was taken; and it was from the same newspaper that, in 1823, newspapers in the United States learned of the " Treaty of Verona," which we now know was a forgery but which then gained enough acceptance to make it a rather important factor in shaping public opinion in that critical period. In the intervening years, the *Morning Chronicle* was time and again quoted in the United States as expressing British views about Latin America. Those views, which helped to shape the American people's own views of Latin America, were represented by the article which furnished Niles's text in 1815 and which warned the British people not to let their enterprising Yankee cousins get ahead of them in Spanish America and concluded with the suggestion that as soon as Britain had completed its task of restoring order in war-torn Europe, it ought to "look across the Atlantic."

In later years, to be sure, when the increasing divergence between England and the Holy Alliance gave many Englishmen an uncomfortable feeling of isolation in Europe, the *Morning Chronicle,* the *Edinburgh Review,* and many other journals discovered that after all their country and the United States had a most important interest in common, their interest in defending liberty against the despotism of the Holy Alliance; and there was never a time when these journals did not give at least some measure of support to the cause of Spanish American independence, which was also supported by the overwhelming majority of journals in the United States. Nevertheless, in the years immediately following the restoration of peace in Europe and the United

States, English journals of all shades of opinion, whether liberal or conservative, stressed the conflict of interest between their country and the United States in Latin America.

The effect of this on opinion and policy in the United States was important. It played into the hands of propagandists in the United States, such as Torres, Duane, and Porter, who were using the spectre of British penetration of Latin America in an effort to bring about the intervention of the United States in favor of Spanish American independence. At the same time, however, it tended to defeat that effort, or at least to delay its success, by strengthening the opinion that the United States must move cautiously in its relations with Latin America and above all must not challenge the important interests of Great Britain in that region too peremptorily, lest the rivalry of the two powers be carried to the point of an open break. The reason for this was obvious. There was a belief (sedulously cultivated by English journals) that the continental powers wished to intervene against the revolution in Spanish America; that England, without whose aid the intervention could hardly be effective, was wavering and might be pushed into the arms of the Continental powers if the United States took too aggressive a stand in favor of Spanish America; and that the United States as well as Latin America might then be made a victim of the intervention.

Other foreign sources also contributed details to the picture of Latin America, though they were less important than the British contribution. Among these were the periodic surveys of world affairs written by the French Abbé de Pradt, whose most notable contribution was probably his emphasis on the idea of hemispheric solidarity between the

United States and Latin America; periodicals published in
Spain and Spanish America, which, by the mutual recrimi-
nations of loyalists and rebels, helped to revive the "Black
Legend" to the discredit of both sides; and official docu-
ments, such as proclamations and letters, issuing from both
the loyalist and rebel camps. Among the latter were Simón
Bolívar's proclamation of war without quarter against the
Spaniards, which was strong medicine even for his most
ardent sympathisers in the United States,[7] and an intercepted despatch from the loyalist Bishop of Valladolid
(Mexico)[8] which gave encouragement to the friends of
Spanish American independence by its admission that the
Spanish regime was crumbling even in Mexico, where
the revolutionists had seemed thoroughly beaten and
demoralized.

II

Books and pamphlets were an important vehicle for
conveying this mass of fact and opinion about Latin America to the people of the United States. Many of these—
such as those by Brackenridge, de Pradt, Pazos, and Walton
—we have already mentioned, and another of some importance, *A Cursory View of Spanish America* written by
William D. Robinson, was published in 1815.[9] It would
seem, however, that publications of this kind reached a
rather restricted audience, for the Americans of that day
were not a book-buying people and they made no exception
in favor of books about Latin America. This was illustrated

---

[7] *City of Washington Gazette*, Dec. 26, 1817, "South American
Independence."

[8] *Aurora*, June 12, 1817, "True Situation of New Spain."

[9] See above, chap. 5, note ?

by the bitter experience of the William D. Robinson just mentioned. In 1820 another book of his, *Memoirs of the Mexican Revolution,* was published through Carey & Lea of Philadelphia.[10] The subject was timely, for popular interest in Spanish America at large had been mounting rapidly in recent years and the long-frustrated movement for Mexican independence, on which this book was focussed, had just been crowned with success. The publisher was one of the best known in the United States. The author had already published another book in the same general field, and had subsequently had an adventurous and highly publicized career,[11] which included trading in munitions with the Mexican rebels whose exploits he was now describing, capture by the Spanish royalists, imprisonment first in the ill-famed Morro Castle at Havana and then at Cadiz, and finally a hairbreadth escape from his Spanish captors. Finally, a rather exacting book-reviewer described the book

[10] This does not appear on the title page of the copy in the American Philosophical Society (which is inscribed " Presented to the Philosophical Society by the Author, 14 Novr. 1820 "). The title page reads, " Printed for the author. Lydia R. Bailey, Printer." However, the Lea & Febiger Papers (HSP) contain a mass of correspondence between Carey & Lea and William D. Robinson for the years 1820 and 1821 which show that this firm handled the book.

[11] For example, in the *Louisiana Courier,* March 22, 1819, news item clipped from the New York *Daily Advertiser,* and Jan. 3, 1820, news item clipped from the *New York Evening Post,* reviewing Robinson's career, reporting his escape from the Spaniards, and stating that their object in imprisoning him had been "to prevent the promulgation of certain facts which they well knew, Mr. R[obinson] had become acquainted with in Mexico." This kind of publicity should have created a good market for the revelations about Mexico published in Robinson's book later on in the same year.

as attractive in both matter and manner, for readers of almost every description.[12] And yet, despite all these favorable circumstances, which should have made it a sure-fire success, the book had an extremely small sale, to the bitter disappointment of its author—and, we may be sure, its publisher as well.[13]

This was not because the American people did not read, but because most of their reading was done in newspapers. An experienced observer, Robert Walsh, remarked that in the enlightened part of Europe books were the main dependence of all those who wished to keep well informed about abstract knowledge, literature and politics, but that " in America, something like the reverse of this yet obtains; we are satisfied or bear with newspapers as sources of intellectual aliment of every description." [14] As he remarked, and as he had learned to his own cost,[15] " periodical journals " of other kinds, such as reviews and magazines, generally failed or at most obtained a limited local circulation. When Walsh wrote, there was not a single national journal of this kind in the United States; and although the *North American Review,* which was soon to win that role for itself,[16] had already been founded, at this time it was still a mere provincial journal which had only a small following in New England and almost none outside of it.

[12] *National Gazette,* Dec. 13, 1820, two items: (a) " Don Xavier Mina," and (b) editorial, no caption.

[13] Correspondence cited above, note 10.

[14] *National Gazette,* April 5, 1820. This was the first issue of this newspaper. For H. M. Brackenridge's comments on this point, see below, note 17.

[15] See article on Robert Walsh in DAB.

[16] H. B. Adams, *Jared Sparks,* I, 231, 232; Frank L. Mott, *A History of American Magazines, 1850-1865* (Cambridge, Mass, 1938), p. 219-227.

Walsh was therefore justified in concluding that throughout the United States newspapers still exerted " an unrivalled influence." This fact gave added significance to the activities of such newspaper propagandists as Porter and Duane, which we have already discussed; but it also made the task of the propagandists more difficult, since there were no newspapers in the country that had a nation-wide circulation, and, of course, no press associations or news syndicates through which one news item or editorial could be assured of reaching the whole country or even a considerable part of it. There were only two factors that tended in any important degree to offset this extreme decentralization of American journalism. The first of these was the common practice of clipping, examples of which are the reproduction of items from the *Boston Patriot* in the *New York Evening Post* and of items from the Wilmington *Delaware Watchman* in the New Orleans *Louisiana Courier*. This practice was, however, haphazard at best and its unifying effect was in turn offset by the multiplicity of newspapers in the large cities and even in many of the towns. The second and more important factor was the universal newspaper practice of reporting more or less extensively the more important utterances of public officials at Washington, such as presidential messages, the reports of heads of departments, and the speeches of members of Congress. Such items were usually clipped from the *National Intelligencer* of Washington but were interpreted by each local editor in his own way.

In view of this situation, the most effective instrument of propaganda that could be used on either side of the Latin American question was an utterance from some official source at Washington that commanded confidence in the nation at large and space in the newspapers. Here, however, as David Porter realized, lay another difficulty: both Congress and the Executive Department required prodding from an aroused public opinion before they would, in any likelihood, make any important statement in behalf of Spanish America; and even after such a statement had been made, there was no assurance that it would be widely and favorably reported in the countless independent newspapers of the country unless local opinion had been educated up to an appreciation of its importance. In other words, the nub of the propaganda problem was to convert the myriad cellular communities of which the United States was composed. It is, therefore, important to recall that there were very few of these communities which had any interest in the maintenance of the colonial regime in Latin America, whereas there were many that had a strong interest in its destruction. This enormously facilitated the task of the Duanes and Porters who were pleading the cause of Spanish American independence, and it laid a hopelessly heavy handicap on the few who opposed them. The only real question at issue—and it was to this issue that the Duanes and Porters mainly addressed themselves—was how far the United States should go in aiding the Spanish Americans. The answer to that question depended mainly on the image of Latin America that had been formed in the minds of the American people by the flood of fact and propaganda that poured in upon them from sources both at home and abroad.

It would be foolhardy to paint an image of Latin America and say, " This is what was in the minds of the people of the United States," for there was not one such image, but many, in their minds. Within two or three years after the restoration of peace, however, they did reach substantial agreement as to certain facts regarding the character of the people of Latin America and its role in relation to the United States and Europe; and perhaps the best way of indicating how far this agreement extended and where disagreement began will be to examine a contemporary portrait of Latin America by a sympathetic painter and then to see how this portrait appeared to his more critical countrymen.

III

For this purpose we could hardly find a better portrait than the one painted by H. M. Brackenridge in his 52-page pamphlet *South America* which was published towards the close of 1817.[17] Like many of his contemporaries, he used the term South America to designate the region that we call continental Latin America, for his pamphlet discussed Mexico as well as South America proper, and Brazil as well as Spanish America. It dealt harshly with Spain and gently with Latin America; but in the main it was singularly temperate, judicious, and well informed, and it gave currency to ideas that were to dominate American thinking about Latin America for many years to come. Finally, while

[17] See above, chap. 5, note 43, and text at that point. The pamphlet was published at Washington, Oct. 15, 1817, and in 1818 was reprinted in the London *Pamphleteer*. Shortly before the pamphlet was published in 1817, Brackenridge said that in the past six or seven years he had read with great attention every book of travel or "statistics" relating to South America and Mexico and that the most valuable accounts of those countries that he had found were in "detached scraps or essays" published in English and American journals, such as the recent article on Pernambuco in the *North American Review* (cited below, note 29). National Archives, SD, "South American Missions . . . 1815-1818," vol. I, Brackenridge to Richard Rush, July 28, 1817.

Brackenridge was not an outstanding political leader and could not be regarded as the spokesman of the administration in this pamphlet, the administration did have enough confidence in him to appoint him secretary to an important mission to South America which set out shortly after the pamphlet was published.[18]

Brackenridge began by stressing the great diversity that characterized the countries and peoples of Latin America. Admitting that they were generally backward, he insisted that the Latin Americans were, like all other human beings, naturally good and that they were probably better fitted for liberty and self-government than most of the people of Europe. Once freed from their bonds of colonial servitude, they would easily rise to the natural standard of their character; and with their rich natural resources and an aggregate population of eighteen million, the new nations would have a great future before them. The present state of the independence movement in Mexico was difficult to ascertain; but elsewhere it was highly encouraging. The rest of Spanish America was already, or soon would be, free. Brazil, through the transfer of the Portuguese court to Rio de Janeiro, had already obtained what the Spanish Americans were still contending for: it was no longer a colony, and it had its own government. All that remained to be done was for the king to sever his connection with Portugal, cease to be European, and identify his interests wholly with those of America.

Turning to the interest of his own country in Latin America, Brackenridge dwelt with equal satisfaction on the thrilling spectacle of eighteen million souls struggling to be free and on the pleasant prospect of larger markets for

[18] The mission is discussed below, chap. 8.

the products and cargoes for the ships of the United States, which, he declared, should also welcome the emancipation of the rest of America from European control.

In conclusion, he discussed the policy of the United States towards Latin America and made the following recommendations: (1) The United States ought not to go to war in behalf of the Spanish Americans, since that might injure both parties by provoking the intervention of the united powers of Europe on the side of Spain. The United States should, however, immediately recognize the independence of La Plata (Buenos Aires) and probably that of Chile as well. Since those countries were already independent in fact, no nation would have any right to take offense at the recognition of their governments, and this act would encourage the independence movement in the rest of Spanish America. (2) The United States ought to abstain from any interference in regard to the political systems of the new American governments. It was to be hoped that they would be republican; but if they were monarchical, as in the case of Brazil, that was their own affair. (3) As for the extent to which the United States should cooperate with the new states, Brackenridge declared that he was no advocate of the "visionary" idea of a great American congress on the isthmus of Panama, but he did believe that the American nations could reach a common understanding on a number of important questions—for example, on the question of neutral rights. He saw no danger that, as "the foxes and wolves" were suggesting, Latin America would fall victim to the ambition of the United States, for it had fixed limits beyond which neither the wishes of its people nor the genius of its government would permit it to stray. The United States would simply be the natural head of the

New World; and if its system should be voluntarily adopted by the new states—as might well be the case, since revolution, which formerly meant little more than a change of masters, now meant the establishment of free government—there would be an end to wars in the Western Hemisphere. On this optimistic and now familiar note the pamphlet came to a close.

In many respects, its contents were not novel but merely presented succinctly and tellingly ideas and information already current in well informed liberal circles. This is one of the reasons why so much space has been given to it here. At the same time, it did mark an advance on what had already been said and written. It helped clarify and popularize the idea of the American system, the " doctrine of the two spheres," which was ultimately incorporated in Monroe's message of 1823. And although its three recommendations of policy related to questions which were being warmly debated at the time, every one of them was followed by the United States government in the course of the next decade. This was not because of Brackenridge's influence with the authorities at Washington, which was probably slight, nor because of his influence on public opinion, which we can not measure. The reason was rather that the basic ideas of his work—such as those regarding the natural goodness of man and the national interests of the United States—were shared by those who controlled the government, and that he was one of the first to make a systematic, comprehensive application of these ideas to the Latin American problem in the light of the best information then available. When his betters came to consider the same problem in the same way, they not unnaturally reached much the same conclusion.

IV

There were, to be sure, many of Brackenridge's contemporaries who had different ideas both about the character of Latin America and about its relation to the rest of the world. As he himself said, " No pains have been spared to represent [the Spanish Americans] in the most hateful and disgusting colors, and there are many of us who now take it for granted that they are the most despicable of the human race." [19] As we have seen, this prejudice was due partly to the " Black Legend " and partly to royalist propaganda; but the patriots themselves were also to blame for it, for in the course of their factional fights they vilified each other so convincingly as to discredit the whole patriot cause in the minds of many foreigners. The most striking example of this was the case of the Buenos Aires exiles of 1816, among whom, besides Vincente Pazos, was Manuel Moreno, brother of the distinguished patriot leader and writer, Mariano Moreno. Expelled from Buenos Aires by Director Pueyrredon, they came to the United States; and when he published a manifesto justifying their expulsion, they published at Baltimore a counter-manifesto in which they accused him, among other things, of trying to place the revolution in the Plata region at the feet of the king of Portugal-Brazil.[20]

According to Niles's *Register,* the effect of this counter-manifesto was to convince people in the United States that true liberty did not exist in the Plata region and to turn some of them against the whole patriot cause. Niles him-

[19] Brackenridge, *South America,* p. 15.
[20] Vicente Fidel López, *Historia de la república argentina* (10 vols., Buenos Aires, 1883-1893), VI, 413, 423-425

self, though decidedly sympathetic to that cause, admitted in August 1817 that he had lost confidence in the Buenos Aires government; [21] and the full significance of this admission will be appreciated when it is remembered that, as even Brackenridge confessed, the Buenos Aires government was the only one in Spanish America that was unquestionably entitled to recognition by the United States. When there was so much doubt about the political talents and civic morality of this ablest exponent of the patriot cause, it is not surprising that there were many in the United States who took a less hopeful view of the present condition and future prospects of Latin America than did Brackenridge.

The result was to increase the existing skepticism about Latin America in general, which John Randolph of Roanoke had already voiced in Congress. " The struggle for liberty in South America," he said in 1816, " will turn out in the end something like the French liberty, a detestable despotism. You cannot make liberty out of Spanish matter—you might as well try to build a seventy-four out of pine saplings." [22] Such doubts were reinforced by considerations that Brackenridge did not mention. One of these was the dawning realization that Latin America might become a serious competitor of the United States in the production of such commodities as flour, tobacco, cotton and beef. Another was Southern dislike of the abolitionist and Negrophil tendencies manifested by some of the new governments.

At the other end of the scale, there were many who were more eager than was Brackenridge to tighten the bonds between the Americas, either because they burned with a

[21] *Register,* XII, 365, and XIII, 185-189.
[22] *Annals Cong.,* 14 Cong., 1 Sess., p. 727, Jan. 20, 1816.

hotter zeal for the Latin American cause, or for some other reason. As Onís warned the Spanish court early in 1815, there were many people in the United States who were dreaming of " a universal republic of the two Americas." [23] One of these dreamers was that distinguished architect and amiable visionary, William Thornton, a naturalized American of English origin who had been federal commissioner of patents since 1802. He designed the national capitol at Washington and he also undertook to design one grand government for the Americas. According to a plan which he drew up in Washington in March 1815, they were to form a voluntary federal union under a " Columbian, Incal or Supreme Government," which was to be divided into thirteen sections or commonwealths and to have as its chief officials one Inca, 26 sachems, and 52 caciques; and the motto of his plan was " Nunc aut Nunquam." [24]

A similar and at the same time strikingly different idea was expressed a year later by a well known figure in American politics who was not a visionary like Thornton but who had the same " nunc aut nunquam " spirit. This was Mathew Lyon, former representative of Vermont in Congress and protagonist in the first famous brawl in the history of the House of Representatives. Moving to Kentucky in 1801 he continued to take an active part in national politics and was always on good terms with Monroe. In

[23] AHN, Est., Legajo 5640, Onís to the Duque de San Carlos, Feb. 4, 1815, No. 7 (LC photostat).

[24] N. Andrew N. Cleven, " Thornton's Outlines of a Constitution for United North and South Columbia," *Hispanic Am. Hist. Rev.*, XII (1932), p. 198-215. For biographical information about Thornton, see *ibid.*, p. 198, and DAB. For his connection with Richard Rush, see below, p. 224-225 and 237, note 22.

a letter that he wrote Monroe in March 1816 [25] and subsequently published at the request of his friends,[26] he said:

I am no fonder of the British nation, or her government than the most flaming partisan against her is. Yet I have long wished to avoid warlike contests with her. Contests in which we are sure to gain nothing, but to waste our strength, and retard the growth of that power which is to pervade this continent, even to Cape Horn. I have long considered that our mode of Government by states confederated for national purposes only, will fit a larger empire than ever yet existed, and I have long believed that such an empire will rise in America, and give quiet to the world.

For the moment, however, Lyon was willing to let this continental union stop short of Cape Horn, and he was as eager for war with Spain as he was for peace with England.

Believing as I do [he continued] that the more of America comes under the controul of the Anglo Americans the better for the world, I care not how soon a rupture [with Spain] takes place. I believe the whole of what is called Terra Firma [northern South America] and the country from there to New Orleans after their struggles and turmoil, are now ready to sit down under the American government. . . . The present is the most favorable opportunity that will offer for perhaps a century. . . .

This idea of "Anglo Americanising the south," as he himself expressed it,[27] was strikingly different from Thorn-

[25] Monroe Papers, NYPL, Lyon to Monroe, March 5, 1816. See article on Matthew Lyon in DAB.

[26] Monroe Papers, NYPL, Lyon to Monroe, April 16, 1816.

[27] In his letter of March 5, 1816, Lyon said: " With my enthusiasm for Anglo Americanising the south, you may possibly wonder that I was not a Burrite." The reason, he explained, was that he was unwilling to interfere with Spanish America without authorization from the United States government, whereas " Burr was in haste to do something, his projects were mere confusion without patriotism; he saw nothing rightly but the weakness of the Spanish government."

ton's idea of a union of the Americas under a plan whose quaint nomenclature, with its Incas and Caciques, shows how far its author was from wishing to Anglo-Americanize our southern neighbors. Yet there were important resemblances between the two ideas, for both of them contemplated the union of the Americas under a federal system of government; and while the voluntary character of the union was more explicit in Thornton's plan, Lyon's too was apparently based on the assumption that the Spanish Americans were " ready to sit down under the American government."

Even when we remember how little reliable information about Latin America was then available in the United States, these plans seem fantastic. Yet they are well worth recording because they express an attitude towards Latin America which, as Onís remarked before either plan was drawn up, was widespread in the United States.[28] They are the more important for this purpose because they were written by men who had very different origins and backgrounds and were living in widely separate parts of the country and who had taken a prominent enough part in public life to entitle their views to more weight than those of the average American. In their different ways they expressed the same underlying idea of the essential unity of the Americas and the need of a new system for the New World. Those who held this mystical faith paid little attention to the diversity

[28] A variant was provided by an advertisement published in various newspapers in 1816 and 1817 (e. g., in *Aurora*, Jan. 1, 1817) inviting subscriptions for a proposed 100-page book containing " An universal constitution of a New Earthly Paradise, or the Elements of the Code of Mankind," by one Joseph Alphonse, in which would be included " a particular Constitution, addressed to the people of New Mexico and South America. . . ." Inquiries were to be addressed to "Mr. Clarke, at the office of the *Western Courier*, Louisville, Ky."

of the Americas; and, by a natural reaction, they were strengthened in it by the growing menace of a union of European despots against the liberty of the Americas.

Let us hasten to add, however, that on the morrow of the restoration of peace in 1815 the great majority in the United States seem to have taken a more common-sense view of Latin America. This view was well expressed by the comments that the *North American Review* made early in 1817 on the republican revolt in Pernambuco. Taking that outbreak in one corner of Brazil as the text for a discourse on " South America " at large,[29] the writer discussed the independence movement in that region with the usual sympathy for the Latin Americans' cause and the usual skepticism about their ability to make good use of their independence, if they won it. He felt, with Abbé de Pradt and John Quincy Adams, that, since the end of the Napoleonic wars in Europe, Latin America had become the scene of the most interesting events in the whole world and that the United States was watching them with lively concern. This concern was natural, he felt, for the Latin Americans were following the example of the United States in its revolution. Not much was to be expected of them politically, for the ability to overthrow a bad government " is no proof that the people are capable of a better," as shown by the recent experience of France; and the Latin Americans, like the French, " are destitute of that moral structure of character, which is the basis and indispensable requisite of a stable, free policy." The Latin Americans, moreover, were even more heavily handicapped than the French, for they had to contend with the heritage of their long colonial servitude, and while all colonial governments

[29] *North American Review* V (1817), 226-239, Art. XI, " Revolution in Pernambuco."

are bad, the Spanish and Portuguese were the worst of all.[30] Yet there was a ray of sunshine: the interests of humanity in general would at least not suffer if the independence of Latin America were established, for its people could not possibly be worse off under any new system whatever than they had been under the imbecile despotisms of Spain and Portugal; and as for the United States in particular, "we shall probably be great gainers on the whole, by having free access to the resources which a revolution will throw open to our commerce."

The comments of this New England journal expressed the sentiments of many people in the United States as they viewed the Latin American scene at that time. Their sentiments were as confused as the scene itself, and that was a jumbled mass of details, many of which were new and strange. It still lacked perspective and composition, and it was marked by a quality of change that suggests the kaleidoscope rather than the cinema. Nevertheless, certain well defined emotional attitudes were developing among the observers. These were suggested by the *Review's* comments on Pernambuco. They were, first, the feeling that the upheaval in Spanish and Portuguese America was the greatest event of the age for the whole Atlantic world—for Europe and the United States as well as for Latin America itself; and second, that this upheaval offered the people of the United States a golden opportunity to serve both humanity and themselves.

[30] Even Jefferson shared these doubts. In 1813 he wrote Humboldt, with special reference to New Spain, that "those countries" visited by Humboldt would doubtless throw off their European dependence, "but in what kind of government their revolution will end I am not so certain. History, I believe, furnishes no example of a priest-ridden people maintaining a free civil government" (Jefferson, *Writings*, XI, 351).

CHAPTER SEVEN

" AN IMPARTIAL NEUTRALITY "

In December 1815 James Monroe wrote that the revolutionary movement in Spanish America " becomes daily more interesting to the United States." [1] A month later public interest in it was given a powerful stimulus by Henry Clay. Discussing it in the House of Representatives in connection with a proposal to reduce both the taxes and the army, which he opposed, he spoke with his already familiar eloquence, with the prestige of his position as Speaker of the House, and (as he had just returned from the peace conference at Ghent) with the authority of an expert on international relations. These combined to gain space for his remarks in newspapers all over the United States and to focus public attention on Latin America more sharply than at any time since the beginning of the upheaval caused by Napoleon's invasion of Spain and Portugal in 1808.

I

In the course of his argument against the reduction of the armed forces of the United States, Clay suggested that they might be needed to aid the cause of Spanish American independence, to defend America against intervention by the united powers of Europe, and to support the position of the United States in its controversy with Spain.

[1] Manning, *Dip. Cor.*, I, 18, Monroe to Adams, Dec. 10, 1815. S. M. Hamilton, ed., *The Writings of James Monroe* (7 vols., New York, 1898-1903), V, 382, prints only a part of the passage in this letter relating to Spanish America.

What [he asked] is the present state of our relations to Old Spain? Who can now say, with certainty, how far it may be proper to aid the people of South America in regard to the establishment of their independence? . . . Besides, is the state of Europe settled? Everyone has heard of the proceedings of the Congress of European potentates at Vienna; we heard, too, that their ideas of legitimate government were carried to an extent destructive of every principle of liberty; we have seen these doctrines applied to create and overthrow dynasties at will. Do we know whether we shall escape their influence? Do we not know, though no such intention may exist at present, we shall, by adopting that policy which recommends a reduction of the Army and Navy, invite their attention to our weakness? Under these circumstances, I am not for exhausting the purse of the country of the funds necessary to enable it to vindicate its rights at home, or, if necessary, to aid in the cause of liberty in South America.[2]

A few days later he added:

This opinion I boldly declare . . . from a deliberate conviction of its being conformable to the best interests of the country, that having a proper understanding with foreign Powers—that understanding which prudence and a just precaution recommend—it would undoubtedly be good policy to take part with the patriots of South America. . . . I consider the release of any part of America from the dominion of the Old World as adding to the general security of the New.[3]

Many of Clay's colleagues thought that he exaggerated the gravity of the situation; some of them regarded him as a reckless incendiary.[4] We know from the publication of

[2] *Annals Cong.*, 14 Cong., 1 Sess., p. 724, Jan. 20, 1816. In this and the following quotation I have, for the sake of clarity, changed the indirect discourse of the report in the *Annals* to direct discourse.

[3] *Ibid.*, p. 790, Jan. 29, 1816.

[4] E. g., Cyrus King (Massachusetts), *ibid.*, p. 809, 810, and Randolph (see below, note 6). Clay himself admitted that there

the secret correspondence of the European governments, that there was solid justification for his fear of European intervention in America, and a leading authority has gone so far as to say that, in this respect, the years 1815-1817 were " the most critical of the whole period," [5] that is, the whole period of the Latin American struggle for independence.

Clay, however, could not be sure of his position. Not possessing any certain knowledge of what was going on behind the scenes in Europe, he was not in a position to insist on the adoption of bold measures by his government. For the moment, he was content to assert general rules of conduct, and did not demand any specific change in the existing policy of the United States towards Latin America. On the contrary, in so far as he discussed that policy, he seemed to approve of it; and he denied the charge—which was made at this time by John Randolph of Roanoke—that he was trying to involve his country in a crusade for liberty in South America and that he had " caught the infection " of war by " snuffing the carnage " at the field of Waterloo.[6] His purpose seems to have been to create a climate of opinion in which he might at some future time gain more direct aid for the Spanish American cause.

Clay had good reason to be satisfied with the existing policy of the United States towards Latin America, for it was about as favorable to his cause as it could have been under the circumstances. The policy towards Brazil can be

---

was " a supineness on this interesting subject throughout the country " which left him " almost without hope " that what he believed to be the correct policy of the country would be pursued.

[5] Webster, *Britain,* I, 14.

[6] Randolph's speech of Jan. 20, 1816, *Annals Cong.,* 14 Cong., 1 Sess., p. 728.

dismissed briefly, for it was not directly contemplated in Clay's remarks and was not an important issue at the moment. Until recently, relations between the United States and the Portuguese court at Rio de Janeiro had been clouded by the latter's predilection for Great Britain, which it had shown by its refusal to grant the United States commercial privileges simliar to those obtained by the British in the Strangford treaty of 1810 and by its benevolent attitude towards Great Britain in the War of 1812. With the return of peace, however, the situation had taken a turn for the better, as the court at Rio began to follow a course that was at the same time more independent of Britain and more friendly to the United States. In 1815 the gradual emancipation of Brazil from colonial subjection was completed by its elevation to the rank of a kingdom.[7] At the end of that year the court was reported to be ready to negotiate a commercial treaty on terms favorable to the United States and was resisting British efforts to induce it to return to Lisbon—a move that was opposed by the United States on the ground that it would in effect reduce Brazil to the status of a colony once more.[8] There was, moreover, reason to hope for a continuance of these favorable developments, since the minister chosen by the Portuguese-Brazilian court to represent it at Washington, the Abbé Corrêa, who was a liberal "philosopher" of the eighteenth-century type,[9] was re-

[7] Oliveira Lima, *Dom João no Brazil*, I, chap. XIII, "Elevação do Brasil a Reino."

[8] *Ibid.*, p. 539-552; Manning, *Dip. Cor.*, II, 693, 697, 699-700, three letters from Thomas Sumter, Jr., United States Minister at Rio de Janeiro, dated respectively March 10, Dec. 29, and Dec. 29, 1815.

[9] Monroe Papers, NYPL, Marquis de Lafayette to James Monroe, Dec. 27, 1811, introducing "Mr. Correa . . . whose uncommon

ported to be too radical to suit the monarchists of Europe and might therefore be presumed to be admirably fitted to promote the cooperation of his government with that of the United States in support of liberal principles.

In its relations with the Spanish empire, on the other hand, the United States faced a prospect that was anything but peaceful. The old controversy over the Louisiana Purchase had never been settled and now ill feeling between Spain and the United States was greatly increased by their sharp disagreement over a number of other questions. These included spoliation claims arising out of the Napoleonic wars, but the most important of them related to the revolution in progress in South America. At this time there was little or nothing in the policy of the United States of which Clay and the other friends of Spanish American independence could complain, for at every one of its four major points this policy was more favorable to the Spanish American revolutionists than to Spain, and on the whole it was about as favorable to the revolutionists as could be reasonably expected under the circumstances. The four major points just mentioned were as follows.

(1) In its controversy with Spain over the boundaries of Louisiana, the United States continued to take a firm and even aggressive stand.[10] It had actually occupied that

merit, liberal sentiments, and amiable temper have endeared him to his very valuable friends in this country [France] "; Gallatin, *Writings,* I, 517, Gallatin to Jefferson, March 10, 1812: " Mr. Correa, an interesting and learned Portuguese . . . lately arrived . . . is recommended to us by Barlow, Humboldt, &c. . . . " For his activities at Washington after 1816, see Joseph Agan, " Corrêa da Serra," *Pennsylvania Mag. Hist. and Biog.,* XLIX (1925), 1-43.

[10] The situation in 1815-1816 is described in Brooks, *Diplomacy and the Borderlands,* chap. III. Onís was finally recognized as minister on Dec. 19, 1815, more than six years after his first interview with the Secretary of State (*ibid.,* p. 14, 62).

part of West Florida which it claimed under the Purchase of 1803 (the Baton Rouge district shortly before the outbreak of the War of 1812, and Mobile during the course of the war) ; it still claimed that Texas was included in the Purchase; and its desire to acquire East Florida, which it had no right to claim on any ground except that of national interest, had been manifested in the War of 1812 and was frankly avowed as soon as diplomatic relations with Spain were reestablished in 1816. Spain, of course, strongly resisted these expansionist efforts of the United States; war threatened to result from the clash of wills, and the threat of war in this quarter tended to aid the Spanish American patriots by embarrassing Spain.[11]

(2) In regard to the struggle going on in Spanish America, the United States government now took a neutral position between the Spaniards and the insurgents. It recognized the belligerency of the latter and issued a neutrality proclamation (September 1, 1815). It admitted that neutrality required it to accord the same treatment to both belligerents and to maintain a strictly impartial attitude towards them;[12] and indeed Monroe insisted that this was

[11] Monroe Papers, NYPL, " J. M." (James Madison) to Monroe, Sept. 22, 1816, replying to a letter from Monroe in regard to rumors of intrigues by Onís at New Orleans and of an impending Spanish attack on that city. Though Madison did not seem to take the rumors very seriously, only three weeks later the Navy Department decided, " that all the ships in the Navy ought to be prepared for active service "; and for the same reason it suspended the voyage of the *Congress* to the Pacific and sent it to the Gulf of Mexico instead. The correspondence on this subject is summarized in a letter from Captain Dudley W. Knox to J. Neilson Barry, April 18, 1932, in the Navy Department Archives, Navy Department Library, Washington, D. C.

[12] *Am. State Papers, Foreign Relations,* IV, 1; Moore, *Digest of International Law,* I, 171; *ibid.,* VII, 860, quoting Adams to

being done. In his first annual message (December 2, 1817) he said that "through every stage of the contest" between Spain and her colonies the United States had " maintained an impartial neutrality "; and two years later, when he was again discussing this contest in his annual message, he asserted even more emphatically that " the greatest care has been taken to enforce the laws intended to preserve an impartial neutrality." [13] Nevertheless, its most responsible spokesman also admitted that the neutrality of the United States operated in such a way as to benefit the insurgents more than the royalists; and in fact they soon gave evidence that they wished it to operate in this way—in other words, that it was not strictly impartial, but decidedly benevolent towards the insurgents. In December 1815 Monroe, in his capacity as Secretary of State, wrote Adams, who was then in London, that he was optimistic of the success of the rebels, and continued:

When it is considered that the alternative is between governments, which, if independent, would be free and friendly, and the relations which, reasoning from the past, must be expected from them as colonies, there is no doubt in which scale our interest lies.[14]

Early the next year Adams explained to one of the insurgent agents in London that the United States was in fact showing its " good will for the South Americans " by remaining neutral, since its neutrality was " more advantageous to them, by securing to them the neutrality also of

Gallatin, May 19, 1818: " By the usual principles of international law, the state of *neutrality* recognizes the cause of both parties to the contest as *just*—that is, it avoids all consideration of the merits of the contest."

[13] *Ibid.*, I, 173.

[14] Manning, *Dip. Cor.*, I, 18.

Great Britain, than any support which the United States could give them by declaring in their favor, the effect of which would be to make Great Britain declare against both," [15] i. e., against both the United States and the South Americans. Subsequently, this interpretation of impartial neutrality was broadened and implemented in orders given to United States naval officers in Latin American waters. In September 1821 the U. S. S. *Franklin,* Captain Charles Stewart, was about to proceed to the west coast of South America for the protection of commerce. The war was still going full blast in that quarter and reports had reached the United States that a paper blockade of the coast of Spanish-dominated Peru had been proclaimed by the patriot government of Chile and was being enforced by the Chilean navy under Lord Cochrane. In his orders to Captain Stewart, Secretary of the Navy Smith Thompson said that the United States denied the validity of this blockade, but that, since the conflict in South America was " a struggle on one side for liberty and independence," the United States must avoid any collision with the patriots and " any act that may, in any manner, have the appearance or admit the construction of favoring the cause of Spain against such a struggle."

I deem it necessary, during the present state of things [continued the Secretary], to caution you to avoid all collision with the Chilean squadron, under the command of Lord Cochrane, and to let nothing but the protection of the honor of the American flag lead you to an open conflict with any of the vessels under his command. Act at present on the defensive only; and for all violations of our neutral rights, let strong and spirited appeals be made, through our public agents, to the government of Chili, impressing it upon the

---

[15] Adams, *Writings,* V, 551-552.

proper authorities [in Chile] that it is from respect to them, and the cause in which they are engaged, that our rights are not protected by force. . . . [16]

(3) Neutrality as thus interpreted was rendered even more helpful to the Spanish American insurgents by the permission which was given to ships flying their flags to make free use of the ports of the United States on the same terms as other foreign ships. This highly important privilege was accorded them in July 1815; and it is interesting to note that although this measure was so provocative to Spain as to endanger the peace of the United States, it was adopted by the Executive Department without consulting Congress and was promulgated in the form of a mere order from the Secretary of the Treasury to the customs collectors at the various ports. The Spanish minister Onís made a vigorous protest against it,[17] and quite properly, for it not only facilitated trade in general between Spanish America and the United States but also made it easier for the insurgents to purchase war materials in this country. They purchased these not only from private individuals but also, on occasion, from the United States government itself. This was illustrated by an incident which occurred in 1816 and was later described by Adams as the " gunpowder plot." The agent of Venezuela was trying to purchased a supply of gunpowder for his government and by an odd coincidence the ordnance department of the United States army discovered just at that time that it had a surplus supply of powder on hand. This was obligingly

[16] *Am. State Papers, Naval Affairs,* II, 538-539.

[17] Moore, *Digest of International Law,* I, 170 (Treasury order); *Am. State Papers, Foreign Relations,* IV, 423, Onís to Secretary of State Monroe, Dec. 30, 1815.

sold to Venezuela on credit, "and," Adams noted drily five years later, "has not been paid for to this day." [18]

(4) So far as Spain was concerned, the rights of the United States as a neutral were defined by the treaty negotiated at San Lorenzo in 1795 by Thomas Pinckney and Manuel de Godoy,[19] which was still in force and which could not be altered without the consent of the United States. Under this treaty Spain was committed to that liberal definition of neutral rights for which the United States had vainly contended against France and fought a war with England. While Spain did not admit that the United States was a neutral in the Spanish American war for independence, she could not give full effect to her view without risking a war, for which she was not prepared, and the treaty at least gave the United States a legal basis for defining its rights in the neutral role which it claimed to be playing. Events were soon to show that the treaty was a two-edged sword, which cut the insurgents as well as Spain, for the United States took the position that it was binding upon the new governments of Spanish America as well as upon Spain.[20] Consequently, when they began to wrest control of the sea from Spain and undertook to place "paper blockades" and other barriers in the way of neutral commerce with the American ports still controlled by Spain, the United States offered as stout a resistance to them as to Spain and based its resistance on the same grounds—its neutral character and the definition of its neutral rights

[18] Adams, *Memoirs,* V, 46.

[19] Bemis, *Pinckney's Treaty,* p. 337-338, discusses this aspect of the treaty.

[20] Moore, *Digest of International Law,* I, 170, and *International Arbitrations,* II, 1574-1575, III, 2737-2738; Robertson, *Hispanic American Relations,* p. 196.

by the treaty of 1795.[21]   This side of the question, however, had little practical significance until the insurgents
acquired enough privateers and warships to challenge Spain
on the high seas.   That did not occur until about 1818, and
in the meanwhile the position taken by the United States
operated almost wholly to the advantage of the insurgents
and the disadvantage of Spain.

II

Thus in 1815 the policy of the United States towards
the Spanish American question was nominally one of strict
and impartial neutrality but actually, in the language of the
present day, one of non-belligerency, since it was deliberately intended to aid the insurgents and since the highest
officers of the government freely expressed their sympathy
with them.   Nevertheless, there was no disposition in any
responsible quarter at Washington to pass from measures
short of war to war itself, and the keynote of the policy
was not aggressiveness but watchful waiting.   Both in Latin
America and among the interested powers of Europe there
were still too many uncertain factors in the situation to
justify a more positive policy.

In Latin America the situation at the close of 1815,
though not without some ground for hope, was on the
whole profoundly discouraging to those who wished to see
it sever its bonds with Europe and achieve independence
under representative governments.   Brazil was governed by
an absolute monarch who was still king of Portugal as well;
and whatever one might hope for the future, so far the net
result of the removal of the court from Lisbon to Rio de

---

[21] For further discussion, see below, chap. 10.

Janeiro seemed to have been to tighten rather than to relax the bond between Europe and that part of America. In Spanish America, the revolutionists seemed to have lost most of the ground they had gained during the French intrusion in Spain. The restored Ferdinand VII had taken advantage of the end of the Peninsular War to reinforce the Spanish armies in America, and these, together with loyalists in the colonies, had crushed or dispersed the patriot forces in Mexico, northern South America, Peru, Chile, and every other important part of Spanish America except the Plata region; and even there the principal government, that of Buenos Aires, had not adopted a declaration of independence, so that its devotion to the cause was open to serious doubt. Whether the patriot forces would be able to rally again, and whether, if they did so, they would strike for independence or effect some kind of composition with the mother country that would keep them within the empire, as some influential persons in the United States had wished to do in the dark days of our own war for independence—these were questions that no one could answer with any reasonable certainty in 1815, and until they were answered it would be foolhardy for the United States to commit itself further.[22]

The situation in Europe was somewhat less uncertain, but for that very reason it imposed an even stronger check upon American policy, not because the risk of error was greater, but because error would be more costly. The ele-

---

[22] This was admitted in effect by Clay himself in the speech of Jan. 29, 1816, cited above, note 3. Even the strongly pro-Spanish American *City of Washington Gazette* admitted as late as Dec. 12, 1817, that the United States "ought to observe the strictest neutrality in the contest between Spain and her colonies" (communication signed "Fair Play").

ment of certainty lay in the general nature of the settlement that the great powers had given to Europe at Vienna,
and the main outlines of this settlement were already quite
clear to informed observers in the United States by the
end of 1815. From their point of view the most important
features of the settlement were, first, that the great powers
had professed to restore the old regime in Europe, and had
actually done so to a great extent; and second, that, in the
field of international relations, they had made an important
innovation by replacing the balance-of-power principle of
the old regime with the new principle of cooperation, which
was denoted by the phrase " the concert of Europe." [23] This
was implemented by the Quadruple Alliance of Russia,
Prussia, Austria, and Britain (to which France was admitted
after it had done penance for its sins under the Revolution
and Napoleon) and was popularly known as the Holy
Alliance.[24]

In both respects the Europe that emerged from Vienna
was a potential menace to the United States, both within
in its own borders and still more in its relations with Latin
America. The restoration of the old regime in Europe was
based on the principle of legitimacy, and this was diametri-

[23] On this subject see W. Allison Phillips, *The Confederation of
Europe* (New York, 1920, 2nd ed.).

[24] See the article, " Holy Alliance," by Charles K. Webster, in
Encyclopaedia of the Social Sciences (15 vols., New York, 1930-
1935), VII, 417-419, and authorities cited there. In the United
States it was variously called Holy Alliance, Sacred Alliance, and
Holy League. The term generally denoted the great powers of the
Continent. It was frequently employed by John Quincy Adams,
who was something of a purist, and I have not hesitated to use it
in this study. In 1817 an obvious twist was given to the term by
Niles, who expressed the hope that " this unholy alliance " might
soon be broken (*Register, XIII, 99*, Oct. 11, 1817).

cally opposed to the principle of revolution, which was the foundation stone of the independence already achieved by the United States, of the independence movement now in progress in Spanish America, and of the policies of neutrality and recognition that the United States was pursuing in relation to Spanish America. The concert of Europe, conceived merely as a type of international cooperation, did not necessarily involve such a conflict of principle; but, as Clay warned in his speech on the army bill in January 1816, there was the possibility that the concert might be employed to extend the principle of legitimacy across the Atlantic.

It was at this crucial point that uncertainty began. What, if anything, did the concert of Europe, the " Holy Alliance," intend to do about Latin America? And, assuming that it intended to intervene there, what degree of harmony might be expected and what degree of discord might be hoped for among its members? Finally, what course of action on the part of the United States would contribute most towards averting such an intervention? These were questions that were ever present in the minds of the authorities at Washington throughout the decade after 1815. Sometimes they seemed urgent, at other times rather remote, but they were never completely lost sight of in the decade following Henry Clay's speech of January 1816 in which he linked Spanish America, the United States, and the " European potentates " in his warning that the Vienna system of legitimacy was " destructive of every principle of liberty."

Several months before Clay's speech was delivered, the Spanish minister at Washington had tried to bring about the extension of the principle of legitimacy to America, with the United States as one of its first victims. In April 1815 he wrote the restored government of Ferdinand VII at Madrid:

The illegal sale of Louisiana to the United States by France was the most obviously traitorous blow that Bonaparte ever dealt the Spanish monarchy; and in view of the fact that in the general peace concluded by the European powers it has been stipulated that things shall be restored to the status quo of 1792, it seems clear beyond all question that the present government of France is obligated to arrange with this country [the United States] for the restitution of Louisiana to the power [Spain] which is its lawful master and was in possession of it at that time.[25]

He had already proposed that the support of England be bought by the cession of Florida,[26] and he now suggested that France might be induced to cooperate by pointing out that " if this republic [the United States] is permitted to go on growing, it will be impossible for the powers of Europe to retain a single foot of territory in this continent or a single island in the Gulf of Mexico." As Abbé de Pradt pointed out a little later, the powers of Europe also had an interest in intervening in America south of the United States in order to keep it attached to the European system of monarchy.[27]

This was cogent reasoning; but the powers of Europe assembled at Vienna soon showed that, whatever they might attempt in the way of piecemeal intervention, they had no intention of undertaking a wholesale restoration of the status quo in America. In the first place, while Onís's

[25] AHN, Est., legajo 5640, Onís to Cevallos, April 16, 1815, No. 33 (LC photostat).

[26] Webster, *Britain,* II, 343-344, Vaughan to Castlereagh, Nov. 16, 1815.

[27] See above, chap. 4.

proposal was not approved by the court in the form in which he made it, the Spanish representative at Vienna actually did demand, on behalf of his government and in the name of legitimacy, that the great powers should aid Spain in recovering Louisiana; but his demand was not even given serious consideration.[28] In the second place, the elevation of Brazil to the rank of a kingdom, which destroyed the status quo in the largest colony in America, was not only accepted by the great powers but was strongly supported if not actually inspired by that arch-legitimist, Talleyrand.[29]

There still remained the danger of limited intervention. Here the outlook was decidedly uncertain. On the one hand, it was known that some of the powers had strong motives for intervening. On the other hand, there was reason to hope that their mutual jealousy and conflicting interests might prevent them from taking any important action, either jointly or severally. Thus, in the case of Brazil, which we have just mentioned, Talleyrand's devotion to the principle of restoration of the status quo had been overcome by his desire to serve the national interests of France by increasing the prestige of the Portuguese monarchy, which he hoped to detach from the British orbit and make a satellite of France. To further this purpose, he sent as French ambassador to Rio de Janeiro one of the most distinguished peers of France, the Duke of Luxembourg. One of the new ambassador's main duties was to

[28] Griffin, *United States,* p. 39; Jerónimo Bécker, *Historia de las relaciones exteriores de España en el siglo XIX* (3 vols., Madrid, 1924-1926), I, 373, 384-387.

[29] Oliveira Lima, *op. cit.,* 519-520, believes that the proposal was inspired by the Portuguese envoy, Palmella.

obtain for his country commercial privileges similar to those already enjoyed by Britain under the Strangford treaty of 1810; but this was only a part of the larger purpose of France, which was to make Brazil predominant in South America, as the United States was in North America, and to convert Brazil from a British to a French sphere of influence,[30] as France had tried to do with the United States in the time of Vergennes.

From this point of view, a survey of the great powers of Europe showed that two of the five—Austria and Prussia—were relatively unimportant, since they possessed no colonies in America and no sea power worth notice. The other three—Britain, France, and Russia—required the most serious consideration; but the best informed observers were in doubt as to what course they were likely to follow in regard to America. The outlook was all the more obscure because each of them might follow a different course and because the question involved their attitude towards each other and the United States as well as towards Spanish and Portuguese America.

Britain, allied with the Bourbon government of Spain since 1808, was understood [31] to favor the restoration of the status quo to the extent of re-establishing the political authority of Spain over Spanish America and of bringing the Portuguese court back to Lisbon. There was no prospect, however, that she would ever consent to the restora-

[30] *Ibid.*, I, 63-64; Robertson, *France and Latin-American Independence*, p. 111, 112.

[31] The policy that the British actually followed is sympathetically described in Webster, *Britain*, I, Introduction. On p. 10, Webster summarizes it as follows: " From 1810-1820 it may be described as *mediation*. . . . From 1820-1824 British policy was a *preparation for recognition*."

tion of the commercial monopolies of Spain and Portugal, which were an essential feature of the old regime in America and on the ruins of which Britain had built up a thriving trade with Brazil and Spanish America. Her attitude towards the United States was unfriendly and even more equivocal; but as Adams viewed the situation from the London legation in the winter of 1815-1816, her whole American policy was clouded with uncertainty because of a sharp division of opinion between the government on the one hand and the mass of the people on the other.

This division presented an interesting and disturbing paradox. As far as Spanish America was concerned, said Adams, many of the British people were at one with the United States in favoring the cause of independence, partly from political sympathy and partly from hope of commercial gain; whereas the cabinet entertained " a different and directly opposite sentiment " since they foresaw " less direct advantage to themselves from a free commercial intercourse with South America, than indirect injury by its tendency to promote the interests of the United States." On the other hand, as far as the United States was concerned, the British people were ready if not eager for war, whereas the cabinet was for peace. ". . . We must not disguise from ourselves," he wrote, " that the national feeling [in Britain] against the United States is more strong and more universal than it has ever been." Hard times had created " a strong wish for a new war in a great portion of the community, and there is no nation with which a war would be so popular as with America [i. e., the United States]." [32]

[32] Adams, *Writings*, V, 487-490, Adams to Monroe, Jan. 22, 1816. A week later, Clay told the House of Representatives, " That man must be blind to the future, who cannot see that we

It was already obvious that the attitude of Britain was more important than that of any other government, because of her naval supremacy, her political and commercial influence at Madrid and Lisbon as well as in Latin America, and her possession of strategically important bases at Jamaica and elsewhere in the Caribbean region. Nevertheless, it was also important to know what attitude France and Russia would take. They too held possessions in America, their naval and maritime strength was not negligible, and Russia was the preponderant power on the continent and the leading member of the concert of Europe. Even if they did not take direct action in America, it was to be expected that they would at least exercise considerable influence upon the wavering policy of Britain.

In 1815 and 1816, however, little that was definite could be learned about the attitude of Russia and France, and the few factors that were known tended to cancel each other and leave the inquirer little better off at the end of his inquiry than at the beginning. On the one hand, the Russian Tsar, Alexander I, was a professed liberal, and he had always shown himself friendly to the United States and had recently expressed a keen sympathy for the Spanish American patriots.[33] On the other hand, he was the guid-

---

are destined to have war after war with Great Britain, until, if one of the two nations be not crushed, all grounds of collision shall have ceased between us" (*Annals Cong.*, 14 Cong. 1 Sess., p. 787).

[33] See above, Chap. 3, and Dexter Perkins, "Russia and the Spanish Colonies, 1817-1818," *Am. Hist. Rev.*, XXVIII (1923), 656-672. Perkins, p. 657, says, "Down to the middle of 1817, the Tsar Alexander does not seem to have concerned himself directly with the restoration of peace and Spanish dominion in the New World." He mentions the matter of the sale of part of the Russian fleet to Spain, points out that the transaction was "veiled

ing spirit of the Holy Alliance, which Americans had already come to regard as the quintessence of the reactionary spirit in Europe, and in any event, one could hardly expect the Autocrat of All the Russias to remain faithful to the liberal cause in a conflict which was coming to be regarded as one between liberty and despotism. Moreover, Russia was an American power, with possessions on the frozen Northwest coast and an evident desire to extend them southward. The threat from that quarter had led to the defensive expansion of Spain into Upper California on the eve of the American Revolution. The United States had now become a claimant in that quarter; and while the administration was not greatly exercised over Russia's designs at the moment, it was easy to believe that she might take advantage of Spain's distress to acquire California.[34]

---

in the deepest secrecy," and cites as his authorities the London *Morning Chronicle* of Dec. 2, 1823, and H. Baumgarten, *Geschichte Spaniens* (Leipzig, 1865), II, 196. Since the foregoing was written, I have read in galley proof an article by William Spence Robertson, "Russia and the Emancipation of Spanish America," *Hispanic Am. Hist. Rev.*, XXI, No. 2 (May 1941). This is an illuminating discussion of Russian policy from 1815 to 1825, but it does not add much to our knowledge of the Russo-Spanish warship deal.

[34] In fact, the Russian ministers at Paris and Madrid, Pozzo di Borgo and Tatischev, were among the strongest supporters of Spain's claims. Speaking of the whole period, Webster, *Britain, I*, 71, says that " The most grandiose project [of European intervention] which was put forward, and which had some countenance from the French and Russian governments, was that of Pozzo di Borgo in 1817." It was in this year that United States newspapers first became definitely suspicious of Russia, and they linked Russian aid to Spain in America with the cession of California to Russia. See for example Niles's *Register*, XIII, 46, Sept. 13, 1817, " European Speculations." For the Russian settlement at Bodega Bay, California, see Dexter Perkins, *The Monroe Doctrine, 1823-1826* (Cambridge, 1932), p. 8.

As for France, her policy was rendered uncertain by an internal division somewhat like that in England, the commercial interests and political liberals sympathising with the Spanish American patriots, and the government with Spain. Though there was some doubt as to whether the old Family Compact between the Bourbons of Versailles and Madrid had been revived by the restoration,[35] the logic of circumstances created a sympathy at Versailles for the legitimist claims of Madrid; and so long as the Allied occupation of France lasted (it was not terminated until 1818) the French government was not likely to show any sympathy that it might feel for revolutionists, in Spanish America or elsewhere.[36]

While the situation in Europe was confused, the lesson that any prudent American statesman could draw from it was simple and clear: the United States must refrain from doing anything that would provoke a concerted European intervention in America. As Adams expressed this thought with special reference to Britain, popular sentiment in that country was at present favorable to the Spanish Americans, but it was also very strong against the United States, so that " if the United States were openly to join the cause of South America, and consequently be engaged in a war with Spain the British people would immediately consider [the United States] as the principals in the contest, all their jealousies and national antipathies would be enlisted against the common American cause," and Britain would join the war on the side of Spain " merely because the United States would be on the other side." [37] Within another year, the situation

---

[35] Robertson, *France and Latin-American Independence*, p. 116, 117, 119, 128.

[36] *Ibid.*, 176, 177.

[37] Adams, *Writings*, V, 551-552.

had been further clarified and the danger from Europe seemed greater than ever, for, as Adams wrote from London in April 1817, shortly before he returned to the United States to become Secretary of State,

There is a perpetual tendency to intervene against the [Spanish American] insurgents in all the councils of the allies, and in none more than in this country [Great Britain] upon the principle of legitimacy.[38]

How the danger from that quarter might be aggravated even by the rivalries among the European powers themselves was illustrated by the controversy over Montevideo and the *Banda Oriental* (the "Eastern Shore" of the Plata River, modern Uruguay).[39] Reviving an old colonial dispute and claiming that disorders in that region justified its intervention, the Portuguese government at Rio de Janeiro occupied Montevideo in 1816. Its position was somewhat similar to that of the United States in regard to Florida a little later, at the time of Andrew Jackson's invasion. Spain reacted as vigorously against Portuguese aggression as it did in the later case of aggression from the United States; and it appeared for a time that the controversy between the two Iberian governments might divide Europe into two camps, Russia supporting Spain, and England, Portugal. In the next stage, however, it developed that the European powers might not only settle the *Banda Oriental* question amicably but might even make it the occasion for a settlement of the whole problem of the Spanish and Portuguese colonies in America.

It was this situation in Europe that made the negative

[38] Adams, *Writings,* VI, 175.

[39] The question of Montevideo and the *Banda Oriental* in this period is discussed in great detail in Oliveira Lima, *op. cit.,* II, chaps. XV-XVII.

policy of not provoking European intervention seem a positive service to the Spanish American cause; and to Monroe, who had even more to do with formulating the policy than did Adams, it seemed all the service that the United States could be expected to render the Spanish Americans at this time. In the first draft of a letter that he wrote to Andrew Jackson in December 1818, with special reference to the Florida crisis, he expressed himself with a frankness that is welcome to the historian but that probably seemed imprudent to him at the time, since he omitted the passage from the final draft of the letter:

I think that the proof which is now in possession of the Government [he said], is satisfactory, that the policy, which was then, and has been since pursued, in regard to Florida, and to Spain and the Colonies in South America, has contributed essentially, to produce the decision of the Allies at Aix-la-Chapelle, not to interfere in favor of Spain against the Colonies, or against us. By this policy we have lost nothing, as *by keeping the Allies out of the quarrel,* Florida must soon be ours, and *the Colonies must be independent, for if they cannot beat Spain, they do not deserve to be free.*[40]

III

Fortunately for the administration, conditions in the United States at the close of the war facilitated its adherence to this cautious, unheroic policy in regard to Latin America. This was mainly because the possible sources of opposition in the United States itself were weakened by

[40] Monroe Papers, NYPL, Monroe to Jackson, Dec. 21, 1818, draft, autograph. Cf. Monroe's letter to Jackson of this date in Monroe, *Writings, VI,* 85-87, and in J. S. Bassett, ed., *Correspondence of Andrew Jackson* (7 vols., Washington, 1926-1935), II, 404-405.

internal divisions. While the restoration of peace had resulted in the dislocation of American commerce and some
mercantile interests sought compensation in independent
Latin America, there was nothing remotely approaching a
union of the commercial interest in favor of intervention
by the United States in favor of Latin American independence. On the contrary, the available evidence indicates
that the more responsible shipowners and merchants were
strongly opposed to intervention on the ground that it
would bring on a war with Spain which would disrupt
the valuable commerce of the United States with loyal Cuba
and expose its whole merchant marine to the depredations
of British and other privateers operating under commissions
from Spain.[41]

The kind of relief that this group desired was indicated
by a memorial [42] drawn up and sent to Congress in January
1817 by Preserved Fish, George and John Griswold, Gardiner G. Howland, Stephen Whitney, and several other
leading merchants and shipowners in a meeting at the
Tontine Coffee House in New York. Complaining that the
commercial and colonial regulations recently adopted by
foreign nations for the protection of their own trade had
" depressed that of the United States to a degree hitherto
unknown," they asserted that their sufferings were increased
by the reciprocity policy of the United States, which operated greatly to the disadvantage of its own citizens, especially in their trade with the colonies of European powers.
The remedy proposed by the memorialists was not that the
United States should promote the independence of those

[41] See " Yard's Pamphlet," cited in Chap. 4, note 39.
[42] *Aurora*, Jan. 23, 1817, " Meeting of Merchants."

colonies, but that it should adopt retaliatory commercial regulations against the mother countries.

As the New York memorialists pointed out, the depression of which they complained threw ships, seamen, and mechanics out of employment; and they might have added that it had a similar effect on agriculture. For a time, however, the slack seems to have been taken up in other ways, so that in the United States there was no such demand for war as an escape from depression and unemployment as Adams was simultaneously noting in England. Privateers and seamen found employment with the Spanish American insurgents, other seamen and mechanics found employment in the new and rapidly growing steamboat industry on the Atlantic coast and in the Mississippi Valley, and farmers and others joined in the post-war migration to the new states and territories beyond the Appalachians.

The political situation, too, favored the administration's Latin American policy. The weakness of the Federalists would have prevented them from offering effective opposition to it, even if they had been inclined to do so. As a matter of fact, most of them seem to have been very well pleased with it, probably because its cautious, pacific character appealed to the conservative commercial group that dominated the party. At any rate, the Federalist members in Congress supported it with their votes, and the opposition to it came from within the administration's own Republican party. This was pointed out in newspaper comment on one of the most important of the early congressional debates on Latin American policy—the debate of March 1818 on a proposal by Henry Clay which contemplated the immediate recognition of Buenos Aires and was understood to be a rebuke to the slow-moving administration. Apropos of this discussion, the Washington *National Intelligencer,* an administration organ, remarked, "No gentleman of the federal party participated in the debate—the republican party in the House has been in danger of a division." Whereupon the independent Republican *City of Washington Gazette* asked why the *National Intelligencer* did not tell the whole truth, and proceeded to supply the deficiency.

It is well known [said the editor of the *Gazette*] that the republican party *is* divided; incurably divided, unless the administration [which has been flirting with Federalism and aristocracy] goes wholly back to sound principles. . . . If the federalists did not partake in the debate referred to, they *voted* with the administration; and it was their votes that swelled the majority against Mr. Clay's motion.[43]

However disquieting this situation might be from the point of view of party discipline, it was reassuring to those

[43] *City of Washington Gazette,* March 31, 1818. An interesting expression of Federalist approval of Monroe's cautious policy at this time came from Rufus King, United States Senator from New York, who had been closely connected with Francisco de Miranda's efforts to revolutionize Spanish America. Writing early in 1818, King said: "So far as I can fathom the system of the Executive [in regard to Spanish America] they mean to act with caution . . . they will not, at least as things are, take any part in their favor. Such indeed are my own views concerning this question. . . . You will not suppose that I have changed any of my former opinions respecting the advantage to this country that will arise out of ye Indep. of ye Span. Colonies, but it is a serious question, and I shd. regard it as an unfortunate decision of it, that we shd. in the actual posture of the world plunge into a war for the deliverance of these Colonies, whose incapacity to manage their own affairs, must for a time be the cause of great confusion & disorder" (Charles R. King, *Life and Correspondence · of Rufus King* (6 vols., New York, 1896-1900), VI, 108-109, Rufus King to ———, Jan. 18, 1818).

who advocated the administration's Latin American policy, for so long as the opposition to that policy was confined to a faction in one of the two parties there was little danger that domestic pressure would force the administration to abandon it in favor of a more aggressive policy.

Indeed, in the first three years after the restoration of peace the principal pressure on the administration came from a very different quarter and was exerted in the opposite direction, in favor of an even more cautious policy. In this period, the first important question was raised by the discovery of serious flaws in the existing neutrality legislation of the United States—flaws which were embarrassing to the government itself as well as highly offensive to Spain and its sympathizers in Europe.

As early as December 1815 the situation was already causing the administration grave concern, as is shown by a letter in which Albert Gallatin discussed the " distressing case " of David Gelston, collector of the port of New York. Acting under orders from Gallatin as secretary of the treasury, Gelston had seized the armed ship *American Eagle,* which was about to be sent from New York to Haiti for use by the revolutionary Pétion government. The authority under which Gallatin's order was issued and the seizure made was the Neutrality Act of 1794, which prohibited the sale of ships of war to any belligerent prince or state; but, although Haiti claimed to be an independent state and in fact had been independent since 1804, it had not been recognized by the United States. Consequently, when the owners of the *American Eagle* brought suit for damages against Gelston, the court found in their favor on the ground that Haiti was not a prince or state within the meaning of the Act of 1794 and awarded them a judgment of $100,000. According to Gallatin, the unfortunate Gelston could not afford the expense of an appeal to the United States Supreme Court, and, indeed, was almost certain to lose if he should appeal. Yet, if his seizure of the ship was illegal, as appeared to be the case, it followed that the Act of 1794 had not provided for the case of vessels intended to be employed by a rebel colony against the mother country. So, concluded Gallatin, " if this decision, which I do not pretend to arraign, be correct, how can the President maintain the neutrality of the United States during the contest between the Spanish colonies and Spain, or any similar one? " [44]

This was bad enough; but subsequent inquiry revealed still another serious flaw in the existing neutrality legislation, namely, that while a citizen of the United States could not send a warship out of the United States for use by a belligerent, there was nothing in either the Act of 1794 or the supplementary Act of 1797 to prevent him from selling such a ship to a foreigner in this country for that purpose.[45]

The question raised by Gallatin in connection with the Gelston case was one of vital importance for the Latin American policy of the United States, for the very essence of that policy was a strict and impartial neutrality. The operation of the policy might—as in fact it did—aid one belligerent more than the other; but the United States could

[44] Gallatin, *Writings*, I, 673-675, Gallatin to A. J. Dallas, Dec. 12, 1815. It appears that David Gelston was at one time considered in connection with the mission to South America on which Poinsett was sent in 1810 (*ibid.*, p. 490-491). This case, *Gelston v. Hoyt,* decided in 1818, is discussed briefly in Charles G. Fenwick, *The Neutrality Laws of the United States* (Baltimore, 1912), p. 74, with a reference to the report of the case in 3 Wheaton, 246.

[45] *Annals Cong.,* 14 Cong., 2 Sess., p. 716-720, report of Committee of the Whole on the neutrality bill, Jan. 24, 1817.

not be held accountable for the unequal operation of the system provided the system itself established equal rights and obligations for both belligerents. That, however, was what the existing system conspicuously failed to do, as the Gelston case demonstrated, for it gave the Spanish American insurgents the privilege of buying warships in the United States and denied that privilege to Spain. This was an inequality of treatment that would have caused ill feeling at any time, and it was especially provocative at this time because the whole American concept of neutrality, even when impartially applied, was highly offensive to Spain and other European powers.[46] One of the most unfortunate results of the system was that it facilitated the arming of a swarm of privateers in American ports which, acting under commissions from the Spanish American governments, preyed on both Spanish and neutral commerce with ports under the jurisdiction of Spain.

IV

In the course of the year 1816 the force of Gallatin's complaints on this score was greatly increased by the clamor raised by foreign envoys in the United States—Abbé Corrêa of the Portuguese-Brazilian Court, Onís of Spain, Bagot of England, and Hyde de Neuville of France—and by merchants of the United States who, under Spanish license or otherwise, engaged in the trade harassed by the privateers. Accordingly, after prolonged debate, Congress enacted a new and more stringent neutrality law. It was to this situa-

---

[43] Frederick L. Paxson, *The Independence of the South American Republics, a Study in Recognition and Foreign Policy* (Philadelphia, 1903).

tion that Duane of the *Aurora* referred when, three years later, he wrote with his usual pungency of

the system of terror and menace which operated so openly upon our administration in 1816, in which Mr. Bagot was the prime but unseen mover; in which the Abbé Correa cast off the cowl of the priest, and the chlamys of the philosopher, and erected himself into a dictator and a bully; in which M. de Neufville acted the part of a subservient instrument to the hereditary enemies of the family compact; and Don Onis appeared with the awkward but confident loftiness of Castile and Arragon; that odious combination of foreign ministers, which an administration of a free people should have made the ground of breaking up all diplomatic establishments but such as were temporary.[47]

"That combination," continued Duane, when he had caught his breath, "produced the odious law of hostility to South American liberty." This was his way of describing the Neutrality Act of March 3, 1817,[48] which corrected the chief defect in the existing laws of 1794 and 1797 by making it illegal to sell warships to the Spanish American insurgents as well as to Spain.

[47] *Aurora,* Aug. 4, 1819, "Political Views.—No. II."

[48] Entitled "An Act more effectually to preserve the neutral relations of the United States." The principal changes were: (1) the scope of the act was extended to include the insurgent colonies as well as Spain by changing the term "foreign prince or state" in the Act of 1794 to "foreign prince, state, colony, district, or people"; (2) armed vessels were required to give bond "in cases where there was reason to suspect that they would be used in violation of the neutrality of the United States"; and (3) collectors and other revenue officers were empowered to seize and detain vessels in cases where there was a strong presumption of an intended breach of the law (as in Gelston's case). See Fenwick, *op. cit.,* p. 37-40. The original House bill was weakened by the rejection by the Senate of a clause relating to the sale of vessels, and this alteration "was destined to impair seriously the strength of the contentions made by the United States in the Alabama controversy with Great Britain fifty years later" (*ibid.,* p. 39).

Duane exaggerated, as usual, for the new act was certainly not conceived in a spirit of hostility to South American liberty. For the rest, however, there was a great deal of truth in what he said, for the passage of the act was largely the result of foreign pressure and of the realization that the most serious foreign complications might ensue unless the inequality of the system were corrected and the excesses of the privateers curbed. Spain was the chief sufferer on both counts, and Baltimore was the chief center of privateering activities in the United States; [49] and this was what gave point to John Randolph's quip to the effect that the neutrality bill (which was still pending at that time) was a bill to make peace between His Catholic Majesty and the town of Baltimore.[50].

Yet there was more to it than this, for it was realized that the probable alternative to a more effective neutrality was war with Spain. As Adams had warned the administration from London, war with Spain would probably mean war with Britain too, and even if Britain did not go to war on the side of Spain, swarms of British privateers under the Spanish flag would play havoc with the seaborne commerce of the United States. Any war at all would defeat the whole purpose of the administration's neutrality policy, which was to maintain peace in the interest both of the United States and also of the Spanish American patriots. Even if the United States did not become involved in war, its refusal to correct the flagrant partiality of its neutrality system might provoke the very thing that it was seeking to avoid and that Spain was trying to obtain—the intervention

[49] Griffin, " Privateering from Baltimore," cited in chap. 4, note 23.
[50] *Annals Cong.*, 14 Cong., 2 Sess., p. 732.

of the concert of European powers against the Spanish American revolution.

It was this situation that led President Madison in December 1816 to recommend the revision of the neutrality laws. In the House of Representatives his recommendation was referred to the Committee on Foreign Relations, of which John Forsyth of Georgia, future minister to Spain and secretary of state, was chairman. Within three weeks Forsyth reported a bill containing the important alterations of the existing law already mentioned; and after warm but comparatively brief debates the bill was passed by a comfortable majority in both houses of Congress and was then signed by the president. The following year, as we shall see, other gaps in the system were closed, again partly at the expense of the Spanish American insurgents. This tightening up of the neutrality system paralleled a similar process in England in the same period; and it caused a good deal of resentment in Spanish America and among the more ardent advocates of the independence movement in the United States. One of the latter inquired during the debate on the bill in Congress:

Suppose Congress pass the bill for preventing the arming and sale of vessels, etc., whilst our richest and most favored merchants, from sheer avarice, supply the forces of *Ferdinand* in South America with all sorts of arms, accoutrements, stores, and munitions—will this be ' equal and exact justice? '

He then went on to ask two questions that we have already quoted in another connection:

Shall the resources of this *republic* be applied in this manner to support the cause of *tyranny?* Is not such conduct a greater violation of our neutrality than the past and present state of trade? [51]

The answers to these two rhetorical questions were the reverse of what the writer evidently expected, for the answer to the first was yes, and to the second, no. To talk about supporting the cause of tyranny was only to obscure the issue, which was simply whether or not Spain should be given equal access with the Spanish Americans to the resources of this republic. To give Spain such access was not to violate neutrality but to remove a flagrant violation of it; to have refused to give it would have been equivalent to forswearing neutrality and courting a war which threatened serious injury to the United States and ruin to the Spanish American cause. That was the considered opinion of Monroe, Adams, and many other well informed, intelligent, and patriotic Americans, and we have no reason to believe that they were mistaken. In other words, they were convinced that the time had not yet come when the United States could afford to take unilateral action in support of Spanish American independence, and there was as yet no good reason to believe that any of the great powers would cooperate with it to that end, but excellent reason to believe that most if not all of them would oppose it vigorously. Consequently there was nothing for it but to reaffirm the existing policy of neutrality and wait for a more favorable turn of events in both Europe and Latin America.

Partly for this reason and partly because national policy is frequently in a state of suspended animation between the election of a new president in the autumn of one year and his inauguration early the following year, American diplo-

[51] *Aurora*, Feb. 5, 1817, item clipped from the *Columbian*.

macy in regard to Latin America came to a standstill in the winter of 1816-1817. The State Department's volume of " Instructions to Ministers " [52] for this period contains not a single document on the subject. On November 23, 1816, Monroe instructed George W. Erving at Madrid to protest to the Spanish government against a recent attack by a Spanish " squadron " of two ships on a " vessel of war of the United States," the *Firebrand,* in the Gulf of Mexico; but that was the only instruction of any importance relating to Latin America in the long period from August 1816 to March 1817. Indeed, few instructions of any kind were despatched during these eight months, and the two topics that were most prominent in them were the affair of the Russian consul at Philadelphia, who was charged with rape and defended himself by claiming diplomatic immunity, and the incident caused by the public denunciation of France by our friend Postmaster Skinner of Baltimore,[53] which led to the temporary closing of the French consulate in that city. From November 24, 1816, to February 4, 1817, neither Monroe nor anyone else in the State Department signed any instruction on any subject whatever. Monroe signed three documents on February 5, 8, and 10, 1817 but none of them was important; and the next document in the series was signed on March 6, 1817, two days after Monroe's inauguration, by the acting Secretary of State, Richard Rush. The next few weeks, however, were to witness developments of great significance in the Latin American policy of the United States.

[52] National Archives, S. D., " Instructions to Ministers," vol. 8.
[53] Skinner's speech and Hyde de Neuville's protest are discussed in Monroe's letter to Gallatin of Sept. 10, 1816 (Monroe, *Writings,* V, 387-390).

CHAPTER EIGHT

WATCHFUL WAITING

When James Monroe was translated from the State Department to the White House in March 1817, even Duane of the *Aurora,* who had found both the domestic and foreign policies of the previous administration almost unbearable, expressed the hope that the new administration would deal more competently with the great questions facing the country. One of these was Duane's favorite theme, " The South American Revolution." [1]   After Monroe had been in office for seven months, another of the leading advocates of the Spanish American cause, David Porter, wrote that in his opinion the views of the administration on that subject were " in some degree (to a great degree) in conformity with our own." [2] With the important difference that Monroe's sympathy was tempered by a realization of the risks involved in unilateral action by the United States and by the conviction that (as he said to Andrew Jackson) if the Spanish Americans could not " beat Spain " unaided, they did not deserve to be free, it was quite true that he sympathized strongly with the Spanish American cause, and it was not long before he showed his sympathy for it and shook off the inertia that had seemed to possess American diplomacy during the past winter.

I

As far as Spanish America was concerned, the initiative in the new administration's diplomacy doubtless came from

[1] *Aurora,* March 5, 1817, editorial.
[2] Poinsett Papers, HSP, D. Porter to Poinsett, Oct. 23, 1817

Monroe himself, who had a long and close acquaintance with its affairs. It certainly did not come from the new Secretary of State, John Quincy Adams, who did not return from England until August 1817. To be sure, Richard Rush, acting Secretary of State in the interval, was at this time " upon terms of personal amity " with Doctor William Thornton, patent commissioner, Spanish American enthusiast, and designer of the plan of 1815 for the federal union of the Americas under an " Incal " government. As Rush wrote a year later from the London legation, he and Thornton

met often, and seldom met without South American affairs being, under some shape or other, brought into view. It was I may say ever the predominant subject. His [Thornton's] zeal in relation to that cause was known to all, and as well the information which he had collected.[3]

Some new information about Spanish America and some fresh zeal for its cause may thus have been communicated from Thornton through Rush to Monroe, but as Thornton was something of a fanatic, it does not seem likely that this had much effect on either the Acting Secretary of State or

[3] National Archives, SD, Despatches from England, Rush to Adams, May 14, 1818. Thornton in turn was in close touch with Pedro Gual, agent until 1816 of the Cartagena (New Granada) government (Griffin, *op. cit.*, p. 127). In an obituary, Sept. 13, 1819, the *Aurora* said that he was a physician whose mind was " stored with the knowledge of modern science " and " an enthusiastic admirer of our country, our government and liberty," and that his death was an " irreparable " loss to his country. It also said that he was descended from an Irish family named Wall (changed to Gual in Spanish). According to Parra Pérez *op. cit.*, I, 46, his home was in Trinidad, where he remained for several years after its acquisition by Britain. See further in *ibid.*, II, consult index.

the President. At any rate, it should be noted that Rush's recollections of his former intimacy with Thornton were given in the course of a letter explaining why he had not communicated to Monroe a proposal of the good Doctor's about Spanish America to which its author attached great importance—and the explanation was that Rush thought the proposal too fantastic to merit the President's attention.[4]

As for Rush's own knowledge of South America, its limitations are suggested by a memorandum of September 1817 in which he spoke of having an American naval vessel " touch at the principal port of Chili (name not recollected) and also at Lima in Peru." [5] When this was written, Rush had been discharging the duties of Secretary of State for more than six months and he could easily have learned from the files of South American correspondence in his office—or for that matter, from any one of a dozen standard works of geography and travel—that Valparaiso was the principal port of Chile and that it would be a remarkable feat of navigation for any ship to touch at Lima in Peru.

It was rather through impulses from other sources that Monroe's interest in Latin America was quickened in the spring of 1817. He may have been influenced by the stronger

[4] The proposal related to Amelia Island. See below in the text, and note 22.

[5] National Archives, SD, Special Agents, vol. 6, memorandum for the new Secretary of State, Adams, dated Sept. 25, 1817, initialled " R. R.," giving the President's views regarding Prevost's mission to Chile and Peru in the *Ontario* (see below). As the memorandum was based on a conversation between Monroe and Rush, it is possible that the former may have been responsible for the boners in it; but the circumstances make this seem very un-likely, especially since Poinsett's mission to Chile had given Monroe reason to be particularly well informed about that country

stand in favor of Latin America that Lord Brougham and other English liberals were taking; but a more definite impulse came from the renewed progress of the movement in Latin America itself. The United Provinces of the Río de la Plata (Argentina) had declared their independence in 1816; San Martín had begun his campaign of liberation in Chile with an important (though not decisive) victory at Chacabuco in February 1817; and further encouragement— all the stronger because it was unexpected—came with the report, received at the end of April, that even Brazil, which had seemed so supine under the monarchy at Rio de Janeiro, was beginning to turn republican and that a republican government had actually been established at Pernambuco.[6]

Even this might not have been enough to stir the cautious Monroe to action if he had not learned simultaneously that there was at last a fair prospect of the fulfilment of one of his prime conditions of action, namely, a rift in the solid European front. He learned this from a series of conferences that Rush had with the French minister, Hyde de Neuville, at the State Department on April 24, 25, and 30, and the results of which he reported seriatim to the president.[7]

[6] *Aurora*, May 2, 1817, extract of three letters from Pernambuco; *ibid.*, May 3, 1817, items clipped from the *Baltimore Patriot*; *ibid.*, May 21, 1817, items clipped from the Boston *Patriot*, reporting the arrival at that port of Antonio Gonçalves da Cruz, "Ambassador" from the provisional government of Pernambuco to the United States. See also Hildebrando Accioly, *O Reconhecimento do Brazil pelos Estados Unidos da América* (São Paulo, 1936), p. 80-84.

[7] An undated 7-page memorandum of these three conferences with Hyde de Neuville, in Rush's handwriting and initialled at the end "R. R.," is in National Archives, SD, Despatches from England, immediately following Adams's despatch from London of

On April 24 the French minister called on Rush, talked mysteriously about important events that were likely to occur in Spanish America within the next few months, hinted that he would speak more plainly if the president was interested and could keep the secret, and said he " would not scruple to add in confidence to me [Rush], that France looked upon this struggle with the same eyes that he presumed we [the United States] did, viz, that if the colonies were destined to become independent, she did not wish England to reap the benefit."

In the second conference, the following day, Rush began by saying that he had reported this conversation to Monroe, who had replied that he would be glad to hear whatever Hyde de Neuville had to say about South America and Spain and (in effect) would treat it as confidential. The Frenchman then unfolded his plan, the essence of which was that if the United States, France, and Spain would form a " concert " (later described by Rush as a " triple-alliance "), " advantageous commercial results might be secured to the *three nations,* from which England could be excluded." He declared that France was " disposed to act on this policy." When Rush objected that there were differences subsisting between the United States and Spain, Hyde de Neuville asked if these could not be " buried in the great scheme of policy suggested."

In their third conference, on April 30, Hyde de Neuville was informed that his " plan for a triple-alliance " had " met no favor from the President." Nevertheless, the two " talked largely about the colonies." Rush admitted that if

---

April 10, 1817, No. 76. The interviews are not discussed in J. G. Hyde de Neuville, *Mémoires et souvenirs* (3 vols., Paris, 1888-1890).

the other powers did not step forward, England would probably run away with the chief profit of the colonies' independence, and countered Hyde de Neuville's proposal with the suggestion that the United States ought to take the lead in acknowledging their independence, so as to keep England from getting all the credit with them. At first the French minister made no reply. "Surely," Rush insisted, "as between England and the United States, the powers of Europe, and France especially, would prefer that the United States should have the best standing with Spanish America." This time, according to Rush, Hyde de Neuville "admitted it." Rush then suggested that in that case the United States would probably let France know its intentions in regard to recognition at the proper time, and thus brought to a close the last of these three conferences.

There was a good deal of room for doubt as to the French minister's purpose in seeking these conferences.[8] Was it really to devise a " great scheme of policy " for the settlement of the whole problem of the Spanish American colonies, as he pretended? Or was it merely to lend Spain a helping hand in its controversy with the United States over Florida, as was suggested by his remark that the differences between the United States and Spain might be buried in that great scheme? Or perhaps he may have had an entirely different purpose; but however that may have been, the incident pointed to two conclusions about which there can be little if any doubt. In the first place, Rush

[8] Robertson, *France and Latin-American Independence,* does not discuss this episode. It is mentioned briefly in Griffin, *United States,* p. 143-144, without reference to the Rush memorandum cited above.

obviously attached a good deal of significance to these conferences, for, besides discussing them seriatim with Monroe,
he made a detailed, seven-page memorandum of them,
which he initialed and filed for future reference. In the
second place, unless Hyde de Neuville was lying, his overture provided striking evidence that a strong antagonism
over Spanish American policy existed between France and
England, the two European powers whose opinion on that
question mattered most.

Consequently, the incident tended to reassure the authorities at Washington about the danger of a joint intervention
by a united Europe in Latin America. This was important,
because the contrary impression that the danger was increasing had just been given by Adams in his despatch from
London of April 10, 1817, in which he wrote with more
apparent alarm than he had shown before that there was
" a perpetual tendency to interference against the [Spanish
American] insurgents in all the councils of the allies " ; and
in this connection it is interesting to note that in the State
Department files Rush's memorandum of his three conferences with Hyde de Neuville follows immediately after
this despatch of Adam's and was apparently attached to it
as a gloss or corrective.[9]

II

In the light of this encouraging information about the
division of counsels in Europe and the progress of the
revolution in South America, Monroe decided on an important step. On April 25, the day of Rush's second conference with Hyde de Neuville, he wrote to Joel R. Poinsett,
former special agent and consul general of the United States

[9] See above, note 7.

in Buenos Aires and Chile, offering him another appointment to South America.

The progress of the revolution in the Spanish provinces, which has always been interesting to the United States [said Monroe], is made much more so, by many causes, and particularly by a well founded hope, that it will succeed." [10]

What the United States now needed, he continued, was reliable information provided by an agent of such character that he would be able to get in touch with the Spanish colonists and that his word would carry weight in the United States. It had therefore been decided to send an agent of this character in a public ship along the east coast of South America at least as far south as Buenos Aires to communicate with the various governments in that region and gather information which would help the United States government determine the part that it might be proper for it to take. " No one," he observed, " has better qualifications for this trust than yourself," and he added that he himself would be particularly gratified by Poinsett's acceptance of the appointment.

Even now Monroe did not plan to take any immediate action in favor of Latin American independence, but the projected mission clearly contemplated the possibility of such action in the not distant future—action which, if we may trust the drift of Rush's simultaneous remarks to Hyde de Neuville, would probably take the form of recognition of one or more of the new governments. That such action was contemplated seems all the more likely when we recall that Poinsett had been an ardent supporter of the inde-

[10] Manning, *Dip. Cor.,* I, 39-40; Poinsett Papers, HSP, vol. 2, Monroe to Poinsett, April 25, 1817.

pendence cause on the occasion of his mission to Buenos Aires and Chile and that he was now closely connected with David Porter and other champions of that cause in the United States.

Poinsett, however, gave the plan a rude check by declining the appointment. Writing from Charleston, South Carolina, on May 6, he explained his declination on the ground that he had recently accepted a seat in the legislature of that state and could not resign it "without some more important motive than this commission presents." What might constitute such a motive was indicated by another passage in this letter in which he said, "Should the result of these enquiries determine the government to acknowledge the independence of the Colonies, and to afford them effectual assistance, I hope that you will give me an opportunity of serving my country in the field." [11]

Two weeks later, at Rush's request, Poinsett provided him with letters of introduction for the commissioner who might be chosen in his stead and with a sketch of the state of the independence movement in some parts of Spanish America. This sketch was not rose-tinted and it contains more than a hint of the adverse effect that the pro-Negro proclivities of some of the patriot leaders were having on opinion in Poinsett's own section, the South; but it is important mainly because it expresses the views of a man whom Monroe regarded as a leading—perhaps the lead-

[11] *Ibid.*, vol 2., Poinsett to Monroe, May 6, 1817, draft. This letter contains a passage which shows that when Poinsett went to South America on his mission beginning in 1810, he expected the United States government to employ him there in a military capacity, that is, to enter the war on the side of the Spanish American patriots. The letter sent to Monroe is dated May 7, 1817, and is in the Monroe Papers, LC.

ing—authority on the subject. In Mexico, wrote Poinsett, there was no independent government

and no reasonable hopes of success can be entertained, from the disunited efforts of the present [insurgent] commanders . . . who would sacrifice the safety of the cause they are engaged in, rather than resign their command. They support their followers by plunder, and the better class of Creoles are united against them. . . . Should the Liberales who are numerous in Mexico and the Creoles of that city unite, the revolution would be speedy and effectual. . . . In Caraccas there is no [independent] government, but the armed force is united under the command of Bolivar. It would be important to know the connection between that Chief and the authorities of San Domingo [i. e., the Negro republic of Haiti]; and of the number of Negroes in arms. . . . In Buenos Aires it will be well to ascertain the stability of the existing government and the probable policy of their successors. It is rare that the same party remains in power two years. It will be necessary to enquire particularly into the extent of their authority, as many of the provinces have established separate and independent governments.[12]

Poinsett's refusal and Monroe's tour of the northern states, which he was about to begin when he received Poinsett's reply, caused a postponement of the projected mission; but it was not abandoned, and in fact later in the year two missions, instead of one, were sent to South America.

In the meanwhile, in July 1817 a mission which was to have important consequences arrived in the United States from Buenos Aires. It consisted of two members, Manuel H. de Aguirre, and his assistant, José Gregorio Gómez, and it represented both the government of Buenos Aires headed

[12] Poinsett Papers, HSP, vol. 2, Poinsett to Rush, May 23, 1817, draft (apparently incomplete). Together with this is Rush's letter of May 15, 1817, asking Poinsett for notes and letters of introduction.

by Juan Martín Pueyrredon and also the leading authorities in Chile, Bernardo O'Higgins and the Argentine liberator of Chile, General San Martín. Aguirre and his companion were charged with two main duties: first, to persuade the United States to recognize the Buenos Aires government, and second, to obtain warships and arms for use in San Martín's impending campaign to liberate Peru.[13]

Aguirre began his work under unfavorable auspices, for the administration at Washington had recently disavowed an agreement concluded with the Buenos Aires government by its special agent, Col. John Devereux, and Consul T. L. Halsey, whereby it was obligated to guarantee a loan to be used by Aguirre in his purchase of ships and arms.[14] Moreover, since Monroe was still absent from Washington on his northern tour and Adams had not yet arrived to take charge of the State Department, Aguirre had to content himself with an interview with Acting Secretary Rush, whose reply to his overtures was not the most encouraging.

[13] An important source for this mission is the *expediente* in AGN, BA, S1-A2-A4, No. 9, marked " 1817-1822, Estados Unidos, Mision Manuel H. Aguirre y Gregorio Gomez." These and other sources were used by Bemis in preparing his excellent account of the mission in his *Early Diplomatic Missions*, p. 41-57. See especially his comment (*ibid.*, p. 42, note 1) on Alberto Palomeque, *Orígenes de la diplomacia argentina, Misión Aguirre á Norte América* (2 vols., Buenos Aires, 1905). The mission is also discussed in Ibarguren, *En la penumbra de la historia argentina,* chap. 7.

[14] AGN, BA, S1-A2-A4, No. 8, Spanish translation of a letter from " Ricardo Ruth " (Richard Rush) to W. G. D. Worthington, April 21, 1817; Bemis, *op. cit.,* p. 43. On Jan. 23, 1817, Worthington had been appointed special agent to Buenos Aires, Chile and Peru. He spent most of his time in Chile. His activities there are described in Eugenio Pereira Salas, *La Misión Worthington en Chile, 1818-1819* (Santiago, 1936).

The question of recognition, said Rush, would have to await Monroe's return, but in the meanwhile he might observe unofficially that, while the people of the United States looked with sympathy on the Spanish Americans' struggle for independence, the policy of the United States government was one of strict neutrality; and that, as for warships, Aguirre could not purchase these from the government or, in view of the recent neutrality act (that of March 3, 1817), from private individuals, although he could purchase ships not armed for war from the latter.[15]

In the matter of recognition, it is enough to say that Aguirre got no more satisfaction from subsequent interviews with Monroe and Adams than he had from Rush. He had better luck with his warships, and thereby hangs a tale that throws a good deal of light on the enforcement of the neutrality legislation of the United States at that time. According to Aguirre's companion, Gómez,[16] the Spanish minister and his consuls (" *estos demonios* ") in every port of the United States were extremely vigilant to prevent any infraction of the law in favor of the Spanish Americans, and if they found any ship that was armed or even appeared to be susceptible of arming, they insisted upon being told its destination. If that was in Spanish America, they either forced the port authorities to put its master under heavy bond not to permit it to be used for improper purposes or else obtained a court order for its seizure. There were, however, ways of getting around these restrictions. For example, the *Araucana*, which was destined for the Chilean navy but was unable to give the

---

[15] Bemis, *op. cit.*, p. 47-48.

[16] AGN, BA, S1-A2-A4, No. 9, Gregorio Gómez to Pueyrredon, Nov. 13, 1817. See also Manning, *Dip. Cor.*, III, 1971-1977.

necessary bond, cleared unarmed for Gibraltar; its guns were taken out in a small boat beyond the three-mile limit and transferred to the *Araucana*, which then proceeded fully armed direct to Chile.

This was the ruse that Aguirre decided to employ. With funds provided partly by his own government and partly by Joseph Skinner of Baltimore and Matthew L. Davis, a New York merchant, he had two disguised frigates of war built at New York. For a while, all went well; but as the disguise was rather thin the consul of Spain was able to procure the seizure of the ships and the arrest and imprisonment of Aguirre. The latter appealed to Washington for diplomatic protection, which was, of course, refused, and in disgust he then threw up his commission. Ultimately he won his case on an appeal, and the two frigates sailed for South America.[17]

This episode did little to promote good feeling between the United States and Spanish America; on the whole, it had the opposite effect. The captain of one of the two frigates converted it into a privateer on his own account, so that neither Buenos Aires nor Chile ever got the benefit of it; and when some years later Skinner and Davis tried to get the Buenos Aires government to repay them the money that they had lent to its agent, it disclaimed any responsibility in the matter and observed that the claim ought to be presented to Chile and was probably illegitimate anyway.[18]

[17] Ibarguren, *op. cit.*, p. 71-73.

[18] AGN, BA, S1-A2-A4, No. 11, copy of an *informe* by M. H. Aguirre, July 8, 1826, with a marginal note of July 28, 1826, containing the decision of the Buenos Aires government. Aguirre's *informe* consisted largely of the quotation of an earlier report that he had made on the same claim to Gregorio Tagle.

Moreover, Aguirre formed an unfavorable opinion of the United States. He found it timid, fearful of the great powers of Europe, and more interested in forming connections with old established states than with new ones. " Consequently," he told his superiors, " I believe that if they do anything in our favor even indirectly, it will be for the purpose of enriching their merchants. . . . " [19]   As late as 1820, two years after his return to Buenos Aires, his unhappy experience in the United States still rankled, for in that year the American consul, John Murray Forbes, described him as one of the many Argentine agents who, " after having duped our fellow citizens, return here and seek to justify their own bad faith by the most studied calumnies on our national and individual character." [20]   The unfortunate effect of the episode was brought out all the more sharply by the fact that a simultaneous effort on the part of Chile to obtain warships from British sources produced excellent results. Two of the East India Company's frigates, the *Whitman* and *Cumberland*, were purchased in England, re-christened respectively the *Lautaro* and *San Martín*, and rendered valuable service to the patriots in the naval warfare along the coast of Chile and Peru.[21]

One result of considerable importance flowed from Aguirre's misfortunes, together with the measures taken by the United States about the same time to enforce its neutrality and maintain order along its southern frontier. These measures were rendered necessary by the embar-

[19] *Ibid.*, No. 9, Aguirre to Pueyrredon, Aug. 17, 1817.

[20] Manning, *Dip. Cor.*, I, 559-560, Forbes to Adams, Dec. 4, 1820.

[21] Vicente Fidel López, *Historia de la República argentina*, VII, 330-338, 341.

rassing activities of Napoleonic exiles and Spanish American agents and their sympathizers in the United States. Prominent among these were Gregor McGregor, who seized Amelia Island from the Spaniards, nominally under the authority of Venezuela and ostensibly with the approval of Acting Secretary Richard Rush;[22] Louis Aury, who operated first on the Texas coast and later at Amelia Island; Jean Lafitte, of Baratarian fame, who also favored the Texas coast with his attentions; and Javier Mina, a refugee Spanish liberal, who for a time made his headquarters at Galveston before setting out on a revolutionary expedition to Mexico that cost him his life.[23] In most cases, these

[22] Griffin, *United States,* p. 111, holds that Rush was at fault in this matter. He represents McGregor as having conferred directly with Rush, and says that Rush's "strong sympathies for the patriots apparently affected his judgment," and that while he refused to have anything to do officially with McGregor's idea of seizing Amelia Island, "he seems to have allowed McGregor to feel that he would not personally be sorry to see such an outcome." The authorities cited by Griffin at this point are Adams, *Memoirs,* IV, 53, and a letter from Thornton to Adams, dated Feb. 9, 1818, which Griffin says was "probably the source of Adams' information" (*op. cit.,* p. 111, note 74). A different and probably more trustworthy version of this affair was given in a subsequent letter written by Rush himself—the letter of May 14, 1818, cited above, note 3. According to this account, McGregor's plan was laid before Rush not by McGregor himself, but by Dr. William Thornton; and Rush thought the plan so fantastic that he did not even mention it to the President. The plan was that the United States government should first let McGregor conquer Amelia Island and the Floridas in the name of the Spanish American patriots and should then buy them for $1,500,000. Alfred Hasbrouck, *Foreign Legionaries in the Liberation of Spanish South America* (New York, 1928), p. 140-142, discusses McGregor's Amelia Island venture and says that he had no valid commission from any insurgent government, as far as is known.

[23] Griffin, *op. cit.,* p. 109-115, discusses these and other similar

activities were carried on in the name of Spanish American independence; but there was one case in which an effort was made to combine the rescue of Napoleon from St. Helena with the revolutionizing of Brazil.[24] Actually, they were generally a screen for smuggling and piracy; and in any case they harassed commerce, kept the border region in a ferment, and compromised the neutrality of the United States. Consequently the administration ordered the occupation of the two principal centers of infection, Amelia Island and Galveston.[25]

Immediately a great hue and cry was raised. Onís protested because both places were in territory still claimed by Spain; but the loudest and most effective protest came from the agents and .friends of Spanish America, who now had the benefit of David Porter's propaganda machine. Still indignant over the passage of the Neutrality Act of March 3, 1817, they asserted that the administration's course in

---

episodes. For further information see H. G. Warren, "The Origins of General Mina's Invasion of Mexico," *Southwestern Hist. Qly.,* vol. 42 (1938), p. 120 ff.; Brooks, *Diplomacy and the Borderlands,* p. 86, and Francisco José Urrutia, *Los Estados Unidos de América y las repúblicas hispano-americanas de 1810 á 1830* (Madrid, 1918), p. 99, 105-143, cited in Brooks, *op. cit.,* p. 102, note 32.

[24] Clarence Edward Macartney and Gordon Dorrance, *The Bonapartes in America* (Philadelphia, 1939), p. 251-262, citing "the Hudson Lowe papers in the British Museum." For the general subject, see Jesse S. Reeves, *The Napoleonic Exiles in America,* a *study in American Diplomatic History* (Baltimore, 1905).

[25] *Annals Cong.,* 15 Cong., 1 Sess., p. 111-113, Jan. 4, 1818, message from President Monroe reporting the suppression of "the establishment at Amelia Island"; Bemis, *op. cit.,* p. 53. In October 1817 Monroe had consulted his cabinet on the advisability of breaking up "the Amelia Island establishment," and the decision was affirmative (Griffin, *op. cit.,* p. 140-141).

the cases of Aguirre and Amelia Island and Galveston now showed a settled hostility to the Spanish American cause.[26] A congressional inquiry was demanded and the movement in favor of immediate recognition of Spanish American independence was revived. By this time, however, Monroe had despatched a mission of inquiry to South America and the administration group was therefore able to make out a strong case for the postponement of further action pending its return.

III

At the same time that this mission was sent to the East Coast of South America, one of a somewhat different character was sent to the West Coast. Both of them were an outgrowth of the mission which Poinsett had declined in May 1817;[27] but the one to the West Coast also had a remoter origin in the Astoria enterprise of John Jacob Astor. Established at the mouth of the Columbia River just before the War of 1812, Astoria was taken over by the British during the war. In June 1815 Astor wrote

[26] For example, the *City of Washington Gazette,* Dec. 12, 1817, letter signed " Fair Play ": " . . . It is unquestionably true, as Mr. Speaker Clay and Col. [R. M.] Johnson have said, that all that has been done by our government is on *one side. . . .* The members of the *Holy League* will be merry enough to dance a jig when they learn that this enlightened republic is the *first,* of all the nations of the earth, actively to interpose against men fighting in favor of liberty; for, be Aury and his companions good or evil, their efforts are in behalf of South American independence."

[27] Aguirre claimed that the mission to Buenos Aires was being sent as the result of a note that he had written the President (Monroe), but the evidence I have seen does not support his claim. (AGN, BA, S1-A2-A4, No. 9, Matías Irigoyen to the Secretario de Estado, etc., March 9, 1818, quoting a letter from Aguirre of Nov. 25, 1817).

Monroe suggesting that the United States ought to do something about Astoria, and Monroe replied expressing interest and asking for further information, which Astor promptly furnished. In August of the following year the U. S. S. *Congress* was ordered to prepare for an expedition to the Pacific and the Oregon country, but before the preparations were completed the danger of war with Spain became so serious that the *Congress* was ordered to the Gulf of Mexico instead.[28] There matters rested for nearly a year, during which time the expedition to the Pacific seemed to have been forgotten.

On July 21, 1817, Captain James Biddle of the *Ontario* was ordered to take a mission to Rio de Janeiro and then to such other ports as they should designate, as far south as Buenos Aires. This mission, which was to play the part declined by Poinsett, finally included three commisssioners, Caesar A. Rodney of Wilmington, Delaware, former member of Congress and attorney general of the United States; Judge Theodorick Bland of Baltimore, father-in-law of Postmaster J. S. Skinner and friend of David Porter; and John Graham, former secretary of legation and chargé d'affaires at Madrid, who had been chief clerk in the State Department since 1807 and who was probably chosen for this mission because of his knowledge of Spanish and his

[28] David Porter was offered the command of the projected expedition of 1816 to the Pacific and the Columbia River. He refused it, and soon wondered whether he had not done wrong in giving up " a command of so much importance and so flattering to me " (Gilpin Papers, HSP, Poinsett Correspondence, Box 1794-1839, folder " Porter, David . . . 1816-1839," Porter to Poinsett, July 28, 1816). For this cruise of the *Ontario*, see Dudley W. Knox, *A History of the United States Navy* (New York, 1936), p. 142-143.

long experience in the field of diplomacy. The pamphleteer H. M. Brackenridge, a close student of Spanish American affairs for several years past, accompanied them as secretary. Following out the plan suggested in his original letter to Poinsett about the mission, Monroe invested it with as much dignity as possible. Besides being sent, with much fanfare, in a public vessel, the members were called commissioners, not special agents, and were paid much higher salaries than the latter usually received. The purpose of the mission, as explained to Congress by Monroe, was to obtain information, to cultivate friendly relations with the authorities on both sides, so far as this might comport with " an impartial neutrality," and to protect American commerce.[29]

At first it was expected that the *Ontario* would sail with the commissioners about August 10; but just when everything else was in readiness it developed that the serious ill-

---

[29] The two main collections of documents relating to this mission are in the National Archives, SD: (1) Despatches to Consuls, vol. II, and (2) "South American Missions: C. A. Rodney, John Graham, Theodore [sic] Bland, 1815-1818, vol. I." The latter is far from complete. Rodney, one of the first appointees, accepted the appointment on June 23, 1817 (*ibid.,* Rodney to Rush, July 13, 1817). The secondary accounts of this mission and Prevost's that I have found most useful are Wriston, *Executive Agents,* p. 220-22, 416-420; Watt Stewart, "The South American Commission, 1817-1818," *Hispanic Am. Hist. Rev.,* IX (1929), 31-59; and Eugenio Pereira Salas, *La Misión Bland en Chile* (Santiago, 1936). Stewart, *loc. cit.,* p. 36, says that "perhaps the strongest" motive for sending this commission was "the desire to gain an excuse for further delay in making a change in the government's policy toward the Spanish American embroglio." In support of this statement he cites Julius Goebel, Jr., *The Recognition Policy of the United States* (New York, 1915) p. 119, 120, but Goebel's statement on this point (p. 120) is not supported by any evidence, and I doubt its accuracy.

ness of Rodney's son would delay his departure indefinitely.[30] The upshot was that the destination of the *Ontario* was changed to the Pacific, and Biddle was ordered to take still another agent, J. B. Prevost (whom Monroe had selected for this purpose in July) to Chile, and to proceed on to the Columbia River to assert the claim of the United States to that country. As for the other party, the *Congress*, which had once been intended for the expedition of 1816 to the Pacific, was now ordered to take them to Rio de Janeiro and points south. The *Ontario* sailed first and was soon followed by the *Congress* after Rodney and his

[30] National Archives, SD, "South American Missions," vol. I, John Graham to Rush, Aug. 7 and Aug. 11, 1817 (two letters). Bemis, *op. cit.*, p. 51, says that Adams persuaded the President to delay the departure of the mission for several months, and cites a despatch from Onís in support of his statement. Onís would appear to have been misinformed. Adams arrived in New York early in August, just before the commissioners were on the point of sailing (as they thought); Graham explained the purpose of their mission, and Adams, far from opposing it, said that "the object in view was very important more especially as the governments of Europe were turning their attention to the affairs of South America" (Graham's letter of Aug. 7, cited above). The subsequent delay was due, first, to the illness of Rodney's son and then to the consequent change in the destination of the *Ontario* and to the decision to send the *Congress* to Buenos Aires. It required a good deal of time to get these ships ready for their long voyages; as Captain Biddle of the *Ontario* objected when abruptly notified of the change in his case, "it is very manifest that a ship which may be in readiness to sail upon such a destination [i. e., to Buenos Aires], may not be in readiness to sail to the Pacific Ocean and the Columbia River" (*ibid.,* Biddle to Adams, Oct. 2, 1817). Onís, who was a landlubber, failed to appreciate this "manifest" nautical difficulty. More than one historian has made the same mistake, and the case seems to illustrate the general tendency to overestimate Adams's influence on the foreign policy of Monroe's administration.

companions had had a satisfactory interview with Aguirre, who promised them a cordial welcome at Buenos Aires.[31]

Before the results of either mission were received at Washington, Clay and his cohorts in Congress threatened to upset the applecart by raising the whole question of policy again. In the background was their dissatisfaction at the administration's conduct in regard to Aguirre and the Amelia Island affair; but the immediate occasion appears to have been their resentment at its effort to procure a further tightening of the neutrality laws. They countered by raising the question of recognition, and as the United Provinces of the Rio de la Plata had the best claim to recognition, Clay made it the test case by offering a resolution making an appropriation for a minister to Buenos Aires.[32] This naturally met with strong opposition from the administration, whose hand it was intended to force. If adopted, its most probable effect would have been to increase the danger of war with Spain, which was feared not for itself but, as we have seen, because of the danger that it might either involve one or more of the great powers of Europe on the side of Spain, or else bring down a swarm

[31] Monroe Papers, NYPL, C. A. Rodney to Monroe, Nov. 22, 1817, reporting that he and Bland had a "free confidential conversation" with Aguirre "yesterday" and that "it left in our minds no doubt of a cordial reception in Buenos Aires." Unlike Rodney, Graham, and Bland, Prevost was expected to remain in South America, where he was to have a general oversight over the other agents of the United States in Chile and Peru. He did remain in Chile and died there in 1825. A recent Chilean writer has praised him highly for his special sympathy for Chile and his services in defense of its rights against the naval officers of the United States (Pereira Salas, *La actuación de los oficiales navales norteamericanos,* p. 23, note 3).

[32] *Annals Cong.,* 15 Cong., 1 Sess., p. 1468, March 24, 1819.

of European privateers on the seaborne commerce of the United States. Monroe believed that war with Spain was a distinct possibility at this time, and he had recently written in a letter to Andrew Jackson, who was threatening to resign his commission as major general in the United States Army:

I need not state that it is my earnest desire that you remain in the service of your country. Our affairs are not settled, and nothing is more uncertain than the time we shall be permitted to enjoy our present tranquillity and peace. The Spanish government has injured us, and shews no disposition to repair the injury; while the revolutionary struggle in the Colonies continues, to which from a variety of important considerations we cannot be indifferent. Should we be involved in another war, I have no doubt, that it will decide the fate of our free government, and of the Independence of Spanish America. I should therefore much lament your retirement.[33]

So the issue was joined in Congress; and the debate that followed in March 1818 is important because, while the recognition of Spanish American independence had been discussed time and again in the United States since 1808, this was the first full dress congressional debate on the subject. The supporters of the policy of watchful waiting accepted Clay's challenge and assailed what they took to be the basic assumptions of his proposal. One of this group, Forsyth of Georgia, denied that there was or could be any community of political interest between the United States and governments as illiberal and ferocious as those of Spanish America had proved themselves to be.[34] Another, Samuel Smith of Maryland, declared that the United

[33] Monroe Papers, NYPL, Monroe to Jackson, Oct. 5, 1817.
[34] *Annals Cong.*, 15 Cong., 1 Sess., p. 1500-1522.

States not only had nothing to gain from promoting Spanish American independence but was actually suffering from competition from the new states, instancing the fact that Chilean flour was underselling that of the United States in Brazil and even in the West Indies.[35]

Clay counter attacked vigorously, repeating his now familiar assertion that the cause of Spanish American independence was the cause of American freedom from the despotism of Europe and hinting broadly that merchant Smith was blind to the justice of that cause because he had received a valuable trading license from the Spanish government. Floyd of Virginia proceeded to remove another portion of Smith's hide by inquiring sarcastically what the price of wheat had to do with the acknowledgment of Spanish American independence; but he then blunted the fine edge of this sarcasm by undertaking to prove that the United States would " gain essentially " by recognizing the independence of Spanish America, since it would thus obtain a free, direct trade with that rich region, which produced many things that the United States needed, possessed inexhaustible stores of the precious metals, and would provide a market for many of the surplus products of the United States.[36] Even this promise that idealism would pay fat dividends left the majority of the House unmoved, and Clay's motion was rejected by a vote of 115 to 45.

Clay's group got some consolation, however, from the new Neutrality Act (April 20, 1818).[37] It codified the

[35] *Ibid.*, p. 1640.

[36] Clay's main speech on the subject is in *ibid.*, p. 1474-1500. He also spoke on it twice subsequently (*ibid.*, p. 1605, 1643). For Floyd, see *ibid.*, p. 1552, 1553.

[37] Fenwick, *Neutrality Laws of the United States*, p. 40-41,

existing legislation on the subject and was the last act of its
kind passed during our period and for many years to come.
While it retained several features of the earlier laws that
Clay's group had found objectionable, it made two alterations that favored the patriot cause.   In the first place, it
corrected an oversight whereby the Act of 1817 had failed
to prohibit a foreign state or prince (such as Spain) from
augmenting the force of their ships of war in the ports of
the United States to commit hostilities against a colony,
district, or people (such as the Spanish American patriots).
In the second place, the Act of 1818 omitted that part of
the Act of 1797 which attempted to prevent the arming of
American vessels beyond the limit of the United States for
hostilities against a power with which the United States
was at peace.   As the Chairman of the Committee on Foreign Relations explained, this stipulation had borne almost
exclusively on the patriot cause.   It was abandoned for that
reason, and its abandonment facilitated the procurement of
warships in the United States through the device employed
by the Buenos Aires agent Aguirre, as described above in
this chapter.

A few days after the defeat of Clay's motion, Adams
wrote this contemptuous obituary for it:

The present session [of Congress] will stand remarkable
in the annals of the Union for showing how a legislature
can keep itself employed when having nothing to do. . . .
The proposed appropriation for a minister to Buenos Ayres
has gone the way of other things lost upon earth, like the
purchase of oil for light houses in the western country.[38]

The proposal was, indeed, gone, but the memory of its
defeat lingered and rankled.   A year later, that gadfly of

[38] Adams, *Writings,* VI, 305.

the administration, Duane of the *Aurora*, asserted "upon the authority of members of Congress" that on this occasion

the department of state did shamelessly interfere to influence a vote in Congress . . . that when the question concerning South America was about to be brought forward in Congress by Mr. Clay, the whole weight, influence and activity of the *executive* was brought to bear upon the members of congress . . . the sole end and purpose in view being to prostrate Mr. Clay, and arrest his popularity . . . that a number of clerks were employed in the department of state to draw up a series of propositions of a political character and intended to act upon the judgment and votes of the members, and that manuscript mandates were circulated by emissaries from the department, the evening before the debate, at the lodgings of members of Congress.[39]

Whether or not Duane was right about the action of the executive, he was very far from doing full justice to its motives, for even if it had entertained the most amiable feelings towards Mr. Clay, it would still have had more than sufficient reason to oppose the immediate recognition of the Buenos Aires government. That the time might be near at hand when it would be entitled to recognition was admitted by Adams himself; but it had not yet given satisfactory evidence of its stability, its illiberal tendencies were notorious, and a large part of the territory that it claimed was successfully resisting its authority. Under the circumstances, it was easy to convince the majority in Congress that action should be postponed, at least until the fact-finding commission sent to South America in the *Congress* in the autumn of 1817 had made its report.

[39] *Aurora*, May 13, 1819, "Robinocracy."

CHAPTER NINE

ANGLO-AMERICAN COOPERATION: A REJECTED BID

When the reports from the South American commissioners, Rodney, Graham, and Bland, at last arrived in 1818, they proved to be less helpful guides for Latin American policy than had been hoped for. Though they covered as broad a field as could have been expected (Chile and Montevideo as well as Buenos Aires), the commissioners disagreed with each other so sharply that, instead of submitting a joint report, as had been planned, each of them filed a separate report. Their secretary, Brackenridge, added to the confusion by publishing a book, *A Voyage to South America,* which described the mission and its results from still a fourth point of view.

On only one important point were the commissioners unanimous, namely, that Spain would never be able to reconquer the Plata region. Their agreement on this point merely confirmed a belief already held by most informed people in the United States and Europe. On other subjects they expressed a diversity of views [1] and to some extent they

---

[1] The existence of a difference of opinion among the Commissioners became known as soon as they returned to the United States, and on July 30, 1818, Adams wrote to Richard Rush: " Their [the commissioners'] unanimous opinion is that the resubjugation of the provinces of La Plata to Spain is impossible. Of their internal condition the aspect is more equivocal " (Adams, *Writings,* VI, 412). By November, in which month their reports were at last submitted, the disagreements among them were causing Monroe sharp irritation. Rodney and Graham first disagreed with Bland, and then with each other. Adams summed up the situation as regarded the main point at issue by saying that

reflected the factional rivalries among the Spanish American patriots. Their total effect was distinctly less favorable to the Spanish American cause than might have been expected from the fact that two members of the group (Bland and Brackenridge) were connected with the David Porter-Joseph Skinner propaganda machine; and their publication brought on recrimination and more controversy in the United States.[2]

Rodney's report was an "apologetic eulogium upon the present Government of Buenos Ayres," while Graham admired that government much less, and Bland held it "in abhorrence and contempt." According to Adams, Monroe "hinted" to him that Rodney's report would be purposely adapted to the views of Clay rather than the administration and that Rodney was under the influence of Brackenridge, "who is a mere enthusiast, and so devoted to South America that he has avowed the wish to unite all America in conflict against all Europe." The characterization of Brackenridge is more probably Adams's than Monroe's, and it is not supported either by Brackenridge's pamphlet of 1817, *South America*, or by his *Voyage* of 1819 (cited in the following note). About the same time, Adams noted that there had been a sharp disagreement between Prevost and Biddle of the *Ontario*. For these topics, see Adams, *Memoirs*, IV, 156, 159, 160, and V, 56-57.

[2] Griffin, *United States*, p. 248-249. The commissioners' reports were published at Washington in 1819 and also appeared serially in the *National Intelligencer* and in newspapers in other cities, e. g., in the Philadelphia *Aurora* in 1819: Jan. 15, 16 (Rodney), Jan. 18-22 (Graham), and Jan. 23-March 29 (Bland); also, April 3-27, a special report from Joel Poinsett, who was, of course, not a member of the mission. The reports of Rodney, Graham, Bland and Poinsett can be consulted conveniently in *Am. State Papers, Foreign Relations*, IV, 217-348, and Manning, *Dip. Cor.*, I, 382 ff. (see *ibid.*, p. 439, note 1). Brackenridge's *Voyage* was published in 2 vols., Baltimore, 1819, and London, 1820. Rodney and Brackenridge also published many letters about the mission in the Wilmington *Delaware Watchman*. Early in 1819 Hullett Brothers had the reports of Rodney and Graham pub-

So, in the end, these missions, which had been intended to clarify the Spanish American question, only obscured it still further. Their very indecisiveness, however, gave a check to the movement for recognition. Since the attitude of the European powers made it dangerous to take that step alone, there was little disposition to take it without the clearest justification. By showing that it was doubtful whether such justification existed even in the case of Buenos Aires and Chile, the most substantial of the new states, the mission put a damper on the enthusiasm for unilateral recognition. In the next stage the question was whether the United States could obtain the cooperation of one of the great powers in recognizing the new states when the time was ripe. In this stage the initiative came not from the critics of the administration in Congress, but from the administration itself.

I

Perhaps the most important piece of information obtained through these missions was one which related to the governments not of South America but of Europe. As the Buenos Aires commissioners were passing through

lished in London " for the information of members of Parliament," together with an introduction and notes by James Russell, the hack whom they were employing at that time to write propaganda for the Buenos Aires government. They omitted Bland's report, partly because they thought it was too favorable to the Carrera faction in Chile (AGN, BA, S1-A2-A2, No. 12, " Anti-Igyptus y Cia." (Hullett Brothers) to Tagle, Dec. 30, 1818, confidential; Hullett Brothers to Tagle, Jan. 26, 1819). This edition is described in Joseph Sabin, *A Dictionary of Books Relating to America* (29 vols., New York, 1869-1936), vol. 17, p. 454. For the London edition of Bland's report, see *ibid.*, vol. 2, p. 220, no. 5865.

Rio de Janeiro on their way south, the Spanish minister at the Portuguese-Brazilian court tried to dissuade them from going on to their destination by informing them that, according to a despatch of November 1817 from the Spanish court, Great Britain had agreed to a general mediation by the European powers to bring about the pacification of Spanish America.[3] This news, if true, was highly important, because it showed that the long-feared joint intervention of the European powers in Spanish America was at hand; and it was presumably true, since it was based on an official communication from the Spanish court.

Adams received this disturbing news in May 1818. It was all the more disturbing because only four months earlier the British minister at Washington, Bagot, had informed him that the European allies were about to interpose in the quarrel between Spain and her American colonies, had promised to keep him informed about the progress of the plan, and had given him some further reassurance, though it was rather vague.[4] The promised information had never been given, and now Adams learned from a totally different source that England had long since committed herself definitely to the intervention. Presumably, the allies were proceeding with their plans for intervention in Spanish America; certainly, they had not consulted the United States, though the question was one of great concern to it.

Adams took the news with apparent calmness, observing that " we have some concern with that question " and that the European powers " ought not to settle it without consulting us."

[3] Adams, *Writings*, VI, 341-342.
[4] *Ibid*, VI, 319 327.

We say [he continued] they ought not to interfere at all; and most especially not to restore any part of the dominions of Spain. We think it impossible that they should interfere with any effect to that end, and we believe that the British government neither expects nor intends it." [5]

The latter belief was the main reason for the calmness with which Adams took the news from Rio. It was based on his conviction that the British, while not yet ready to recognize the independence of Spanish America, were nevertheless determined to protect the commercial advantages which they had gained through the Spanish American independence movement and would consequently oppose the restoration of the Spanish colonial system, whether through the intervention of the Continental powers or otherwise. Adams also hoped that any united action on the part of Europe would be rendered impossible by the rivalry between Britain, mistress of the seas, and Russia, which had succeeded Napoleonic France as the preponderant power on the Continent.[6]

He realized, however, that this was a decidedly optimistic view of the situation. For one thing, it was based partly on his impression that the British government was moving towards the same kind of liberal commercial policy that underlay the friendly attitude of the United States towards Spanish American independence;[7] but further reports from Rush at London disillusioned him on this score late in May 1818,[8] at almost the same time that he received the disturbing news from Rio de Janeiro. Moreover, he realized that European intervention in Spanish America would not necessarily take the form of direct military intervention

[5] *Ibid.*, VI, 342.
[6] *Ibid.*, VI, 452.
[7] *Ibid.*, VI, 327.
[8] *Ibid.*, VI, 344.

which might be resisted by the United States and by Great Britain as well. It might equally well take the form of a pacific intervention, such as that recently suggested by Russia, which would reconcile the Spanish Americans to Spain by granting them certain privileges upon condition of their return to obedience. The settlement would then be confirmed by general European treaties similar to those recently concluded at Vienna for the suppression of the African slave trade,[9] and would thus rivet Europe's hold on Spanish America more firmly than ever.

Finally, Adams himself had some doubts about the protective value of that rivalry between Britain and Russia of which he sometimes spoke so hopefully. Like many other Americans, he was beginning to question the liberalism of the Russian Tsar, Alexander I, and his good will towards the United States. Russia's recent sale of warships to Spain, which was assembling an armada at Cadiz for use against the Spanish American patriots,[10] gave good ground for this skepticism, and Adams was also fretted by the efforts of the Reverend Noah Worcester and other pacifists in the United States to cultivate the friendship of Alexander I. Comparing the situation to the one in Athens at the time when Athenian pacifists were assailing Demosthenes for his philippics against the ruler of Macedon, Adams wrote:

Alexander of the Neva is not so near nor so dangerous a neighbor to us as Philip was to the Athenians, but I am

[9] *Ibid.*, VI, 324-325.
[10] A report to this effect was published in Niles's *Register*, XIII, p. 46, Sept. 13, 1817. See Webster, *Britain*, II, 364-365, for a despatch from the British minister at Madrid announcing the arrival of the Russian squadron at Cadiz on Feb. 21, 1818, and enclosing an official article published at Madrid which coupled that event with the war in Spanish America.

afraid his love of peace is of the same character as was that of Philip of Macedon. . . . While Alexander and his Minister of Religious Worship, Prince Galitzin, are corresponding with Rev. Noah Worcester upon the blessedness of peace, the venerable founder of the Holy League is sending five or six ships of the line, and several thousand promoters of peace armed with bayonets to Cadiz, and thence to propagate good will to man elsewhere. Whether at Algiers, at Constantinople, or at Buenos Ayres, we shall be informed hereafter.[11]

At this time Adams did not apprehend any difficulty with Russia over the Oregon country, where he thought England would probably be the only serious rival of the United States; [12] but he did conclude from Russia's sale of warships to Spain and her memorial of November 17, 1817, that her disposition, which until recently had seemed to favor Spanish American independence, was inclining "strongly against the South Americans." [13] In view of Russia's preponderant power on the Continent and her leadership in the Holy Alliance, this was an ominous change. In order to guard against its possible consequences, the policy makers at Washington had to rely mainly on detaching England from the Continental allies and using her influence on the side of Spanish American independence to counterbalance the influence that Russia was now exerting on the side of Spain. The prospect was not encouraging, but there seemed to be no other weak spot in the armor of a Europe that was increasingly united, reactionary, and hostile to the Spanish American patriots as representatives of the revolutionary spirit against which the European allies were contending.

Accordingly, Monroe and Adams increased their efforts

[11] Adams, *Writings*, VI, 280-281.
[12] *Ibid.*, VI, 372.   [13] *Ibid.*, VI, 324-325.

to draw England into a joint demonstration with the United States on behalf of Spanish American independence. These efforts, which were made most vigorously in 1818 and 1819, are especially interesting because, only a few years later, in 1823, joint action for the same purpose was proposed to the United States by England and the proposal fell through, although effective control of American foreign policy still lay largely in hands of Monroe and Adams. The reasons for this apparent reversal of attitude will appear in due course. Here we need only note that in the earlier period Monroe and Adams took the initiative in proposing the plan to the British government and renewed the proposal with increasing urgency. Thus, on May 20, 1818, Adams wrote in a letter to Richard Rush, now American minister at London, about the proposed interposition of the European allies in Spanish America:

It cannot have escaped the recollection of Lord Castlereagh how often he has been assured of the wish of this Government to proceed in relation to South American affairs, in good understanding and harmony with Great Britain; most especially so long as their mutual policy should be neutrality. . . . It may be an interesting object of your attention to watch the moment when this idea [i. e., the idea that the recognition of Spanish American independence is an " act of friendship to Spain herself "] will become prevalent in the British councils, and to encourage any disposition which may consequently be manifested to a more perfect concert of measures between the United States and Great Britain towards that end—the total independence of the Spanish South American provinces.[14]

When this overture was duly made by Rush, Castlereagh

[14] *Ibid.*, VI, 323, 326. See also Manning, *Dip. Cor.*, I, 66-70, and Richard Rush, *Memoranda of a Residence at the Court of London* (Philadelphia, 1833, first ed.), p. 209-213, 246-252, 300-302, and 323-328.

replied rather frigidly, observing, with appropriate expressions of regret, that the views of the United States and his own government on the Spanish American question were not identical.[15] The overture was to be renewed some months later in a still more interesting form, but in the meanwhile two important developments occurred which require our attention.

II

In February 1818 the Buenos Aires government appointed two new agents to the United States in place of Aguirre. One of these was David Curtis DeForest,[16] an American business man who had resided at Buenos Aires for a good many years past and had made a fortune out of privateering and other more conventional forms of business enterprise. He was appointed consul general with the usual powers and was also instructed to urge the United States to recognize the independence of the Buenos Aires government. In his negotiations regarding recognition he was instructed to act in concert with the other agent appointed at this time, General William H. Winder of Baltimore, a veteran of the War of 1812 who had already manifested his sympathy for the Spanish American patriots and was regarded by them as a man of great influence in the United States. After some hesitation, Winder declined the appointment.

Arrived in the United States, DeForest applied to Adams

[15] Adams, *Writings*, VI, 523.

[16] Bemis, *Early Diplomatic Missions*, p. 71-89, gives an account of his mission, with other biographical data, based partly on hitherto unexploited papers (p. 71, note 2). In the Buenos Aires documents in Spanish, DeForest's middle name, Curtis, appears as Cortes or Cortez.

in May 1818 for an exequatur for his commission as consul general and also for formal recognition of his government. Both requests were rejected. The application for the exequatur was refused partly on the ground that its issuance would be equivalent to recognition of the independence of the Buenos Aires government [17]—an interesting argument, in view of the fact that the United States had only a few years since been represented at Buenos Aires by Joel R. Poinsett with the title of consul general, despite the fact that the government of Buenos Aires had not even declared its independence at that time.

In the course of the conferences and correspondence that followed between Adams and DeForest, the former elaborated the reasons for which the United States still withheld recognition. Aside from the considerations of a general nature with which we are already familiar, the most important reasons applying particularly to the case in hand were, first, that the Buenos Aires government claimed sovereignty over regions over which it obviously had no effective control (such as the modern Uruguay and Paraguay) and, second, that the commercial policy of the Buenos Aires government raised serious doubts as to whether it actually was or would remain independent. Explaining the latter point, Adams reminded DeForest that his government had refused to accord the United States most-favored-nation treatment and had justified the refusal on the ground that it might need to give Spain preferential treatment as the price of recognition. Moreover, it had decided to offer special commercial advantages to the first nation that recognized its independence—a step which, Adams observed, might only transfer the dependence of Buenos Aires from

[17] Bemis, *op. cit.*, p. 80; Adams, *Writings*, VI, 524-525.

one government to another. He then described to DeForest, as an example worthy of imitation, the commercial policy of the United States, which was one of " perfect equality and reciprocity," based on most-favored-nation treatment.[18]

Although all of DeForest's overtures for recognition were rejected, the rebuff was softened as much as possible and his mission was by no means futile. It not only offset, at least in the United States, the unfortunate effect of the mission of his predecessor, Aguirre, but it also appears to have created a more favorable opinion of the Buenos Aires regime than had yet been held by the authorities at Washington. This should probably be set down as a personal achievement of DeForest's. His success was due partly to his personality and partly to his connections in the United States.[19] He was no fly-by-night adventurer of the kind so common among the foreigners who flocked to Latin America in that period, but a man of substance who came of a good Connecticut family, had made his mark as well as his fortune in Buenos Aires, and while there had been the agent of John Jacob Astor,[20] who, as we have seen, was a correspondent of James Monroe's. In short, DeForest was exceptionally well qualified to serve as an intermediary between his adopted country on the Plata and his native country, the United States. Enveloped in an aura of respectability that inspired confidence, he was able to strengthen the Buenos Aires case at the point at which it had been weakest by convincing the Washington authorities that his government was responsible and stable.

So, even while Adams was repeatedly warning DeForest

[18] *Ibid.,* VI, 518. [19] Bemis, *op. cit.,* p. 72, 79.
[20] Porter, *Astor,* II, 650, describes DeForest as " Astor's agent at Buenos Aires."

that the United States was not yet ready to recognize the independence of the United Provinces, he was saying enough in other quarters to show that it was moving in that direction. Thus, on August 15, 1818, he sent cipher instructions to the ministers of the United States in England, France, and Russia to inquire of those governments how they would view an acknowledgment of the independence of the Spanish colonies by the United States, and what position they would take if Spain declared war on the United States in consequence of such recognition.[21] A few days later he wrote that, if the Buenos Aires government would make the proper modification in its territorial claims and commercial policy, " I should think the time now arrived when [it] might be recognized without a breach of neutrality." [22] And at the close of the year his detailed statement to DeForest of the reasons for withholding recognition was followed a few days later by his instructions to Rush to inform the British government that the United States would probably recognize DeForest's government " at no remote period." [23]

The other important development of 1818 was the check given to the project of European intervention in Spanish America. This was administered at the Congress of Aix-la-Chapelle in the autumn of 1818, mainly through the opposition of England to the plan of intervention proposed by France and Russia.[24] According to this plan, the great powers were to agree with Spain on reasonable terms to be offered the insurgent colonies. The latter were to be

[21] Adams, *Writings,* VI, 433.

[22] *Ibid.,* VI, 443.   [23] *Ibid.,* VI, 525.

[24] Webster, *Britain* I, 14-15; Robertson, *France and Latin-American Independence,* p. 150-154.

coerced into accepting them—not by force of arms, but first by threats and then, if that failed, by economic sanctions.

At every stage in these proceedings the United States was an important factor in the calculations of the five great powers. The Franco-Russian plan of intervention was drawn up because it had been learned that the United States was contemplating the recognition of one of the revolutionary governments (that of Buenos Aires). One feature of the plan was the intervention of the Allied powers in the United States to prevent this; and one of the chief arguments advanced in favor of the whole plan was that a republican New World, headed by the United States, would be a constant menace to monarchical Europe, a *point d'appui* for " all that remains in Europe of the spirit of discontent, of faction, and of discord." [25] Finally, in opposing the imposition of economic sanctions on the Spanish colonies, the English argued that even if " by a miracle " a contraband trade could be prevented from growing up in place of the prohibited direct trade with Europe, still " the only results would be that the same amount of trade would pass circuitously through the United States to the Provinces in revolt." [26]

III

The result of this congress in turn produced some important results in the field of Spanish American affairs. For one thing, it confirmed Monroe's faith in the policy of watchful waiting that he had been pursuing in regard to Latin America, for it was on this occasion that he said, in the letter to Andrew Jackson of December 1818 from which

[25] *Ibid.*, p. 153.
[26] Webster, *Britain*, II, 65, Castlereagh to Bathurst, Nov. 2, 1818.

we have already quoted,[27] that that policy had "contributed essentially, to produce the decision of the Allies at Aix-la-Chapelle, not to interfere in favor of Spain against the Colonies, or against us." At the same time, however, Monroe believed that the very success that had so far attended his cautious policy justified him in venturing on a bolder one. The stand taken by Britain at Aix-la-Chapelle suggested the direction of the new policy, and in January 1819 Monroe made his most definite bid for Anglo-American cooperation in promoting the independence of Latin America.

It will be easier to understand not only this episode but also the events of 1823 if we emphasize here the fact that this idea of Anglo-American cooperation was Monroe's, not Adams's. Monroe had long been a persistent advocate of Anglo-American amity and he lacked Adams's first-hand acquaintance with the Europe of the Restoration, in which even the British government accepted the principle of legitimacy. During Jefferson's administration he had shared in the negotiation of a treaty with England which was so advantageous to the latter power that it was not even submitted to the Senate. He had entered Madison's cabinet on the eve of the War of 1812 as a champion of a good understanding with England. Now that most of the old causes of friction had disappeared with the end of the Napoleonic Wars, it was easy for him to believe that an entente might be reached between the two powers in regard to Latin America, although this involved an underestimate of the new causes of friction growing out of their rivalry in that region.

Adams, on the other hand, was equally persistent in his

[27] See chap 7, note 40.

Anglophobia. Since he had recently returned from London believing that the classes in England which were most sympathetic towards Latin American independence were also the most hostile to the United States and that the English government, which was more friendly towards the United States, was opposed to Latin American independence, he found it hard to believe that there was any real possibility of Anglo-American cooperation in regard to Latin America. If his instructions to Rush in London seem to show that he did believe in it, that is only because he deferred, however, reluctantly, to his chief.

How the views of Monroe and Adams on this subject clashed is illustrated by an incident that occurred in July 1818.[28] One day Monroe "very abruptly" asked Adams to see the British minister Bagot and "propose through him to the British Government an immediate cooperation between the United States and Great Britain to promote the independence of South America." In a cabinet meeting some two months earlier Adams had openly objected to a proposal of the same nature, but now his gambit was merely to ask, "What part of South America?" "All South America, and Mexico, and the islands included," replied Monroe. Adams then observed, with obvious self-restraint, that in his opinion Britain was not yet ready for such a direct proposition. As he tells the story, further conversation showed that Monroe's idea was "crude," and he immediately abandoned it—but not for long.

Throughout the rest of the summer and autumn Monroe bided his time. Though he gave encouragement to De-Forest, his annual message to Congress towards the end of the year gave no reason to believe that any important

[28] Adams, Memoirs, IV, 118.

step was about to be taken in Latin American affairs. Such
a step was taken, however, at the beginning of the new
year, 1819. On January 2 Adams showed Monroe the
draft of a despatch he had prepared for Rush at London
in which the latter was instructed to inform the British
government that it was the "intention" of the United
States to recognize the Buenos Aires government. Under
the circumstances, this was a provocative statement since in
effect it bluntly announced that the United States intended
to take alone and, presumably, at once a step that the Allied
powers of Europe, including England, had condemned.
Monroe read the draft in the morning and called a cabinet
meeting on it for that afternoon.[29]

It was a nearly full meeting. The other members present,
besides Monroe and Adams, were William H. Crawford
(Treasury), John C. Calhoun (War), and the Attorney
General, William Wirt. Only the Secretary of the Navy
was absent.

When the draft of the despatch to Rush was read, all the
members were startled at the word "intention." Wirt
asked whether this was not inconsistent with the refusal to
recognize Buenos Aires last winter and with the President's
message even at the beginning of the present session of
Congress. Two members of the cabinet—Crawford and
Adams—replied that circumstances had changed since then.
The South American mission had returned, additional proof
of the stability of the Buenos Aires government had been
received, and the united forces of the patriots of Buenos
Aires and Chile had won a great victory over the royalists
at Maipú. Moreover, even since the President's message it
had been ascertained that the European allies would take

[29] *Ibid.*, IV, 203-205.

no part with Spain against the colonies—an allusion to the proceedings at Aix-la-Chapelle.[30]

The most important contribution during the whole discussion came from Calhoun, who made the allusion to Aix-la-Chapelle still clearer by pointing out that the views of Great Britain were now better known and more clearly stated than last winter. With the obvious implication that the views of the British government as thus established were believed to be in harmony with those of the United States, he went on to urge cooperation with it. According to Adams, of all the cabinet members, Calhoun " expressed the most earnestness to avoid acting unless in concert with England."

Adams characteristically objected to this " deference to England "; but Calhoun had evidently voiced the sentiments of the rest of the cabinet as well as the President himself. In the form in which it was finally sent, the despatch to Rush differed from Adams's draft in two important respects. First, the statement of intention to recognize Buenos Aires (and possibly Chile and Venezuela, at a later period) was qualified by the clause, " if no event occurs that would justify postponement." Second, and more important, the despatch expressed the hope that the difference between the views of England and the United States (which Castlereagh had stressed in 1818) was one of form rather than substance, and continued,

[30] Adams, *Gallatin,* p. 573, calls attention to the fact that Gallatin's advices to the home government furnished much of its best information about the Congress of Aix-la-Chapelle and its transactions in regard to Spanish America; but he does not develop this point or illustrate it, and most of Gallatin's despatches of this period are omitted both from his edition of Gallatin's writings and also from Manning, *Dip. Cor.* The despatches are in the National Archives, SD, Despatches from France.

If it should suit the views of Great Britain to adopt similar measures at the same time and in concert with us, it will be highly satisfactory to the President.[31]

This was a definite proposal of not merely parallel but concerted action on the part of the two powers. That it was made without the least encouragement from Castlereagh is striking evidence of the eagerness of the administration to detach Britain from the Continental allies. It was not well adapted to its purpose, however, for the proposal was made conditional upon Britain's adopting " similar measures at the same time" with the United States. Since the despatch to Rush contained a rather detailed and explicit statement of what those measures were to be, the proposal was in effect an invitation to the British government to underwrite the Spanish American policy of the United States.

Castlereagh gave the proposal a cold reception, as might have been foreseen, and thereby proved Adams a better analyst of British policy than Monroe and his other advisers. When Rush read him the despatch a little more than a month later, Castlereagh expressed his surprise at the passages which " seemed to import that the government of England was, at bottom, inclining to our [the United States'] view of the subject, as regarded the recognition of the colonies." On the contrary, said Castlereagh, England had always acted "upon the basis of a restoration of the supremacy of Spain, on an improved plan of government indeed, especially as regarded the commercial interests of the colonies, but still her entire supremacy." [32]

[31] Adams, *Writings*, VI, 524-525; Manning, *Dip. Cor.*, I, 87.

[32] Rush's account of the interview of Feb. 12, 1819, at which he read Castlereagh the despatch in question, is in his *Memoranda*

This frank statement showed the American government that the fruits of Aix-la-Chapelle were less sweet than had been hoped. It showed, indeed, that there was no real basis for Anglo-American cooperation in Latin America, for the American government, in order to create such a basis, would have had to reverse its policy of the past decade and subscribe to a policy which looked to the restoration of the " entire supremacy " of Spain over her American colonies.

IV

If we may trust a report received through Gallatin, there was a close connection between the Congress of Aix-la-Chapelle and the surrender of Spain to the United States in the controversy over Florida and other questions dating back to the period of the Napoleonic wars. The details of this long-drawn-out negotiation need not detain us here, for our only concern is with its bearing on the movement for independence in Spanish America.

As is well known, Spain long refused to agree to any settlement of the points at issue which was acceptable to the United States, and, as we have had occasion to observe, more than once in the years from 1815 to 1818 the controversy threatened to bring on a war between the two powers. Suddenly, late in 1818, the Spanish minister for foreign affairs, the Marqués de Casa Irujo,[33] sent the

---

of a Residence at the Court of London (Philadelphia, 1845), p. 13-20. In this case, as in others, Rush's book follows his despatches almost verbatim; compare the foregoing quotation with his despatch of Feb. 15, 1819, in Manning, Dip. Cor., III, 1451.

[33] Former Minister to the United States (where he married the daughter of Governor Samuel M'Kean of Pennsylvania) and to the Portuguese court at Rio de Janeiro. See Griffin, United States, p. 173.

Spanish plenipotentiary in the United States, Onís, instructions under which he negotiated with John Quincy Adams a treaty (signed February 22, 1819) conceding most of the points contended for by the United States. The latter was confirmed in the possession of the parts of Florida that it already held, and acquired the rest of that strategically important colony; gave up its claim to Texas but acquired Spain's claim to the territory on the Pacific coast north of the forty-second parallel (the Oregon country); and paid Spain five million dollars, which sum was ear-marked for the satisfaction of the spoliation claims of its own citizens against Spain.[34]

The reasons for this sudden surrender by the Spanish court of a position that it had long maintained with great tenacity have been a subject of much study and speculation. For many years it was believed that Andrew Jackson's invasion of Florida early in 1818, skilfully exploited by Adams in his negotiation with Onís, was mainly responsible for Spain's decision to barter away a colony that she was in imminent danger of losing in any case. So many other factors and so many other issues besides Florida were involved, however, that this explanation would hardly seem adequate. Recent research [35] has clarified this question, first, by confirming the belief that Jackson's invasion had " an electric effect " on the negotiation; second, by showing that Adams's exploitation of it in his famous despatch to Minister Erving at Madrid came too late to affect the course

[34] *Ibid.*, p. 187. Brooks, *Diplomacy and the Borderlands*, p. 160, says that the claims question and the boundary question "were debated and decided separately."

[35] Griffin, *op. cit.*, p. 176-177, 182. The problem is discussed more briefly and with a somewhat different conclusion in Brooks, *op. cit.*, p. 137.

of the Spanish court; and third, by showing that the new head of the Spanish government, Irujo, hastened the conclusion of the negotiation with the United States in order to give Spain a free hand for the reconquest of its American colonies by means of the great expeditionary force which it was assembling at Cadiz at this time.

To one important question, however, no satisfactory answer has been given: what relation, if any, did the Spanish surrender to the United States bear to the failure of the determined effort that Spain made in 1818 to obtain the intervention of the great powers in its behalf in Spanish America?

Such an explanation is suggested by a despatch from Albert Gallatin which has not, so far as is known, come to the attention of previous students of this problem. Writing in May 1819 from Paris, which was the diplomatic center of Europe and was in very close touch with Spain, Gallatin said:

Marquis Dessole [the French minister of foreign affairs] informed me that the Spanish Government had delayed for a considerable time to transmit to Onís the final instructions by virtue of which the treaty [with the United States] was concluded, and which had been prepared by Yrujo's predecessor. The determination was taken only after the failure of obtaining at Aix la Chapelle the mediation of the allied powers with the colonies, under a feeling of irritation against Great Britain as the author of the failure, and from a conviction that any attempt to subjugate [the colonies] by force was hopeless whilst the danger of a rupture with the United States continued to exist.[36]

[36] National Archives, SD, Despatches from France, Gallatin to Adams, May 5, 1819, No. 102, endorsed " Rec'd 8th July." This despatch is not printed in Manning, *Dip. Cor.* So far as I can find, it is not mentioned and the explanation of Spanish policy

Literally construed, the explanation reported by Gallatin was not correct, for the Congress of Aix-la-Chapelle was still in session when Irujo sent Onís the instructions of October 10, 1818,[37] under which he negotiated the treaty with Adams. Nevertheless, the adverse decision of the Congress on the intervention desired by Spain was made a foregone conclusion by the very strong letter written to the British ambassador at Madrid by Castlereagh on September 1, 1818, as he was on the point of setting out for Aix-la-Chapelle.[38] Although this was a private letter, the substance of it was clearly intended to be communicated to the Spanish court. Consequently, while the question requires further study, it seems probable that Spain surrendered to the United States partly because her hopes of an intervention by the powers assembled at Aix-la-Chapelle had been blasted; and the episode provides one more illustration of the intimate triangular relationship that existed between the affairs of Europe, Latin America, and the United States in the period of the present study.

The immediate result was a resounding diplomatic victory for the United States. Adams recorded it in his diary [39] with deep satisfaction and with reverent though slightly puzzled gratitude to the " all-beneficent Disposer of events " who had " brought it about in a manner utterly

---

contained in it is not discussed in either of the two works cited in the preceding note.

[37] The date when the instructions of Oct. 10, 1818, were actually despatched from Madrid is not altogether certain. In one place, Griffin gives the date as Oct. 10; in another, as Oct. 23 (*op. cit.*, p. 175, note 58, and 185). Brooks merely says that Irujo " sent it [the instruction] along dated October 10 " (*op. cit.*, p. 155).

[38] Webster, *Britain*, II, 369-370, Castlereagh to Sir Henry Wellesley, Sept. 1, 1818.

[39] Adams, *Memoirs*, IV, 274-275.

unexpected and by means the most extraordinary and unforeseen." It was certainly a highly important treaty, for, aside from the fact that it settled many vexatious problems, it greatly strengthened the position of the United States in the Gulf of Mexico and gave it its first treaty claim to territory on the Pacific coast. This " Transcontinental Treaty," [40] as it has been appropriately named, marked one of the principal stages in the territorial expansion of the United States and in its rise to world power.

Nevertheless, the treaty had some most unfortunate repercussions in the field of Latin American relations. The surrender of the United States' claim to Texas provoked sharp criticism at home and gave rise almost at once to a demand for the reannexation of Texas.[41] Coinciding with the establishment of Mexican independence, this demand clouded the relations of the United States with its new neighbor to the south from the very beginning of its national existence, and set in motion a train of events that by the end of the next generation had antagonized Spanish Americans everywhere against the United States.

More immediately unfortunate was the resentment that the very negotiation of the treaty aroused against the United States in Spanish America. This resentment arose from the belief that the United States had deliberately

[40] This is the name given it in Samuel Flagg Bemis, *A Diplomatic History of the United States* (New York, 1936). Other recent writers (e. g., Griffin and Brooks) call it the Adams-Onís treaty. All of them condemn the name Florida treaty as misleading. They are right from the point of view of a modern appraisal of its significance; but so far as my observation extends, contemporary commentators generally called it the Florida treaty and regarded the settlement of the Florida question as its most important feature.

[41] Griffin, *op. cit.*, p. 189-190.

sacrificed the Spanish American cause in order to further its own national interests. In its extreme form this belief was based on the assumption that the treaty contained a secret clause by which, as a part of the price that it paid Spain for Florida, the United States had obligated itself not to recognize or otherwise aid the Spanish American revolutionists. In its milder form, the belief was based on the conviction that, whatever the intention of the United States might have been, its settlement of its difficulties with Spain made it possible for the latter to concentrate all her energies on the subjugation of her colonies.

In one form or another, this belief was widespread in Europe and America. In May 1819 Gallatin reported that it was held in usually well informed quarters in Paris; [42] and a month earlier the American vice-consul at Buenos Aires, W. G. Miller, listed it as one of the chief reasons for the rapidly rising resentment of the people of that city against the United States.

We are no longer looked up to [by the people of Buenos Aires] as Americans, the protectors of liberty and the supporters of the independence and of the cause of our South American brothers [concluded Miller], but rather as *neutrals* determined to assist Spain in the reconquest of the country.[43]

[42] In his despatch to Adams of May 5, 1819, cited above, note 36, Gallatin said, " I found that both this government and the Spanish ambassador were under the impression that the treaty [i. e., the Adams-Onís treaty] if not by any positive stipulation, at least by a tacit understanding, implied on our part an obligation not to recognize the independence of Buenos Ayres."

[43] Poinsett Papers, HSP, Miller to Poinsett, April 27, 1819. See also Griffin, *op. cit.,* p. 260. It is not easy to see why Griffin believes that the articles attacking the United States that appeared in the Buenos Aires press on this occasion were probably due in

The flames of resentment were fanned by British rivals of the United States; for example, the Buenos Aires government was told by its London agents, Hullett Brothers, that the treaty was a betrayal of the Spanish American cause.[44]

There can be no doubt that the treaty would have injured that cause if the Spanish government had been able to take advantage of the opportunity afforded by it; but it would be difficult to sustain the further charge that the United States deliberately sacrificed the interests of Spanish America to its own. For one thing, there was no truth whatever in the charge that the United States had obligated itself, by a secret article or otherwise, not to recognize the independence of the new Spanish American states. Indeed, its refusal to make any commitment to that effect was one of the main reasons for Spain's long delay in ratifying the treaty,[45] the ratifications of which were not exchanged until February 22, 1821, precisely two years after Adams and Onís signed it.

---

large measure to personal grudges against individual Americans, and should be discounted to some extent" (*loc. cit.*).

[44] AGN, BA, S1-A2-A2, No. 12, "Anti-Igyptus y Cia." (Hullett Brothers) to Gregorio Tagle (Foreign Secretary of the Buenos Aires Government) April 23, 1819, suggested that the conversion of the London *Times* to the Spanish American cause gave reason to hope for a similar change in British policy, and continued, "Lo cierto es que la causa de la independencia podrá ganar tanto terreno en esta politica, quanto ha perdido por la felonia de Norte América"—i. e., of the United States in negotiating the treaty "sobre la cesion de las Floridas." Replying to this, Tagle wrote, "La conducta de los Estados Unidos, relativam[en]te á nuestra causa, aparece qual jamàs se esperó, por la identidad de intereses de ambos Estados" (*ibid.*, Tagle to "SSres. Anti-Igyptus y Compa.," Sept. 9, 1819).

[45] Griffin, *op. cit.*, p. 201-205, 222; Brooks, *op. cit.*, p. 179, 181, 188.

Again, there appears to be no foundation for the assertion, which has been repeated by historians in the United States itself, that the American government postponed recognition of Spanish American independence until the treaty had been safely negotiated and ratified. Statements made by Adams himself can be cited in support of this view, but they must be discounted heavily, for they were obviously made for political and diplomatic effect, to appease the unrecognized governments of Spanish America and their impatient champions in Congress.[46]

The fact is that, as the present chapter and the two preceding chapters should have made abundantly clear, the policy which delayed recognition had been decided upon long before the beginning of Adams's negotiation with Onís and was based upon considerations which had little if anything to do with it; and it is not easy to see how recognition could have been hastened appreciably even if there had never been a Spanish negotiation. After the negotiation was completed by the exchange of ratifications at Washington (February 22, 1821) more than a year elapsed before President Monroe sent the message to Congress that committed his administration to recognition. It would seem, therefore, that in the long story of the cautious, tentative, intermittent advance of the United States towards the recognition of the new states, the retarding influence of the Spanish negotiation was relatively unimportant.[47]

The postponement of recognition was mainly due to two other factors: first, to the situation in Spanish America,

[46] For a different view, see Griffin, *op. cit.*, p. 142-143.

[47] A very different conclusion was reached by Goebel in his *Recognition Policy*, p. 141-142; but his argument is based on coincidence and Spanish suspicion and I find it unconvincing.

where there was no government that was clearly entitled to recognition; and second, to the attitude of Europe, which, the administration believed, made it dangerous to recognize any Spanish American government, no matter how meritorious its case might be. Until the latter part of 1818 both factors remained fairly constant and both were adverse to recognition. Then they became somewhat more favorable as a result of the stand taken by England at Aix-la-Chapelle, the progress of the revolution in South America, and the good impression created by DeForest's mission. The administration at Washington promptly made unmistakable though cautious preparations to abandon its policy of watchful waiting and begin its recognition of Spanish American independence.

It is important to note, however, that these preparations contemplated recognition by the concerted action of the United States and Great Britain, as proposed in Adams's instructions to Rush of January 1819. There is no good reason to believe that the administration was ready to brave the hazards of recognition alone; and when Castlereagh again, as in 1818, turned a cold shoulder to the invitation to concerted action, the rebuff was only another warning to Washington to make haste slowly along the road to recognition. Progress was not renewed again until nearly three years later, under profoundly different circumstances.

Chapter Ten

THE RÔLE OF THE NAVY (1815-1823)

As Adams pointed out to the British government through his instructions to Rush in January 1819, an important reason in favor of the recognition of the new Spanish American states was that only by recognizing them could other nations compel them to observe the ordinary rules of international law in their intercourse with the civilized world. In other words, he explained, it was the only way of suppressing piracy and other unwarranted interference with the shipping of the United States and other foreign nations by armed vessels flying the flags of the new Spanish American governments, which could not be held to the obligations of sovereignty if they were not accorded the privileges of sovereignty through recognition.

I

Adams was not only quite sincere in advancing this consideration as an argument in favor of recognition; he also attached great importance to it. Yet the truth of the matter is that the protection of the commerce of the United States, which was the chief purpose that Adams had in mind, operated against the recognition of Spanish American independence as well as in favor of it. This was partly because Spanish American interference with the commerce of the United States aroused much ill feeling in this country and consequently created an atmosphere unfavorable to immediate recognition of the offending states. It was also because, in an effort to provide more adequate protection for its commerce, the United States greatly extended and intensified the operations of its navy in Latin American waters, with results that for a time still further clouded its relations with its neighbors to the South.

For a variety of reasons, as we shall soon see, this vexatious question reached a climax in the very same year in which Adams sent Rush the instructions mentioned above. To be sure, it embroiled the United States with Spain as well; but for our purpose this was less important, because there were already many other grounds for controversy with that power, whereas with most of the Spanish American states the only serious cause of difference lay in the use of the navy to protect the interests of the United States and its citizens.

In the early days of the republic—and, indeed, until the administration of John Adams—the United States had had no navy worthy of the name; but by the period with which we are now concerned it had built up a very respectable establishment, which had given an excellent account of itself in the War of 1812, and the great importance of sea power to the United States was clearly recognized.[1] In a letter written in 1813 and published in Niles's *Register* in 1818, John Adams, who took a paternal pride in the navy, wrote:

[1] But its lessons had not been well learned. This is the point stressed in the account of the post-war decade in Harold and Margaret Sprout, *The Rise of American Naval Power, 1776-1918* (Princeton, 1939), p. 86 ff. On the other hand, Knox, *History of the United States Navy*, p. 139-152, stresses the extension of naval protection to commerce in this period. See the discussion of these points at the close of the present chapter. For the period of the war, see Alfred Thayer Mahan's classic account, *Sea Power in its Relations to the War of 1812* (Boston, 1905).

The foundation of an American navy . . . is a grand era in the history of the world. The consequences of it will be greater than any of us can foresee. Look to Asia and Africa, to South-America and Europe, for its effects. . . . The four quarters of the world are in a ferment. We shall interfere everywhere. Nothing but a navy, under Heaven, can secure, protect or defend us.[2]

And, he might well have added, nothing but a navy, under Heaven, could protect and extend the interests of the United States in Latin America and give effect to the policy of excluding the political and commercial influence of Europe from the New World. The interests of the United States in Latin America, which were mainly political and commercial, were great and growing; but they were threatened by European rivals, by the warfare between colonists and mother country, and by the depredations of adventurers and freebooters who came in droves to fish in these troubled waters. In most of this vast region, the situation recalled the smaller-scale anarchy in the West Indies in the days of Henry Morgan and other seventeenth-century buccaneers, and in the western Mediterranean before the Barbary corsairs were tamed by Commodore Bainbridge. The Gulf of Mexico and the Caribbean and the Atlantic and Pacific coasts of South America and Mexico were under the rule of force, not of law, or at best under a rule which was so often capricious and irresponsible that it could not be dignified by the name of law. Under these circumstances, diplomatic representations were futile even when they could be made at all, and the only effective means by which the United States could protect its interests and the property and lives of its citizens was by the direct

[2] *Register*, XIV, 33-34, March 11, 1818.

interposition of force, that is to say, through its navy. In this respect it only followed the example of France and England, which were the first foreign powers to station warships in Latin American waters and which made the same use of them as did the United States.[3]

The two most important direct services rendered by the United States navy in Latin American waters were, first, in protecting merchant vessels against unlawful seizures and exactions, whether by pirates or by privateers and warships of the belligerents (for example, in the enforcement of " paper " blockades), and second, in facilitating commerce by transporting specie from Latin American ports either to some other Latin American port or to the United States. Furthermore, by transporting despatches and agents (such as the commissioners sent to Buenos Aires and Chile in the autumn of 1817) the navy gave important support to the State Department in the Latin American sector; and the mere presence of United States warships in Latin America waters gave some measure of protection to American citizens on land as well as on the high seas and strengthened the prestige of their country in all quarters, royalist and revolutionary alike.

[3] English naval protection to commerce has been mentioned above in preceding chapters, and other instances are given below in this chapter. French naval protection is discussed in Robertson, *France and Latin-American Independence,* e. g., p. 126-127, describing the Caribbean cruise of Commander Le Bozée under orders from Paris dated Aug. 1, 1817. In this respect both England and France enjoyed an important advantage over the United States through their possession of colonies and seaports in the Caribbean and on the east coast of South America. The advantage to England was noted in the London *Quarterly Review,* XXVI (1822), 527, in an article on " Colonial Policy."

II

For several years after the War of 1812, the protection afforded to American commerce by the navy was sporadic and limited. Complaints on this score had begun with the beginning of the Spanish American struggle for independence and in the course of the next few years they poured in from every quarter. They were directed against both the Spanish authorities and the revolutionists, and they were accompanied by the suggestion that the United States follow the example of Great Britain in providing regular naval protection for its ships and citizens. In 1810 Robert K. Lowry, commercial agent of the United States at La Guaira on the coast of Venezuela, urged the authorities at Washington to send a warship to cruise on that coast for the protection of commerce against privateers and pirates, thus putting the United States on a footing with England, which already had two brigs of war at La Guaira.[4] In 1812 William G. Miller, United States consul at Buenos Aires, wrote that a frigate ought to be stationed in the River Plate to protect not only American shipping in the river but also the American citizens residing in Buenos Aires who had been threatened with extermination in a recent uprising.[5]

As the number of privateers multiplied after the end of the War of 1812, there was a corresponding increase in the number and vehemence of the complaints from American merchants, consuls, and naval officers. In 1817 a group of about thirty New Orleans merchants presented a memorial in which they asserted that freebooters under the flags of

[4] Manning, *Dip. Cor.*, II, 1145.
[5] *Ibid.*, I, 329-330.

Buenos Aires, Venezuela and Mexico were ruining their extensive commerce with Vera Cruz, Campeche, and " other places in the Gulf of Mexico" and requested the naval officer in command at New Orleans to provide convoys for their ships.[6] Commenting on their request, this officer said, " Under the existing orders from the [Navy] Department, I do not feel myself authorised to afford [a convoy], beyond our own limits."

But [he continued] unless convoy should be afforded to vessels pursuing a fair and legal commerce, to the Spanish ports on the Maine, and the Island of Cuba, the intercourse, which is highly lucrative to our citizens, will necessarily be suspended, to the injury of this Port.[7]

Two years later, the captain of the U. S. S. *John Adams,* which had just returned from a mission to Mexico and Cuba, wrote in even stronger terms:

The frequency of murders & piracies among the W[est] India Islands, on American vessels, scarcely one passing without molestation, has been represented to me in the strongest terms, by American Merchants at the different places, where I have touch'd & I was urged to represent the

---

[6] *City of Washington Gazette,* Dec. 24, 1817, memorial dated July 28, 1817. This memorial was one of the documents relating to Amelia Island and Galveston transmitted to the House by the President. One of the New Orleans firms signing the memorial was " Vincente Nolte & Co." For Vincent Nolte, see above, Chap. 1. For an account of some of the hazards to shipping in this region, see A. Curtis Wilgus, " Spanish American Patriot Activity along the Gulf Coast of the United States, 1811-1822," *Louisiana Hist. Qly.,* VIII (1925), 193-215.

[7] Navy Archives, Captains' Letters, vol. 3, Commodore Daniel T. Patterson to Secretary of the Navy B. W. Crowninshield, July 28, 1817.

same to the Department, that if practicable some cruizers might be sent for the protection of the trade in those seas.[8]

The same kind of complaints poured in from the west coast of South America, where Lord Cochrane's Chilean navy and the royalist warships of Peru vied with each other in harrying neutral commerce. In 1818 the merchant ship *Macedonian*,[9] in which John S. Ellery, Israel Thorndike, Samuel Parkman, Jr., Thomas Parsons, Daniel Appleton, and other leading merchants of Boston were interested, sailed from that port on a voyage to Chile, Peru, and Canton. After trading first at Valparaiso, Chile, and then at Callao, Peru, the captain of the *Macedonian* was seized and deprived of most of the proceeds of his sales by Cochrane's Chilean forces, whose action was subsequently justified by the Chilean government largely on the ground that that part of the coast which was in royalist hands was in a state of blockade. The owners of the *Macedonian* protested that this was only a paper blockade and that any seizure under it was a violation of neutral rights which they were confident the United States government would not tolerate.

And [they continued] while the usual branches of commerce afford little or no profit to the merchants, it is peculiarly necessary that a fostering care and protection should be

[8] Navy Department Archives, Masters Commandant, 1819, No. 71, Capt. Alex S. Wadsworth to Secretary of the Navy Smith Thompson, May 2, 1819.

[9] *Am. State Papers, Naval Affairs,* II, 554-556; Pereira Salas, *La actuación de los oficiales navales,* p. 57-59. The master of the *Macedonian*, Eliphalet Smith, appears to have carried on an arms trade with the royalists, and was described by San Martín as having done the greatest injury to the cause of liberty (*ibid.,* p. 63). This merchant ship should not be confused with the U. S. S. *Macedonian,* Capt. John Downes, which was on the west coast about the same time.

extended to the enterprising, who are traversing the globe to discover new channels, through which they may benefit themselves and their country.

Cochrane and his Chileans were only following the example of the royalists, for already, early in 1818, J. B. Prevost had written to Adams from Santiago denouncing the " ships of war of Lima " which were " affecting to hold the entire coast under blockade," attacking only unarmed ships, and committing " outrages in defiance of every principle of the law of nations and even of the modern doctrine of blockade." [10] In his opinion the Spanish authorities at Lima seemed " determined to annihilate our commerce in this ocean." Even the whaling ships which were flocking to the South Pacific from Nantucket and New Bedford and which never approached the mainland of South America except in case of necessity were constantly exposed to indignities and detention and sometimes to confiscation.

Prevost reached the same conclusion as most of the other observers who had a first-hand acquaintance with this problem in any part of Latin America: the United States must take a leaf out of England's book and provide permanent and adequate naval patrols for the protection of its commerce. If this were not done, the United States would soon, he feared, lose the preponderance it had been enjoying for several years past in the trade with Chile. Rodney's observations on the east coast of South America led him to write Monroe to the same effect in September 1818 advising him to station some warships in the principal ports of South America, which, returning home once in a while,

[10] National Archives, SD, Special Agents, vol. 6, Prevost to Adams, Feb. 9, 1818.

" would divert to this country some of the golden streams
that now flow into England: Besides giving respect and
attention to our flag, in these seas and ports." [11]

To illustrate the dangers to which United States commerce was exposed for lack of adequate naval protection,
Prevost cited the cases of the merchant ships *Beaver* of New
York and *Canton* of Salem, which had recently been seized
by the Peruvian royalists. The outcome of these cases soon
provided a striking illustration of the benefits that such
protection could afford. Only the case of the *Beaver* [12] will
be discussed here, as it attracted more attention at the time
and has been more fully reported, and the case of the
Canton was very similar to it.

The *Beaver* was owned by John Jacob Astor. In 1817 he
loaded it with a cargo worth $140,000, consisting mainly
of European manufactures and partly of arms and ammunition, and obtained clearance papers for " Canton and the
Northwest." Its real destination was the coast of Chile and
Peru; its master was Richard J. Cleveland, an experienced
sailor who was already acquainted with that coast, having
visited it with William Shaler in 1802; and its supercargo
was one Francisco Ribas, whose name adequately suggests
his special qualification for such a voyage. It should also be
noted that when Astor insured the cargo with the National
Insurance Company of New York for $80,000 against all
risks, he specifically included the risks arising from partici-

[11] Monroe Papers, NYPL, Rodney to Monroe, Sept. 19, 1818.
[12] The following account is based mainly on Porter, *Astor* II,
648-653. Porter discusses the sources in *op. cit.,* II, 676, note 43.
The principal sources are in National Archives, SD, Claims on
Spain, 1819, Allowed Claims, Vols. 13 and 15A. The latter and
vol. 13 contain a mass of papers relating to the *Canton*.

pation in illegal trade. Arrived on the west coast of South America, the *Beaver* put into the port of Talcahuano, ostensibly to obtain food and water. The port authorities, who were Spanish royalists, promptly seized the ship on the ground, first, of illegal entry, and second, that the presence of arms and ammunition on board proved the intention of trading with the enemy. The ship was condemned and $100,000 worth of its cargo removed.

Captain Cleveland and Supercargo Ribas promptly launched a host of appeals—to the viceroy at Lima, to the American consul at Buenos Aires, to J. B. Prevost, special agent at Santiago, and to Secretary Adams, who promptly instructed George W. Erving, American minister at Madrid, to take the matter up with the Spanish government. If any of these appeals had ever obtained redress, which seems doubtful, it would have been long delayed. Fortunately, the U. S. S. *Ontario*, Captain James Biddle, which had sailed from New York the preceding September to bring Prevost to Chile and assert the United States' claim to the mouth of the Columbia River, was at Valparaiso at this time. An appeal was made to Captain Biddle, too, and he obliged by sailing in June 1818 from Valparaiso to Callao, where, from the quarterdeck of the *Ontario* he conducted a negotiation which ended in November in the viceroy's reversing the decree of condemnation of the *Beaver*, ordering the ship to be restored to its owner with the remainder of its cargo, and authorizing him to sue for the value of that part of the cargo which could not be recovered.[13]

This was quite properly regarded as a signal achievement

[13] Porter, *Astor* II, 651. Pereira Salas, *La actuación de los oficiales navales,* p. 22-40, gives an account of Biddle's cruise that is based in part on fresh manuscript sources.

and together with similar services that Captain Biddle
rendered to other merchant vessels, such as the *Lion* of
Providence, the *Canton* and *Indus* of Salem, the *Levant* of
Boston, and the *America* of Philadelphia, it won him public
letters of thanks from John Jacob Astor, a group of merchants of Boston, and a group of masters, supercargoes, and
agents at Valparaiso.[14] In July 1818, long before all the
returns were in, Niles's *Register* reported that Biddle had
saved a million dollars worth of property in this way, besides checking the desertion of seamen and protecting
American citizens from arrest and maltreatment at the
hands of the authorities of Chile and Peru.[15] Nor was this
all, for, as we shall see, Biddle also rendered Astor and
other merchants a highly valuable service by using the
Ontario to safeguard and transport specie belonging to
them.

III

Biddle's achievements, which were already a matter of
common knowledge in the United States by the summer
of 1818, indicated the proper means for coping with the
depredations from which American commerce was suffering
in the West Indies, the Gulf of Mexico, and the Caribbean,
and on both coasts of South America. These were, first, to
clarify and increase the authority of the navy in protecting

[14] Niles's *Register,* XIV, 358, July 18, 1818; *Aurora,* June 4,
1819, "From the Philadelphia Gazette." On the other hand,
Biddle's conduct on this cruise aroused sharp resentment among
Spanish American sympathizers in the United States and seems to
have given a strong impulse to the demand for a more careful
regulation of naval activity. See Clay's speech of May 10, 1820,
in *Annals Cong.,* 16 Cong., 1 Sess., p. 2223-2224.

[15] *Register, loc. cit., supra.*

commerce, and second, to broaden the scope of naval operations. An important measure towards the first of these two ends was the act of Congress of March 3, 1819, for protecting commerce and punishing piracy.[16] Though intended partly to deal with the problem, which we have discussed in an earlier chapter, of privateering from the ports of the United States itself, its other and more important purpose was to enable the navy to give more effective protection to American ships in distant waters against commerce raiders of all kinds. Among other provisions, it gave the naval vessels of the United States the power, which they had not previously possessed, to convoy merchant vessels of the United States on the high seas; and it even went so far as to give them the broad power to retake any vessel of the United States or its citizens " which may have been unlawfully captured upon the high seas."

This act provided the legal basis [17] for a great extension of the operations of the navy in Latin American waters in the course of the next few years; and aside from its legal significance, it is important because it expressed the growing determination to make a more dynamic use of sea power in promoting the interests of the United States among its

[16] *Annals Cong.*, 15 Cong., 2 Sess., vol. 2, p. 1418, Feb. 26, 1819, passage of the bill on its third reading. The bill originated in the Senate and aroused little discussion in either house. The text is in *ibid.*, p. 2523-2524, " An Act to protect the commerce of the United States, and punish the crime of piracy," approved March 3, 1819.

[17] Thus, in 1823, in reviewing the use of the navy to protect commerce in the West Indies and the Caribbean, Adams said that the President's authority was the Act of Congress of March 3, 1819 (Manning, *Dip. Cor.*, I, 167, in Adams's instructions to Hugh Nelson, Minister to Spain, April 28, 1823).

southern neighbors. It should be emphasized that the primary concern of the United States in this matter was the promotion of its own interests, not the promotion of Latin American independence or inter-American solidarity or any other larger or altruistic or extra-national purpose.

In short, this extension and intensification of naval action was carried out in the spirit of the existing policy of neutrality. Insofar as its obligations as a neutral were concerned, the United States was benevolent towards the revolutionists; but as for its rights as a neutral, it interpreted these as broadly and enforced them almost as rigorously against the revolutionists as against Spain,[18] asserting them to the fullest extent even when they obviously operated to the disadvantage of the independence cause. Thus in 1820 Secretary Adams refused to make the slightest concession to Chile in the matter of paper blockades,[19] although such a concession would have been of material assistance to the Chilean navy in its crucial struggle with the royalist forces of Peru. He still refused to budge even when the experience of the next few years fully revealed the great value that such a concession would have for Chile; he sanctioned the use of the American navy to break the Chilean paper blockade, and in 1823 he defended his course by saying that "This principle is too important to be surrendered to any belligerent

[18] The Navy Department's orders to Captain Stewart quoted below in this chapter directed him to make a sharp distinction in practice in favor of the revolutionists, but it does not appear that either he or the other naval officers did so and, as stated below in the text, Adams refused to make any distinction at all. This apparent divergence between the State Department and the Navy Department constitutes a problem that deserves further study.

[19] Am. State Papers, Naval Affairs, II, 557, Adams to John M. Forbes, July 6, 1820, extract.

party, however favorably disposed we may be to his cause; for we cannot concede it to him without yielding it alike to his enemy." [20]

Adams had no intention whatever of yielding this or any other principle to either side, although the course of their conflict served as a vivid reminder that the defence of neutral rights may easily involve a neutral nation in war. Adams's clear realization of this fact was expressed in his comments on this same question of paper blockades as it had been raised by the proclamation of a blockade of 1200 miles of the coast of Venezuela by the Spanish General Morales who had only one frigate, one brig, and one schooner with which to enforce the blockade:

They [paper blockades] were in violation of the laws of nations [wrote Adams]. They were in conflict with the law of Congress [i. e., the act of March 3, 1819] for protecting the commerce of the United States. It was impossible that ships of war of the United States with commanders instructed to carry that law into execution, and Spanish privateers commissioned and instructed to carry into effect the atrocious decree of General Morales, should meet and fulfil their respective instructions without hostile collision. The decree of General Morales constituted all those Spanish subjects who acted under it in a state of war *de facto* with all neutral nations; and on the sea it was a war of extermination against all neutral commerce.[21]

Morales' decree was revoked in time to prevent the conflict between the United States and Spain which Adams

[20] *Ibid.*, Adams to J. B. Prevost, Dec. 16, 1823. In this letter Adams defended the action of Capt. Charles Stewart in protecting the American merchant ship *Canton* against a warship of the Chilean navy which tried to seize it for violation of the paper blockade of Peru. For further information about Stewart, see below in this chapter.

[21] Manning, *Dip. Cor.*, I, 183. See also *ibid.*, p. 166.

had feared would result from it; but there still remained many other problems of the same sort, which occupied the attention of the authorities at Washington for several years to come. In an effort to solve these the government first employed diplomacy in the hope of avoiding armed conflict; [22] it also employed the navy to protect its interests pending a diplomatic settlement and the restoration of peace; and it sometimes combined the two by sending naval officers on quasi-diplomatic missions.[23] It is only with the naval aspects of this effort that we are concerned here. For our purpose, three examples will suffice to illustrate the effort. These are the missions of Commodore Oliver Perry to Venezuela and Captain James Biddle to the West Indies, and the establishment of the Pacific Station on the West Coast of South America.

In May 1819, a few weeks after the passage of the act for the protection of commerce and the suppression of piracy, the State and Navy Departments collaborated in sending Commodore Oliver Perry on a mission which was intended to take him first to Venezuela and then to Buenos Aires. In both places he was directed to discuss, in his capacity as a naval officer, certain political questions with the heads of

[22] The South American mission of Rodney, Graham, and Bland in 1817-1818 may be placed in this category, since one of its purposes was to induce both sides to accord better treatment to American commerce. See above, chap. 8.

[23] A very useful pioneer work in this field is Charles O. Paullin's *Diplomatic Negotiations of American Naval Officers, 1778-1883* (Baltimore, 1912), but it contains only a brief account of these negotiations in Latin America in the period of the present study. A great deal would be added to it by further study of the relevant sources in *American State Papers, Naval Affairs*, in the archives of the Navy Department, and elsewhere.

the revolutionary governments. He carried out the first part of his mission, but not the second, as he died while in Venezuela.[24]

The first part of his mission was the more immediately important and there were several reasons why it was urgent for the United States government to come to an understanding with Bolívar's Venezuelan government. The recent rapid progress of Bolívar's arms had given his government a leading rôle among the new Spanish American states whose friendship the United States wished to cultivate, but in this case the establishment of friendly relations was threatened in various ways. The freebooters under Gregor McGregor who had recently seized Amelia Island [25] and had been expelled from it by the United States claimed to be acting under the authority of Venezuela; and although the action of the United States in this matter had been explained to Bolívar and he had disavowed the freebooters, his sympathisers in the United States were still so indignant over the affair that there was reason to fear that he himself was not entirely satisfied with the explanation he had received. Moreover, Adams and Monroe had made Bolívar's disavowal of McGregor one of the grounds for its refusal to hold any official communication with the representative of Venezuela in this country, Lino de Clemente, who had authorized McGregor's seizure of Amelia Island; and this refusal had not yet been explained to Bolívar.[26]

[24] Besides the sources noted below, this account of Perry's mission is based on the article on Perry in DAB, and on Wriston, *Executive Agents*, p. 421-422, 426. The latter erroneously dates the mission in 1820 (instead of 1819).

[25] See above, chap. 8.

[26] Navy Department Archives, Private Letters, 1813-1840, p. 266-281, Adams to Secretary of the Navy Thompson, May 20,

Most important of all, privateers commissioned by the Venezuelan government were prominent among those scourges of American commerce that the authorities at Washington were now determined to suppress. Even in cases in which Bolívar admitted that his privateers were at fault, he refused to make restitution, and Baptis Irvine, the first agent sent to take up the matter with him, had recently returned to this country in disgust after an acrimonious and futile correspondence with him on the subject.[27] Perry's instructions covered these points and also directed him to " report all interesting information respecting the condition of the countries [Buenos Aires as well as Venezuela], their internal situation and prospects, and to assure the governments and people of the friendship of the United States." [28]

Though Perry was sent in the warship *John Adams* and his instructions were drawn with care by Adams himself, the results of his mission to Venezuela were disappointing. He obtained no real satisfaction on the main question, privateering, and the chief impression that emerged from his observations was that, partly as a result of hostile propaganda from British sources, the people of Venezuela regarded the United States as indifferent to the struggle of

---

1819. Extracts from this letter have been published in Manning, *Dip. Cor.,* I, 101-107.

[27] *Ibid.* Adams, who had a low opinion of Irvine, said that he had been appointed to Venezuela on the recommendation of Samuel Smith, DeWitt Clinton, and " many other habitual recommenders," and that he had returned to the United States " assuredly without having done any good " (*Memoirs,* V, 57). Some of Bolivar's letters to Irvine are about to be published, with an introduction by Lewis Hanke, in the *Hispanic Am. Hist. Rev.,* May 1941. For Irvine's report on his mission, see above, chap. 5, note 38.

[28] Wriston, *op. cit.,* p. 421-422.

Venezuela for liberty, and even to its commerce, and as far behind England in contributing to the success of the Venezuelan cause. The best that Perry could say in defense of his country was that when greater security had been established " the merchants of the U. S. would not fail to embrace so lucrative a traffic [as that with Venezuela], when at the same time that their prospects of pecuniary benefits were realized, the best feelings of the human heart would be interested in furnishing supplies to a people oppressed and struggling for existence." [29]

A few months after Perry's death in Venezuela, Senator Dana of Connecticut proposed to derive some benefit from the affair by publishing Adams's letter of instructions to Perry, which, he told Adams, was " the best thing [he] had ever written." With a view to increasing its effect, Dana suggested that some of the opposition in Congress should be stimulated to call for the document, so that it might be made public with an air of reluctance; but Adams, who felt that this suggestion had in it too much of Dana's familiar " winding-stair quality, cunning," refused to adopt it.[30]

Captain James Biddle's mission to the West Indies was of

[29] Manning, *Dip. Cor.*, II, 1178-1182, Charles O. Handy (purser of the *John Adams*) to Adams, Sept. 29, 1819, a report on the mission based on Perry's original notes.

[30] Adams, *Memoirs*, IV, 515. Perry's mission was keenly resented by Bolívar's more ardent supporters in the United States. For example, the *Aurora* spoke of it as " in its inception and character, one of the most curious affairs that governmental infatuation and wantonness ever adventured," and said (alluding to James Stephen's famous book) that Perry had been sent to demand the restitution of the American ships " under the English construction of *war in disguise* " (*Aurora*, Aug. 10, item commenting on a letter from the West Indies; *ibid.*, Aug. 11, comment on item " From the Philadelphia Gazette ").

a different character and wider scope, for, although he too was assigned quasi-diplomatic duties, the main purpose of his mission was to protect American commerce, his field of activities extended throughout the West Indies and the Caribbean, and he was given command of a squadron of eight ships, including his flagship, the *Macedonian*. His mission was more important, too, because it marked the establishment of a permanent West India squadron.[31]

His instructions,[32] drawn up by the secretary of the navy, Smith Thompson, and dated March 26, 1822, ordered him to use the ships placed under his command for the protection of commerce and the suppression of piracy in the West Indies and the Gulf of Mexico. Among the places specifically mentioned as lying within the zone that he was to patrol were Cuba and Haiti in the West Indies and La Guaira, Cartagena, Vera Cruz, and Chagres on the mainland, and he was instructed to afford convoys for the protection of commerce and citizens of the United States to and from all ports whenever required. By this time the United States was demanding the privilege of pursuing pirates and privateers in the West Indies not only into territorial waters but also on land—as General Andrew Jackson had recently pursued hostile Indians and bandits across the international

[31] Sprout, *Rise of American Naval Power*, p. 94. For the establishment of other permanent squadrons or "stations," see below in the text.

[32] Navy Department Archives, Private Letters, 1813-1840, Secretary Thompson to Biddle, March 26, 1822. In 1823 the West India squadron was reinforced by 8 schooners, 5 barges, and the steam galliot *Sea Gull*, which was the first steamer of any navy to engage in warfare (Knox, *History of the United States Navy*, p. 140). See also references in note 34.

border in his famous invasion of Spanish Florida.[33] Accordingly, Biddle was given the quasi-diplomatic duty of negotiating with the Spanish captain general of Cuba, which was, of course, still a Spanish colony, and with President Boyer of Haiti, whose independence had not been recognized by the United States, with a view to obtaining from them the rare privilege of landing armed forces in their territory for this purpose.

Biddle discharged his manifold duties in this vast region with great zeal but only limited success. He was soon transferred to another post and Commodore David Porter, the former propagandist for Spanish American independence, who took his place in the West Indies, found the region infested with a swarm of pirates and privateers. Throwing himself into his task with characteristic impetuosity, he seized the privilege, which Biddle had been unable to persuade the Spanish colonial authorities to grant, of landing parties in pursuit of pirates. For this and other reasons his West Indies campaign caused an international crisis, raised a great hue-and-cry in the United States, and led to an official inquiry into his conduct which in turn involved him in a duel and brought about his resignation from the navy and his subsequent entry into the naval service of Mexico.[34]

[33] The parallel with Jackson's case was drawn by David Porter (Knox, *op. cit.*, p. 140), who succeeded Biddle on the West India station (*v. inf.*).

[34] For Porter, see the article on Porter in DAB, and Archibald D. Turnbull, *Commodore David Porter, 1780-1843* (New York, 1929). For both Biddle and Porter, see Gardner W. Allen, *Our Navy and the West Indian Pirates* (Salem, Mass., 1929), p. 24-81. Several letters from Porter to Joel Poinsett describing his service

IV

One of the most important extensions of naval activity occurred on the west coast of South America, culminating in the establishment of the Pacific Station. As we have seen, the United States had shared in the commerce of this region since the closing years of the eighteenth century. By 1818 its share had grown to exceed that of any other foreign nation and was important not only for itself, but also because it facilitated trade between the United States and Asia; but it was threatened with ruin by the conflict between Chilean patriots and Peruvian royalists for supremacy at sea. The conflict was growing in intensity at this time and the Chilean navy, which was gradually gaining the upper hand, was under the command of Lord Cochrane, who, though he had been cashiered from the British navy, was apparently using his control of the Chilean navy to build up the commerce of Great Britain at the expense of the United States and its other competitors in this region. The situation was developing in such a way as to threaten not only important commercial interests of the United States but also principles of international law in defense of which it had recently fought a three-year war with the world's greatest sea power. Chief among these principles was the doctrine of effective blockade, which was now challegend by the paper blockade proclaimed by both Chile and royalist Peru.

Although American interests in this region had seldom been without some measure of naval protection since the

---

in the Mexican navy are in the Gilpin Papers, HSP, Poinsett Correspondence. For a brief discussion of the episode, see below, chap. 19.

arrival of Captain James Biddle in the *Ontario* in 1817,[35] it was the opinion of all observers that this protection ought to be increased and made more systematic. Steps toward this end were taken as the result of an episode which occurred in 1820 and which provides interesting evidence that President Monroe was more keenly alive to the interests of his country in this region than was his secretary of state, John Quincy Adams, within whose immediate jurisdiction they lay.

The episode in question had its origin in a letter that Adams received from General Parker of New York. According to Parker, Isaac Byers, a New York merchant, had told him that new land had been discovered in the Pacific Ocean at 61° 40′ south latitude, that some twenty whaling and sealing vessels were setting out from that port for this new "land or continent," and that they would need naval protection. In commenting on this discovery, Adams described it as very important; but for him its importance seemed to be that of a probable cause of fresh diplomatic controversy with Great Britain. English adventurers might be expected to flock to the new land too, and in that case, he advised Monroe, who was at his home in Virginia at the time,

Nootka Sound and Falkland Island questions may be expected. . . . The British government just now have their

[35] Biddle sailed from Valparaíso for the United States on the same day that Cochrane's Chilean squadron put to sea (Dec. 30, 1818). A few days later the U. S. S. *Macedonian* arrived at Valparaíso, having been sent under rush orders in response to the advice of Biddle and Prevost (Knox, *op. cit.*, p. 143). For the resentment caused in Chile by Biddle's conduct and for the Chilean government's protest to the United States, see Pereira Salas, *La actuación de los oficiales navales*, p. 36-40.

hands so full of coronations and adulteries . . . high treasons and petty treasons, pains, penalties, and paupers, that
they will seize the first opportunity they can to shake them
all off; and if they can make a question of national honor
about a foothold in latitude 61° 40′ upon something
between rock and iceberg, as this discovery must be, and
especially a question with us, they will not let it escape them.

The prospect of such a " question " did not by any means
disturb Adams, who loved a war of words, especially when
the British government was his antagonist. " The idea," he
continued, " of having a grave controversy with Lord Castlereagh about an island latitude 61° 40′ south is quite fascinating." As for the protection of American interests in
the new land, he contented himself with asking General
Parker to advise Mr. Byers to see the secretary of the navy
about sending a frigate to take possession.[36]

Monroe, who was at his home in Virginia at the time,
looked at the matter very differently. As soon as he received Adams's report about it, he replied, " Communicate
the documents to the Secretary of the Navy and suggest the
motive, asking how far it would be practicable to send a
frigate there, and thence to strengthen our force along the

[36] Adams, *Writings*, VII, 66-68, Adams to Monroe, Aug. 26,
1820. It should be noted, however, that Adams did describe the
subject as one of "very considerable importance" in this letter.
The new land was Graham Land. In reporting its discovery, J. B.
Prevost said it was wonderful how Cook and other early explorers
had avoided it. Prevost, who was a southerner, was inclined to
think that the United States might as well let England have it,
"for it appears that during the last month corresponding with our
June, the whole was covered with ice and snow." But he added,
on second thought, "it offers a new field to the adventure of our
countrymen in the number of seals and whales that abound on its
coast. National Archives, SD, Special Agents, vol. 6, Prevost to
Adams, Jan. 10, 1820, duplicate.

[South] American coast. I shall write him on the same subject." [37] The difference between the responses of the president and his secretary of state to the news from the South Pacific is striking. Where Adams, who was in Washington, with the Navy Department just around the corner, merely sent a message at second hand to a private individual in New York to take up the matter with the secretary of the navy, Monroe, who was in Virginia, promptly instructed Adams to communicate directly with the secretary of the navy and followed this up with a letter of his own to the latter. What is more important, he made the request for naval protection in the new land in the South Pacific the occasion for strengthening the existing naval force on the west coast of South America.

It was probably this letter of Monroe's, together with pressure from merchants and shipowners in the United States, that led to the establishment in 1821 of the Pacific Station,[38] that is a permanent naval force based on ports in Chile and Peru from which they regularly patrolled the coast of South America and often extended their activities northward to Mexico and California and westward to Hawaii and the islands of the South Pacific. Maintained throughout the rest of the century, the Pacific station not only rendered services of inestimable value to navigation and commerce in the whole of this vast zone but also paved the way for the extension of the dominion of the United States across the Pacific to Hawaii and beyond. If Adams found fascination in the idea of a grave controversy

[37] Adams, *Writings,* VI, 67, note 1, Monroe to Adams, Sept. 1, 1820.

[38] Paullin, *Diplomatic Negotiations of American Naval Officers,* p. 332.

with Lord Castlereagh over a frozen island in latitude 61° 40′ south, we today may find food for thought in the fact that the person who made that island the point of departure for a dynamic navalism which promoted American commerce and dominion in the Pacific was not Adams himself, product of maritime New England and son of the founder of the navy, but the Virginia farmer, James Monroe.

Two other naval stations of a similar character were established within the next few years.[39] The mission assigned in 1822 to Captain Biddle and his formidable squadron marked the establishment of the West India Station, which embraced the Caribbean as well as the West Indies. In 1826 the Navy Department created a permanent Brazilian or South Atlantic Squadron, which patrolled the east coast of South America. These three stations, together with the naval vessels operating in the Gulf of Mexico from the New Orleans base, protected American commerce throughout the Latin American zone. The fact that only one other foreign station (the one in the Mediterranean) had been established by this time is an indication of the importance attached to American commerce with Latin America as well as of the dangers to which it was exposed.

---

[39] Sprout, *op. cit.*, p. 94-95. The need for American warships on the Brazilian coast was stressed by Raguet, consul at Rio de Janeiro, in a letter to Adams of Oct. 1, 1822, in which he said there were six French " national ships " in that port and that British vessels were always kept " in this quarter," to protect the persons and property of French and British subjects (Manning, *Dip. Cor.*, II, 149).

V

Whether on the Pacific Station or elsewhere, one of the most important services rendered by United States warships in Latin American waters was in receiving and transporting specie. In doing so, they made themselves useful in a variety of ways. In the first place, they acted in effect as banks of deposit. For example, ships stationed on the coast of Chile and Peru frequently provided the only place of safekeeping for the funds of merchants in those countries, where the incessant turmoil was a constant menace to property of all kinds, and especially to specie, which, once lost, was exceptionally difficult to identify and recover by legal process even if the owner should be so fortunate as to find it again.[40]

In the second place, such deposits were made the basis of a kind of paper currency which made it easier to continue ordinary business transactions in Latin America in spite of the general confusion and insecurity of property. Thus, the U. S. S. *Franklin*, commanded by Captain Charles Stewart, who was the first commander of the Pacific Station (1821-1824), made it a practice to give receipts or bills of lading for the money or bullion deposited on board, and these bills passed " as so much cash " throughout the whole region,[41] since they provided the easiest as well as the safest means of transferring funds.

In the third place, the warships gave a direct stimulus to commerce by transporting specie from one place to another in Latin America and from Latin America to the

[40] *Am. State Papers, Naval Affairs*, II, 498, 506, 507, 512.
[41] *Ibid.*, II, 548.

United States.[42]. Among other things, this enabled merchants in Latin America to make safe remittances to the United States in payment for goods received from it, and provided cash for circulation in the United States and for re-exportation to Asia.

For a variety of reasons, which will appear below, the activities of these United States warships provoked a great deal of criticism at home and ill feeling in Latin America. Yet the service they rendered was so valuable that in the long run they were not only not curbed but were on the whole given even greater freedom of action. How this came about is so important for our story that it must be related in some detail.

In transporting specie on private account, the United States Navy was again following British practice. This was brought out very clearly by the inquiry into Captain James Biddle's conduct on the cruise to the Pacific of which we have already spoken in another connection. When he returned from that cruise late in 1818, Biddle's ship, the *Ontario*, brought $41,000 in money from Lima to New York and $160,000 from Lima to Rio de Janeiro. This money was consigned to John Jacob Astor and Archibald Gracie of New York and to various merchants in Boston and Rio.[43] Since Lima was then in royalist hands, Biddle's

[42] For example, during its cruise on the coast of Chile and Peru in 1822, the *Constellation* kept on deposit for Eliphalet Smith, subject to his order, some $320,000 in " money." When relieved by the *Franklin* in 1822, the *Constellation* transferred about $120,000 to that ship and brought the remaining $200,000 to the United States (*ibid.*, II, 505, 506). On this cruise of the *Constellation*, see Pereira Salas, *La actuación de los oficiales navales*, p. 51-61.

[43] *Am. State Papers, Naval Affairs*, I, 871-762, Biddle to the Secretary of the Navy, April 2, 1820.

action was thought to have given important aid to the royalists in their struggle with the South American patriots. Partly for this reason, he was sharply criticized in independent Chile and in certain quarters in the United States. Defending his action, he said:

The law of the United States permits specie to be received on board. The English men of war, with whom the law is the same as with us, do it constantly. Our own ships have done it constantly. Commodore Shaw, who is now in Washington, informs me, what indeed I previously knew, that the Saranac, the Boxer, and our other vessels in the Gulf of Mexico, have always brought specie from Vera Cruz and other ports.[44]

There was much truth in what Biddle said; but the practice of transporting specie on private account in naval vessels had not always been so clearly and uniformly sanctioned as he claimed. Indeed, the Act of Congress of April 1800, which he cited and which he described as " borrowed from the British," sanctioned the practice only by implication, since it prohibited naval officers from receiving on board any goods or merchandise except gold, silver, or jewels. Biddle's interpretation of this act as authorizing what it did not prohibit may seem reasonable, but it was not the interpretation adopted by the Navy Department in the first years following the restoration of peace. In November 1815 Commodore Daniel T. Patterson, commanding naval officer at New Orleans, wrote to the

---

[44] *Ibid.*, I, 668, Biddle to the President of the United States, Aug. 16, 1819. One of Biddle's critics was J. B. Prevost, who said that Biddle's conduct on his last visit to Valparaíso (ending in December 1818) had turned Chilean opinion against the United States (National Archives, SD, Special Agents, vol. 6, Prevost to Adams, March 20, 1819).

secretary of the navy, Benjamin W. Crowninshield, and suggested that naval vessels be permitted to "convoy" specie from Spanish and patriot ports in the Gulf of Mexico to the United States. In January 1816 Secretary Crowninshield vetoed the suggestion.[45] In October of that year the instructions to Captain Charles Morris of the frigate *Congress*, which was to cruise in the Gulf of Mexico, ordered him not to allow any public vessel of the United States to transport "any private mercantile property, of which description specie and bullion are considered. . . ." A few months later Captain Morris asked the secretary to authorize the transportation of specie and bullion in naval vessels "agreeably to the provisions of the law for the government of the navy."

The British cruisers at present are deriving all the advantages of a similar arrangement [wrote Morris], and they are, by no means, inconsiderable. It is openly and publicly done by them, and not considered as impairing, in any degree, their neutral or their national character.[46]

Again (February 1817) Crowninshield rejected the recommendation, on the ground that "such employment of our national ships" might tend to "produce a collision of interests"—that is, presumably, collisions with the belligerents in Spanish America. "The course pursued by the British," he concluded, "cannot be considered a precedent for the United States." [47]

Despite Crowninshield, the course pursued by the British was considered a precedent for the United States; and the authorization which was so resolutely withheld by this son of mercantile Salem was soon given by another Southern

[45] *Am. State Papers, Naval Affairs*, I, 673.
[46] *Ibid.*, I, 674.   [47] *Ibid.*

planter, John Calhoun of South Carolina. In October 1818, Calhoun, as acting secretary of the navy, instructed Commodore Patterson at New Orleans that United States warships would henceforth be permitted to touch at Kingston and Port Royal, Jamaica, and Nassau, New Providence, and, with the permission of the local authorities, to take on board specie belonging to merchants of the United States in virtue of previous transactions.[48]

This was a small breach; but it was soon widened. In January of the following year the commander of the *John Adams* was instructed to aid a certain private citizen in bringing a " large amount of specie " to the United States from Vera Cruz as well as Jamaica.[49] Another step forward was taken shortly after the passage of the act of March 3, 1819, for the protection of commerce, under which cruising vessels were instructed towards the termination of their cruises " to touch at such ports as may be designated by the banks or commercial houses of the principal cities as points where it is probable that specie may be deposited on their account, and to receive on board and bring to the U. S. whatever amount may be delivered to them." [50] In August

[48] *Ibid.* The relaxation of policy at this time may have been influenced by a letter to Monroe from Caesar A. Rodney in which he advised the stationing of warships in the principal harbors of South America which " would divert to this country some of the golden streams that now flow into England" (Monroe Papers, NYPL, Rodney to Monroe, Sept. 19, 1818). A few weeks later, Poinsett developed the point in his report on South America to Adams. See below in text.

[49] Navy Department Archives, Private Letters, 1813-1840, Secretary Thompson to Master Commandant Alexander S. Wadsworth, Jan. 9, 1819.

[50] Samuel Smith Papers, LC, William H. Crawford to Samuel Smith, April 3, 1819.

of the same year (1819) the bars were let down when Captain John Downes, of the *Macedonian*, which was about to begin a cruise in the Pacific, was given a general authorization to take on board " specie, which you have permission to bring to the United States." [51] Two years later substantially the same order was given to Captain Stewart of the *Franklin* when he was sent to establish the Pacific Station.[52] Both Downes and Stewart interpreted the order as authorizing them to receive and transport specie not merely at the termination of their cruises but at any time during their course; and it was Stewart (or his officers) who made it a general practice to issue against these specie deposits bills of lading which circulated as money along the Pacific coast of South America.

VI

By this time the practice of receiving and transporting specie on board naval vessels of the United States had, as Captain Biddle asserted, become a general, regular and recognized practice. The change had come about mainly in the period 1818-1821 and appears to have been due to four factors:

(1) The rapid increase of privateering and other perils to the commerce of the United States with Latin America.[53] As we have already seen,[54] this situation produced the act of Congress of March 3, 1819, for the protection of com-

[51] *Am. State Papers, Naval Affairs*, I, 674.

[52] *Ibid.*, II, 539.

[53] Between 1815 and 1823 nearly 3000 cases of piratical aggression against merchant ships were reported (Knox, *op. cit.*, p. 139).

[54] Above, in this chapter.

merce; and it was in conformity with the general policy of affording more effective protection to commerce that the government extended the use of naval vessels for the transportation of specie, which was the life blood of commerce.

(2) Hard times, as dramatized by the panic of 1819. In 1818 and 1819 many people in the United States believed that the economic depression, which was becoming acute, was due in large measure to the shortage of gold and silver coin; Latin America was the principal source of supply of these metals, and naval vessels offered much the safest means of bringing them to this country. Advice to this effect poured in upon the government from many sources, both friendly and hostile to the administration. One of these was no less a person than Langdon Cheves, president of the Bank of the United States. In March 1819 he wrote Secretary of the Treasury Crawford about the critical situation in which the Bank found itself for lack of specie. After remarking that the transportation of specie in naval vessels offered great advantages, especially when it was to be brought from Havana and the Spanish continental colonies, he continued, " In looking to the restoration of the active powers of the Bank some pretty large operations of this kind in some way must be contemplated." [55] Crawford replied that in his opinion specie ought to be imported by private individuals rather than by the Bank of the United States, but that in either case the cooperation of the navy could be counted on.[56] A few months later, the anti-ad-

[55] Monroe Papers, NYPL, Cheves to Crawford, March 20, 1819, " Private & confidential."

[56] *Ibid.*, Crawford to the President of the Bank of the United States, March 27, 1819. At the end of this year Cheves wrote Poinsett politely rejecting a plan that the latter had proposed for

ministration *Aurora* spurred the government to action by abusing it roundly for neglecting an opportunity to procure many million dollars' worth of gold and silver from Mexico and South America, " which would have averted the *present distresses* of the nation." [57]

(3) Rivalry with Great Britain. This had existed from the beginning of the independence movement in Spanish America, but for a variety of reasons—such as the revelations of the Perry mission to Venezuela—it became keener in the period now under consideration. That British warships in Latin American waters transported specie and thereby gave the commerce of their country a distinct advantage over its competitors had long been known at Washington, which now received some forcible reminders of the fact. For example, in November 1818 Joel Poinsett, one of the government's most trusted advisers on Latin American affairs, called Secretary Adams's attention to the fact that since 1810 the British frigates maintained on the Buenos Aires station, which were relieved every six months, had carried home nearly $10,000,000 in specie, part of which was for the government and part on private account.[58]

(4) The private interests of naval officers. This was frankly avowed by Captain Charles Morris of the *Congress*, who, in his letter of January 1817 to Secretary of the Navy Crowninshield requesting that naval vessels be permitted to transport specie from Spanish American ports, said that

---

supplying the Bank of the United States with specie, presumably from Latin America, since a naval officer, Captain Charles Morris, was concerned in the plan. Poinsett Papers, HSP, vol. 2, Langdon Cheves to Poinsett, Dec. 20, 1819. See also Adams, *Memoirs,* IV, 345-349.

[57] *Aurora,* Sept. 20, 1819.   [58] Manning, *Dip. Corr.,* I, 455

this privilege "might be of considerable pecuniary advantage to the officers." [59] The advantage to them was sometimes quite considerable. Captain Biddle stated that he charged $2\frac{1}{2}\%$ freight on the $201,000 that he brought away from Lima, in 1818; [60] whether he kept all or any part of this fee does not appear from his statement. The officer who received deposits on board Captain Stewart's ship, the *Franklin*, along the west coast of South America in 1821-1824 testified that, besides the $2\frac{1}{2}\%$ charge for freight, he collected a handling commission of 1% which he kept for himself.[61] With this incentive, it is not surprising that all the naval officers, without any known exception, favored the transportation of specie on naval vessels; and since the prestige of the navy was great through this period, their opinion was no doubt an important factor in establishing and extending the practice.

It was not maintained without a fight. Reports from more or less responsible sources in Latin America and revelations at trials in the United States created rather widespread dissatisfaction with the navy. This had been brewing for a long time. Clay had expressed it in 1820 in a speech that showed clearly one of the chief grounds for it, namely, the belief that the navy's protection of American commerce in Latin American waters was aiding the royalists to the detriment of the patriot cause. Criticism was centered on the transportation of specie on private account and in the session of 1823-1824 a determined effort was made in Congress to prohibit the practice.[62]

[59] *Am. State Papers, Naval Affairs*, I, 674.

[60] *Ibid.*, I, 671.   [61] *Ibid.*, II, 495-496, 498.

[62] *Annals Cong.*, 18 Cong., 1 Sess., p. 48, 320-321, 337. For contemporary newspaper discussion, see *National Gazette*, March

The friends of the navy, however, had gained strength in the recent election and in the end they won a sweeping victory. The new Navy Act passed at this session imposed some minor restrictions on the practice,[63] but their signifinance lies not in their restrictive character but, on the contrary, in the fact that they put the practice on a firmer basis than ever before by giving it the first positive legislative sanction it had ever received. The reports filed in accordance with the act show that naval officers in Latin American waters continued at least for a few years to make a tidy income from deposits of money on board their ships.[64]

29, 1824, " Interesting Case in Chancery," clipped from the *Albany Argus* of March 23; *Richmond Enquirer,* April 2, 1824, " The Navy." On Sept. 1, 1823, Richard Alsop wrote Henry Clay from Lima, Peru, complaining that the conduct of the United States naval officers on that coast was turning the patriots against the United States. He enclosed an account of the cruise of the *Franklin* written by Platt H. Crosby (translator of Pazos' *Letters to Henry Clay*) which he described as " a history of truth abjured, good faith violated, and justice trampled to earth." (This manuscript is now in LC, Manuscript Division.) He also said that Prevost had repeatedly informed the State Department of these abuses in the past four years, but that no attention had been paid to him (Jeremy Robinson Papers, LC, Box 1821-1832, copy of Alsop's letter " made from the original by J[eremy] R[obinson] "). For Clay's speech of May 1820, see above, note 14.

[63] These required naval officers to report periodically to the Navy Department the deposits of specie received and prohibited them from receiving on board specie or other property belonging to foreigners. Navy Department Archives, Letters to Officers, Ships of War, Secretary Southard to Captain Charles G. Ridgeley, Commander of the West Indies Squadron, Nov. 25, 1826. For other discussion and legislation relating to the navy at this session, see below, chap. 17.

[64] For example, reports sent by Captain Isaac Hull from Callao, Peru, showed that from July 11, 1825, to Jan 18, 1826, his ship, the *United States,* received on board some $255,000 in coin and

The conditions of insecurity in Latin America which had given rise to the practice still existed.

VII

The results of the expansion of naval activity in Latin American waters during this critical period were decidedly mixed. On the one hand, the mere demonstration of power throughout these far-flung seas was gratifying to the people at home and created a certain amount of useful prestige in Latin America itself. By transporting and guarding specie, the navy undoubtedly rendered an important service. It also achieved considerable success in its main function of protecting commerce, although the most important results were obtained after the end of the period discussed in this chapter. The delay is hardly surprising, since the establishment of the permanent squadrons or stations which were so essential to the protection of commerce came so late in the period.

On the other hand, the increase in the power, prestige, and scope of action of the navy in Latin America was bought at a rather high price, if only because of the resentment it aroused in Latin America. As has already been suggested, this resentment was caused mainly by the action of the navy in breaking paper blockades and in trans-

---

bullion on private account, for which he collected deposit fees amounting to $2534.23; and that from Sept. 15, 1825, to (presumably) Jan. 18, 1826, his subordinate, Captain Thomas ap Catesby Jones, received on board the *Peacock* $102,725.50, for which he collected deposit fees amounting to $1,207.79 (Navy Department Archives, " Capts. Hull and Biddle, Jan.-Dec. 1826," Hull to Secretary Southard, June 25, 1826, No. 38). For Hull see Gardner W. Allen, *Papers of Isaac Hull, Commodore United States Navy* (Boston, 1929), Chap. V, " The Pacific Station."

porting specie. It was felt by both belligerents, though it was probably keener with the patriots than the royalists, since the former assumed that a common interest in the cause of freedom ought to induce the United States to make an exception in their favor.

To a very limited extent, the validity of this assumption was admitted by the United States. Thus, the Navy Department's orders to Captain Charles Stewart as he was about to sail in the *Franklin* to the Pacific Station in September 1821 stated that the conflict in South America was " a struggle on one side for liberty and independence " and that the United States must therefore avoid any act that might " in any manner, have the appearance or admit the construction of favoring the cause of Spain against such a struggle." [65]

Stewart's orders on this point could hardly have been more explicit; nor considering the fact that the United States still claimed to be observing " the strictest neutrality," could they have been more favorable to the Spanish American patriots. Yet the conduct of the *Franklin* on this cruise provoked indignant protests from the Spanish American governments on the ground that it was persistently favorable to Spain, and these protests were supported by the United States' own agent in Chile, J. B. Prevost.[66] They were lodged at Washington not only by the governments of

[65] See above, note 18.

[66] The fact that Prevost had preferred charges against Stewart and was himself under fire, and that an inquiry into the charges was still in progress, was partly responsible for President Monroe's refusal of the request of the House of Representatives in January 1825 for papers relating to the conduct of naval officers in South America (*Am State Papers, Naval Affairs*, II, 20-21).

Chile and Peru, which were immediately concerned, but also by remote Colombia [67] and Buenos Aires. The protest of the Buenos Aires government is particularly noteworthy because it was made in the name of continental solidarity and contained the categorical assertion that Stewart had given "open protection to the royalist army in Upper and Lower Peru" and had shown "direct hostility to the American system." [68]

When Stewart returned from his cruise he was tried by court martial. One of the principal charges against him was that he had violated the neutrality of the United States. The trial, which was long and sensational, ended in his complete vindication by the court. Its sentence was promptly approved by Adams, who was now President.[69]

[67] Manning, *Dip. Cor.*, I, 218-219, Adams to José María Salazar, Colombian Minister to the United States, Dec. 5, 1823, replying (in part) to the latter's note of Sept. 6 enclosing a complaint on behalf of Peru against the commander (Stewart) of the *Franklin*. Adams asked if, conversely, Colombia made itself responsible for the complaints which the United States might have to make against Peru.

[68] Emilio Ravignani, *Correspondencias generales de la provincia de Buenos Aires relativas à relaciones exteriores* (Buenos Aires, 1921), p. 445-447, Rivadavia to Rodney, Feb. 12, 1824. There is a translation of this note in Manning, *Dip. Cor.*, I, 635-636.

[69] *Am. State Papers, Naval Affairs*, II, 521. See *ibid.*, p. 487 ff. for the proceedings of the court martial in Stewart's case. It was fully reported in many newspapers, e. g., *Columbian Centinel*, which reported in its issue of Sept. 7, 1825, Joseph Hopkinson's preliminary speech in defense of Stewart, at the close of which "many congratulations were exchanged, many eyes glistened, and some tears were shed." Adams's *Memoirs* contain several references to the trial (e. g., VI, 429, 449-450, 461-462, and VII, 40, 45), but nothing about the sentence or his approval of it. The sentence was dated Sept. 3, 1825, he approved it two days later, and there is a gap in his *Memoirs* from Aug. 29 to Oct. 25, 1825.

The point that concerns us here is not whether Stewart was innocent or guilty, but that his conduct, which was endorsed by the highest authority in the United States, caused the liveliest indignation in patriot circles throughout South America. This illustrates an important fact about the role of the United States navy in the Latin American wars of independence, namely, that while the United States and the new states of Latin America had much in common, they were in sharp and apparently irreconcilable disagreement as to the way in which the navy of the former ought to be employed in Latin American waters.

While this disagreement would doubtless have been serious under any circumstances, it was aggravated by the unfortunate circumstance that the Latin American states employed, either in their regular navies or as privateers, a good many persons whom the United States regarded with a jaundiced eye. Foremost among these was that "titled freebooter," [70] Lord Cochrane, who, while still an officer in the British navy, had taken part in the assaults on Washington and New Orleans during the War of 1812.

[70] *New York Evening Post,* Jan. 19, 1821, letter clipped from the *Boston Daily Advertiser* of Jan. 16, signed "A Merchant," referring to Cochrane as "the titled freebooter." The writer suggested that "*old iron sides*" and one or two other ships ought to be sent to the coast of Peru and Chile, where they "would do more good than a regiment of ambassadors." See also note 73. Cochrane's side of the story is told in the laudatory sketch of his life in the *Dictionary of National Biography* (see under Cochrane, Thomas, 10th Earl of Dundonald) and in his own *Narrative of Services in the Liberation of Chili, Peru and Brazil, from Spanish and Portuguese Domination* (London, 1859). The parts of the *Narrative* relating to Chile and Peru have been published in a Spanish translation, *Memorias de lord Cochrane,* Lima, Peru, 1863, and Madrid, n. d., (1917).

This made it virtually impossible for the two parties to reach a mutual understanding on naval problems. According to the Spanish Americans, the United States ought, if not to aid them, at least not to interfere with them in their struggle for freedom; but to the United States it seemed that abstention from interference meant giving freebooters like Cochrane a free hand to despoil its own citizens.[71] According to the United States, its navy was merely trying to compel the new states, in Adams's phrase, to observe the ordinary rules of international law in their intercourse with the civilized world; but it was difficult for Spanish Americans to appreciate the nobility of this purpose when they were sure that the naval officers charged with its execution were lining their own pockets and aiding the hated Spanish royalists in the process. So it was that the sea, which was the strongest link between the two Americas, became an abundant source of discord between them; and one of the main points of disagreement was the use that the United States made of its naval power to protect its national interests in Latin America.

Finally, the United States navy itself was moulded by the part that it played in Latin American relations during this period. The extension of its operations gave its officers a far better knowledge than they had ever had before of the conditions affecting navigation and warfare in the whole vast Latin American zone. This knowledge would, of course, be of the greatest value in case European inter-

[71] *Columbian Centinel,* April 30, 1823, " From a correspondent," dated Valparaíso, Jan. 20, 1823: " These Patriots are considered by Europeans little better than pirates; and the *Franklin* keeps them but in little awe. . . . Unless more authority is given to our commanders, our ships might as well be laid up at the Charlestown navy yard. You can form no idea of the repeated insults which are daily offered here to American merchant vessels. . . ."

vention in Latin America should be attempted and the United States should undertake to resist it.

In another important respect, however, the navy was becoming not better but worse prepared to meet such an assault, and its operations in Latin American waters were probably responsible in part for the deterioration. As a recent authority has said, after 1815 the United States disregarded the lessons of the War of 1812, neglected its capital ships, and concentrated on the building of smaller ships, which, in time of war, would be unable to stand up against an enemy fleet and would be useful mainly for commerce raiding. The same authority has suggested that this policy was adopted under the influence of the myth of a United States victory in the naval War of 1812 and of the regime of economy forced on the navy by Congress.[72] This is doubtless true, but it seems probable that the policy was also a result of the navy's function in Latin American waters. That function was essentially to protect commerce in a vast area against pirates, privateers, and the third-rate navies of Spain and the new states. For this purpose, many small ships were better than a few large ones; indeed, for the inshore work so often required, large ships were almost useless. When we recall the importance of its Latin American operations in the sum total of the operations of the navy at this time—three of its four foreign squadrons were stationed in Latin America—the force of this factor can be appreciated.

Whatever the reasons for the naval policy followed by the United States navy in the period 1815-1823, it was not a sound policy from the point of view of the defence of America against a first-rate naval power. Indeed, the hard

[72] See above, note 1.

times following the Panic of 1819 created a fresh zeal for economy in Congress that threatened to impair the efficiency of the navy still further.[73] Yet this was precisely the period when the threat of European intervention in America became most alarming, and even a child could understand that only a battle fleet could repel a blow from that quarter. It remained to be seen whether the obvious conclusion would be acted on when the threat from overseas reached its climax, or whether the United States would rely on something besides its navy to secure, protect, and defend it.[74]

[73] Sprout, *op. cit.*, p. 96-98. For example, in 1821 an effort was made in Congress to reduce the Navy. One of the chief arguments against the proposed reduction was the need for additional protection for American commerce in the West Indies, on the Spanish Main, and on the coast of Chile and Peru. Stress was laid on the complaints of respectable Boston merchants against " the paper blockade of Lord Cochrane, as the outrage of an unprincipled freebooter" (*Annals Cong.*, 16 Cong., 2 Sess., p. 1060, Feb. 8, 1821).

[74] The danger of the myth of naval victory over England and the need for larger warships were clearly understood by Richard Rush, Minister to England 1817-1825, and his correspondents on this subject. Among these were President Monroe, Secretary of the Navy Smith Thompson, Commodore Stephen Decatur (a member of the Navy Board at Washington), and Samuel Humphreys, United States Naval Constructor. Thus, Humphreys wrote, " However much we may value ourselves upon our naval superiority [over England], & the results of actions fought the last war; it does not comport with sound policy to hug too closely this idea of superiority" (Rush Papers, Folder 1823, Humphreys to Rush, March 1, 1823). With the same thought in mind, Rush had already advised Monroe to send a secret agent to England to gather information on naval affairs (*ibid.*, Letter Books, vol. I, diary-letter from Rush to Monroe, Nov. 26-Dec. 4, 1817). For Humphreys, see Howard I. Chapelle, *History of American Sailing Ships* (New York, 1935), p. 112, 128 (I am indebted to Prof. Robert G. Albion, Princeton University, for this citation). For other recommendations by Rush, see below, chap. 15, note 37, and chap. 17, note 29.

CHAPTER ELEVEN

THE SPECTER OF THE HOLY ALLIANCE

It was in January 1819 that Adams informed the British government that the United States contemplated the early recognition of Spanish American independence and invited Great Britain to cooperate with it in the process; but it was not until more than three years later that the United States took the first step towards recognition and when it did so it took unilateral action, without consulting Great Britain or any other power.

This three-year interval was marked by events in both Europe and Latin America that profoundly affected the policy of the United States towards both regions. Among the most important of these events were the liberal revolutions that occurred in Spain and elsewhere in Europe; the aggressive reaction of the Holy Alliance against these revolutions; and the revelation that a strong leaning towards the European system existed among the patriots of the Plata region. So far as the policy of the United States was concerned, the most important development of the period consisted first, in a cautious but substantial advance along the road of recognition, and second, in the check that was administered to the earlier trends towards Anglo-American cooperation and towards embarking on a crusade for liberty. The check was administered in 1821 by no less a person than the Secretary of State, John Quincy Adams, in one of the most dramatic speeches that he ever made and some of the ideas contained in it dominated American foreign policy until the close of the century.

The present chapter will discuss the events that led up to Adams's address and the next chapter will discuss the address itself.   How Adams's ideas were subsequently modified will appear in later chapters.

I

As we have seen, the bid that Adams and Monroe made in January 1819 for British cooperation in Spanish America contained the categorical declaration that the United States contemplated the recognition of the Buenos Aires government at no remote period, unless some event should occur which would justify a postponement, and hinted that the recognition of Buenos Aires would be followed by that of Chile and Venezuela.   The main reason for the long delay that followed this brave declaration was probably Castlereagh's refusal to cooperate; but there were other reasons as well.   One of these, which, though imponderable, certainly had some weight in delaying recognition, was political rivalry in the United States.   This factor was noted by Duane's *Aurora* in March and again in October 1819.

. . . *The policy of the United States government* [said Duane] *was made to bend* against the cause of American liberty, because it was apprehended that if Mr. Clay carried any measure in congress *favorably to South American liberty,* those who were jealous of him apprehended that his *success in congress* would lead to his success as a competitor for the presidential chair.[1]

This was probably an extreme statement of the case, and certainly oversimplified it.   Yet there was a great deal of truth in it, for by his ardent advocacy of recognition and

[1] *Aurora,* May 13, 1819, " Robinocracy."

his scathing criticism of the administration for withholding it, Clay had made that cause peculiarly his own and had created a situation in which its success would be regarded as a defeat for Monroe's administration unless the case for recognition should be greatly strengthened by some new development, such as conspicuous progress in the liberation of Spanish America and in the stabilization of its governments.

In the spring of 1819, however, no such progress was recorded and the most important development was the revival of strong doubt in the United States as to the fitness of any of the Spanish American governments for recognition. It cannot be too often repeated that recognition was not an abstract question, but a very concrete one, and the form in which it presented itself was, which, if any, of the Spanish American governments was entitled to recognition. When Adams made his bid for British cooperation in January 1819, the answer to this question seemed to be, the government of Buenos Aires. But, beginning in that month and continuing on through April, the newspapers of the United States published serially the reports of the commissioners sent to South America (Caesar Rodney, John Graham, and Theodoric Bland), together with Joel Poinsett's report to Adams of November 1818 on the situation in Spanish America at large; [2] and the effect of these diverse but generally unfavorable reports was to dampen enthusiasm for the Spanish American cause and to create the widespread conviction that none of the new governments, not even Buenos Aires, was yet entitled to recognition. Consequently, the need for the protection

[2] For the publication of these reports, see above, chap. 9, note 7.

of American commerce with Spanish America was met not by recognizing the new governments in order that, as Adams had said, they might be compelled to observe the ordinary rules of international law in their intercourse with civilized nations, but by direct action, that is, by the passage of the act of March 1819 under which, as we have seen, the United States government greatly extended the operations of its navy in Latin American waters.

To be sure, Bolívar's victories in northern South America soon made news which, as the *Aurora* noted in October 1819, was " more auspicious to the cause of South American independence than any that [has] been received for three years past," [3] and a few months later even the unimpressionable Adams observed that the recent union of Venezuela and New Granada " certainly now presents the most remarkable and the most powerful of the revolutionary South American governments." [4]   Yet when he and President Monroe surveyed the state of the Union in a two-hour conference at the beginning of the new year, 1820, Adams expressed great uneasiness over the relations of the United States with Latin America as well as with the European powers that were most directly interested in the affairs of the New World.

With England, he told Monroe,[5] " we stood upon terms . . . as favorable as can ever be expected, but with a state of things dissatisfactory for the present and problematical for the future, with regard to our commercial intercourse with her American colonies." With France, the situation was " much less pleasing and more unpromising "; with Spain, the situation was uncomfortable for the United

[3] *Aurora,* Oct. 9, 1819, " South America."
[4] Adams, Memoirs, V, 44.   [5] *Ibid.,* IV, 497-498.

States; and with Portugal there was an angry dispute, mainly over the depredations committed on Portuguese-Brazilian commerce by privateers fitted out in ports of the United States. As for Latin America, said Adams, " although we have done more than any other nation for the South Americans, they are discontented because we have not espoused their cause in arms, and, with empty professions of friendship, they have no real sympathy for us." Finding the situation even more threatening at home than abroad, he warned Monroe that, while the latter's first term had been one of unprecedented tranquility, " it appears to me scarcely avoidable that the second term will be among the most stormy and violent " in the history of the United States.

II

The events of the year 1820 did not quite justify Adams's universal pessimism, but it was marked by two developments which further complicated the problem of policy towards Spanish America. The first of these was a revolution in Spain itself which had immediate repercussions in both hemispheres and which in its ultimate effects changed the alignment of the European powers and the political map of America. This revolution,[6] which ushered in the new year, was instigated in part by agents of the South American Governments, and it began in the expeditionary force that Spain was assembling at Cadiz for the reconquest of Buenos Aires and Montevideo. Led by an officer in that force, Rafael del Riego, from whom it takes its name, it soon won support among civilians throughout the country and in an incredibly short time the absolute monarchy of Spain was converted

[6] Ballesteros, Historia de España, VII, 163-173.

into a liberal monarchy under the revived Constitution of Cadiz of 1812. Ferdinand VII retained his crown by bowing to the revolutionists, but his powers were sharply curtailed by the creation of a representative assembly called the Cortes. Since this was the most striking feature of the new regime, the latter was often referred to simply as the Cortes.

Liberals everywhere rejoiced over the news from Spain and a newspaper in the United States which on April 5 had spoken of the " incurable rottenness and the proverbial ' slow-paced Saturnian movement' of the Spanish court," only three weeks later hailed the news of the revolution with the statement that " the general prospect of so many millions of the most sagacious, ardent, and persevering part of the human race, serving as new labourers in the cause of civilization " was " one of the most brilliant and delightful that could dawn upon the liberal mind." [7] At first this prospect bade fair to include a peaceful and rapid solution of the Spanish American question, for it was widely believed that the new government of Spain would prove its liberalism by either granting the colonies independence or at least offering them such generous terms of reconciliation that they would gladly return to the fold. In the latter case, speculated one editor, the Spanish American provinces would probably be reunited to Spain " upon a plan of equality and indulgence, which would enable them and the world to reap mutually all the advantages which are in the order of nature and reason." [8]

[7] *National Gazette,* April 5, 1820, " The Florida Question," and April 26, " The Spanish Revolution."

[8] *Ibid.,* April 26, 1820; *ibid.,* May 10, 1820, " South America." See also Ballesteros, *op. cit.,* VII, 425-426.

Early in 1820 occurred another event which, though it had less far-reaching consequences than the Spanish revolution, caused a sensation in both Europe and America at the time and exerted no little influence on policy and opinion in both regions for some time to come. This was the revelation, through one of the frequent upheavals in Buenos Aires, of an intrigue carried on in 1818 and 1819 between the government at that city and the French government for the purpose of establishing a Bourbon monarchy in the United Provinces of the Río de la Plata.[9] The first, circumstantial reports of this affair appeared in newspapers in the United States about the beginning of June 1820 and by the end of July many of them had published documents that were widely accepted as conclusive proof of the existence of the intrigue.[10]

For the United States this revelation threw a rather confused light on the Latin American problem. It increased the gravity of that problem by justifying the skepticism that Adams and many of his countrymen had long entertained about the professed republicanism of the South Americans [11] and also by proving that at least one of the European allies had attempted to extend its political and commercial influence over a large part of South America—an attempt

[9] The British Ambassador at Paris, Sir Charles Stuart, reported on July 10, 1820, that publication of news of the affair had "created a great sensation" there (Webster, *Britain and the Independence of Latin America,* II, 103). The episode has been discussed briefly in Robertson, *France and Latin-American Independence,* p. 162-175, and at length in Belgrano, *La Francia y la monarquía en el Plata,* 109-225.

[10] *Baltimore Federal Gazette,* June 10, 1820; *National Gazette,* June 21, 1820; *Louisiana Courier,* July 17 and July 31, 1820.

[11] *National Gazette,* June 10, 1820.

in which that power, France, appeared to have had the support of Russia and the Portuguese-Brazilian House of Braganza. On the other hand, this revelation simplified the problem by furnishing important evidence of a division in the counsels of the European allies about Spanish America,[12] for France had carried on the intrigue against Spanish authority in America while pretending to support the united front of European legitimists against revolutionary Spanish America, and the revelations included a strong suggestion of rivalry between the continental powers and England over Argentina. An agent of Buenos Aires was quoted as having told his government, after conferences with high officials of the French government:

. . . It is important for all of the states on the [European] continent that a throne should be raised in the provinces of Rio de la Plata, on which may be seated a monarch independent of England, who may some day counterbalance her power on the ocean and diminish the importation into those provinces of English merchandize by granting a free intercourse to other nations. France particularly would like to have this market for her manufactures, in preference to the English.

Commenting on this document, the *National Gazette* said, "We are inclined to think that [the continental powers] care not so much for establishing a monarchy *as*

[12] Castlereagh was outraged by the revelation of the intrigue: Webster, *The Foreign Policy of Castlereagh, 1815-1822* (London, 1925), p. 566-567. Under his prodding the British Ambassador at Paris told Baron Pasquier, the French Foreign Secretary, that the affair indicated a disposition on the part of France " to abandon the principle which connects the chief states of Europe, and to separate the interests of France from those of the Alliance " (Webster, *Britain*, II, 107).

such in any portion of South America, as for securing there
an influence tending to counteract that of England." [13]

This rift in the European front let in a welcome ray of
sunshine, but it fell only on the European side of the
picture. On the South American side, the picture seemed
darker than ever. Even before the full revelation of the
intrigue was received, Robert Walsh of the *National Gazette*
said, " Old Spain makes a better figure in her revolution,
than her revolted colony [Buenos Aires] "; and after the
intrigue had become a matter of common knowledge, he
pointed the finger of scorn at his colleague of the *National
Intelligencer* who, at last disillusioned about Buenos Aires,
was turning with unabated zeal to " our Sister Republic of
Columbia." " There can be no *genuine* republics in that
quarter [Spanish America]," commented Walsh. " Whatever form of polity may be admitted there, European
influence will predominate." [14]

III

The first effect of the news from Spain and Buenos Aires
was to strengthen the case for the administration's policy
of watchful waiting. Walsh spoke for many of his fellow
countrymen when he described it late in April 1820 as proof
of " the wisdom of the American cabinet in avoiding
hitherto any close connexion with the South American
provinces " and of the " good sense which . . . taught
them to doubt and to await results as the rule of judgment." [15]   Events were moving fast, however, and within

[13] *National Gazette,* June 21, 1820, " Buenos Ayres."
[14] *Ibid.,* June 28, 1820, " South America."
[15] *Ibid.* April 29, 1820, " South America."

little more than a year the cabinet had decided to abandon the course that he praised so warmly. Hope of a peaceful settlement by mutual agreement between Spain and its former colonies soon disappeared, the Cortes forfeited much of the sympathy it had first enjoyed in the United States, and the colonies that had remained in Spanish possession at the beginning of 1820 were soon falling from the parent stem like leaves in autumn.

This was largely because, for all its vaunted liberalism, the Cortes followed a policy towards Spanish America that savored strongly of the old regime, opposing not only political independence [16] but also the liberation of colonial commerce and offering the colonies a degree of parliamentary representation that they regarded as quite inadequate. Speaking of the latter point, the agent of Venezuela, Manuel Torres, told Adams as early as May 1820 that by excluding from representation all persons of African origin, even in the remotest degree, the Cortes had disfranchised a large part of the population of Spanish America, including the armies of liberation in Chile, La Plata, New Granada, and Venezuela, and had raised an insurmountable obstacle to reconciliation.[17]   When the Cortes did attempt to introduce

[16] For a careful study of Spanish policy, with copious references to the sources and secondary works, see William Spence Robertson, "The Policy of Spain toward its Revolted Colonies, 1820-1823," *Hispanic Am. Hist. Rev.*, VI (1926), 21-46.

[17] Manning, *Dip. Cor.*, II, 1189-1190, Torres to Adams, May 20, 1820. In March of this year Torres had presented himself at Washington in the capacity of chargé d'affaires of Venezuela. Though he was not recognized in that capacity until 1822, this marked the beginning of the period when, as noted above, he exercised a marked influence upon Adams and Monroe. Adams remarked that he "soothed and coaxed" where his predecessors, Vicente Pazos and Lino de Clemente, had "bullied and insulted" (Adams, *Memoirs*, V, 51) and while Adams distrusted him as

genuinely liberal measures into the colonies, such as measures intended to curb the privileges of the Church and the army, their main effect was to alienate the colonial upper classes who had hitherto been the strongest prop of Spanish authority in America.[18]

Weakened by dissension at home and by increasing resistance overseas, Spain was able to exert even less force in America after the Riego revolution than before it. At the beginning of 1820 only Argentina, Chile, and parts of Venezuela and New Granada were free; by 1822 Bolívar had completed the liberation of Venezuela, New Granada, and Ecuador, Mexico had won its independence almost overnight, and San Martín had begun the liberation of Peru, the only colony left to Spain on the American continent. No less important was the fact that stable governments seemed at last to be emerging in Venezuela and New Granada (now united as Colombia) and in Buenos Aires; and the latter, apparently repenting of its dalliance with Bourbon princes, had set up a regime which promised to be liberal as well as stable.[19]   Moreover, Portugal had caught the revolutionary contagion and had established a liberal government which, like that of Spain, proved far from liberal in regard to colonial commerce and government— and with the same result, for in 1822 Brazil proclaimed its independence.[20]

---

well as all the other "South American gentlemen," his honey caught more flies than their vinegar. His mission is described in Nicolas García Samudio, *Capítulos de historia diplomática* (Bogotá, 1925), p. 43-98.

[18] Ballesteros, *op. cit.*, VII, 440; Carlos A. Villanueva, *Fernando VII y los nuevos estados* (Paris, n. d.), 56-58.

[19] Manning, *Dip. Cor.*, I, 582-583, 585-587.

[20] João Pandiá Calogeras, *A History of Brazil* (Chapel Hill,

Before the end of 1820 it was already obvious that the case for recognition was greatly strengthened by the changes that were taking place in Latin America; and in November those who advocated it received cautious but valuable support from President Monroe in his annual message to Congress. For many years past Monroe had taken a warmly sympathetic interest in the Spanish American movement for independence. The reader will recall that as early as 1811, when he was secretary of state, he had informed the ministers of the United States in Europe that our government was contemplating recognition of Venezuela and had instructed them to persuade the European governments to take the same step. But (to use an expression that was very common at that time) Monroe was never quixotic in his devotion to the Spanish American cause. He still glowed with the ardor for universal emancipation which had made him so welcome to republican France when he arrived there as minister of the United States in 1794; but he had learned to restrain his ardor since his humiliating recall from France in 1796. With the passing years he became less doctrinaire and more practical and he also became less and less the exponent of a sectional interest and sought to reconcile the conflicting interests of the various sections in a national synthesis.[21]

It was in this spirit that he surveyed the ever-shifting Latin American scene in the long period from 1810 to 1825,

---

1939, tr. and ed. by Percy Alvin Martin), p. 81. The declaration was made at Ypiranga on Sept. 7, 1822, by Dom Pedro. His subsequent acceptance of the title of " Constitutional Emperor of Brazil " and his coronation " were in reality mere consequences " of this declaration (*ibid.*, p. 82).

[21] This is pointed out in the article on Monroe by Dexter Perkins in DAB, XIII, 91.

when, first as secretary of state and then as president, he exercised a greater and more sustained influence than any other person in shaping the policy of the United States with regard to Latin America. With changing circumstances, his course and that of his government were frequently altered; but his ultimate goal and his rules of navigation remained the same. For him, the Latin American cause was only one phase of the universal problem of liberty. The chief factor in that problem was the United States, which was the stronghold of liberty. His first task, then, was to strengthen the United States at home and increase its influence abroad.

He approached the task in a very practical spirit, for while he may have thought that his country's strength was as the strength of ten because its heart was pure, he never for a moment lost sight of its material interests; and like many of his fellow countrymen he believed that the United States would promote its own material interests as well as the cause of liberty by encouraging the movement for Latin American independence. But such encouragement involved risks as well as benefits, and the course of Monroe and his cabinet was shifted as the one or the other of these opposing forces was stronger at the moment.

Until 1820, the risks of encouraging Latin American independence far outweighed its probable benefits—the risk of embroilment with the great European powers, of loss of the valuable trade with Cuba and other loyal Spanish colonies, and of grave dissension in the United States itself, where powerful interests opposed any sacrifice for the benefit of the remote and alien South Americans.[22] On the

[22] This idea was developed in an outspoken article, "South America," in the *National Gazette*, June 28, 1820, which con-

other hand, even selfish national interest, if it were far-sighted, must see that, once the success of the independence movement was reasonably certain, the United States ought to manifest at least enough solicitude for the welfare of the new states to assure itself of friendly relations with them and of a good share of their future favors.

The latter consideration was to prove decisive in 1822. At the end of 1820 it was already important because of the great progress made by the independence movement during that year. Coupled with this was another considera-tion which, while not new, was acquiring greater importance than ever before and was also to have great influence in the shaping of American policy in the years immediately ahead: namely, the fear that the Holy Alliance might soon undertake to suppress free governments everywhere, in America as well as in Europe, and in the United States as well as in Spanish America.[23]

It was in this atmosphere that Monroe sent Congress his

---

cluded that the United States " are not, certainly, called upon, by any motive of profit or defence, to incur the least risk, to admit the least disquietude, touching dispositions and events in that quarter [" South America "]."

[23] As noted in chap. 7, this consideration had been given promi-nence as early as January 1816 in Clay's speech on the army appro-priation bill. It seems to have caused little uneasiness for nearly two years after the Congress of Aix-la-Chapelle. The revival of the threat in 1820 and 1821 is discussed below in the present chapter. Manuel Torres may have done something to revive apprehension on this score in the United States. He certainly tried to do so, for early in 1820 he stressed the political diversity and conflict of interest between Europe and America and said that it was " not altogether impossible that a war against the new world on the part of the sovereigns who compose the holy alliance, may issue from the present or future political situation of Europe and America " (Manning, *Dip. Cor.,* II, 1186-1188).

annual message in November 1820. With regard to Spanish America, the message said that the struggle for independence in that region was being carried on with improved success and that the new governments were acquiring a reputation for the order of their internal administration. It also expressed the opinion that the revolution which had just taken place in Spain would aid the independence movement in Spanish America and that the great powers of Europe would not intervene to suppress it; and it concluded with the suggestion that those powers might better take into consideration the recognition of the new Spanish American states.[24]

This was certainly not a bold blast in favor of the Spanish American cause, but it did render that cause an important service by dispelling the cloud under which it had rested since the results of the missions to South America were made known in the winter of 1818-1819. And if, with regard to Spain and the great powers of Europe, the message breathed an optimism which few people in this country shared, that fact only increased the significance of the central thought of this part of the message. This was that the time was approaching when the United States must recognize the independence of the new Spanish American governments.

IV

That, at any rate, was the central thought that opponents as well as advocates of recognition found in it. Among the former was the Philadelphia *National Gazette,* which questioned the authenticity of the information on which

[24] J. D. Richardson, *Messages and Papers of the Presidents, 1789-1900* (10 vols., Washington, 1896-1899), II, 77.

Monroe's favorable picture of condition in Spanish America was based, and reminded its readers that the Buenos Aires government had recently engaged in a monarchist intrigue with France and that other South American patriots had issued manifestos containing "strictures on our institutions." Why then, asked Editor Walsh, had Monroe so suddenly and unjustifiably revived the issue of recognition?

The *Gazette* was generally favorable towards the administration at this period, particularly in questions of foreign policy; but in answering this question Walsh used language which reflected grave discredit upon the president and also upon his secretary of state, who presumably shared the responsibilty for this part of the message. The clear implication of the passage was that the administration was seeking to provoke a war with Spain in order to furnish itself with a pretext for seizing Texas, the claim to which, it will be recalled, had been surrendered by the United States in the still unratified Adams-Onís Treaty of 1819.

The paragraph of the message concerning the Spanish colonies [said the *Gazette*] has, we must confess, produced alarm as well as dissatisfaction in our minds. We suspect these gentle breathings on their [the South Americans'] side, and the supererogation in "friendly counsels" with the European powers, for the acknowledgment of their independence. The people of the Northern and Middle States of the Union ought not to consent to risk a war with Spain *for the acquisition of Texas.* . . The policy of securing it [Texas] has, we believe, become more general and systematic with those who have the ascendancy in our national affairs.[25]

On the other side, Clay and his cohorts found encouragement in the message, as well they might. Early in 1821,

[25] *National Gazette,* Nov. 24, 1820, "The President's Message."

they obtained the adoption by the House of Representatives of a resolution expressing the " deep interest " of the United States in the successs of the Spanish American struggle for independence and looking towards early recognition of the new states.[26] This was no small achievement for the friends of Spanish America; for, mild as it was, the resolution was the first definite step towards recognition taken by any organ of the American government. Recognition still had its dangers. It was not, as our government asserted, an entirely neutral act—a mere photographic process, so to speak— for it was sure to give aid and comfort to the Spanish American rebels; and it might provoke retaliation against the United States by the increasingly aggressive Holy Alliance.

To opponents of recognition, however, the terms of Clay's resolution were less distrubing than the crusading zeal of some of its advocates. In the course of the debate upon it in the House of Representatives, Stevens of Connecticut said that republics ought to take care of themselves as kings were doing[27]—a reference to the Holy Alliance and a suggestion that the challenge from this united front of the monarchical powers of Europe ought to be met by the formation of a united front of the republican powers of America. Trimble of Kentucky made the appeal to arms more explicit by saying frankly that he would not stand by as an idle witness of " political homicide " while free governments were put down (as the liberal government of Naples had just been put down by one of the Holy Allies, Austria), but would aid them.[23]

[26] *Annals Cong.*, 16 Cong., 2 Sess., p. 1081.
[27] *National Gazette*, Feb. 10, 1821, quoted in editorial.
[28] *Ibid.*

This was a large and generous view; but the suggestion that the United States ought to go crusading for democracy met with strong opposition. One of its most determined opponents was, of course, Walsh's *National Gazette,* which had protested against even the mild encouragement offered to the Spanish American cause by Monroe's message. Trimble's proposal it now branded as " Quixotic "; and, alluding to the business depression which had begun in the Panic of 1819 and was still going on, it said, " We should attend exclusively to our own concerns before we go a ' colonelling ' in pursuit of independence for South American provinces." [29]

The success of Mr. Clay [continued the *Gazette*] is the triumph of rhetoric, aided by the force of a liberal and natural, though not, perhaps, well applied sympathy. Liberty and independence are magic words in this country, and objects which we think ourselves bound to wish to all distant communities of men, who may appear to be struggling for them, without consulting their disposition and capacity to put them to a good use.[30]

Two months later a far stronger blast in the same key was blown by the *North American Review,* which was then edited by Edward Everett. In an article entitled " South America," written by Everett himself and published in the number for April 1821,[31] it described the " appeals resting

[29] *Ibid.*

[30] *Ibid.,* Feb. 13, 1821, " South America."

[31] *North American Review,* No. XXXI (vol. III, No. 1, New Series, 1821), p. 432-443, " South America," a review article on Dean Gregorio Funes, *Ensayo de la historia civil del Paraguay, Buenos-Aires, y Tucuman* (Tom. 3, Buenos Aires, 1816-1817). In a letter of June 2, 1821, to Joel Poinsett, Everett said in reference to this article, " Nothing but the seeming necessity of not leaving it [South America] longer untouched

on the community of the American name, or the partnership
of one continent " as " fallacious " and suggested that talk
about continental solidarity was a convenient cloak for a
Yankee imperialism similar to the imperialism of Russia
and England in Asia, India, and Africa.   In some respects
the article reflected Puritan New England's distrust of
Latins, Roman Catholics, and all people who lived in a less
rigorous climate than that of Boston.   In many respects,
however, it expressed misgivings about the political and
social virtues of the Latin American people that were widely
felt throughout the United States.   A special interest attaches
to the article because its tone was strikingly different from
that which the same journal was soon to take under the
editorship of that hardy pioneer in the field of inter-American cultural relations, Jared Sparks.

The truth is [wrote Everett], that the policy, which has been
at various times most powerfully recommended in the
United States, of a vigorous interference on our part, in the

---

c[oul]'d have induced me, with the little detailed knowledge I
have on the subject, to risk the remarks I made in the last
number " (Poinsett Papers, HSP, Everett to Poinsett, June 2,
1821).   Everett prefaced this with the remark that he had been
constantly reproached for not prevailing on Poinsett to write
something on this important subject.   He had tried to do so.   In
August, 1820, he had invited Poinsett to review Brackenridge's
Voyage to South America, the publications to which it had given
rise, and the subject generally, requesting, " for obvious considerations that Mr. Brackenridge should not be treated with undue
severity."   Poinsett evidently declined and took exception to the
request, for in September Everett renewed the invitation and
said, " . . . Nothing was farther from our design, than to excuse
or conceal the manifest spirit of party, in which his [Bracken-
ridge's] work is written, and which we hope . . . you will take
occasion duly to expose " (*ibid.,* Everett to Poinsett, Aug. 3 and
Sept. 29, 1820).   Presumably, Poinsett declined again.

South American contest, is a policy highly anti-republican; a policy which has wasted Europe from the middle ages to the present day. We have no concern with South America; we have no sympathy, we can have no well founded political sympathy with them. We are sprung from different stocks, we speak different languages, we have been brought up in different social and moral schools, we have been governed by different codes of law, we profess radically different codes of religion. Should we espouse their cause, they would borrow our money and grant commissions to our privateers, and possibly extend some privileges to our trade, if the fear of the English, which bringeth a snare, did not prevent this. But they would not act in our spirit, they would not follow our advice, they could not imitate our example. Not all the treaties we could make, nor the commissioners we could send out, nor the money we could lend them, would transform their Pueyrredons and their Artigases, into Adamses or Franklins, or their Bolivars into Washingtons.[32]

Though he was aware that Abbé Corrêa and the British poet-historian, Robert Southey, had spoken well of the Brazilians, Everett saw a great variety of insurmountable obstacles to " our feeling a sympathy " with any of the Latin Americans. At one extreme, he could not conceive how " our industrious frugal yeomen " could " sympathise with a people that sit on horseback to fish." At the other, he observed that " The various tyrannies, political, feudal, and ecclesiastical of Europe, are the auspices under which these provinces have grown up; and in many of them the seductions of equatorial and tropical climates, and the possession of the mines of the precious metals have come in aid of human oppression, to insure the degeneracy of the inhabitants." From such premises he moved naturally to his conclusion: " South America will be to North America,

[32] *North American Review, loc. cit.,* p. 433-435.

we are strongly inclined to think, what Asia and Africa are
to Europe."

The two basic assumptions of this article were widely
accepted. These were that the United States ought to
cultivate its own garden and that it ought to be particularly
wary of any course that might entangle it with the alien
peoples of Brazil and Spanish America. On the latter point,
indeed, it rather understated the case, for there were other
writers who believed that if the myth of inter-American
solidarity was not the product of shallow sentimentalism
and of such political maneuverings as those of Henry Clay,
it was the creature of paid propaganda carried on by the
agents of the Spanish American revolutionists and other
interested persons in the United States. Towards the end
of 1820 appeared W. D. Robinson's *Memoirs of the
Mexican Revolution,* in which the author complained at
length about the activities of " Spanish agents " in the
United States who were creating prejudices in the public
mind against the Spanish American cause. To this one critic
promptly replied that it would be easy to indulge in equally
loose talk about the activities of the agents of the Spanish
American cause itself; and, he continued, " if suspicion
should attach in any quarter, it should be to that where most
ardor and activity are displayed for foreign interests." [33]

Adams, who had long shared this skepticism, felt it very
keenly at this period. Commenting in March 1820 on the
current effort of Manuel Torres to buy 20,000 stand of arms
from the United States government on credit, Adams was
reminded of the " gunpowder plot " of 1816 and noted
that " by one of those back-stair proceedings which I often

[33] *National Gazette,* Feb. 9, 1821, South America."

feel without seeing," the Ordinance Department had most opportunely reported that it had arms available for sale, and that the pro-Spanish American Duane was fully informed about this report.

> To this complexion [he said] ninety-nine-hundredths of the South American patriotism, and which has for these three years been flaunting in such gorgeous colors in this country, must come at last.[34]

So, he frankly told Monroe, he felt some distrust of everything proposed by " these South American gentlemen," both the agents of the South American governments and their sympathisers in the United States.[35]

V

And yet at this very time the Holy Alliance was beginning to give such startling evidence of its power and agressiveness that even those Americans who were devoted to isolationism and skeptical about the ostensible liberalism of Latin America began to wonder whether liberals could afford to sit quietly at home while the European despots destroyed liberal institutions in one country after another. The work of destruction had already begun in Europe: might not America's turn come next?

This sector of opinion is well represented by the Philadelphia *National Gazette,* whose editor, Robert Walsh was one of the most talented, most judicious, and best informed of the conservative commentators on foreign affairs. On April 18, 1821, the *Gazette* quoted with approval the *North American Review's* unsympathetic article on South America, from which we have just quoted a long and characteristic

[34] Adams, *Memoirs,* V, 45-46.   [35] *Ibid.,* V, 51.

passage.[36]   The very next day, however, the *Gazette* noted with concern that Austria had invaded the kingdom of Naples for the purpose of putting down constitutional government and restoring absolute monarchy there.[37] Naples seemed remote from Philadelphia; but two days later the *Gazette* noted other items that brought the danger closer home: first, because the Holy Allies' Troppau Circular and Laibach Manifesto condemned the liberal government of Spain as well as that of Naples, thus giving ground for apprehension that they might intervene in Spain as well, and, through Spain, in Spanish America; and second, because the Circular and Manifesto also condemned the right of revolution, so that, said the *Gazette*, " our American theory of government is . . . put under the ban." [38]

Another aspect of the same problem was brought out in Walsh's coment on a memorial of the Russian government denouncing the new constitutional government in Spain.

These American States [commented Walsh] need not fear that they will ever be reached by the arm of Russia; they may deride the suggestion that their destinies are involved in any European Revolution: But they have a general concern in the political system of Europe, with which they will always maintain important, though never, we trust, *vital,*

[36] *National Gazette,* April 18, 1821, editorial on the article, a long extract from which was published in this issue. This extract included the passage quoted above in the text (see note 32). Walsh said that the extract "furnishes several just and striking observations on a subject that has been most industriously attempted, both in and out of Congress, to be made one of deep concern to the United States," and that, as the effort would "no doubt, be incessantly renewed . . . the sound ideas of the Boston writer [Everett] must therefore be at all times seasonable."

[37] *Ibid.,* April 19, 1821, " The Foreign News."

[38] *Ibid.,* April 21, 1821, " The Holy Alliance.

relations; and in the fate throughout the world, of human and political liberty, which Russia has now openly proscribed in Europe.[39]

In a very real sense, then, the interests of the United States as well as those of Spanish America were involved in the European crisis and the two Americas were aligned on the same side. Editor Walsh did not, however, show any immediate inclination to buckle on his crusading armor. Like lovers of liberty before and since, he took comfort in the reflection that liberals in other lands would defend the cause of liberty, and he contented himself with finding reasons for their doing so. According to some reports, he said, the French people and soldiery would not consent that their government should " connive or merely gaze at the efforts of despotism against free institutions." As for England, inaction on her part in this crisis would be even worse than on the occasion of the dismemberment of Poland, when Edmund Burke had " properly styled her an accessory after the fact," for, as one member of Parliament had just said in the debate on Laibach and Naples, " whilst such doctrines [as those of the Holy Alliance] were put forth, England was not safe." [40]

If Americans could expect every Englishman to do his duty, they had little immediate cause for worry about their own hemisphere; but there was always the doubt whether every Englishman would see his duty as clearly as his American cousins saw it for him, and this doubt fed the growing conviction that the United States itself might have

[39] *Ibid.,* Sept. 23, 1820. For the Russian memorial, see W. P. Cresson, *The Holy Alliance* (Washington, 1922), p. 100.

[40] *National Gazette, loc. cit., supra,* note 37, and the issue of April 24, 1821, " Holy Alliance."

to do something in the premises. As the months passed and England disappointed the hopes of liberals by failing to take a stand against continental despotism, the *Gazette's* sense of the peril in which its country stood became acute. On August 2, 1821, it considered the possibility that France and England might even join with the other great powers of Europe in an "imperial conspiracy," and continued:

The destruction of this republic [the United States] must enter into the plan of the monarchical league, which is one that looks to the dominion of particular principles, as well as of particular thrones. After the subjugation of Europe, the existence of our republican institutions will be deemed the only obstacle to the perpetuation of that order of things there, and the extension of royal rule over the whole civilized world.[41]

Robert Walsh was a man of letters, and keenly aware of the many cultural bonds that united his country to western Europe. It is all the more interesting, then, to observe how he was beginning to feel—as Clay, Brackenridge, and other partisans of Spanish America had long been feeling and saying—that Europe and America were becoming separate and even antagonistic entities, separated not only by the Atlantic Ocean, but also by what in modern parlance is called a conflict of ideologies.

Even as early as January of this year he had already shown that his mind was moving towards that conclusion. In 1820 a Danish Counsellor of State, Dr. Konrad Friedrich von Schmidt-Phiseldeck, had helped swell the torrent of writings on America with a book written in German and published at Copenhagen, entitled *Europe and America, or the Relative State of the Civilized World at a Future*

[41] *Ibid.*, Aug. 2, 1821, "Imperial Conspiracy."

Period. The work was soon translated into English as well as French and Danish, and by the end of the year it was offered for sale in Philadelphia.[42] Reviewing it,[43] Walsh found the earlier parts " somewhat repulsive " since they were " in a degree abstruse "; but the feeling of repulsion wore off as he advanced to the practical and more intelligible later chapters. He was struck by the optimism of the author regarding the future of America—a future as magnificent, Walsh remarked, as anything conceived even by the most enthusiastic of our own politicians.

[42] The English translation, by Joseph Owen, was published at Copenhagen, 1820. According to the *National Gazette,* Jan. 18, 1821, " Political Philosophy," a second German edition had already been published and the book had been translated into Danish and French as well as English. Among other things, it stressed the influence of the American Revolution on the European revolutions of the past forty years. The *Gazette* praised it highly, said that it ought to be read throughout the United States, and described Schmidt-Phiseldeck as enjoying a high reputation for learning. He had already written a commentary in Latin on Kant's Critique of Pure Reason and a study of Danish neutrality, and later wrote on European union and the Holy Alliance. See the biographical sketch in *Allgemeine Deutsche Biographie,* vol. 32 (Leipzig, 1891), p. 23-24. The character of the author and of his *Europe and America* and its reception illustrate the widespread recognition in Europe of the revolutionary effect of America on Europe. The book also expresses the contemporaneous German interest in American affairs, which deserves more attention than it has received. A valuable contribution to this subject is Fritz Baumgarten, " Hamburg und die lateinamerikanische Emanzipation (1815-1830)," in Fritz Baumgarten and others, *Ibero-Amerika und die Hansestädte: Die Entwicklung ihrer wirtschaftlichen und kulturellen Beziehungen* (Hamurg, 1937), p. 153-194; but the bibliography (p. 192-194) indicates how little had been written on the subject previously.

[43] *National Gazette,* Jan. 18, 1821, " Political Philosophy." The same issue contains three columns of extracts from the English translation of the book.

What impressed Walsh most of all was a passage in which the author said that Europe's only salvation lay in imitating America, which enjoyed the plenitude of liberties combined under a common tie, and that Europe must consider itself one grand state, for otherwise its national rivalries and wars would carry it piecemeal to ruin, whilst America, through its unanimity and the legally free development of its vast resources, would go on consolidating its dominion. This passage, concluded Walsh, " may serve as a useful admonition to the American statesman."   A significant conclusion, coming from the same editor who endorsed the *North American Review's* article against Spanish America; most significant because in that context it typifies the indecision and confusion of thought of most of Walsh's countrymen in this great world crisis and because it illustrates the emergent sense of continental solidarity that was taking hold of them, often in spite of themselves.

The declarations of Troppau and Laibach and the invasion of Naples provoked a bolder response from Henry Clay; but it was hardly a clearer one, and its significance lies mainly in the retort that it elicited from John Quincy Adams, in connection with which we shall consider it.

CHAPTER TWELVE

THE REPLY TO LEXINGTON AND EDINBURGH

I

On the afternoon of May 19, 1821, between two and three hundred guests assembled at Higbee's Tavern in Lexington, Kentucky, to do honor to Henry Clay. The occasion was notable one, for it marked Clay's retirement to private life after a decade of conspicuous public service. Most of the guests were citizens of Fayette, Woodford, and Jessamine Counties, in the district that Clay had long represented in Congress, but some of them were " strangers " (as they were described in Lexington) who had come from a distance by special invitation.

At three o'clock the company sat down to an excellent and plentiful dinner prepared by Mr. Higbee. When they had eaten their fill, the guest of honor regaled them with his familiar eloquence.[1] Since his speech was in the nature of a farewell address, a political testament, he could hardly have failed under any circumstances to mention the Spanish American question, to which he had devoted so much time and so many speeches in the course of the Congressional

---

[1] *New York Evening Post,* June 9, 1821, " Dinner to Mr. Clay," item dated " Lexington, May 24," describing the dinner. The speech was reported at length in the *Argus of Western America* (Frankfort, Ky.), June 7, 1821, and the *Richmond Enquirer,* June 26, 1821, " Speech of Mr. Clay, at the late dinner given to him by his constituents in Kentucky, on his retiring from public life." The editorial comment on the speech in this same issue of the *Enquirer* is remarkably unsympathetic to the Spanish American cause, considering the warm support that the *Enquirer* had once given it.

career just closed. Under the existing circumstances, the
sense of an impending crisis in the affairs of Spanish
America required him to discuss the question soberly, even
in the wake of a Kentucky banquet.

Clay gave Spanish America all the prominence that its
most zealous partisan could have expected. In most respects,
he merely reaffirmed the position that he had long since
taken, but the total effect of his speech was to give new and
stronger emphasis to his rôle as critic of the administration's
Spanish American policy. In this part of his speech he stressed three points. First, he asserted that the Executive Department had delayed to conform to the known sentiment of
the whole Union in favor of the recognition of Spanish
American independence. Next, he renewed his recommendation that the United States should countenance " by
all means short of actual war " the great cause of Spanish
American independence, for, he declared, it would thereby
" give additional tone, and hope, and confidence to the
friends of liberty throughout the world." Finally, he advised that " a sort of counterpoise to the holy alliance
should be formed in the two Americas, in favor of national
independence and liberty, to operate by the force of example,
and moral influence . . ."

Clay's suggestion that the two Americas should form a
counterpoise to the Holy Alliance was actually much less
startling than it might seem at first sight. Indeed, it was
less decisive and showed less development of thought than
might have been expected. Already in 1820 he had advocated in Congress the formation of an American system,
citing Abbé de Pradt in support of his recommendation.[2]

<hr/>

[2] *Annals Cong.*, 16 Cong., 1 Sess., p. ????-????, May 10, 1820.
Clay " quoted a few passages from the work of the Abbe de

Now, a year later, although the threat of the Holy Alliance had become more serious in the interim, he made no corresponding change in his proposal for a counterpoise to it. If there was any important change, it lay in the greater care that he took to disclaim any intention of involving the United States in war.

Since the threat of the Holy Alliance was generally understood to be a military threat, it would seem to have been rather meaningless to talk about forming a counterpoise to it unless one contemplated the use of force, at least as a last resort; and yet Clay declared emphatically that his proposal was not a call to arms, that he wished to aid Spanish America only by "means short of actual war." Whether this was because he did not face the issue or because he was unwilling to bring it out into the open, or for some other reason, we cannot say. In any case it is interesting to note that, as Robert Walsh's isolationism was tempered by a dawning sense of continental solidarity, so Clay's enthusiasm for the American system was held in check by something that we may perhaps identify as the traditional isolationism of his countrymen and their love of peace.

However inconclusive this part of Clay's Lexington speech may seem to the hindsight analyst, to his contemporaries the speech was a political event of exceptional

---

Pradt . . . on the importance of the commerce of South America, when freed from its present restraints, &c." Clay then went on to describe the advantages of "the course which I propose," namely, the creation of "a system of which we shall be the centre, and in which all South America will act with us." This was to be both a commercial system and also "the rallying point of human wisdom against all the despotism of the Old World." The speech can also be consulted in Calvin Colton, *The Life, Correspondence and Speeches of Henry Clay* (6 vols., New York, 1864), V, 238-244.

interest. Quite aside from the character of the speaker, what he said was important because of the place where he spoke. For over a generation Lexington had provided a political leadership for the Western World that had been respected throughout that region.[3] The West had, moreover, shown more sympathy than any other section of the country for Spanish America;[4] and now the most eminent of the Lexington leaders, speaking at Lexington itself, was leaving a political testament that was designed to consolidate this sympathy and perhaps also (though he himself denied this) to make it more militant. Consequently, the speech attracted nationwide attention and was featured in newspapers on the eastern seaboard as well as in Kentucky.

The opponents of any given policy usually represent it to be more clear-cut and more extreme than it actually is. So it was with the *North American Review's* assertion, in its article of April 1821, that the policy of a "vigorous interference on our part" in the South American contest had been "most powerfully recommended in the United States";[5] for it would be difficult to say by whom or in what form any such powerful recommendation had been made. Clay was the only man of first rank in public life who had made anything approaching such a recommendation, and the measures that he advocated—recognition, and

[3] Bernard Mayo, "Lexington: Frontier Metropolis" (in Eric F. Goldman, ed. *Historiography and Urbanization: Essays in American History in Honor of W. Stull Holt,* Baltimore, 1931), p. 37.

[4] This is indicated by the vote in Congress in 1818 on Clay's resolution in favor of the recognition of Buenos Aires. The West voted for it 15 to 8 and was the only section that cast a majority of its votes in favor of the measure (Griffin, *United States,* p. 136, note 67).

[5] Passages quoted in chap. 11 and cited in note 32.

other aid short of war—could scarcely be regarded as constituting a " vigorous interference." The term clearly connoted direct military aid, probably even open war; and that was far more than Clay had ever recommended. The most that could be fairly said was that Trimble and other second-rate politicians had talked as if they wished to engage the United States in a crusade for democracy; but even they had never, by resolution in Congress or otherwise, made what could be called a formal recommendation of such a policy, and it would be paying Trimble and his kind too high a compliment to describe any recommendation of theirs as " powerful."

The same misinterpretation was put upon Clay's Lexington speech of May 1821. On July 4, less than two months after it was delivered, no less a person than John Quincy Adams took Clay's vague proposal of a " counterpoise to the Holy Alliance " and, disregarding Clay's denial that it was an appeal to arms, made it the text of a dramatic warning to his countrymen against crusading for democracy. Even that was only one of many striking things that Adams said on this occasion, and perhaps it was only poetic justice that his speech, like Clay's, was misinterpreted. Indeed, his address was so spectacular a performance, is so important in the history of our relations with Latin America, and has been so frequently misunderstood from the day of its delivery to our own time, that it requires our most careful attention.

II

Towards the latter part of June 1821 a citizens' committee of Washington invited Adams to deliver the Fourth-of-July oration at that place. Although the time was short

and he knew that the committee had first tried to engage
Attorney General William Wirt and William Pinkney, one
of the leading lawyers of that generation, he accepted after
some hesitation and for reasons that will shortly appear.[6]
Once he had given his consent, he devoted himself with
characteristic thoroughness to the preparation of the oration
or " address," as he preferred to call it. Nothing perfunc-
tory would do. He was determined to make this a memor-
able occasion, and we may well believe that he succeeded
even beyond his expectations.

The address was delivered on the morning of the Fourth
in the House of Representatives before an audience that
one eyewitness described as " large and brilliant " and
another as " a very respectable assemblage of ladies and
citizens." [7] Fortunately, as it turned out, the British minister was not among those present. Adams began to speak at
eleven o'clock, and one of his auditors who arrived a few
minutes after the hour said that the hall was so crowded
that he could get only a few feet inside the door; even then
there was so much noise of scraping feet and whispering
that for some time he could hardly hear a word. Finally
the speaker caught the close attention of his whole audience, and he held it until the end, when his extraordinary
address was greeted with a great burst of applause.[8] According to the *National Intelligencer,*[9] Adams had not only prepared his address with great care, but had even " so far
studied [it] as to deliver [it] with action suited to the

[6] Adams, *Writings,* VII.

[7] *Baltimore Patriot,* July 7, 1821; *National Intelligencer,* July 6,
1821.

[8] *Richmond Enquirer, July* 17, 1821, " Mr. Adams's Oration,"
clipped from the *Baltimore Federal Gazette*

[9] Issue of July 6, 1821.

word "; in short, it was " a finished oration." Another critic was less indulgent. If this speech had come from common lips, he said, it would not have been trumpeted forth with such enthusiasm, " but a Secretary of State, of course, particularly if he had been once a Professor of Rhetoric, must be expected to deliver a ' finished oration.' " [10]

The allusion to the fact that Adams had once been a professor of rhetoric at Harvard was altogether justified and it suggests an important point. Whether the American people liked the address [11] or not, they all discussed it eagerly. Indeed, it still stands as one of the few really striking speeches ever made on Independence Day and one of the most sensational ever made by an American Secretary of State on any occasion. Discoursing on liberty in various aspects, he asserted principles in regard to colonialism and American foreign policy that will be discussed below; and a good deal of his time was devoted to answering the supercilious British question, " What has America

[10] *Richmond Enquirer*, July 17, 1821, communication, " The ' Finished Oration ' "; signed " A Brief Reviewer."

[11] The address was published in many of the newspapers that I have consulted, e. g., *National Intelligencer*, July 10, 1821; *Baltimore Patriot*, July 12; *New York Evening Post*, July 14; *Richmond Enquirer*, July 17; *National Gazette*, July 14. I have followed the text published in the last-named journal, whose editor, Robert Walsh, was a correspondent of Adams's at this time. In this issue, the address filled 8 1/3 columns (the whole front page, 6 columns, and 2 1/3 columns on the last page). The address was also published separately as a pamphlet by Davis and Force at Washington, and a second edition was published at Cambridge, 1821 (Sabin, *op. cit.*, I, 37, No. 267). A one-column summary of the address, with a brief and favorable introductory statement, was published in the Buenos Aires newspaper *Argos de Buenos Aires*, No. 32, Nov. 17, 1821, p. 319, " America. Estados Unidos."

done for mankind? "—a question involving the use the American people had made of their liberty.[12] In part, however, the address was a regular Fourth-of-July oration,[13] containing the customary eulogy of the Declaration of Independence and the heroes of the Revolution and the routine denunciation of Great Britain, and this was what made it a sensation both at home and abroad. For denunciation of Great Britain was to be expected of Fourth-of-July orators in general, but not of an American Secretary of State, at least in time of peace. Adams, who intended his address to make an impression but not to create a scandal, sought to disarm criticism on this score by protesting that his speech was made in his private character; [14] and it was probably in

[12] Two years earlier, Robert Walsh of the *National Gazette* had published a book, *An Appeal from the Judgments of Great Britain Respecting the United States of America: Part First* (Philadelphia and London, 1819), in which he took the British to task for their supercilious attitude towards the United States. In the *Edinburgh Review* for January 1820 Sydney Smith asked his famous questions, " In the four quarters of the globe, who reads an American book? or goes to an American play? or looks at an American picture or statue? " (See below, note 26.) Adams now wrote Walsh that if even the " Aristarchs of Edinburgh " (the *Edinburgh Review*) had taken this castigation kindly, he himself would not have disturbed the truce in his Independence Day address (Adams, *Writings,* VII, 116-117). Walsh used some of the phrases from Adams's letter in his article on the address in the *National Gazette,* July 18, 1821. For the *Edinburgh Review's* comments on Walsh's book, see below, note 25.

[13] *National Gazette,* July 16, 1821, " Mr. Adams's Address," remarking that it had been long since any expectation had been aroused " by what is called specifically ' a Fourth of July Oration.' " Walsh, a friendly critic, regarded Adams's address as being wholly unlike " a Fourth of July Oration," but it was only partly so.

[14] Adams, *Writings,* VII, 113. As far as I have been able to

the hope of emphasizing this point that he delivered it in his robe of professor of rhetoric. But most of his countrymen seem to have missed the point and to have regarded the wearing of the professorial robe as just another of the Secretary's New England crotchets.[15]

It was consequently these largely retrospective and thoroughly commonplace passages in the address—passages remarkable only because of the office held by the speaker—that attracted attention. The part that Adams himself considered novel and highly important—important because it laid down principles for the guidance of future policy—was, to his great distress, largely ignored. Posterity has done little to right the wrong of which he complained. Even Mr. Dexter Perkins, who is the leading authority on Adam's career as secretary of state and who rightly observes that this address contains "a fierce attack upon the whole colonial principle," asserts that it makes "no reference to South America, no assertion of any general principle"[16]—a statement that would have pained Adams keenly if he had lived to read it. Another recent writer, Mr. E. H. Tatum, properly stresses Adams's opposition to the United States' engaging in a foreign war for freedom; but he falls into the old error of overemphasizing the challenge-to-England aspect of the speech and gives a mis-

---

discover, Adams did not consult Monroe or any of his colleagues in the cabinet in preparing the address.

[15] The writer of the report (a favorable one) in the *Baltimore Federal Gazette,* quoted in the *Richmond Enquirer* of July 17, said that Adams was "dressed in a professor's gown—always worn on such occasions in the part of the country from which he came, but seldom among us, except by Episcopal clergymen."

[16] Dexter Perkins, *The Monroe Doctrine, 1823-1826* (Cambridge, Mass., 1932), p. 10.

leading account of its relation to contemporaneous public opinion. "It was spoken," he says, "to a nation whose temper had been steadily rising for years and whose hostility to England had been worked up by the bitterest of journalistic controversies." In his opinion, it "represents the complete fusion of the personal views of Adams with those of his countrymen." [17]

This interpretation of the address is not supported by the evidence. In the first place, Adams himself did not regard the speech as an expression of a rising national temper or as the culmination of a bitter journalistic controversy with England, but rather as a much needed spur to a sluggish national temper and to a journalistic controversy which, in his opinion, had not been half bitter enough on the side of the United States. According to his own statement, he was reluctant to make the speech and his reluctance was overcome only when he learned that some twenty newspapers in the United States had noticed meekly and without protest a recent statement by an English writer to the effect that certain principles of warfare which were too cruel for legitimate use against the people of a monarchy could and should be used against the people of the United States since they were mere republicans.[18] In the second place, we have Adams's own admission (which, as we shall see, is abundantly supported by other evidence) that he did not completely express the temper of the American people in regard to England, for, nearly three weeks after his speech

[17] Edward Howland Tatum, *The United States and Europe, 1815-1823* (Berkeley, Cal., 1936), p. 241, 246, 247.

[18] Adams, *Writings,* VII, 121. See also note 12, above. The offending British book was written by George R. Gleig (see Sabin, *op. cit.,* VII, 284-285, Nos. 27568, 27569), and discussed the Washington and New Orleans campaigns in the War of 1812.

was delivered, he remarked that that feature of it which
" seems to have been most extensively censured " was " the
temper towards Great Britain." [19]   And nearly a year later
he spoke of the " tempest of critical animosity " in the
United States through which the speech was still passing.[20]
Nevertheless, Adams's chief complaint in regard to the
reception accorded it by his countrymen was not that it
had been censured but that nearly all the commentators,
friendly and hostile alike, had failed to grasp what he
considered its most important point.[21]

III

What, then, is the correct interpretation of this spectacular and much misunderstood oration?   And what, in
particular, is its significance in relation to the Spanish
American problem?   The answers to these questions must
be fashioned from material drawn from many sources,
mainly from the oration itself, the circumstances under
which it was delivered, and, above all, Adams's own letters
of the next six months, which contain his own invaluable
explanation of what he meant by that Delphic utterance.

These sources show that, at least as Adams himself
understood it, his address does contain a statement of principle and does refer to Spanish America; that the address
was not so much a challenge to England as a warning to his
countrymen to be on their guard against the blandishments
of the British Delilah, who was seeking to seduce them
from their policy of isolation, and against Henry Clay and
the other champions of Spanish America and crusaders for

[19] Adams, *Writings*, VII, 121.
[20] *Ibid.*, VII, 265.   [21] *Ibid.*, VII, 199-200.

democracy, who were striving towards the same goal; and that, for all his surface bitterness towards what England had done in the past, Adams expected the fundamental ideas set forth in his address to militate more strongly against the Holy Allies than against England.

Among the fundamental ideas of the address were two principles which were only implicit in the speech but which he stated explicitly in his subsequent exegesis of it. These two principles were, first, that "colonial establishments cannot fulfil the great objects of government in the just purpose of civil society," and, second, that the United States must never become embroiled in wars between other countries, not even in defence of liberty and its own principles of government. Given these principles and the background of domestic politics and world affairs against which the address was delivered, it obviously had an important bearing upon the Spanish American problem then confronting the United States.

The essence of Adams's own explanation of his address is contained in two letters that he wrote to Robert Walsh, editor of the Philadelphia *National Gazette*, on July 10 and 27, 1821,[22] and in a letter of January 31, 1822 to Edward Everett, editor of the *North American Review*.[23] In the first letter to Walsh, after speaking of a recent article in the *Edinburgh Review* which had descanted largely upon the importance of a good understanding between the United States and Great Britain and upon the supposed duty of

[22] *Ibid.,* VII, 113-118, Adams to Walsh, July 10, 1821, and p. 127-137, Adams to Walsh, July 27, 1821. Unfortunately there is a gap in Adams's *Memoirs* from May 5 to Oct. 7, 1821, that is, during the whole period of the preparation of the address and for three months after it was delivered (*ibid.,* V, 354-355).

[23] Adams, *Writings,* VII, 197-207.

the United States to take an active part in the impending conflict between liberty and despotism in Europe, Adams wrote:

[This article] inculcates a political doctrine in my opinion of the most pernicious tendency to this country [the United States], and the more pernicious because it flatters our ambition—the doctrine that it is the duty of America to take an *active* part in the political reformation of Europe. It is most especially to that doctrine that a passage alludes in the address, which the hearers generally understood as referring only to the South American contest. The principle applies to them both, and my intention in pronouncing it was to reply to both Edinburgh and Lexington.[24]

By " Lexington," of course, Adams meant Henry Clay and, more specifically, the speech delivered at Lexington in May of this year, in which Clay had suggested that " a sort of counterpoise to the Holy Alliance should be formed in the two Americas in favor of national independence and liberty." The specific doctrine of " Edinburgh " that Adams was attacking was contained in the May 1820 number of the *Edinburgh Review*.[25] It was set forth so clearly

[24] *Ibid.*, VII, 117.

[25] *Edinburgh Review*, LXVI (1820), p. 395-431, " Dispositions of England and America." This was a review of Robert Walsh's recent book, *An Appeal from the Judgments of Great Britain* (see above, note 12). The reader may find a certain quiet amusement in noting that, as a matter of fact, the *Edinburgh Review* treated Walsh's book rather kindly and that one of its sharpest barbs was aimed at no less a person than John Quincy Adams. Walsh had objected to the *Review*'s earlier criticisms of certain American books, including Adams's *Letters on Silesia*; the *Review* now replied that its criticism was temperate and it had nothing to retract on that score (*ibid.*, p. 413-414). This contrasted rather sharply with the conciliatory tone of the article as a whole. As for Walsh's book, the *Review*'s main criticism was that he had failed to note that the party in Great Britain which was hostile to

and persuasively and our eminent secretary of state challenged it so directly and uncompromisingly that it deserves to be quoted at length.

It is impossible [said the *Edinburgh Review*] to look to the state of the Old World without seeing, or rather feeling, that there is a greater and more momentous contest impending, than ever before agitated human society. In Germany—in Spain—in France—in Italy, the principles of Reform and Liberty are visibly arraying themselves for a final struggle with the principles of Established abuse,— Legitimacy, or Tyranny,—or whatever else it is called, by its friends or enemies. . . . We conceive, that much will depend on the part that is taken by America. . . . It is as an associate or successor in the noble office of patronizing and protecting general liberty, that we now call upon America . . . to unite herself cordially with the liberal and enlightened part of the English nation, at a season when their joint efforts will in all probability be little enough to crown the good cause with success . . . [America's] *influence,* as well as her example, will be wanted in the crisis which seems to be approaching. . . .[26]

---

the United States was hostile to liberals in every other country as well, including Britain itself. It argued that in the current world crisis the United States ought not to engage in recrimination with Britain but cultivate a good understanding with it, since its sensible, educated, and liberal people would surely control it sooner or later (*ibid.,* p. 395-402). Finally, the *Review* quoted against Walsh his own pamphlet of 1810, *A Letter on the Genius and Dispositions of the French Government,* in which he had said that the American people derived the best elements of their character and institutions from the British, and that if the British were destroyed, Freedom would fall with them (*ibid.,* p. 423-425). To drive this point home, the *Review* took the word "dispositions" from the title of Walsh's pro-British pamphlet of 1810 and used it in its review of his anti-British book of 1819.

[26] *Ibid.,* p. 403-405. In his interesting chapter, "Travellers and Observers," *Cambridge History of American Literature* (4 vols., New York 1917-1921) I, 207, Lane Cooper quotes some of the irritating questions put by Sydney Smith in the *Edinburgh Review*

In other words, the *Edinburgh Review* proposed to meet the threat of the Holy Alliance by Anglo-American cooperation; Clay proposed to meet it by inter-American cooperation. Adams rejected both proposals. His own device for meeting the threat was stated in his second letter to Robert Walsh, and the passage which contains it shows that the prospective part of his speech was directed against the Holy Allies rather than England. His Independence Day address, he said, was spoken

to and for *man*, as well as to and for my own country, [though] like the famous Epistle to Posterity it may never reach its address. The *legitimacy* of colonial dominion and of *chartered* [as opposed to constitutional] liberties are questions of deeper and more overwhelming interest to other nations than to Britain at this time, and if the Holy Allies of Laybach and their subjects do not hear the sound of the trumpet upon Zion, it shall be for the want of dimensions to the instrument that bore the blast, and not of willingness in the breath that inspired it.[27]

To put the matter plainly, "the trumpet upon Zion" was Adams's Independence Day address in the House of Representatives, his blast was directed towards Europe as well as his own country, and he hoped to cripple the Holy Allies by spreading liberal propaganda among their subjects. He was not only wary of England and wedded to the non-intervention policy of Washington and of his own

---

in 1820 (see above, note 12) and says that the literary strife between England and the United States was at its height from 1814 to 1825. The same journal's article of 1821, which I have quoted in the text, seems to have escaped his attention. His statement needs some qualification in view of this and other efforts of British literati to promote a better understanding with the United States. Adams's explanation of their efforts is worth considering.

[27] Adams, *Writings*, VII, 136.

father, John Adams; he also had in an unusually high degree the calm confidence of his generation in the ultimate triumph of liberty over despotism, and less than two years later he was writing that the "rage" for making constitutions would infallibly overturn every throne in Europe.[28] So why involve the United States in the broils of Europe, why grapple with the difficulty of uniting the two Americas, which were so utterly different from each other, and why expose our own America to the perils of a foreign war, when with a little patience the same result could be obtained by sounding the trumpet upon Zion?

A valuable statement of the way in which Adams applied the principle of his address to the Spanish American question is contained in the third of the three letters mentioned above—the letter that he wrote Edward Everett on January 31, 1822, on the eve of the administration's decision to recognize the new states of Spanish America. His anti-colonial principle, he told Everett, looked forward to the downfall of the British empire in India, pointed to the principle that colonial establishments are incompatible with the political institutions of the United States, and showed the duty of the human family to abolish colonial establishments as it was already abolishing the slave trade; it also placed on new and solid ground the right of the United States' own struggle for independence, and (he continued immediately) "it settles the justice of the struggle of South America for independence, and prepares for an acknowledgment upon the principle of public law of that independence, whenever it shall be sufficiently established by the fact."[29]

[28] *Ibid.*, VII, 488.   [29] *Ibid.*, VII, 200.

It is important to note that Adams regarded his anti-colonial principle as novel.[30] To be sure, he had previously asserted the right of the United States to recognize the independence of the Spanish colonies whenever that should be established in fact; but his novel principle now provided a justification more satisfying to his legalistic mind than any he had yet discovered. In view of the state of world opinion, past and present, regarding recognition, there was real need for some such justification. The need was likely to be most strongly felt by those who, like Adams, were most fully aware of their country's debt to European culture and were accordingly respectful of what they regarded as the best European opinion. For it had long been and still was the almost unanimous opinion of European authorities that recognition of a belligerent during the course of hostilities was an unneutral act. The opposite rule supported by the United States was therefore an innovation upon the generally accepted rules of international law.[31] To many Americans, the novelty of their government's position only made it the more attractive, for they believed that in the New World everything ought to be new—new governments, new social customs, even a new spelling of the English language, and, of course, a new international law as well.[32] Even conservatives such as Adams shared this feeling to some extent; but they were more inclined

---

[30] *Ibid.* Adams spoke of his " novel " demonstration " from the moral and physical nature of man that colonial establishments cannot fulfill the great objects of government in the just purpose of civil society."

[31] Paxson stresses this in his *The Independence of the South American Republics.*

[32] Albert K. Weinberg, *The Idea of Manifest Destiny* (Baltimore, 1935, p. 29, 134-135.

to put the burden of proof on the innovation, and in the case of this particular innovation in international law, they were not disposed to apply it unless the cause was clearly just.

In these considerations lies the immediate significance of Adams's new anti-colonial principle. If, as he claimed, it put the right of the United States' own struggle for independence on new and solid ground, *a fortiori* it must strengthen the case for the independence of the Spanish Americans, whose apparent unfitness for rational liberty had left room for doubt in many minds as to their right to any liberty at all. Moreover, Adams had at last persuaded himself of something that he had hitherto been unable to perceive, namely, that an ideological bond united the cause of Spanish American independence to our own; and now for the first time he was fully convinced of the justice as well as the legality of the Spanish American cause.

IV

Here, however, he stopped; and the same letter to Everett contains a passage, explaining his anti-crusading doctrine, which should be pondered well by students of the Monroe Doctrine and by all who are interested in our foreign policy at any period. Discussing his Fourth-of-July reply to Lexington and Edinburgh, which, he said, presented a novel [33] "view of a question in political morality transcendently important to the future destiny " of

[33] Adams, *Writings*, VII, 201-202: "Had this view of a question in political morality transcendently important to the future destiny of this country ever been presented before? Certainly not to my knowledge." This follows immediately after, and refers to, the passage quoted below in the text, ending " . . . to change the very foundations of our own government from *liberty* to *power*."

the United States, Adams wrote that the Edinburgh-Lexington doctrine that the United States ought to take part in foreign conflicts between power and right

has already twice in the course of our history brought the peace and the permanent welfare of the Union into jeopardy: under Washington's administration at the early stage of the French Revolution; and under the present administration in the efforts to entangle us in the South American conflict. The address has presented a principle of *duty* directly the reverse as that which ought forever to govern the Councils of the Union, and has assigned as a reason for it the inevitable tendency of a direct interference in foreign wars, even wars for freedom, to change the very foundations of our own government from *liberty* to *power*.[34]

[34] *Ibid.*, VII, 201. In the address itself, Adams said, in discussing this point, that America (which he used in place of " the United States " throughout his address) had abstained from interference in the concerns of others even when the conflict was for principles to which she herself clung, for she knew that such interference would involve her beyond the power of extrication in wars of intrigue and ambition. " The fundamental maxims of her power," he continued, " would insensibly change from *liberty* to *force*. The frontlet upon her brow would no longer beam with the ineffable splendour of Freedom and Independence; but in its stead would soon be substituted an Imperial Diadem, flashing in false and tarnished lustre the murky radiance of dominion and power. She might become the dictatress of the world. She would be no longer the ruler of her own spirit." This passage (quoted from the *National Gazette* of July 12, 1821) illustrates the stylistic peculiarities of the address, which even the friendly Walsh described as " of too rhetorical and vehement a cast for our taste " (*ibid.*, July 16, 1821, " Mr. Adams's Address ") ; but many who criticized it on this ground believed, as Walsh did, that " the general spirit and purport of the performance possess so transcendent an interest and are eminently entitled to our sympathy and concurrence " (*ibid.*). The Boston *Columbian Centinel* of July 21, 1821, obviously referring to this part of the address, praised " the sound wisdom of that policy which refuses to stalk abroad in search of monsters to destroy them." See the following note.

A more solemn or irrevocable statement of political principle has seldom if ever been made; and Adams could hardly have found language to make its application to Spanish America more explicit. In modern parlance, what he advocated was isolationism or non-intervention. He based his advocacy of it partly on the ground that it was a traditional policy which had been justified by experience; but he gave the policy a new application and a much broader one than it had had before. That is to say, he linked it to Washington's policy of avoiding entanglement in the wars of the French Revolution; but, whereas Washington's policy, as summed up in the Farewell Address, might be interpreted as applying only to Europe (that is, as a regional policy) or at any rate as not applying to Latin America (where no independent nations existed in Washington's day), Adams erected it into a universal policy to which no exceptions were to be admitted. To make it unmistakably clear that the policy which he advocated was absolute, Adams refused to make an exception to it even in the case of peoples inhabiting the same continent as the United States and engaged in a struggle for independence and free institutions.[35]

[35] This sensational and much discussed isolationist address is briefly noted (though without specific mention of the occasion or citation of the text) in the first of Dr. Albert K. Weinberg's two recent articles on isolationism in the United States: "The Historical Meaning of the American Doctrine of Isolation," *Am. Polit. Science Rev.*, XXXIV (1940), 542 ff., and "Washington's 'Great Rule' in its Historical Evolution," in *Historiography and Urbanization* (*cit. supra*, note 3), p. 109-138. In the latter article, p. 116, 119, Dr. Weinberg considers the ideas expressed by Adams four years later and concludes, "Adams's message on the Panama Congress appeared to limit the rule [Washington's "Great Rule"] to Europe." In 1821 Adams

V

Adams's account of the reception of his Fourth-of-July address in the United States is borne out by the contemporary newspaper comment on it, and this is worth describing in some detail since it indicates the state of public opinion on the important questions relating to Latin America and Europe raised in the address.

While the address met with enthusiastic acclaim in many newspapers,[36] this was offset by a chorus of denunciation which, as one of Adams's most loyal supporters admitted, was raised by a " host of cavillers " and was heard " from Maine to Georgia." [37] Indeed, the very same part of the address that won the warmest praise on the one hand provoked the sharpest criticism on the other. This part was Adams's challenge to England, which was his retort to the taunting British question, " What has America done for mankind? " His retort was most gratifying to many of the American people, who were already deeply irritated by the smug superiority of their British cousins.

Even the temperate and discriminating Robert Walsh

---

applied the same rule to Latin America as to Europe and apparently believed that in doing so he was continuing Washington's policy. He had provided it with a new basis in " political morality " (see above, note 33), but the policy was the same. For the subsequent development of Adams's ideas, see below in chaps. 16 and 18.

[36] For example, the *Baltimore Patriot,* July 12, 1821, expected the address to rank first among the many productions of its kind, to serve as a model to future orators, and to defy even the carpings of European criticism. Other highly laudatory comments appeared in the *National Intelligencer,* July 6, and the *Columbian Centinel* (Boston), July 21 and Sept. 5. See above, note 34.

[37] *National Gazette,* Aug. 18, 1821, " The Old Leven."

applauded this part of the address; and well he might, for he himself had recently published a book which anticipated Adam's reply to the British question; and we have (and Walsh himself had) Adams's own word for it that the unsatisfactory reception that Walsh's book met with in Great Britain was the main reason for Adams's plain speaking in this address.[38] Walsh's enthusiasm, however, was shared by few of the other conservative urban newspapers of the North Atlantic and New England states—the old stronghold of Federalism. Generally speaking, their attitude is better represented by the *Boston Daily Advertiser,* which found the challenge to England not only highly improper in the mouth of an American secretary of state but " disgusting " in itself, and declared that the last two pages, beginning " Stand forth, ye champions of Britannia," were " written in such extremely bad taste, that the rest of the piece appears almost good by comparison." [39]

Criticism of the address came not only from conservative Federalist sources in the Northeast which might be suspected of an Anglophil bias. It came also from the *Richmond Enquirer,*[40] which certainly did not belong in that category, from Duane's Philadelphia *Aurora,*[41] a free-lance Republican newspaper notorious throughout the land for its Anglophobia, and from other papers in the South and West.[42] Even Duane's dislike of England was not enough

[38] See above, notes 12 and 25.

[39] *Boston Daily Advertiser,* Aug. 14, 1821, quoting and commenting on a pamphlet, *A Review of the Address by Mr. Adams.*

[40] *Richmond Enquirer,* July 17, 1821, communication " The ' Finished Oration,' " signed " A Brief Reviewer."

[41] See below, note 43.

[42] The *National Gazette* of Aug. 28, 1821, published a list to prove its assertion (which had been denied by the *Boston Daily*

to make him applaud Adams's challenge to it, which the
Aurora charged was a transparent effort to win votes in the
next presidental election by making people forget that
Adams and his father were really devoted to England.

One of the grounds on which both the *Aurora* and the
Enquirer took exception to the address shows that after all
it was not so completely misunderstood as Adams thought.
The *Enquirer* complained that in recounting what America
had done for mankind Adams had omitted some of the
most telling points that might have been made, and among
these omissions it mentioned particularly the stimulus that
the United States had given to the movement for liberty in
South America. The *Aurora,* which had long complained
bitterly of the administration's unsympathetic policy towards the Spanish American struggle for independence and
which found no promise of amendment in Adams's address,
made the sarcastic suggestion that

it might as well be made a standing rule that the annual
oration [on Independence Day] be delivered by the secretary of state, so that the policy of the administration may be
in that way apologized for, and the anniversary which derived so much eclat from the enthusiasm and admiration of
European nations, may be made use of to discourage all
future rebellions; and to inculcate the doctrine, that man,
as soon as he has no longer need for the *sympathy* or
generosity of others, shall be told, ' let every man be left
to paddle his own canoe.' [43]

Advertiser, a hostile critic of the address) that Adams's address
had been widely censured. Among the papers that had censured
it, the *Gazette* listed the New York *Commercial Advertiser* and
the *Daily Advertiser*; "one or two" Philadelphia newspapers;
the *Richmond Enquirer,* the *Alexandria* (Va.) *Gazette.* and
Charleston papers. It said that the *Washington City Gazette* of
July 21 had published a number of these hostile pieces; and in its
issue of Aug. 31 it added the Nashville (Tenn.) *Clarion* to its list.

[43] *Aurora,* July 18, 1821, editorial.

Other orations delivered and toasts offered on that day show that Adams's Fourth-of-July address was by no means a perfect expression of the temper of his countrymen, either in its subject matter or in its spirit of exultant nationalism. Two weeks later, Duane published in the Aurora a survey of the toasts offered on the Fourth, observing that they were significant of public opinion. He found that they related to three principal topics: (1) the principles of the Revolution, (2), the cause of South America, and (3) internal industry, and he declared that public interest in the second topic (the cause of South America) had not abated even under all the vicissitudes of public adversity— by which he meant the current economic depression. In regard to the general spirit that had marked the Fourth, the *Aurora* said: [44]

The national holiday has not been celebrated as generally, nor with that animation that has been usual. . . . The public suffering is, no doubt, great and unprecedented, and a state of *poverty* cannot be a state of enjoyment; but the principles of the revolution, and the day fixed for its anniversary celebration, ought to be held in such sacred reverence, that no adversity should cloud, or abuse of power bring it into indifference.

This may have been an excessively gloomy view of the recent celebrations; but an independent study of the reports of many of them confirms its substantial accuracy and shows that most of them breathed a very different spirit from that of Adams's address. Though some of the orations and toasts contained the same routine abuse of England, their main concern was with other matters. What seemed to trouble these speakers most was not the misconduct of Eng-

[44] *Ibid.*

land, past or present, but the danger of domestic discord
in the United States itself, for the bitter controversy over
the Missouri question had just sounded, in Jefferson's
phrase, like a fire bell in the night, sending a chill to the
hearts of those who loved the Union.[45] On the brighter
side, the orations stressed the democratic mission of the
United States. Said one of the orators, " I conceive our
country as about to be, under Heaven's direction, the instrument of the political and moral regeneration of the
world . . ." [46] That was a spirit which, when translated
into foreign policy, Adams deeply deplored and, in his own
Fourth-of-July oration, sought to arrest.

To sum up what has been said about this extraordinary
and sensational address, it would seem that the first of the
two principles laid down in it—the anti-colonial principle—
prepared the way for the early recognition of the new governments by unilateral action of the United States, regard-
less of the offense that this might give to the great powers
of Europe. Here, however, Adams was determined to stop,
for at the same time he let it be known by the enunciation
of his second principle—the principle of isolationism or
non-intervention—that he was firmly opposed to the in-
volvement of the United States in any foreign war, even a
war for freedom; and he explicitly applied this principle
to the war for independence then in progress in Spanish
America. Finally, the tone of his address made it seem
unlikely that the government of which he was so important
a part would continue further along the path, which it had

[45] For example, the address delivered by E. L. Finley in Baltimore: *Baltimore Patriot,* July 5, 1821.

[46] *Ibid.,* July 10, 1821, address at Abington by William H. Allen,
delegate to the Maryland legislature from Harford County.

not long since begun to explore, of cooperation with England in regard to Latin America.   And while his tone had been disagreeable to many of his fellow countrymen, the reception that his address met with gave no reason to believe that public opinion would push the administration along that path.   All the indications were that in its relations with its southern neighbors the United States would pursue an independent course.

CHAPTER THIRTEEN

RECOGNITION

I

While the American Secretary of State was getting himself in the right frame of mind for immediate and unilateral recognition of the new Spanish American states, their cause was making such rapid progress that the time was evidently at hand when prudent policy as well as justice would require the United States to recognize them. Aided by the inability of the new government of Spain to give proper support to its armies overseas and by the opposition which its colonial policy had aroused even among royalists in America, the rebels were storming the last strongholds of Spanish authority in Peru and Mexico. By the beginning of 1822 a large part of Peru was still in royalist hands, but its capital, Lima, had been taken by the liberator from the South, San Martín, who was operating from a base in already emancipated Chile, had the support of Cochrane's formidable naval force, and was soon to be joined by the liberator of the North, Bolívar.[1]

In Mexico, the success of the rebels had been even more sweeping. The conservative upper classes, which had been loyal to the Spanish government as long as it protected their privileges, revolted against it as soon as these were threatened by the otherwise tepid liberalism of the new Cortes. Appropriately led by the turncoat Agustín Iturbide, quondam scourge of the insurrectionists, it joined forces

[1] For the situation in Peru from the beginning of 1822, see Jorge Basadre, *Historia de la República del Peru* (Lima, 1939).

with the latter, gave them leadership, and immensely strengthened their cause. From that moment, its success was assured, and by the end of the year 1821 practically the whole country was in their hands and it was known in the United States that Mexico was in fact independent.[2]

That the long struggle for independence was now completed in most of the Spanish American countries and apparently on the verge of completion in the rest of them, was highly gratifying to its many sympathizers in the United States. And yet in the very moment of victory the movement was revealing tendencies which could not fail to disturb the well informed observer. The existence of some of these tendencies was already known but new evidence of their strength poured in, old hopes were disappointed, and new grounds for uneasiness were created. Even when the monarchist negotiation between the Buenos Aires government and France was exposed in 1820, many Americans hoped that the exposure would lead to a prompt and thorough reformation in that country; but in 1821 the new agent, John Murray Forbes reported to Washington that " this *Republic,* if it ever merited that name, is now in

[2] *Argus of Western America* (Frankfort, Ky.), Oct. 11, 1821, " Mexico." For the situation in Mexico at this time, see Herbert I. Priestley, *The Mexican Nation, A History* (New York, 1923), and José Vasconcelos, *Breve historia de México* (3rd ed., Mexico, 1937), p. 347-357. The latter is a work of interpretation rather than erudition. The sudden reversal was also keenly appreciated in Buenos Aires. As recently as the beginning of 1820 its people had feared that it might at any time be assailed by the grand armada assembling at Cadiz. By Sept. 19, 1821, the newspaper *El Patriota* of Buenos Aires was writing loftily that there was nothing Spain could do about the new states except recognize their independence. " Las Américas," it boasted, " exigirán cuanto quieran, y todo tendrá que otorgárselas.

the most utter darkness of despair. . . . " [3]   As for Chile, complaints were multiplying that its navy was being used by its British commander, Cochrane, to build up the interests of Britain at the expense of those of the United States on the west coast of South America.[4]   In Peru the liberator San Martín was understood to be working for the establishment of a monarchy.[5]   In Venezuela a regime which was at least nominally republican had been established; but it continued to show a strong predilection for the trade and friendship of Great Britain.[6]

Most disquieting of all was the situation in Mexico, which was becoming the main focus of American interest in Latin America.   In the earlier phases of the struggle for independence, Americans had for a time taken a keen interest in the successive uprisings led by the Mexican priests Miguel Hidalgo and José María Morelos and the Spanish adventurer Javier Mina, who had won a great deal of sympathy and had even obtained some aid in the United States; but with disheartening regularity these uprisings had been suppressed and their leaders executed.   Now with startling suddenness the cause of independence triumphed—only to confront its American sympathizers with the equally

[3] Manning, *Dip. Cor.,* I, 573.

[4] See above, chap. 10.

[5] Manning, *Dip. Cor.,* I, 573. Forbes to Adams, April 1, 1821: ". . . No one believes in the sincerity of San Martin's republican professions."

[6] See for example Manning, *Dip. Cor.,* II, 1255-1261, Charles S. Todd, confidential agent of the United States, to the Acting President of Colombia, June 1, 1823, complaining of the Colombian tariff act of Sept. 25, 1821, and other acts which seemed to show an unfriendly disposition on the part of Colombia towards the United States. See also the report on Perry's mission in chap. 10.

unexpected but less agreeable spectacle of an American monarchy in their back yard.

The reception this news met with in Kentucky illustrates the conflict of emotions with which the American people regarded the independence movement among their southern neighbors. It was a Kentuckian, Henry Clay, who had most effectively publicized the struggle of those eighteen million people to be free, and generally speaking his fellow Kentuckians shared his sympathy for it. But now that the struggle was won in Mexico, the first thought of one of the more important Kentucky newspapers, the Frankfort *Argus of Western America*,[7] was that the erection of a " new and powerful empire " on its borders was a serious thing for the United States, and above all for the West, whose weakest and most important point, Louisiana, was exposed to Mexico. " Some day," warned the *Argus,* " the sons of America will be called on to defend New Orleans against some ruler or king of Mexico, and Texas . . . will become the Flanders of America. . . . "

II

These misgivings, and others as well, were felt at Washington too. Yet on March 8, 1822, President Monroe sent a message to Congress stating that five of the Spanish American states—La Plata (i. e., Argentina), Chile, Peru,

---

[7] Issue of Oct. 11, 1821, "Mexico." It should be pointed out that in this article and also in previous issues (e. g., Dec. 7, 1820, " Treaty with Spain," and March 8, 1821, " The Florida Treaty ") the *Argus* had protested against the surrender of Texas, which it described as worth ten Floridas. Aside from military defence, the consideration that it stressed most strongly was the South's need for Texas in order to maintain the balance between free and slave states.

Colombia, and Mexico—were entitled to recognition and asking that Congress make an appropriation for that purpose.[8] The message was soberly if not drably worded and the action that it recommended was not heroic, for Monroe made it clear that recognition of the new states was not intended as a step towards war on their behalf but that, on the contrary, his administration intended to adhere to its policy of neutrality. Yet the occasion had a certain dramatic quality, for Monroe was at last proposing to end the suspense in which the policy of his government had remained ever since it first seriously considered recognition in 1811, to take the lead over all other governments in welcoming the new Spanish American states into the family of nations, and to take that step alone and in the face of European disapproval.

The Spanish minister at Washington, Joaquín de Anduaga, realizing the importance of Monroe's modestly garbed message, filed a strong protest against it.[9] Though perhaps too vehement, his protest was well argued from the point of view of the older international law; but Adams, who had thought out his novel anti-colonial principle in good time to serve him in this emergency, replied

[8] The message is in Richardson, *Messages and Papers of the Presidents*, II, 116-118. For the general subject, see William Spence Robertson, " The Recognition of the Hispanic American Nations by the United States," *Hispanic Am. Hist. Rev.*, I (1918), 239-269; Griffin, *The United States and the Disruption of the Spanish Empire*, chap. IX, " Recognition of Spanish American Independence." Although the latter seems to me to overemphasize the legal aspects of the question, I have found it very helpful. Adams's rôle in the matter of recognition is magnified in Dexter Perkins, " John Quincy Adams " (Bemis, ed., *American Secretaries of State*, vol. 4), p. 53-55.

[9] Moore, *Digest of International Law*, I, 86-87.

loftily that in recognizing the independence of the former
Spanish colonies, the United States was only complying
with " an obligation of duty of the highest order." [10]

Reasoning on a somewhat lower level, Monroe explained
his recognition message in a letter to James Madison.[11]

The time had certainly arrived [he wrote], when it became
our duty to recognize, provided it was intended, to maintain friendly relations with them [the Spanish American
countries] in future, and not to suffer them, under a feeling of resentment towards us and the artful practices of
the European powers, to become the dupes of their policy.
I was aware, that the recognition was not without its dangers, but as either course had its dangers, I thought it best to
expose ourselves after the accession of Mexico, and of Peru,
to such as were incident to a generous and liberal policy.

That Monroe had in mind the maintenance of friendly
commercial as well as political relations with the new
Spanish American states is hardly open to question. First
among the dangers to which he alluded was the familiar
danger that the European powers would be " much excited
by the measure [recognition], from its bearing on *legitimacy*," and that if too much " éclat " were given to the
measure, it might be

inferred that our object is to organize these new Governments, against the Governments of Europe and thus do
the provinces more harm than good, by organizing Europe
against them, if not against ourselves. The object is to
serve the provinces essentially, by promoting the independence of all, with the establishment of free Republican Governments, and with that view, to obtain their recognition by

[10] *Ibid.*, I, 88.

[11] Monroe Papers, LC, Monroe to Madison, May 10, 1822, copy.
Printed in Monroe, *Writings*, VI, 284-291.

other powers, as soon as possible. If we alarm these powers, we may defeat our own objects.[12]

These explanations of recognition by the person immediately responsible for the measure possess great interest for the student. They illustrate once more the way in which national interest and republican zeal were intertwined in American policy. They also show how cautiously and with what anxious glances towards the great monarchies of Europe the United States developed its policy towards Latin America. Perhaps it was bold to take the step at all,[13] but Monroe was eager to keep it from seeming bold, and the spirit in which he took the step was no bolder than that of any man who, when forced to choose between two evils, chooses the lesser of them.

The latter point was stated explicitly by Monroe, and it should be emphasized. He had recommended recognition not of his own free will and not merely because the new states deserved recognition, but mainly because, if the United States withheld recognition any longer, its " friendly relations " with them might suffer and they might become the " dupes " of European policy.

There was only too much reason for Monroe's fears on this score. He knew that the Spanish Americans were already resentful towards the United States because it had so long refused them aid as well as recognition, because of the Florida treaty, because of the injury which they thought

[12] Monroe Papers, LC, Monroe to (Jonathan) Russell, March 12, 1822, " Private," copy. Printed in Monroe, *Writings*, VI, 211-212. See *ibid.*, p. 212, note 1. Russell was chairman of the House Committee on Foreign Relations, to which this part of the message was referred. See below, note 20.

[13] Perkins, *Monroe Doctrine, 1823-1826*, p. 50-51.

the American navy had inflicted upon their cause, and for other reasons. Monroe knew, too, that many of them were already the "dupes" of European policy and that their number was probably increasing; that monarchical sentiment was strong among them and that British trade was preferred by many of them. The most recent, immediate, and forcible reminder of this danger had just been provided by Mexico, which was not only establishing a monarchy but also looking for a European prince to occupy the throne. But the most eloquent expression of Spanish American coolness towards the United States was the fact that, whereas there had formerly been a number of Spanish American representatives in the United States, now there was only one; [14] and that one, Manuel Torres, the representative of Colombia, had remained because he was permanently domiciled in Philadelphia, where he had been living for more than a quarter of a century.

As Monroe conceived it, his Spanish American policy at this stage was much closer to Jefferson's policy of 1808 than it was to the policy underlying the famous pronouncement which he himself was to make in December 1823. He was continuing Jefferson's effort to exclude European influence from America; but in contrast to his warning to Europe of 1823, his present policy was shaped for the express purpose of giving as little alarm as possible to the European powers—above all, they must not think that it was "our object" to organize the new governments against

[14] In his letter of March 12 to Russell cited above, note 12, Monroe remarked that Torres (who was living in Philadelphia) was believed to be the chargé d'affaires of Colombia, that a minister from Mexico was expected, and that there was no representative of any grade from Buenos Aires or Chile (or, he might have added, Peru) at this time.

them, or, as Monroe might have expressed it a year and a half later, to set the American system against the European system.

Since it was also the purpose of Monroe in recognizing the new states at this time to promote " the establishment of free republican governments " among them, it is not a little remarkable that the first of the new governments to which he proposed to send a minister, and perhaps the only one, he said,[15] to which a minister would be sent for some time to come, was precisely the government of Mexico. This was remarkable partly because Mexico was the newest and least known of the new states and consequently the one whose fitness for recognition was most debatable. It was remarkable still more because one of the few things known about the new regime in Mexico was that it was monarchical.

This paradox may seem puzzling. In reality, it only helps to clarify Monroe's policy. In the first place, it furnishes additional evidence that national interest, not political idealism, was the mainspring of that policy: however much Monroe might desire to see republican governments established in the new states, his first purpose was to maintain " friendly relations " with them, whether they were republics or monarchies. In the second place, it suggests that he was all the more willing to tolerate monarchies among them at the outset because he believed that

[15] In his letter to Russell cited above, note 12, Monroe, after remarking that a minister from Mexico was expected, went on to say that it might perhaps be proper to send one to Mexico and to that place only, for the present. At this as at other important periods in the development of Latin American policy, there is a gap in Adams's diary. In this case the hiatus extends from Jan. 7 to April 1, 1822 (Adams, *Memoirs,* V, 484). For relevant entries after the latter date, see *ibid.,* V, 491-493, and VI, 111.

ultimately they would all become republican. Even when the Mexicans, unable to find a European prince for their throne, made Agustín Iturbide their emperor, Monroe did not lose heart. " The prospect is discouraging for the present," he wrote on August 25, 1822, " but I have no doubt that he [Iturbide] will find it necessary to change his course & relinquish all pretention to hereditary power, or be finally driven from it, & perhaps from the country." [16]

The same issue was to be raised again in 1824 in the case of Brazil,[17] which also had a monarchical government. Again the administration at Washington refused to let the form of government stand in the way of recognition. And again it showed its confidence that any tendency on the part of the Latin Americans to run after the false gods of monarchy would be corrected by the free genius of America. Thus, even Adams wrote in May 1823 that he expected the Montevideo question to embroil republican Buenos Aires and monarchical Brazil in the near future; " and then will soon be seen," he continued triumphantly, " that the republican hemisphere will endure neither emperor nor king upon its shores." [18]

To be sure, this expression of mystical faith in the republican destiny of Latin America does not sound a bit like John Quincy Adams and was probably dictated by Monroe. If that was the case, the fact gives added support to the present interpretation of American policy, for it reminds us of another fact which has been too often overlooked but which seems hardly open to serious question, namely, that the administration's Latin American policy was Monroe's

[16] Monroe Papers, LC, Monroe to Madison, Aug. 25, 1822.
[17] See below, chap. 18.
[18] Adams, *Writings*, VII, 451-452.

rather than Adams's. As we shall see, the latter admitted in 1823 that on all important questions of foreign policy he made it a rule to yield his judgment to that of his chief;[19] and it seems clear that in the Latin American field, as in the other fields of foreign policy, the decisive voice in the administration was at all times that of Monroe. The prudence which restrained the unfolding of that policy was as much Monroe's as Adams's; within the bounds set by prudence, the policy was shaped mainly by Monroe's greater eagerness to promote American interests abroad, his greater faith in the republican destiny of Latin America, and his firmer conviction that the promotion of the interests of the United States and the liberation of Latin America were complementary aspects of one great historical development.

III

When Monroe at last prepared to recognize the first of the new Spanish American states, he still listened attentively to the voice of prudence. It was this that led him to suggest that for the present the United States should send a minister to Mexico alone. For a mission to Mexico would be the least likely to alarm Europe, since its government was monarchical, and it was the only one of the states that bordered upon the United States, and also the only one that was then sending a minister to Washington. It was also prudence that led Monroe to seek the sanction of Congress before he recognized the new states. The constitution and precedents set since Washington's second administration would have justified his recognizing them at his own discretion; but since the act was highly important on many

[19] See below, chaps. 14 and 16.

accounts and might even involve the United States in war
(though he did not intend it to do so), he was unwilling
to bear the whole responsibility for it.[20]

The importance that he attached to the support of Congress is shown by a letter that he wrote to Robert Selden
Garnett, a member of Congress from Virginia, on March
29, 1822.[21] The letter is also interesting because the charge
had often been made in the past few years that the executive
department tried to influence the votes of members of
Congress; and in his letter to Garnett, Monroe did just
that.   On the previous day, the former had cast the only
negative vote against the appropriation bill which was to
signify Congressional support of recognition. Now Monroe
wrote him asking him to change his vote, since the question
was one that should be carried in Congress by a unanimous
vote.

The report of it to the world [wrote Monroe] will produce a very strong effect everywhere, particularly with
Spain, and the provinces; with the former, by announcing,
that if she resents it, that we shall be united in meeting her

[20] The unanimous report of the House Committee on Foreign
Relations is in *Annals Cong.*, 17 Cong., 1 Sess., p. 1314-1321.
Five thousand copies of it were ordered to be printed for the use
of members of the House, in addition to the usual number (*ibid.*,
p. 1314). For Poinsett's opinion of it, see below, note 30.

[21] Monroe Papers, LC, Monroe to Garnett, March 29, 1822,
autograph letter, signed. Printed in Monroe, *Writings*, VI, 214-
215. See *ibid.*, p. 215, note 1. Garnett came of a prominent Virginia family, was a graduate of the College of New Jersey (Princeton), and represented his district in Congress from 1817 to 1827.
His wife was Olympia Charlotte, daughter of the French general
Jean Pierre DeGouges. See article "Robert Selden Garnett" in
Biographical Directory of the American Congress, 1774-1927
(Washington 1928), p. 1002, where he is described as a Democrat,
and the article on his son of the same name in DAB, VII, 158.

resentment; with the latter, by shewing the deep interest which the whole American people, take in their welfare. For you to stand, alone, against that sentiment will deprive your country of that advantage, and without the possibility of any indemnity. The incident, in my opinion, affords you an excellent opportunity of conciliating the public opinion, as well as of Congress towards you, which may be done by stating in your place, that you had thought, on great reflection, that the measure was hazardous, but seeing that your country had taken its step, you were resolved to go with it, and therefore changed your vote.

Unmoved by Monroe's suggestion that, having shown his " firmness and independence " by voting against the recognition bill, he ought now to show his " moderation and conciliation " by voting for it, Garnett persisted in his contumacy; but he stood almost alone. Though some delay was caused in the Senate [22] by the Spanish minister's pro-

[22] This delay illustrates the point, made in earlier chapters, that the Spanish American question cut across party lines. The Senators who were mainly responsible for the delay were the ultra-Federalist Rufus King (New York) and the ultra-Republican Nathaniel Macon (North Carolina). They proposed an amendment to the effect that the appropriation for ministers to the new states should not be used until the President was fully satisfied that this would not interrupt peaceful relations with other powers (*Annals Cong.*, 17 Cong., 1 Sess., p. 430, 431). For King's earlier approval of Monroe's policy of watchful waiting, see above, chap. 7, note 43. On March 17, 1822, he wrote, " On the whole the time seems to have arrived for this act [recognition] on our part; and somehow I feel glad that it has been done before any *nation* had given us the example. England must, I think, follow our example, and even France cannot hold back. The pride of Spain may be hurt, but she will not take any step to show it " (*Life and Correspondence of Rufus King*, VI, 462, King to C. Gore, March 17, 1822). His subsequent change of front was due to the receipt of news that the Spanish Cortes had passed a strong resolution against recognition (Adams, *Memoirs*, V, 489).

test and by rumors to the effect that Spain was about to come to terms with the revolutionists, the bill was passed with little opposition and on May 4, 1822, it received the President's signature.[23]

The measure was warmly applauded both at home and in liberal circles abroad. Writing to Monroe from Paris in July 1822 Lafayette said that "the acknowledgment of South American independence by the U. S. has been to us [French liberals], and particularly to me, a great cause of joy," and added the hope that, with this encouragement from the United States, the South Americans would put aside the follies of protectorship and imported monarchy and would follow "the more enlightened advices of experienced republicanism in the North."[24]

In contrast to Lafayette's romantic liberalism, the British minister at Washington, Stratford Canning, took the news with a dash of cynicism. Just after he heard that the new states were to be recognized, he met Adams and said, "So Mr. Adams, you are going to make honest men of them?" "Yes, Sir," was the answer. "We proposed to your government to join us some time ago, but they would

[23] For the progress of the bill through Congress, see the preceding note and *Annals Cong.*, 17 Cong., 1 Sess., p. 430, 431, 825, 1395, 1404.

[24] Monroe Papers, NYPL, Lafayette to Monroe, July 13, 1822. As was to be expected, Monroe's recognition message made a very different impression at the allied courts. The British Ambassador at St. Petersburg reported that it was considered there "in its true light of an attempt to strike a great and dangerous political blow" (Webster, *Britain,* II, 298). The Spanish government made it the occasion of a canvas of the attitude of the great powers towards the Spanish American question (*ibid.,* II, 298). For the British government's reply, see *ibid.,* II, 387-389. See also Robertson, *France and Latin-American Independence,* p. 207, 210.

not, and now we shall see whether you will be content to *follow* us." [25]

In the press of the United States, as in Congress, recognition won general support, even in quarters where the opposition to it had been strongest only a year previously. For instance, the Philadelphia *National Gazette* admitted—rather grudgingly, to be sure—that " To the measure of recognition, there will be, we apprehend, but little opposition. . . . No harm, we think, can result [from it], under the present circumstances of the world." [26] The *North American Review* now persuaded itself that this once distasteful measure might actually prove beneficial to the United States by promoting its trade with Spanish America.[27]

How are we to explain the sudden popularity of a measure to which there had until recently been such strong, well-reasoned, and deepseated opposition? Perhaps the best explanation lies in the fact that the measure was now supported by the administration. It had solidly established its reputation for prudence in its conduct of Spanish American relations, and its approval was therefore for many people the best guaranty of the wisdom of recognition. Added to this was the fact that the rapid progress of the independence movement had deprived the opponents of

[25] Stanley Lane-Poole, *Life of Stratford Canning* (2 vols., London, 1888), I, 309.

[26] *National Gazette,* March 11, 1822, editorial on Monroe's message of March 8.

[27] *North American Review,* XIV (1822), 420-446, review article on Monroe's message of March 8, 1822, with running title, " Mexico." The conclusion (p. 446) was that the independence of Spanish America would " give a spring and animation to commerce scarcely, if at all inferior, to that which resulted from the original discovery of this religion [*sc.* region]."

recognition of one of their most telling arguments against it. But perhaps the best explanation of the change of sentiment is to be found in the " present circumstances of the world " alluded to by the *National Gazette*. Here the most important point was the position of Spain in relation both to the great European powers and to America.

This had an obvious bearing upon the question of recognition. Early in 1821 Spain's position was rather uncertain in both aspects; by the spring of 1822 it had been clearly defined, and the change strengthened the hands of the American champions of recognition. In the interval, the constitutional government of Spain had been branded as a pariah by the great powers of the Continent. They might even attack it as they had already attacked the liberal government of Naples, and they would certainly not help it reestablish its authority in America.

At the same time, efforts at reconciliation between Spain and Spanish America had failed. Even the colonies hitherto loyal and still nominally obedient to Spain, such as Cuba, were actually paying little attention to orders from Madrid; and some of the Cuban people were beginning to talk again about independence and were sending agents to discuss the matter in the more congenial atmosphere of the United States.[28] Consequently, if Spain should decide to make recognition of the continental American governments by the United States a cause of war, there would be much less danger than two or three years previously that such a war would wipe out the profitable trade of the United States with Cuba and the other loyal colonies of Spanish America.

[28] Portell Vilá, *Historia de Cuba*, I, 197, describes this situation in detail. For further discussion of relations between Cuban revolutionists and the United States, see below, chap. 14.

In short, in the "present circumstances of the world," the perils of recognition that had alarmed so many Americans in 1817 and 1818 and even as recently as the beginning of 1821 had by this time greatly diminished.

Economic interest was still an important ingredient of American sympathy for Latin American independence. Whether it had increased within the past year and whether this increase contributed to the change of sentiment regarding recognition, it would be hard to say. At any rate, there are some indications that the continuance of the economic depression and the loss of other markets made some Americans appreciate more keenly the value of the Latin American market, both actual and potential. It was this line of thought that now enabled even the *North American Review* to take some pleasure in the decision to recognize the Latin American states,[29] although only a year earlier this same journal had barely conceded that, in case the United States should espouse their cause, the Spanish Americans might "possibly extend some privileges to our trade, if the fear of the English, which bringeth a snare, did not prevent this."

The debate on the appropriation bill in Congress contains evidence to the same effect. Especially notable was the speech by Joel Poinsett,[30] who, although he had opposed

[29] See above, note 27.

[30] *Annals Cong.*, 17 Cong., 1 Sess., p. 1395-1402. After stressing the natural wealth of Spanish America, Poinsett said that independence would raise its standard of living and "produce a demand for all the manufactures of this country [the United States], and for all the objects of trade" (*ibid.*, p. 1400). He described the report on recognition by the Committee on Foreign Relations as "clear and convincing" and "highly honorable to the committee," but questioned their assurance that Spain would now consent to the independence of its colonies (*ibid.*, p. 1401).

recognition at an earlier period,[31] nevertheless strongly advocated it now on the ground that it would give American commerce a much needed stimulus by opening new channels for it in Spanish America. His support of recognition on this ground is all the more significant because he stated at the same time that he expected Spain to regard recognition as a hostile act; and his picture of the commercial possibilities of Spanish America was impressive because he had served the United States for several years in Buenos Aires and Chile.

The hopeful view expressed by Poinsett was by no means universally accepted. In some quarters, it was believed that the business possibilities of Latin America had already been sufficiently explored to prove that they were extremely limited, and that recognition was not likely to improve them. "We do not see the probability of any particular benefit to [the Spanish Americans] or to the United States, from the act," sighed the *National Gazette* (March 11, 1822). The *New York American* [32] saw only a faint ray of hope. The manufacturers of the United States, it said, were incompetent to supply the South American market as yet, though some day they would do so; this country therefore should admit European goods for re-exportation to South America in American ships without the payment of transit duties, thus giving the United States a larger share of the carrying trade. "In this way, it is, and in this alone," said the *American,* "that our commerce can materially be benefited by the independence of the South American nations."

[31] In 1818. At a still earlier period, on the occasion of his mission to South America beginning in 1810, he had warmly supported the independence movement.

[32] Quoted in the *National Gazette,* March 14, 1822.

IV

With the endorsement of Congress and the support of articulate public opinion, Monroe proceeded to carry out his recognition policy. There was at first a disposition in the Cabinet to await the arrival of representatives from the new states before sending representatives to them.[33] Consequently, the first state to be recognized was Colombia, whose chargé d'affaires, Manuel Torres, was, as already stated, the only accredited agent of a Spanish American power in the United States at this time.

For Torres, this signal honor was a fitting reward for the long, devoted, and effective service that he had rendered to the cause of Spanish American independence. It came to him just in time. His health was breaking rapidly, and illness forced one postponement of his formal presentation to the President. The second time he was barely able to keep his appointment; and when at last the Secretary of State escorted him to his audience with the President (June 19), an audience which symbolized the admission of the first Latin American state into the family of nations, Torres was already at death's door. Weak and overcome with emotion, he could hardly speak. Monroe said a few kind words to him; but he and Adams, too, were deeply affected, and the interview was soon over.[34]

Torres dragged himself back to Philadelphia, and from that place on July 15, less than a month later, William Duane wrote Monroe a hasty note informing him that on

[33] As late as Nov. 28, 1822, the question of principle had not yet been settled. See Adams, *Memoirs,* VI, 110, and note 15, above.

[34] Adams, *Memoirs,* VI, 23, 27-28.

the same day had died Manuel Torres, " the friend of all America, of humanity, and virtue." [35]   From what we know of Torres, the eulogy was deserved.[36] Without wishing to detract from it, but rather to suggest one of its connotations, we should note that the central theme of his many contributions to Duane's *Aurora* and his voluminous notes to Adams was the development of commerce between the United States and Spanish America, and that the most important work that we have from his pen is entitled *An Exposition of the Commerce of Spanish America.*

The second of the new states to be recognized was Mexico. On second thought, Monroe had sent Joel Poinsett on a mission of inquiry to that country [37] similar to those sent

[35] Monroe Papers, NYPL, Duane to Monroe, July 15, 1822.

[36] He was highly esteemed in Philadelphia where he had spent nearly half his life. An obituary in *Poulson's American Daily Advertiser*, July 17, 1822, reported the death of Torres, " Minister " of Colombia, at Hamilton Ville, near Philadelphia, on July 15, and described him as being in the fifty-eighth year of his age. Another obituary in *ibid.*, July 18, reported his burial in St. Mary's churchyard, Philadelphia, with military honors. Officers of the United States army and navy took part in the " numerous and brilliant " military procession. The " first mourner " was " Com. O'Daniels, in the Colombian service," who was " accompanied by his officers." The funeral was also attended by the city authorities, the members of the bar, and " a large concourse " of citizens. " The shipping in the harbour had their colours half-mast during the day." " This spontaneous tribute to talent, patriotism, and personal worth," commented the *Advertiser*, " will be duly appreciated by his countrymen."

[37] Rippy, *Poinsett*, p. 90-103, chap. VII, " Condemning an American Monarch," discusses this mission, mainly on the basis of Poinsett's *Notes on Mexico, Made in the Autumn of 1822* (Philadelphia, 1824; London, 1825). Early in 1824 Poinsett wrote: " My book has been delayed much longer, than I had anticipated; the fault is to be divided between the Printer and myself; for I rewrote it this winter, and you will hardly know

to Buenos Aires and Chile in 1817; but without waiting for his report Monroe recognized the Mexican imperial government by formally receiving its minister on December 12, 1822, very shortly after his arrival at Washington.[38] Apparently the fear that the Mexicans might become the " dupes " of European—particularly British and French— policy again goes far to explain Monroe's course.

When Poinsett returned from Mexico and found that its imperial government had already been accorded recognition, he wrote Monroe a letter in which he said politely but firmly that he disapproved of what had been done. The letter is all the more interesting because it registered Poinsett's refusal to accept the administration's fiction that recognition is a mere photographic process for recording accomplished fact, and expressed his own more realistic view that recognition is an instrument of policy for shaping future events. European critics had already expressed this view in relation to the external struggle of the Spanish Americans for independence from Spain. Poinsett now applied it to the domestic conflict within one of the Spanish American countries and showed how recognition had made

the historical part or indeed the narrative, for I have interwoven a good deal of information on the Agriculture, Commerce, &c. Mr. Walsh [probably Robert Walsh of the *National Gazette*], who urged me to publish, says the book will be out next week " (Gilpin Papers, HSP, Poinsett Correspondence, 1794-1839, Poinsett to Joseph Johnson, May 4, 1824).

[38] Isidro Fabela, *Precursores de la diplomacia mejicana* (Mexico, 1926), p. 153. The Mexican minister was José Manuel Bermúdez Zozaya. Though well received officially, he sensed the general hostility at Washington to the imperial regime in Mexico and wrote his government a despatch (Dec. 26, 1822) bitterly denouncing the United States for its arrogance and territorial ambitions (*ibid.*, p. 154).

the United States a party to the factional conflict in that country and had aided the wrong faction. Discussing the strong opposition in Mexico to Iturbide's regime, Poinsett wrote to Monroe:

I am disposed to believe Iturbide cannot maintain himself many months on the throne. At all events it becomes an important question whether the United States ought to sanction his usurpation and recognize as legitimate a government erected & supported by violence and oppression. By recognizing the Emperor during the present contest we give him an advantage over the republican party. We take part against the majority of the nation; for I hazard nothing in asserting that the people of Mexico were not more unanimous for the establishment of their Independence than they are for a liberal & constitutional form of government.[39]

If any advantage had been gained by Monroe's precipitate haste in recognizing the imperial government (which, as Poinsett had prophesied, was overthrown almost immediately) it would have been lost by the long delay of the United States in sending a minister to Mexico—a delay which offended the Mexicans and was caused by political intrigues in the United States connected with the coming presidential election of 1824. Andrew Jackson, one of the likeliest candidates, was offered the appointment, but refused it, partly on the ground that Iturbide's government was monarchical. His declination was subsequently used to forward his presidential campaign.[40]

[39] Poinsett Papers, HSP, Poinsett to Monroe, Jan. (day missing), 1823, endorsed on back, "Copy of a letter addressed to President Monroe upon my return from Mexico in 1823."

[40] William R. Manning, *Early Diplomatic Relations between the United States and Mexico* (Baltimore, 1913), p. 31; *Correspondence of Andrew Jackson*, III, 187-189, 191-193. On Jan. 8, 1824, a number of citizens at Washington presented an address

In recognizing the other three of the group of five states named in Monroe's recognition message, the United States took the initiative by sending ministers to them without awaiting the arrival of their representatives. In this way were recognized Buenos Aires and Chile (1823) and Peru (1826). Central America (1824), which had just broken away from Mexico, and Brazil (1824), another imperial government, were the only other Latin American states recognized before 1830.[41] The case of Brazil, already mentioned briefly, deserves special notice; but it arose later than that of the first Spanish American states and stood on somewhat different ground, and it will be discussed separately in a later chapter.

V

The final commitment of the United States to the recognition of Spanish American independence marks so important a stage in the history of its Latin American policy that it is interesting to see how the situation appeared to the two principal architects of that policy, Adams and Monroe, just after the commitment was made. As for Adams, his satisfaction seems to have been unalloyed and to have been considerably enhanced by the reflection that his own department had so many more achievements to its credit than the

---

to Jackson in which they said: " You refused to accept an Executive appointment of high importance and trust because you disdained the tyrant, who, (thank God, but for a short period,) ruled with a rod of iron the country to which you were appointed." This address and Jackson's reply, which was in the same strain, were published in an item without caption in the *National Gazette,* Jan. 16, 1824.

[41] Robertson, " The Recognition of the Hispanic American Nations," *loc. cit.,* p. 261-269. A detailed study of " The Recognition of the South American Nations " by Bernice B. Tompkins, Stanford University, was recently reported to be in progress.

departments headed by his two rivals for the presidential succession—the Treasury, under William H. Crawford, and the War Department, under John C. Calhoun. "Of the public history of Mr. Monroe's administration," he wrote in October 1822, "all that will be worth telling to posterity hitherto has been transacted through the Department of State." By way of illustration, he mentioned among other things the transcontinental treaty with Spain, by which the United States had acquired Florida and extended its territory to the Pacific, and "the whole course of policy with regard to South America," which, he remarked, had been under the immediate management of the State Department. On the other hand, as for the departments presided over by Crawford and Calhoun, "an army reduced to a peace establishment, and a Treasury reduced to loans in profound peace, form hitherto the only history of those two Departments under Mr. Monroe." [42]

It was with much less than complete satisfaction that Monroe himself viewed the situation, and one of the many things that troubled him was what had happened to the military establishment. Even the approval of his recognition policy by Congress did little to appease his discontent. Only a few days after he signed the bill making the necessary appropriation for that purpose, he wrote Madison:

I have never known such a state of things, as has existed here, during the late session, nor have I personally ever experienced so much embarrassment, and mortification. Where there is an open contest with a foreign enemy, or with an internal party, in which you are supported by first principles, the course is plain, and you have something to cheer and animate you to action. But we are now blessed with peace, and the success of the late war, has overwhelmed the federal party, so that there is no division of that kind,

[42] Adams, *Writings,* VII, 316-317.

to rally any persons together, in support of the administration.[43]

At least one of the main sources of his personal " embarrassment and mortification " was indicated in a letter that he wrote to Andrew Jackson three weeks later:

I was exposed in the course of the last session [he said], to much embarrassment. The lessons of the late war seem to have been forgotten, and the efforts, since made to put the country in a better state of defense, for another [war], happen when it may, have been tortur'd into crimes, and those who have been most active, treated as the greatest criminals.[44]

These two letters are valuable not only to the biographer of Monroe, but also, since he was the chief policy-maker of his administration, to the historian of foreign policy. They reveal Monroe's state of mind at the moment when, having completed one stage in the development of his policy towards Latin America and Europe by the unilateral recognition of Spanish American independence, he was contemplating his course of action in the next stage. They show that he was suffering keenly from the feeling that his administration lacked popular support and that he attributed this lack to the absence of any great and pressing issue, foreign or domestic, to focus public sentiment and to cheer the administration and animate it to action.

Where was such a focus, such encouragement, to be found? These letters do not provide a direct answer to the question; but they suggest it. One of the two alternatives considered by Monroe—a contest with an internal

[43] Monroe Papers, LC, Monroe to Madison, May 10, 1820, copy. This is the letter cited above, note 11, in which Monroe explained his decision to recognize the new states at this time.

[44] Monroe Papers, LC, Monroe to Jackson, May 30, 1822.

party—was out of the question, for the Federalist party had disintegrated and the prospect was that no effective opposition party would rise to take its place in the near future. This prospect, it is important to note, pleased Monroe. In his letter to Madison from which we have just quoted, he went on to say: " Surely our government may get on, and prosper without the existence of parties. I have always considered, their existence, the curse of the country. . ."

However laudable this sentiment may have been, it reduced him to his only alternative, namely " an open contest with a foreign power." That did not necessarily mean war; on the contrary, he was doubtless sincere in describing peace as a blessing and he doubtless wished to maintain it. Moreover, even if he had ever thought of provoking a foreign war, he would have been forced to give up the idea in view of the strong opposition that, as he told Jackson, had just encountered his efforts to " put the country in a better state of defense." But many foreign quarrels do not lead to war, and on his own showing such a quarrel offered Monroe his only means of escape from the embarrassing and mortifying situation in which he found himself and his administration in 1822.

It is not implied that Monroe deliberately sought a foreign quarrel; but it is suggested that he was in a frame of mind to welcome one, provided it were a contest in which he would be " supported by first principles " but which he could reasonably hope to wage without going to war, and through which he might rally the American people behind his administration. In 1823 a kind fate provided him with a contest that met these specifications as fully and precisely as if Monroe himself had planned it, and with the aid of his advisers he made brilliant use of the opportunity.

CHAPTER FOURTEEN

"PEACE IN OUR TIME"

I

In April 1823 the Bourbon king of France sent an army into Spain to destroy the constitutional government called into being by the Riego revolution of 1820 and restore the absolute authority of his royal cousin, Ferdinand VII. The invasion followed shortly after the Allies' Congress of Verona and hard on the heels of the Spanish government's rejection of their demand that Ferdinand VII be restored to absolute power.[1] Consequently France appeared to be the agent of the Holy Allies in Spain as Austria had recently been their agent in striking down the liberal regimes established in Piedmont and Naples.

Liberals everywhere were deeply alarmed, for the French invasion of Spain seemed to prove the truth of current reports to the effect that the Holy Alliance had adopted a grand plan of destroying liberalism everywhere by armed intervention. In the United States and the rest of America liberals were doubly alarmed because, while the Holy Allies were willing to tolerate the denatured liberalism of a

[1] Robertson, *France and Latin-American Independence,* p. 259. For the Congress of Verona, with special reference to France and the Spanish American question, see *ibid.,* chap. VIII. The Protocols of the Congress are in Webster, *Britain,* II, 79-83. The false treaty of Verona is discussed in Perkins, *Monroe Doctrine, 1823-1826,* p. 52-53, and T. R. Schellenberg, "The Secret Treaty of Verona: a Newspaper Forgery," *Jour. Mod. Hist.,* VII (1935), 280-291. The "treaty" apparently originated in the London *Morning Chronicle.* The activities of this newspaper in relation to Latin America are discussed in chap. 6.

charter granted by a king of his own free will, they were determined to suppress any constitution (such as that of Spain) imposed upon a ruler by his people and they openly condemned the right of revolution on which every independent government in America (except perhaps that of Brazil) was based. An attack on liberalism in Spain seemed to presage an attack on liberalism in Spanish America; and it was easy to believe that the United States itself would be the next victim.

In the United States some comfort was found in the fact that the French invasion of Spain had widened the rift between Great Britain and the Continental powers. Fearing that France would try to obtain undue advantages for herself in Spain and the colonies, Britain opposed the intervention,[2] and this fact was known in Washington even before it was known that the invasion had actually begun. As Adams phrased it at the time, England had " now for the first time . . . seceded from the political system of the European alliance." [3] It was good to know that the crack long since perceived in the solid European front had now widened into a definite rupture; but this knowledge gave rather cold comfort to the authorities at Washington for they realized that, in view of the circumstances under which the rupture had occurred, it might hasten European intervention in America by precipitating a scramble among the great powers for the remnants of the Spanish empire. Moreover, even Adams admitted that the United States might be dragged into the European conflict itself.[4]

[2] Webster, op. cit., I, 18-19.
[3] Adams, Writings, VII, 369-370, instructions to Hugh Nelson, April 20, 1823.
[4] Ibid., VII, 371.

As he described it at this time, the situation was a perplexing one for his government. On the one hand, the United States could never be indifferent to the cause of those struggling for civil liberty and independence; on the other hand, its first duty was to maintain peace and (as he had said in his spectacular address of July 4, 1821) never to fight in any cause but its own. Yet if, as then seemed likely, England should go to war with France over the latter's invasion of Spain, there was great reason to apprehend that the resulting maritime war would soon involve the United States. As for Spanish America, said Adams, it had " not yet been sufficiently disclosed " whether " the purposes of France, or of her continental allies, extend to the subjugation of the remaining ultramarine possesions of Spain "; but the only reasons for doubting whether France would invade Cuba were " the probable incompetency of the French maritime force to effect the conquest and the probability that its accomplishment would be resisted by Great Britain." [5]   A few weeks later he noted another danger, which had long given him serious concern but which loomed larger than ever now that Spanish American independence seemed assured, namely, the " tampering " of the European powers with " internal parties " in Spanish America in an effort to " turn to their own account the issue which they could not control." British agents had been " feeling their way for exclusive privileges of commerce "; Portugal had been " chaffering for a fragment of territory "—Montevideo and its hinterland; and France, with Portuguese connivance, had been " darkly plotting a monarchy [at Buenos Aires] for the Prince of Lucca, which she seems to have considered

[5] *Ibid.,* VII, 374.

as a sort of compromise between political legitimacy and bastardy, to be purified by crossing a breed of the Bourbon and Braganza blood." [6]

II

At the beginning of the French invasion, however, the greatest threat to Spanish America, in Adams's opinion, came from England and the threat was focussed on Cuba. England had already avowed her determination to defend Portugal against the application of the principles on which the French invasion of Spain was justified; [7] and English opinion was so strongly opposed to France and English interests were so deeply involved in the Spanish conflict that it was " scarcely possible that the neutrality of Great Britain should be long maintained." Adams therefore concluded that Britain would probably soon enter the war on the side of Spain, but would do so only for a price, and the price would be the acquisition of Cuba and Puerto Rico. [8]

Its commercial and strategic importance made Cuba a valuable prize for any nation and Adams noted several indications that Britain was interested in it. During the past two years there had been many rumors that the transfer had already beeen consummated; confidential information from the French government hinted that Britain had even

[6] *Ibid.*, VII, 453.

[7] *Ibid.*, VII, 376; Harold Temperley, *The Foreign Policy of Canning, 1822-1827* (London, 1925), p. 83-84.

[8] Adams, *Writings*, VII, 376. On March 30, 1823, Calhoun wrote Andrew Jackson linking the Cuban question with the " mighty contest " impending in Europe, " commenced there not for commerce, or territory, but to crush any vestige of liberty on the continent." Calhoun dwelt on English designs on Cuba and the importance of the Island to the United States (*Correspondence of Andrew Jackson*, III, 193-194).

offered Gibraltar in exchange for Cuba; and the acquisition of Florida by the United States and the establishment of the independence of Mexico gave the British additional reasons for wishing to acquire the island. The British government had recently given France a disclaimer of any designs on Spanish territory; but Adams discounted this because it applied to peace time, and now the situation had been completely changed by the French invasion of Spain. The British could easily find a pretext for occupying Cuba on behalf of Spain, and, Adams remarked, " It is not necessary to point out the numerous contingencies by which the transition from temporary and fiduciary occupation to a permanent and proprietary possession may be effected." [9]

Since Adams believed that Cuba had " an importance in the sum of our national interests, with which that of no other foreign territory can be compared, and little inferior to that which binds the different members of this Union together," he naturally believed that the United States could not afford to let Cuba fall into British hands; and his view was shared by the rest of the administration.[10] Accordingly, on April 28, 1823, he solemnly instructed the American minister to Spain:

The question both of our right and our power to prevent it [the acquisition of Cuba by England], if necessary, by force, already obtrudes itself upon our councils, and the administration is called upon, in performance of its duties to the nation, at least to use all the means within its competency to guard against and forfend it. [11]

[9] Adams, *Writings,* VII, 378-379.

[10] Adams, *Memoirs,* VI, 112, 138. See the following note.

[11] Adams, *Writings,* VII, 379. Adams, however, did not believe that the United States either would or could " prevent by war the British from obtaining possession of Cuba, if they attempt to take it " (Adams, *Memoirs,* VI, 138).

As Adams noted, rumors of British designs on Cuba had been circulated in the United States for a long time past, and in September 1822 its status—with reference to its independence, its acquisition by England or the United States, or its continuance under Spanish control—had been the subject of long discussions in Monroe's cabinet. The discussions were based on a proposal made by a certain Bernabé Sánchez of Havana, who claimed to be the agent of an important group of revolutionists in Cuba, that the island should be admitted into the Union. Considering how little information the cabinet had about the agent and his principals, it gave a surprising amount of attention to his proposal. It appears that Sánchez brought a letter of introduction to Peter S. Duponceaux of Philadelphia from a French officer at Havanna who had served at New Orleans in the War of 1812, that Duponceaux introduced him to General John Mason of Georgetown, Virginia, and that Mason put him in touch with the administration.[12]

In the first cabinet discussion [13] Calhoun showed himself eager to annex Cuba ultimately and said that Jefferson shared his desire and had told him in 1820 that the United States ought to take the island even at the cost of war with England; but he felt that, since the United States was not at

[12] *Ibid.*, VI, 69-70. See also Portell Vilá, *Historia de Cuba,* I, 213-216. Caesar A. Rodney, Joel Poinsett, Capt. James Biddle of the *Macedonian,* and Michael Hogan and other United States consular and commercial agents in Cuba all contributed to building up the administration's interest in Cuba and its fear of English designs on Cuba in the period 1820-1823. See the interesting account of this subject in *ibid.*, I, 198-232. See also James Morton Callahan, " Cuba and Anglo-American Relations." American Historical Association Report (1897) p. 198-199.

[13] Adams, *Memoirs,* VI, 70-72, Cabinet meeting on Sept. 27, 1822.

present prepared to fight and its object was to gain time, the Cubans should be advised to adhere to their present connection with Spain. In his opinon, the annexation of Cuba by the United States would avert two dangers; first, its acquisition by England; and second, a revolt ending in domination of the island by Negroes. He suggested that a secret message on the subject be sent to Congress at its next session; but Adams objected that secrecy was out of the question, and so was war with England, which could only result in that power's acquisition of Cuba. In the end, it was agreed merely to tell Sánchez that the United States could not encourage the revolution; and perhaps the most important result of the discussions was to clarify the minds of the cabinet members about Cuba and to prepare them for the crisis that developed over it in 1823. Adams's own conclusion from the discussion was that the affair was one " of deeper importance and greater magnitude than had occurred since the establishment of our independence." [14]

Three months after this cabinet discussion took place and four months before the French invasion of Spain began, a fresh warning about British designs on Cuba was sent from Paris by the trusted Gallatin. In a despatch dated January 6, 1823, Gallatin wrote in regard to the sending of a British fleet to stamp out piracy in and around Cuba:

There is nothing very alarming either in this or in the nature of the armament sent by Great Britain to the West Indies. But various reports are afloat respecting her ultimate views; and without attaching to them more weight than they deserve, I think that the possibility of her trying to obtain possession of Cuba deserves consideration. Such an acquisition would compensate the expenses of war, and might

[14] *Ibid.*, VI, 72-73, Cabinet meeting on Sept. 30, 1822.

conquer the reluctance heretofore evinced by the British
ministry to depart from the pacific system adopted since the
year 1815 or to break altogether the ties which unite her
with the continental powers.[15]

The war alluded to in this passage was the war in which
England might become involved with France if the latter
should invade Spain—a possibility that was already being
seriously considered; and Gallatin added that the Spanish
government might be willing to cede Cuba to England in
return for its aid against France and the Holy Alliance.
Received in the State Department on March 11, 1823,
Gallatin's despatch brought home forcibly to the administration the fact that the impending invasion of Spain was
full of danger as well as promise to the New World; that
while the schism it was likely to cause among the powers
of Europe might aid America by weakening them, it was
just as likely to injure America by precipitating a scramble
among them for possession of the remnants of the Spanish
empire; that the main focus of danger was in Cuba and that
the chief threat to Cuba—and therefore to the United States,

[15] National Archives, SD, Despatches from France, Gallatin to
Adams, Jan. 6, 1823, No. 242, endorsed, " Rec'd 11 March."
For the mutual suspicions of England and the United States in
regard to Cuba in 1822-1823, see Rippy, *Rivalry*, p. 78-84. In his
cabinet memorandum of Nov. 15, 1822, Canning wrote of the
danger of the United States' obtaining Cuba: " It may be questioned whether any blow, that could be struck by any foreign
power in any part of the world would have a more sensible effect
on the interests of this country or the reputation of its government." The acquisition of Cuba would give the United States
possession of " both shores of the Channel through which our
Jamaica trade must pass " and in time of war would bring about
the " total ruin of a great portion of the West Indian interests "
of Britain (Webster, *Britain*, II, 393-394).

which was vitally interested in Cuba—came from Great Britain.

The gravity of this situation was understood not only in administration circles, which had the benefit of confidential advices from Gallatin and its other agents abroad; it was also widely and earnestly discussed in the newspapers. For example, a writer in the Boston *Columbian Centinel* of March 12, 1823, saw in the reported British naval expedition to the West Indies a " cover to a scheme on the carpet, *for the transfer of Cuba to England."* Ten days later the editor of the same newspaper wrote in a more skeptical mood that the rumor of the transfer " appears to have been one of the numerous speculations of which the newspaper soil of France and England is more prolific, than that of *Cuba* is of sugar and coffee." [16]   On April 2, however, the *Centinel* published another communication in which the writer took the British threat to Cuba quite seriously and urged that the United States itself should annex the island in order to forestall England. To the commentators who were objecting that the constitution did not authorize its annexation, he replied that if this was true, the constitution should be amended to provide the authority, for the United States simply could not tolerate the acquisition of Cuba by Great Britain. In time of war, the latter, using Havana as a naval base, could play havoc with American shipping, and even in time of peace the now valuable commerce of the United States with the island would suffer serious injury, and " the greatest sufferers " would be " the New-England states."

Nothwithstanding our dislike to colonies [concluded the writer], let us look to the consequences of their falling into

[16] *Columbian Centinel,* March 22, 1823, " Island of Cuba."

other hands; particularly our great commercial rival [England], who now nearly surrounds us by sea and land. And Cuba is an important link in the chain, that would make our commerce tributary to her own.[17]

III

This sense of the gravity of the situation in Europe and its importance to the United States was fully shared by President Monroe. Early in April he was approached by George W. Erving, former minister of the United States to Spain, who expressed a desire to revisit Europe, " impelled by the urgency of the present crisis, which is perhaps not less important to us, than to those who are the immediate partners in it." Monroe naturally welcomed the suggestion, for he needed all the information he could get about the situation in Europe, and the reports of a semi-official observer who was familiar with the Spanish background might be particularly valuable. Accordingly, on April 14 he made the following suggestion to Erving, apparently on his own initiative:

It has occurred to me, that letters from me to our ministers abroad, or from the Secretary of State, intimating that you leave the country in the confidence of the Government . . . might be agreeable to you, and perhaps useful.[18]

Erving carried out his plan of revisiting Europe and, as we shall see, sent home reports that may have helped to shape the administration's policy in the greater crisis that developed at the end of the year. If his reports did influence the administration, their influence was exerted through

[17] *Ibid.*, April 2, 1823, " Cuba." This long communication was continued in the issues of April 12 and 16.

[18] Monroe Papers, LC, Monroe to Erving, April 14, 1823.

Monroe and through Erving's paticular friend in the cabinet, Secretary of the Treasury Crawford, and not through Adams, who apparently did not relish Erving's semi-official commission and had no very high opinion of Erving himself.[19]

To the preparations for meeting the crisis through the regular diplomatic establishment Adams addressed himself with great zeal in the latter part of April and May. Important among these preparations was the drafting of instructions for a new minister to Spain and for the first ministers from the United States to Buenos Aires and Colombia.

The main purpose of the instructions to the new minister to Spain, Hugh Nelson, was to discharge the administration's duty, as Adams expressed it,[20] " to use all the means within its competency to guard against and forfend " the acquisition of Cuba by Great Britain. In these instructions, which fill more than fifty printed pages,[21] Adams wrote at length about the apprehension caused in the United States by the French invasion of Spain, which he described as " ere this probably commenced " and as likely to be immediately if only temporarily successful, and about the far-reaching changes that it might bring about in Spanish America. He then entered upon a detailed discussion of the Cuban question, at the close of which he instructed Nelson to inform the Spanish government that the United States could not permit the transfer of Cuba to England, since that would infringe upon the rights of the Cubans and would injure vitally important

[19] Adams, *Memoirs*, VI, 196. Erving appears to have sought an appointment as successor to Gallatin at Paris (*ibid.*, VI, 139, 160).

[20] See above, note 11.

[21] In Adams, *Writings*, VII, 369-421, dated April 28, 1823.

interests of the United States. He added the solemn warning, which Nelson was to communicate to the Spanish government, that if the cession should be made despite this protest, the United States would regard the Cuban people as fully justified in declaring their independence and itself as equally justified in aiding them to obtain it. Then, blandly assuming that the cession would not be made, he devoted the remaining four-fifths of these voluminous instructions to a remonstrance against the depredations on United States commerce in the West Indies and the Caribbean, for which he held Spain largely responsible, and to an explanation of the use of the United States navy in defence of its commerce, concluding with a renewal of the request, already made so many times in the past generation, that American consuls be admitted to Cuba and Puerto Rico.

In view of the urgency of the crisis to which these instructions related and the importance that Adams attached to them, their principal features require some comment. In the first place, they were based not upon the general policy of the United States in relation to Spanish America but upon its particular policy in relation to a special region, centering in Cuba.[22] In the second place, in these instructions Adams did not undertake to apply the universal anticolonial principle so strongly and uncompromisingly stated in his address of July 4, 1821.[21] On the contrary, their chief purpose was to maintain the existing status of Cuba, as a colonial possession of Spain, for an indefinite period. In the third place, while the instructions did not assert the general principle that no European colony in America

[22] On this point and the place of these instructions in the evolution of the Monroe Doctrine, see Perkins, op. cit., 54-55.

[23] See above, chap. 12.

should be transferred from its present owner to another power, the principle was adumbrated by the warning that the United States would not permit the transfer of Cuba to England, since that was the only case in which the United States government then believed that such a transfer was likely to be attempted and, if attempted, was likely to succeed. In the fourth place, the instructions help us to understand how the threat from Europe appeared to the authorities at Washington and how they planned to meet it. While the threat from France and the other powers was recognized as a possibility, it was completely overshadowed by the threat from Great Britain, and this was directed mainly at Cuba and was to be met first by diplomacy and, if diplomacy failed, by force. Finally, in announcing the determination of the United States to resist the threat from Europe at this most likely point, the instructions justified its position not so much by an appeal to any ideal principles of right or justice or even of the separation of the European and American spheres, as, in the last analysis, on the ground of national interest— an interest arising mainly from the " transcendent " commercial and strategic importance of Cuba to the United States.

The crisis in Spain also accelerated the completion of arrangements for sending the first ministers from the United States to Buenos Aires and Colombia—the first, indeed, to any independent Latin American country [24]—and their instructions were drawn up with a view to guarding against

[24] The United States had had a minister at Rio de Janeiro most of the time since 1810, and Brazil had been a kingdom since 1815, but it had remained bound to Portugal by the personal union of the crown. When its independence was declared in 1822 the United States did not have a minister at Rio, and it had not yet recognized the new government.

certain aspects of the threat from Europe which were quite properly ignored in the instructions to the new minister to Spain. It will be recalled that in 1822, when the administration committed itself to the recognition of the new Spanish American states, Monroe wished to avoid giving " a distinguished éclat to the recognition " lest it provoke the European powers by its implied condemnation of their principle of legitimacy. At first he thought of sending a minister to only one of the new states, Mexico, " for the present " and of making it a general rule to send a minister —or other diplomatic agent—to a new government only after one had been received from it at Washington.

Although a year had passed since Congress and the Executive Department committed themselves in principle to recognition, no ministers would have been sent to South America even now if the principles of 1822 had been adhered to strictly. Torres had been received as the envoy of Colombia, but he had died almost immediately after his reception and had never been replaced; and neither Buenos Aires nor any of the other South American governments had yet sent a duly accredited diplomatic representative to Washington.[25] As for the attitude of the European powers, Monroe had every reason to believe that they were more aggressively legitimist now than when he had sought to placate them by retarding the process of recognition; but that very fact had now become a reason for hastening the process. The aggressiveness of the Neo-Holy Alliance [26]

[25] As noted above, chap. 13, a Mexican minister had been sent to Washington and formally received by Monroe in December 1822.

[26] Temperley applied this term to the Holy Alliance after the Congress of Troppau, where the principle of intervention was adopted by Austria, Russia and Prussia. France for a time adhered

made it less likely than ever that he could gain anything by further efforts to placate them on this score, and more likely than ever that they would make a vigorous effort to extend their influence in Spanish America. They might resort to force for this purpose, or, more probably, persuasion. In the latter case, as Monroe realized, there was a real danger that they might succeed in making many of the Spanish Americans, in his phrase, the dupes of European intrigue. In either case, it was important for the United States to have diplomatic representatives on the spot to give the Spanish Americans wholesome advice and keep their own government informed of developments.

IV

Adams's next task was to draw up the instructions for the ministers whom the administration was on the point of sending to Buenos Aires and Colombia. Setting to work on them at once, he completed the instructions for Caesar A. Rodney (Buenos Aires) on May 17 and those for Richard C. Anderson (Colombia) ten days later.[27] The interest of these instructions lies mainly in the fact, first, that, taken together with the instructions recently prepared for the minister to Spain, they help define the European

---

to it, but Britain refused to do so. See Temperley, *Foreign Policy of Canning,* p. 16-17, 22-24.

[27] The instructions to Hugh Nelson were dated April 28, 1823. On May 10 Adams sent Monroe the draft of the instructions to Rodney and said that he would now prepare the instructions to Anderson and would incorporate in the latter a review of the Spanish American policy of the United States, as suggested by Monroe in a note of April 30. The instructions to Rodney were put in final form on May 17; those to Anderson, on May 27. See Adams, *Writings,* VII, 422-424, 441.

menace to America as it was conceived by the United States government at the beginning of this crisis; and second, that they illuminate the government's attitude and policy towards Latin America as these were developing under the pressure of the menace from Europe. For the latter purpose the instructions to Anderson [28] are particularly important, since Adams inserted in them, at Monroe's suggestion, a review of the conduct of the United States towards the struggle for independence in Spanish America and since he drafted them with an eye to the future as well as the past and as a guide to the policy of the United States towards not merely Colombia but the whole of Spanish America. As he himself expressed it, the instructions to Anderson were designed to lay " the foundations of the future intercourse political and commercial between the United States and the new Spanish American nations." [29]

The instructions to Rodney and Anderson strengthen the impression, created by the instructions to Hugh Nelson, that the administration saw no immediate danger of an armed attack from Europe on continental Spanish America, and they contain no proposal for military cooperation between the United States and Spanish America to repel such an attack. Indeed, Adams went so far as to say that, while the first result of the French invasion of Spain might be to draw England to Spain's side, the ultimate result would probably be to promote the recognition of Spanish American independence by England as well as by the rest of the powers.

So far as the continent was concerned, the danger was

[28] They are printed in *ibid.*, VII, 441-487. The instructions to Rodney are in *ibid.*, VII, 424-441.
[29] *Ibid.*, VII, 423.

conceived of as lying in Spanish America itself and as arising from the strong inclination of many of its people
towards European connections and institutions—an inclination which, it was feared, the European powers would now
redouble their efforts to exploit. Thus, Adams cautioned
Rodney that monarchist sentiment was strong in Buenos
Aires, probably stronger there than anywhere else in Spanish
America, and that England enjoyed a preferred position in
the foreign trade of that important port. Even Bernardino
Rivadavia, the head of the government, who was reputedly
a good republican, had recently given evidence of a strong
leaning towards Europe; and Adams emphasized the fact
that the triumph of European influence at Buenos Aires
would be prejudicial to the United States both politically
and commercially.

He was less disturbed about Colombia than about Buenos
Aires on this score and, commenting on the activities of
Gaspard Mollien, an undercover agent of France who had
recently tried to stir up ill feeling in Colombia against the
United States, he remarked that "while the French government pursues its new career in the affairs of the world
with such designs, it is to be hoped the development of
them will be entrusted to such performers " as Mollien.[30]
Yet even in this case he found occasion to protest against
the maintenance of a European tie of what he regarded as
a very dangerous kind, namely, the establishment of the

[30] *Ibid.,* VII, 472-473. Mollien's mission is briefly described in
Robertson, *op. cit.,* p. 222, 315, 318. After his return to France
Mollien published a book, *Voyage dans la république de Colombie
en 1823* (2 vols., Paris, 1824; English translation, London, 1824).
M. S. Sánchez, *Bibliografía venezolanista,* says that it contains
many errors and confusions of fact but that some of his generalizations about the character and customs of the people are valuable.

Roman Catholic Church as the state church of Colombia
on terms that gave no adequate protection to other sects.
Though this pained Adams, it did not greatly surprise him.
As he remarked in a passage in his draft of the instructions
to Anderson, the people of Colombia were a heterogeneous
mass of creoles, Indians, and Negro slaves, who had been
subdued in mind and body by centuries of Spanish oppression, and "there was no spirit of freedom pervading any
part of this population, no common principle of reason. . . . " [31] Though this passage was prudently deleted in
the final revision, the latter retained an interesting homily
on the relations between religious freedom and the American system which was drawn up for the edification of
the Colombian government. Freedom of conscience, said
Adams,

is in truth an essential part of the system of American
independence. *Civil, political, commercial* and *religious*
liberty are but various modifications of one great principle
founded in the unalienable rights of human nature, and
before the universal application of which, the colonial
domination of Europe over the American hemisphere has
fallen, and is crumbling into dust. Civil liberty *can* be
established on no foundation of human reason which will
not at the same time demonstrate the *right* to religious
freedom; and the control of a Bishop of Rome and a
conclave of cardinals on the banks of the Tiber over the
freedom of action of American nations on the shores of the
Orinoco, or the Magdalena, is as incompatible with their
independence, as the arbitrary mandate of a Spanish monarch and a Council of the Indies at Madrid.[32]

[31] Adams, *Writings,* VII, 442.
[32] *Ibid.,* VII, 466. This is reminiscent of the passage from
Everett's *North American Review* article of 1821 quoted in chap.
11, in which he said that "The various tyrannies, political, feudal,
and ecclesiastical of Europe, are the auspices under which these
[Latin American] provinces have grown up."

This passage illustrates an important point which has already been suggested: that while at this stage the United States government did not seriously apprehend the use of force by the European powers against continental Spanish America and (as a natural consequence) did not seek to enlist the cooperation of the Spanish American governments in resisting such an attack, it did have a lively and well defined fear of the susceptibility of Spanish America to European influence and it did try to enlist the cooperation of the Spanish American governments in checking that influence. This was formidable because it was exercised through three important channels—political, economic, and ecclesiastical—in each of which it was favored by the European predilections of strong elements in Spanish America. Several specific instances were cited by Adams in these instructions—in the case of Buenos Aires, monarchist intrigues with France and commercial preference for Great Britain; in the case of Colombia, ecclesiastical ties with Rome—and many other instances of the same kind could easily have been added if Adams had extended his survey to include Mexico, Brazil, and the rest of Latin America.

If Latin American independence had been firmly established, these connections with Europe might have been regarded with equanimity as normal manifestations of friendly intercourse between civilized nations; but that was not the case. Given the weakness of the new-born states, the strength and aggressiveness of the European powers and the anti-republican character that their program was assuming, there was only too much reason to fear that unless the further progress of European influence were checked, Latin America would be only nominally independent and would for all practical purposes relapse into a condition of colonial servitude to Europe. Thus, by peaceful penetration and without firing a shot, the European powers could defeat the purpose of the United States, which Jefferson and his cabinet had formulated as far back as 1808, of excluding the political and commercial influence of Europe from the New World.

Assuming that Latin America could be kept from relapsing into the grasp of Europe, what plans did the United States government have at this time for the new order that it wished to establish in America? Adams's instructions to Rodney and Anderson contain some interesting information on this point. To Rodney, he said:

With relation to *Europe,* there is perceived to be only one object, in which the interests and wishes of the United States can be the same as those of the South American nations, and that is that they should all be governed by republican institutions, politically and commercially independent of Europe.[33]

In other words, Adams looked forward (apparently with perfect equanimity) to the establishment of a new order which would be characterized by a high degree of diversity. From other passages in the instructions, we know that he hoped to persuade the new states to adopt the United States' system of commercial reciprocity and its definition of neutral rights, and to enlist their cooperation in suppressing piracy; but the only two points of cardinal importance on which uniformity was expected (or, at any rate, desired) were republicanism and independence of Europe, both politically and commercially. Even in regard to these two points some important reservations must be noted. As for republicanism, the desire of the United States to see this

[33] Adams, *Writings,* VII, 428-429.

established in Latin America had not prevented it from recognizing the imperial government of Mexico in 1822, and was not to prevent it from recognizing the imperial government of Brazil in 1824. In the light of these facts, we may conclude that the desire to see republican institutions established in Latin America had not hardened into a policy of promoting their establishment at all costs, and that even on this point the United States was fully prepared to tolerate a wide divergence from its own system on the part of the new nations.

In stating that it was the interest and desire of the United States to make all the nations of America politically and commercially independent of Europe, Adams not only reaffirmed in substance the Jeffersonian policy of 1808 but also expressed the idea of the "American system," which, when he drafted these instructions, was receiving widespread attention and support in Latin America as well as in the United States.[34] It is important to note, however, that in these instructions the idea received only a very limited endorsement, which was strongly tinged with skepticism. For example, Adams had just learned through John Murray Forbes of the arrival at Buenos Aires of Joaquín Mosquera y Arboleda, minister plenipotentiary of Colombia, with the general object of engaging the independent governments of Spanish America to "settle a general system of *American policy* in relation to Europe."[35] This news was the imme-

[34] Joseph Byrne Lockey, *Pan Americanism, Its Beginnings* (New York, 1920), p. 292-303.

[35] Adams, *Writings,* VII, 427. Mosquera's mission was not successful, and did not leave a favorable impression in government circles at Buenos Aires. Writing early in 1825 the latter government spoke of a proposal regarding boundaries which it had made to Mosquera and which he had rejected, "acaso solo porque no

diate occasion for Adams's observations on the idea of an American system.

The idea was not new, of course, nor was Adams's skepticism about it. Implicit in the Jeffersonian policy of 1808, widely discussed in later years, and publicized by Clay in 1820 and 1821, it was proposed to Adams in the former year by the Portuguese-Brazilian minister, Abbe Corrêa; but Adams's rather scornful comment on it at the time was, " As to an American system, we [the United States] have it—we constitute the whole of it." [36] Since then several developments had occurred which seemed to entitle the idea to more respectful consideration. The rapid progress of the independence movement in the past two years had made it seem more practicable; and the increasing aggressiveness of the European powers in support of their system made many Americans feel that, as Clay had suggested at Lexington in 1821,[37] the nations of the New World ought to draw closer to one another in defence of their own system.

Even so, the instructions to Rodney and Anderson gave

---

entramos en la idea colombiana de formar un Congress general de todos los nuevos Estados á uso de Europa." It spoke of the project as " un paso tan vano " and said that in Colombia " parece que la guerra no ha dado mucho tiempo para dedicarse á la política " (AGN, BA, S1-A2-A4, No. 10 (the Minister of Foreign Relations) to Carlos Alvear, Jan. 15, 1825, draft). There seems to have been a good deal of truth in the suggestion that the idea of an American system was borrowed from the idea of the concert of Europe.

[36] Adams, *Memoirs,* V, 176, entry for Sept. 19, 1820. Adams continued: ". . . there is no community of interests between North and South America. Mr. Torres and Bolivar and O'Higgins talk about an American system as much as the Abbé Correa, but there is no basis for any such system."

[37] See above, chap. 12.

little encouragement to the proposal to implement the system through political cooperation, whether in the form of a Spanish American confederation or a larger confederation embracing the United States as well as Spanish America. Rodney was instructed that

To any confederation of Spanish American provinces for that end [republicanism and independence of Europe], the United States would yield their approbation and cordial good wishes. If more should be asked of them, the proposition will be received and considered in a friendly spirit, and with a due sense of its importance.[38]

In his instructions to Anderson, which were drawn up with unusual care, Adams discussed this subject even more guardedly and less sympathetically.

Floating, undigested purposes of this great American confederation [he wrote] have been for some time fermenting in the imaginations of many speculative statesmen, nor is the idea to be disdainfully rejected, because its magnitude may appal the understanding of politicians accustomed to the more minute but more complicated machinery of a contracted political standard.[39]

Again he endorsed the proposed confederation of Spanish American states for the purpose of establishing complete independence and representative government; and again he further qualified this limited endorsement by saying that the United States would have to have more specific information before it could agree to take part in a meeting which it had been proposed to call for the purpose of assimilating the policies of South America to those of North America.

Adams's coolness to the idea of inter-American political cooperation was no doubt due in part to his respect for the

[38] Adams, *Writings*, VII, 429.
[39] *Ibid.*, VII, 471-472.

isolationist tradition of his government. It was also due
to the fact that he still retained some of his earlier prejudices against the Latin American people, as is evidenced
by his statement, made with special reference to Colombia,
that the Spanish American people were a heterogeneous
mass of creoles, Indians, and Negro slaves, who were subdued in mind and body by centuries of Spanish tyranny and
who had " no spirit of freedom " and " no common principle of reason." Nevertheless, this familiar note of skepticism was sounded with less assurance than in the past;
and other passages in the instructions to Rodney and Anderson suggest that Adams regarded the Latin Americans more
sympathetically, and the common destiny of America more
hopefully, than he had ever done before. Thus, while he
still differentiated between the American Revolution, which
was declared " in defence of our *liberties*," and the Spanish
American movement for independence, which was forced
upon the people of Spanish America by external events, he
now conceded that as a general movement in human affairs,
the latter movement was perhaps a development of the
principles of the American Revolution.[40]

Whatever may be said of the logical validity or historical
accuracy of Adams's new position, it is important because
it marks another advance along the path of sympathy with
the Spanish American cause, comparable to the one that he
had made in his Independence Day address in 1821. Even
more striking are the passages which show his sense of the
destiny of America. In one of these he wrote: [41]

The emancipation of the South American continent opens
up to the whole race of man prospects of futurity, in which

[40] *Ibid.*, VII, 442-443, 466.   [41] *Ibid.*, VII, 486.

this Union will be called in the discharge of its duties to itself and to unnumbered ages of posterity to take a conspicuous and leading part. It invokes all that is precious in hope and all that is desirable in existence to the countless millions of our fellow creatures, which in the progressive revolutions of time this hemisphere is destined to rear and to maintain. That the fabric of our social connections with our southern neighbors may rise in the lapse of years with a grandeur and harmony of proportions corresponding with the magnificence of the means, placed by providence in our power and in that of our descendants, its foundations must be laid in principles of politics and of morals new and distasteful to the thrones and dominations of the elder world, but co-extensive with the surface of the globe and lasting as the changes of time.

V

Greater hopefulness about the future of Latin America was justified by recent developments in its two largest nations, Mexico and Brazil. In Mexico the monarchy established in 1822 was overturned in 1823 and those in power promptly set about creating a republic in its place.[42] In Brazil the independent imperial government established in 1822 still maintained itself; but at this time it was regarded as a decidedly liberal government which had little in common with the autocratic system of the Holy Allies.[43]

[42] Priestley, *The Mexican Nation*, p. 256, 259-264. This development was all the more warmly applauded in the United States because it was believed that the republicans in Mexico were taking the United States as their model. For a discussion of this question, with special reference to the Mexican Constitution of 1824, see J. Lloyd Mecham, "The Origin of Federalism in Mexico," *Hispanic Am. Hist. Rev.*, XVIII (1938), 164-182. This article was also published in *The Constitution Reconsidered*, ed. Conyers Read (New York, 1938), p. 349-365.

[43] In support of his request for the recognition of the imperial government of Brazil by the United States, the Brazilian agent

More important still, it was believed in the United States that the republican element in Brazil, which had given evidence of its strength in the Pernambuco revolt of 1817, was now gaining ground, and in May 1823 Adams wrote that if the controversy over Montevideo should embroil Brazil in war with Buenos Aires, as seemed probable, it would " soon be seen that the republican hemisphere will endure neither emperor nor king upon its shores." [44]

In one of the most perfect anti-climaxes ever composed by a former professor of rhetoric, Adams then continued: " Of this mighty movement in human affairs, mightier far than that of the downfall of the Roman Empire, the United States may continue to be, as they have been hitherto, the tranquil but deeply attentive spectators." The historian will leave the anti-climax to professors of rhetoric and will dwell upon the tranquillity of the American Secretary of State in the face of this incomparably mighty movement which was taking place next door. A brief review of what has been said above regarding the crisis of the first half of 1823 as it appeared to the authorities at Washington may help explain both the strange tranquillity of Adams and also the measure by which he sought to meet the crisis in which America had been involved by the French invasion of Spain. At first sight, that measure, too, may seem

---

Rebello stressed the fact that the Emperor was ruling by the consent of his people and with the cooperation of " a legislative Body in two chambers," like that of the United States (Manning, *Dip. Cor.*, II, 788). As Webster remarks (*op. cit.*, I, 57), " The title of Emperor derived from the Napoleonic example. . . . On the one hand, it recognized an elective element, such as Napoleon had always taken care to secure by plébiscite. In one sense the Empire in Brazil was a protest against legitimacy."

[44] Adams, *Writings*, VII, 471.

strange, for it was nothing more or less than a communication to the imperial government of Russia.

As we have seen, Adams believed at this time that, so far as direct intervention was concerned, the threat from Europe was confined mainly to Cuba and that it came from two quarters: first, from France, which, after overrunning Spain, might try to seize Cuba by force of arms; second, from England, which might obtain Cuba either by outright cession from Spain or else under cover of a "temporary" occupation, nominally in the interest of Spain, which would later be converted into permanent possession. The threat to Cuba seemed immediate and very real. For protection against it, Adams relied mainly upon the welcome rift that had recently appeared between England on the one hand and the continental powers (especially France) on the other. As for the measures that the United States itself was to take to forestall the danger, these were for the moment confined to diplomatic representations—notably, the instructions to the new minister to Spain, Hugh Nelson, to warn the Spanish government against letting England obtain even a temporary foothold in Cuba; but these were accompanied by the intimation that the United States would, if necessary, resort to war and the revolutionizing of Cuba to prevent the island from passing into the hands of either England or France.

The threat to continental America was of a very different kind. It was hardly, if at all, a threat of direct intervention by armed force, but rather one of peaceful penetration through diplomatic, commercial, financial, and ecclesiastical channels, which would leave Latin America nominally independent but would actually reabsorb it into the European system. The danger was all the greater because peaceful penetration was so intangible, because it was operating simultaneously at so many points along the whole vast Latin American front, and, above all, because there existed among the Latin American people themselves so strong a predilection for Europe.

Consequently, what the situation called for was not military mobilization (since a military attack was not anticipated) but moral mobilization—in other words, a bold and convincing assertion of American principles, another sounding of the trumpet upon Zion, which would rally the republican forces of America against Europe and against the dupes of European intrigue in America itself. The occasion that Adams seized for this purpose was the current controversy with Russia. There is nothing surprizing about this, for we know that in Adams's opinion the occasion and place of a trumpet blast were far less important than the blast itself. It will be recalled that in 1821, when he was preparing a blast for the ears of the peoples of Europe, the occasion that he chose for it was a Fourth of July celebration in which he addressed himself immediately to a Washington audience and spoke not in his official capacity but as a private citizen. Now his blast was contained in a communication to the Russian Tsar; but both he and Monroe had every expectation that the communication would be published in the United States, and from the United States it would be circulated in Latin America, where its tonic effect was so much needed.

The controversy with Russia was not a new one. It had been going on since the latter part of 1822 and it related to an ukase issued in 1821 in which Russia undertook to exclude the ships of other nations from a zone running down the coast of Alaska and extending out to sea a distance of one hundred Italian miles.[45]   The immediate objections of the United States to this ukase were, first, that it involved a claim to exclusive trading rights in territory which was also claimed by the United States, and second, that the Russian claim to jurisdiction over the high seas, far beyond the territorial waters of Alaska, was contrary to international law.

In the background, there were two other objections of a still more serious character.   For one thing, Adams, developing the non-colonization principle asserted in his Independence Day address of 1821, was prepared to challenge the right of Russia to any colonial possessions at all in America.[46]   For another (and this was the most important consideration of all), the once-liberal Tsar was now working hand in glove with the other members of his Holy Alliance who were endeavoring to suppress the revolutionary principle—the principle on which the United States and the new nations of Latin America were founded—and for that purpose had intervened in the affairs of independent nations to put down revolutionary governments; and to Adams the ukase of 1821 seemed of a piece with the Tsar's other recent acts " bearing hard upon the liberties of nations."   Consequently, in the summer of 1823 he prepared a counterblast against the ukase which he intended to serve as " a warning voice to check and control " the Tsar.[47]

---

[45] Perkins, *op. cit.*, p. 7-8. For the extent of the United States' territorial claim at this time, see *ibid.*, p. 22, note 47.

[46] *Ibid.*, p. 10-11.

[47] Adams, *Memoirs,* VI, 170. Entry for Aug. 9, 1823.

VI

The counterblast was contained in the instructions to the minister to Russia, Henry Middleton, and was to be communicated by him to the Tsar. These instructions were not sent to Middleton in the form in which Adams originally drafted them, and the circumstances under which the most important change was made are worth narrating, because they bring out a point not sufficiently appreciated by historians of this period, namely, that the important decisions on foreign policy were made not by Adams but by Monroe. In his original draft, Adams undertook to demonstrate (as an *argumentum ad hominem*, he said) that Russia's course was contrary to the principles of the Holy Alliance itself. Monroe objected to this passage on the ground that it might possibly be construed by readers in the United States as giving some sort of approval to the Holy Alliance. Adams replied that he had guarded against such misunderstanding by inserting in the instructions a distinct allusion to the acts of the Holy Alliance as liable to censure; but Monroe thought the guard inadequate, and Adams accordingly struck out the offending passage, though he thereby gave up what he considered "the mainspring of the argument to the Emperor." [48] The importance that he attached to the passage is easy to understand if we keep in mind the purpose of the instructions, for there was hardly anything that would have bolstered the morale of republican America more effectively than to prove that Europe, as represented by the head of the Holy Alliance, was not even faithful to its own system.

In explaining his deference to Monroe on this occasion,

[48] *Ibid.*

Adams recorded in his Memoirs: " In this case, as in all others for which Mr. Monroe as the head of his Administration is responsible, I submit my own judgment to his." [49] In another case, which occurred some three months later and which also related directly to Russia and indirectly to Latin America, he repeated the substance of this statement, and made it even more emphatic. The case will be discussed again in a later chapter, and here it need only be noted that although the difference of opinion between Monroe and Adams involved a note which the latter considered " the most important that ever went from my hands " and although the alteration desired by Monroe involved the deletion of a paragraph containing what Adams regarded as " the soul of the document," he nevertheless concluded by assuring Monroe that he would " cheerfully acquiesce in his decision," whatever that might be. And again he explained his course of action: " I was the agent of his [Monroe's] administration, the general responsibility of which rested upon him." [50]   Such deference to the head of the executive department on the part of the secretary of state may be entirely natural and normal; but still it is not superfluous to emphasize the fact that it was shown by Secretary Adams to President Monroe, that twice within a period of four months in one of the most critical years in the history of American diplomacy Adams yielded his judgment to that of Monroe, and that this involved, in one case, the sacrifice of " the mainspring " of an argument addressed to the head of the Holy Alliance and, in the other case, the sacrifice of " the soul " of " the most important document " that Adams had ever drawn up as secretary of state.

In June 1823 Adams discussed the Russian problem in a letter to a Philadelphia correspondent, Charles Jared Inger-

[49] *Ibid.*, VI, 171.   [50] *Ibid.*, VI, 211.

soll. The letter is interesting partly because it throws further light on the relationship between Adams and Monroe and still more because it breathes the spirit of calm assurance which, strange as it may seem, pervaded the administration at that time and made it seem unnecessary to take more vigorous measures to meet the threat from Europe. The calmness of the administration was shared by the public at large, and in both cases it was a product of wishful thinking about the conflict in Spain—of the belief that the side with which the United States sympathized was bound to win. As the British chargé, Henry Addington, wrote from Washington towards the end of this year,

From the beginning of the contest [the French invasion of Spain], the people of this Republic seem to have mistaken their own ardent wishes for a secure conviction of the discomfiture of the invading Power, and the triumph of the invaded.[51]

Adams's own view of the conflict between liberty and despotism in Europe was a larger one, but it gave him the same comfortable feeling about the .future that was entertained by most of his fellow countrymen.

. . . The influence of our example [he said in his letter to Ingersoll] has unsettled all the ancient governments of Europe. It will overthrow them all without a single exception. I hold this revolution to be as infallible as that the earth will perform a revolution around the sun in a year.[52]

[51] Webster, *op. cit.,* II, 499, Addington to Canning, Dec. 1, 1823, no. 22.
[52] Adams, *Writings,* VII, 488. Adams to Charles Jared Ingersoll, June 19, 1823. Ingersoll was a prominent Philadelphia lawyer who had long taken a keen interest in foreign affairs. In 1808 he broke with his Federalist associates over foreign policy. He maintained close relations with Monroe, Adams, Richard Rush and

From this long-time point of view, one did not need to worry greatly about defending the American system against Europe, since Europe was already on the eve of a revolution that would assimilate it to the American system. To be sure, there were at the moment some annoying and even disturbing things in the European situation, such as the Spanish conflict and the Russian ukase of 1821. In recent letters to which Adams was now replying, Ingersoll had urged the administration to take a spirited stand against the ukase. These sentiments, wrote Adams, "I would call . . . wise had not my own entirely concided with them." But, he continued,

They yielded to a system more cool, probably more profound, certainly more safe, upon the principle of preserving peace *in our time*. This administration has been in a period of uncommon tranquility in Europe, and has itself partaken of that character. *Servatur adimum* is now its motto, and the ambition of the incumbent is to deliver over the trust in peace as well as in prosperity to his successor. I share so much in this feeling that although my first impressions were very distinctly avowed and agreed perfectly with your advice, I have more than acquiesced in the course determined upon after full advisement. . . . [53]

Less than six months later all this was changed. The hope of maintaining " peace in our time " seemed a pathetic illusion; the rôles of Adams and Monroe had been reversed, and now it was Adams who sought to restrain his chief from going to bid defiance to the Holy Allies in the heart of Europe.

---

other leading Republicans. For his record of an interesting conversation with Joel Poinsett in 1823 just after the latter's return from his special mission to Mexico, see William M. Meigs, *The Life of Charles Jared Ingersoll* (Philadelphia, 1897), p. 111-113, 116. See also the article on Ingersoll in DAB.

[53] Adams, *Writings*, VII, 488-489.

CHAPTER FIFTEEN

CANNING, RUSH, AND MONROE

I

The mid-summer tranquility described by Adams was only the calm before the storm. Even as he wrote, the French army was completing its lightning invasion of Spain; and as quickly as the constitutional government of that country had been set up in 1820, it was destroyed in 1823. Within three months after the French invaders crossed the Pyrenees the restoration of the absolute monarchy of Ferdinand VII was virtually complete. Cadiz, at the southernmost tip of Spain, was the only important city that still held out against him, and most of the liberal leaders who had not bought his pardon by betraying their cause were in flight or in prison or dead.

In the United States—and in England, too—the unexpectedly rapid and sweeping success of France created deep uneasiness. This was the more profound because the invasion had demonstrated not only the military prowess of France but also the weakness and demoralization of her liberal opponents. Might not France, either as the agent of the Holy Alliance or acting only for herself with the acquiescence of the grateful Ferdinand, try to repeat in Spanish America what she had just accomplished with such terrifying efficiency in Spain? And was there much reason to hope that the liberals of Spanish America would be more steadfast than those of Spain in withstanding the double-barrelled French campaign of force and propaganda?

To be sure, those who wished to find comforting answers

to these questions could do so; but realists could not close their eyes to the fact that the French had long been casting hungry glances at Latin America and—especially in their present rôle of champion of monarchy and order—might count upon important support among its people. At least since 1820, if not longer, it had been a matter of common knowledge that France had a keen political interest in that region, and that this was based on a solid foundation of economic interest. It was also known that France had had— or still had—agents in Mexico, Argentina, Colombia, and Brazil, and that in at least one case, that of Buenos Aires, its advances had met with warm response in the highest quarters.[1]

In whatever form it might be conceived, the French menace began to be taken very seriously by many well informed people in the United States after France won its quick victory in Spain. As early as August 13, before the full extent of the victory was known, the menace was made the subject of a long editorial by one of the sanest commentators in the United States, Robert Walsh of the Philadelphia *National Gazette*. As evidence of its gravity and urgency, Walsh asserted that in a recent diplomatic note the French minister of foreign affairs, Chateaubriand, had said that the fleets as well as the armies of France would be placed at the disposal of the king of Spain. " The *fleets*," observed Walsh, " could be meant to be employed only against the revolted colonies." [2]

[1] See above, chap. 11.
[2] *National Gazette,* Aug. 13, 1823, editorial. Walsh did not identify the note in question. He may possibly have had in mind Chateaubriand's instructions of June 9 to the new French Ambassador to Madrid; but while these expressed a lively sympathy for Spain's cause in America, they " made no mention of the use

The knowledge that the situation was disquieting to England only made it doubly so to the United States, for there was no telling how England might go about protecting her interests in this crisis. She had fleets of her own with which, if she thought it worth while, she could easily check any French move in the direction of Latin America; but in the United States people were asking whether she would use her fleets to checkmate France or merely to help herself to a slice of Spanish America, or whether she would use them at all. Commenting on a statement in the Venezuelan newspaper *El Colombiano* of Caracas to the effect that England's well known jealousy of France guaranteed American security against the designs of the latter, Walsh remarked, in the editorial just quoted, that the liberal government of Spain had very recently put its trust in that same jealousy and had been woefully disappointed.

Indeed [continued Walsh], deeming them [the British government], as we do, scarcely less the enemies of ' essentially republican ' systems than the members of the Holy Alliance, we do not find extravagant the idea that they may connive at the attempts of France to bring the late Spanish colonies again under the yoke of European monarchy, as they have at her crusades against the free institutions and national independence of Portugal. . . . The distracted condition of Mexico and Peru will enable them to accomplish much in those countries with a comparatively small force. . . . Let the people of our Union be on their guard against such neighbors. This subject is fruitful and *momentous*.[3]

---

of armed force by France in Spanish America " (Robertson, *France and Latin-American Independence*, p. 261).

[3] *National Gazette*, Aug. 13, 1823, editorial.

II

In government circles, however, the dominant note in Anglo-American relations at this moment was not the one of mutual suspicion sounded by Walsh, but of a desire for a better understanding and mutual support. The feeling was almost equally apparent at both London and Washington. In both cases it was in part the product of the deepening crisis over the Spanish American question, though, in the case of the United States, it also marked the revival of a hope long felt by Monroe. By an interesting coincidence it received its most striking expression almost simultaneously in the two capitals in July and August 1823.

At Washington even Adams, as Stratford Canning observed in May of this year, had "caught a something of the soft infection" of growing Anglo-American friendship.[4] The infection spread as the administration matured its plans for the important general negotiation that was about to be entrusted to Richard Rush in London. The negotiation was designed to settle all the outstanding disputes between the United States and Great Britain, such as those relating to trade with the British West Indies and the Northwest boundary; and the administration hoped that it would not merely remove causes of irritation but would also lay the foundations for a lasting entente between the two governments. As Adams wrote Rush on July 29 at the close of a series of instructions relating to it, "the final result anxiously looked to from it" was "a more permanent and more harmonious concert of public policy and community of purpose between our two countries, than has

[4] Perkins, *Monroe Doctrine,* p. 60.

ever yet existed since the period of our Independence." [5]
This urgent invitation to an entente contained no specific
reference to Spanish America, which, for obvious reasons,
was not included in the agenda of the general negotiation;
but the " concert of public policy and community of purpose " of which Adams spoke could hardly fail to extend
to an international problem of such deep concern to both
governments as the Spanish American question.

The establishment of such an entente with Great Britain
might well seem a revolutionary change in the foreign relations of the United States; but it was intended to be carried
out within the framework of the existing policy. That no
substantial change in the latter was contemplated at this
time is shown by another despatch to Rush, dated some
three weeks later, in which Adams took an appeal for aid
from the Greek patriots as the text for a disquisition on the
foreign policy of the United States. Because of its manifest significance for the policy of the United States in
regard to both Great Britain and Spanish America, the
despatch is worth quoting at length.

The policy of the United States, with reference to Foreign
Nations [wrote Adams], has always been founded upon the
moral principle of Natural Law—Peace with all Mankind.
From whatever cause, war, between other Nations, whether
foreign or domestic, has arisen, the unvarying Law of the
United States has been *Peace* with both belligerents. From
the first war of the French Revolution, to the recent invasion
of Spain, there has been a succession of wars, national and
civil, in almost every one of which *one* of the parties was
contending for Liberty or Independence. To the first
[French] Revolutionary war, a strong impulse of feeling

[5] Richard Rush Papers, Folder 1823, Adams to Rush, July 29,
1823, No. 72. The receipt of this despatch was acknowledged by
Rush on Aug. 30, 1823.

urged the people of the United States to take side with the Party, which, at its commencement, was contending, apparently, at least, for both. Had the policy of the United States not been essentially pacific, a stronger case to claim their interference, could scarcely have been presented. They, nevertheless, declared themselves neutral, and the principle then deliberately settled, has been invariably adhered to ever since.

After remarking that the experience of the past thirty years had served to ascertain the proper limits for the application of these principles, Adams continued:

Precluded, by their neutral position, from interfering in the question of right, the United States have recognized the *fact* of foreign Sovereignty, only when it was undisputed, or disputed without any rational prospect of success. In this manner the successive changes of Government in many of the European States, and the Revolutionary Governments of South America, have been acknowledged. The condition of the Greeks is not yet such as will admit of the recognition upon these principles.[6]

It would be a great mistake to regard this as a mere brief in defence of *de facto* recognition. Its significance lies in its assertion of the principle from which that defence was deduced—the principle that the United States must never interfere in any foreign war, no matter what its character—and in the universal application of this principle to the relations of the United States with all parts of the world, with Spanish America as well as with Europe. Given the turbulent state of both regions when the despatch was written, it was a highly important statement of policy; and it did indeed serve to ascertain the existing limits both of the

[6] Richard Rush Papers, Folder 1823, Adams to Rush, Aug. 18, 1823, No. 74.

United States' aid to Spanish America and also of its projected " concert of public policy " with Great Britain.

Some three weeks after Rush was instructed that his
government anxiously desired such a concert of policy, and
some two weeks before he received the instructions, an
even more explicit overture for Anglo-American cooperation
was made by George Canning, the new British secretary
for foreign affairs.   On his side, too, there had been many
recent signs that the time for such cooperation was fast
approaching.   On March 31 he had warned the French
government that its intervention in Spain would not be
permitted to extend to Spanish America.[7]   Though this
warning contained not the slightest allusion to the possibility of cooperation with the United States, it indicated
that at least the basis for such cooperation existed.   It
marked another long step on Canning's part away from his
predecessor Castelreagh's system of cooperation with the
Continental Allies and, indeed, completed that secession
of England from the concert of Europe which Adams had
somewhat prematurely hailed at the time of the Congress of
Troppau.   At Washington it seemed not unreasonable to
believe that every step that Canning took away from the
concert of Europe would bring him closer to a concert with
the United States.

Other signs pointed in the same direction.   In April, at
the Foreign Secretary's annual dinner for the diplomatic
corps to celebrate the King's birthday, Rush offered the
toast, " Success to neutrals! " and Canning agreeably sur-
prized him by not only applauding the sentiment but also
pointing his applause with a flattering reference to Jeffer-

[7] Webster, *Britain,* I, 19, and II, 111-112.

son's doctrines of 1793.[8]   Coming from the head of a government that had always conspicuously flouted these doctrines, Canning's remarks seemed to betoken, if not a shift in British policy, at least a novel tenderness for Yankee susceptibilities.   Then in July Canning corrected with his own hand some newspaper accounts of an important speech he had recently made on British policy and sent them to Rush—one copy for himself and the others for President Monroe and Secretary Adams—" for the purpose of recording more clearly, than a newspaper could do, the principles of our conduct and policy."   This was a delicate attention and, despite the fact that Canning mispelled the name of the man who had been President of the United States for the past six years, as well as an envoy to London itself on an earlier occasion, its significance was further enhanced by the engaging modesty with which the great man made his friendly gesture.

[8] Richard Rush Papers, Letter Books, vol. VII, Rush to Monroe, April 24, 1823. Rush's report of Canning's soft breathings was strongly tinged with skepticism.   After mentioning the fact that Canning had already publicly praised the neutral doctrines of the United States in a speech in the House of Commons on April 16, Rush added, " We shall see by and by how they [Canning's statements in praise of Jeffersonian neutrality] stand with the praises of Sir William Scott, which he [Canning] had uttered in Parliament two days before."   Sir William Scott (Lord Stowell) was best known in the United States for the part he had played in the Court of Admiralty in combatting the neutral doctrines of 1793. For example, it was he who handed down the notorious *Essex* decision of 1805, in connection with which Henry Adams says that Scott " made himself and his court a secret instrument for carrying out an act of piracy " (*History of the United States,* III, 45-46).   In citing Rush's letter to Monroe, Perkins, *op. cit.,* p. 61, note 65, erroneously dates it April 4; he also cites it in support of his statement that relations between Rush and Canning were quite cordial at this time.

Your personal kindness [he wrote Rush] will supply the value wanting in the present itself. But I cannot venture to hope that, without your friendly intervention Mr. Munro & Mr. Adams would receive with like indulgence the copies which I take the liberty to inclose to you for their acceptance.[9]

III

The ground was thus well prepared for Canning's now famous proposal, made a month later, for a joint declaration by Great Britain and the United States on the Spanish American question. The proposal was made informally in a conference on August 16, and Canning followed this up with three " personal and confidential " notes to Rush on August 20, 23, and 31.[10] The conference of August 16 had

[9] Richard Rush Papers, Folder 1823, Canning to Rush, July 11, 1823, "Private."

[10] The originals of these famous notes are preserved in the Richard Rush Papers, Folder 1823. They are accompanied by two brief, undated memoranda in Richard Rush's handwriting, initialled " R. R." One memorandum refers to Monroe's " celebrated message "; the other, to " The ' Monroe Declaration.' " The location of Canning's original notes is a bibliographical item of considerable importance, since it has apparently not been widely known. For example, the leading British work on Canning's foreign policy, Temperley, op. cit., p. 110-112, quotes the notes in part but does not cite the source of the text. Webster, Britain, I, 46, merely remarks that Canning's letters " are not in the British archives "; and the leading work on the side of the United States, Perkins's Monroe Doctrine, p. 65, notes 72 and 74, follows the text of the notes of Aug. 20 and 23 as published in T. B. Edgington, The Monroe Doctrine (Boston, 1905), p. 7-9, and the paraphrase of the note of Aug. 31 in Rush, Court of London, p. 425. Worthington C. Ford published Canning's notes from the copies forwarded to Adams by Rush (both in Mass. Hist. Soc., Proceedings, 2 Series, XV (1902), 415-417, and also in Am. Hist. Rev., VII (1902), 682, 683, 686-687), as did also Manning, Dip Cor., III, 1478-1479, 1482, 1485-1486.

been arranged for the discussion of a different matter, the general negotiation recently entrusted to Rush. After that matter had been disposed of for the time being and the conference seemed about to come to a close, Rush " transiently " raised the question of the French invasion of Spain and its possible bearing on Spanish America. Alluding to Canning's warning to France of March 31, he said that even if France should complete the overthrow of constitutional government in Spain, " there was at least the consolation left, that Great Britain would not allow her to go further and stop the progress of emancipation in the colonies." [11]

With seeming casualness, Canning thereupon asked Rush what he thought his government would say to going hand in hand with England in such a policy. The two nations possessed so large a share of the maritime strength of the world, he said, that a mere joint declaration on their part would be enough to arrest any designs France might have on Spanish America, without the need for resorting to force. Canning hoped that the powers recently received by Rush

[11] Rush, *op. cit.*, p. 399. I have ventured to retell the story of Canning's negotiation with Rush about the proposal because the principal account of it previously published is quite misleading in some important respects. I refer to Worthington C. Ford's account in his well known article, " John Quincy Adams and the Monroe Doctrine," *Am. Hist. Rev.*, VII (1902), 680-691. For example, Ford makes the quite erroneous statement (p. 687) that on receiving Canning's note of Aug. 31 Rush regarded the incident as closed, and (p. 688) that Canning made only " one or two subsequent incidental references to the matter." He also fails to make it clear either that Rush offered to join in the proposed declaration on condition of British recognition of the new states, or that through Rush's despatch of Oct. 10, 1823, Monroe and his cabinet were well aware while they were framing the Monroe Doctrine that Canning had virtually abandoned his proposal (see below, chap. 16).

for the general negotiation would permit him to join in such a declaration without consulting his government. Rush told him that that was not the case; but otherwise his reply, though non-committal, was distinctly encouraging.[12] On August 20 Canning followed up his oral suggestion with the first of his three "personal and confidential" notes on this subject,[13] in which he outlined the character of the proposed declaration.

In effect, the declaration was to contain a warning to the European powers not to attempt the reconquest of Spanish America or the transfer of any part of it from Spain to another power. It was also to contain a self-denying ordinance by which Great Britain and the United States pledged themselves not to acquire any part of Spanish America. "I am persuaded," wrote Canning, "there has seldom, in the history of the world, occurred an opportunity, when so small an effort, by two friendly governments, might produce so unequivocal a good, and prevent such extensive calamities." His eagerness to conclude the business was indicated by his closing sentence, in which he said that, while he was about to go out of town, he would not be gone more than three weeks and would never be so far distant but that he would receive and reply to any communication within three or four days.

Without waiting for Rush's reply, Canning wrote him again from Liverpool on August 23.[14] He had just been informed by the French government that when the war in Spain was over (and its end was already at hand) a

---

[12] Rush, *op. cit.*, p. 400-404. For Rush's despatches to Adams reporting the various stages of his discussion of the proposal with Canning, see Manning, *Dip. Cor.*, III, 1475 ff.

[13] *Ibid.*, III, 1478-1479.   [14] *Ibid.*, III, 1479-1480.

European congress would probably be called to deal with the colonial question. He knew how deeply the United States had been disturbed in the past by the mere rumour of such European congresses, and he made the most of the news from Paris. Urging it upon Rush as an additional motive for the prompt issuance of the joint declaration, he concluded rather ominously, " I need not point out to you all the complications to which this proposal [for a European congress], however dealt with by us, may lead."

These overtures to Rush were, of course, private and confidential; but two days after the date of his second note Canning gave striking public expression to his zeal for Anglo-American solidarity. The occasion was a dinner at Liverpool on August 25, which was attended not only by Canning but also by the new American envoy to Sweden, Christopher Hughes, who was on his way to his post. This gave Canning his opportunity and he made the most of it. Proposing a toast to Hughes, Canning made a speech (which was duly published) in which he described the United States and Great Britain as united " by a common language, a common spirit of commercial enterprise, and a common regard to well-regulated liberty." They had had their disputes in the past, but these were now forgotten. " The force of blood again prevails," he feelingly declared, " and the daughter and the mother stand together against the world."[15]

[15] Temperley, *op. cit.,* p. 112, says, " There can be no mistaking the importance of this utterance in the mouth of a diplomat speaking outside the walls of Parliament." It is interesting to compare this with Rush's statement, made in a private letter to Monroe, Oct. 22, 1823, that he himself attached no importance whatever to Canning's speech. " He [Canning] happened to fall in with Mr. Hughes at the very moment when he was making his advances

On August 27 Rush replied [16] to Canning's notes of the 20th and 23rd. He repeated what he had already told Canning—that in order to establish a common basis for the proposed declaration of common policy, Great Britain must recognize the independence of the new states, as the United States had already done, and that he had no specific authority to commit his government to the proposed declaration. At the close of his letter he hinted that he would nevertheless assume the resposibility of so committing it if the British government on its part would agree to immediate recognition. Canning either did not see the hint or did not choose to notice it. The gist of the last of his three " private and confidential " notes, written from Storrs, Westmorland, on August 31,[17] was that in view of the long delay that must now intervene, his overture was not to be regarded as a binding proposal and that he would feel free to act as the rapidly changing situation might require.

Although this note "betrayed coldness and disappointment," it was not understood on either side as terminating the discussion.[18] Rush received it on September 7, and a week later he wrote Monroe that he expected to be invited to an interview with Canning "very shortly" after the latter's return to London. " The topick of Spanish American affairs," he continued, " will doubtless be resumed in

---

to me respecting Spanish American affairs," continued Rush, " and I have always considered this fact as the key to his speech " (Rush Papers, Letter Books, vol. VII). See below, chap. 17, note 7.

[16] Manning, *Dip. Cor.*, III, 1482-1483.

[17] *Ibid.*, III, 1485-1486.

[18] Temperley, *op. cit.*, p. 112, describes Canning's note of Aug. 31 as betraying coldness and disappointment and then makes the unsupported assertion that Rush regarded the overture as definitely ended.

our conversations, and it is my intention to urge upon him the immediate and unequivocal recognition of those new States by Great Britain. Upon no other footing whatever, shall I feel warranted in acceding to the proposals he has made to me." [19] Canning had, in fact, already returned to London by this time, and three days later (September 18) the expected interview was held at his invitation. It was followed by another on September 26. On both occasions Canning urged his proposal upon Rush with a zeal that belied the coldness of his written communication of August 31.

The interviews of September 18 and 26 marked the climax (and, as Rush subsequently learned to his great chagrin, the end) of the discussions. On the eighteenth,[20] Canning again stressed the seriousness of the menace to Spanish America and the imperative need for despatch in forestalling it. Rush did not deny this, but observed that the decision he was called on to make was one of extreme gravity, since his consent to join in the proposed declaration would involve the abandonment of the United States' settled policy of " preserving peace and harmony with all nations, without offending any, or forming entangling alliances with any," and particularly of abstaining from interference in the affairs of Europe. Canning replied that " powerful and controlling circumstances " made this policy " inapplicable upon the present occasion." The question at issue was " full as much American as European, to say no more." The United States, he continued,

[19] Rush Papers, Letter Books, vol. VII, Rush to Monroe, Sept. 15, 1823.

[20] This interview is described in Rush's despatch to Adams of Sept. 19, No. 331, printed in his *Court of London,* p. 429-443.

were the first power established on that continent, and now confessedly the leading power. They were connected with Spanish America by their position, as with Europe by their relations; and they also stood connected with these states by political relations. Was it possible they could see with indifference their fate decided upon by Europe? . . . Had not a new epoch arrived in the relative position of the United States towards Europe, which Europe must acknowledge? Were the great political and commercial interests which hung upon the destinies of the new continent, to be canvassed and adjusted . . . without some proper understanding between the United States and Great Britain, as the two chief commercial and maritime States of both worlds? He hoped not, he would wish to persuade himself not.[21]

This was a powerful appeal, partly because the reasoning was cogent and partly because it was expressed in terms that were flattering to Rush's country. It was, indeed, the very kind of blandishment against which Adams had sought to put his fellow countrymen on their guard in 1821. We have no reason to believe that Rush was taken in by it, for, as we shall shortly see, he maintained a salutary skepticism with regard to Canning's advances throughout this whole affair; and his reply on this occasion was precisely what he had already told Monroe it would be.

Nevertheless, we must emphasize the fact that Rush's reply involved the assumption of a grave responsibility on his part, for he now offered to join Canning in the proposed declaration without awaiting specific instructions from his government, provided the British government would accord immediate and unequivocal recognition to the new states. Canning, describing this interview subsequently, reported Rush as saying to him that " *if we* [the British] *would place ourselves on the same line* with the *United States* by ac-

---

[21] *Ibid.,* p. 431-432.

knowledging the S[outh] A[merican] States, he would say, swear, sign, anything *sub spiritu.*" [22]

As Rush himself admitted, his action would involve a departure from the settled policy of the United States; and he had good reason to believe that Canning would agree to the condition attached to his offer. As he pointed out to Canning in this interview, Britain had already legalized her trade with the new states, was ready to support it with her squadrons, was on the eve of sending out commercial agents to some or all of the new states, and had publicly admitted that their independence was assured. "Why then," he asked, "should Britain longer forbear to acknowledge this independence? She had already done so in effect, and why should she not in form?" [23]

Canning did not reply to the question at this interview, possibly because, as Rush reported, it was apparently now now that he learned for the first time that Rush was prepared "to come fully into his views, if this [the British] Government would immediately acknowledge the new states." [24] A week later (September 26) the discussion was resumed. In reply to an inquiry from Canning, Rush said that he had not received any further instructions from Washington, but added that he was "still willing to go forward with him in his proposals, upon the terms I had made known." Canning replied that England felt "great embarrassment as regarded . . . immediate recognition," and countered with an offer of "*future* acknowledgment." Rush was adamant

[22] Temperley, *op. cit.,* p. 110, quoting from a letter from Canning to Bagot, Jan. 9, 1824. Though the language is different, the sense tallies rather closely with what Rush himself reported that he said (*Court of London,* p. 436-437).

[23] *Ibid.,* p. 441.   [24] *Ibid.,* p. 443.

and the interview—the last on this subject—came to an inconclusive close. He expected the discussion to be renewed,[25] but in this he was disappointed.

Almost immediately after this last interview with Rush, Canning reached a satisfactory understanding with France herself and promptly lost all interest in the joint declaration that he had proposed to the United States. The understanding was arrived at in a series of conversations between Canning and the French ambassador, Prince Polignac, in September and early October and was embodied in a memorandum (the Polignac Memorandum) in which Polignac declared, among other things, that

France disclaimed, on her part, any intention or desire to avail herself of the present state of the Colonies, or of the present situation in France towards Spain, to appropriate to herself any part of the Spanish possessions in America, or to obtain for herself any exclusive advantages . . . that she abjured, in any case, any design of acting against the Colonies, by force of arms.[26]

[25] In the course of his despatch of Oct. 2, 1823, No. 334, reporting the interview of Sept. 26, Rush said that it was " ended by his [Canning's] saying that he would invite me to an interview in the course of a few days "; and since Rush expected the interview to deal with Spanish America, he delayed reporting to Adams on the interview of Sept. 26 with the intention of dealing with both of them in the same despatch. He waited until Oct. 2 without hearing from Canning and then decided that he ought not to delay further. These facts do not appear in the truncated and misleading account of the interview of Sept. 26 published in Rush, *op. cit.*, p. 443 ff.

[26] For a brief discussion of the negotiation, see Webster, *Britain*, I, 19-20, and for the text of the Memorandum, *ibid.*, II, 115-120. Robertson, *France and Latin-American Independence*, p. 269-272, compares the Memorandum with Polignac's account of the interchange of views with Canning in his despatch of Oct. 10 to Chateaubriand, and finds that the latter " stressed more than did

It would seem that if Canning's proposal of a joint declaration had been animated by a sincere desire for cooperation, or merely for a better understanding, with the United States, he would have found some means of letting Rush know at least the general drift of his conversations with Polignac and the substance of their result; but he did not do so until the end of November. By that time Monroe was on the point of making his decision and the Polignac Memorandum was a matter of common knowledge in European diplomatic circles.[27] Rush did, however, suspect what was going on; and, as we shall see, he communicated his suspicious to Washington early in October and his communication was received at a crucial moment in the formulation of American policy.

IV

This brief but earnest effort at Anglo-American cooperation is one of the most important episodes in the history of the relations of the United States with Latin America as

the Polignac Memorandum the intention of France not to intervene in Spanish America" (*ibid.*, p. 270).

[27] Temperley, *op. cit.*, p. 114, states that the substance of the Memorandum "was certainly known to Austria and to Russia, as well as to France, by the third week of October," and it was circulated to them in November. He adds that though Canning communicated it to Rush by word of mouth on Nov. 24, it was not circulated to him until Dec. 13. As a matter of fact, it was not actually circulated to Rush until Dec. 26, and he received it the following day (Rush Papers, Letter Books, vol. VII, Rush to Adams, Dec. 27, 1823, No. 354). Along with the Polignac Memorandum and an official covering letter, Canning sent Rush a "confidential" note dated Dec. 13 (*ibid.*, Folder 1824) in which he explained his negotiation with Polignac on the grounds of Rush's lack of power and the pressure of events.

well as with Great Britain. If it had succeeded, it might
well have averted a whole series of misunderstandings and
controversies that disturbed the relations of the United
States with both the former and the latter in the course of
the next generation. It would have improved relations with
Great Britain because the ensuing rivalry with her related
in considerable part to Latin America. It would have
improved relations with Latin America too, if only because
the growing antagonism of its people towards the United
States was in part a by-product of this Anglo-American
rivalry, which generated a highly effective British propaganda among the new states against their northern neighbor and occasionally betrayed the United States into taking
steps to get ahead of its British rival which resulted in
frightening and affronting the people of Latin America.

The responsibility for the failure of the effort rests
squarely on the shoulders of its author, George Canning.
As far as the United States was concerned, its chances of
success were excellent. Rush's offer to commit the United
States to it was made subject to only one condition, which
Canning might well have accepted. If the commitment had
been made on these terms, there is good reason for believing
that Rush's action would have been approved by the government at Washington. Rush seems to have been justified in
his belief, expressed while the question was still pending,
that his offer was made in accordance with the President's
policy.[28] To be sure, it met with strong opposition in
Washington, but it also received strong support there. If it
had been already accepted by Canning and if the joint
declaration had been presented to Monroe as an accomplished
fact, there is good reason to believe that he would have

[28] Rush, *op. cit.,* p. 441.

accepted it. Canning, however, refused to wait for word from Washington. He not only abandoned his proposal but in the following weeks veered to the opposite course of of Anglo-American rivalry. Rush, immediately, and his government, ultimately, took the same course by a natural reaction; and rivalry was the keynote of relations between the two governments—especially of their relations in regard to Latin America—during most of the rest of the century.

Canning's abandonment of his proposal may therefore be regarded as a turning-point in the history of Anglo-American relations. His conduct in this affair was marked by a levity and shortsightedness that seriously mar his record as a statesman. His conduct is all the more exceptional because in 1823 he realized the importance of cultivating friendly relations between the two great English-speaking nations, " the leading maritime and naval powers of the world." The Canning who deliberately chose the path of rivalry with the United States after his need for its support had passed, and followed that path to the end of his career, was the same Canning who in August 1823, when his need was greatest, publicly proclaimed that " the force of blood again prevails, and the daughter and the mother stand together against the world."

Why Canning abandoned his proposal seems fairly clear. Why he ever made it is, according to a recent British authority, C. K. Webster, still a matter of doubt. Although Canning, too, was alarmed over the quick success of France in Spain and the designs she was suspected of having on Spanish America, Webster thinks that " it is not easy to account for Canning's desire to associate the United States [with Great Britain] in the defense of the New States." He points out that Britain's supremacy at sea was so great that she had no need of aid from the United States. Adams though that the proposal was designed to prevent the United States from annexing Cuba; but Rush, who was in a much better position to judge, does not seem to have believed that that was Canning's purpose. Adams also suspected that Canning's object was to keep the United States from remaining neutral and absorbing the carrying trade in case Britain should go to war over the Spanish American question; but Webster remarks that "war was not very likely and there is no evidence of this motive." [29]

Rush himself, who had been in London more than five years and thought he understood British policy fairly well by this time, was at no loss as to Canning's motive. Writing to Monroe on September 15, 1823, at a time when he had had a month to reflect on the proposal and when he thought Canning was still eager for its acceptance by the United States, he found the motive in the fact that England had recently broken with her former confederates of the Holy Alliance and was now afraid she would have to fight them single-handed unless she could gain the support of the United States.

. . . Britain has been from the very beginning [he said], positively or negatively, auxiliary to the evils with which this alliance, under the mask of Christianity, has already afflicted the old, and is now menacing the new world. It is under this last stretch of ambition [the French invasion of Spain] that she seems about to be roused, not . . . from any objections to the arbitrary principles of the Combination [i. e., the Holy Alliance] . . . but rather from the apprehensions which are now probably coming upon her, touching her own influence and standing, through the formidable and encroaching career of these Continental

[29] Webster, Britain, I, 46-47.

potentates.   She at last perceives a crisis likely to come on, bringing with it peril to her own commercial prospects on the other side of the Atlantic, & to her political sway in both hemispheres.   Hence probably some of her recent and remarkable solicitudes.   The former war of 20 years more than once shook her prosperity, and brought hazards to her existence, though for the most part she was surrounded by allies.   A second war of like duration, and with no ally for her in Europe, might not have a second field of Waterloo for its termination.   Such are the prospective dangers that possibly do not escape her.[30]

For our purpose, it makes no difference whether Rush was right or wrong as to Canning's motives.   What is important is the opinion that he formed and communicated to his government.   In this connection two points should be noted.   The first is that the skepticism of his letter to Monroe from which we have just quoted was not the result of a snap judgment based on transient circumstances but reflected a settled opinion formed shortly after Rush's arrival in London and reinforced by his whole subsequent experience there.   This was the opinion that the whole governing class of Great Britain, Whig and Tory alike, was dominated by a supercilious and antagonistic attitude towards the United States that made the development of genuinely friendly relations between the two countries difficult if not impossible.   In April 1818, four months after his arrival, he wrote Monroe that in relation to the United States

There is in the atmosphere of them [the British governing class], a coldness not to be thawed, and I solemnly believe that it will forever remain incapable of nourishing into life either friendship of kindness. . .   A man like Lord Hol-

[30] Rush Papers, Letter Books, vol. VII, Rush to Monroe, Sept. 15, 1823.

land [a liberal peer, who frequently entertained Rush] may, personally, be an exception to the remark, but those of his political family, Lords, commoners, and all, are, according to my most deliberate opinions thus far formed, under the same systematic belief of our being nothing but degenerate English . . . Stupid as well as dangerous, I would add fatal delusion, for at last it will come to this in recoils upon themselves . . . In fundamental dislikings of our system (private, publick, and all that belongs to each) there is no difference whatever to my observation between the whig and the tory aristocracy.

To illustrate the point, Rush quoted a remark made to him very recently by an influential Englishman to the effect that " it was unnecessary to disguise it—our two countries were at heart opposed and fight it out upon the ocean we must." The sentiment was uttered, said Rush, " with entire urbanity, and a sort of nonchalance, as if it had been a first truth." What made it the more striking was that " the same gentleman has been personally civil to me, and invited me to his house." [31]

Five years later he still held substantially the same opinion.[32] In his letter of September 15 to Monroe, he

[31] *Ibid.,* vol. I, Rush to Monroe, April 22, 1818, " Private."

[32] Particularly galling to Rush was " the ignorance, real or affected, which still continues to prevail in England of the character of our country," an ignorance which " habitually puts on the most offensive forms . . . in the aristocratic caste." He illustrated the point by telling how the Lord Chancellor had recently refused to permit certain children, wards of the Court of Chancery, to be taken to the United States until he received a satisfactory certificate that " the means of educating the children " existed there. " In relating this anecdote," said Rush, " I am very naturally reminded of one I have heard you tell of Sir Wm. Scott. ' The taste and fashion of Africa! ' Par nobilum fratrum! " Rush's remarks may also remind the reader of Henry Adams's anecdotes of Palmerston. Rush's letter is in Rush Papers, Letter Books, vol. VII, Rush to Monroe, June 20, 1823.

said that the estimate he had formed of the British government and the character of its governing class did not lead
him to hope for any material change in the part which
Britain had acted in the world for the past fifty years whenever the cause of freedom was at stake—" the part which
she acted in 1774 in America, which she has since acted in
Europe, & is now acting in Ireland."

I shall therefore [he continued] find it hard to keep from
my mind the suspicion, that the approaches of her Ministers
to me at this portentous juncture, for a concert of policy
which they have not heretofore courted with the United
States, are bottomed on their own calculations.

Nevertheless—and this is the second point to be noted—
Rush said that whatever the motives of the British might be,
if their " approaches " promised to benefit the United
States, " I grant that a dispassionate & friendly ear should be
turned to them." " Such," he said, " shall be my aim in the
duties before me." Indeed, for all all his skepticism about
Canning's motives, Rush seems to have been sorely tempted
by the proposal; and he might well have been. Britain was
the greatest naval power in the world and also the chief
rival of the United States in Latin America. In her former
rôle, the joint declaration would assure the United States of
her aid in the impending crisis. In her latter rôle, the
declaration would to a certain extent neutralize her; and if
the proposal could be used as a lever to obtain the immediate recognition of the new states by Britain (a step
which Rush made a sine qua non), then the vexatious and
long-drawn-out Spanish American question would at last be
brought to a happy ending. Moreover, while Rush had no
specific authority to join in such a declaration, yet he had
just been instructed that his government anxiously desired

a concert of policy with Britain. And, finally, it would have been only human for him to wish to set his name to as important a document as this declaration would assuredly be.

How he reconciled his lively suspicions of the British with his readiness to join with them in this epochal declaration is explained in his own words, written on October 2:

I cannot be unaware that, in this whole transaction the British Cabinet are striving for their own ends; yet if these ends promise in this instance to be also auspicious to the safety and independence of all Spanish America, I persuade myself that we cannot look upon them but with approbation. England it is true has given her countenance, and still does, to all the evils with which the holy Alliance have afflicted Europe; but if she at length has determined to stay the career of their formidable and despotick ambition in the other hemisphere, the United States seem to owe it to all the policy and to all the principles of their system to hail the effects, whatever may be the motives of her conduct.[33]

V

When Rush's reports of the proposal and his first conversations with Canning about it reached Washington on October 9,[34] Adams was not in town. Several weeks earlier he had quitted the mosquito-infested capital with its torrid climate for more salubrious Massachusetts; and it is a measure of his tranquility during this period that he spent a large part of the late summer and early autumn of this critical year nearly five hundred miles away from his office,

[33] Manning, *Dip. Cor.,* III, 1495.
[34] Rush's despatches received at the State Department on Oct. 9 were his No. 323, Aug. 19, reporting his interview of Aug. 16 with Canning; No. 325, Aug. 23, enclosing Canning's note of Aug. 20; and No. 326, Aug. 28, enclosing Canning's note of Aug. 23.

from which it required more than a week for a letter to reach him by ordinary post. So it was the President who first read Rush's reports, and they completely destroyed the tranquility which he, too, had felt.

Monroe had a great deal of respect for Rush, with whom he carried on a regular private correspondence during the latter's residence in London. On one of these private letters, written in May 1822 and containing a discussion of the Russian ukase of 1821, he made the following notation: "*All* Mr. Rush's letters afford some points of interest to an American citizen and to *all* who are concerned in the policies of the U. States." [35]

In the current crisis Rush's letters, both official and private, were particularly valuable. He was not only an experienced diplomat, having served more than five years at his present post: he was the only experienced diplomat of first rank now representing the United States in Europe, for Gallatin, the only other envoy who belonged in that category, had left the Paris legation and was on his way back to the United States.[36] Aside from the intimate knowledge of the European situation that he had acquired by this time, Rush possessed special qualifications as an adviser on a problem that involved Latin America and sea

[35] Monroe Papers, NYPL, Rush to Monroe, May 24, 1822, "Private." The notation quoted in the text is written on the back of the letter. It is not signed or initialed, but the handwriting appears to be Monroe's.

[36] Gallatin arrived at New York in June 1823. His successor, James Brown, was not appointed until the end of the year. The British minister at Washington, Stratford Canning, also returned home in the summer of 1823, leaving the legation in the hands of a chargé d'affaires for the rest of the year. Thus the crisis that developed in the late summer seems to have taken the British as well as the American government unawares.

power, for, as Monroe knew, he had paid close attention to both subjects [37] while still in Washington and had kept up his interest in them since his appointment to London. He was in close contact with the Spanish American agents in London,[38] and, as he wrote Adams on October 10, 1823, with reference to his discussion of the joint declaration, " Throughout the progress of our discussion [i. e., Rush's discussion with Canning] on Spanish American affairs, I thought it proper to apprize Mr. Ravenga [the envoy of Colombia] confidentially of all that was going on."[39]

[37] For Rush's earlier interest in Spanish America, see above, chap. 8; for some indications of his continued interest in it, see below, notes 38 and 39. Some information about his interest in sea power is given above, chap. 10. Of the many other illustrations that might be added, the following passage from his letter of July 28, 1823, to Smith Thompson, Secretary of the Navy, will suffice: " During my residence at the Court, I have steadily regarded and still regard the navy of England as a more important subject for our observations, than any other establishment of the country, or, in short, than any other one point in the whole compass of European affairs. . . . We live in an age of steam. The late improvement in the engine . . . must assure us that we have not yet witnessed a tithe of the vast results which this new and mighty agent in navigation is big with; a reflection which I make the rather, from my belief that those in power in this country are beginning to think of it more and more as an instrument of war upon the ocean " (Rush Papers, Letter Books, vol. VII).

[38] In a private letter of June 20, 1823, to Monroe, Rush spoke of " the intimacy which I maintain with the deputies from them [" the South American States "] here " (ibid.). In 1822 and 1823 Rush also received a number of letters from Jeremy Robinson at Valparaiso (ibid., Rush to Robinson, June 26, 1823, acknowledging five of these letters, which contained charges against Commodore Charles Stewart and J. B. Prevost).

[39] Manning, Dip. Cor., III, 1803. The Colombian envoy José R. Revenga (the correct spelling) had been imprisoned for debt in London in March 1823 and had appealed to Rush, who helped him obtain his release. The action related to a loan made to the Colom-

Despite the skeptical tone that pervaded Rush's comments on British policy, his despatches left little room for doubt that the British government was genuinely alarmed by the threat from continental Europe to Spanish America; and since the British were presumably better informed, and certainly far more powerful, than the United States, it is small wonder that to Monroe and many of his advisers the danger seemed grave.

Monroe's first step was to consult his two immediate predecessors in the presidency, Jefferson and Madison, whose administrations, together with his own, spanned the whole period of the independence movement in Latin America, which was the nub of the present question. In submitting Rush's reports to Jefferson, he wrote a covering letter [40] in which he said that, while the maxim of " no foreign entanglements " was a sound one, the present case might justify a departure from it; that it was his own " impression " that the United States " ought to meet the proposal of the

---

bian government. This affair was discussed in relation to the recognition question in the Rush-Canning conversations regarding the proposed joint declaration. Several documents relating to Revenga's arrest are in the Rush Papers, Folder " Miscellaneous, XXVI."

[40] Dated Oct. 17, 1823, at Oakhill, Virginia. The text of the letter was printed by Ford in *Mass. Hist. Soc. Proc., loc. cit.,* p. 375, and *Am. Hist. Rev., loc. cit.,* p. 684-685. Oakhill was Monroe's " country-seat," to which he repaired (" for a rest," says Ford), on Oct. 11. He took copies of Rush's despatches with him. Ford thinks it indiscreet of Monroe to have sent copies of these confidential documents to Jefferson and Madison, and strange that he should have consulted them without either notifying Adams beforehand that he was doing so or informing Adams of their replies until two weeks after he received them. What Adams thought of all this is not recorded. His *Memoirs* are silent for the period Sept. 11-Nov. 7.

British government"; that the proposed declaration ought to be directed against any interference with Spanish America, especially against an attack on it by the European powers; and that such interference or attack would be regarded as an attack on the United States, since it was to be presumed that if the European powers succeeded with Spanish America, they would extend their attack to the United States.

On the main question, whether Canning's proposal should be accepted, Jefferson took substantially the same view as Monroe. In his reply,[41] he admitted that " our first and fundamental maxim should be, never to entangle ourselves in the broils of Europe "; but, he said, " the war in which the present proposition might engage us, should that be its consequence, is not her [England's] war, but ours. Its object is to introduce and establish the American system, of keeping out of our land all foreign powers, of never permitting those of Europe to interfere with the affairs of our [American] nations. It is to maintain our principle, not to depart from it." The principle was founded not only on the " first and fundamental maxim " of non-entanglement in Europe but also on a second maxim, " never to suffer Europe to meddle with cis-Atlantic affairs "; and this led him to the assertion of an ideal which was only faintly suggested in Monroe's letter to him and which constituted his main contribution to Monroe's political thinking at this period: the idea of the American system.

America, North and South [he wrote], has a set of interests distinct from those of Europe, and peculiarly her own. She should therefore have a system of her own, separate and apart from that of Europe.

[41] Jefferson, *Writings* (Memorial ed.), XV, 477-480.

In the present crisis the way to maintain the principle based on these two maxims was to accept Canning's proposal, even if that should lead to war, for " Great Britain is the nation which can do us the most harm of any one, or all on earth; and with her on our side we need not fear the whole world."

" Thus," observes a distinguished historian,[42] " did Jefferson reconcile cooperation with Canning with the notion of America for the Americans." Thus also, we may add, did Jefferson recapitulate and synthesize the apparently conflicting policies recommended in three of the most important pronouncements made by him during his own administration. In his great inaugural address of 1801, he had counseled against "entangling alliances ": he now repeated that we ought " never to entangle ourselves in the broils of Europe." In 1802, in his well known letter to Dupont de Nemours, he warned that if France reoccupied New Orleans, the United States would marry itself to the British fleet and nation: he now advised that if Europe (meaning France) attempted to intervene in Spanish America, the United States ought to fight " side by side " with Great Britain to prevent it. In 1808, he asserted that it was the object of the United States and Spanish America to exclude all European influence from this hemisphere: he now asserted that North and South America had an American system, separate and apart from that of Europe, in which Europe should never be suffered to interfere.

His letter to Monroe is, therefore, an important one and deserves the widespread attention it has received, for it summed up and applied to the great crisis of 1823 the policies of the first president of the United States to advocate

[42] Perkins, *op. cit.*, p. 97.

the development of the American system.   And, as we shall see, it is important also because of the part that it played in the formulation of the Monroe Doctrine.

On October 24 Jefferson forwarded to Madison the Rush documents and Monroe's covering letter, together with a letter of his own.   A few days later Madison wrote the President a letter [43] containing his advice on the course to be followed.   He too concurred " in the policy of meeting the advances of the British government," though he added the suggestion that the administration have " an eye to the forms of our Constitution in every step in the road to war." He too believed that " with the British power and navy combined with our own we have nothing to fear from the rest of the world "; but here he began to part company with Jefferson, for he conceived of the present crisis not in hemispheric but in universal terms, that is, not merely as an occasion for promoting the establishment of the American system and its severance from the European system, but as a phase of " the great struggle of the Epoch between liberty and despotism."   In this great struggle, he said, " we owe it to ourselves to sustain it [liberty] in this hemisphere at at least," and he then completed his doctrinal divergence from the Jeffersonian system by suggesting that the United States invite Great Britain to join in aiding the cause of liberty in Spain and Greece.

It doubtless gave Madison a certain puckish pleasure to retort to the British invitation to aid liberty in America by by inviting Britain to aid liberty among its own neighbors in Europe, for Madison shared the feeling of many of his countrymen that Britain had shamelessly abandoned the liberal cause in Spain and was now aiding the Spanish

[43] Monroe, *Writings,* VI, 394.

Americans only in order to extend her commerce with them; but, whatever his reasons for making it, the important point is that his suggestion that the United States interfere in the affairs of Europe was contrary to the basic principle of the American system advocated by Jefferson.

VI

Before Jefferson and Madison wrote their replies to Monroe's request for advice, Adams, who had now returned to Washington, received the first of two communications from the Russian court which increased the gravity of the situation. This took the form of an oral communication from the Russian minister, Baron Tuyll, which he reinforced by an official note to Adams the same day (October 16).[44] The gist of its was that the Tsar complimented the United States (rather too pointedly, it seemed) on its declared intention of remaining neutral in the Spanish American conflict, and stated that, "faithful to the political principles which he follows in concert with his allies," he could not "under any circumstances receive any agent whatsoever" from Colombia or any of the new states of Latin America.

There was nothing very novel or immediately threatening in this, and if it had been said at another time it might have attracted little notice; but coming on the heels of the French victory in Spain and of Canning's urgent warning against the threat from France and her Continental allies, it fell upon Washington with the effect of a time bomb. It asserted the solidarity of the Continental allies, of whom France was one; it also asserted Russia's fidelity to the political principles of the allies, which had just been strik-

[44] Ford in *Am. Hist. Rev., loc. cit.,* p. 685-686.

ingly illustrated by France's intervention in Spain; and its direct and unsparing condemnation of the new governments of Colombia and its sister states fed the growing fear that the united allies, with France as their spearhead, might undertake to apply their political principles overseas by direct intervention in Spanish America.

All this, of course, was conjectural; but its plausibility was increased by the arrival a month later of a note direct from St. Petersburg,[45] in which the Russian court gloated over the succes of the French intervention in Spain. Even Adams, who was less alarmed by the threat from Russia and Europe at large than were most of his colleagues in the Cabinet, described the note as " an ' *Io Triumphe* ' over the fallen cause of revolution, with sturdy promises of determination to keep it down," and as " bearding us to our faces upon the monarchical principles of the Holy Alliance." [46]   If, as Madison and many other Americans thought, the struggle in Latin America was only a phase of a universal conflict between liberty and despotism, it was easy to read into this note a threat from the allied despots of Europe to strike down liberty in Spanish America, and ultimately in the United States itself.

[45] Adams, *Writings*, VIII, 29-32.

[46] Adams, *Memoirs*, VI, 190. Perkins, *op. cit.*, p. 72, note 5, points out that another warning about the designs of Russia and France on Spanish America came in a letter of Sept. 25, 1823, from G. W. Erving, then traveling in Europe, to Secretary of the Treasury Crawford, and that Monroe certainly knew of the letter and on Nov. 21 mentioned it to Adams. As we have seen, Adams did not have a high opinion of Erving; and he spoke rather disparagingly of the letter. Perkins considers the letter " worth noting " but of distinctly secondary importance as compared with the overtures of Canning and the language of the Russian minister Tuyll.

Though the military threat from Europe was increasingly alarming, the danger did not seem imminent. There was no good reason to believe that any hostile expedition was yet being assembled in Europe and the attitude of England seemed to make it doubtful, at least for the present, whether such an expedition would be permitted to cross the Atlantic. What the situation required was not immediate action but the charting of the course to be followed when the time for action arrived.

At any rate, that is what Monroe and his advisers seemed to think, for they conducted their deliberations without any appearance of haste. Rush's first report of Canning's proposal, which was the focal point of these deliberations, had been in Monroe's hands nearly two months when the President and his cabinet finally decided what to do about it. In view of the gravity and complexity of the issues they had to consider, however, one could certainly not say that their pace was too slow or their caution excessive. As Adams observed when the British chargé at Washington pressed him for as quick a decision as possible, the question

was of such magnitude, such paramount consequence as involving the whole future policy of the United States, as far at least as regarded their own hemisphere, that the President was anxious to give it the most deliberate consideration, and to take the sense of his whole Cabinet upon it. That magistrate [President Monroe] considered it . . . the most interesting and important incident of his whole administration.[47]

When once the issues were brought together for formal cabinet discussion, the pace became almost dizzying, for in

[47] Webster, *Britain*, II, 543.

a series of meetings beginning on November 15 and ending only eleven days later, November 26, the whole vast problem was discussed from beginning to end and every important issue was decided so far as the cabinet was concerned; and the President's message embodying the substance of his final decision in paragraphs that posterity has called the Monroe Doctrine was communicated to Congress only a week later (December 2, 1823).

CHAPTER SIXTEEN

HOW MONROE'S MESSAGE WAS WRITTEN

I

The starting-point of the momentous cabinet discussions of November 15-26 was Monroe's submission to his advisers of the replies that he had received from Jefferson and Madison in regard to Canning's proposal. The latter, which was the first major theme of these discussions, and the disturbing communications from Russia, which also played a prominent part in them, were answered in detail in notes addressed to the British and Russian governments; but the administration's decisions in these cases, as well as on all the other important questions considered at this time, were summed up in the Monroe Doctrine.[1] Consequently the formulation of that pronouncement will serve as the focus for the following account of the great debate on foreign policy that took place in these cabinet meetings.

The chronological narrative is so familiar that it need not be repeated here, and the following account of it, in this chapter and the next, will be presented in the form of answers to certain important questions which have attracted much attention from historians but about which something still remains to be said.

The first of these questions relates to the authorship of the Doctrine. As the reader will recall, the Doctrine consists of two distinct parts, which were presented separately

[1] Perkins, *Monroe Doctrine,* p. 74, has already pointed out that " All these matters taken together engaged the attention of the Cabinet during the momentous sessions of November, 1823. All of them have a direct relation to the enunciation of the Monroe Doctrine."

in the message. In the first part, Monroe asserted the non-colonization principle: "the American continents, by the free and independent condition which they have assumed and maintain, are henceforth not to be considered as subjects for future colonization by any European powers." The second part contains the doctrine of the two spheres and the warning to Europe to keep within its own sphere.

In the wars of the European powers in matters relating to themselves [said Monroe], we have never taken any part, nor does it comport with our policy so to do. . . . With the movements in this hemisphere we are, of necessity, more immediately connected. . . . The political system of the allied powers is essentially different in this respect from that of America. This difference proceeds from that which exists in their respective governments. . . . We owe it, therefore, to candor, and to the amicable relations existing between the United States and those powers, to declare that we should consider any attempt on their part to extend their system to any portion of this hemisphere as dangerous to their peace and safety. With the existing colonies or dependencies of any European power we have not interfered and shall not interfere. But with the Governments who have declared their independence and maintained it, and whose independence we have, on great consideration and on just principles, acknowledged, we could not view any interposition for the purpose of oppressing them, or controlling in any other manner their destiny, by any European power, in any other light than as the manifestation of an unfriendly disposition toward the United States. . . . It is impossible that the allied powers should extend their political system to any portion of either continent without endangering our peace and happiness; nor can anyone believe that our southern brethren, if left to themselves, would adopt it of their own accord. It is equally impossible, therefore, that we should behold such interposition, in any form, with indifference.[2]

[2] The text of the Doctrine can be consulted together with the rest of the message in Richardson, *Messages and Papers of the Presi-*

Our main concern is with the second part of the message, which related directly to Latin America and asserted a new policy. The first part related directly to the Northwest coast and was designed to check the advance of Russia in that region; and the non-colonization principle contained in it, while novel from the point of view of international law, had already been asserted as a part of the administration's foreign policy several months earlier.[3] Yet it should be noted that this part of the message, too, was related to the larger situation that produced the doctrine of the two spheres and the warning to Europe. For the first formal, written assertion of the non-colonization principle was contained in the instructions to Rush (July 1823) for his general negotiation with Great Britain; and in the message the principle was justified partly on the ground that "the American continents"—that is, not merely the United States, but the new states to the south as well—had established their independence.

II

The complex question of the authorship of the Monroe Doctrine has long been debated by historians and other interested persons. Many different answers to it have been given; but in the past generation careful study has narrowed the debatable ground so greatly that only a few of them need to be considered here.

Some historians, especially Latin Americans, have sought to trace the leading ideas of the Doctrine to earlier sources

dents, II, 209, 217-219, and separately in Manning, *Dip. Cor.*, I, 216-218.

[3] Perkins, *op. cit.*, p. 3, 11-12, 19-26.

in Latin America.[4]   The similarities are striking and they
have an interesting place in the history of ideas; but their
significance for the present question is doubtful, since the
same ideas can be traced to earlier sources in the United
States as well and no one has shown the process by which
any specifically Latin American idea found its way into the
Monroe Doctrine.   Probably the most that can be said is
that the intensive propaganda conducted in the United
States from 1815 to 1823 by Latin American agents (such
as Manuel Torres) and by American citizens who were in
close touch with Latin America (such as David Porter) did
a great deal to popularize some of the ideas that were
subsequently gathered up in the Monroe Doctrine.

By hammering away at the ideas of continental solidarity
and the great potential value of Latin American trade to the
United States, and by their strenuous efforts to break down
the Black Legend and build up in its place a belief in the

[4] Thus, J. M. Yepes, *Le Panaméricanisme au point de vue his-
torique, juridique et politique* (Paris, 1936), p. 26-27, writes:
". . . On est en droit d'affirmer . . . que le président Monroe
puisa largement les idées essentielles et le texte même de son message dans les notes que le premier diplomate d'une république
latino-américaine auprès des Etats-Unis, M. Manuel Torres, minis-
tre de Colombie, lui addressa pour lui suggérer l'attitude que
Monroe se décida finalement à prendre.   Ceci est un point his-
torique suffissament éclairci aujourd'hui sur lequel il est inutile de
revenir ici.   L'origine latino-américain de la doctrine de Monroe
ne fait point de doute pour ceux qui ont étudié l'histoire diplo-
matique américaine avec un esprit vraiment critique."   The case
for Torres is set forth in detail and interestingly, but not (to my
mind) at all convincingly, in Nicolás García Samudio, *Capítulos
de historia diplomática*, p. 77-86.   Perkins, *op. cit.*, p. 97-98, considers and rejects the claim for Latin American authorship of the
Doctrine as set forth in Charles Lyon Chandler, *Inter-American
Acquaintances*, and F. J. Urrutia, *Páginas de la historia diplomática*.

civic virtue and political aptitude of the Latin American people and their devotion to republicanism, these propagandists helped create the climate of opinion that in turn produced the Monroe Doctrine. They doubtless made an impression upon Monroe himself. Throughout this period he gave much thought to the probable effect of the acts and declarations of the United States on public opinion in Latin America. It is not likely that he lost sight of this consideration in framing the most important pronouncement of his whole administration; [5] and for a knowledge of what would make a favorable impression in Latin America he was to a considerable extent dependent upon its propagandists in the United States. Of direct Latin American influence in the formulation of the Doctrine, however, there is no satisfactory evidence.

There was a time when many commentators on the problem before us simplified it by ascribing the Doctrine to a single author, such as John Quincy Adams or (strange as it may seem) George Canning. Only in recent years has the weight of opinion shifted strongly in the direction of the man whose name the Doctrine bears.

The time is long past, if it ever existed, when Canning's claim required serious consideration. As Perkins has observed with commendable restraint, the case for him is " pitifully weak." [6] Nevertheless, the feeling still persists

---

[5] That he did not lose sight of it at that time is indicated by the letter that he wrote Jefferson in December 1823, in which, referring to his recent message, he said: " Had we moved in England, it is probable that it would have been inferr'd that we acted under her influence, and at her instigation, and thus have lost credit with our Southern neighbors, as with the allied powers" (quoted in Perkins, *op. cit.*, p. 75).

[6] *Ibid.*, p. 97.

in some quarters that Canning deserves part of the credit (or, to put it another way, must bear part of the responsibility) for the Monroe Doctrine. The feeling finds support in a recent work by a leading British historian, Professor C. K. Webster, who notes with apparent disapproval that " American historians have tended to depreciate the influence of Canning on the Monroe Doctrine." He admits that Canning " disagreed profoundly " with most of the sentiments expressed in it; but, he asserts, Canning provided " the occasion and opportunity for expounding those very sentiments " and " had he not made his offer to Rush, it seems very unlikely that any declaration about America would have been made in the form of Monroe's message." [7]

Even if we agree to Webster's statement of the case, it is not easy to see how he has helped it very much. Employing the same process of reasoning and even the same phraseology, one could say that Daniel Webster's famous " reply to Hayne " was influenced by the latter in the same way that Monroe's message was influenced by Canning. Hayne disagreed profoundly with the sentiments expressed in Webster's reply; but he provided the occasion and opportunity for expounding those very sentiments, and had he not made the speech against which Webster's reply was directed, it seems very unlikely that any declaration about the American Union would have been made in the form of Webster's reply.

But must we agree that no declaration about America would have been made in the form of Monroe's message if Canning had not made his offer to Rush? This is mere conjecture—a might-not-have-been that is entitled to the same respect as the might-have-beens of history of which

[7] Webster, *Britain*, I, 45.

the exponents of the art are generally skeptical. In this case, skepticism is strengthened when we analyze the two assumptions on which the conjecture seems to rest, namely, that Canning's proposal led to Monroe's declaration because it preceded it, and that Monroe was indebted to Canning for the idea of making a declaration of Spanish American policy.

The first assumption is open to two objections: first, that it involves one of the most obvious of logical fallacies, the *post hoc* fallacy, and second, that the form of Monroe's declaration, which was unilateral, was essentially different from the form of the declaration proposed by Canning, which was joint. As for the second assumption, one may counter by asking whether it is seriously maintained that Canning's proposal suggested to Monroe for the first time the idea of making a declaration of policy in regard to Spanish America and of using a message to Congress as the vehicle for that purpose. The fact is that every president of the United States from Washington to Monroe had made public declarations of foreign policy, and Monroe himself had frequently used his messages to Congress as vehicles for the discussion of his Latin American policy. Moreover, we know that as early as June 1823, two months before Canning first broached his proposal to Rush, Monroe was already considering the advisability of taking a bolder stand in favor of Spanish American independence.[8] He did not say that this new boldness would be expressed in the form of a message; but knowing his penchant for frank and manly declarations and Adams's for trumpet blasts, and

[8] Monroe, *Writings*, VI, 309-310, Monroe to Jefferson, June 2, 1823.

the caution of both men in deeds, we may be confident that bold action was less likely than a bold pronouncement.

The main reason for Monroe's pronouncement of December 2, 1823, lay not in Canning's proposal but in the increasing gravity of the situation in regard to Latin America. This increased throughout November as the time for the submission of the message to Congress approached, and made it ever more desirable for the President to incorporate in his message, as a warning to possible aggressor nations, a statement of the policy of the United States in regard to Spanish America. Consequently, Professor Webster's assumption seems no more reasonable than the contrary assumption that the idea of making a declaration of policy by the perfectly familiar vehicle of a message to Congress would have occurred to Monroe, and would have been adopted by him, at some time in the uneasy month of November, even if he had never received Canning's proposal of a joint declaration.

The point to be emphasized, however, is that when Monroe made his declaration, it was fundamentally different in content as well as in form from the declaration proposed by Canning. Since even Professor Webster, who believes that Canning somehow influenced the Doctrine, admits that he " disagreed profoundly " with most of the sentiments expressed in it,[9] we need not labor the point. It is enough to say that the sentiments in it which most offended him were its republicanism (he was a militant monarchist) and the idea of an American system headed by the United States and separate and different from, and possibly antagonistic to, the European system of which England was a part.

[9] Webster, *Britain*, I, 45.

If any of the credit or responsibility for the Monroe Doctrine belongs to Canning, it is remarkable how little pleasure he took in his handiwork. Indeed, from the very beginning he waged relentless war on the basic principle of the Doctrine, the American system, resisting the new order that the Doctrine purported to establish in America with as much vigor and tenacity as the United States has shown, in our own time, in resisting the new order that Japan has undertaken to establish under its "Monroe Doctrine" for Asia. As Professor Webster himself has written,

Henceforward his [Canning's] policy in Latin America was to undermine by every possible means the position of the United States. During the next three years, with great energy and skill, he used every opportunity to destroy the contention that the New States [of Latin America] had in any way special relations to the United States rather than to Britain. Jealousy of France continued, but it was never allowed to interfere with the other object of countering the blow which Adams had struck.[10]

III

The "blow" in question was, of course, the Monroe Doctrine. Was it Adams who struck it? Was he the real author of the Monroe Doctrine? The case for him once seemed overwhelmingly strong, and it still requires respectful consideration; but in recent years the careful studies of Professor Dexter Perkins and other scholars have considerably reduced the extent of his claim. That he was the principal author of the first of the two parts of the doctrine (the part containing the non-colonization principle) is universally admitted,[11] and the question therefore relates

---

[10] *Ibid.*, I, 50.
[11] Even T. R. Schellenberg, in the article cited below, note 14,

only to the second part, which contains the doctrine of the two spheres and the warning to Europe. Early in the present century the question seemed to be resolved in Adams's favor by W. C. Ford's well known articles,[12] which brought to light important new evidence and subjected it to a microscopic scrutiny. In 1927, however, Perkins reopened the investigation, discovered that Ford's microscope had been somewhat out of focus, and reported that " a reasonable view " must " incline the balance, which has been so heavily tipped in favor of the New Englander, back toward Monroe." Specifically, he found that it was Monroe, not Adams, who decided that the South American question should be discussed in the message and who " penned the words in which that question was discussed " and " assumed responsibility for the policy enunciated "; as for Adams's contribution, he found only that " in the clear line which the message draws between the Old World

---

in which Adams's claims are considered with a minimum of sympathy, admits that " for this [non-colonization] principle Adams is unquestionably responsible " (loc. cit., p. 2). Perkins, op. cit., p. 8, writes that the development of this principle " was due almost exclusively " to Adams.

[12] Mr. Ford published two articles on the subject: (1) " Some Documents on the Origins of the Monroe Doctrine," Mass. Hist. Soc. Proceedings, 2 Series, XV (1902), 373-476, a poorly constructed article which was nevertheless very valuable at the time because of the many documents published in it for the first time; and (2) an article in two parts in Am. Hist. Rev., VII (1902), 676-696, and VIII (1902), 28-52. While Mr. Ford deserves great credit for his fruitful spade work, the use that he made of the new materials left a great deal to be desired. For example, on the Rush-Canning negotiation of 1823, see Chap. 15, note 11. He subsequently surrendered approximately half of the ground claimed in these articles, for in his article on Monroe in the Dictionary of American Biography he wrote that the credit for the message was equally divided between Adams and Monroe.

and the New the President, in large part at least, probably followed Adams's views." After presenting this impressive bill of specifications in favor of Monroe, Perkins weakened its effect somewhat by the negative conclusion that " it is not necessary to assume " that Monroe " played a subordinate rôle, that he was dictated to by a stronger and more dominant personality [i. e., Adams's personality]." [13]

Dissatisfied with Perkins's conclusions, which seemed to him still too heavily weighted in Adams's favor, Mr. T. R. Schellenberg in 1934 carried the war into the enemy's country in an article [14] in which he sought to deprive Adams of credit for the idea of the American system as presented in the message. His reasons are, briefly, that Adams had certain basic ideas about Latin America that were irreconcilable with those on which the doctrine of the two spheres was founded—for example, that he had no faith in the republicanism of the Latin American people and did not

[13] Perkins, op. cit., p. 102-103. An earlier critique of Ford's articles, James Schouler, " The Authorship of the Monroe Doctrine," Am. Hist. Assn. Report (1905), I, 125-131, contains a brief but very effective statement of the case for Monroe. As Schouler pointed out, Stanislaus M. Hamilton had recently published (1902) an exhaustive and valuable " note " on " The Genesis of the Monroe Doctrine " in his edition of Monroe's correspondence (Monroe, Writings, VI, 346-444). The " note " consists almost entirely of documents, many of which had just been published earlier in the same year by Ford (see the preceding note). One of the best contributions prior to the publication of Perkins's book was made by Samuel Eliot Morison in his article, " Les origines de la doctrine de Monroe," Revue des sciences politiques, XLVII (1924), 52-84, which continued to tip the scales too heavily in favor of Adams, but otherwise gave an exceptionally well balanced account of the subject and is still very useful.

[14] T. R. Schellenberg, " Jeffersonian Origins of the Monroe Doctrine," Hispanic Am. Hist. Rev., XIV (1934), 1-31.

believe that there was any real community of interest between the United States and Latin America; and that while he spoke with approval of an "American system," the system he had in mind was one which was "*exclusively national* in character" and "limited strictly to the *direct interests* of the United States."[15]

Schellenberg was not, however, seeking to abase Adams merely in order to exalt Monroe; and the main contention of his article is that, for the doctrine of the two spheres and even for much of the very phraseology in which it was incorporated in his famous message, Monroe was indebted to Jefferson, who in turn was indebted for it to no less a person than our old friend the French publicist Abbé de Pradt.[16]

There is a good deal of truth in what Schellenberg says, but it can be accepted only with some important reservations. In the first place, he leaves the reader with the impression that Abbé de Pradt was the real author of the doctrine of the two spheres and the American system,[17] which is the most characteristic part of the Monroe Doc-

[15] *Ibid.*, p. 25.

[16] "The paragraph [in Monroe's message] which contained the statement of the doctrine of two spheres bore the imprint of Jefferson's letter [of Oct. 24, 1823, to Monroe], just as this letter bore that of the Abbé de Pradt's remarkable prediction of an American system in his *L'Europe après le Congrès d'Aix la Chapelle* . . . [published in 1819]" (*ibid.*, p. 30-31). Schellenberg's detailed discussion of de Pradt's book and its influence on Jefferson is in *ibid.*, p. 3-8.

[17] Although Schellenberg concludes that "Jefferson, then, more than any other individual, was responsible for the basic doctrine of Monroe's message of 1823," this statement is preceded by the sentence quoted in the preceding note, which (together with the discussion on p. 3-8) leaves the impression that Jefferson was indebted to de Pradt for this idea.

trine. As a matter of fact, de Pradt himself got the doctrine from a French newspaper, the *Moniteur Universel* of November 24, 1818, which in turn got it from an unsigned editorial published in an American newspaper, the *City of Washington Gazette* of October 12 of the same year.[18] Since Schellenberg maintains that the Abbé's phraseology influenced Jefferson and found its way into the Monroe Doctrine through Jefferson's letter of October 24, 1823, to Monroe, the editorial from which the Abbé's idea came is worth quoting. It first mentions the apparent failure of Gallatin's recent efforts to negotiate commercial treaties with France and Holland, and continues:

No one in the least acquainted with the political reputation of Mr. Gallatin will attribute any share of his failure to a want of diplomatic skill on his part: it more likely grows out of the peculiarity of his instructions from his own government, or the present conceit of the Holy Alliance on their ability to abridge the commercial prosperity of America, thinking this the most favorable opportunity for accomplishing it. If our cabinet understands its true interest, in the advantages offered our commerce with the republics of South America, it will no longer permit its ministers to be knocking at the door of an European sovereign to seek a commercial treaty, and be dismissed empty handed. This, if anything can, will convince us of the necessity of adopting a policy purely American. . . . [19]

[18] Schellenberg himself states this fact in a footnote (*ibid.*, p. 5-6, note 12), but fails to consider its significance either there or in the text of his article.

[19] *City of Washington Gazette*, Oct. 12, 1818, p. 2, editorial column headed "The Gazette" and dated Oct. 12, 1818. The editor of this newspaper was Jonathan Elliot. See the article on Elliot in DAB, and Adams, *Memoirs*, VI, 56-57. In 1817 and 1818 the *Gazette* was almost as friendly to Spanish America and critical of the administration's policy as was Duane's *Aurora*.

Here we find clearly expressed the basic ideas of the doctrine of the two spheres: antagonism to the Holy Alliance, the community of interest between the United States and " South America," and a " purely American " policy oriented away from Europe and towards South America. These ideas were not new when the *City of Washington Gazette* advocated them in 1818. The *Moniteur Universel* and de Pradt could have found them as clearly stated and often better expressed in other American publications of the period.[20] Why they took them from this particular newspaper is a question we do not need to answer. The important point is that the underlying ideas of the doctrine of the two spheres were familiar in the United States before de Pradt borrowed them from a Washington newspaper and still longer before he sent them back to the United States restated in the form in which Jefferson seems to have passed them on to Monroe.

---

[20] Notably in H. M. Brackenridge's pamphlet *South America,* published at Washington in 1817, which is discussed in detail in chap. 6. The idea of the American system embraced two distinct though related principles: first, the severance of America from the European system, and second, cooperation among the states of America. Brackenridge's pamphlet expressed both ideas. There was, of course, a wide difference of opinion as to the degree of cooperation that was desirable or practicable. Some of the opinions on the subject in 1815 and 1816 are discussed in chap. 6. See further in Lockey, *Pan Americanism: Its Beginnings,* p. 263-302. Anticipations of the idea of severance are discussed in Daniel Coit Gilman, *James Monroe* (Boston, 1888), p. 162-170, and J. F. Rippy and Angie Debo, " The Historical Background of the American Policy of Isolation," *Smith College Studies in History,* IX (1924), 75-165. Two valuable articles on the history of American isolationism by Albert K. Weinberg are cited in chap. 12, note 35. Dr. Weinberg has in progress a comprehensive study of the subject.

Why Jefferson, who was no mean phrase-maker himself, should have borrowed a French publicist's formulation of a thoroughly American idea, is another question that we do not need to answer. It was certainly not the novelty of the thought that attracted the man who, as far back as 1808, had declared that it was the object of the United States and Spanish America to exclude all European influence from this hemisphere; and there is plenty of evidence that the idea had again been uppermost in his mind in more recent years before he read the book in which de Pradt discussed it. It was likewise familiar to Monroe long before he received Jefferson's letter of October 24, 1823, and was indeed a commonplace of political discussion in both North and South America.[21]

IV

Adams, too, was familiar with the idea of the American system; but, unlike Jefferson and Monroe and, of course, Clay, he had no great enthusiasm for it in the broader, hemispheric sense of the term. Nevertheless, it would not be safe to say that he still regarded it in 1823 with the same impatient scorn of earlier years. In the past two years, as we have had occasion to note,[22] he had come to take a somewhat more sympathetic and hopeful view of Spanish America and this doubtless disposed him more favorably towards the American system. To be sure, his

[21] As pointed out in earlier chapters, the idea was publicized in the United States by Clay in 1820 and 1821 and was the main inspiration of the mission of the Colombian envoy Mosquera to Buenos Aires in 1822. In 1821 and 1822 it was also a favorite theme of the Colombian envoy in the United States, Manuel Torres (see above, note 4). See also Perkins, *op. cit.,* p. 98-100.

[22] See above, chaps. 12 and 14.

new attitude could hardly be called enthusiastic and he seemed quite ready to revert to the older one. Thus, when Calhoun, who was "moonstruck" (according to Adams) by the surrender of Cadiz to the French, expressed the fear that the Holy Alliance with a mere ten thousand men could restore all Mexico and South America to Spain, Adams's comment was that " if the South Americans were really in a state to be so easily subdued, it would be but a more forcible motive for us to beware of involving ourselves in their fate"; and a few days later he raised the question "whether we had not, after all, been overhasty in acknowledging the South American independence." [23]

Another member of the cabinet, Attorney General William Wirt, was, however, the only one who offered direct opposition in these discussions to the warning to Europe and the closely allied doctrine of the two spheres. The main reason for his opposition was that " he did not think this country would support the government in a war for the independence of South America." [24] Though Adams did not support Wirt,[25] he did draw him out on the subject in the final meeting of November 26; [26] and when Wirt

[23] Adams, *Memoirs,* VI, 186 (Nov. 15), and 197 (Nov. 22).

[24] *Ibid.,* VI, 205 (Nov. 26). Wirt had already raised this question at the meeting the day before (*ibid.,* VI, 202).

[25] Adams states, however, that it was he himself who first raised the question: ". . . Mr. Wirt made a question far more important, and which I had made at a much earlier stage of these deliberations. It was, whether we shall be warranted in taking so broadly the ground of resistance to the interposition of the Holy Alliance by force to restore the Spanish dominion in South America" (*ibid.,* VI, 202, Nov. 25).

[26] Adams said that the note to Russia, the message, etc., were only various parts of the same question, "and the only really important question to be determined, as it appeared to me, was

had finished, Adams, while dissenting,[27] said that he considered Wirt's objections " of the deepest moment " and
that he " trusted the President would give them full consideration before coming to his definitive decision." [28]
Adams had already confided to his diary the preceding day,
after Wirt first raised this question and discussed it briefly,
that " it is, and has been, to me, a fearful question," and
" the only really important question." [29]

It is easy to understand why Adams regarded this as a
fearful question: it is by no means easy to understand how
he brought himself to support a message which, as Wirt
declared and as Adams himself conceded, might involve the
United States in a war for the independence of South
America.[30] The difficulty lies in the fact that in this respect

---

that yesterday made by Mr. Wirt, and which had been incidentally
discussed before, namely, whether we ought at all to take this
attitude as regards South America; whether we get any advantage
by committing ourselves to a course of opposition against the Holy
Alliance " (ibid., VI, 204-205).

[27] Adams said, " If they [Wirt's objections] prevailed, neither
the paragraph in the message nor my draft would be proper. . . . I
did believe, however, that both would be proper and necessary "
(ibid., VI, 207). In introducing the question at this meeting,
Adams had already said, " My own mind, indeed, is made up that
we ought thus far to take this stand; but I thought it deserved
great deliberation, and ought not to be taken without a full and
serious estimate of the consequences."

[28] Ibid., VI, 207.   [29] Ibid., VI, 202.

[30] It is important to stress this point because certain passages in
Adams's Memoirs expressing his disbelief in the Holy Allies' intention of attacking the United States might be misconstrued to mean
that he did not believe there was any real danger of war at all.
The fact is that in the crucial final discussion of Nov. 26 Adams's
position was based on the premise, first, that the danger of an
attack by the Allies on Spanish America was real, and second, that
Monroe's message would (to the extent of the President's power)

the message ran counter to the fundamental policy, the
"principle of *duty* . . . which ought forever to govern the
Councils of the Union," to which Adams had given the
most solemn public expression in his Independence Day
address of 1821.[31]   That speech was a blast against Lexington as well as Edinburgh—against Henry Clay, who had
ventured to suggest that the United States aid the independence cause in Spanish America, as well as against the
Edinburgh Review, which wished to enlist the United States
in a struggle for liberty in Europe; and Adams had said
that his principle forbade the interference of the United
States in any foreign war, "even wars for freedom," because such wars had an inevitable tendency "to change the
very foundations of our own government from *liberty* to
power."

How, then, did Adams bring himself to support in 1823
a course that he had denounced so solemnly and so unreservedly in 1821? This question would be difficult to answer even if we knew that we had all the extant evidence
before us.   In fact, the only important evidence we have is
contained in Adams's published diary, and we can be reasonably certain that additional evidence, possibly of great
importance, is contained in his correspondence for this
period, the bulk of which is preserved with the family
papers, has never been published,[32] and is closed to all
students.

---

commit the United States to war with the Allies if that attack
were made (see chap. 17, note 32).   It is only in the light of this
fact that we can understand why he attached so much importance
to the "fearful question" posed by Wirt at this time and anticipated by himself in an earlier session.

    [31] See above, chap. 12.

    [32] Ford's edition of Adams's letters (*Writings, cit. supra*) stops

Admitting that in view of this difficulty only a tentative answer can be given to the question, we may nevertheless venture to suggest what seems the most probable answer. This is that Adams first convinced himself that the war in which the message of 1823 might involve the United States was not the kind of war against which he had spoken in his address of 1821; and that, although the conviction was not complete, he then resolved whatever doubt lingered in his mind by a process with which we are already familiar, that is, by telling himself that it was his duty to submit his judgment to that of the head of the administration, President Monroe.

The first point is illustrated by his reluctance to come to grips with the question, to admit that there was any real danger of war by act of Europe; and as late as November 25 he declared that he " thought the Holy Alliance would not ultimately invade South America." [33] The point is also illustrated by Adams's determination to regard the hypothetical war as a war not for freedom abroad but in defence of the national interests of the United States. To be sure, he tacitly assented to Wirt's view that the war would aid the independence movement in Spanish America; but when Wirt's strong statement brought the discussion to a sharp focus on this " fearful question," Adams made it perfectly plain that, in his own mind, aid to Spanish America would

---

abruptly and most tantalizingly with June 1823, on the very threshold of this critical period in the development of American foreign policy. The Adams family papers are on deposit with the Massachusetts Historical Society. They were used by W. C. Ford in preparing the articles cited above, note 12, but are now closed to all students.

[33] Adams, *Memoirs*, VI, 201.

be merely incidental and that the main purpose of any war he was prepared to support would be to defend the United States itself. If, he said, the Holy Allies should attack and conquer Spanish America, it was " not in human absurdity " to imagine that they would do so to re-establish the old Spanish colonial system: their purpose would be to partition the former colonies among themselves. England would take Cuba; Russia, California; France, Mexico; and, he added, Gallatin, who had recently returned from Paris, had told him only a few days earlier that France was even threatening to recover Louisiana, where she had a strong party in her favor.[34]

" The danger, therefore," he concluded, " was brought to our own doors, and I thought we could not too soon take our stand to repel it." [35] This was his main reason for deciding against Wirt and in favor of Monroe on this " fearful question." His only reason which related to Spanish America at large was based not on his desire to promote the independence of that region but to prevent Britain from adding it to her already overgrown empire. If the Holy Allies should attack Spanish America and the United States should remain aloof from the contest, Britain would probably resist them single-handed and, through her overwhelming naval superiority, would probably defeat them; and in that case, he said,

[34] Hyde de Neuville, writing to the Duke de Richelieu in January 1817, suggested that in case of war with the United States, France might reopen the Louisiana question and employ the French element in Louisiana in attacking the United States. He made some uncomplimentary remarks about these creoles but said that at least they were loyal to France and might be useful in such a crisis. See Hyde de Neuville, Mémoires et souvenirs, II, 267-268.
[35] Adams, Memoirs, VI, 207-208.

as the independence of the South Americans would only be protected by the guarantee of Great Britain, it would throw them completely into her arms, and in the result make them her colonies instead of those of Spain.[36]

In this danger Adams found an additional reason for acting " promptly and decisively," that is, for supporting the threat of war that Monroe had proposed to make. Yet even now Adams did not accept either for himself or for the cabinet as a whole the responsibility of making the final decision. As we have already seen, he accompanied this statement of his reasons for supporting the pronouncement with the admission that he considered Wirt's objections to it as " of the deepest moment " and with the advice to Monroe to " give them full consideration before coming to his definitive decision." [37]

The phrase " before coming to his definitive decision " deserves special emphasis, for the cabinet meeting in which Adams used it was the last of this momentous series of meetings in which the Monroe Doctrine was discussed before it was communicated to Congress; and yet, although the Secretary of State and (so far as the evidence shows) all the other members of the cabinet, except Wirt, had approved of the passages bearing on the " fearful question," it was Adams's view that the question had not yet been decided and that the decision rested with Monroe alone. Whatever Monroe's decision might be, Adams would be able to accept it with a clear conscience, for, as he had said in August of this year and repeated in another connection at this very time,[38] he acquiesced cheerfully in

---

[36] *Ibid.*, VI, 208.   [37] *Ibid.*, VI, 207.

[38] See above, chap. 14. It was probably this spirit, and not impatience, that inspired the well known passage in Adams's diary

the decisions of his chief even when they conflicted sharply
with his own.

Thus it was, apparently, that Adams reconciled the conflict between the foreign policy that he advocated in 1821
and the one to which he gave his adherence in 1823. The
question has been discussed at length because it involves
not only the views of one of the leading American secretaries of state and the most important pronouncement in
the history of American foreign policy but also a conflict of
principle that has run through the whole history of the
United States—a conflict which, at the risk of oversimplifi-
cation, may be called one between isolationists on the one
hand and interventionists on the other. As Adams said
when he discussed this conflict in 1821, it had already
appeared in Washington's administration over the issue of
aiding republican France and was now being pressed by
Clay in relation to Spanish America; and in our own time
it has reappeared on two conspicuous occasions—in connection with the Wilsonian effort to make the world safe
for democracy, and in the present world crisis.

The interest of the phase of this conflict that developed
in 1823 lies partly in the fact that most of the pros and
cons of the question as it has been debated subsequently
were stated, or at least suggested, on that occasion. It lies
partly also in the fact that Adams followed a course which
has subsequently been followed by many of his countrymen, for he first committed himself on theoretical grounds
to a policy of non-intervention, and then, when faced by

for Nov. 13, 1823: " We [Monroe and Adams] discussed the proposals of Canning, and I told him if he would decide either to
accept or decline them, I would draft a dispatch conformable to
either decision for his consideration" (*Memoirs*, VI, 185).

a crisis which demanded action, abandoned the policy without confessing the abandonment and, perhaps, without even being clearly conscious of it. At any rate, it is difficult to read his challenge to Lexington and Edinburgh of 1821, and his subsequent commentaries on it, without concluding that in November 1823 he went a long way towards capitulating to Lexington; but a careful reading of his diary for that month fails to reveal anything more than a vague hint, implicit in his anxious comments on the objections raised by Wirt, that he realized what he was doing.

V

These considerations make it easier for us to answer the question whether Adams contributed anything at all to the second part of the Monroe Doctrine. As we have seen, the researches of Perkins and Schellenberg have reduced this to the question whether Adams contributed materially to drawing a clear line between the Old World and the New, and thus clarifying the idea of the American system. Before we answer this question, we must first recall the form in which Monroe presented this part of the Doctrine to his cabinet.

In this first draft, Monroe embodied ideas drawn from the replies of both Jefferson and Madison to his inquiry regarding Canning's proposal. From Jefferson's reply he took the idea of an American system separate and distinct from the European system; but with a catholicity of republican zeal that does more credit to his heart than his head, he borrowed from Madison's reply the conflicting idea of undertaking to sustain liberty in Spain and Greece as well as in Spanish America. In both replies he found support for his own predisposition to accept Canning's proposal.

It was his intention to couple a joint declaration along the lines proposed by Canning with a unilateral statement of policy in his forthcoming message to Congress; and the idea of inserting such a statement in his message was almost certainly his own [39] and he was not indebted for it to Jefferson or Madison any more than he was to Adams.

Adams began his contribution at this point. His prudence recoiled from the suggestion that the United States should undertake to sustain liberty in Spain and Greece, for, he said, this would make the message " a summons to arms against all Europe, and for objects of policy exclusively European," whereas our true policy was " to meet, and not to make " an issue with the Holy Allies.[40] Yet the suggestion held a strong attraction for his chief, and unless Adams was prepared for an open break with him, he must make some concession on his own part in return for the sacrifice he was asking Monroe to make.

It was under these circumstances that Adams undertook his vigorous advocacy of a policy based on the idea of the American system— a system for which he had never before shown comparable enthusiasm. Even now he had no great enthusiasm for it, in the hemispheric sense in which it was understood by Jefferson and Monroe, and he justified his support of it on essentially nationalist grounds and mainly as a means of reducing the scope of Monroe's declaration. This was accomplished by eliminating the ideological principle contained in the passages relating to Spain and Greece, suggested by Madison, and by basing the declaration squarely upon the geographical concept of the American system, suggested by Jefferson.

[39] Perkins, op. cit., p. 14-45.
[40] Adams, Memoirs, VI, 195.

There was thus nothing original in Adams's contribution, since he was in effect merely supporting Jefferson against Madison in the cabinet discussions of this question; but it was important, for he was an effective advocate and unquestionably did much to convince Monroe that, on both logical and practical grounds, a choice must be made between the two and that the preference should be given to Jefferson.

The question of Adams's influence on the decision regarding Canning's proposal requires clarification, as does the nature of the decision itself. There has been a tendency to exaggerate Adams's influence in this matter. Even his severest critic, Schellenberg, credits him with having " effectively prevented a bilateral declaration of policy." [41] Perkins properly notes that " the idea of association with a European power was not . . . entirely repudiated " at this time. But he goes on to say that Adams himself " whose vigorous mind and will had much to do with the decision that was taken, favored cooperation on the basis of Canning's acknowledgment of colonial independence," and he also remarks that, in the instructions to Rush of November 30, " the question of at once accepting the British overtures was virtually decided in the negative." [42]

In order to understand what Monroe and his cabinet actually decided and what share Adams had in the decision, the following facts should be kept in mind. First, the decision was made in the knowledge that Canning had in effect abandoned his proposal. This knowledge was derived from Rush's despatch of October 10, 1823, which was received by Adams on November 16, at the beginning of

[41] Schellenberg, *loc. cit.*, p. 17.
[42] Perkins, *op. cit.*, p. 93-94.

this momentous series of Cabinet meetings.[43] It is therefore inaccurate to say that Monroe and his advisers rejected
Canning's proposal, for they would have stultified themselves by accepting a proposal in which, as Rush's despatch
made unmistakably clear to them, Canning had lost interest
completely. (2) In this situation, the only alternative
immediately open to Monroe and his advisers was to make
a unilateral declaration or none at all. The decision in
favor of making a unilateral declaration in the forthcoming message was unquestionably Monroe's, not Adams's.
(3) The question then remained whether subsequently the
United States should attempt to revive the project of
cooperation with England, despite Canning's sudden coldness towards it, and, if so, on what terms. Adams's influence in the decision of this question was negligible compared with that of Rush and Monroe. It was Rush who
first recommended the principles finally adopted by his
government, namely, that cooperation with the British government in this crisis was desirable and that it should be
effected on the basis of British recognition of Spanish
American independence.[44] It was Monroe who kept the
door open to cooperation with England by overruling
Adams's effort to make prior recognition a sine qua non.[45]

In summing up what has been said about the authorship
of the Monroe Doctrine, it should be repeated that this
consisted of two distinct parts. The first part, containing
the non-colonization principle, presents a relatively simple

[43] This despatch is cited below in chap. 17, note 5, and is
discussed at length in that chapter.

[44] For a more detailed discussion of this important point, see
below, chap. 1 /.

[45] Perkins, *op. cit.*, p. 93.

problem. It merely repeated in public, and with special reference to Russia, what had already been said in private, and with special reference to Great Britain, in the instructions to Rush of July 1823. At every stage the influence of Adams appears to have been decisive. It was he who drafted both the instructions to Rush and also the first part of the message and who recommended the discussion of the subject in the message. His recommendation was accepted, and his very phraseology was followed almost without change. For all practical purposes, then, he was the author of the first part of the message.

The problem presented by the second part is more difficult, for it was the work of several hands. The value of each contribution cannot be fixed precisely, but some approximations may be ventured. First, it should be noted that Richard Rush's contribution was more important than has been generally recognized. Though he did not urge the unilateral declaration that was finally made, he gave information and advice which pointed in that direction, as will appear more fully in the following chapter.

Adams's share in establishing the policy was less important than his share in formulating the unilateral declaration that constituted the leading feature of it. When all the evidence has been balanced and due allowance has been made for his lack of originality and his mental reservations, the fact remains that, by his insistence that the administration should "make an American cause, and adhere inflexibly to that," he was largely responsible, as Perkins has said, for "the clear line which the message draws between the Old World and the New." If the original ideas of Jefferson, Madison, and Monroe himself had prevailed, the line would have been less clear. But this is the limit of

Adam's contribution. Whatever its ultimate value in clarifying ideas on American policy, its immediate practical value would seem to have been rather small, for it is difficult to see how the Cabinet could have adopted the alternative policy of a joint declaration in the face of Rush's plain statement that Canning was no longer interested in making it.

Moreover, if Adams's original idea had prevailed, the second part of the Monroe Doctrine would not have been stated at all. The message would have contained only the first part, the assertion of the non-colonization principle, which, while it was novel if not bizarre from the point of view of international law, was a far less important statement of policy than the second part of the Doctrine, both at the moment of its publication and subsequently. In drawing up the plans for this part, which contains the doctrine of the two spheres, the idea of the American system, and the warning to Europe, Adams rendered some valuable assistance as draftsman; but its chief architects were Jefferson and Monroe, and it reflects their greater sympathy for Latin America and their more dynamic republicanism.

Chapter Seventeen

WHAT MONROE MEANT

In the preceding chapter we saw how the parts of Monroe's great message which constitute the Monroe Doctrine were drafted by him in consultation with his constitutional and unofficial advisers. We also saw how the Doctrine asserted two broad principles—the negative principle of non-colonization and the positive principle of the American system—and how it contained a warning to the European powers not to violate these principles. We have not, however, discussed the important question of the intent of the Doctrine as proclaimed by Monroe—what, precisely, he meant by it, and what, if anything, he meant to do about it. Against which of the European powers was it primarily aimed? Was it a war message? If so, what military preparations were made to back it up? If not, what was the purpose of the message? Did Monroe seek the cooperation of the Latin American states in supporting the American system, which lay at the heart of the message and of which they formed an essential part? Finally, was the Doctrine merely an *ad hoc* declaration designed to apply only to the current crisis, or was it intended as a statement of permanent policy and, if so, was there anything novel in the policy? These are the questions that will occupy us in the present chapter, and the answers to them will incidentally throw further light on the origin of the pronouncement.

I

The question, against which power or powers the Monroe Doctrine was principally aimed, brings us to the consideration of another conspicuous effort to correct Perkins's standard account of the subject. In the latter, as in most of the previous accounts, the Doctrine is represented as having been aimed principally against the Holy Alliance, particularly against France and Russia; but in 1935 Mr. E. H. Tatum published a book in which he argued ingeniously and at length that its target was England herself. His argument, based mainly on circumstantial evidence, runs to the effect that the years 1821-1823 were marked by a rising tide of anti-British sentiment in the United States, which was expressed as early as 1821 by Adams's spectacular Independence Day address; that the so-called menace of the Holy Alliance to America in 1823 was a British invention which did not deceive either Monroe or Adams, both of whom were suspicious of England and convinced of her hostility to the United States; that the real threat to America in 1823 came not from France, either alone or as the agent of the Holy Alliance, but from England; that all the factors which prompted Monroe's decision to proclaim the Doctrine were related to the central idea that England was not sincere in her offer to join the United States in making the declaration proposed by Canning; that Monroe accordingly decided to make an independent declaration; and that this declaration, the Monroe Doctrine, was intended to prevent " any Power whatsoever " from interfering in the Western Hemisphere, but was aimed primarily against England and above all against England's designs on Cuba.[1]

This novel interpretation of the Monroe Doctrine was effectively criticized by Perkins, who pointed out among other things how the record of the cabinet discussions of

[1] Tatum, *The United States and Europe, 1815-1823*, p. 254-270.

November 1823 and the terms of the Doctrine itself show that it was aimed primarily against the Continental powers. He also pointed out that the warning to Europe, which spread a mantle of protection over the independent states of Spanish America, could not have been aimed at England's designs on Cuba, which was still a colony.[2]

At another point— and it is one of very considerable importance—Perkins's rebuttal was much less effective. He undertook to show that the tide of anti-British feeling in the United States had begun to recede by the early part of 1823 and that, although there was still some remnant of this feeling in administration circles in the latter part of that year, it was not an important factor in the November discussions in which the Doctrine was framed.[3]   On this point Tatum seems to be nearer the truth than Perkins, and the former's position is supported by a piece of evidence the importance of which has not been duly appreciated.[4]

[2] In Perkins' review of Tatum's book, *Am. Hist. Rev.*, XLII (1936), 156-157.

[3] *Ibid.*, p. 155-156.

[4] Even Perkins fails to bring out the full significance of this evidence (Rush's despatch of Oct. 10, 1823, cited in the following note). He points out that the despatch created an atmosphere of suspicion of England and that it shows that the Monroe Doctrine was not " launched in the secure knowledge that it would be made good by the British navy" (*op. cit.*, p. 82). But he distinctly understates the case, for whereas he says that "the overtures of Canning . . . had suddenly ceased," what Rush actually reported was that Canning had in effect abandoned them. He spoke explicitly of the " termination " of the discussions by Canning and said " Canning and I stand as we were before his first advance to me." On this point see further chap. 16, notes 41-43, the discussion in the text at that point, and note 9 in the present chapter. I also feel that Perkins does not sufficiently emphasize the extent and intensity of Rush's suspicions on this occasion or

This evidence is furnished by Richard Rush's despatch No. 336 of October 10, 1823,[5] which was received at the State Department on November 16, at the beginning of the momentous series of Cabinet discussions out of which the Monroe Doctrine emerged. We have already [6] called attention to the fact that this despatch eliminated Canning's proposal for a joint declaration from practical consideration by showing that he was no longer interested in it; but the despatch contained other information of an even more disturbing character. For it not only showed that Canning had abandoned his overtures for cooperation with the United States but also created a strong presumption that he was reverting to the earlier policy of cooperation with the Holy Alliance and to the earlier attitude of indifference if not antagonism towards the United States.

In other words, throughout virtually the whole critical period of the formulation of the Monroe Doctrine the dominant feeling in administrative circles was not one of trust in England based upon Canning's desire for cooperation but of vigorously reawakened suspicion of England based upon Rush's despatch of October 10, 1823. Canning's subsequent course confirmed Rush in his main conclusions. Returning to the United States in 1825 he

---

relate them properly to Rush's previous and subsequent opinions of British policy.

[5] National Archives, SD, Great Britain, Rush to Adams, London, Oct. 10, 1823, No. 336. On the first page of the despatch is the notation "Recd 19 Nov.," but according to Adams, *Memoirs*, VI, 187, this despatch No. 336 (together with No. 334) was received on Nov. 16. The text of No. 336 was published by Ford in *Mass. Hist. Soc. Proceedings*, 2 Series, XV (1902), 424-428, and extracts of it are in Manning, *Dip. Cor.*, III, 1500-1503, and Monroe *Writings*, VI, 388-390.

[6] In chap. 16.

became a leading member of Adams's Cabinet, as Secretary of the Treasury, and while he held that position he again asserted [7] the opinion, formed as the result of Canning's tergiversation in the autumn of 1823 and forcefully expressed in his despatch of October 10, 1823, that Canning's policy was essentially antagonistic towards the United States. As this view was one that Adams, the head of the new administration, was predisposed to accept, the effect of the despatch endured long after the end of the crisis to which it related.

[7] In a letter of June 23, 1827, to Henry Clay, Rush mentioned a recent speech by Earl Grey on Canning and the recognition of the Spanish American states, gave the credit for their recognition to Clay, and continued: "I give Mr. Canning no credit for the part he acted. It was forced upon him by our lead. . . . He esteems civil and political liberty no more than Lord Londonderry [Castlereagh] did . . . as regards the United States, he has been, of all British statesmen, the least disposed to do us justice. . . . Was it not he who in 1823 infused the unfriendly tone into that long [general] negotiation at London . . . ? . . . Mr. Canning never liked the United States or their institutions, and never will, his Liverpool speech [of 1823], and the conclusion of his late despatch, notwithstanding" (Colton, *Life, Correspondence and Speeches of Henry Clay*, IV, 165-166). Rush took the same view in his essay, "Character of Mr. Canning," written at the time of Canning's death and republished in Rush's posthumous *Occasional Productions, Political, Diplomatic, and Miscellaneous* (Philadelphia, 1860), p. 183-195. For example, he said: "His [Canning's] very speech at Liverpool, that went the joyous rounds of our newspapers in the autumn of 1823, in which he threw his compliments over the United States, as the powerful daughter of Great Britain, had no other object, and originated in no other feeling, than the hope of leading them captive, for the time being, in order to subserve purposes upon which he had deeply meditated, and which he was then ardently following up, as exclusively British" (*ibid.*, p. 194). For Canning's Liverpool speech of 1823, see above, chap. 15, note 15, and the discussion in the text at that point.

The despatch is, therefore, worth quoting at length. It is one of the most important that Rush ever wrote, and obviously more important for the history of the Monroe Doctrine than the earlier despatches in which he reported Canning's desire for cooperation with the United States. It deserves full quotation all the more because it paints Rush's antipathy towards the British government in far livelier colors than those that he used in his memoirs, which were published a score of years later in an effort to improve Anglo-American relations [8] and which appear to have been the main reliance of most historians of this subject. The despatch records the views that Rush held and communicated confidentially to his government in October 1823 and not those that he deemed it fitting to publish under very different circumstances many years later.

Rush began his despatch of October 10 by telling how, although he had seen Canning twice in the past two days, the latter had " said not one single word relative to South America," although the second occasion had been " altogether favorable for resuming the topick." After suggesting that the questions involved in their earlier discussions of August and September might have been essentially changed by the favorable news just received from South

[8] In his *Court of London* (1845), p. 1-2, "Introductory Remarks," Rush spoke of the " less and less friendly " aspect that relations between the United States and England were assuming, especially because of the Oregon controversy, and continued: " I have therefore been induced to publish an account of negotiations . . . which I conducted with England . . . including the whole subject of the Oregon; and if by doing so, I may be able to contribute a mite towards awakening dispositions to calmer inquiry on both sides of the water, I should consider myself truly fortunate. I desire to pour oil on angry waves which seem beginning to heave. . . "

America (news of the surrender of the last Spanish army in Colombia), he continued:

The termination of the discussion between us may be thought somewhat sudden, not to say abrupt, considering how zealously as well as spontaneously it was started on his [Canning's] side. As I did not commence it, it is not my intention to revive it.[9]

Canning's pointed silence was all the more disturbing because Rush had been expecting him to resume the topic ever since their last discussion of it on September 26. He suspected (as was the case) that it might have been " fresh explanations " with France that had brought Canning to " so full and sudden a pause with me "; and he was certain that nothing had been accomplished by his discussions with the latter.

Canning and I [he wrote] stand as we were before his first advance to me, except for the light our discussions may have shed on the dispositions and policy of England. It appears that having ends of her own in view, she has been anxious to facilitate their accomplishment by invoking my auxiliary offices . . . but as to the independence of the new states of America, for their own benefit, that this seems

[9] Ten days after the date of this despatch to Adams, Rush returned to this subject in a private letter to Monroe. " The Spanish American topic," he wrote, " has been dropped by Mr. Canning in a most extraordinary manner. Not another word has he said to me on it, since the 26th of last month, at the interview at Gloucester lodge, which I have described in my despatches to the department and he has now gone out of town to spend the remainder of this and part of the next month. I shall not renew the topic, and should he, which I do not expect, I shall decline going into it again, saying that I must now wait until I hear from my government " (Rush Papers, Letter Books, vol. VII, Rush to Monroe, Oct. 22, 1823, " Private ").

quite another question in her diplomacy. It is France that must not be aggrandized, not South America that must be made free.

After suggesting that Canning would never renew the discussions unless England needed the aid of the United States for her " schemes of counteraction against France or Russia," he delivered himself of as hot a blast against the British governing class as was ever penned by an American official in that generation.

That the British cabinet, and the governing portion of the British nation, will rejoice at heart in the downfall of the constitutional system in Spain [wrote Rush], I have never had a doubt and have not now, so long as this catastrophe can be kept from crossing the path of British interests and British ambition. This nation, in its collective, corporate, capacity has no more sympathy with popular rights and freedom now, than it had on the plains of Lexington in America; than it showed during the whole progress of the French revolution in Europe, or at the close of its first great act, at Vienna, in 1815; than it exhibited lately at Naples in proclaiming a neutrality in all other events, save that of the safety of the royal family there; or, still more recently, when it stood aloof whilst France and the Holy Alliance avowed their intention of crushing the liberties of unoffending Spain. . . . With a king in the hands of his ministers, with an aristocracy of unbounded opulence and pride, with what is called a house of commons constituted essentially by this aristocracy and always moved by its influence, England can, in reality, never look with complacency upon popular and equal rights, whether abroad or at home. She therefore moves in her natural orbit when she wars, positively or negatively, against them. For their own sakes alone, she will never war in their favor.[10]

Rush concluded his despatch with a disturbing bit of

[10] See the similar passage in Rush's letter to Clay written nearly four years later, quoted above, note 7.

information about British activities in Latin America: the British government was sending consuls to some of the Spanish American countries, but to Mexico it was sending three commissioners, one of whom, according to Canning himself, might remain there as minister. Why, asked Rush, had Britain singled Mexico out for such "provisionary" diplomatic representation? Was it because Mexico had rich mines and a large population, or because of its proximity to the United States?

Bristling with dislike of England's governing class and distrust of her government, Rush's despatch had an effect upon the cabinet discussions of late November which is easier to sense than to measure, but which must have been powerful. At two points its effect is entirely clear and precise. In the first place, as already noted, by showing that Canning had in effect abandoned his proposal of a joint declaration, it left the administration with the alternative of issuing a unilateral declaration or none at all. In the second place, it confirmed Adams in his belief that the British government's alarm over the designs of the Holy Alliance against Spanish America was pretended and that the real purpose of Canning's proposal was to keep the United States from acquiring Cuba.[11]

The most unequivocal evidence of the effect of Rush's despatch on the administration before Monroe's message was communicated to Congress is contained in Adams's reply of November 30. It had been observed, said Adams, that in all his conferences and correspondence with Rush on this subject, Canning

did not disclose the specific information on which he apprehended so immediate an interposition of the European

[11] Adams, *Memoirs*, VI, 187-188.

Allies, in the affairs of South America, as would have warranted or required the measure which he proposed to be taken in concert with you, before this Government could be advised of it. *And this remark has drawn the more attention, upon observing the apparent coolness and comparative indifference with which he treated the subject at your last conferences after the peculiar earnestness and solemnity of his first advances.* It would have been more satisfactory here, and would have afforded more distinct light for deliberation, if the confidence in which his proposals originated had at once been entire. This suggestion is now made with a view to the future. . . . [12]

Beyond this we can only say with certainty [13] that the despatch contained information and advice that pointed towards the decision finally reached by Monroe in consultation with his cabinet. It strengthened the case for a " purely American " policy, for it emphasized the fact that England, the only European power with which the United States might conceivably cooperate, was controlled by a governing class which was scarcely more sympathetic to the political ideals of the United States than were the Holy Allies themselves. It also contained a sharp reminder that in Latin

[12] Rush Papers, Folder 1823, Adams to Rush, Nov. 30, 1823, No. 77. Italics inserted. The preceding despatch (No. 76, Nov. 29) contained the reply to Canning's proposals. This despatch No. 77 was intended, explained Adams, to give Rush the President's views with regard to a more general consideration of South American affairs, to guide Rush and to be used at his discretion in any further intercourse that he might have with the British Cabinet on the subject.

[13] There are, however, other indications of the effect produced by the despatch at Washington. For example, it was mentioned in a letter that Monroe wrote Madison on Dec. 4, 1823, and Madison replied, " The reserve of Canning, after his frank and earnest conversations with Mr. Rush, is mysterious and ominous " (Monroe Papers, LC, Madison to Monroe, Dec. 6, 1823).

America the chief rival of the United States was not France or any other Continental power, but England. The latter fact also strengthened the case in favor of a strongly worded pronouncement which, even at the risk of war, would maintain the prestige of the United States in the new Spanish American states [14] lest, as Adams said, they should fall so completely under the influence of Britain as to become in effect British colonies.

This is not to say that Monroe was induced, either through Rush's despatch or otherwise, to aim his declaration against Britain, which came within its range only as a part of the European system from which Monroe proclaimed the severance of the American system. What Rush's despatch did was to remind the administration, strongly and at a crucial moment, that Britain was essentially a part of the European system.

II

Further evidence that the Monroe Doctrine was not directed primarily against British designs on Cuba or on Latin America at large is furnished by Monroe's own statement that it was directed primarily against France. This evidence seems to have escaped the attention of many students of the question; but that is not surprising, for it is contained in a report [15] by a diplomatic agent of the Buenos

[14] See Monroe's reference to this point in his letter to Jefferson of December 1823 quoted above, chap. 16, note 5.

[15] AGN, BA, S1-A2-A4, No. 9, report by Carlos de Alvear, entitled " Conferencia à que se refiere la Nota No. 10, entre S. E. el Sor. Presid[en]te de los E. U. y el Min[istr]o Plenip[otenciari]o que suscrive," dated Washington, Oct. 14, 1824. The "Nota No. 10 " was Alvear's despatch No. 10, Oct. 18, 1824, to the Buenos Aires government (*ibid.*), in which Alvear explained

Aires government, General Carlos de Alvear, which has not been easily accessible in the northern hemisphere. It was not written by Monroe himself, but it is probably trustworthy since it is based on a long interview that Alvear and his secretary had with Monroe in October 1824, and the conversation was carried on in Spanish (which Monroe had learned in Spain) and was recorded at the time, and, we have no reason to doubt, was reported in good faith and with substantial accuracy. It was held at the instance of Alvear, who wanted to get an authoritative statement of the foreign policy of the United States, and most of the report is devoted to Monroe's remarks on that subject. Its opening sentence bears directly on the question before us:

The President [Monroe] said that fearing that France, after its success in Spain, might undertake an expedition against South America, he made the solemn declaration contained in his annual message of 1823, by which he committed himself in an unequivocal manner to protect the

that he would present his report of his conference with Monroe in person, since it contained important and confidential information and he did not have a cipher in which to send it. For some unexplained reason, Alvear did send it to Buenos Aires with his despatch No. 14, Jan. 1, 1825, though it was still not in cipher. The report is printed in Carlos Correa Luna, *Alvear y la diplomacia de 1824-1825 en Inglaterra, Estados Unidos y Alto Perú* (Buenos Aires, 1926), p. 43-56. This work also contains the instructions of the Buenos Aires government to Alvear (*Apéndice*), and some useful bibliographical information, *e. g.,* an the account of the interview published by Alvear's secretary, Tomás Iriarte, in *Revista de Buenos Aires,* IX (1866), 526 ff. The instructions to Alvear will also be found in Ravignani, ed., *Correspondencias,* p. 453-458. Another account of the interview is contained in Carlos Ibarguren, *En la penumbra de la historia argentina* (Buenos Aires, 1932), p. 87-96. Alvear's mission is the subject of a doctoral thesis in preparation by Mr. Thomas B. Davis under the supervision of Professor S. F. Bemis at Yale University.

cause of the new states of America in the case referred to in that message; and that he also required the English government to state what course it would follow in case any other nation than Spain should undertake to intervene in the subjugation of the former colonies . . . that the British government replied in a most satisfactory manner through the declaration and speeches of Mr. Canning in Parliament, adopting the principle established by the government of the United States [in Monroe's message] and thereby disconcerting completely the hostile plans of France. . . .

Except that (for easily understandable reasons) Monroe omitted to mention Canning's proposal, its abondonment, and the atmosphere of suspicion of England in which the Doctrine was formulated, his statement to Alvear is supported by the available evidence. There are two points in it that require special emphasis. In the first place, it states categorically that the warning to Europe was directed at France and was designed to prevent the military intervention of France against the new states of Spanish America. In the second place, it shows Monroe's understanding of the significance of his pronouncement in Anglo-American relations: whereas the acceptance of Canning's proposal would have made the United States the junior partner of Great Britain in Spanish American affairs, Monroe's unilateral declaration and its subsequent support (as Monroe claimed) by Canning reversed the rôles and yet (though Monroe did not point this out to Alvear) left the United States with entire freedom of action in regard to both Spanish America and Europe, including England.

Russia, too, played an important rôle (though one which was subordinate to that of France) in the cabinet discussions of the second part of the Doctrine. It did so mainly because the Russian notes received at Washington in October and November 1823 [16] had made the Tsar seem the ideological champion of the Holy Alliance, although there was also some apprehension that Russia might give military support to French intervention in Spanish America. It was the general sense of the Cabinet that the situation called for a direct reply to the monarchical manifesto from St. Petersburg; but there was considerable difference of opinion as to the tone that should be given to the reply. Adams had an extraordinarily robust faith in the Tsar's essential goodness and liberalism—a faith which perhaps rested on the kindness shown him by the Tsar when he was minister at St. Petersburg [17] and which resisted the efforts of Gallatin (now back from France) to convince him that the Tsar had long since forgotten the liberalism of his salad days.[18]

Adams therefore believed that his great and good friend's present course was the result of a temporary aberration and that a verbal chastisement might be enough to bring him back into the path of rectitude.[19] The note that he drafted

[16] See above, chap. 15.

[17] In cabinet meeting, Nov. 26, Adams, repeating what he had told Baron Tuyll about his "high opinions of the Emperor's moderation," said, "I had told him that, having, while residing at his Court, witnessed the many acts of friendship for the United States of the Emperor Alexander, I had formed sentiments of high respect for his character, and even of personal attachment to him. This was true. I thought better of him than perhaps any other person at this meeting . . ." (Adams, *Memoirs*, VI, 209).

[18] In a conversation with Adams on Nov. 27, Gallatin said that liberty was nothing to the Tsar Alexander and "as to independence, it was his habit to meddle and interfere with everything . . . [He] had at one time inclined to liberal opinions; but that was now much changed" (*ibid.*, VI, 215-216). I have not found any indications that this modified Adams's opinion of the Tsar.

[19] Of the most controverted paragraph in his draft, Adams said, "I had much confidence in the effect of that paragraph—first, as

for this purpose was not a little remarkable, for its language was so provocative that it startled even those members of the Cabinet who were much less well disposed towards the Tsar than Adams. Wirt called one passage in it a " hornet of a paragraph." [20] Monroe himself counselled moderation, and in the end Adams again yielded to his chief, though most reluctantly.[21] The upshot of all these discussions was a much milder reply to Russia than the one Adams had proposed to make.

III

How did Monroe propose to support the principles and back up the warning contained in his message? To begin with, did he contemplate the use of armed force? His warning to Europe certainly contained a definite threat of war, as Wirt complained and Adams admitted in the cabinet discussions, and as newspaper commentators in the United States pointed out upon the publication of the message. Thus, a sympathetic and discerning commentator, Robert Walsh, wrote in the Philadelphia *National Gazette*:

Those paragraphs of the President's Message, which refer to the extension of the political system of the Holy Alliance to any part of this continent, are of most serious import. . . . It was not a distant and improbable danger, which would have induced him to dwell so emphatically upon the urgent necessity, at this time, for patriotism and union in the public servants and their constituents, and to

---

persuasion to the Emperor, and, if that failed, as our manifesto to the world " (*ibid.*, VI, 211).

[20] *Ibid.*

[21] *Ibid.*, VI, 210-212. For a discussion of this episode as an illustration of Adams's deference to Monroe on questions of foreign policy, see above, chap. 14.

give so round and menacing an admonition to the Allied powers. He must have studied with severe attention the omens abroad, and probably possessed means of judgment more certain than those which are found in recent events and public declarations, before he undertook to rouse in this nation, the feelings and fears which his language is adapted to excite. . . . The danger, then, being thought real and urgent, it is to be expected that the President will submit plans for rendering the country more secure, and that Congress will exert energy and liberality in providing additional means of carrying the *new policy* into effect. Should France send an armament to Mexico or Colombia, it must be intercepted at once. . . . Negotiation will accomplish nothing for us.[22]

It was entirely reasonable to expect the administration to prepare for the eventuality of war so clearly contemplated in the message, and in fact Monroe claimed in his interview of October 1824 with Alvear that this had been done, asserting that when the Doctrine was proclaimed the government of the United States

had taken all the measures necessary to render it effective, fortifying its coasts, increasing its navy, and sending part of it to other seas; and that in making this show of force its purpose had been to show other nations that it was ready for action in case of necessity.[23]

Whether the fault lay with Monroe, who made the statement, or with Alvear, who reported it, this assertion grossly exaggerated the activity of the administration in preparing for war. In the kind of war in prospect, it was clearly understood that naval power would be decisive; and yet in the message in which he issued his warning to Europe, all that Monroe had to say about the naval power of the United States was summed up in these words:

[22] *National Gazette,* Dec. 9, 1823, editorial.
[23] Alvear's report, cited above, note 15.

It is a source of great satisfaction, that we are always enabled to recur to the conduct of our Navy with pride and commendation. As a means of national defence, it enjoys the public confidence, and is steadily assuming additional importance. It is submitted whether a more efficient and equally economical organization of it might not in several respects be effected.[24]

This might well have been said of the navy in a period of profound peace and tranquility; it was hardly the kind of thing to say if Monroe expected to have to fight in support of his Doctrine. There was no urgency in it, no sense of an impending crisis, no recommendation that the navy should be greatly increased or even that the existing navy should be placed on a war footing. Nor do the subsequent actions of Congress in relation to the navy during this session indicate any greater zeal for preparedness than appeared in Monroe's message. This is rather surprising since it had been noted, as Congress was assembling and before it received Monroe's message, that the " friends of the Navy " had received an accession of strength in it and that the " patronage " of the navy was anticipated.[25] On December 15, 1823, the House of Representatives adopted a resolution requesting the President to submit to it a plan for a *peace* establishment of the navy.[26] In due course, but without any indication of haste, the President

[24] Richardson, *Messages and Papers of the Presidents,* II, 214.

[25] *Columbian Centinel,* Dec. 3, 1823, " Extract of a letter. Washington, Nov. 26." Reporting that the new members were flocking in, the letter continued, " The friends of the *Navy* are said to have received a large acquisition in the new Congress, and its patronage is anticipated."

[26] *Annals Cong.,* 18 Cong., 1 Sess., p. 830. The resolution was offered on Dec. 12 by Representative Timothy Fuller of Massachusetts (*ibid.,* p. 827).

submitted such a plan, drawn up by the Secretary of the Navy. In his message [27] accompanying it Monroe stressed the devotion of the United States to peace, spoke of the value of the navy as an instrument for the protection of the neutral rights of the United States (a purpose for which extensive use had been made for it for the past four years, against the Spanish American states as well as against Spain), and said not one word about the threat of the Holy Alliance to America.

On the same day on which the above resolution was adopted by the House, Joel Poinsett introduced another resolution instructing the Committee on Naval Affairs to inquire into the expediency of constructing ten additional sloops of war; but again no reference was made to the Holy Alliance or Spanish America, and Poinsett offered his resolution on the ground that more ships were needed to provide active service for the officers of the navy and to keep them from forgetting all they had learned. To illustrate his point he said that at present the navy had thirty masters commandant and only five sloops of war, with the result that an officer of this grade could expect to be employed only one year in six.[28] It should also be noted that a sloop of war was one of the smaller warships,[29] and that the

---

[27] *Ibid.*, p. 1292-1296.   [28] *Ibid.*, p. 830-831.

[29] For a brief discussion of the question of the size of warships in relation to general naval policy at this period, see above, chap. 10. In 1822 Rush, whose keen interest in naval affairs has already been mentioned, sent Monroe a memorandum on naval construction in which he said that the size of warships had increased steadily ever since the sixteenth century and would probably go on increasing, and advised that the United States should get the advantage of other nations by jumping the maximum size of its ships from 3000 to 4000 tons, with a similar increase in the calibre of the guns. He admitted that the idea of building ships of such

construction of ten of them would have made little difference in the defense of Spanish America against the French
navy, which was then ranked second among the navies of
the world. That, however, was apparently a purpose for
which neither the new sloops nor the existing naval force
was to be used.

In the final debate [30] on the navy bill in the House, in
which several members participated, there was still no reference to defence against the Holy Alliance. The bill appro-
priated only $225,000 for "contingent expenses, including
all extra allowances," and more than one-fourth of even
this modest sum was lopped off before the final passage of
the bill, which came at last some five months after Congress received the President's message containing the warning to Europe. The topic that seems to have aroused the
keenest interest in the debates on naval affairs in this critical
period was the familiar question of the transportation of
specie on private account in naval vessels. As we have
seen,[31] this practice had been widely condemned in the
United States on the ground that it tended to coarsen the
"fine and chivalric" feelings of the naval officers who
profited from it, and it had aroused a good deal of resentment among the new states of Latin America. Neverthe-

---

enormous size might seem fantastic, but argued that it could be
done and that it would give the United States the strongest navy
in the world. This proposal put Rush on the side of a fighting
navy. The other side, which favored a police navy, was represented by Poinsett's proposal to add ten sloops. The latter side
had its way in the period of the present study.

[30] *Annals Cong.*, 18 Cong., 1 Sess., p. 1875-1877. On April
27, after a disagreement with the Senate and a conference, the
House passed the bill as agreed on in the conference (*ibid.*, p.
2498).

[31] In chap. 10.

less, the result of the debates was the passage of an act which placed some limitations on the practice but at the same time gave it distinct encouragement by providing it for the first time with an explicit legal sanction.

Of course, neither Monroe nor his cabinet thought that his message would automatically commit the United States to war, for they knew perfectly well that the message left the power to declare war precisely where the Constitution placed it—in the hands of Congress.[32] The conclusion indicated by the evidence we have cited, and by other evidence that might be cited, is that Monroe did not expect war to come at all, either through a declaration by Congress or by aggression on the part of France or any other power.

IV

This may seem paradoxical, since, as we have seen, Monroe and some of his cabinet (notably Calhoun) believed the danger of French aggression was very real and since Monroe's message definitely pledged the United States (to

---

[32] On Nov. 25 Adams said that his "paper" (the draft of the reply to Russia) and "the paragraph" (of Monroe's message containing the warning to Europe) "would certainly commit us [to war] as far as the Executive constitutionally could act on this point; and if we take this course, I should wish that a joint resolution of the two Houses of Congress should be proposed and adopted to the same purpose" (*Memoirs,* VI, 202). A little later he said that "at all events, nothing that we should do now would commit us to absolute war" (*ibid.,* VI, 203), and (on Nov. 26) that "the act of the Executive could not, after all, commit the nation to war . . . anything now done by the Executive here [will] leave Congress free hereafter to act or not, according as the circumstances of the emergency may require" (*ibid.,* VI, 208). This was, of course, constitutionally correct, but it was a legalistic rather than a realistic view of the situation.

the extent of the President's constitutional powers) to meet such aggression with force. The explanation is that Monroe counted upon his very threat of war to forestall actual war, that he relied upon the moral force of his message to save the United States from the necessity of employing physical force for the defence of America against European aggression. From this point of view, the moral force of the message was designed to operate most strongly upon England, France, and Russia: upon England, in the hope of bolstering up her wavering resistance to the Holy Alliance;[33] upon Russia, in the hope of detaching her from the Holy Alliance in so far as the Spanish American question was concerned; and upon France, in the hope of bluffing her government into abandoning any plan it might have for intervening in America. The message was also designed for moral effect in Spanish America, where it was intended to strengthen the prestige of the United States as the best friend and protector of the new states and also to foster republicanism among them. The latter point was not explicitly stated in the message, but it was clearly implicit in the passage dealing with the American system. It was a point to which Monroe attached great importance, and in his interview of October 1824 with the minister from Buenos Aires, Carlos de Alvear, in which he explained his Doctrine, he laid great stress on the necessity of the universal adherence of Spanish America to republican institu-

[33] On Nov. 25 Adams represented Monroe as saying that he thought the financial and commercial interest of Great Britain would finally force her to take the side of Spanish America against the Holy Allies, and that he was eager to avoid giving any *political* offence to England that might shock her into the opposite course.

tions as the only means of putting an end to European interference in America.[34]

While Monroe's message contained a warning that carried with it a threat of war with France and while it also contained a statement of the American system that was in effect a challenge to the whole of Europe, he did not by any means proclaim it in a spirit of reckless defiance. On the contrary, he tried to make it as inoffensive as possible and he also tried to keep the door open to cooperation with England. In pursuance of the former purpose, he presented his declaration in the form of a message addressed not to the European powers but to the representatives of his own people. He made it a " fireside chat "; as Calhoun remarked during the cabinet discussions of November, " The message was a mere communication to our own people. . . . It was like a family talking over subjects interesting to them by the fireside among themselves." [35] That was its form, at least; and the form did something to temper the substance. It should also be noted that while the substance of the message which related to England and Russia was communicated directly to their governments, the warning to Europe, which was in effect a warning to France, was not communicated directly to the French government. Indeed, of the three notes despatched to these powers at the time of Monroe's pronouncement, the one addressed to France was the most colorless and the least provocative.[36]

Monroe did not even close the door to cooperation with the British, despite Canning's equivocal conduct and the logic of his own message. Indeed, the idea of cooperation

[34] Alvear's report, cited above, note 15
[35] Adams, *Memoirs,* VI, 200, Nov. 25.
[36] Perkins, *op. cit.,* p. 89-90.

was recommended, though with important reservations, in instructions to Rush written both immediately before and immediately after the message was sent to Congress. On November 30 Adams instructed Rush that the United States thought it "most advisable" that the two powers should act "separately" in regard to Spanish America, but said that the United States was "willing to move in concert with Great Britain" on condition that the latter should first recognize Spanish American independence.

Should an emergency occur [continued Rush's instructions] in which a *joint* manifestation of opinion by the two Governments may tend to influence the Councils of the European Allies, either in the aspect of persuasion, or of admonition, you will make it known to us without delay, and we shall according to the principles of our Government, and in the form prescribed by our Constitution, cheerfully join in any act, by which we may contribute to support the cause of human freedom and the Independence of the South American Nations.[37]

The recommendation was made more strongly in the instructions sent to Rush on December 8. He was told that the President was "anxiously desirous that the opening to a cordial harmony in the policy of the United States and Great Britain, offered on this occasion" might be "extended to the general Relations between the two Countries." Since the arrival of news of the fall of Cadiz to the French, rumors had been prevalent that the Holy Alliance was about to send an army of 12,500 men to reconquer Spanish America. Even if this were true, said Adams, it would take time to prepare the expedition. "And that time," he con-

[37] Rush Papers, Folder 1823, Adams to Rush, Nov. 29, 1823, No. 76. Endorsed, "Received January 27, 1824." Printed in Manning, *Dip. Cor.*, I, 210-213.

tinued, " may yet be employed, if necessary, by Great Britain and the United States, in a further concert of operations, to counteract that design, if really entertained." [38]

It is to be noted that Adams spoke of a concert not merely of sentiments and policy but also of operations. This would seem to indicate that the United States was ready to support a joint declaration by joint military action, if necessary.[39] Whether it would actually have done so will never be known; and there is some reason to suspect that perhaps Monroe did not expect the concert with Great Britain to be effected at all and that his purpose in offering it was merely to penetrate more deeply into the mystery of British policy. At any rate, the condition attached to his offer of cooperation—namely, British recognition of Spanish American independence—was one which Rush's latest despatches had given him no reason to expect Great Britain to fulfill

[38] Rush Papers, Folder 1823, Adams to Rush, Dec. 8, 1823, marked " No. 1. 77 " and " Secret "; endorsed " Recd Jan. 27th, 1824." Not printed in Manning, *Dip. Cor.* For Canning's attitude when Rush took up the question with him in January 1824, see below, chap. 18.

[39] There are, moreover, indications that such a course would have had important support in the United States. For example, on the very day of Monroe's message Senator James Barbour of Virginia, Chairman of the Senate Committee on Foreign Relations, wrote Madison suggesting the advisability of a treaty of alliance between the United States and Great Britain to prevent the interference of the Holy Alliance in Spanish America, and asked Madison's opinion. In his reply (Dec. 5) Madison suggested that while Barbour's treaty proposal might be of great avail, a joint resolution of the two Houses of Congress would be of still greater avail. Nevertheless, he stated explicitly that he thought the United States ought to move " hand in hand " with Britain in this " experiment of awing the confederated powers into forbearance." Barbour's letter and the draft of Madison's reply are in the Madison Papers, LC.

in the immediate future, and the thing he did ask for immediately and as a prelude to a concert of sentiments and operations was a frank statement of the "ulterior views" of the British government. ". . . To the end of concert and cooperation," Rush was instructed, "the *intentions* of Great Britain, under all the contingent aspects which the subject may assume, should be as unequivocally known to us [as ours are to the British government]." [40]

Another possibility of cooperation with Europe was presented by the general congress which, it was understood, was to be called for the settlement of the Spanish American question. Canning had suggested that Rush himself should attend this congress as the representative of the United States; but Rush refused to do so and the administration not only approved his decision but also declared that it would not take any part in such a congress. "We would not sanction by our presence any meeting of European potentates to dispose of American Republics," it instructed Rush.[41] Monroe did, however, send a secret and unofficial agent, Alexander MacRae, to report on the proceedings of the congress.[42] It was never held and MacRae's commission was terminated in August 1824.[43]

[40] Instructions of Dec. 8, 1823, cited above, note 38.

[41] Rush Papers, Folder 1823, Adams to Rush, Nov. 30, 1823, No. 77. Printed in Manning, *Dip. Cor.,* I, 213-216. Yet even after these instructions were sent, Monroe seems to have thought of sending "a special mission, of the first consideration" to England "with power, to attend, any Congress, that may be convened, on the affrs. of So. Am: or Mexico" (Monroe, *Writings,* VI, 345, quoted in Perkins, *op. cit.,* p. 94, note 62).

[42] Rush Papers, Folder 1823, Adams to Rush, Dec. 17, 1823, No. 2/77, "Secret." Not printed in Manning, *Dip. Cor.*

[43] Wriston, *Executive Agents,* p. 574, note 4. The mission is described in *ibid.,* p. 572-574, 696-697. See also Rush's despatch

V

It is sometimes said that the Monroe Doctrine contained nothing essentially novel, that it merely restated familiar ideas and at most gave a new application to existing policies; that it was, in short, merely an extension of the basic foreign policy established in Washington's administration and consecrated in his Farewell Address.[44]

Such statements combine a portion of truth with a larger portion of error. On the one hand, it is true that the message did not contain a single idea that had not been

---

of July 10, 1824, in Manning, *Dip. Cor.*, III, 1525. As Wriston observes, " MacRae was not, in any sense, a participant in a conference " and " was intended to be more nearly a spy " (*op. cit.*, p. 574). The government's precautions in the interest of secrecy were carried to the point of forbidding MacRae to draw drafts on either Rush or the United States' bankers in London, Baring Brothers, although he was to receive through Rush his traveling expenses and his princely allowance of six dollars per diem (Rush Papers, Folder 1823, Adams to Rush, Dec. 17, 1822, No. 2/77, " Secret," enclosing a copy of the instructions to MacRae of Dec. 15). MacRae's letters, with other related papers, are in National Archives, SD, Special Agents, vol. 9. His first report is dated April 16, 1824; his last, Jan. 4, 1825 (*sc.* 1826; the letter is addressed to Henry Clay, Secretary of State).

[44] For example, Frederick Jackson Turner, *Rise of the New West* (New York, 1906), p. 220, says, " This classic statement of the position of the United States in the New World, therefore, applied an old tendency on the part of this country to a particular exigency." Thomas A. Bailey, *A Diplomatic History of the American People* (New York, 1940), p. 186, says, " The fundamental ideas of the Monroe Doctrine were neither new nor original. They go back to the colonial period, and they had been repeatedly foreshadowed if not definitely formulated by Washington, John Adams, Jefferson and others. Monroe, so to speak, merely codified such existing ideas as those of the two hemispheres, no transfer of territory, nonintervention, and nonentanglement."

explicitly stated again and again in the public discussions of the past eight years. On the other hand, it is equally true that the message gave one of the most important of those ideas the first official sanction it had ever received. This was the idea that the United States would, if necessary, fight for the independence of a foreign nation. Coupled with this was the highly important limitation of the new principle to the nations of North and South America.

The fact is that the Monroe Doctrine, far from being a mere restatement of familiar and generally accepted principles, registered a choice between different and conflicting principles. And far from being a mere extension of existing policy, it marked the emergence of a new policy, namely, a special policy towards Latin America which was based on different principles from the policy of the United States towards the rest of the world.

That a conflict of principles was involved is evident when the Monroe Doctrine is compared with John Quincy Adams's reply of July 4, 1821, to Lexington and Edinburgh. For our present purpose, the main point at issue in Adams's address was whether the United States should adhere to Washington's policy of non-intervention in foreign wars for freedom and independence, or whether it should make an exception in favor of the new states of Latin America that had arisen since Washington's day.[45]

---

[45] Weinberg, "Washington's 'Great Rule' in its Historical Evolution," loc. cit., p. 127, writes: "A corollary which isolationist and anti-isolationist alike drew from the great rule is the Monroe Doctrine . . . John Quincy Adams . . . was the first officially to derive its principles from the Farewell Address." This statement calls for two comments: (1) Whether the Monroe Doctrine is to be regarded as a corollary of the Farewell Address or a departure from it depends upon whether one has in mind the

At that time Adams was resolutely opposed to making the exception; and it is important to note that, down to 1823, the whole course of the United States in regard to Latin America conformed to the policy that he advocated, namely, that in its relations with Latin America the United States should be guided by the same principles that it followed in its relations with Europe.

This uniformity was exhibited in the conduct of the United States in regard to neutrality, the traffic in arms, maritime commerce, recognition, and every other question involving the new states.[46] The policy was interpreted benevolently in their case; but it was the same policy. Even as late as August 1823, less than four months before the Monroe Doctrine was proclaimed, this principle of uniformity was reasserted in the instructions to Rush on the Greek question,[47] which stated that the United States had followed the same policy in recognizing " the Revolutionary Governments of South America " as in recognizing " the successive changes of Government in many of the European States." Similarly, these instructions reasserted the principle, " invariably adhered to " ever since Washington established it, that the United States would never inter-

principle of the exclusion of Europe from American affairs or the principle of the non-intervention of the United States in foreign wars for freedom and independence. In the former case the Doctrine was a corollary; in the latter, a departure. (2) While the Adams of 1825 derived the principle of the Doctrine from the Farewell Address, the Adams of 1821 derived the contrary principle of absolute non-intervention from the same address. Like many others throughout the ages, Adams was skillful in deriving convenient principles from the Farewell Address.

[46] These topics are discussed at length in the preceding pages, especially in chapters 6-13.

[47] See above, chap. 15.

fere in any foreign war, even a war for "Liberty and Independence."

The novelty of the Monroe Doctrine stands out sharply against this background. With regard to the new states of Latin America the message placed the United States in a role that it had hitherto uniformly refused to take with regard to any other nation or nations, including the new states themselves—the role of protector of their independence. The message also pointed to the continuance of this specifically Latin American policy beyond the present crisis by stressing the severance between the European system and the American system. The point was driven home in Rush's instructions of November 30, which were drawn up in connection with the message to Congress and in which he was told that, while on the one hand it was " the unaltered determination " of the United States not to interfere in the affairs of Europe, on the other hand " American affairs, whether of the Northern or the Southern Continent, *can* henceforth not be excluded from the interference of the United States." [48]

This was a wide departure from previous policy and it was apparently as far as Monroe was prepared to go, at least for the present. He did nothing to implement either of the two leading positive principles implicit in his American system, which were republicanism and inter-American solidarity. He did not even call upon the other American states to join with the United States, either by word or deed, in providing for their mutual defense against European aggression.

Indeed, although Monroe regarded the Doctrine as in-

[48] Instructions cited above, note 41.

volving " the whole future policy of the United States, as far at least as regarded their own hemisphere," [49] a great deal of doubt remained as to what he meant by these principles and how they should be applied in practice. It was not long before some light was shed on these questions by two important test cases—the application of the Brazilian monarchy for recognition in the spring of 1824, and the invitation to the Panama Congress in 1825. For the present, however, the all-absorbing question was the threat from Europe, which continued to ala.m the authorities at Washington well into the following year.

[49] Addington's despatch cited above, chap. 15, note 47.

CHAPTER EIGHTEEN

SECOND THOUGHTS

I

On the very day of Monroe's message, Adams had a conversation about it with Clay, who had returned to the House of Representatives after two years of restless retirement and had been promptly reelected Speaker. It was Adams who sought the interview, but he tells us that his purpose was to discuss the arrangements for the funeral of the late Prussian minister, and that it was Clay who broached the subject of the message.[1]

His way of broaching it was to put a burr under the saddle of the Secretary of State. " The message seems to be the work of several hands," he began. " The War and Navy Departments make a magnificent figure in it," adding as he pushed the burr home, " as well as the Post Office." That rather pointedly left only two departments unnoticed, one of which was Adams's, and the latter obliged by bridling at the omission. " There was also an account of a full treasury," he replied, " and much concerning foreign affairs, which is within the business of the Department of State."

Clay had had his fun and was ready to be gracious. " Yes," he said, " and the part relating to foreign affairs

[1] In the following account of the conversation between Adams and Clay, I have followed the former's report of it in his *Memoirs,* VI, 224, with a change from indirect to direct discourse. It is hardly necessary to add that the comments with which the conversation is interlarded are not Adams's but mine.

is the best part of the message. The government weakened itself and the tone of the country by withholding so long the acknowledgment of South American independence. I believe even a war for it against all Europe, including even England, would be advantageous to us."

If Clay was putting out a feeler to discover which of the several hands that had drafted the message was responsible for this part of it, he must have got very little satisfaction from the answer. "I believe a war for South American independence may be inevitable, and, under certain circumstances, may be expedient," said Adams. "But I view war in a very different light from you. I view it as placing high interests of different portions of the Union in conflict with each other, and thereby endangering the Union itself."

"Not a successful war," replied Clay, "But a successful war, to be sure, creates a military influence and power, which I consider the greatest danger of war."

With Clay striking a note that Adams had sounded in his Independence Day address of 1821, and with Adams treading the Lexington trail, there was not much occasion for disagreement between them on this topic. The conversation was the most friendly they had had on any question for a long time past, and it was the first time they had ever come close to an agreement on the Spanish American question, which had been the main focus of their rivalry since Adams's return from London to take over the State Department in 1817. This conversation marks a turning-point in their relations and the beginning of a friendship which was crowned by Adams's appointment of Clay as his secretary of state fifteen months later at another critical juncture in the affairs of Latin America.

Clay's gratification over the part of the message that came

to be known as the Monroe Doctrine is easy to understand, for it asserted principles that he had long advocated. Generally speaking, public opinion in the United States divided along the lines suggested by his comments on it. Those who had the least sympathy for the Spanish American cause were the most critical of the message, and it was most warmly applauded by the opposite party.

Congressional opinion will be discussed in another connection. The opinion of the public at large was probably well expressed by the newspapers, and on the whole their response to it seems to have been enthusiastic.[2]

Even Walsh's *National Gazette,* which had long resisted every effort to involve the United States in the Spanish American wars for independence, described it as " superior . . . to any of his [Monroe's] preceding messages, and well adapted to the times and the tone of public sentiment." [3] " It is, we know," Walsh added a few days later, " the idea of some politicians that he [Monroe] has

[2] See the brief analysis of newspaper opinion, based on an examination of a score of newspapers, in Perkins, *Monroe Doctrine, 1823-1826,* p. 144-146. On Jan. 5, 1824, the British chargé at Washington, Henry Addington, wrote Canning: " The President's message to Congress seems to have been received with acclamation throughout the United States. Although naturally commented on in detail according to the political prepossessions and views of each individual, it has enjoyed, as a whole, unqualified approbation." This exaggerated somewhat the initial popularity of the message. In this letter Addington spoke of " the public prints " as " the best, indeed, in ordinary circumstances, the only, criterion of public opinion "; but for a survey of newspaper opinion outside of Washington he seems to have relied largely, if not wholly, on the pro-administration *National Intelligencer* of that city. Extracts of Addington's despatch are in Webster, *Britain,* II, 508-509. Brief extracts are in Perkins, *op. cit.,* p. 144.

[3] *National Gazette,* Dec. 5, 1823.

gone too far, and thrown down the gauntlet to the Holy Alliance, rashly and prematurely. We trust and believe that they are wrong. . . ." [4]

Walsh's comments on the message are particularly important because he was one of the few journalists who noticed the non-colonization principle.

This, asserted as '*a principle* in which the rights and interests of the United States are involved' [he said], has a very comprehensive meaning; forms quite an epoch in our relations with Europe, and cannot fail to have produced a new sensation in all her leading courts.[5]

Most of the other commentators confined their attention to the second part of the message. Walsh himself regarded this part of the message, which contained the President's "round and menacing admonition to the Allied powers," as "of most serious import." It was in this connection that he expressed the expectation that Monroe would "submit plans for rendering the country more secure" and that Congress would "exert energy and liberality in providing additional means of carrying the *new policy* into effect." [6]

The new policy met with surprisingly little articulate opposition in the press. The best example of this was a communication published in the *Boston Daily Advertiser* early in December.[7]

Is there anything in our Constitution [asked the writer] which makes our Government the Guarantors of the Lib-

[4] *Ibid.*, Dec. 9, 1823.

[5] *Ibid.*, Dec. 5, 1823.

[6] For a discussion of this point, see above, chap. 17.

[7] *Boston Daily Advertiser,* Dec. 12, 1823, communication entitled "Queries for Statesmen." Perkins, *op. cit.*, p. 146, quotes a part of this communication as quoted in the Salem *Gazette* of Dec. 16.

erties of the World? of the Wahabees? the Peruvians? the Chilese? the Mexicans and Colombians? . . . Could the black, red, yellow and white populations of the Southern Continent return the favor if we were attacked? Is there any perceptible, clearly distinguishable difference between despots invading a neighboring State, on the sole and horrible ground, that the *principles* set up by a minority or majority, of such a state, are dangerous to their *own* peace, and a free nation's undertaking to interfere to sustain *free* principles in a *foreign* state, because despotic principles would be dangerous to us? In short, to reduce it to the actual case, though we acknowledged the disturbed and unsettled Governments of South America as being de facto independent, did we mean to make that act equivalent to treaties offensive and defensive? I hope not.

II

In Europe, the message met with the response that might have been expected. Liberals lauded it. Lafayette was reported to have called it "the best little bit of paper that God had ever permitted any man to give to the World." [8] Francis Jeffery, one of the aces of the Edinburgh squadron, lavished high praise on it in a notable public speech. Rush, more than ever skeptical of all British professions of friendship for the United States, whatever their source, regarded Jeffery's speech as only an interesting oratorical exercise; but he reported that the message had in fact made a strong appeal to English liberals, and he himself was delighted with it.[9]

[8] National Archives, SD, Special Agents, vol. 9, MacRae to Adams, Nov. 3, 1824. Also quoted in Perkins, *op. cit.,* p. 165, note 78. For French opinion, see further in Robertson, *France and Latin-American Independence,* p. 288-292.

[9] Jeffery's speech was made at a dinner in Edinburgh in commemoration of Charles James Fox, and followed his toast, "The President of the United States, and may there be a speedy union

Opinion in government circles was, of course, decidedly hostile, and there was a strong disposition, especially in France and Austria, to regard such strong language, coming from such a weak power, as rather ridiculous.[10] Canning made no such mistake. He, too, thought that the claims asserted in the message were absurdly pretentious; but he did not underrate its significance for that Anglo-American rivalry in Latin America of which he was so keenly conscious. Indeed, although the message was directed mainly against France and Russia, it seems to have been this British minister who conceived the most deep-seated aversion for the Monroe Doctrine and made the most determined effort to nullify it.[11]

---

of all free countries against the United Association of Despots." Reporting this dinner the Boston *Columbian Centinel* said that encomiums on the United States had recently become "*all the rage*" in England and that the fashion had been set by Canning himself. Transmitting the *Morning Chronicle's* report of Jeffery's speech, Rush wrote Monroe: "I must cordially confess . . . that the longer I stay here . . . the less disposed am I to set any value on any praise of us which proceeds from either side of the aristocracy, tory or whig, no matter what the apparent motive or occasion" (Rush Papers, Letter Books, vol. VIII, Rush to Monroe, Feb. 3, 1824).

[10] Perkins, *op. cit.*, p. 167-168. "The extraordinary language of Monroe called forth no formal representations from any European court . . . Ferdinand [King of Spain], it appears, never bothered to read the message, and the Foreign Minister, the Conde de Ofalia, never gave Nelson [United States Minister at Madrid] the slightest intimation of his displeasure" (*ibid.*, p. 168). But on Jan. 4, 1824, Ofalia did give the British ambassador at Madrid "a long dissertation upon the growing influence and power of the United States of America," warning him that "*old* England would also do well to reflect that a *new* England was rising rapidly on the other side of the Atlantic, which, ere a century elapsed, would probably exceed her in population in the proportion of at least three or four to one" (Webster, *Britain*, II, 411).

[11] *Ibid.*, I, 50.

Perhaps this was because, as Webster suggests,[12] Canning realized, as early as October 1823, that his proposal to Rush was a blunder. Rush had at once taken advantage of it to maneuver Canning into the admission that his government was not yet prepared to recognize the new states. Monroe had then seized the occasion to make a ringing declaration in favor of their independence. Both developments, properly exploited by the United States, might give it a decided advantage over its British rival in their contest for the affections of Spanish America.

Canning's irritation at these consequences of his blunder would have been only natural; but in any case there was more than enough in the message itself to explain his hostility to it. The points to which he took the strongest exception were the non-colonization principle and the American system, with its overtones of republicanism and the hegemony of the United States in the New World.

Hence it was that from this time to the day of his death nearly four years later Canning's efforts to defeat the Monroe Doctrine were vigorous and unremitting. They began at once with the general negotiation entrusted to Richard Rush in July 1823. Postponed by Canning for several months, the negotiation had now at least got under way. The British plenipotentiaries were Stratford Canning and William Huskisson. Since the former had just returned from a successful mission to the United States and the latter was a proponent of commercial liberalism, a friendly and fruitful negotiation might have been expected. In fact, its course was marked by increasing asperity and it ended in pretty complete failure. The explanation of this unhappy turn of affairs lies partly in the Monroe Doctrine. As we

[12] *Ibid.*, I, 49.

have seen, the non-colonization principle of the Doctrine had already been embodied in the instructions to Rush for this negotiation. When he told Huskisson and Stratford Canning that he had been instructed to insist upon it, they responded with an " utter denial " of this " extraordinary principle." The unoccupied parts of America, they asserted, were " just as much open as heretofore to colonization by Great Britain as well as other powers," and " the United States would have no right to take umbrage at the establishment of new colonies from Europe in any such parts of the American continent." [13]

In such an atmosphere there was little hope of effecting that concert of policy and operations with Great Britain that Rush had been directed to seek by instructions sent even after the Monroe Doctrine was proclaimed. Ready to broach the subject in an interview that took place on February 2, 1824, Rush began by reading Canning Adams's despatch containing the direct answer to the proposal for a joint declaration. Canning's only comment was to the effect that " the intervening events had put an end to the state of things " on the basis of which his proposal had been made; and he repeated the request, which he had already pressed strongly on Rush, that his confidential notes containing the proposal should not be given publicity.[14] He then let Rush read his despatch of January 30 to Sir William à Court, British ambassador

[13] Anna Lane Lingelbach, " Huskisson and the Board of Trade," *Am. Hist. Rev.*, XLIII (1938), 769. This illuminating account of the general negotiations is based mainly on manuscript reports of the conferences in the Public Record Office, London. Another voluminous collection of documents relating to this negotiation is in the Rush Papers (see Bibliographical Note).

[14] Rush Papers, Letter Books, vol. VIII, Rush to Adams, Feb. 9, 1824, No. 361.

at Madrid, urging Spain to recognize Spanish American independence.

The interview left Rush with the belief that the British government now had a "steady desire . . . to avoid any further advance to a political cooperation with our system." Consequently, he did not even inform Canning of the contents of his instructions of November 30 and December 8 which expressed the President's anxious desire for a concert of policy and operations with Great Britain. He also reported that he was quite unable to obtain a franker avowal of British policy than had already been made.[15] Thus again, as in the time of Castlereagh, efforts from Washington to bring about cooperation and a better understanding with Great Britain were brought to a standstill by British indifference. This time Washington took the hint and the effort was never made again in the period with which we are concerned.

These facts suggest the nature of the most important immediate result of Monroe's declaration, namely, that it opened a new and more intense phase of Anglo-American rivalry over Latin America. It did not save America by striking terror to the hearts of the allied despots, as Monroe's countrymen were beginning to assert in his own lifetime [16] and continued to assert until the present century. The two most immediate dangers—that France and her allies would invade America, and that a European Congress would be held to settle the Spanish question—had already been exorcised by the time that Monroe's message reached

[15] *Ibid.*

[16] Alexander H. Everett, *America* (1827), p. 287, is the best early example of this myth that I have been able to find. He speaks of "the sort of shivering sensation with which it [the message] shook like an ague fit the old continent of Europe."

Europe. In both cases England had contributed to the result—in the first case, by Canning's conversations with Polignac, and, in the second, by his refusal to take part in the proposed Congress.

It would, however, be easy to exaggerate the value of the service thus rendered America by Canning. In France, which would necessarily be the spearhead of any such enterprise, opinion in government circles as well as in the country at large was sharply divided and it seems very doubtful whether France would have prosecuted either design even if Canning had not opposed them both. French officials at this time and for half a centruy to come undoubtedy gave more or less serious thought to the possibility of picking up something in Latin America—in the West Indies, in Argentina, in Mexico and elsewhere. Early in 1824, however, their plans probably did not extend beyond the recovery of Haiti, whose independence had not yet been recognized by the United States.[17] Certainly no concerted design of the Allies against the freedom of America was on foot at this time.

The nearest approach to such a design was the fascinating but fantastic enterprise of the quondam financial wizard of Napoleonic France, the banker Ouvrard.[18] The profitable dealings that he had with the Spanish empire at that time doubtless explain his continued interest in it. His associates included the House of Rothschild and, as formerly, David

[17] Robertson, op. cit., p. 341-342, 458.

[18] The brief account of this affair in the text is based on Webster, Britain, II, 405, 407-409. See also Gabriel Julien Ouvrard, Mémoires . . . sur sa vie et ses diverses opérations financières (3 vols. in one, Paris, 1827), II, 225-240, where Ouvrard discusses his project for a compagnie armée du nouveau monde and refers to his earlier Mexican enterprise.

Parish, now an agent of the Rothschilds. What he proposed was the application of capitalist enterprise to the Spanish American problem. He and his associates were to form a company to which the King of Spain would cede all the crown properties in America, both in the new states and in the loyal colonies. Using its influence with the other European governments and employing mediation and the threat of force, the company would salvage for the King as many of his colonies as possible and obtain possession of the crown properties in America for itself. Instantly rejected by both France and Britain, the scheme apparently never had a chance of success; but the incident deserves to be recorded as an evidence of the zeal for Latin American investments that was beginning to sweep over western Europe and that soon produced in England a second South Sea Bubble.[19] The incident also indicated that in the opinion of hard-headed business men as well as politicians the political problem of Spanish America was virtually settled and that in at least a large part of it the dominion of Spain was gone beyond recall.

[19] Benjamin Disraeli made his bow as a writer in connection with this Bubble. He published several pamphlets in support of a Mexican mining company and lost a small fortune when the bubble burst. See William F. Moneypenny and George E. Buckle, *Life of Benjamin Disraeli, Earl of Beaconsfield* (6 vols., London, 1910-1920), I, 54-60. An interesting contemporary comment on the bubble is contained in David Barry's edition of Jorge Juan and Antonio de Ulloa's *Noticias Secretas de América* (London, 1826), p. 603-605. For a brief general account of British investments in Latin America in this period, see Leland H. Jenks, *The Migration of British Capital to 1875* (New York, 1927), p. 44-49.

III

The specter of European intervention continued to haunt the authorities at Washington and a few of the Latin American capitals for some time to come; but after the first few weeks of 1824 the threat was never constant or substantial. Even as early as December 1823 some newspapers in the United States were skeptical about its reality. One of them went so far as to suggest that it was only a " gull trap " fabricated by stock-market manipulators in London [20]—the kind of thing for which (whether justly or not) Lord Cochrane had been cashiered from the British navy. By the latter part of January 1824 Monroe had received a report from Paris which seemed to show that the worst of the crisis was over.[21] In April his fears were vigorously reawakened by French naval activities along the coast of Brazil; but within a fortnight they were allayed

[20] *Columbian Centinel,* Dec. 3, 1823, editorial, " European affairs." This skepticism about alarmist reports from London is all the more significant because the same issue of the *Centinel* contained such a report from the *Morning Chronicle,* which stated that on Oct. 16 France, Spain, and Portugal had signed " a treaty for the restoration of the American colonies to the two latter powers." It also quoted the London *Morning Herald* to the effect that " perhaps it would be rash to pronounce against the success of this new crusade of the French Cabinet, after the marvellous successes of the campaign in Spain."

[21] Madison Papers, LC, vol. 72, Monroe to Madison, Jan. 26, 1824. Monroe referred to a report recently received from Daniel Sheldon, chargé d'affaires at Paris, which strengthened " the presumption that they [the allied powers] would make no attempt in favor of Spain for their subjugation of the new governments. . . . Mr. Sheldon thinks, that the attitude assumed by England, and that that [*sic*], which is anticipated on the part of the U. States, will have a decisive effect in preventing it."

again by fuller reports from that quarter.[22] In July, Rush wrote from London that the danger of armed intervention by the European powers in Latin America no longer existed.[23] On this ground he suggested the recall of secret agent MacRae, whom Monroe had sent to Europe at the height of the crisis the preceding December; and in August MacRae was recalled.[24]

While the alarm in the United States had been very genuine, it had been rather vague and the threat from Europe had never assumed a definite enough shape to call forth a preparedness program—much less a preparedness effort— from the administration. Under these circumstances, the most important question regarding Monroe's pronouncement was what character was to be given to the new order in America that he had described so glowingly but in such general terms. The answer to this question depended partly on the attitude of the new states towards the message, and still more on the attitude of the United States itself—of Congress as well as the Executive Department.

In our own time, there has been a tendency to exaggerate the enthusiasm with which the new states received the Monroe Doctrine. Whatever may have been the motives of other writers, certain Latin American critics of the neo-Monroe Doctrine as an instrument of Yankee imperialism have found such exaggeration useful for their purpose.[25] For

[22] For a fuller discussion of this episode, see Whitaker, " José Silvestre Rebello," *loc. cit.,* p. 388. At the height of the flurry Monroe considered making the French threat the subject of a special message to Congress.

[23] Manning, *Dip. Cor.,* III, 1525, Rush to Adams, July 10, 1824.

[24] See above, chap. 17.

[25] See for example Luis Cuervo Márquez, *Independencia de las colonias hispano-americanas, Participación de la Gran Bretaña y*

by overdrawing the picture of a naively trusting Latin America receiving Monroe's pronouncement with unrestrained and universal acclaim, they have been able to heighten the effect of their picture of the Latin Americans' subsequent disillusionment over the Doctrine.

As a matter of fact, in some circles in Latin America, the reception accorded Monroe's message was decidedly cool. This was partly because the threat from Europe seems to have aroused much less apprehension in Latin America than in the United States.[26] It was partly also because many Latin Americans looked to Great Britain for protection and by the time the pronouncement was made, had already become indifferent, if not positively hostile, to the United States.

---

de los Estados Unidos. Legión Británica (2 vols., Bogotá, 1938), I, 272-274, where he first describes the "júbilo y entusiasmo" with which the Monroe Doctrine was received in Latin America and then develops the theme that, because of the narrow and selfish interpretation given the Doctrine by the United States, "Poco tiempo duró el júbilo, la confianza y la alegría de los primeros días" (*ibid.*, I, 274-283). By contrast with this, he says that "en los países de la América Latina se conserva el recuerdo de Canning como el de un protector de su Independencia y su Libertad" (*ibid.*, I, 192).

[26] Perkins, *op. cit.*, p. 149-154. It should be noted, however, that, whereas Perkins says (p. 149-150) that "it is not likely that the confidences of George Canning to Richard Rush . . . had any counterpart in the relations of the representatives of the new republics with the British or American government," we have Rush's own word for it that he kept the Colombian envoy in London, José Revenga, fully informed of his discussions of the proposed joint declaration with Canning in August and September 1823 (see above, chap. 15, note 39, and text at that point). Also, on Nov. 29, 1823, Adams told the Colombian Minister, Salazar, something about the Canning-Rush conversations and said that Revenga "would inform his government how earnestly we were pressing the acknowledgment of it by Great Britain" (*Memoirs*, VI, 220).

The reasons for this were many—resentment over the Adams-Onís treaty, over the neutrality of the United States in the struggle for independence, and over the use of the United States navy to protect its commerce to the positive detriment of the independence cause.[27]   In the case of Mexico, there was also fear of the territorial ambitions of its more powerful neighbor.[28]   Ill feeling had been increased by a number of disagreeable incidents, such as the unhappy mission of the Buenos Aires agent, Manuel de Aguirre,[29] and the European rivals of the United States were already beginning to fan the flames of discontent.

It was only natural that even in the first flush of pleased surprise at Monroe's ringing pronouncement in favor of their independence, some of the Latin Americans eyed it with a detachment verging on dislike.   Among their number were Lucas Alamán and other prominent Mexicans, the illustrious Bolívar of Colombia, and most of the conservative upper class in Buenos Aires.[30]   Striking evidence of the

[27] For a discussion of these topics, see above, chaps. 9, 10.

[28] See for example the letter of the Mexican Minister Zozaya quoted in chap. 13, note 38.

[29] This is described above, chap. 8.

[30] Perkins, *op. cit.*, p. 156-161, reviews the evidence on this point, observes that it is rather scanty, warns that "from the exaggerated view of its [the Doctrine's] significance common to the conventional historical narrative, it is easy to fall into a contrary error," and concludes that while in general Latin American opinion attached considerably more importance to the attitude of England than to that of the United States, "Monroe's declaration was by no means disregarded." For earlier studies of the question, see William Spence Robertson, "South America and the Monroe Doctrine," *Polit. Science Qly.*, XXX (1915), 82-105, and Lockey, *Pan Americanism,* p. 223-262. For a more recent special study, see Watt Stewart, "Argentina and the Monroe Doctrine, 1824-1828," *Hispanic Am. Hist. Rev.,* X (1930), 26-32.

displeasure of the latter was furnished by Consul John
Murray Forbes, who had been living in Buenos Aires
for the past three years and was presumably in a position
to know what its people were thinking. Writing to Monroe
on March 22, 1824, shortly after the arrival of the message,
he said: [31]

I must frankly say that one of the principal motives of my
disgust towards this Country is the overweening partiality
of the dominant party and of the highest classes of Society
here for the English. I can plainly foresee that all we
have done for this people is poorly appreciated and that we
are condemned to be in this Country, *' hewers of wood '* and
' drawers of water ' to the English who are daily becoming
Lords of the Soil by Proprietorship as well as influence.
Your *Splendid Message* at the opening of Congress, so
justly classed in point of character and interest with our
Declaration of Independence, produced an electrical effect
on the Republican Party, whose numbers I am sorry to say
are few, but was received with an unwelcome apathy by the
men in power, because it so far outshone the faint glim-
merings of the British Cabinet, the Shrine before which they
all bend the knee. By the sanction of the Minister, I caused
it to be faithfully and elegantly translated and printed and I
disseminated it through the Provinces and beyond the
mountains.

It is quite true, however, that the Monroe Doctrine
seems to have been cordially received by the more liberal

[31] Monroe Papers, LC, Forbes to Monroe, March 22, 1824.
This letter may be compared with the account in Perkins, *op. cit.,*
p. 159. Forbes hardly exaggerated the extent of British economic
penetration. According to the British consul at Buenos Aires,
Woodbine Parish, at the end of 1823 British residents in that
city owned half the domestic debt of $2,500,000 and "the best
part of the most valuable property in the city" (Jenks, *Migration of British Capital,* p. 353, note 39). See also Forbes's letter
of Jan. 24, 1824, to Adams in Manning, *Dip. Cor.,* I, 632.

elements in Latin America. It was also officially endorsed by two of the new governments, Colombia and Brazil,[32] and in some respects it aroused an enthusiasm that embarrassed its author. The reasons for both the enthusiasm and the embarrassment are brought out by the experience of Heman Allen, the first United States minister to Chile.

Minister Allen and Monroe's message arrived in Santiago about the same time in the spring of 1824. Finding the Chileans under the impression that the threat from the Holy Alliance had been averted by the joint action of England and the United States, Allen sought to correct the misconception by telling the new foreign minister of Chile, Rafael Egaña, how Canning had grown cold as soon as Rush suggested the recognition of Spanish American independence. Replying that this was the first time he had heard the true story of the Rush-Canning negotiation, Egaña went on to propose an alliance between Chile and the United States. Much embarrassed by this proposal, which he had no power even to discuss, Allen hastily turned the conversation with the remark that Monroe's message meant only that the United States reserved the right to act " as its own interest might hereafter require." [33]

---

[32] For Colombia, see Lockey, *op. cit.*, p. 243-244, and Perkins, *op. cit.*, p. 157; for Brazil, see Whitaker, " José Silvestre Rebello," *loc. cit.*, p. 382-384.

[33] Henry Clay Evans, Jr., *Chile and its Relations with the United States* (Durham, N. C., 1927), p. 38-39. See Allen's report of this interview with Egaña in Manning, *Dip. Cor.*, II, 1092-1094.

IV

The idea that the American system was to be implemented by the negotiation of inter-American alliances was a natural inference from Monroe's message if one read it hastily and apart from the context of the diplomatic history of the United States. To the people of the United States itself the meaning of this part of the message was not clear, and one of the few objections raised against it at the time of its publication was precisely this possibility that it might lead to the conclusion of such alliances.[34]

For reasons that have already been suggested, the question of alliances, whether with the new states or Great Britain, was not brought to a decision at once, and the first points relating to the Doctrine to which attention was given were first, Congressional endorsement of it, and, second, the Greek question. Both points had already been discussed in the Cabinet meetings of November 1823. At that time Adams had strongly urged that Congressional support should be obtained for the administration on the " fearful question " of the warning to Europe. Even earlier, in his letter regarding Canning's proposal, Madison had suggested the same thing by advising Monroe to " have an eye to the forms of the Constitution in the road to war." Now he recommended it explicitly, for in reply to an inquiry from Senator Barbour regarding the advisability of concluding a treaty alliance with Britain, he said that in his opinion it would be better to obtain the support of *both* houses of Congress for the President's pronouncement.[35]

[34] See the communication cited above, note 7

[35] For Barbour's inquiry and Madison's reply, see above, chap. 17, note 39.

With regard to the Greek question, it was observed in the November cabinet sessions that unless the message spoke out strongly enough on that subject, the Hellenic bloc in Congress might bring forward a resolution on the subject. That is just what happened, for within three days after the delivery of Monroe's message Daniel Webster had decided to propose such a motion and was engaged in correspondence about it with Edward Everett, who was about to publish an article on the Greeks in the *North American Review*.[36]

As Webster understood the situation, the administration had sacrificed Greece to Latin America in the message, and he was not pleased.

The pinch is [he told Everett], that in the message, the President has taken, as is supposed, pretty high ground as to this continent; and is afraid of the appearance of interfering in the concerns of the other continent also. This does not weigh greatly with me; I think we have as much community with the Greeks as with the inhabitants of the Andes, and the dwellers on the borders of the Vermilion Sea.[37]

Webster did offer his resolution; and perhaps the strongest (though not the most vociferous) opposition to it came from Joel Poinsett, who was an earnest though moderate supporter of the Spanish American cause and was pleased with the " high ground " taken by the President's message in regard to America. ". . . We are running wild

[36] *Writings and Speeches of Daniel Webster* (18 vols., Boston, 1903), XVII, 332.
[37] *Ibid.*, XVII, 332-333.

about the Greeks," he wrote on Christmas day.[38] Two weeks later he wrote again: [39]

We are in hourly expectation of the discussion on the Greek question, which I have once succeeded in postponing being well assured, that as the excitement subsided the members would see the absurdity of running any risk in a cause, that does not even remotely affect the interests of this country. Especially too at this crisis, when we may be called upon to defend our own shores . . . There never was so absurd a proposition made and seriously entertained by a nation. If my health or rather my breath will permit I shall speak upon it in opposition to Mr. Webster . . .

The Greek question and the Spanish American question were again linked together in an important debate in Congress in January 1824. This was no accident, for they were closely related to each other in American policy. To Webster's resolution in favor of the Greeks Clay now added a resolution explicitly committing Congress to the support of Monroe's warning to Europe. In order to nail down the committment already made in favor of Spanish America, Poinsett offered an amendment to Webster's resolution and also proposed a resolution similar to Clay's, but soon withdrew it.[40]

All three questions (the two resolutions and Poinsett's amendment) were considered together by the speakers in the debate that followed late in January. Besides the principals, John Randolph and several other members took part in it. "To judge from the representations of the Washington correspondents of the newspapers," said the

[38] Gilpin Papers, HSP, Poinsett Correspondence, Poinsett to Col. John Johnson (Dec. 25, 1823).

[39] Ibid., Poinsett to Dr. Joseph Johnson, Jan. 7, 1823 (sc. 1824).

[40] Annals Cong., 18 Cong., 1 Sess., vol. I, p. 1115, note.

Philadelphia *National Gazette*, " every orator, pro and con, in this debate, has proved a Cicero or Demosthenes." [41] The *Richmond Enquirer* found it " the most interesting debate which has occurred during the present session— interesting not only from the eloquence it calls forth, but from the points and principles it embraces." [42]

A broad statement of principles, comprehending both hemispheres, was contained in Webster's opening speech.[43] His resolution, he said, raised an *American* question, for " we, as a nation, have precisely the same interest in international law as a private individual has in the laws of his country." His resolution in favor of Greece was directed against the system of the Holy Alliance, which was subversive of international law, and " the same reasons of an abstract kind, that would lead us to protest in the case of the whole Southern continent, bind us to protest in the case of the smallest Republic in Italy." Appealing to pride of race, he said that if the Holy Alliance " is not resisted here, and in one other spot [England], it will be resisted nowhere. If there is no vigor in the Saxon race to withstand it, there is none to be looked for elsewhere."

Poinsett's temperate remarks were directed towards preventing even the suggestion of a commitment to action in favor of the Greeks.[44] Clay spoke patronizingly of Webster's "simple, modest, unpretending, harmless proposition," but he nevertheless urged its adoption, declaring that it did not conflict either with the commitments already made in

[41] *National Gazette*, Jan. 27, 1824.

[42] *Richmond Enquirer*, Jan. 27, 1824.

[43] The following quotations are taken from the report of Webster's speech published in the *National Gazette*, Jan. 22, 1824.

[44] *Ibid.*, Jan. 24, 1824.

favor of Spanish America by the President, or with his own resolution, and that its adoption would be in conformity with the well established policy of de facto recognition.[45]

Randolph wanted no commitment in favor of either Greeks or Spanish Americans. The doctrines broached in this debate, he said, were fraught with disastrous consequences and implied " a total and fundamental change of the policy pursued by this government *ab urbe condita.*"

Not satisfied with attempting to support the Greeks, our world, like that of Pyrrhus or Alexander, is not sufficient for us. We must have yet another world for exploits: we are to operate in a country [Chile] distant from us eighty degrees of latitude, and only accessible by a circumnavigation of the globe, and to subdue which we must cover the Pacific with our ships, and the Andes with our soldiers. Do gentlemen seriously reflect the work they have cut out for us? Why, Sir, these projects of ambition surpass those of Bonaparte himself.

Thus did Randolph pay his respects to the " myth of the continents." As for Webster's eulogy of the " Saxon race," he remarked that " along with some most excellent attributes and qualities . . that we have derived from our Anglo-Saxon ancestors, we have got not little of their John Bull, or rather bulldog spirit." " England," he declared, " has been for centuries the game cock of Europe." [46]

To some observers of this debate, it seemed that the American people had entirely too little of the bull-dog spirit. Clay, noting that it was admitted by all that there was " impending over our country a threatening storm, which is likely to call into action all our vigor, courage, and resources," chided his more timid colleagues by asking

[45] *Ibid.,* Jan. 26, 1824.   [46] *Ibid.,* Jan. 28, 1824.

whether it was " a wise way of preparing for this awful event to talk to this nation of its incompetency to resist European aggression." Robert Walsh, who was surely no crusader but who was disgusted by the defeatism of some of the speakers, applauded Clay's speech and drove his point home by remarking that in this debate " alarms have been sounded which would have come with more propriety from members of the public councils of a Republic like St. Marino, than from any American representative." [47]

Perhaps the most striking thing about the debate is that it ended in the failure of Congress to endorse the Monroe Doctrine. Clay's resolution of endorsement was not defeated, but he permitted it to lie unnoticed on the table for several months, and then abandoned it [48] and the Senate did not debate the question at all.

This is surprising in view of the warm and general public acclaim that greeted the message. The debates do not seem to support the thesis that Congress differed markedly with the general public on this point,[49] for the only important objection to the warning to Europe came from John Randolph, who was a lone wolf. Nor do the debates indicate any marked disagreement between Congress and Executive on the seriousness of the threat from Europe. It should be noted, however, that the first trustworthy report from Europe that the crisis was passing reached Monroe while this debate was going on.[50] It is possible that this

---

[47] *Ibid.*, Jan. 27, 1824.

[48] *Annals Cong.*, 18 Cong., 1 Sess., vol. 2, p. 2763-2764, May 26, 1824. Clay explained that his resolution was offered at a time when the threat from the Holy Alliance seemed very alarming, and that as the danger now no longer existed he would allow his resolution " to sleep where it now reposes, on the table."

[49] Cf. Perkins, *op. cit.*, p. 147-148.

[50] See above, note 21.

report was passed on to members of Congress and diminished the pressure for Congressional support of the warning to Europe.

This possibility should be considered in connection with another fact which appears to have been generally overlooked. This is the fact that Clay's resolution relating to Spanish America was not considered solely on its own merits, but, as already stated, had become involved with Webster's resolution in favor of Greece. On the one hand, the latter was disliked by some of the Spanish American sympathizers such as Poinsett, who regarded it as absurd and mischievous. Yet, on the other hand, the Hellenic bloc was, by Poinsett's own admission, a strong one—possibly strong enough to defeat Clay's resolution if its votes were added to those of the thoroughgoing isolationists. By joining forces the two groups might possibly have procured the passage of both resolutions and that was apparently the strategy that lay behind Clay's support, at once magnanimous and patronizing, of Webster's resolution as amended by Poinsett. But, as Webster himself had admitted before the debate began, and as Randolph asserted far more emphatically during its course, the idea of challenging the Holy Alliance over both Greece and Spanish America simultaneously seemed rather appalling. Since neither resolution could pass without the other, both were dropped.

Some such feeling seems to have inspired the remarks that were made on the debate by the *Richmond Enquirer*, which was then in rather close touch with the Administration. These were to the effect that, so far as mere declarations about Spanish America were concerned, the President had already said enough, and Congress's contribution could be made when the time came to act; and that in such a crisis as the present one the United States ought not to meddle in the affairs of Greece, since by doing so it would only invite Europe to meddle in the affairs of Spanish America. So, said the *Enquirer,* let us give the Greeks our good wishes, but " let us resolve to *act* in the defence of South America against the unholy designs of the unholy allies." [51]

V

A few weeks after this interesting but inconclusive political debate petered out, the economic relations of the United States with Latin America were the subject of a highly significant discussion in Congress. The subject was a very timely one. Monroe's pronouncement had just underlined the general importance of Latin America to the United States and the recent sharp increase in the trade between them [52] seemed to promise the fulfilment of the hope, long entertained in this country, that the emancipation of Latin America would yield cash dividends to the United States. The significance of the discussion of 1824 lies in

[51] *Richmond Enquirer,* Jan. 27, 1824, "The Greeks." It is worth noting that the *Enquirer* (issue of Dec. 4, 1823) had described Monroe as taking "bold ground" in the part of his message in which he "chalked out" "the policy . . . in relation to the states of South America," but that it praised this part of the message highly (issue of Dec. 6), justifying Monroe's boldness on the supposition that the Holy Allies were bent on restoring legitimacy and the rule of Spain in South America, that Britain was determined to prevent this and had asked the United States to join with it in "staying the hand of despotism from this quarter of the globe," and that Monroe had reason to believe that, after South America, "we should be the next to be devoured."

[52] Charles Lyon Chandler, "United States Commerce with Latin America at the Promulgation of the Monroe Doctrine," *Qly. Jour. Econ.,* XXXVIII (1923), 466-487.

the fact that it led to a more searching analysis of the foundations of this hope than had ever been made before, at least in Congress.

Again the main discussion took place in the House of Representatives, not the Senate, and again Henry Clay took a leading part in it. This time, indeed, he percipitated the whole discussion. The speech in which he did so is particularly notable because, while it accorded a prominent place to Latin American relations, it gave a very different meaning to the term " American system " from that which was attached to it in Monroe's great message of the preceding December. This was, of course, Clay's well-known speech of March 31, 1824,[53] in which he urged the adoption of a system of tariff protection for American manufacturers.

He began with a description of the economic distress that pervaded " every part of the Union, every class of society," and attributed it to the fact that " during almost the whole existence of this government, we have shaped our industry, our navigation, and our commerce, in reference to an extraordinary war in Europe, and to foreign markets, which no longer exist." The remedy, he said, lay in the

[53] *Annals Cong.*, 18 Cong., 1 Sess., vol. 2, p. 1963-1981. The speech can also be consulted in Coulton, *Life and Speeches of Henry Clay*, I, 219-266. In 1824, after his return from a trip to Colombia, William Duane published a pamphlet, *The Two Americas, Great Britain, and the Holy Alliance* (Washington, 1824) in which he described the rapid growth of British trade with Latin America and urged the United States to protect its manufactures partly in order to be able to compete more successfully with the British in that region. For British trade with Latin America in this period, see Leonard A. Lawson, *The Relation of British Policy to the Declaration of the Monroe Doctrine* (New York, 1922), chap. IV.

modification of "our foreign policy" and in the adoption
of "a genuine American system," namely, the establishment
of a protective tariff in order to create a home market.

The nature of the United States' relations with Latin
America provided Clay with some of his ammunition. So
far, he said, our exports to Latin America had consisted
mainly foodstuffs; but he warned that with the end of the
wars of independence, which seemed to be near at hand,
Latin America would feed itself. The only hope of maintaining and developing an extensive export trade to it lay
in the promotion of manufactures in the United States.
"We know," he said, "that our cotton fabrics have been
recently exported, in a large amount, to South America,
where they maintain a successful competition with those
of any other country."

Throughout the following month the debate continued to
call forth repeated references to the bearing of Clay's
proposal on the relations of the United States with Latin
America. Among those who discussed this aspect of the
question were, besides Clay himself, Webster of Massachusetts and Hayne of South Carolina.

The inter-relation of economics and politics and the
bearing of the tariff question on the threat from the Holy
Alliance was brought out in a speech by Robert Garnett,
the contumacious member from Virginia who had stood out
alone against the recognition of the new states in 1822.
Speaking in answer to the argument that tariff protection
was necessary for national defense, he asserted that the
United States had no reason to expect to be at war with any
power, least of all England, for the next twenty years,
unless it undertook "to go 'a colonelling' for universal
liberty." In the improbable case of an attack on America
by the Holy Allies, he said,

I believe, next to our own valor, our best security is the attachment of the people of England to the principles of free government. Yet the policy recommended [by Clay] is, to weaken the ties subsisting between the two countries, and to destroy our mutual interest in each other's prosperity.[54]

Some important conclusions regarding the economic relations of the United States with Latin America emerged from this protracted discussion and their total effect was not very encouraging. It was shown that Latin America was an invaluable source of supply of specie for the payment of trade balances in Europe, China, and India, and that in the carrying trade between Latin America and other parts of the world the United States enjoyed certain advantages over its chief rivals, the British, even in trade with British India. One of the most important of these advantages, however, was almost certain to be lost since it arose from flaws in Great Britain's own legislation and from the "sluggishness" of the monopolistic East India Company, and it was only too likely that both of these defects would be corrected by the British sooner or later.[55]

Elsewhere the outlook was even darker. It was almost universally admitted that the considerable demand which had long existed in Latin America for foodstuffs and munitions from the United States was an accident of wartime and would diminish greatly, if it did not, as Clay warned, vanish completely with the restoration of peace.[56] Clay and other optimists [57] hoped that compensation would be found in

[54] *Annals Cong.*, 18 Cong., 1 Sess., vol. 2, p. 2095.

[55] See especially Webster's discussion of these points in his speech of April 2 in *ibid.*, p. 2050-2051. The same point was made by Williams of Mississippi (*ibid.*, p. 2113).

[56] *Ibid.*, p. 1969.

[57] E. g., Webster (who, however, was still opposed to protection

the development of a market for United States manufactures in Latin America; but Hayne punctured this
balloon by producing figures which showed that at present
this branch of the export trade of the United States was
insignificant and by pointing out that, as for the future, the
manufacturers of the United States could not hope to
compete with England abroad at a time when, as Clay
himself admitted, they could not do so even at home except
behind the protection of a high tariff wall.[58]

To make matters even worse, Latin America was already
competing directly with the United States in the production
of foodstuffs and raw materials, such as cereals, beef,
livestock, tobacco, and cotton. With the restoration of
peace, this competition was likely to increase rapidly.
European capitalists were already showing a keen interest in
the development of the natural resources of Latin America,
and in the case of England, which was already the world's
chief banker and had already made some investments in
Latin America, a spur to further activity would be provided
by the adoption of Clay's American system.[59] Though the

at this time), James Strong of New York, and Cassedy of New
Jersey (*ibid.*, p. 2058, 2060, 2129-2132, 2146-2147). On Jan. 6,
1824, Samuel Slater and other Rhode Island manufacturers had
submitted a memorial to Congress in which they argued that a
protective tariff would increase the sale of manufactures of the
United States in Latin America (*Annals Cong.*, 18 Cong., 1 Sess.,
vol. 2, p. 3123).

[58] *Ibid.*, vol. 1, p. 636-637, Hayne's speech of April 30, 1824,
in the Senate debate on the tariff bill.

[59] This point was made, with special reference to the competition of Brazilian cotton, by Rankin of Mississippi and Hamilton
and McDuffie of South Carolina (*ibid.*, vol. 2, p. 2011, 2195,
2426). The argument had already been anticipated and rebutted
in a memorial of March 10, 1824, by the Pennsylvania Society
for the Encouragement of Manufactures (*ibid.*, p. 3180-3181).

point does not seem to have been mentioned in this debate, experience had already shown that the United States, itself a debtor nation, was not in a position to supply capital for this purpose.

Some of these points were brought out even more clearly in the presidential campaign of 1824, in which the Latin American policy of the United States was an issue of considerable importance. Since Monroe, who was officially responsible for the policy now in effect, was not a candidate for re-election, Henry Clay was naturally the candidate on whom most of the discussion centered, for both friend and foe seemed to regard him as mainly responsible for the adoption of the policy. Two of the campaign pamphlets will illustrate the general trend of the argument on both sides.

A pro-Clay pamphlet [60] of fifteen pages devoted one page to his services to the " South American " cause, which were listed as one of the reasons why he ought to be elected president. The consideration that was stressed was the value of these services not to the material interests of the United States but to the cause of liberty.

Under the influence of an ardent patriotism, of the most exalted benevolence [said the writer], he [Clay] appealed from the cold calculating policy of the Cabinet, to the people of the United States. They responded to the appeal, and his generous efforts were crowned with triumphant success.

The supporters of the rival claims of Andrew Jackson to the suffrages of his countrymen argued that Clay's benev-

[60] *Some Reasons Why the Votes of the State of New York Ought to be Given to Henry Clay, For President of the United States* (New York, 1824), signed " Millions " and dated Oct 7, 1824 (p. 15).

olence had been too exalted and that the Cabinet should have been even more coldly calculating in its Latin American policy. They evidently believed that they could win votes by stressing this issue, for " Philo-Jackson " devoted the whole of a twenty-four page pamphlet to it.[61] He, too, held that this policy was in large measure Clay's policy, and he criticized it on two grounds. In the first place, by promoting Spanish American independence, it had injured the United States by stimulating the development of a competing region, which not only produced many of the same articles as the United States but also was able to sell them at a far lower price. In the second place, the policy had aroused the hostility of Spain and her European allies, with the result that, having no other friend, the United States must now protect itself by forming an alliance with Great Britain. Since the danger of war was great, the American people ought of course to elect as their president that experienced soldier and brilliant general, Andrew Jackson.

" Philo-Jackson " was particularly irritated because the administration was spending $100,000 a year on its diplomatic missions to Latin America. Two of the new posts, he said, were held by Kentuckians, who were doubtless " very worthy " men; " but I am well assured that no trade can be driven between Kentucky and the countries to which they are accredited, which will ever yield to Kentucky as much benefit as their salaries and other expenditures will amount to."

[61] *The Presidential Election . . . Relating also to South America, A War with the Holy Allies, and to an Alliance with Great Britain. Fifth Series.* By *Philo-Jackson* (Frankfort, Ky., 1824). Dated March 25, 1824 (p. 25).

Latin America did in fact bulk large in the diplomatic service of the United States at that time. In the State Department's budget for 1824 [62] it accounted for five of the ten ministers to foreign countries and three of the five were already at their posts in Buenos Aires, Colombia, and Chile.

VI

In the administration itself there seem to have been no serious misgivings about the new Latin American policy, and the remainder of Monroe's administration was signalized mainly by the definition and reaffirmation of the policy. These developments are illustrated by four incidents that occurred between May and November 1824, namely, the recognition of Brazil, the reply to the Colombian government's suggestion of an alliance, Monroe's interview with the Buenos Aires minister Carlos de Alvear, and his last annual message to Congress.

Early in 1824 the imperial Brazilian government commissioned José Silvestre Rebello chargé d'affaires to the United States and sent him to Washington to obtain recognition and to purchase warships for the Brazilian navy.[63]

[62] National Archives, SD, Domestic Letters, vol. 20, p. 250-251, "Estimate of Appropriations for the year 1824." This included salaries for ministers at London, Paris, St. Petersburg, Madrid, Lisbon, Buenos Aires, Bogotá, Santiago de Chile, Mexico, and Lima at $9000, and for chargés d'affaires at Madrid, Stockholm and the Hague at $4500.

[63] The following account is condensed from my article, "José Silvestre Rebello, loc. cit., p. 384-389, which is based partly on unpublished manuscript sources in the Brazilian foreign archives in the Itamaraty Palace, Rio de Janeiro, and partly on printed materials. Among the latter there are two items that deserve special mention: (1) Hildebrando Accioly, O Reconhecimento do Brasil pelos Estados Unidos da America (São Paulo, 1936) and

Though Rebello's mission had already been decided on before Monroe's message of December 1823 reached Rio de Janeiro, it arrived in time to shape Rebello's instructions. These cited the Monroe Doctrine in support of the request for recognition and constituted the first response to the message from any South American government.

For the present purpose, the most important part of Rebello's mission related to recognition. His request for recognition was discussed at length by Monroe and his Cabinet, for it involved the meaning of that part of the Doctrine which might be understood to proscribe monarchy from America. Attorney General William Wirt was the only member of the Cabinet who wished to invoke this intepretation against the recognition of the new monarchy at Rio de Janeiro. Calhoun retorted that this did violence to the language as well as the spirit of the message, which asserted the independence of the new states and left it to them to set up whatever form of government they chose, whether republican or monarchical. Substantially the same view was stated at a subsequent meeting by Secretary of the Treasury William H. Crawford, who was absent from the first discussion; and it was accepted by Monroe and apparently by every member of the Cabinet except Wirt,[64] for after a brief delay Rebello was received by the President in

---

(2) *Archivo diplomatico da independencia*, vol. V (Rio de Janeiro, 1923), which contains selected documents from the Itamaraty archives relating to Rebello's mission, and also an account of the mission by Zacarias de Góes Carvalho (p. vii-xlvii).

[64] The cabinet discussion of this question is recorded in Adams, *Memoirs*, VI, 281-282, 314, 328-329. Adams quotes Monroe himself as saying that "the essential principle for us was independence. The form of government was not our concern . . ." (*ibid.*, VI, 319). For a different view see Perkins, p. 95-96, note 66.

a formal audience which signified the recognition of his government.

This episode is all the more important because the Brazilian government was not only a monarchy but also in a sense a European monarchy, since the emperor was a member of the Portuguese House of Braganza and was closely related to the dynasties of Spain and Austria. Inded, this fact seems to have been one of Monroe's main reasons for recognizing the new empire, for he felt, as in the case of the Mexican empire in 1822, that he could make his recognition policy less offensive to the European powers by showing his readiness to recognize monarchical as well as republican governments in the new states. Whether or not this was the decisive consideration, the fact remains that within five months after the Monroe Doctrine was proclaimed, the same President and Cabinet who formulated it showed that the proscription of monarchy from America was not a part of the new policy. Indeed, Monroe gave positive aid to the establishment of monarchy in America. For no other government outside of Latin America had yet recognized the Brazilian empire, and by taking the lead in the process of recognition the United States helped the imperial government at Rio to consolidate its position in Brazil and obtain admission to the family of nations.

The same desire to avoid too provocative an attitude towards Europe that had marked the formulation of the Doctrine and its application to Brazil also characterized the reply to the Colombian government's inquiry as to the meaning of the Monroe Doctrine. The inquiry was contained in a note addressed to Adams on July 2, 1824, by the Colombian minister at Washington, José María Salazar.[65]

[65] Manning, *Dip. Cor.*, II, 1281-1282. As stated by Perkins,

According to his note, there was still a real danger of armed intervention by the Holy Alliance in America, especially by the action of France through Spain, which was still occupied by French troops. The most interesting point in the note, however, was that it fixed attention on a less obvious but possibly more serious aspect of the threat from Europe, which had been noticed only by implication in Monroe's message. This was the danger that the European powers would exert pressure on the new states to establish monarchical in place of republican governments. According to Salazar, the Holy Alliance objected less to their independence than to " the principles which they profess, and to the republican form " of their governments.

Consequently, said Salazar, his government wished to know (1) in what manner the United States intended to resist interference by the Holy Alliance in the " political forms " of the new states as well as its efforts to reconquer them; (2) whether the United States would enter into a treaty of alliance with Colombia to defend America; and (3) whether it would regard as "foreign interference " the employment of Spanish forces against America at a time when Spain was occupied by French troops and its government was under the influence of France and her allies.

Adams replied to the inquiry a month later,[66] after discussing it in a rump cabinet meeting attended only by

---

op. cit., p. 186, Salazar's note was " first given due importance by the fruitful researches of Professor [William Spence] Robertson." See the latter's article, " South America and the Monroe Doctrine," loc. cit., p. 88-92. He has subsequently brought to light much new information about the French agent Benoît Chasseriau, whose mission to Colombia was given an important place in Salazar's note (France and Latin-American Independence, p. 323-330).

[66] Manning, Dip. Cor., I, 224-226.

Monroe and Calhoun, besides himself.[67] Taking Salazar's
questions in the order in which they have been stated
above, we may summarize Adams's reply to them as
follows: (1) In effect, Adams refused to regard the possibility of European pressure on the new states to convert
their republican governments into monarchies as constituting a serious danger. As for the other aspect of the threat
from Europe—an effort at reconquest—he pointed out that,
if the attempt were made, it would raise the question of a
declaration of war, the power to make which was vested
by the constitution not in the President, but in Congress.
" The sentiments of the President," he continued, " remain
as they were expressed in his last annual message to Congress." If the crisis which gave rise to the message should
recur, the President would recommend appropriate action to
Congress, and if Congress concurred, the action would be
"efficaciously maintained." However, he added, "the occasion
for this resort could arise only by a delberate and concerted
system of the allied Powers to exercise force against the freedom and Independence of your Republic." Consequently,
the United States "could not undertake resistance to them by
force of arms, without a previous understanding with those
European powers, whose interests and whose principles
would secure from them an active and efficient cooperation
in the cause." (2) There was no reason to doubt that this
cooperation could be obtained; but it would have to be
obtained before, or at least at the same time with, the
negotiation of any alliance with Colombia. (3) The employment of Spanish forces in America during the French
occupation of Spain would not " constitute a case upon

[67] Adams, *Memoirs*, VI, 399.

which the United States would feel themselves justified in departing from the neutrality which they have hitherto observed."

Adams's note has been described as constituting a " distinct retreat " from the Monroe Doctrine.[68] It is difficult to see wherein the retreat consisted, even if one considers only the text of Monroe's message. If one considers also the contemporaneous and closely related notes to England and Russia, and the cabinet discussions of November 1823, it would seem that the reply to Salazar substantially reaffirmed the policy established at the time of Monroe's pronouncement. Caution marked the note to Salazar, but it had also marked even the reply to Russia's absolutist manifesto, and still more the note to France. The fact that Monroe's message did not and could not constitutionally commit the United States to war had been stated by Adams as clearly and forcefully in the cabinet meetings of November 1823 as it was now stated in the note to Salazar. And the desire for the cooperation of England in the defense of Spanish America against any attack by the Holy Alliance, which was broadly hinted in the note to Salazar, had been the subject of instructions sent to Richard Rush at London only five days after the publication of Monroe's message.[69]

The only important difference was one of definition, for it consisted in the fact that the reply to Salazar defined the limits of Monroe's American system more clearly by discouraging, though not unconditionally rejecting, the

[68] Perkins, *Monroe Doctrine*, p. 192: " If the Adams note to Salazar was not the abandonment of the Doctrine, it was, I think it must be conceded, a distinct retreat."

[69] See the discussion of these topics in chap. 17.

suggestion of an alliance with Colombia. This showed more clearly than Monroe's message had done that the aspect of the American system in which he was most interested was not cooperation with the other American states but the severance of America from Europe. It also showed that the traditional opposition against entangling alliances had been carried over into the new Latin American policy and was acting as a brake upon its development. The demonstration was completed the following year when a similar proposal for an alliance with Brazil was flatly rejected by Adams, who was now President, and his secretary of state, Henry Clay.[70]

If, therefore, the reply to Salazar marked any retreat from the policy of December 1823, it was a retreat from cooperation with Latin America, not from opposition to Europe; but even in the former case the retreat was only from a position which was at most implicit in Monroe's assertion of the American system. He had never said that his system included cooperation with the new states; he had not, even at the height of the crisis, sought their cooperation; and if he now rebuffed the overture of one of them for cooperation, he only made clearer a position that he seems to have maintained from the beginning. Now that the threat from Europe was no longer causing great uneasiness at Washington, the chief care of the administration was to avoid involvements with the new states that might prove embarrassing at a later period.

The mission of the Buenos Aires agent, Carlos de Alvear, threw fresh light on Monroe's attitude towards the problem of republicanism and monarchy in Latin America. The

[70] Manning, *Dip. Cor.*, I, 233-234, Clay to Rebello, April 13, 1825.

reply to Salazar had shown pretty conclusively that Monroe
had no intention of intervening in the domestic conflict in
Latin America over the issue; but his interview with Alvear
showed that he was deeply interested in it, and that he
attached great importance to the consolidation of republican
regimes in the new states. Indeed, he told Alvear that in
his opinion the belief that a strong monarchical element
existed in Latin America was the only thing that kept
interventionism alive in Europe. In their own interests,
therefore, the new states ought to make a convincing
demonstration of their devotion to republicanism. Alvear
took these paternal admonitions in good part, passing them
on to his government with evident approval and with warm
praise for Monroe himself and evident satisfaction with his
Doctrine.[71]

VII

In his annual message of December 1824,[72] which was in
effect his farewell address, Monroe reasserted the basic
principle of his warning to Europe of the preceding year—
the doctrine of the two spheres—but there were some
important differences between the two messages. In the
first place, whereas the message of 1823 was oriented
towards the danger of the European intervention to " re-
subjugate " the new states, the present message seemed to
assume that that danger had passed, and dealt mainly with
the internal problem of republicanism and monarchy in

[71] Alvear's report of this interview is cited above, chap. 17,
note 15.

[72] Richardson, *Messages and Papers of the Presidents,* II, 260.
The message was dated Dec. 7, 1824. Again, as in the message
of Dec. 2, 1823, Monroe discussed this topic in a paragraph
separated by several pages from the part of the message dealing
with normal diplomatic relations.

Latin America. In the second place, the present message asserted a new principle—the principle of non-intervention in this internal problem of the new states. Echoing the opinion that had led to the recognition of the Brazilian empire earlier this year, Monroe said that in this internal question " we have not interfered, believing that every people have a right to institute for themselves the government which, in their judgment, may suit them best "— " in the expectation," he added, " that other powers will pursue the same policy," In the third place, while the earlier message had spoken as if the United States alone among established powers supported the principles enunciated in it, the present message noted with pleasure that " some of the powers with whom we enjoy a very friendly intercourse, and to whom these views have been communicated, have appeared to acquiesce in them."

If, as seems unlikely, this last statement meant that some of the European powers had approved of the Monroe Doctrine *in extenso,* it was a product of mere wishful thinking, for not one of them had done so. From the context, however, the statement appears to have referred only to the views of the United States on the subject of intervention—to its condemnation both of armed intervention for the reconquest of Latin America and also of interference in the internal question of republicanism and monarchy. In this sense the statement was to a large extent justified by the facts.[73] Armed intervention had been condemned by Britain and disavowed by France; and however much Canning might prefer monarchy to republicanism, it was now as much his policy as Monroe's to let the new

[73] For a different view, see Perkins, *op. cit.,* p. 194.

states make their own choice between these forms of government.[74]

Consequently, Monroe had good reason to feel the solid satisfaction expressed in this part of his last annual message to Congress. By and large, the Latin American problem was the most persistent, the most difficult, and the most important of all the problems of foreign policy with which he had had to deal. It had required constant attention throughout his two terms. It was complicated by sharp divisions of opinion in the United States and among the new states themselves, as well as by the threatening attitude of the European allies. Directly or indirectly, it involved almost all of both the Old World and the New, including the regions with which the United States carried on nine-tenths of its total foreign commerce and every state with which it maintained diplomatic relations. It also involved immediately the momentous issue of war and ultimately, as Adams quoted Monroe as saying in November 1823, " the whole future foreign policy of the United States, at least as regards their own hemisphere."

In steering his ship of state on its long voyage through the reefs and shoals that beset it at every turn, he had shown himself a skilful navigator. To be sure, his success was not complete. For all the caution that marked the early years of his administration, he took at last a course that some of his fellow-countrymen thought was overbold. In Latin America, on the other hand, there were many who thought his policy too timorous, even after his great pronouncement of 1823, and too regardful of the national interests of the United States. But it would not have been possible to

[74] Webster, *Britain,* I, 33.

please everybody and he had succeeded in his major purpose, which was to promote the independence of the new states without involving the United States in war. Until the very end, he was careful not to commit his country to a too-ambitious program—either to a military program beyond its present powers or to a program of inter-American co-operation beyond its present desires. For the moment, he contented himself with doing what seemed practicable; for the future he set up the ideal of a new order of freedom for the New World and sent it ringing down through the ages in a message that most appropriately bears his name.

CHAPTER NINETEEN

TEMPEST OVER PANAMA

I

As the evolution of policy at Washington and London gave the new states greater security and enhanced their charms for foreign capitalists and entrepreneurs, the presses of all nations poured fourth an increasing stream of books and articles to supply that want of correct and timely information about Latin America of which there had been so much complaint as recently as 1820. Many of these publications—such as Peuchet's continuation of Raynal, John Miers' travels in Southern South America, Benjamin Disraeli's pamphlets on Mexican mining, and William Duane's travels in Colombia[1]—had an obvious business bias. Others[2]

[1] William Duane, *A Visit to Colombia in the Years 1822 and 1823* (Philadelphia, 1826); John Miers, *Travels in Chile and La Plata* (2 vols., London, 1826). For Peuchet, see p. 106; for Disraeli, chap. 18, note 19.

[2] For example, Charles Waterton, *Wanderings in South America . . . with Original Instructions for the Perfect Preservation of Birds, etc. for Cabinets of Natural History* (London, 1825); J. B. von Spix and C. F. P. von Martius, *Reise in Brasilien* (3 vols., Munich, 1823-1831). For evidences of the continued interest of the Lyceum of Natural History of New York in Latin America, see its *Annals,* I (1825), 400, 402, and II (1828), 467-472. In 1825 the Academy of Natural Sciences of Philadelphia received and published several communications on the birds of Mexico, Brazil and other parts of South America by Charles Lucien Bonaparte (*Report of the Transactions of the Academy . . . during the years 1825 and 1826,* Philadelphia, 1827, p. 7-8), and among the corresponding members of the Academy were Mariano de Rivero of Arequipa, Peru (1821), José Hipólito Unánue of Lima, Peru

reflected the continuation of that interest that scientists and scientific societies had taken in Latin America since the eighteenth century and which in 1817 had led Dr. Samuel Latham Mitchill to employ Jeremy Robinson as the field agent of the New York Lyceum of Natural History in South America. Still others were designed for the general reader [3] and some were written for the larger purpose of shaping public opinion and policy in regard to the new states.

To the latter group belong the numerous articles on Latin America published in the *North American Review* after 1823. They were on the whole decidedly sympathetic towards the new states, and their publication marks a change of attitude on the part of the *Review* which is one of the most interesting signs of the changing climate of opinion in the United States, for though the *Review* was beginning to acquire a nationwide influence, it was still essentially a New England periodical, and until recently New England had shown less sympathy than any other section of the country for the Latin American cause. This is all the more interesting because a contrary shift was taking place in the opinion of another section, the South. It will be recalled that in Jefferson's administration the South showed a sympathy for the Spanish American cause that New England

(1821), and Andrés del Río and José María Bustamante, both of Mexico City (1829) (*List of Members and Correspondents of the Academy* . . . Philadelphia, 1841).

[3] In this category may be placed, besides such works as Poinsett's *Notes on Mexico* and Maria Graham's *Journal of a Residence in Chile,* the memoirs, etc., of naval and military officers, such as Basil Hall's *Extracts from a Journal, written on the Coasts of Chili, Peru, and Mexico, in the Years 1820, 1821, 1822* (2 vols., Edinburgh, 1824), and H. L. V. Ducoudray Holstein's *Memoirs of Simon Bolivar* (Boston, 1829).

deemed excessive; but by the period with which we are now concerned a new and less Jeffersonian South was emerging and the Haynes and McDuffies who were its spokesmen showed a conspicuous coolness towards both Latin America and the pro-Latin American policy of the administration.

Perhaps it was not a mere coincidence that the reversal of attitude on the part of the *North American Review* began in the same year in which the Monroe Doctrine was proclaimed,[4] for it was due mainly to Jared Sparks, who was appointed editor of the *Review* in that year. He had already held the post for a short time in 1817 and 1818, but had then resigned to become pastor of the Unitarian church in Baltimore, where he remained for the next five years.[5] Baltimore seems to have done something to the young New Englander. The city was fired by the fervent nationalism that swept over much of the country after the close of the War of 1812. What is more to our purpose, it was one of the main centers of commerce with Latin America, of privateering in the interest of the new states, and of propaganda on behalf of their cause; and prominent among Sparks's Unitarian flock was Judge Theodorick Bland, who had been one of the members of the South American mission of 1817-1818.[6]

[4] The number of important articles on Latin America published in the *North American Review* was only one each in 1821 and 1822; in 1823, two; in 1824, two; in 1825, five; in 1826, seven; and in 1827, five. As interest in Latin America declined, the number dropped to three in 1828 (including one article dealing primarily with relations between the United States and Great Britain); one in 1829 (a review of Ouvrard's *Mémoires,* which relate mainly to Europe); and two in 1830.

[5] Adams, *Sparks,* I, 98, 108.

[6] *Ibid.,* I, 209.

All this while the *North American Review* was edited by
Edward Everett, who modelled it on English lines and
whose principal article on Latin America in these five years
developed the thesis that " we have no spmpathy with the
South Americans; we can have no well founded political
sympathy with them." [7]   Although Sparks was pushing
the interests of the *Review* in Baltimore and helping to
give it a national influence,[8] he was complaining to Everett
himself of its " want of Americanism." Though admitting
the justice of the criticism, Everett replied that " there is
really a dearth of American topics " and that " the people
round here . . . have not the raging Americanism that
reigns in your quarter." [9]

When Sparks resumed the editorship of the *Review* in
1823, he promptly set himself to the task of correcting its
want of Americanism. Interpreting the term broadly, he
gave Latin America far more prominence than it had ever
received before in this journal, and he belied Everett's
words by treating it with sympathy. As he said of himself
a few months after taking over the editorship, he was " a
warm friend of what is called the South American cause." [10]
He was also a conscientious laborer in the vineyard. He
learned Spanish; [11] in search of information and contributors,
he carried on a far-flung correspondence with persons both
in the United States and Latin America; [12] and he himself

[7] See above, p. 336.   [8] Adams, *Sparks*, I, 231-232.
[9] *Ibid.*, I, 242-243, Everett to Sparks, May 17, 1821.
[10] *Ibid.*, I, 295-296, Sparks to Caesar A. Rodney, June 28, 1824.
[11] *Ibid.*, I, 297.
[12] *Ibid.*, I, 293-299, 310-317, where many of these correspondents
are named and some extracts from the correspondence are given.
Most of the documents utilized by Adams are preserved in the
Sparks MSS., Harvard College Library, vol. 153. This contains

contributed many of the articles on the new states.[13] In his zeal for the cause he undertook tasks that fairly appalled some of his correspondents. John Bailey, a clerk in the State Department to whom he had written for documents relating to the history of the independence movement, replied: [14]

Dare you enter that labyrinth of history? I confess to you, I would not undertake to get and give a distinct view of events in South America, since 1805, under many thousands. It must be a task of Hercules. I am glad, however, if it is to be done, that a Hercules has it in hand.

Among Sparks's correspondents in Latin America were Lucas Alamán of Mexico, José Manuel Restrepo of Colombia, and Manuel Moreno of Buenos Aires, all of whom were distinguished writers as well as statesmen; and several diplomatic and consular agents of the United States, such as Joel Poinsett (Mexico), Heman Allen (Chile), Richard C. Anderson (Colombia), and William Tudor (Peru). Much information and advice and many subscriptions were obtained in this way. Anderson contributed a valuable article on the government of Colombia. Moreno was probably responsible for the 26 subscriptions that were received at one time from Buenos Aires.[16] Even Alamán, who was associated with British mining interests in Mexico and was

---

some letters in both Spanish and English that Adams apparently did not use, but on the whole his work was done with admirable skill. An interesting letter from Sparks to Joel Poinsett, March 12, 1828, which Adams did not see, is in Poinsett Papers, HSP, vol. 5.

[13] For particulars, see Adams, *Sparks,* I, 299-308 and 319-327.

[14] *Ibid.,* I, 292-293.   [15] See above, note 12.

[16] Adams, *Sparks,* I, 314, where it is also stated that the *Review* had many subscribers in South America.

never noted for his friendliness towards the United States, responded warmly to Sparks's overtures and declared himself eager to do his part towards promoting cultural relations between " the countries of America, which nature has made neighbors and which the similarity of their institutions has bound together even more closely." [17]

As for Sparks himself, he wished to bring the Americas closer together politically as well as culturally. To this end, he published in his *Review* for January 1826 an article based on Bernardo Monteagudo's pamphlet, " The Necessity of a General Federation between the States of Spanish America." [18] The article was a timely one, for an inter-

---

[17] Sparks MSS., vol. 153, Alamán to Sparks, March 25, 1826: " Muy deseoso de contribuir por mi parte a todo cuanto pueda servir a multiplicar las relaciones entre los payses de America que la naturaleza ha hecho vecinos y que la semejanza de las instituciones ha ligado aun mas estrechamente afianzando en ellos el dominio de los principios justos y liberales, y persuadido de que nada conduce tan directamente a este fin como el conocimiento intímo de los intereses mutuos y de la situacion peculiar de cada una de estas naciones tendré el mayor placer en remitir a V. por conducto de Sr. Poinsett cuanto pueda recojer de impresos que puedan serle interesantes . ." One obstacle to the success of this cultural interchange, noted by Alamán in a subsequent letter, was the high postage on printed matter (*ibid.*, Alamán to Sparks, Nov. 10, 1827, in French). Alamán's latest biographer hails him as the man who, more than anyone else, saved Mexican independence when it was threatened by the United States and as " una muralla sólida, impenetrable," against Poinsett's designs: José C. Valadés, *Alamán, estadista e historiador* (Mexico, 1938), p. 203-205. Alamán's connection with British investment in Mexican mining was maintained through Hullett Brothers of London (*ibid.*, p. 139, 141, 187, 355).

[18] *North American Review*, vol. 22 (1826), p. 162 ff. Monteagudo's pamphlet, *Ensayo sobre la necesidad de una federación jeneral entre los estados hispano-americanos*, was published at Lima

national Congress which was expected to result in the establishment of a confederation of American States, and to which the United States had been invited, was about to open at Panama. Sparks thought that it would be inexpedient at present for the United States to join the confederacy, since by doing so it might become involved in war; but he said that there were many reasons why it ought to send representatives to the Congress.

The article proved a boomerang, for to Sparks's disgust it strengthened the opponents of participation in the Panama Congress. He was still hot with indignation when he described the situation some months later.[19]

You can hardly imagine how much folly, bombast, and ignorance came out upon this subject. You say rightly that one or two strong articles in the 'Review' would have done good. But the truth is, we were taken unawares; no one dreamed of such a contest; the mission to Panama was universally popular among the people; and no one supposed Congress would go mad, or fall into its dotage, upon so simple a matter. A pamphlet on the Panama Congress, written by the ill-fated Monteagudo, of Lima, with considerable ability, came into my hands at a late hour, out of which I made a short article, confining my remarks exclusively to the designs of the South Americans themselves in assembling this Congress, without touching on the reasons why the United States ought to take part in the business.[20] This review did great mischief, for it furnished many of the representatives with nearly all the facts they possessed on the subject, and enabled the oppositionists to turn what few arrows they could gather against the cause.

---

in 1825. An English translation of the essay by Platt H. Crosby, with explanatory notes by the translator and the Peruvian editor, is in the John Sergeant Papers, HSP, Box 1821-1832. For Sergeant, see below, note 32.

[19] Adams, *Sparks*, I, 326, Sparks to Everett, Sept. 12, 1826.

[20] This was not strictly true. See *ibid.*, I, 325.

Was the mission to Panama "universally popular among the people" of the United States, as Sparks asserted? If so, why was it that the mission met with bitter opposition in the Congress of the United States, despite the extensive reservations with which the Executive Department had accepted the invitation to participate in the meeting at Panama? In order to answer these questions, we must review briefly the origin of the Congress and the way in which the question of participation was first debated and then solved in the United States. The whole question deserves close attention, for, although the commissioners finally sent from this country never took part in the Panama Congress and the Congress itself failed to accomplish any of its immediate purposes, the episode illuminates opinion and policy in the United States. It also helped to shape Latin American opinion regarding the United States.

II

Simón Bolívar more than any other individual, was responsible for the Panama Congress.[21] He originally

---

[21] Relevant documents can be conveniently consulted in James Brown Scott, ed., *International Conferences of American States, 1889-1928* (New York, 1931), p. xix-xxix, and *Am. State Papers, Foreign Relations*, V, 883 ff. Among the more important studies in English on this subject are Lockey, *op. cit.*, p. 312-433; Perkins, *op. cit.*, p. 204-222; Rippy, *Rivalry*, p. 227-246; E. Taylor Parks, *Colombia and the United States, 1765-1934* (Durham, N. C., 1935), p. 137-147; and Frances L. Reinhold, "New Research on the First Pan-American Congress Held at Panama in 1826," *Hispanic Am. Hist. Rev.*, XVIII (1938), 342-363. These contain references to other works, among which should be mentioned Reginald F. Arragon's "The Panama Congress," a manuscript doctoral dissertation (in the Harvard College Library) of which

planned it as an essentially Latin American Congress, and its purpose was to promote the unification of Latin America —a process already initiated by a series of treaties negotiated by Colombia with its South American neighbors. According to the original plan, the United States was not to be invited to participate in the Congress. Late in 1825, however, an invitation was extended to it by the government of Colombia, mainly through the efforts of Vice President Santander, who had more faith than Bolívar in republicanism and hemisphere solidarity. Similar invitations were received about the same time from the governments of Mexico and the United Provinces of Central America, which had separated from Mexico on the collapse of Iturbide's short-lived empire. The guest-list also included Great Britain and the Netherlands, which, through commerce, finance, and their territorial possessions in the Caribbean region and the Guianas, were in a sense more closely connected with the new states than was the United States itself.

As Adams observed in his message to Congress on the Panama mission, " objects of the highest importance . . . bearing directly upon the special interests of this Union " were on the agenda of the Panama Congress.[22] As a recent writer has expressed it, one of the purposes of the Latin American participants in the Congress was to " pluralize "

Mr. Arragon kindly lent me his copy. Among the older works in Spanish, special mention is made of Fabián Velarde, *El congreso de Panamá en 1826* (Panama, 1922). Of the recent works in Spanish, the most important, because it deals with the hitherto neglected part of Central America in the Congress, is José Rodríguez Cerna, *Centro América en el congreso de Bolívar, Contribución documental, inédita* . . . (Guatemala, 1938).

[22] *Am. State Papers, Foreign Relations,* V, 883.

or Pan Americanize the Monroe Doctrine [23]—as, indeed, Brazil had already sought to do by direct negotiation with the United States through Rebello at Washington.[24] Other items related to the defence of Latin American independence, to which the United States was already committed; the definition of the maritime rights of neutrals, which had been the foremost problem in the foreign relations of the United States in the forty years since the establishment of its own independence; the liberation of Cuba and Puerto Rico, a point on which the United States did not by any means see eye to eye with their would-be liberators in Latin America; and the creation of a permanent system of treaties of alliance, commerce, and friendship, with provision for an international council for the adjudication of disputes arising out of the treaties.

The importance that Adams attached to the Panama mission is shown by the fact that he tried to persuade Albert Gallatin, who might be called the dean of American diplomats at that time, to represent the United States at the Congress.[25] It was not that Adams was proposing to commit the United States to any political or military obligations towards the new states, for, as he assured the Senate, the

[23] Rodríguez Cerna, *op. cit.,* p. 36.

[24] Whitaker, " José Silvestre Rebello," *loc. cit.,* p. 390-391.

[25] National Archives, SD, Instructions to Ministers, vol. 10, Clay to Gallatin, Nov. 8, 1825, " confidential." Clay said that the President was offering the appointment to Gallatin because he wished to " give to the mission . . . a distinguished character," that Richard C. Anderson would be associated with Gallatin, and that the latter would not be expected to leave for Panama before Dec. 15-20. A notation on this document states that the same invitation was sent to John Sargeant (*sic*) on Nov. 16 and that Jan. 20 was then indicated as the probable date of departure.

purpose of the mission was "neither to contract alliances, nor to engage in any undertaking or project importing hostility to any other nation." [26]

Nevertheless Adams did describe Latin America as standing in a different and closer relation than Europe to the United States. His language at this point was reminiscent of the Monroe Doctrine and it reaffirmed the fact, which we have noted in connection with Monroe's message, that the United States now had a special policy towards Latin America, which was based upon closer geographical proximity and political similarity. His language showed that he did not regard the rule of isolation as applying with the same force to Latin America as to Europe,[27] and many members of Congress construed it as suggesting that the community of interests so glowingly described in his message might be made the basis of inter-American cooperation.

The American colonies of Spain and Portugal, he said, had been transformed into eight independent nations:

[26] *Am. State Papers, For. Rels.,* V, 834, in Adams's message to the Senate, Dec. 26, 1825. For the adverse of the Committee on Foreign Relations, see *ibid.,* p. 857-865.

[27] Weinberg, "Washington's 'Great Rule' in its Historical Evolution," *loc. cit.,* p. 119, says that "Adams's message on the Panama Congress appeared to limit the rule to Europe" and that Clay's instructions to the delegates made the limitation explicit. Opposing the Panama mission, James Buchanan of Pennsylvania quoted this part of Adams's message, charged that he had "attempted to explain away the principles of the Farewell Address," and called for a return to "the policy of Washington" and the maxims of "union at home and independence of all foreign nations" (*Register of Debates in Congress,* 19 Cong., 1 Sess., p. 2175, 2182). He also charged that Clay had changed the policy of the United States by inviting Mexico, through his instruction to Poinsett, to "act in concert" with the United States in asserting the principles of the Monroe Doctrine (*ibid.,* p. 2173).

Seven of them [are] Republics like ourselves, with whom
we have an immensely growing commercial, and must have,
and have, already important political connections; with
reference to whom our situation is neither distant nor
detached; whose political principles and systems of government, congenial with our own, must and will have an action
and counteraction upon us and ours to which we cannot be
indifferent if we would . . . *America* has a set of primary
interests which have none or a remote relation to Europe
. . . and if she [Europe] should interfere, as she may . . .
we might be called, in defence of our own altars and fire-
sides, to take an attitude which would cause our neutrality
to be respected, and choose peace or war, as our interest,
guided by justice, should counsel.[28]

Adams was still basing his policy squarely on the national
interests of the United States; but his conception of those
interests was manifestly different and broader than it had
been a few years earlier. In 1823 he had taken one step
along the Lexington trail and now he took another. Indeed,
he now took a more advanced position than even Monroe
had reached, for the latter's conception of the American
system was limited to the exclusion of Europe and the pious
hope that the independent states of America would all
adopt the same—i. e., republican—institutions. Now Adams
clearly, though cautiously and with important qualifications,
stressed a hitherto neglected aspect of the American system,
namely the positive principle of inter-American consultation.
The conversion of the once-cautious Adams to bold advocacy of this aspect of the American system astonished his
contemporaries and was the subject of many jibes by those
who were opposed to participation in the Panama Congress.
" He has started from a caution cold as marble, into the
vernal fervors of love at first sight for the South Amer-

[28] *Am. State Papers, Foreign Relations*, V, 885-886.

icans," said one of them; and they were sure that he had caught "this Spanish American fever" from Henry Clay.

This *American System* [said Rives of Virginia] is not confined to the Secretary of State and his diplomatic pupils. The President himself is a proselyte! This system has a peculiar *nomenclature* of its own. It is distinguished by certain *cabalistic* phrases . . . Of these phrases, the President has made the most copious use in his message to this House, and has, indeed, added some new samples to the original stock. ' The fraternity of freedom ', ' sister Republics ' (including the Emperor of Brazil, I suppose), ' nations of this *hemisphere*,' ' the Powers of America,' dance through his pages.[29]

With the issue presented to Congress in this way, it is not surprising that the mission encountered widespread opposition; and Sparks would not have been so unprepared for it if he had followed more attentively the tariff debates and presidential campaign literature of 1824, in which so much was said about the obstacles confronting the commerce of the United States with Latin America, and so little was said in support of the thesis of inter-American solidarity.[30] To be sure, many of the objections raised against the Panama mission proceeded from quite different sources —for example, from resentment that the United States had not been consulted about the preparations for the Congress; from factional politics, which had been exacerbated by Adams's defeat of Jackson in the recent presidential election; and from the determination of certain pro-slavery

[29] *Register of Debates in Congress,* 19 Cong., 1 Sess., p. 2079-2080, 2163. Theodore E. Burton, " Henry Clay," in Bemis, ed., *American Secretaries of State,* IV, 137, attaches great importance to Clay's role in shaping the administration's policy in regard to the Panama Congress.

[30] See above, chap. 18.

Southern leaders to prevent the United States from partici-
pating in an international conference in which, it was
believed, anti-slavery measures would be adopted and the
black republic of Haiti, founded on a slave revolt and mass
massacre of the white population, would be represented by
a Negro.

In addition to these objections, however, and probably
underlying some of them, was the conviction, so plainly
stated in the discussions of 1824, that Latin America was
a poor customer and a dangerous competitor of the United
States. Though this issue does not appear prominently in
the debates on the Panama mission, it must have been an
important premise of many of the speakers, for what had
been said so often and so emphatically in 1824 could hardly
have been forgotten so soon, and its relevance to the present
question was perfectly obvious. Those who had complained
in 1824 of what the United States had already done to promote the development of a region that was perhaps its
most dangerous competitor in the production of wheat,
tobacco, livestock, and cotton, were not likely to approve of
a policy which would, if successful, encourage the further
development of the competitor's resources and would perhaps involve the assumption of risks for his benefit. It
is no mere coincidence that Hayne of South Carolina, who
in 1824 developed most carefully the theme of Latin American competition with the United States, was in 1825-1826
one of the most determined opponents of the Panama
mission. This economic factor, as well as the slavery question, must be taken into account in explaining the fact that
opposition to the mission was to a large extent localized in
the South.

On the other hand, in 1824 representatives of the North

Atlantic seaboard had shown the greatest faith in the possibilities of Latin America as an outlet for American manufactures, and it was from this region that the Panama mission now received its warmest support. A recent survey of newspaper opinion in this region has shown, first, that while there was disagreement on some of the subsidiary questions, there was general agreement that the United States ought to participate in the Congress and, second, that the dominant motive was the advancement of the commercial interests of the United States.[31] These facts help explain why Sparks was caught unawares by the opposition to the Panama mission and why he asserted, even after the opposition in Congress had proved formidable, that the mission was " universally " supported by the general public; for he was evidently basing his judgement on public opinion in the North Atlantic States, with which alone he seems to have been familiar.

III

After Gallatin's refusal of the mission, John Sergeant, former member of Congress from Pennsylvania, was chosen to join Richard C. Anderson, minister to Colombia, in representing the United States at Panama.[32]   Adams might

[31] Reinhold, *op. et loc. cit.*, p. 343-350.

[32] John Sergeant was a Philadelphia lawyer who had won considerable prominence by the time of his appointment to Panama. He was an acknowledged leader of the Philadelphia bar, member of Congress from 1815 to 1823, a director of the Second Bank of the United States and its " chief legal and political adviser," and president of the board of canal commissioners of Pennsylvania in 1825-1826 (article on John Sergeant in DAB, XVI, 588-589). There are five volumes of Sergeant MSS. in the Historical Society of Pennsylvania. For Anderson, see the article in DAB, I, 271.

have saved much time and trouble by sending them there in the capacity of executive agents,[33] in which case the appointments would not have required confirmation by the Senate. But in a matter of such moment he felt the need of the moral as well as the financial support of Congress and consequently asked the Senate to confirm the appointments. The House was expected to initiate an appropriation for their expenses.

The long debate that followed covered many other points besides those mentioned above; but for our purpose the major conclusions that emerged from it may be summarized briefly. In the first place, although the mission was finally approved, the approval was given so tardily and opposed so strenuously by a highly articulate minority that it had the effect of a rebuff both to the administration and to the Latin American sponsors of the Panama Congress. In the second place, the debates themselves contained some remarks that were likely to offend the Latin Americans if brought to their attention, for some of the opponents of the mission spoke unkindly of our southern neighbors,[34] and many

[33] Though Anderson and Sergeant were formally nominated to the Senate as ministers plenipotentiary and envoys extraordinary, some of the Senators insisted on debating the issue as if the question of executive agents were involved. See Wriston, *Executive Agents*, p. 224-237.

[34] Thus, in the Senate debate Berrien of Georgia opposed involving "the interests of this Union in a foreign association, composed of States, with whom we have no natural connection" (*Register of Debates in Congress*, 19 Cong., 1 Sess., p. 277, March 1826). Invidious remarks of this kind were, however, few and brief, and the shafts of the opposition were directed much more against Adams and Clay than against Latin America. John Randolph's principal reported speech in this connection was his famous Blifil-Black George, Puritan-blackleg blast against Adams and Clay.

of its supporters said quite frankly that their main purpose was to promote the national interests—mainly the economic interests—of the United States. In the third place, there was general agreement that the United States ought to adhere to its traditional policies of neutrality and abstention from entangling alliances. That there must be no deviation from these policies in favor of Latin America was one of the points most strongly urged by the opponents of the mission, including not only Southern members but also James Buchanan of Pennsylvania and other Northerners.[35] The net result was a warning to the administration against further progress in the path of cooperation with Latin America.

As is well known, the representatives of the United States never reached Panama. Anderson died on the way, and before Sergeant left the United States he was informed that the Congress had adjourned to meet again at Tacubaya, Mexico. It has been suggested that it was just as well they did not attend the Congress, since the policies of the United States and the Spanish American states represented at Panama conflicted at some points (especially in regard to slavery and Cuba) and some Spanish Americans, under British prodding, may have taken offense at the " intemperate and ungenerous " remarks made by some of the congressional critics of the mission and Latin America.[36] On the other hand, it would seem that, from the long-time

[35] See above, note 27.

[36] Rippy, *Rivalry,* p. 240-241, quoting in note 31 a despatch from Beaufort T. Watts to Clay, Nov. 7, 1826 (Manning, *Dip. Cor.,* II, 1302-1303). Watts was United States chargé at Bogotá. It should be noted, however, that Watts said that the English effort to make trouble had failed.

point of view, much would have been gained by the mere presence of the representatives of the United States at the meeting, for this would have silenced the criticism, which was made at the time and has been repeated many times subsquently,[37] that the United States was coldly indifferent to the first great effort at inter-American cooperation, by which many influential Latin Americans set great store.

There has also been a tendency to condone the absence of the United States delegation from Panama on the ground that the Congress was a fiasco, since only four Latin American states attended it and none of its acts was ever given effect. As a matter of fact, considering the circumstances the Congress was very well attended. Of the established and recognized states of Latin America, only three (Argentina, Brazil, and Chile) failed to attend, and the four that did attend (Mexico, Central America, Colombia, and Peru) embraced territory that has subsequently been divided into twelve independent states.[38]

While it is true that the immediate achievements of the Congress were nil, the moral effect of merely having made the effort was great. The fact that the precedent was established at the very beginning of their independent existence would seem to explain in part the deep and continuing interest that the Latin American states have taken

[37] E. g., Jorge Pérez Concha, *Bolívar internacionalista* (Quito, Ecuador, 1939), p. 54-59. At this point the author leans heavily on Carlos Pereyra and Rafael Ramos Pedrueza, who are confirmed critics of Yankee imperialism; but his views are worth noting because they are of very recent date and because he is a member of the *Centro de Estudios Internacionales* (Quito) and the *Centro de Investigaciones Históricas de Guayaquil.*

[38] Mexico, Guatemala, Honduras, Nicaragua, El Salvador, Costa Rica, Panama, Colombia, Venezuela, Ecuador, Peru, and Bolivia.

in international cooperation; and their respect for the precedent has deepened with the passage of time as they have discovered in subsequent efforts at international cooperation elements which, rightly or wrongly, they attribute to Bolívar and those who were associated with him in the design of the Panama Congress.

For the United States, at least, the Congress had one immediate result of great importance; and a most unfortunate result it was. This was the success that Canning met with in his effort to use the Congress as a means of increasing the prestige of Britain and lowering that of the United States in Latin America.[39] For this purpose he sent Edward J. Dawkins, a man of considerable ability, as commissioner to Panama and drew up carefully worded instructions for his guidance.[40] It may be doubted whether the agents of the United States could have counteracted Dawkins if they had been present at Panama; but at any rate they were absent, and Dawkins had a clear field. He made the most of his opportunity.[41] Taking advantage of an indiscreet avowal made to the Spanish government by the American minister at Madrid, Alexander Everett, to the effect that the

[39] Webster, *Britain*, I, 52. The United States was better prepared for the projected congress at Tacubaya, Mexico, to which place the Panama Congress adjourned and at which it was to have been represented by Joel Poinsett; but the projected congress was never held. Sergeant went to Mexico late in 1826 as a delegate to the congress at Tacubaya, but soon returned to the United States. His reports are in the papers relating to the Panama Congress, 1825-1827, in the National Archives, SD, Miscellaneous. Extensive use was made of them by Mr. Arragon in his excellent study cited in note 21.

[40] The text of the instructions is given in *ibid.*, I, 406-409.

[41] Rippy, *Rivalry*, p. 240-246, discusses Dawkins's activities at Panama.

United States was opposed to the liberation of Cuba by Mexico and Colombia, Dawkins used the information to stir up the resentment of those two countries against the United States through their representatives at Panama. On the other hand, he was able to disprove the charge, made by Wasnington, that Britain was trying to protract the war between Spain and her former colonies in the interests of British trade; and he had some success in checking the efforts of the United States to win the Latin American states over to its definition of neutral rights as opposed to that of Britain.[42]

As one authority has remarked, Dawkins owed much of his success to Canning, and Canning in turn owed much of his success to the fact that Britain, with her superior commercial and financial resources and maritime power, had more to offer the new states.[43] It might be added that so far as the main point in his program of rivalry with the United States was concerned, Canning was successful because the United States did not oppose him. That was his effort to prevent the United States from placing itself at the head of a league of American states, which, he said, " would too probably at no very distant period endanger the peace both of America and of Europe." [44] As a matter of fact although Canning's suspicions on this point seemed to be well founded, since they were based on statements made by Joel Poinsett,[45] who was now minister to Mexico, Poinsett's

---

[42] Webster, *Britain*, I, 51-52.

[43] *Ibid.*, I, 52.

[44] *Ibid.*, I, 404, Canning to Dawkins, March 18, 1826.

[45] *Ibid.*, I, 486, 489, Henry George Ward to Canning, Sept. 27-28, 1825, quoting Poinsett as claiming for the United States the headship of " the great American Federation." Ward was British chargé to Mexico.

zeal for Pan Americanism at this time far outran that of his government. If there had been any doubt on the question, the debates in Congress on the Panama mission made it abundantly clear that the United States had no desire whatever to join an American league, even as its head.

For whatever reasons, Canning met with a very considerable measure of success in his efforts to " avert the blow " struck by the Monroe Doctrine. He had good reason to feel the satisfaction that he expressed when, in 1825, he rounded out his policy by at last persuading the Cabinet to recognize the new states, thus nullifying one of the most important advantages that the United States had enjoyed.

The Yankees will shout in triumph [wrote Canning]; but it is they who lose most by our decision. The great danger of the time . . . was a division of the world into European and American, Republican and Monarchical; a league of worn-out Gov[ernmen]ts, on the one hand, and of y·uthful and stirring nations, with the U[nited] States at their head, on the other. We slip in between; and plant ourselves in Mexico. The Un[ited] States have gotten the start of us in vain; and we link once more America to Europe. Six months more—and the mischief would have been done.[46]

Canning and his government had, indeed, " slipped in between "; but that did not require so much agility as Canning would have us believe, and it is doubtful if the game was worth the candle. If he had had better judgment and a broader vision, he might have added still another link, and an even stronger one, between Europe and America.

[46] Temperley, " The Later American Policy of George Canning," *Am. Hist. Rev.*, XI (1906), 781, note 1.

IV

Commerce constituted one of the principal points of friction in the rivalry of the United States and Great Britain over Latin America. Even if that had not been the case, it would still have been one of the chief factors in the development of American policy towards the new states. This was partly because the administration's Latin American policy and its policy of commercial reciprocity were twin products of the same liberal rationale of emancipation—the emancipation of man and the emancipation of commerce.[47] The establishment of Latin American independence served both purposes, for at the same time that it freed the people of that region from European political domination, it also destroyed the commercial monopolies that had characterized the old regime. Moreover, one of the inducements most persistently offered to their fellow countrymen by Clay and other advocates of the Latin American cause in the earlier stages of the movement had been the rich commercial rewards that its success would bring to the United States. Now that independence was won, it was only natural that the United States should seek both to secure these rewards and also to prevent the erection of new barriers to the free flow of international trade.

Unwilling—as the discussion of the Panama Congress showed—to enter into multilateral agreements on this or any other subject, the United States sought to promote its commercial policy among the new states by the negotiation of bilateral treaties. Seeking no special privileges for itself and determined not to permit them to be granted to

[47] Setser, *Commercial Reciprocity Policy*, p. 243-244.

other nations, it proposed to the new states— as it had already proposed to the old states of Europe—that these treaties should be based upon the principle of complete reciprocity.

Although the foreign commerce of the United States was vigorously supported by the government until the end of Adams's administration, this policy met with only limited success in Latin America.[48] With four of the seven continental states—Buenos Aires, Chile, Peru, and Mexico— no treaty at all was negotiated. The Buenos Aires government, as Forbes had noted, was under British influence, and through the early part of this period British policy was dominated by Canning's effort to checkmate the United States. Caesar A. Rodney, the first American minister, was well liked, but he died shortly after his arrival without accomplishing anything. Forbes, who had continued as consul and succeeded Rodney as chargé, protested vigorously against the government's exclusion of American flour; but his protest succeeded only in changing the exclusion to a prohibitive duty. This atmosphere was not propitious to the negotiation of a commercial treaty; and from 1825 to 1828 it became even less so because of the Buenos Aires government's absorption in its war with Brazil over the Uruguay question. In Chile and Peru,[49] where the United

[48] Except as otherwise noted below, I have in the main followed Dr. Setser's excellent account of this subject in *ibid.*, p. 243-251.

[49] Louis C. Nolan, "The Diplomatic and Commercial Relations of the United States and Peru, 1826-1875," discusses the difficulties of this early period in detail and quotes Clay's complaint early in 1829 that recent decrees of the Peruvian government threatened to "put an end to all commerce between the two countries." I am indebted to Mr. Nolan for the privilege of reading this manuscript study.

States, though outdistanced by Britain, still had important commercial interests, the failure to obtain a treaty seems to have been due mainly to the instability of the new governments.

The failure in the case of Mexico calls for special comment, because in the past few years the commerce of the United States had grown with such rapidity as to alarm the agents of Great Britain [50] and because the minister of the United States was its leading Latin American specialist, Joel Poinsett. One of the main purposes of his mission was to obtain a commercial treaty, and he did in fact negotiate two such treaties, one in 1826 and the other in 1828; but neither was ratified. The former was in effect rejected by both governments; the latter, by Mexico alone. British influence may explain in part the attitude of the Mexican government, for Canning's boast that he was slipping in between the United States and Latin America was made with special reference to Mexico, and the British agents in Mexico were making every effort to widen the breach. As we shall see, however, Poinsett's own indiscretions were partly responsible for his disappointments.

With the other three continental states—Colombia, the United Provinces of Central America, and Brazil—the United States was more successful. The commercial treaty of 1824 with Colombia was the first treaty concluded by the United States with any of the new States. Negotiated by Richard C. Anderson and Pedro Gual, it contained a

[50] In 1824 the British consul at Vera Cruz wrote that a large part of the goods brought to Mexico in American ships were of British origin, and expressed the fear that the Americans might " engross the greater part of the carrying trade " of Mexico (Humphreys, *British Consular Reports*, p. 313-314).

most-favored-nation clause which removed a long-standing cause of complaint on the part of the United States by putting an end to the preferential treatment of British commerce in Colombia.

The treaty of 1825 with Central America possessed an importance out of all proportion to the small volume of commerce between the two countries, for it was the first treaty to contain the complete reciprocity rule and it became a model for later treaties. In accordance with the general trend of policy at Washington in that period, it stressed navigation rather than trade, and it implemented more fully than any of its predecessors the policy of commercial emancipation. As Clay said of it in 1826:

This is the most perfect freedom of navigation. We can conceive of no privilege beyond it. All the shackles which the selfishness or contracted policy of nations had contrived, are broken and destroyed by this broad principle of universal liberality. The president is most anxious to see it adopted by all nations.[51]

The Argentine-Brazilian war, which delayed the negotiation of a treaty between the Buenos Aires government and the United States, had the opposite effect in the case of Brazil. Harassed by the war with its southern neighbor, dependent to some extent upon the United States for naval supplies, and uneasy at the decided preference shown by the American people for the success of republican Buenos Aires, the imperial government at Rio de Janeiro at last agreed to enter into the commercial negotiation with the United States which it had persistently evaded hitherto.[52]

[51] Quoted in Setser, *op. cit.,* p. 247.
[52] Whitaker, "José Silvestre Rebello," *loc. cit.,* p. 398-399; Hill, *United States and Brazil,* p. 70-71. According to Rebello,

The negotiation was conducted by William Tudor, formerly consul at Lima and now chargé at Rio, who brought it to a successful conclusion in December 1828. The treaty was modeled on the Central American treaty, for in spite of the Brazilian tariff discriminations in favor of Great Britain under the Strangford treaty, which were now terminated, the United States had built up a thriving trade with Brazil. So far as the trade of the United States with the states and colonies of Latin America was concerned, it was exceeded in value only by the trade with Cuba, and it was nearly four times as large as that with Buenos Aires.

In these negotiations with the new states, one of the chief problems that confronted the United States was the persistent effort in some of them to establish a customs union, or at least preferential tariff treatment, among themselves.[53] Since the United States as well as the European powers were to be excluded from the arrangement, and since its political implications were obvious, it was vigorously opposed by the authorities at Washington. It received equally vigorous support from the Mexican government, which actually concluded a preferential tariff treaty with

---

Clay told him that the United States was "perfectly satisfied" with the treaty and that it removed the impression, given by the reports of the American chargé, Condy Raguet, that the Brazilian government treated the United States with disrespect because the latter was a republic (Archives of the Ministry of Foreign Affairs, Rio de Janeiro, "Legação Imperial nos Estados Unidos," Rebello to the Marques de Aracaty, March 26, 1829, No. 100).

[53] It was in this connection that Poinsett said (according to Ward) that the President of the United States would never consent to "be excluded from a federation of which he ought to be the head" (Webster, I, 486). Poinsett's Mexican mission is discussed at length in Parton, op. cit., and briefly in Rippy, Poinsett.

Colombia; and the effort to consolidate and extend the system was abandoned not out of consideration for the United States or devotion to any Pan American ideal, but because Colombia subsequently negotiated a conflicting treaty with Great Britain. The system was, indeed, doomed to failure in any case, for it did not correspond to the realities of the situation. Then, as now, the bulk of the foreign commerce of the Latin American states was carried on not among themselves, but with the United States and Europe.

V

The Mexican government's effort to establish a Latin American customs union to which the United States would not be admitted is one evidence of the coolness that developed between the two Americas in the course of Adams's administration. The sharpest drop in temperature occured in Mexico during Poinsett's mission, which is worth describing not only for that reason but also because the rest of the Latin American states were already acquiring the habit of appraising the policy of the United States towards them in the light of its conduct towards Mexico.

In this phase of his career Poinsett was an ardent advocate of inter-American cooperation under the leadership of the United States. He also believed that the British government was trying to stir up discord between the two Americas and that it was his duty to combat this fell design vigorously.[54] His suspicions were justified and some of his

[54] For an account of the ensuing contest between Poinsett and the British chargés, H. G. Ward and Richard Pakenham, see Rippy, *Rivalry,* p. 253-302. This contest led to the publication of two pamphlets setting forth the views of the rivals: (1) a British

measures were well conceived; but the net effect of his mission on inter-American relations was deplorable

Even before he left for Mexico, Poinsett obtained a commission in the Mexican navy for David Porter.[55] Perhaps he was only doing an old friend a good turn, but it was probably also his purpose to extend the influence of the United States in Latin America. At any rate, Porter thought of himself as playing the same rôle that Lord Cochrane had played in the naval service of Chile.[56] For a while, all went well, and in 1826 and 1827 Porter commanded a Mexican squadron in a highly successful cruise in the Gulf of Mexico. Summarizing his achievements on this occasion, he claimed that he had " saved Colombia from a counter revolution " by immobilizing in the west a fleet which was to have aided the counter-revolutionists, that he had compelled Spain to reinforce Cuba at " enormous expense," had paralysed its commerce and caused great discontent among the inhabitants of Cuba, and had " established a character of activity for the Mexican Marine, which if the gov[ernment] thought proper to take advantage of would

---

pamphlet, *Spanish America. Observations on the Instructions given by the President of the United States . . . on the conduct of Mr. Poinsett . . . and generally on our Relations with Spanish America . . .* (London, 1829) ; and (2) *Mexico and Mr. Poinsett* (Philadelphia, 1829), which contained a reply to the foregoing and attributed the misfortunes of Mexico to its wasteful and prodigal system of finance, its internal dissensions, and the deep traces left by the despotism and superstition of the colonial government.

[55] Gilpin Papers, HSP, Poinsett Correspondence, Box 1794-1839, folder endorsed " Porter, David . . . 1816-1839," Porter to Poinsett, Aug. 21, 1825, and copy of letter from Porter to Pablo Obregón (Mexican minister at Washington), Oct. 6, 1825.

[56] *Ibid.,* Porter to Obregón, Oct. 6, 1825.

be highly injurious to the interests of Spain." [57]   Soon, however, he became involved in a series of disputes with the Mexican authorities, who seem to have transferred to him some of their dislike for his sponsor, Poinsett; and in the end Porter threw up his commission and returned to the United States in disgust.

Poinsett's contributions to his own unpopularity in Mexico were numerous and important. In some instances he was not to blame, for he was only acting under instructions from Washington. This was true of the Cuban question, about which, moreover, Adams made some indiscreet revelations that caused Poinsett great embarrassment.[58]   It was also true of the Texas question, which was already arousing Mexican fears of Yankee aggression, and of the long and futile effort to conclude a treaty of commerce and friendship, in the course of which Poinsett had to insist on clauses that were distasteful to the Mexicans. In other cases the fault was clearly his. He gave the impression that the United States was ready for a union with the Latin American states, that it expected to hold a position of primacy over them, and that it expected to be rewarded for its trouble by commercial advantages in Latin America.[59]

[57] *Ibid.*, undated 8-page memorandum in Porter's handwriting, beginning, " In November 1826 information reached this place that Labord's squadron had been dismantled by a gale of wind in September."

[58] *Ibid.*, Poinsett to Dr. Joseph Johnson, May 25, 1826, expressing his regret that Adams had published his correspondence about a negotiation with Mexico that was still pending. He continued, " These people are very angry about the language held by Mr. Adams respecting Mexico."

[59] This point is stressed in the manuscript study of Poinsett's carreer by C. L. Chandler and E. J. Pratt.

If not erroneous, this was at least offensive to Mexican sensibilities.

Even more serious were the blunders that he committed in his effort to counteract British machinations in Mexico. He was deeply alarmed by them, for, as he himself expressed it, ". . . When I arrived here the English men were completely master of the field, and I really feared that Mexico would never become a member of the American family." [60] Attributing this situation largely to British meddling in the domestic politics of Mexico, he decided to fight fire with fire. One of his devices was the organization of York rite Masons, which were designed to neutralize the pro-British Scottish rite Masons and to serve as political clubs. Whatever advantage such methods yielded at the beginning was offset by the resentment that they ultimately aroused. This reached such a pitch that finally the Mexican government demanded and and obtained his recall.

It would be easy to judge Poinsett's conduct too harshly and there is much that can be said in defense of it.[61] The point to be stressed, however, is not his personal defects or shortcomings, but the fact that his trials in Mexico were a fair sample of those that the United States faced in most of the new states on the morning after the end of their struggle for independence. Generally speaking, politica

[60] Gilpin Papers, Poinsett Correspondence, Box 1794-1839 Poinsett to Dr. Joseph Johnson, Oct. 31, 1825.

[61] Poinsett himself attached great importance to his achievement in Mexico. Writing in 1827 about "the extreme peril" in whic its government had stood because of "the machinations of th monarchical party," he said, "Most unquestionably had it no been for my foresight and conduct this gov[ernmen]t would hav been overthrown and this country deluged in blood." Ibid., Poinsett to "Dear Jos" (i. e., Dr. Joseph Johnson), Aug. 15, 1827.

control was vested in the creole upper classes, in which the strongest element was a landed aristocracy and which, as the liberal enthusiasm of the wars of independence died down, found themselves in closer affinity with aristocratic Great Britain and France than with the increasingly democratic United States. As regarded Britain this proclivity was reinforced by her pre-eminence in certain matters of deep concern to the new states, such as commerce, finance, and sea power. Applying these considerations to Poinsett's case, we can more readily understand why his meddling in the domestic affairs of Mexico aroused so much more resentment among its people than did that of the British chargé and his cohorts, though theirs seems to have been quite as extensive and notorious.

Poinsett's conduct in Mexico had its repercussions in South America, despite the difficulty and infrequency of communication among the Latin American states. Early in 1828 a Lima newspaper published an extract of a letter from Mexico containing " severe strictures " on the policy of the United States towards that country and on Poinsett personally, and the item was then clipped in the semi-official gazette of Santiago, Chile.[62]

Poinsett was not the only American agent in Latin America whose mission ended in disappointment — disappointment not only over his own failure to advance the legitimate national interests of his country but also over the strength shown by conservative and reactionary elements in the new states. Forbes at Buenos Aires had never had much faith in the liberalism of the ruling classes in that city; in

[62] Poinsett Papers, HSP, Samuel Larned to Poinsett, Santiago de Chile, July 15, 1828.

his ten-year residence there he devoted a large part of his energy to a futile effort to counteract the dominant influence of Great Britain and to obtain more favorable terms for American commerce; and he lived just long enough to see the fulfilment of his gloomy prediction that the incessant domestic strife in Argentina would lead to the establishment of a dictatorship—the dictatorship of Juan Manuel Rosas, which was to last for more than a score of years.

Condy Raguet's experience at Rio de Janeiro was very similar, with the differences that at this imperial capital there was even less liking for the republican system of the United States than at Buenos Aires, and that Raguet had far less forbearance than Forbes.[63] Promoted from consul to chargé not long after the recognition of Brazil, he chafed at the scant respect which, as he felt, was shown by the monarchy at Rio to the republic that he represented; and in 1826 he made a relatively minor dispute the occasion for demanding his passports, which were promptly delivered to him, thus terminating the first diplomatic mission from the United States to Brazil.

In Colombia the situation was scarcely more encouraging

[63] Hill, op. cit., p. 49-52. The Brazilian government, which had already complained of Raguet's instability, was deeply offended by his precipitate withdrawal; and subsequently it attributed his action to the fact that he was under the influence of the American consul at Rio de Janeiro, who, it asserted, had a pecuniary interest in the majority of the cases so insistently supported by Raguet (Archives of the Ministry of Foreign Affairs, Rio de Janeiro, "Estados Unidos," Registo, vol. I, Marques de Inhambupe to Rebello, Oct. 26, 1826, no. 71; Marques de Queluz to Rebello, March 27, 1827; same to same, April 6, 1827, no. 4; Francesco Carneiro de Campos to José de Araujo Ribeiro, March 16, 1831, no. 3).

from the point of view of Spanish American enthusiasts in the United States. In the year of Monroe's pronouncement, Colombia was the Latin American country for whose progress in the path of rational liberty many people in the United States had the highest hopes. Only six months before that pronouncement was made, even the cool scrutiny of John Quincy Adams found that

the Republic of Colombia is, of all the nations which have arisen from the ruins of the Spanish power in America . . . . that which amidst the convulsions of the revolutionary tempest has assumed the most encouraging appearance of consistency and stability; and that in which the principles of civil liberty have apparently made the most successful progress towards a final triumph over the prejudices of inveterate ignorance, despotism, and superstition.[54]

By the end of the decade, even the appearance of civil liberty had vanished; and so had the Republic of Colombia. It had broken up into the three jarring states of Venezuela, New Granada, and Ecuador; and even before its disintegration had undone an important part of the Liberator Bolívar's work, the achievements of this " Lion of Colombia " and the state of his nation were made the subject of a scathing criticism by a United States agent at Bogotá, the capital of Colombia. He wrote from this city in 1829:

You ask in vain, what good has he [Bolívar] done? No roads are repaired or made, no bridges built—no schools established—no vice discouraged—nor is there an improved administration of justice. The Treasury is empty, and no encouragement is extended to internal or external trade. The agricultural industry is withdrawn to recruit the ranks

[54] Adams, *Writings*, VII, 453-454. This passage occurred in the draft of Adams's instructions to R. C. Anderson of May 27, 1823, but was deleted.

of the army . . . . I had formed an opinion, which I have discovered was erroneous, that Colombia was, in many respects, in advance of Mexico. The same degree of ignorance, and an equal share of vanity prevail in both countries, but fanaticism deeper rooted in this [country], and republican liberty is trodden down by the *expansive* weight of military despotism.[65]

These were strong words—all the stronger since the writer had recently lived in Mexico and Mexico was emerging as the country of the egregious Antonio López de Santa Anna. With such a scroll unfolding before them, people in the United States might well ask what had been the advantage of excluding monarchy from Latin America. Some even doubted whether anything had been gained by its liberation.

VI

In many respects, as any informed and candid judge would have had to admit, the United States had met with disappointment in its effort to carry out the Latin American policy outlined by Jefferson in 1808 and brought to its full development by Monroe in 1823. It had failed to exclude either the political or the commercial influence of Europe from America; and if its efforts had helped prevent the establishment of any more European monarchies in America on the model of Brazil, no one could claim that this was due to the unaided efforts of the United States alone or that the success of this negative measure had been followed by that progress of rational liberty and republicanism which it had been designed to promote.

It was now apparent that only two alternatives were open

[65] Poinsett Papers, HSP, Edward T. Tayloe to Poinsett, Bogotá, March 24, 1829. Tayloe was secretary of legation at Bogotá.

to the United States: either the retrenchment, tacit or avowed, of its large policy towards Latin America, or else a far more aggressive effort to carry that policy into effect. The latter alternative was not so completely out of harmony with the dominant political ideas of that generation as might be imagined; but the subsidence of the menace from Europe and, still more, changes in the economic and political pattern of the United States itself destroyed whatever chance of adoption this alternative might otherwise have had.

Until the independence of Latin America was established, all classes alike in the United States—farmers, merchants, ship-owners, manufacturers — could, and many of their members did, hope that the independence of Latin America would open up a bonanza to them. This was a hope that could not exist without a good deal of optimism; but it was a hope that all could share. The event was most disappointing to two of these interests. For while farmers continued to find a modest market in some parts of independent Latin America, what they sold there was an insignificant part of their total product and, above all, the hope of further increase had vanished; and the manufacturers suffered an even more complete disillusionment, for they could not compete with English and other European manufacturers in foreign markets. Only the mercantile interest still had an important stake in Latin America.

Here the changing economic and political pattern came into play. The mercantile interest, even in its New England stronghold, was losing ground; the rising industrial interest was looking to the home market, protected by a tariff wall; and the agricultural interest was showing a jealousy of its handmaid, commerce, which had seldom been in evidence in the formative period of our Latin American policy. One instance will serve to mark the latter change. In 1820 the Virginia planter James Monroe had prodded his New England secretary of state into making a more active use of the United States navy to protect and extend American commerce in the Pacific; but at the end of the decade the South Carolina planter Robert Y. Hayne made a report to the Senate that breathes a very different spirit. A proposal of the Adams administration for a naval expedition to the Pacific, the purpose of which was to gather data for scientists and navigators and to open new sources to American commerce, had been referred to a committee of the Senate. As chairman of this committee Hayne reported in February 1829 that the proposed expedition bore " an interesting relation to the foreign policy of this country," as well as to its commerce, and continued:

However desirable it may be to open new sources to our commerce, or to give greater security to those who navigate our seas, the committee cannot perceive why those objects should be deemed of more value than to ' open new sources ' to agriculture, or to give security to those who may be engaged in other branches of industry—objects which may be safely left to the enterprise of individuals, which, with an instinctive sagacity that puts to shame the assumed wisdom of governments, is invariably directed to the pursuits most profitable to themselves, and most to the welfare of the country.[66]

In this new economic development, with all its rich and at times sombre political overtones, the protective tariff played an important part. A recent Brazilian writer, lamenting the fact that the economy of his country is still colonial, has envied the protectionist system that brought the United

[66] *Am. State Papers, Naval Affairs,* III, 339.

States so early to economic maturity. Whether or not his envy is merited, it should be recognized that this development, by turning American enterprise into domestic channels for half a century, accelerated the decline of interest and the relaxation of policy on the part of the United States with respect to Latin America. It was only in the last quarter of the century, when the United States had reached a greater degree of economic maturity, that it once more took Latin America into serious account. And once more, as in the hopeful and expansive period from 1808 to 1823, a strong ingredient of its Latin American policy was economic interest, real or fancied.

It would be a great mistake, however, to regard the efforts of that earlier period as wasted. The rather tenuous cultural ties established by Mitchill, Poinsett and Sparks were strengthened in the next generation by such men as the *Norteamericanos* Louis Agassiz in Brazil and J. C. Squire in Central America and Peru, and the Argentine Domingo Faustino Sarmiento in the United States. As for commerce, while the United States did not realize the expectations of 1808 or even hold all the gains that it made in the next two decades, nevertheless its net gain through the establishment of Latin American independence was very considerable and in the next generation it traded far more extensively with its Southern neighbors than it had done at the end of the colonial period.

In the political field, the pattern was much the same as in the economic field, for even after the *détente* of the late 'twenties, much remained that had not existed at the beginning of the period. The legacy of this generation included not only the conviction that the United States had a special interest in Latin America, but also a unique policy in relation to it. Both the conviction and the policy were most strikingly embodied in the Monroe Doctrine and the very discusions of the next few years that ended in a strict construction of the Doctrine also helped to fix the idea of its permanent significance and to make it, what Monroe intended it to be, the determining factor in " the whole future policy of the United States, as far at least as regards their own hemisphere."

The legacy included also a reciprocal feeling on the part of the new states that they stood in a special relation to the United States. The feeling was not always a source of pleasure to our Southern neighbors; but when all due allowances and qualifications have been made, the fact remains that at the end of the period covered in this study there existed in Latin America both a considerable sense of gratitude to the United States for its sympathy and aid during the struggle for independence, and also the belief that the two Americas possessed common interests based on their geographical propinquity and the similarity of their political institutions.

There was also a desire for cooperation among the independent states of America, not excluding the United States. Then, as in our own day, there were many persons in both the United States and Latin America who found the same desire expressed in the " American system " of Monroe's famous message; but on this point Monroe and his contemporaries left it to future generations to forge their own policy.

It would be hard to find a better epilogue for this story than one that was composed by John Quincy Adams in the year after the fiasco of the Panama mission. This is contained in a private letter, written in reply to one from

Richard Rush enclosing a letter that he had recently received from James Monroe, in which the latter had expressed his uneasiness over the deterioration in the United States' relations with Latin America. Commenting on Monroe's letter, Adams wrote: [67]

That our relations with South America have been weakened, is I think an erroneous opinion. Of our *commercial* relations I am sure it is. They have greatly increased and been strengthened. Of our political relations it may be partially true that they have been weakened, and from many obvious causes, as well as from some not so apparent. As *friendly* Relations however they cannot have been much weakened, for they never were very strong. Whether they ever will or can be strong must be doubtful to those who look forward to human action only by combining the probable results of human motives. Certain it is that to preserve those Relations in Amity, which is the unquestionable interest of all parties, will require on the part of the United States, an observing and persevering system of kindness, moderation, and forbearance, which was emphatically the Policy of Mr. Monroe, and which has been and will continue to be that of his successor.

Evidently convalescing from his recent attack of "the Spanish American fever," Adams once more appraised the Latin American relations of the United States in a spirit of cool, objective realism. Though somewhat too pessimistic about the past and perhaps a trifle too optimistic about the present, his appraisal was substantially correct in both respects; and an invaluable prescription for future statesmen was contained in his warning that the preservation of friendly relations with Latin America would require of the United States "an observing and persevering system of kindness, moderation, and forbearance."

[67] Gratz Papers, HSP, Adams to Rush, Aug. 16, 1827.

BIBLIOGRAPHICAL NOTE

I. BIBLIOGRAPHICAL AIDS

The present note is intended to indicate only the more important sources of information and ideas on which I have drawn in writing this book. Also, in the case of printed works it deals mainly with those that have been published within the past few years. The older works are so familiar that they do not need to be listed here. These, together with all the other works that I have cited in the footnotes, can be located through the Index of Authors. Students who wish to explore the bibliography of this subject more fully should consult the following works:

Samuel Flagg Bemis and Grace Gardiner Griffin, *A Guide to the Diplomatic History of the United States, 1775-1921* (New York, 1935).

Handbook of Latin American Studies (Cambridge, Mass., 1936—), an annual publication, under the general editorship of Lewis Hanke until 1940 and of Miron Burgin since that date.

Special bibliographies of exceptional value for the subjects indicated are contained in the following:

Charles Carroll Griffin, *The United States and the Disruption of the Spanish Empire, 1810-1822*, p. 289-302.

Dexter, Perkins, *The Monroe Doctrine, 1823-1826*, p. 263-269.

II. MANUSCRIPT SOURCES

The government archives consulted are as follows: In Spain, the Archivo Histórico Nacional (Madrid) and the Archivo General de Indias (Seville), for the years 1800-1815. In Argentina, the Archivo General de la Nación (Buenos Aires). In Uruguay, the Archivo General de la Nación (Montevideo). In Brazil, the archives of the Ministerio de Relacões Exteriores (Rio de Janeiro). In the United States, the archives of the Department of State in the National Archives, and the archives of the Navy Department.

Among the private papers consulted, the following deserve special mention both because of their intrinsic importance and also because relatively little use has been made of them by previous students of this question:

Poinsett: The Correspondence of Joel Roberts Poinsett in the Gilpin Papers, Historical Society of Pennsylvania. This correspondence, which is not to be confused with the better known collection of Poinsett Papers in the same Society, contains a large body of the correspondence of this outstanding specialist on Latin America. It is described in a printed guide about to be issued by the Society.

Porter: A folder containing a considerable number of letters from David Porter is in the Poinsett Correspondence just cited, and a number of his letters are scattered through the separate collection of Poinsett Papers. They relate mainly to his propaganda on behalf of Spanish America and his service in the Mexican Navy.

Robinson: The Papers of Jeremy Robinson, Library of Congress, contain his correspondence and diaries, which throw much light on the cultural, commercial, and political relations of the United States with Chile and Peru. Apparently the only previous writer who has made extensive use of them is Dr. Eugenio Pereira Salas (see below, VI, B, 1).

Rush: The Papers of Richard Rush, owned by Mr. Benjamin Rush of "Chesteridge," West Chester, Pennsylvania, to whom I am most grateful for his generosity in placing this rich collection at my disposal. Besides valuable collectors' items such as the originals of George Canning's famous notes to Rush regarding the proposed joint declaration of 1823, it includes: (1) Rush's letter books (containing both official and private letters) for the whole period of his London mission, 1817-1825, (2) miscellaneous correspondence (mainly letters received), arranged in folders by years, for almost the whole period of this study, and (3) several bundles of papers relating to Rush's general negotiation of 1824 at London. Though many of these documents are available in one form or another elsewhere (e. g., his despatches, in the National Archives; some of his letters to Monroe, in the Monroe Papers), this collection, by bringing them all together, gives a better idea than could be obtained in any other way of the sustained, sympathetic, and fruitful interest that this talented public servant took in Latin America. So far as I am aware, the collection has not been used by any previous student of this question. It is described in a general description (typescript) of " The Rush Family Papers at ' Chesteridge '," prepared in 1938 by Mr. J. H. Powell.

Sparks: The Jared Sparks Papers, Harvard College Library, contain a large number of letters written to Sparks when he was editor of the *North American Review* by agents of the United States in Latin America and by a few leading Latin Americans. Discriminating, but by no means exhaustive, use of them was made by H. B. Adams in his life of Sparks.

Other collections that I have consulted include the papers of John Quincy Adams, Thomas Jefferson, James Madison, James Monroe, and Samuel Smith (all in the Library of Congress) ; the Monroe Papers in the New York Public Library; the Letter Books of John Stoughton in the New York Historical Society; and the Condy Raguet Papers, the John Sergeant Papers, and the Lea and Febiger Papers (containing many letter from Baptis Irvine and William D. Robinson to Matthew Carey) in the Historical Society of Pennsylvania.

III. Documentary Collections

The only recent items of importance in this group are the very valuable work, *Britain and the Independence of Latin America, 1810-1830* (2 vols., London, 1938), edited by C. K. Webster, and *British Consular Reports on the Trade and Politics of Latin America, 1824-1826* (London, 1940), edited by R. A. Humphreys. For the rest I have relied on such long familiar works as *American State*

Papers (Foreign Relations, Commerce and Navigation, and Naval Affairs) ; William R. Manning, ed., *Diplomatic Correspondence of the United States concerning the Independence of the Latin American Nations* (3 vols., New York, 1925) ; and the *Annals of Congress*.

IV. CORRESPONDENCE, DIARIES, MEMOIRS

So far as the United States is concerned, most of the works in this group come under the rubric of correspondence. Our leading public men in the generation covered by this study seem to have been lusty extroverts who were not given to the production of diaries and memoirs. No important additions to the published correspondence of these political leaders has been made in recent years.

There are only three items in this group that call for special comment. The first is the *Memoirs* of John Quincy Adams, who was an exception to the rule noted above. While he earned the undying gratitude of future historians by keeping a voluminous diary, it suffers from some conspicuous lacunae at some of the most interesting periods in the early history of our relations with Latin America— for example, in the summer of 1821, for some weeks before and after Adams's spectacular Independence Day address; early in 1822, on the eve of the recognition of the new states; in October and the first days of November 1823, shortly before Monroe's great pronouncement was made; and in 1825 at the time of the trial of Captain Charles Stewart, which involved important questions relating to the neutrality policy of the United States and the use of its navy in Latin American waters. And while the *Memoirs* contain many references to the Panamá mission, they tell us relatively little about the main questions raised in the debate over it.

The second item is Adams's *Writings,* edited by W. C. Ford. These stop with the summer of 1823, with the result that for the rest of his public career Adams is the only important public man of this period whose correspondence has not been published. This is all the more regrettable since the Adams Papers (on deposit in the Massachusetts Historical Society) are not open to students.

The third item is Richard Rush's *Memoranda of a Residence at the Court of London* (Philadelphia, 1845), covering the period 1818-1825 (not to be confused with the author's earlier book covering the first two years of his mission and first published in 1833). Since this well known book has been a main reliance of historians of this period, often to the neglect of Rush's public and private correspondence during his London mission, it should be noted, first, that the book consists mainly of paraphrases of parts of Rush's despatches, and second, that in selecting the despatches to be paraphrased, Rush followed consistently his declared purpose of promoting better relations between England and the United States (see above, p. 497, note 8). Consequently the book omits some of the most characteristic and important passages in Rush's public despatches (as well as his private letters) and fails to reflect the Anglophobia that he felt so strongly throughout his residence at " the Court of London."

V. CONTEMPORARY PUBLICATIONS: MAGAZINES, NEWSPAPERS, BOOKS AND PAMPHLETS

For the subject of this study, the *North American Review* was by all odds the most important magazine published in the United States. Most of its articles dealing with Latin America were published after Jared Sparks became its editor for the secod time in 1823. After that date it reflected Sparks's warm sympathy for " the South American cause," contrasting sharply in this respect with the coldness of Sparks's predecessor, Edward Everett, towards our southern neighbors.

Among newspapers, the two that I examined most carefully were William Duane's *Aurora* and Robert Walsh's *National Gazette,* both of Philadelphia. These papers were chosen partly because their editors were outstanding in the field of journalism and took widely different views of the Latin American problem. Duane is probably the best known American journalist of that generation; he was an ardent supporter of the Latin American cause and sharply critical of Monroe's cautious policy in regard to it. Robert Walsh was a man of respectable attainments in the field of letters and a civilized and discerning commentator on domestic and foreign politics. Possibly because he was a Roman Catholic and the Vatican was slow to give its *Nihil obstat* to the independence movement, he viewed the new states with cool detachment; and he was generally sympathetic towards the administration's policy. He was, in fact, a correspondent of John Quincy Adams's; and though Adams said some unkind things about him in his *Memoirs*, these lose most of their sting when it is recalled that Adams thought well enough of Walsh and his newspaper to write him many letters explaining his own course and that of the administration.

I have also made considerable, though much less extensive, use of many other newspapers in various parts of the country, such as that old standby, Hezekiah Niles's *Register* (Baltimore), and also the *National Intelligencer* (Washington), *City of Washington Gazette, Boston Daily Advertiser, Columbian Gazette* (Boston), *New York Daily Advertiser, New York Evening Post, Baltimore Patriot, Baltimore Federal Gazette, Richmond Enquirer, Charleston Courier, Louisiana Courier* (New Orleans), and *Argus of Western America* (Frankfort, K.).

As for contemporary books and pamphlets, there seems to have been a good deal of truth in Robert Walsh' remark, which was made in 1820 and is quoted in the text, that the American people of that day relied mainly on newspapers for intellectual aliment of every description. Probably because books were so little read, few were written; and very few of real importance were written about Latin America. The inarticulateness (in this form) of the Americans who visited Latin America in the period of the present study is indeed astonishing, especially when it is compared with the opposite characteristic displayed our British cousins who visited it at that time. The American naval officers in particular seem to have been of the strong, silent type. Of the many who served in Latin American waters while that fascinating region was being rediscovered, only one, Captain David Porter, wrote a really important book about his experiences there, and even he discussed it incidentally in a book that was primarily concerned with his part in the naval war of 1812. The diplomatic and commercial agents did not do much better. Except for official reports, of which the most notable are those of Rodney, Graham, and Bland on their South American mission of 1817-1818, only two important works about Latin America came from their pens. One of these was Brackenridge's *Voyage to South America*; the other, Poinsett's *Notes on Mexico in 1822.*

Of the other principal books and pamphlets on this subject published in the United States in our period, two were written by Latin Americans (Pazos and Torres), one (Brackenridge's pamphlet *South America*) was published before the author's first visit to Latin America, and two (Yard's pamphlet on the commerce of Spanish America and Alexander Everett's *America*) were written by men who never visited it at all. Consequently, when W. D. Robinson and William Duane published books about their observations and experiences in Mexico and Great Colombia respectively, they did something which, for an American of that day, was exceptional. The enterprising Mathew Carey published a section on Spanish America and Brazil in his American geography (1822) and statistical data about their commerce with the United States were included in the familiar works of Timothy Pitkin and Adam Seybert. On the whole, however, the number of such books and pamphlets is comparatively small; and while the few that were published are very useful to the student, it is mainly to other sources, such as newspapers, debates in Congress, and the reports and correspondence of government officials, that we must look for the information and ideas of the people of the United States in that generation regarding Latin America.

VI.   GENERAL AND SPECIAL WORKS

Full citations of the books and articles listed below can be found in the footnotes with the aid of the Index of Authors. With a few exceptions, they have appeared since the publication of Bemis and Griffin's *Guide*. Among earlier works, I am most indebted to those of John Bassett Moore, Frederick L. Paxson, Isaac J. Cox, William Spence Robertson, Joseph B. Lockey, Charles Lyon Chandler, J. Fred Rippy, Henry M. Wriston, and Dexter Perkins. The latter's scholarly and penetrating monograph, *The Monroe Doctrine, 1823-1826*, requires special mention, for it was exceptionally useful to me; and while I sometimes found myself in disagreement with the author, I was always conscious of my deep indebtedness to him.

A.   General Works

Among the more recent works of relatively broad scope, there were three that I found particularly useful. One of these was the 80-page historical introduction to Professor Webster's *Britain and the Independence of Latin America,* already mentioned. Written by an acknowledged master in the field, this may be taken as summarizing the conclusions reached by the best British students of the subject under consideration and it is invaluable to the student of the relations between the United States and Latin America. I ought to add, however, that, for all its many merits, I believe that Professor Webster's introduction glosses over some of the less edifying aspects of British policy and exaggerates the British contribution to the establishment of Latin American independence. It also shows a lack of familiarity with the recent literature of the history of the Monroe Doctrine. Different in kind but of the same order of importance is Professor W. S. Robertson's *France and Latin-American Independence,* which is an exhaustive study of the diplomatic history of the period and is based on extensive use of manuscript sources in France. It would have been still more useful for the purposes of the present study if the author had paid more attention to the correspondence of the French ministers in the United States and the American ministers in France and to the economic and cultural aspects of French interest in Latin America. The third work, Professor Charles C. Griffin's *The United States and the Disruption of the Spanish Empire, 1810-1822,* covers a part of the ground covered in the present study and contains a store of information, bibliographical and otherwise, that I have found most useful. It is, however, written from a different point of view from the one I have taken, and its main focus is the negotiation that was crowned by the so-called " Florida Treaty " of 1819 with Spain. For the latter subject the reader should also consult Dr. Philip C. Brooks's recent study, *Diplomacy and the Borderlands: the Adams-Onís Treaty of 1819.*

Another recent work, which bears a title very much like that of the present work but is of a very different character, is *The United States Government and Latin American Independence, 1810-1830* (London, 1937), by James Johnston Auchmuty, who is described on the title page as " Lately Scholar of Trinity College Dublin." It seems to be based almost entirely on Manning's *Diplomatic Correspondence*; it deals largely with the policy of the United States government and the activities and reports of its agents; and the arrangement is largely regional (five of the eight chapters deal successively with Greater Columbia, the Provinces of La Plata, the Western Coast—Chile and Peru, the Brazilian Empire, and Mexico). There is an appendix consisting of three documents reprinted from Manning. In my opinion, the book does not give an adequate account of the development of public opinion and policy in the United States in regard to Latin America; but it will be found useful by those who wish to follow the activities of agents of the United States in Latin America.

B. Special Works

Among recent special works I have found the following most useful for the topics indicated:

1. Relations between the United States and individual countries: Ludwell Lee Montagu, *The United States and Haiti*; Herminio Portell Vilá, *Cuba en sus relaciones con los Estados Unidos y España*; E. Taylor Parks, *The United States and Colombia.* Special mention should be made of the work of the distinguished Chilean scholar Dr. Eugenio Pereira Salas, who in the past decade has published many articles on the political, economic, and cultural relations of the United States with Chile in the period covered by the present study. As a result we have a better picture of the relations of the United States with Chile than with any other Latin American country in this period.

2. Missions from Latin America to the United States and vice versa: Accioly, *O reconhecimento do Brasil*; Bemis, *Early Diplomatic Missions from Buenos Aires*; Parra-Pérez, *Historia de la primera república*; Whitaker, " José Silvestre Rebello "; Wriston, *Executive Agents*; Stewart, " South American Mission "; Nichols's two articles, " Trade Relations " and " William Shaler "; and the several studies of Poinsett's career by Parton, Rippy, and Chandler.

3. Commerce: Dorothy Burne Goebel, " British Trade to the Spanish Colonies "; John Rydjord, " Napoleon and Mexican Silver "; Vernon L. Setser, *Commercial Reciprocity Policy*; and Simonsen, *Historia economica do Brasil.*

4. Privateering, the protection of commerce, the United States Navy: Bealer, *Corsarios de Buenos Aires*; Griffin, " Privateering from Baltimore "; Knox, *History of the United States Navy*; and Harold Sprout and Margaret Sprout, *Rise of American Naval Power.*

5. Cultural relations and the intellectual background: Belaúnde, *Bolívar and the Political Thought of the Spanish American Revolution*; Bernstein, " Primeras relaciones intelectuales "; Mott, *History of American Magazines*; Pueyrredon, *Dominique de Pradt*; and Weinberg, *Manifest Destiny* and two articles on isolationism.

6. Monroe Doctrine, Panama Congress, Pan Americanism: Schellenberg, " Jeffersonian Origins of the Monroe Doctrine "; Tatum, *United States and Europe, 1815-1823*; Ibarguren, *En la penumbra de la historia patria* (on Alvear and Monroe) ; Reinhold, " New Research on the Panama Congress "; Rodríguez Cerna, *Centro América en el congreso de Bolívar*; Valadés, *Alamán*; and Yepes, *Le panaméricanisme.*

INDEX OF AUTHORS

This list includes the names of editors and translators as well as authors. The numbers refer to the page and note where the first full citation will be found.

GENERAL INDEX

A

Adams, Henry, on Jefferson and Spanish America, 41-46, 48, 62, n. 1.

Adams, John, on Spanish Americans and democracy, 37; and navy, 276-277.

Adams, John Quincy, on foreign wars for freedom, viii, 479-486.

Mission to Russia, 59, 81; on commercial agents, 64; on consuls and recognition, 66, 257; on public interest in Latin America, 111, 187; on commerce with Latin America, 118, 132; on Cuba, 127, 131; letter to, quoted, 135-136; qualifications in Latin American field, 147-149; and "Black Legend," 148, n. 12, 419; and consular service, 155; on neutrality, 195-196; on British attitude towards U. S. and Latin America, 206, 209-210; on South American mission (1817), 242, n. 30; on defeat of Clay's motion (1818), 246; on South American mission and reports, 248, n. 1; to Rush on Anglo-American cooperation, 255; relations with DeForest, 256-259; dubious about cooperation with England, 261-264; negotiates treaty with Onís, 267, 269-270; on protection of commerce, 275, 298-299; on Dana, 292, on new land in South Pacific, 296-299.

Address of July 4, 1821, 317, 348-363, 398-424, 518; text cited, 350, n. 11; extract quoted, 362, n. 34; misunderstood, 351-354, 366; principles of non-colonization and isolation, 355; explained in letters to Walsh and Everett, 355; reply to Clay of Lexington and *Edinburgh Review*, 355-359; directed against Holy Allies rather than England, 358-359; application to Spanish America, 359-363; opposition to foreign wars, 362; reference to Washington, 362, 363; reception, 364-368.

Surveys U. S. foreign relations (1820), 320-321; critical of Spanish American agents, 337-338; on achievements of State Department (1822), 392-393; on French invasion of Spain and international situation, 397-399; fears British designs on Cuba, 400; on the four freedoms, 413; on American system, 415-419; growing sympathy for Latin America, 419-420; on U. S. as tranquil spectator, 421; reply to Russian ukase, 423-428; deference to Monroe on questions of foreign policy, 425-428; "peace in our time," 428; catches "soft infection," 432; on concert with England, 432-433; on U. S. policy of peace, 433-435.

Contribution to Monroe Doctrine, 472-475, 486-491; on American system, 478-479; on warning to Europe, 479-488; reconciliation with Independence Day address, 480-486; importance of his policy in regard to Panama Congress, 574-576; on Colombia (1823), 596; letter to Rush on Latin America, quoted, 602.

Adams-Onís treaty, discussed, 100, relation to Congress of Aix-la-Chapelle, 266-269; concluded, 269-272; relation to recognition, 273-274; adverse effect on U. S. relations with Latin America, 270-272; ratified, 273.

Agrarian class, 36, 87-89.

Aguirre, Juan Pedro, Venezuelan agent, 67, 68-69.

Aguirre, Manuel H. de, mission to U. S., 232-236, 246; unfriendly to U. S., 236.

Aix-la-Chapelle, Congress of, 169, n. 3, 211, 259-260, 264, 266-269.

Alamán, Lucas, 536; writes to Sparks, 568; quoted, 569.

Alexander I, tsar of Russia, 60, 253-254.

Allen, Heman, U. S. minister to Chile, cited, 538; correspondent of Sparks, 568.